D1556239

Digital Public Administration and E–Government in Developing Nations:

Policy and Practice

Edward Francis Halpin
Leeds Metropolitan University, UK

David Griffin
Leeds Metropolitan University, UK

Carolynn Rankin
Leeds Metropolitan University, UK

Lakshman Dissanayake
University of Colombo, Sri Lanka

Nazmunnessa Mahtab
University of Dhaka, Bangladesh

A volume in the Advances in Electronic Government, Digital Divide, and Regional Development (AEGDDRD) Book Series

An Imprint of IGI Global

Managing Director:	Lindsay Johnston
Production Editor:	Jennifer Yoder
Development Editor:	Austin DeMarco
Acquisitions Editor:	Kayla Wolfe
Typesetter:	Kaitlyn Kulp
Cover Design:	Jason Mull

Published in the United States of America by
Information Science Reference (an imprint of IGI Global)
701 E. Chocolate Avenue
Hershey PA 17033
Tel: 717-533-8845
Fax: 717-533-8661
E-mail: cust@igi-global.com
Web site: http://www.igi-global.com

Library of Congress Cataloging-in-Publication Data

Digital public administration and e-government in developing nations : policy and practice / Edward Francis Halpin, David Griffin, Carolynn Rankin, Lakshman Dissanayake and Nazmunnessa Mahtab, editors.
     pages cm
  Includes bibliographical references and index.
   ISBN 978-1-4666-3691-0 (hardcover) -- ISBN 978-1-4666-3692-7 (ebook) -- ISBN 978-1-4666-3693-4 (print & perpetual access) 1. Internet in public administration--Developing countries. I. Halpin, Edward F.
   JF1525.A8D549 2014
   352.3'802854678--dc23
                               2014018195

This book is published in the IGI Global book series Advances in Electronic Government, Digital Divide, and Regional Development (AEGDDRD) (ISSN: 2326-9103; eISSN: 2326-9111)

British Cataloguing in Publication Data
A Cataloguing in Publication record for this book is available from the British Library.

For electronic access to this publication, please contact: eresources@igi-global.com.

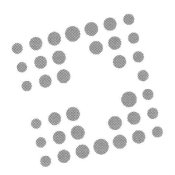

Advances in Electronic Government, Digital Divide, and Regional Development (AEGDDRD) Book Series

Zaigham Mahmood
University of Derby, UK & North West University, South Africa

ISSN: 2326-9103
EISSN: 2326-9111

MISSION

The successful use of digital technologies (including social media and mobile technologies) to provide public services and foster economic development has become an objective for governments around the world. The development towards electronic government (or e-government) not only affects the efficiency and effectiveness of public services, but also has the potential to transform the nature of government interactions with its citizens. Current research and practice on the adoption of electronic/digital government and the implementation in organizations around the world aims to emphasize the extensiveness of this growing field.

The Advances in Electronic Government, Digital Divide & Regional Development (AEGDDRD) book series aims to publish authored, edited and case books encompassing the current and innovative research and practice discussing all aspects of electronic government development, implementation and adoption as well the effective use of the emerging technologies (including social media and mobile technologies) for a more effective electronic governance (or e-governance).

COVERAGE

- Digital Democracy
- E-Citizenship
- Electronic & Digital Government
- ICT Adoption in Developing Countries
- ICT within Government & Public Sectors
- Knowledge Divide
- Public Information Management
- Regional Planning
- Urban & Rural Development
- Web 2.0 in Government

IGI Global is currently accepting manuscripts for publication within this series. To submit a proposal for a volume in this series, please contact our Acquisition Editors at Acquisitions@igi-global.com or visit: http://www.igi-global.com/publish/.

Titles in this Series

For a list of additional titles in this series, please visit: www.igi-global.com

Emerging Mobile and Web 2.0 Technologies for Connected E-Government
Zaigham Mahmood (University of Derby, UK & North West University Potchefstroom, South Africa)
Information Science Reference • copyright 2014 • 332pp • H/C (ISBN: 9781466660823) • US $205.00 (our price)

E-Governance and Social Inclusion Concepts and Cases
Scott Baum (Griffith University, Australia) and Arun Mahizhnan (National University of Singapore, Singapore)
Information Science Reference • copyright 2014 • 300pp • H/C (ISBN: 9781466661066) • US $205.00 (our price)

Design, Development, and Use of Secure Electronic Voting Systems
Dimitrios Zissis (University of Aegean, Greece) and Dimitrios Lekkas (University of Aegean, Greece)
Information Science Reference • copyright 2014 • 270pp • H/C (ISBN: 9781466658202) • US $195.00 (our price)

Digital Access and E-Government Perspectives from Developing and Emerging Countries
Peter Mazebe II Mothataesi Sebina (University of Botswana, Botswana) Kgomotso H. Moahi (University of Botswana, Botswana) and Kelvin Joseph Bwalya (University of Botswana, Botswana & University of Johannesburg, South Africa)
Information Science Reference • copyright 2014 • 356pp • H/C (ISBN: 9781466658684) • US $195.00 (our price)

Technology Development and Platform Enhancements for Successful Global E-Government Design
Kelvin Joseph Bwalya (University of Botswana, Botswana & University of Johannesburg, South Africa)
Information Science Reference • copyright 2014 • 511pp • H/C (ISBN: 9781466649002) • US $235.00 (our price)

IT in the Public Sphere Applications in Administration, Government, Politics, and Planning
Zaigham Mahmood (University of Derby, UK & North West University, South Africa)
Information Science Reference • copyright 2014 • 359pp • H/C (ISBN: 9781466647190) • US $200.00 (our price)

Globalization and Governance in the International Political Economy
Ümit Hacıoğlu (Beykent University, Turkey) and Hasan Dinçer (Beykent University, Turkey)
Information Science Reference • copyright 2014 • 435pp • H/C (ISBN: 9781466646391) • US $175.00 (our price)

Developing E-Government Projects Frameworks and Methodologies
Zaigham Mahmood (University of Derby, UK & North West University, South Africa)
Information Science Reference • copyright 2013 • 460pp • H/C (ISBN: 9781466642454) • US $180.00 (our price)

701 E. Chocolate Ave., Hershey, PA 17033
Order online at www.igi-global.com or call 717-533-8845 x100
To place a standing order for titles released in this series, contact: cust@igi-global.com
Mon-Fri 8:00 am - 5:00 pm (est) or fax 24 hours a day 717-533-8661

List of Reviewers

Antony Bryant, *Leeds Metropolitan University, UK*
Margaret Chawawa, *Leeds Metropolitan University, UK*
Amanda Foster, *Sheffield Hallam University, UK*
John Lannon, *University of Limerick, Ireland*
Nehal Mahtab, *Leeds Metropolitan University, UK*
David Moore, *Leeds Metropolitan University, UK*
Shane O'Hanlon, *University of Limerick, Ireland*

Table of Contents

Section 1
Technological and Political in Developing E-Government: Administration, Policy, Politics, and Management

Detailed Table of Contents

Section 1
Technological and Political in Developing E-Government: Administration, Policy, Politics, and Management

Chapter 1
Laura Alcaide Muñoz, University of Granada, Spain
Manuel Pedro Rodríguez Bolívar, University of Granada, Spain

Many countries have implemented changes in public sector management models based on the strategic and intensive use of new information and communication technologies. However, most research has focused on developed countries, with the area of emerging economies being neglected. This chapter offers a framework to help public administrators and researchers evaluate the field of e-Government research in emerging economies, identifying research gaps and possibilities for improvement in the context of e-government research in developing countries. The findings reveal the existence of various research gaps and highlight areas that should be addressed in future research, especially in developing countries. Indeed, the research approach to e-government remains immature, focusing on particular cases or dimensions, while little has been done to produce theories or models to clarify and explain the political processes of e-government.

Chapter 2

JungHo Park, Korea Institute of Public Administration, South Korea
Greg Prombescu, Northern Illinois University, USA

The objective of this chapter is to critically evaluate the e-governmentization of administrative processes, which many developing nations have come to enthusiastically espouse. From a theoretical perspective, such a trend is ostensibly positive, as e-government serves to promote transparency and efficient information exchange, which in turn serves to stimulate more equal distributions of power, inside as well as outside the bureaucracy, and perhaps most importantly (efficiently) solicit greater citizen participation. However, such benefits associated with the proliferation of e-government are often contingent upon a host of prerequisite conditions that, often times, developing nations do not meet. Therefore, such enthusiastic attempts by developing nations to e-governmentize administrative processes may be misplaced. As such, the primary thesis of this research is that the e-governmentization of administrative processes are likely to stimulate positive effects only after a certain level of democracy has been achieved. To explore this thesis, this chapter focuses on exploring the evolution and ensuing effects of the proliferation of e-government in South Korea.

Chapter 3

Fuat Alican, Central American Scientific Research and Education Center, Costa Rica

Political and cultural aspects of digital public undertakings in developing countries are often neglected as more emphasis is placed on the technological components. The mutual impact between political or cultural issues and emerging trends such as cloud computing and social networks exacerbate the problem. This chapter analyzes political and cultural issues which have a significant impact on digital public administration and e-government initiatives in developing countries, also taking into consideration the emerging tendencies and technologies. It combines theory and practice, including studies that demonstrate different political or cultural issues involved in the digital undertakings in these countries, examples from different contexts and nations, and a case study from Turkey. The chapter starts with examples of different political issues, analyzing and summarizing some of the most relevant of these issues, including existing literature related to each subject. It continues with cultural issues. The subsequent section contains a discussion of how political and cultural issues relate to the tendencies of the Information and Communication Technologies (ICTs) sector, and why this context is important for digital initiatives in developing countries, as an initial guide to existing and future challenges. The chapter ends with the case of Turkey, which demonstrates political and cultural issues faced on both national and regional levels, in the context of digital public administration and emerging trends in ICTs.

Emerging trends in Information and Communication Technologies (ICTs) in governments around the globe suggest that developing countries should embrace e-government as an enabler of efficient and effective service delivery. The Government of Zimbabwe, which is a case study in this chapter, is acutely aware of the critical role that ICTs play in socio-economic development. This chapter discusses Zimbabwe's e-government policies and programmes and maps them against the e-government architecture framework by Ebrahim and Irani (2005). The e-government architecture framework defines the standards, infrastructure components, applications, technologies, business models, and guidelines for electronic commerce among and between organisations that facilitate the interaction of the government and promote group productivity. The study is theoretically based upon the socio-technical theory, whose view suggests the existence of a technical sub-system and a social sub-system in an organisation. This theory has been adopted in this study to explain the complex relation between the government as an institution and e-government as an artifact. Drawing from the e-government architecture framework and the social-technical theory, an integrated e-government assessment framework is developed to explain the nature of relationships among government, citizens, and technology.

The ICT-blessed e-governance is transforming public administration systems worldwide and forcing a paradigm shift. E-governance renders a new way and style in each and every aspect of public administration. It brings about changes in the structure, functions, and processes of public service delivery, ushering transformation in the system through effectively connecting, engaging, and streamlining the relations among government, businesses, citizens, and other relevant stakeholders. Irrespective of certain obvious limitations and challenges, it not only attempts to ensure economy, efficiency, and effectiveness in service delivery, but also offers unlimited potential for combating corruption and many other bureau-pathologies in public administration. Based on secondary sources, this chapter offers brief theoretical discussions on e-governance, including, among others, its emergence, types of service delivery, and transformation stages.

Chapter 6

There is a growing recognition among scholars, practitioners, and elected officials that e-government success is not a deterministic outcome of entrepreneurial design or exacting implementation. In fact, constructing cost-efficient and policy effective e-government platforms has proved to be much more challenging than originally expected. In many instances, failed e-government experiments have led to significant financial losses and to increased dissatisfaction levels among citizenry. These latter experiences have nuanced the need for a much more thorough understanding and appreciation for the difficulties faced within the conceptualization and application of e-government platforms in successfully achieving the expected administrative and democratic outcomes. This chapter, by tracing the evolution of e-government both as a concept and as an administrative trend within the transformation of governance, delineates the main challenges in achieving the core goals and the democratic scope of e-governance. It is argued that in e-governance, success is a function of three fundamental vectors – security, functionality, and transformation.

Chapter 7

The arrival of Rafael Correa in Ecuador is leading to a structural transformation of the Ecuadorian economy and society with the arrival of e-Government and the introduction of the digital economy in the country. The objective of this chapter is to design a strategy based on entrepreneurship, e-Government, and higher education for creating a digital society in Ecuador (the triple helix strategy). To achieve it, the authors analyse the Ecuadorian's National Plan for Good Living 2013-2017 linked to higher education reforms and the influence of the European-based e-Government policies in Ecuador. The authors finish with some perspectives and the foreseeable impact of a digital society in this developing nation.

Chapter 8

The aim of this chapter is to discuss how the emerging process of gamification can impact the production of public services. Gamification is a relatively recent phenomenon that relates, in broad terms, to the introduction of game elements in non-game contexts. After reviewing the concept, design principles and techniques, and effects of gamification, the chapter discusses the extent to which gamification may affect the production and delivery of public services. The conclusions discuss the possible role of gamification in reshaping the identity and role of citizens and their relationship with public authorities.

Chapter 9

María de Miguel Molina, Universitat Politècnica de València, Spain
Carlos Ripoll Soler, Universitat Politècnica de València, Spain

In this chapter, the authors explore the different literature that analyses the application of Social Network Sites (SNSs) in e-government to help government managers to improve citizens' communication and participation. The use of Web 2.0 tools is perceived as a new way of communication not only in the political arena but also on the government level to improve civic engagement, to coproduce public services, and to increase service personalization. Citizens still like traditional communication tools, and it is important not to overload them through SNSs. The authors show possible new trends for future analysis on the application of SNSs.

Section 2
Evidence: Case Studies and Issues of E-Government in Practice and Reality

Chapter 10

Ronan de Kervenoael, Sabanci University, Turkey & Aston Business School, UK
Vasileios Yfantis, Ionian University, Greece

For the last several years, mobile devices and platform security threats, including wireless networking technology, have been top security issues. A departure has occurred from automatic anti-virus software based on traditional PC defense: risk management (authentication and encryption), compliance, and disaster recovery following polymorphic viruses and malware as the primary activities within many organizations and government services alike. This chapter covers research in Turkey as a reflection of the current market – e-government started officially in 2008. This situation in an emerging country presents the current situation and resistances encountered while engaging with mobile and e-government interfaces. The authors contend that research is needed to understand more precisely security threats and most of all potential solutions for sustainable future intention to use m-government services. Finally, beyond m-government initiatives' success or failure, the mechanisms related to public administration mobile technical capacity building and security issues are discussed.

Chapter 11

Noore Alam Siddiquee, Flinders University, Australia
Md Gofran Faroqi, Flinders University, Australia

This chapter reviews the state of e-government development and associated changes to service delivery in Bangladesh. Using the "stage model" as a frame of reference, the authors show the progresses Bangladesh has made in terms of informational, interactive, transactional, and integrated services. They argue that although Bangladesh's overall progress is still modest for it allows only limited advanced levels of services, there are encouraging trends underway. In its conclusion, the chapter highlights some of the impediments and challenges that hamper e-government initiatives undermining their potentials and benefits in the country.

Chapter 12

Nazmunnessa Mahtab, University of Dhaka, Bangladesh
Nehal Mahtab, Leeds Metropolitan University, UK

This chapter focuses on how e-Governance empowers women, specifically poor rural women. ICT for Development emerged as a new area of work in the mid-1990s at a time when the potential of new technologies was starting to be better understood. In poor countries, particularly rural women in Bangladesh, access to ICTs is still a faraway reality for the vast majority of these women as they are further removed from the information age, as they are unaware of the demonstrated benefit from ICTs to address ground-level development challenges. The barriers they face pose greater problems for the poor rural women, who are more likely to be illiterate, not know English, and lack opportunities for training in computer skills. Access to ICT can enable women to gain a stronger voice in their government and at the global level. ICT also offers women flexibility in time and space and can be of particular value to women who face social isolation, especially the women in the rural areas in Bangladesh. To represent the use of ICT, this chapter focuses on the use of "Mobile Phone" by the rural women of Bangladesh and how the use of mobile phones have helped in empowering rural poor women in Bangladesh.

Chapter 13

Md. Rokon-Ul-Hasan, Bangladesh Public Administration Training Centre, Bangladesh
Mobasser Monem, University of Dhaka, Bangladesh

In Bangladesh, there is an undeniable wave of awareness about e-governance at present. Therefore, it is high time that government prepare itself in terms of implementing e-governance in order to cope with the requirements of the fast changing global environment. As bureaucracy is one of the most vital pillars of government, it is imperative that it is well prepared to face the upcoming challenges of technological boost. This chapter assesses the preparedness level of bureaucracy from the perspective of e-governance implementation. Analysis of primary data reveals that the frequency of computer and Internet usage for official activities is also very low. Most of the officials do not have any formal ICT training, and those who have such training have covered only very elementary aspects. The overall readiness in terms of technical skills is found to be unsatisfactory. Existing laws, rules, and regulations are found to be very insufficient for smooth implementation of e-governance in Bangladesh.

This chapter explores the interplay between society and Internet technology in the context of the developing former socialist country of Mongolia. This chapter goes beyond questions of access to the Internet and explores three factors of the global digital divide. First, this chapter explores how language factors such as non-Roman domain names and the use of the Cyrillic alphabet exacerbate the digital divide in the impoverished country of Mongolia. ICANN's initiation of international domain names is an initial development toward achieving linguistic diversity on the Internet. Second, this chapter explores how post-communist settings and foreign investment and aid dependency afflict Internet development. A rapid economic growth in Mongolia has increased access to mobile phones, computers, and the Internet; however, the influx of foreign capital poured into the mining, construction, and telecommunication sectors frequently comes in non-concessional terms raising concerns over the public debt in Mongolia.

This chapter presents an enhanced eGovernment stage model based on citizens' participation for improvements in the delivery of governmental services by putting citizens' insights and their requirements in the context of e-government development and the potential use of a multi-channel delivery of services for regional governments in developing countries. The model proposed is based on research done in the Kurdistan region of Iraq. This research identified missing elements in traditional eGovernment models that would prove essential for implementation in developing countries. These models usually propose five stages of development spanning from emergence to integration. The proposal here considers most of the limitations in two stages, namely initial and an enhancement stage with the advantage of decreasing the uncertainty of e-government implementation in the public sector by recognising the consequence of the institutional readiness, adoption processes, the needs of ICT tools, and the factors that influence the implementation process.

Chapter 16

Suran Dissanayake, Leeds Metropolitan University, UK
Lakshman Dissanayake, University of Colombo, Sri Lanka

Evolution of e-Governance concept in Sri Lanka can be traced back to 1983 because the Government of Sri Lanka for the first time recognized its obligation for ICT development by creating the National Computer Policy of 1983. The Information and Communication Technology Act No. 27 of 2003 came into existence in 2003 and the Information and Communication Technology Agency of Sri Lanka was established. In 2004, "e-Sri Lanka Development Project" was initiated. It included information infrastructure building, improvement of human resources in ICT, citizen-specific service delivery, creating a modern government using ICT for social and economic development, and endorsing Sri Lanka as a destination for ICT. The e-Sri Lanka initiative expects to use ICT to develop the economy of Sri Lanka by reducing poverty and thus improving the quality of life of its citizens. Presently, the government makes an effort in realizing this vision through six programme strategy schemes. This is explored in this chapter.

Chapter 17

Virgil Stoica, Alexandru Ioan Cuza University of Iasi, Romania
Andrei Ilas, Independent Researcher, Romania

The last two decades witnessed the sudden raise in importance of Information and Communications Technology (ICT). Some societies have been quick to embrace the benefits of ICT, while others have used the new technologies in a rather limited way. A new term, "digital divide," was coined to describe the gap between the societies using ICT on a large scale and those with limited access. Much was written with respect to the causes of this gap. Factors such as socioeconomic conditions, geographical position, tradition, social and individual values are considered to play major roles in the creation of the digital divide. The vast majority of the studies have focused on the digital performance of cities with far less attention being paid to what was happening in the villages. Arguably, the villages would greatly benefit, and the existent data shows that in many societies a significant rural-urban digital divide is already in place. The goal of this chapter is to assess the urban-rural digital divide in Romania in terms of official website performances by evaluating five components: security and personal data protection, usability, content, type of services, and digital democracy. The authors conclude that in Romania the rural-urban digital divide is extremely large. Based on their conclusions, they offer suggestions for future studies and policies.

Chapter 18

The Internet is definitely the most complex and dynamic technical and cultural phenomenon that humanity ever experienced. Nevertheless, despite its positive impact on the Western world, Web 2.0 has yet to prove its power in the undeveloped regions of the globe, where the Internet Era is still at its dawn. In developing countries, the barriers that women face, such as poverty or social imbalances, establish significant challenges that hinder connectivity and access to modern technologies. In this context, the chapter discusses the evolution of gender speech in relation to new Information and Communication Technologies (ICTs). The authors determine whether the declarations and plans for action that were issued subsequent to the 1995 Fourth World Conference on Women in Beijing enhanced the establishment of gendered policies on ICTs, particularly in the undeveloped regions of the world, and whether, in this way, they empower women, contribute to combating women's poverty, and promote gender equality.

Chapter 19

Government initiatives in the United States have been passed in an effort to increase citizen usage of e-government programs. One such service is the availability of online health insurance information. However, not all demographic groups have been equally able to accessing these online services, primarily the poor and rural American. As more legislation is passed, including the advancement of broadband services to remote areas, infrastructure barriers are being removed, opening access to Medicare and Medicaid websites for these vulnerable groups. The purpose of this chapter is to analyze factors predicting the impact of recent government actions on citizen access to health insurance information online. This topic is explored using multivariate regression analysis and individual level data from the Internet and American Life Project. The findings suggest that healthcare needs and quality of Internet access may be playing a more important role in health insurance information services than other factors.

Chapter 20

Many developing nations have begun to introduce elements of e-Health to improve service provision. This chapter provides an account of work in the area including case studies where pioneers have utilised modern mobile technologies to quickly and efficiently introduce new mHealth interventions, despite being resource-limited and having a heavy disease burden. Telemedicine has become well established, linking these nations with specialists in centres of excellence. Obstacles such as cost, inadequate infrastructure, data security, and the lack of a trained health informatics workforce need to be resolved. Several innovative solutions have been put forward: satellite broadband access for the most remote areas, international sponsorship initiatives, use of open source software, and exchange programmes for staff education. There is strong support from the World Health Organization and other international bodies, as development of the eHealth agenda has the potential to help ease access barriers and improve provision of healthcare in developing countries. This is explored in this chapter.

Preface

At the origins of this book, we, the editors set out to examine e-government from the perspective of the developing regions of the world and to explore issues of e-government policy and practice in these regions, combining scholarly research alongside practitioner case studies, with the aim to provide a critical current perspective on e-government progress in the developing regions and an evaluation of challenges for the future. In the time that followed, there have certainly been applications of technology in many areas of politics and governance, including the Arab Spring; there are continually new examples of e-Government, e-Governance, and the implementation of new technological resources, with guiding principles provided by governments around the world, and with the United Nations (UN) providing or applying an oversight. Therefore, as a reference point, it is worth reflecting upon the United Nations E-Government Survey 2012, in which imperatives are made for the way forward, including the following:

As the way forward the first imperative is to recognize the role of national governments in tapping into the transformative nature of e-government for sustainable development as it relates to whole-of-government approaches and multichannel service delivery. In this regard countries must at a minimum establish a persistent online presence with at least basic services in order to build trust in government. (United Nations, 2012)

It is perhaps with these imperatives in mind that we should view the chapters in this book. The chapters cover many facets of e-Government, and offer valuable insights from many countries including case studies from Morocco, Bangladesh, Kurdistan (Iraq), Sri Lanka, Turkey, Romania, Ecuador, Zimbabwe, South Korea, China, and Mongolia. These case studies provide richness and an opportunity to critically reflect upon the UN imperative. Similarly, there are chapters on health, gender, and the digital divide.

Before considering the chapters and structure of the book, it is worth viewing some recent research, which might not appear immediately related to e-Government or e-Governance. Between July and November 2012, Plan International, through the researchers Dr. John Lannon and Professor Edward Halpin, undertook a study of the "feasibility of a technologically enabled system to help respond to the phenomenon of cross-border child trafficking in South Asia, and makes recommendations on how to proceed with a pilot project in the selected areas of Bangladesh, Nepal and India" (Lannon & Halpin, 2013). The idea of an alert is not new. There are a number in operation; therefore, in terms of a technological solution, this seems perhaps a simple task: e-Government implementation with the support of governments. The issue is considerably more complex though, even with the good offices of governments and support of many good people, there were many administrative and political issues that required addressing, ranging from the processes for recording who is a missing child at local level by police to the political issues surrounding borders, migration, and repatriation. The development therefore is bureaucratic, legal, and political; it crosses political borders and administrative division, involves multiple actors, and requires a "whole-of-government approach." This is a complex e-Government and e-Governance issue, with real impact on communities, families, and vulnerable children. It certainly appears to fall within the imperative of the UN and requires cross border or regional intervention. In this case, the governments are working to together in working parties to address these issues and South Asia Initiative to End Violence Against Children (SAIEVAC), which is a South Asian Area for Regional Cooperation Apex body. This example serves to briefly illustrate how levels of complexity impact the introduction of a technological e-Government project, and the difficulty in achieving the imperative of the UN, even when, as is the case here, governments and NGOs are working hard to provide a solution, and it shows some coordinated success as there are now bilateral discussions in progress to use an existing system (DNAIndia, 2013).

With the issues of reality and practical application in mind, the editors have attempted to present the chapters in just two sections; the first deals with the technological and political issues associated with e-Government, administration, policy, politics, and management, whilst the second provides insights into specific rich case studies relating to countries and to issues. The division is probably false as allocating chapters is always difficult, as many could fit into other categories. It is also worth considering the argument presented by Professor Bannister (2012), when reflecting upon publication:

Research that investigates and describes practice in a rigorous and informative manner will always be of value in its own right and, being blunt, is often more useful to both academics and practitioners than abstruse and hard to operationalise theoretical concepts.

TECHNOLOGICAL AND POLITICAL IN DEVELOPING E-GOVERNMENT: ADMINISTRATION, POLICY, POLITICS, AND MANAGEMENT

In the first chapter by Muñoz and Bolívar, "Comparing E-Government Research in Developed vs. Emerging Economies: A Bibliometric Study," we are provided with an informative and thoughtful critical review of research in e-Government. The chapter suggests that many countries have implemented changes in public sector management models based on the strategic and intensive use of new information and communication technologies. However, most research has focused on developed countries, with the area of emerging economies being neglected. This chapter offers a framework to help public administrators and researchers evaluate the field of e-Government research in emerging economies, identifying research gaps and possibilities for improvement in the context of e-government research in developing countries. The findings reveal the existence of various research gaps and highlight areas that should be addressed in future research, especially in developing countries. Indeed, the research approach to e-government remains immature, focusing on particular cases or dimensions, while little has been done to produce theories or models to clarify and explain the political processes of e-government. There are important challenges provided to researchers and practitioners in the conclusions, including the following, which addresses the UN imperative and the issues raised in the foregoing introduction.

The authors of this chapter believe that a useful area for future study could be that of the policy-making processes in e-government projects in a complex political environment, and that the results of such future studies could strengthen the connection between e-government and the traditional concerns of public administration (Yildiz, 2007).

If Muñoz and Bolívar provide a challenge in the opening chapter, then Im, Park, and Prombescuask ask a very pertinent question in their chapter "E-Governmentization: A Panacea for the Democratization of Developing Countries?" The authors indicate that the objective of this chapter is to critically evaluate the e-governmentization of administrative processes, which many developing nations have come to enthusiastically espouse. From a theoretical perspective, such a trend is ostensibly positive, as e-government serves to promote transparency and efficient information exchange, which in turn serves to stimulate more equal distributions of power, inside as well as outside the bureaucracy, and perhaps most importantly (efficiently) solicit greater citizen participation. However, such benefits associated with the proliferation of e-government are often contingent upon a host of prerequisite conditions that, often times, developing nations do not meet. Therefore, such enthusiastic attempts by developing nations to e-governmentize administrative processes may be misplaced. As such, the primary thesis of this research is that the e-governmentization of administrative processes are likely to stimulate positive effects only after a certain level of democracy has been achieved. To explore this thesis, this chapter focuses on exploring the evolution and ensuing effects of the proliferation of e-government in South Korea.

In the conclusion, they assert that a consistent theme throughout the case of e-government discussed by this research is that, while e-governmentization offers the potential for enhancing citizen participation in government, this enhanced participation is allowed by existing organizational elites selectively to advance existing agendas, as was the case in China and South Korea, or opposed for the reason that the use of e-government services is perceived by government leaders as a threat to their legitimacy, as was suggested by the Indian case. However, while the use of e-government was assessed in only three nations, what is suggested is that it may be difficult to find instances where e-government was adopted strictly for the sake of enhancing democracy. Rather, what their analysis of three very different cases suggests is that success and failure of e-government projects is often a result of responses made by leaders at various levels of government attempting to consolidate their authority vis-à-vis other actors in society.

Next Alican, in the chapter "Political and Cultural Issues in Digital Public Administration" examines how the political and cultural aspects of digital public undertakings in developing countries are often neglected as more emphasis is placed on the technological components. The mutual impact between political or cultural issues and emerging trends such as cloud computing and social networks exacerbate the problem. This chapter analyzes political and cultural issues which have a significant impact on digital public administration and e-government initiatives in developing countries, also taking into consideration the emerging tendencies and technologies. It combines theory and practice, including studies that demonstrate different political or cultural issues involved in the digital undertakings in these countries, examples from different contexts and nations, and a case study from Turkey. The chapter starts with examples of different political issues, analyzing and summarizing some of the most relevant of these issues, including existing literature related to each subject. It continues with cultural issues. The subsequent section contains a discussion of how political and cultural issues relate to the tendencies of the Information and Communication Technologies (ICTs) sector, and why this context is important for digital initiatives in developing countries, as an initial guide to existing and future challenges. The chapter ends with the case of Turkey, which demonstrates political and cultural issues faced on both national and regional levels, in the context of digital public administration and emerging trends in ICTs.

In conclusion, the chapter suggests that the research data from Turkey illustrates clearly the importance and relevance of the political and cultural issues in digital public administration and e-government initiatives in developing countries, which are often considered and treated as a solely technological question. Here again we encounter the complexity of development of e-Government.

Ruhode provides the next chapter on "Integrated Architecture Framework for E-Government: A Socio-Technical Assessment of E-Government Policy Documents." He posits that emerging trends in Information and Communication Technologies (ICTs) in governments around the globe suggest that developing countries should embrace e-government as an enabler of efficient and effective service delivery. The Government of Zimbabwe, which is a case study in this chapter, is acutely aware of the critical role that ICTs play in socio-economic development. This chapter discusses Zimbabwe's e-government policies and programmes and maps them against the e-government architecture framework by Ebrahim and Irani (2005). The e-government architecture framework defines the standards, infrastructure components, applications, technologies, business models, and guidelines for electronic commerce among and between organisations that facilitate the interaction of the government and promote group productivity. The study is theoretically based upon the socio-technical theory, whose view suggests the existence of a technical sub-system and a social sub-system in an organisation. This theory has been adopted in this study to explain the complex relation between the government as an institution and e-government as an artifact. Drawing from the e-government architecture framework and the social-technical theory, an integrated e-government assessment framework is developed to explain the nature of relationships among government, citizens, and technology. At the conclusion of the chapter, an e-government architecture framework that underpins a successful e-government implementation is offered and could provide a valuable tool to examine the challenges explored in other chapters.

Islam and Ehsan provide us with a theoretical and conceptual chapter titled, "E-Governance as a Paradigm Shift in Public Administration: Theories, Applications, and Management," in which they suggest that an effort to claim for a paradigm shift in an academic discipline is daunting. Without a firm-rooted trend, distinguishing characteristics and evidence-based transformation, the claim for a paradigm shift would be futile. How far e-governance has provided and managed a space for a shift in paradigm is still debatable in the academic circle. However, the trends and applications are so widespread, inevitable, and visible that a modest claim for a paradigm shift is timely and due. The fundamental reasons and clues for such a "claim" are justified by the transformation that occurred not only in the processes and practices of public administration, policy, and management, but also in the structure that shapes it. From a systems approach, the changes are evident in inputs, throughputs, and outputs, thus bringing out a holistic transformation in public administration functionaries. No doubt that a system of public administration is all-pervasive and has been ubiquitous since times immemorial. Today, what we understand as the public administration existed even before the birth of modern states. The nature, functions, and mode of public service delivery, however, have gone through radical changes from those earlier times. This chapter offers an extension of public administration paradigms proposed and postulated by Henry (1995) and Gotembiewski (1977). It also deals with the basic theoretical backgrounds of e-governance, its types of ICT-driven service delivery, and transformation phases.

From their research, Islam and Ehsan indicate that, as is evident, e-governance facilitates development and offers many benefits to the citizens. It has the potential that made governments around the world initiate innovative changes in the delivery of public services. The issues of poverty reduction, economic underdevelopment, illiteracy, and pervasive corruption can be minimized, if not completely eliminated, through the skilful application of e-governance initiatives. Despite its enormous potential, it is also true that the benefits of e-governance are not duly reaped by the governments, both in developed and developing countries. The main stumbling blocks in the way are the political leadership and bureaucratic inertia. Another major concern for global equitable access of e-governance is the "digital divide," often called an "information black hole." As indicated, e-governance can very positively direct a paradigm shift, from traditional bureaucratic administration to a more responsive, accountable, and effective public administration that many governments around the world are aspiring to obtain. This is perhaps a more utopian and positive perspective than some of the previous or later chapters, but it is valuable in creating a theoretical perspective.

Roman next offers an interesting and valuable perspective that provides some further analysis of the maturity of e-Government development in the chapter "Realizing E-Government: Delineating Implementation Challenges and Defining Success." The assertion by Roman is that there is a growing recognition among scholars, practitioners, and elected officials that e-government success is not a deterministic outcome of entrepreneurial design or exacting implementation. In fact, constructing cost-efficient and policy effective e-government platforms has proved to be much more challenging than originally expected. In many instances, failed e-government experiments have led to significant financial losses and to increased dissatisfaction levels among citizenry. These latter experiences have nuanced the need for a much more thorough understanding and appreciation for the difficulties faced within the conceptualization and application of e-government platforms and in successfully achieving the expected administrative and democratic outcomes. This chapter, by tracing the evolution of e-government both as a concept and as an administrative trend within the transformation of governance, delineates the main challenges in achieving the core goals and the democratic scope of e-governance. It is argued that in e-governance, success is a function of three fundamental vectors – security, functionality, and transformation. In concluding, Roman suggests that functionality is most often emphasised as the primary factor within the design of e-Government projects, that security is often only considered later in the implementation process, and that transformation is rarely considered but is more often than not unwarrantedly expected to be a deterministic outcome of technology adoption.

Alvarez and Crespo provide a chapter that considers the "Design of a Triple Helix Strategy for Developing Nations Based on E-Government and Entrepreneurship: An Application to Ecuador." The chapter provides a case study of Ecuador, taking us from the arrival of Rafael Correa in Ecuador and the delivery of a structural transformation of the Ecuadorian economy and society, with the implementation of e-Government and the introduction of the digital economy in the country. The objective of this chapter is to design a strategy based on entrepreneurship, e-Government, and higher education for creating a digital society in Ecuador (the triple helix strategy). To achieve this, the authors analyse the Ecuadorian's National Plan for Good Living 2013-2017 linked to higher education reforms, and the influence of the European-based e-Government policies in Ecuador. They finish with some perspectives and the foreseeable impact of a digital society in this developing nation. In this conclusion, there is allusion to the UN whole-government approach and also the conception of an emerging international e-Government relationship.

In the following chapter, we are challenged by Asquer, who takes us into the realm of "gamification" in a chapter titled "Not Just Videogames: Gamification and its Potential Application to Public Services." In this chapter, the aim is to discuss how the emerging process of gamification can impact the production of public services. Gamification is a relatively recent phenomenon that relates, in broad terms, to the introduction to game elements in non-game contexts. After reviewing the concept, design principles and techniques, and effects of gamification, the chapter discusses the extent to which gamification may affect the production and delivery of public services. The conclusions discuss the possible role of gamification in reshaping the identity and role of citizens and their relationship with public authorities. This alternative perspective brings a new opportunity and is already attracting interest within the world of practice and academia, providing a new perspective through which to view the development and delivery of e-Government.

Molina and Soler, in the next chapter, offer us the opportunity to explore "The Use of Social Network Sites to Market E-Government to Citizens." In this chapter, the authors explore the different literature that analyses the application of Social Network Sites (SNSs) in e-government to help government managers to improve citizens' communication and participation. The use of Web 2.0 tools is perceived as a new way of communication not only in the political arena but also on the government level to improve civic engagement, to coproduce public services, and to increase service personalization. Citizens still like traditional communication tools, and it is important not to overload them through SNSs. The authors show possible new trends for future analysis on the application of SNSs. In their conclusion, a very strong point made is that beyond the benefits that a higher interaction with citizens can have, governments should also consider that these tools are used to define a new kind of society, a Network Society (Castells, 2009), in which new forms of self-organizational processes appear. In this context, governments "fear to lose the control of information and communication in which power has always been rooted" (Castells, 2005), so a new wave of democratization of communication should always be considered when defining Web 2.0 strategies. In this single point, the authors take us past the issues of technology into e-Governance and also into e-Politics, where perhaps some future challenges await.

EVIDENCE: CASE STUDIES AND ISSUES OF E-GOVERNMENT IN PRACTICE AND REALITY

In their chapter "Articulating Wider Smartphone Emerging Security Issues in the Case of M-Government in Turkey," Kervenoael and Yfantis, take us straight to an implementation issue from the previous section and provide us with insight from their example. They claim that for several years mobile devices and platform security threats, including wireless networking technology, have been top security issues. A departure has occurred from automatic anti-virus software based on traditional PC defense: risk management (authentication and encryption), compliance, and disaster recovery following polymorphic viruses and malware as the primary activities within many organizations and government services alike. While private services will surely continue to take the lead, others such as government and NGOs are also becoming prominent m-players, reflecting on the meaning of Smartphone-based security threats.

Enhanced data services through smart phones raise expectations that governments will finally deliver secured services in line with consumer ICT lifestyles. To date, it is not certain which form of technological standards will take the lead. Yet, with the introduction of interactive applications and fully transactional services via 3G smart phones, many currently untapped segments of the population (without computers) have the potential to gain access at low cost to government services, but they also expose themselves to unknown threats. This chapter covers research in Turkey as a reflection of the current market – e-government started officially in 2008. This situation in an emerging country presents the current situation and resistances encountered while engaging with mobile and e-government interfaces. The authors contend that research is needed to understand more precisely security threats and most of all potential solutions for sustainable future intention to use m-government services. Finally, beyond m-government initiatives' success or failure, the mechanisms related to public administration mobile technical capacity building and security issues are discussed. In concluding, the authors take us to ethical questions related to security and privacy that are significant, known, but sometimes perhaps overlooked.

In the chapter by Siddiquee and Gofran, "A Road Far Too Long? E-Government and Service Delivery in Bangladesh," we begin to explore development in some of the countries that are considered to be developing; we are fortunate to have more than one perspective on e-Government in Bangladesh, which will provide good opportunity for comparison and conjunction. In this chapter, we are provided with a review of the state of e-government development and associated changes to service delivery in Bangladesh. Using the "stage model" as a frame of reference, the authors show the progresses Bangladesh has made in terms of informational, interactive, transactional, and integrated services. They argue that although Bangladesh's overall progress is still modest for it allows only limited advanced levels of services, there are encouraging trends underway. In its conclusion, the chapter highlights some of the impediments and challenges that hamper e-government initiatives undermining their potentials and benefits in the country. Appositely, the authors declare that, since Bangladesh's problems are complex and multi-dimensional, there is no quick fix to such enormous challenges. What is needed is a sustained commitment on the part of the country's leadership and continuous drives to move the agenda forward with a robust implementation strategy in place. Given the arduous and stretched nature of the task, e-government must be seen as a journey rather than a destination.

Mahtab and Mahtab next offer us a perspective of e-Government that considers gender, development, and the socio-economic and cultural issues encountered by women in Bangladesh, in their chapter "Understanding ICT: The Potential and Challenges for the Empowerment of Rural Women in Bangladesh." This thorough examination of the various aspects of these issues provides valuable insights into the digital divide in real terms, as well as the gender divide. The concluding comment, taken from a quote, is a powerful indicator of the significance of empowerment for women and needs to be incorporated into the development of e-Government if Millennium Development Goals and the UN imperatives are to be achieved:

It is important to point out that empowerment is typically conceptualized as a process, and therefore change is at its very essence. Once a resource, capacity, or form of agency becomes commonplace, it no longer distinguishes more empowered women from the less empowered women. Therefore, it is relevant that the measurement of empowerment must change and adapt to keep up with the elusive phenomenon. (Schuler, Islam, & Rottach, 2010)

A third chapter on Bangladesh by Rokon-Ul-Hasan and Monem provides a further lens or perspective on "E-Governance Preparedness of Public Bureaucracy in Bangladesh." They suggest that in Bangladesh, there is an undeniable wave of awareness about e-governance at present. Therefore, it is high time that government prepare itself in terms of implementing e-governance in order to cope with the requirements of the fast changing global environment. As bureaucracy is one of the most vital pillars of government, it is imperative that it is well prepared to face the upcoming challenges of technological boost. This chapter assesses the preparedness level of bureaucracy from the perspective of e-governance implementation. Analysis of primary data reveals that the frequency of computer and Internet usage for official activities is also very low. Most of the officials do not have any formal ICT training, and those who have such training have covered only very elementary aspects. The overall readiness in terms of technical skills is found to be unsatisfactory. Existing laws, rules, and regulations are found to be very insufficient for smooth implementation of e-governance in Bangladesh.

The three chapters, taken individually, provide a very interesting insight and reflection upon e-Government development in Bangladesh, but if analysed collectively, they provide a magnificent insight into the complexity of the demands placed upon a developing country as it attempts to meet the needs of external arbiters, such as the UN, its own political and administrative needs, whilst also trying to engage and include its populous in real ways in the significant changes it is encountering, not only in terms of governance but also socio-economic, cultural, and most importantly, in addressing both digital and other divides that exist.

Next, we move to Mongolia, in the chapter provided by Baasanjav titled "Beyond the Digital Divide: Language Factors, Resource Wealth, and Post-Communism in Mongolia." This chapter explores the interplay between society and Internet technology in the context of the developing former socialist country of Mongolia. This chapter goes beyond questions of access to the Internet and explores three factors of the global digital divide. First, this chapter explores how language factors such as non-Roman domain names and the use of the Cyrillic alphabet exacerbate the digital divide in the impoverished country of Mongolia. ICANN's initiation of international domain names is an initial development toward achieving linguistic diversity on the Internet. Second, this chapter explores how post-communist settings and foreign investment and aid dependency afflict Internet development. A rapid economic growth in Mongolia has increased access to mobile phones, computers, and the Internet; however, the influx of foreign capital poured into the mining, construction, and telecommunication sectors frequently comes in non-concessional terms raising concerns over the public debt in Mongolia. The chapter exemplifies a very different set of issues of digital divide and political decision making providing us with another layer of complexity, which needs to be addressed in policy, practice, and the implementation of e-Government.

In the next chapter, the authors, Jahankhani, Dastbaz, Shareef, and Pimenidis, provide research findings from work in the Kurdistan Region of Iraq, which is titled "Developing a Citizen-Centric E-Government Model for Developing Countries: Case of Kurdistan Region of Iraq." This chapter presents an enhanced eGovernment stage model based on citizens' participation for improvements in the delivery of governmental services by putting citizens' insights and their requirements in the context of e-government development and the potential use of a multi-channel delivery of services for regional governments in developing countries. The model proposed is based on research done in the Kurdistan region of Iraq. This research identified missing elements in traditional eGovernment models that would prove essential for implementation in developing countries. These models usually propose five stages of development spanning from emergence to integration. The proposal here considers most of the limitations in two stages, namely initial and an enhancement stage with the advantage of decreasing the uncertainty of e-government implementation in the public sector by recognising the consequence of the institutional readiness, adoption processes, the needs of ICT tools, and the factors that influence the implementation process. The research concludes that current models of e-Government do not meet the needs or situation of Kurdistan, and the authors offer a new approach.

In Sri Lanka, the development of e-Government has been a long process, starting as early as 1983, but also having to be undertaken throughout an internal conflict, and now the country is in a post-conflict development state, still dealing with and responding to redevelopment required to recover, though with strong economic growth. Dissanayake and Dissanayake, in their chapter, "Development of E-Governance in Sri Lanka," provide a historical overview and the ongoing commitment to deliver e-Government in this context.

In the next chapter, titled "Rural-Urban Digital Divide in Romania," Stoica and Ilas provide valuable reflection upon e-Government and rural Romania. Their work describes how the last two decades witnessed the sudden raise in importance of Information and Communications Technology (ICT). Some societies have been quick to embrace the benefits of ICT, while others have used the new technologies in a rather limited way. A new term, "digital divide," was coined to describe the gap between the societies using ICT on a large scale and those with limited access. Much was written with respect to the causes of this gap. Factors such as socioeconomic conditions, geographical position, tradition, social and individual values are considered to play major roles in the creation of the digital divide. The vast majority of the studies have focused on the digital performance of cities with far less attention being paid to what was happening in the villages. Arguably, the villages greatly need and would benefit from e-Government, but the existing data shows that in many societies have a significant rural-urban digital divide is already in place. The goal of this research is to assess the urban-rural digital divide in Romania in terms of official Websites performances by evaluating five components: security and personal data protection, usability, content, type of services, and digital democracy. The authors conclude that in Romania, the rural-urban digital divide is extremely large. The digital divide in Romania clearly has more to do with the size of the conurbation and location than any other factor, which might be similar in other e-Government development projects in the developing world.

A second Romanian chapter deals with "ICTs and their Impact on Women's Roles and Evolution within Developing Societies" (Ionescu). In the chapter, Ionescu suggests that the Internet is definitely the most complex and dynamic technical and cultural phenomenon that humanity ever experienced. Nevertheless, despite its positive impact on the Western world, Web 2.0 has yet to prove its power in the undeveloped regions of the globe, where the Internet Era is still at its dawn. In developing countries, the barriers that women face, such as poverty or social imbalances, establish significant challenges that hinder connectivity and access to modern technologies. In this context, the chapter discusses the evolution of gender speech in relation to new Information and Communication Technologies (ICTs). The authors determine whether the declarations and plans for action that were issued subsequent to the 1995 Fourth World Conference on Women in Beijing enhanced the establishment of gendered policies on ICTs, particularly in the undeveloped regions of the world, and whether, in this way, they empower women, contribute to combating women's poverty, and promote gender equality. In conclusion, Ionescu fervently expresses her view on the gender imbalances and divides that exist.

The final two chapters both deal with the implementation of e-Government in health fields, providing us with a view that of a practitioner field. First, Schmeida and McNeal, offer a chapter titled "Medicare and Medicaid Services Online: Government Initiatives Narrowing Online Access Inequalities." They discuss government initiatives in the United States that have been passed in an effort to increase citizen usage of e-government programs. One such service is the availability of online health insurance information. However, not all demographic groups have been equally able to accessing these online services, primarily the poor and rural American. As more legislation is passed, including the advancement of broadband services to remote areas, infrastructure barriers are being removed, opening access to Medicare and Medicaid websites for these vulnerable groups. The purpose of this chapter is to analyze factors predicting the impact of recent government actions on citizen access to health insurance information online. This topic is explored using multivariate regression analysis and individual level data from the

Internet and American Life Project. The findings suggest that healthcare needs and quality of Internet access may be playing a more important role in health insurance information services than other factors. The concluding thoughts posited indicate that no matter what the technology is there is a key place for literacy and information literacy that needs to be addressed through education, approaches to supplying information online, or a combination of both.

In the final chapter, O'Hanlon considers "The Role of E-Health in Developing Nations." The chapter provides an excellent account of the current issues within the field of e-Health, providing us with a clear definition: e-Health is the use of information and communication technologies for health services. O'Hanlon contends that many developing nations have a government-operated health system and have introduced elements of e-Health to improve service provision. Despite being resource-limited and having a heavy disease burden, certain pioneers have shown that lack of funding is not an obstacle to leveraging technology. In addition, the leapfrog effect has allowed some developing countries to skip the fixed-line infrastructure development of the late 20th century and utilise modern mobile access to quickly and efficiently introduce new interventions. M-Health, or mobile information technology applications, has been shown to be an effective tool for the citizens of these countries. Telemedicine, or the practice of medicine at a distance, has also been used to introduce new services in developing countries by linking with specialists in centres of excellence.

Obstacles do exist: inadequate infrastructure cost of equipment and software, maintenance of data security, and the lack of a trained health informatics workforce. Several innovative solutions have been put forward: satellite broadband access for the most remote areas, international sponsorship initiatives, use of open source software, and exchange programmes for staff education. There is strong support for the development of this e-Health agenda from the World Health Organization and other international bodies. Significant ethical considerations impact the use of e-Health in developing countries. The issue of cost effectiveness of e-Health is also important, as the opportunity cost of providing it means that funding for other areas must be reduced. Unless there is good evidence for the efficacy of e-Health projects, this cannot be justified. There is a clear need for more research in this important area so that informed decisions can be made. In the concluding thoughts, O'Hanlon suggests that in order to help further development, steps must be taken to increase the informatics workforce and for developed nations to exchange knowledge and skills. Achieving this may make e-Health a very fruitful area in the developing world.

CONCLUDING THOUGHTS

At the start of the project, the editors set out to examine e-government from the perspective of the developing regions of the world and to explore issues of e-government policy and practice in these regions, combining scholarly research alongside practitioner case studies to provide a critical current perspective on e-government progress in the developing regions plus an evaluation of challenges for the future. The chapters, broad in coverage but focused in depth, have painted a rich analysis of a wide range of e-Government issues. Our audience, hopefully practitioners, e-Government developers, politicians, policy makers, decision makers, those who implement e-Government, students, and academics, should all be able to find significant new thought, challenges, and knowledge; Albert Einstein is said to have offered the following thought that might be useful to all of us in considering what we read here and what we do with the information we gain:

Any fool can know. The point is to understand.

Albert Einstein (1879 - 1955) Physicist & Nobel Laureate

The editors hope that this book will add to understanding, and to the development and implementation of e-Government and e-Governance in developing and developed countries in the future.

Edward Francis Halpin
Leeds Metropolitan University, UK

Carolynn Rankin
Leeds Metropolitan University, UK

REFERENCES

Bannister, F. (2012). *Case Studies in e-Government*. Reading, MA: Academic Publishing International.

Castells, M. (2005). The Network Society: From Knowledge to Policy. In M. Castells, & G. Cardoso (Eds.), *The Network Society: From Knowledge to Policy* (pp. 3–22). Washington, DC: Center for Transatlantic Relations.

Castells, M. (2009). *The rise of the network society: The information age*. Chichester, UK: Wiley-Blackwell. doi:10.1002/9781444319514

DNAIndia. (2013, October 5). Retrieved April 28, 2014, from http://www.dnaindia.com/world/report-bangladesh-nepal-to-use-indian-system-for-missing-children-1898872

Ebrahim, Z., & Irani, Z. (2005). E-government adoption: Architecture and barriers. *Business Process Management Journal*, *11*(5), 589–611. doi:10.1108/14637150510619902

Gotembiewsky, R. T. (1977). *Public Administration as a developing discipline, part I: Perspectives on past and present*. New York: Marcel Dekker.

Henry, N. (1995). *Public administration and public affairs*. New York: Prentice-Hall, Inc.

Lannon, J., & Halpin, E. (2013). *Responding to cross border child trafficking in south Asia: An analysis of the feasability of a technological enabled missing children alert system*. Bangkok, Thailand: Plan International.

Schuler, S. R., Islam, F., & Rottach, E. (2010). Women's empowerment revisited: A case study from Bangladesh. *Development in Practice*, *20*(7), 840–854. doi:10.1080/09614524.2010.508108 PMID:20856695

United Nations. (2012). *United Nations e-government survey 2012 e-government for the people*. New York: United Nations.

Yildiz, M. (2007). E-government research: Reviewing the literature, limitations, and ways forward. *Government Information Quarterly*, 646–665. doi:10.1016/j.giq.2007.01.002

Acknowledgment

The editors would like to acknowledge the help of all of those involved in the drafting and review process of this book. Without their input and support the book could not have been developed and delivered.

In particular, thanks are due to our colleagues at IGI, especially Austin DeMarco, Managing Editor-Book Development, for his patience, determination, and wise counsel, and also to Christine Smith, Development Editor, who stuck with us through some difficult times.

We would like to thank all of the authors for their excellent contributions to this book. Without their insight and expertise it would not have been possible to provide a book with such breadth and detail in this rapidly changing and challenging world of e-Government.

Finally, thanks to Carolynn Rankin, who joined the editorial team at a point when we faced many challenges for a variety of reasons. Her fortitude, skill, and quiet determination have been significant in bringing this book to publication.

Edward Francis Halpin
Leeds Metropolitan University, UK

David Griffin
Leeds Metropolitan University, UK

Carolynn Rankin
Leeds Metropolitan University, UK

Lakshman Dissanayake
University of Colombo, Sri Lanka

Nazmunnessa Mahtab
University of Dhaka, Bangladesh

Section 1
Technological and Political in Developing E–Government:
Administration, Policy, Politics, and Management

Chapter 1
Comparing E–Government Research in Developed vs. Emerging Economies:
A Bibliometric Study

Laura Alcaide Muñoz
University of Granada, Spain

Manuel Pedro Rodríguez Bolívar
University of Granada, Spain

ABSTRACT

Many countries have implemented changes in public sector management models based on the strategic and intensive use of new information and communication technologies. However, most research has focused on developed countries, with the area of emerging economies being neglected. This chapter offers a framework to help public administrators and researchers evaluate the field of e-Government research in emerging economies, identifying research gaps and possibilities for improvement in the context of e-government research in developing countries. The findings reveal the existence of various research gaps and highlight areas that should be addressed in future research, especially in developing countries. Indeed, the research approach to e-government remains immature, focusing on particular cases or dimensions, while little has been done to produce theories or models to clarify and explain the political processes of e-government.

INTRODUCTION

The emergence of information and communication technology (ICT) in the field of public administration has aroused widespread interest in the search for mechanisms enabling the public administration to make a more positive impact on daily life. This tendency is understood to be one of the forms of expression of the information society, in addition to being a central part of the process of the modernization of public administration (Park & Joo, 2010), allowing a strategic and intensive use of

DOI: 10.4018/978-1-4666-3691-0.ch001

ICT (Dunleavy et al., 2005), both in the internal relations of public administrations (Edelenbos & Klijn, 2007) and in terms of the relationship of these organizations with citizens (Kim et al., 2011) and with companies in the private sector (Callanan, 2005).

In consequence, e-government has become a key issue in political agendas concerning public administration reform (Jaeger, 2005). To date, most e-Government research has focused on developed countries, neglecting the area of emerging economies. Indeed, up to now, e-Government research on emerging economies seems to have been neither meaningful nor homogeneous. In addition, the large number of studies and research projects published in this respect draws upon various reference disciplines, including public administration, computer science, political science, management, and library and information science (Manoharan, 2013). Since its appearance, e-government researchers have explored the past, present and future development of the field (Bannister & Connolly, 2012).

In view of this heterogeneity on the question of e-Government in emerging economies, and in the belief that scientific evidence is not the result of a single research study but rather the aggregation and accumulation of knowledge supported by the foundations of prior research (Rodríguez et al., 2010; Alcaide et al., 2012), in our opinion it is necessary to perform critical integrative reviews of literature in this field in order to enhance our knowledge of e-Government and to acquire a broad view of the current state and possibilities in e-Government research in the future. For this purpose, we propose a descriptive bibliometric methodology (Cocosila et al., 2011) that has been comprehensively tested in the field of information science (Chang & Huang, 2012; Tseng & Tsay, 2013), and more currently used in the field of public administration (Lecy et al., 2013; Raadschelders & Lee, 2011).

Accordingly, this paper constitutes a bibliometric study analysing the journals with greatest international impact (according to Journal Citation Reports) listed in the fields of Information Science and Library Science and of Public Administration. This review process involved the analysis of 114 journals catalogued by the ISI as belonging to the areas of *Public Administration* or *Information Science & Library Science,* published between 2000 and 2013. This procedure highlighted, among other factors, the most significant approaches, the subjects which have aroused most interest, the journals in which studies have been published and the methodologies used to analyse this phenomenon.

The remainder of this chapter is organized as follows. In the next section, a literature review related to relevant bibliometric studies is performed. In section three, the research methodology used is outlined, and then the results obtained in the empirical research are analysed. Finally, the main conclusions of this study are summarized and some questions on future trends in this area are highlighted for discussion.

LITERATURE REVIEW ON BIBLIOMETRIC STUDIES

Bibliometric reviews enable members of the academic community to identify the historical roots of a particular field of study (Atkins, 1988), to predict future research trends (Löfstedt, 2005), and to discern the direction taken in a discipline, possible inadequacies in methodology, weaknesses, trivial approaches, etc., - in summary, they provide a starting point which greatly facilitates the enhancement of knowledge.

This tool has been widely used in research field such as Library Information Science (LIS) (Chang & Huang, 2012; Tseng & Tsay, 2013), allowing the knowledge of the evolution of this interdisciplinary field, journals taken as a reference by researchers, the input knowledge, research gaps, trends and future opportunities. Similarly, there are studies that present the profile of the researchers, the pattern for scientific collaboration and the knowledge organization in the area of Information Science, contributing to a better understanding of the characteristics of this academic field (Gomes de Souza & Azevedo Ferreira, 2013).

In the field of public administration, there has been a great deal of research, leading to lively debate and discussion network-focused research in the public administration (Lecy et al., 2013). Lecy et al., (2013) organize the network literature in public administration using compact citation networks to identify coherent subdomains focused on policy formation, governance and policy implementation. Thus, it is identified promising research avenues focused on the wider adoption of methods derived from social networks analysis. In addition, Raadschelders and Lee (2011) show a marked increase in the application of more sophisticated quantitative statistical methodology in Public Administration field, and a sharp reduction in the number of practitioner authors. Also, they highlight the main topics analyzed by researchers and central challenge in the years ahead.

In the field of e-Government, until recently very few bibliometric studies had been carried out. Yildiz (2007) discusses the limitations of prior research in this area, such as vagueness in the definition of e-Government, and points out the need for empirical studies which would lead to new theoretical arguments in addition to new concepts and categories. Heeks & Bailur (2007) focus their analysis on perspectives regarding e-Government, research philosophy and the use of theory, analysing only academic talks given at scientific conferences in Europe and articles published in two journals listed on the JCR index, thus giving a partial analysis of this question. However, we intend to go further, making a complete and thorough review with the ambition that researchers may make use of our results to establish relationships that promote the maturity of this topic, and exploit possible synergies.

Similarly, Rodríguez et al. (2010) provided an overview of previous research into e-government,

making a detailed analysis of the contributions published in public administration and information science journals from 2000 to 2009. These authors concluded that quantitative research methodologies should be applied so that theoretical frameworks may be established (Bailey, 1992; Land & Anders, 2000), because if a field of study is to reach maturity, more sophisticated and objective quantitative methodologies must be used. Only thus can theoretical approaches be tested, validated, and definitively accepted. By this means, an interdisciplinary field of study such as e-government can be assigned specific, targeted theories, derived from different areas of research, and the successful implementation of public policies can be promoted.

Nevertheless, the above type of bibliometric study is under-represented in academic literature, and many possibilities are neglected of predicting future research trends, of determining the direction a discipline should take in order to achieve maturity and thus of improving understanding in a given area of research. In the case of e-Government, the findings from such studies could be used by researchers, government managers and decision takers to better plan for e-Government, to compare the different situations found in developed countries, to examine how strategic e-Government plans are being addressed, and to analyse successes made and failures suffered. These findings would be of use to leaders and managers in emerging countries, facilitating development and enabling them to achieve the maturity of more favoured economies.

EMPIRICAL ANALYSIS OF RESEARCH IN THE FIELD OF E-GOVERNMENT

Sample Collection

This study is focused on analysing journal publications, in the view that they constitute a resource that is often used by academics as a source of new knowledge and as a medium for its disclosure (Nord & Nord, 1995), and at the same time, as an indicator of scientific productivity (Legge & Devore, 1987). Symposia, summaries of communications, letters to the editor, articles of a professional nature and book reviews were excluded from this analysis because, in our opinion, they offer a limited view of the subject. However, we did take into account articles included in special issues of journals, considering that these reflect a greater interest in the study of a particular issue and in the need to examine it further (Rodríguez et al., 2010).

We have used objective criteria such as the citation rate, impact factor, immediacy index and number of source items (Gordon, 1982) as references to select the journals with which to carry out our analysis. The reason for this choice is to avoid the bias found when subjective criteria are used (Vocino & Elliott, 1982), although it is true that objective indicators, too, have their critics (Cameron, 2005). Nevertheless, Garfield (1972) defended the use of indicators based on the citation methodology because they provide useful data. For this reason, and taking into account the findings of previous studies (Plümper & Radaelli, 2004), we excluded listed journals of marginal importance, i.e. those with an impact factor of less than 0.25 or with fewer than 50 total citations for the year 2012.

According to the International Statistical Institute (2012), Malaysia, Romania and the countries of Latin America were all defined as developing countries in 2012 because they did not meet World Bank requirements (2011) to be defined as developed countries. Furthermore, except for Chile and Uruguay, all of these countries obtain fewer than 50 points on the latest Corruption Perception Index (CPI) published by Transparency International in 2012 (http://www.transparency.org/cpi2012). In this regard, although the CPI has been much criticised, it has been shown to exercise great influence both in academic research and in anti-corruption policies (Andersson & Heywood, 2009).

In recent years, governments in all of these countries have taken steps to foster the information society (United Nations, 2003 and 2012), developing programmes and initiatives to implement ICTs in diverse areas in order to enhance the transparency of management, reduce corruption and promote and expand citizens' participation. These initiatives have not yet been fully implemented, according to research carried out in these countries – for Latin American countries, see Caba et al. (2010), for Malaysia, see Seng et al. (2010) and for Romania, see Velicu (2012) – and this was also confirmed in the latest UN E-government Report (United Nations, 2012). Therefore, although there has been some growth in e-government in these countries, much remains to be done.

Our book chapter seeks to include all journals indexed in the year 2012 and which achieve the stipulated impact factor in the areas of Public Administration and of Information Science & Library Science and also, irrespective of the impact factor achieved and even if they have received fewer than 50 total citations. The inclusion of these journals in the present study provides a more precise view of the status of e-government research being conducted in less developed countries on initiatives and experiences undertaken in these countries, enabling a more complete and up-to-date view and enriching the comparison and differentiation of research into e-government in developing *versus* developed countries

In determining the articles to be included in the sample, we analysed all the articles published in the journals that met the above-described criteria for inclusion. To do this, we first examined the title and the keywords of each one (Lan & Anders, 2000; Plümper & Radaelli, 2004). These descriptors provided an initial idea of the topic addressed in the article. If the keywords offered were generic and did not provide a clear idea about the research topic discussed, we then read the abstract, to obtain a better view of the article.

If doubts remained, we then read the introduction to identify the research goals and to determine the main factors analysed. Finally, in the very few cases when these discriminant criteria were insufficient, we read the whole article.

As a result, we obtained a database composed of 932 articles published during the period 2000-2013, in 114 journals catalogued by the ISI as belonging to the areas of *Public Administration* or *Information Science & Library Science*. In the first of these areas, there were 45 journals, of which 32 (71.11%) published articles on e-government, while in the second, there were 69, of which 29 (42.03%) published articles on e-government. In this sense, 932 met the selection criteria established and focused on e-Government in the two field analysis, with 592 articles in Information Science and Library Science journals (63.42%) and 340 articles in Public Administration journals (36.48%).

Meanwhile, in the two groups of results analysed below emerging and developed countries –twelve of the articles take into account data for both types of countries, 105 non-empirical stud-ies, 29 informetrics analysis, 24 studies in European countries and 48 studies with internacional perspectives. Therefore, we review 559 articles examining e-Government in developed countries and 179 articles examining the questions from the standpoint of emerging countries –see Figure 1.

Research Methodology

To fulfil our goals for this chapter, each of the articles included in the data base was classified, using MS Excel software, by year of publication, journal title, the institutional affiliation of the authors (departments and universities), the main subject addressed and the principal methodology used. When the articles examined multiple research topics and/or used multiple methods, double counting was avoided by focusing exclusively on the main research item and methodology used. To ensure this approach, it was essential to identify the main aim of the paper. In addition, to determine the number of departments and universities of origin, each article is considered as a single unit, and divided among the number

Figure 1. Studies in developed countries vs. studies in emerging countries

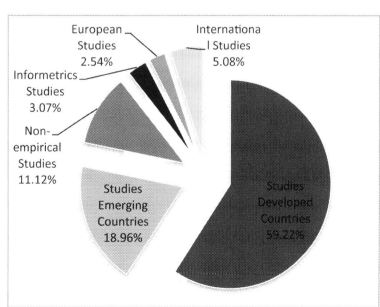

of authors. Therefore, if an article is signed by three authors from different universities, each University is assigned one third of this article; if the article is authored by four persons from three different universities, then two universities are each assigned one quarter, and the other is assigned the remaining two quarters. The same process is applied to the departments.

To determine the subjects addressed and methodologies applied, the authors conducted a content analysis of each article separately. The content analysis method is considered appropriate because it exhibits the following characteristics: (a) it is systematic, following a planned approach, such as selecting export-related articles in accordance with explicit and defensible rules and examining their content in exactly the same way; (b) it is objective, adopting an explicit set of rules that minimize the possibility of the findings' reflecting the analyst's subjective predispositions, rather than the content of the articles under analysis; and (c) it is quantitative, measuring the extent of emphasis or omission of any given analytic category, thus enhancing the precision of the conclusions drawn and permitting a more accurate description of results (Krippendorff, 1980).

In order to determine the main categories to be analysed in our study, first, categories were selected and adapted from those previously used in public administration research by Bingham & Bowen (1994), Lan & Anders (2000) and, recently, by Rodríguez et al, (2010) and Alcaide et al., (2012) (Figure 2).

Comparative Analysis of the Results in Developed Countries vs. Emerging Economies

1. Chronological evolution of e-government research topics and JCR journals.

Growing interest in the implementation of ICTs in the area of public administration has been reflected in a gradual increase in the amount of research carried out in the field of e-Government in recent years (Rodríguez et al., 2010; Alcaide et al., 2012), especially regarding modernization in the management of public administration and institutional change (25.43%), deliberative democracy and Web 2.0 (24.79%), delivery of public services (14.27%), accountability, transparency and dissemination of information (12.34%) and

Figure 2. The main research topic about e-Government

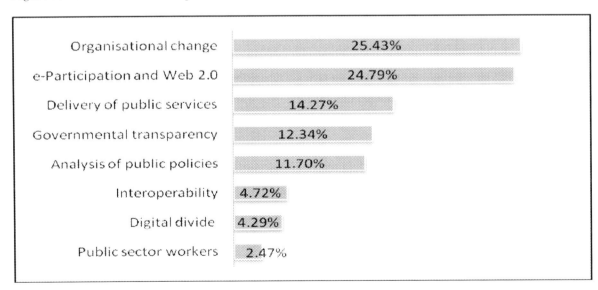

e-Government programme/project evaluation and policy analysis (11.70%) –see Figure 2.

On the chronological evolution of given research topics (Figures 3 and 4), among the main topics covered in the literature on e-Government, the participation of citizens in decision making show a clear upward trend over the year, mainly due to the importance attached by Government to promoting e-democracy and the reducing political corruption, encouraging transparency and the accountability of public managers (Lio et al., 2011), as well as, the increasingly frequent use of Web 2.0 technologies by public administrations (Mergel, 2013) –see Figure 3. Hence, research studies dealing with accountability, transparency and the dissemination of information have been conspicuously present from 2000 to 2013, with researchers being mainly concerned with analysing the openness, access and information transparency of developed governments. However, researchers have not paid so much attention to information transparency among less developed countries.

Similarly, studies on the usefulness of e-Government as a tool for improving service delivery showed a decreasing trend from 2005 to 2008, although this trend has changed from 2009 to a moderate growth until 2013. This is mainly due to the discussion made in the first studies regarding the reasons for the development of the provision of online services through supply-side indicators in order to evaluate government Web sites (Gouscos et al., 2007). However, recent studies show the demand perspective, using the Technology Acceptance Model (TAM) or the Theory of Planned Behaviuor (TPB) (Wang & Lo, 2013), determining the factors that influence the intention of citizens to use government Web sites (Susanto & Goodwin, 2013), as the user satisfaction is crucial to the continued use of e-Government service factor, and thus the success or failure of e-Government projects (Alawneh et al., 2013).

On the other hand, articles on the modernization of governments have always been present, although there is a rising trend with respect to

Figure 3. Chronological distribution of e-Participation, delivery of public services and government transparency studies

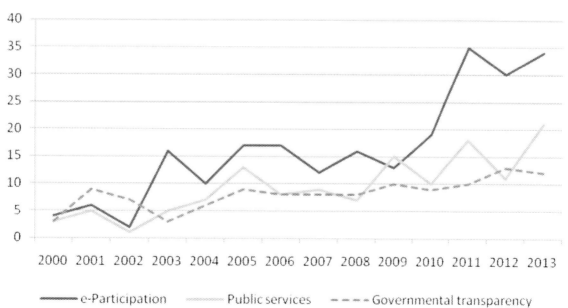

Figure 4. Chronological distribution of organizational change and public policies studies

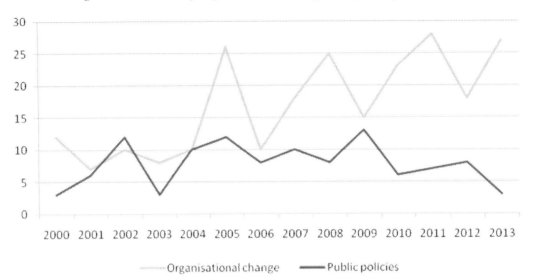

change in organizational structure and institutional factors in developed countries –see Figure 4-. In this sense, there are studies that have treated how Customer Relationship Management (CRM) has represented an organizational change in local government (Reddick, 2011), as well as other studies showing that the implementation of new technologies entails decentralization, differentiation and division of departments in the management of government institutions (Gao et al., 2013). In the case of public policy in e-Government, we can see that this research topic has shown a decreasing trend since 2005 with an upward spike in 2009 before falling again until 2013 – see Figure 4. In this regard, recent studies evaluate whether the development of e-Government in emerging and transition countries is being consistent with the principles set (Yuan et al., 2012), examining whether these countries have the strategic and financial resources needed, and whether they have the support and international assistance (Kromidha, 2012).

Meanwhile, some subjects have not been thoroughly examined in the JCR journals analysed, such as intergovernmental relations (4.72%),

digital divide and barriers of resistance to e-Government (4.29%) and e-Government and human resources (2.47%) – see Figure 2. The reason for the apparent lack of interest in these subjects, on the whole, is not their lesser importance but rather the fact that they are often published and listed in different research fields, e.g., studies of organization theory or human resources may be included in management journals.

Nevertheless, the presence of e-Government research is still scarce, with the articles published in this field in JCR-listed journals (Rodríguez et al., 2010; Alcaide et al., 2012), and the majority of these (63.42%) are in the field of Information Science and Library Science. In this regard, whereas there is a clear preference for one journal in the field of Information Science and Library Science to publish this type of research, with more than 46% being published in *Government Information Quarterly* –see Figure 5. In the field of Public Administration there is a preference for two journals, *Public Administration Review* and *Journal CLAD. Reform and Democracy*, which together account for 23.89% of the articles published –see Figure 5.

Figure 5. The main Information Science and Library Science journals and Public Administration journals which published articles about e-government

Abbreviations: GIQ (Government Information Quarterly); SSCORE (Social Science Computer Review); IS (The Information Society); IJIM (International Journal of Information Management); ASLIB (Aslib Proceedings); ITD (Information Technology for Development); EJIS (European Journal of Information Systems); PAR (Public Administration Review); CLAD (Revista CLAD. Reforma y Democracia - Journal CLAD. Reform and Democracy); ARPA (American Review of Public Administration); IRAS (International Review of Administrative Sciences); AS (Administration & Society); PA (Public Administration); LGS (Local Government Studies) and JPART (Journal of Public Administration Research and Theory).

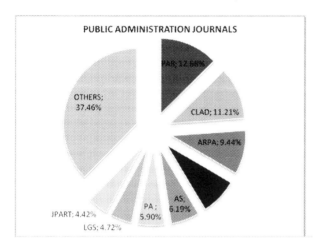 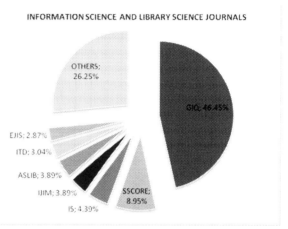

2. Methodologies used in e-government articles.

Focusing on the methodology used in the articles published on e-Government, we observe a preference for the use of empirical research methods (827/932; 88.73%), over non-empirical ones (105/932; 11.27%). In the case of studies on developed countries, the percentage of empirical studies (85.74%) is lower than that corresponding to studies of emerging countries (100%) –see Figure 6-. In both cases, there is a clear preference for the use of qualitative tools (55.06% in studies of developed countries and 72.63% in studies of emerging countries), although this trend seems to be weakening as time passes (see Figure 7), i.e. researchers are increasingly relying on quantitative methodologies for analysing the phenomena of e-Government, at the expense of qualitative methodologies, as shown in Figure 7. In this sense, the quantitative methodologies used in the studies in developed countries has undergone a rapid

increase since 2010, while in the case of studies in emerging countries show a slowdown in 2009, although it has increased since 2010.

With regards to qualitative methodologies, we can see that the cases studies are the main methodological tools in the analysis of developed and emerging countries, followed at a great distance by content analysis and comparative analysis –see Figure 8. Also, the researchers use a wider variety of qualitative methodologies to analysis e-Government experiences in developed countries, such as ethnographic study, exploratory study, life history study, social network analysis or Webometric approach. However, to examine e-Government initiatives in emerging countries the scholars use a limited variety of qualitative techniques, such as legislature approach, feasibility study or holistic approach.

To analyse e-Government experiences in developed and emerging countries, the most widely used quantitative methodology is regression analysis (44.50% and 38.78%) –see Figure 9. In

Figure 6. Methodologies used in studies in developed countries vs. studies in emerging countries

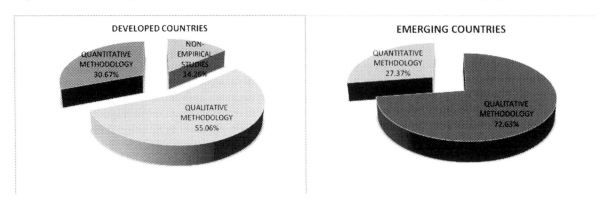

Figure 7. Temporal trends in the use of methodologies in studies of emerging countries and studies of developed countries

Abbreviations: QUAL MET EMER (Qualitative methodologies in emerging countries); QUAL MET DEVE (Qualitative methodologies in developed countries); QUAN MET EMER (Quantitative methodologies in emerging countries); QUAN MET DEVE (Quantitative methodologies in developed countries)

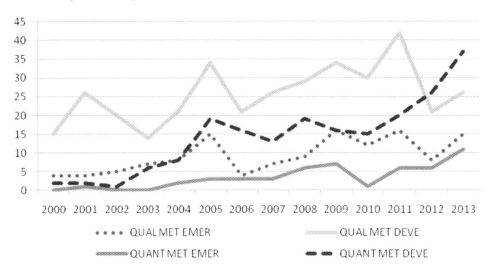

the case of e-Government practices in emerging countries, the most another widely used quantitative methodologies are structural equation models (26.53%), followed at a considerable distance by other methodologies. In this sense, factorial methodologies are also frequently used tools in the analysis of e-Government initiatives in this case. Meanwhile, logistic regressions are used by researchers in the analysis of e-Government practices in developed countries.

In summary, investigators tend to make more use of qualitative than quantitative methodologies in both cases, but in studies of developed countries the use of qualitative methodologies is lower. With respect to emerging countries, over time greater use is also being made of quantitative methodologies; moreover, no theoretical studies have been published. Accordingly, we conclude that whilst studies carried out in developed countries reflect an advanced phase of research into e-Government,

Figure 8. Qualitative methodologies used in studies of developed countries and studies of emerging countries

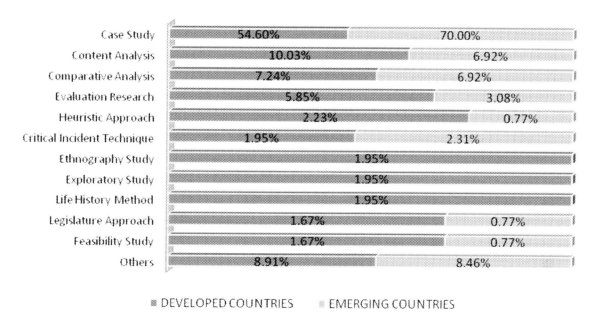

Figure 9. Quantitative methodologies used in studies of developed countries and studies of emerging countries

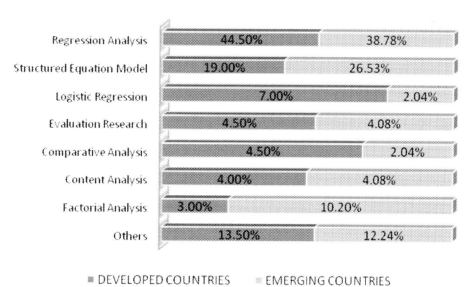

in emerging countries, the work carried out remains insufficient. Therefore, in this chapter, we are focusing on quantitative empirical studies, so that the results obtained may highlight the degree of progress achieved in e-Government research.

3. The most important contributions in the field of e-government research and the main journals that published articles about e-government in emerging countries.

With respect to the year of publication of e-government articles with great impact (see Appendix 1), most were published in the early years of research in this field (2001-2002) by leading international journals. These articles, to a large extent, laid the foundations for e-government research, documenting the main aspects of the public administration reforms carried out to date. Since then, these articles have been cited regularly in later studies. As e-government was initially developed in the USA, the authors of these studies were mainly located in US universities and focused their studies on the evolution of e-government in the US context.

Other areas that have been addressed in e-government research are those of technological innovation and public services delivered through the internet; the latter is a newer area of research and articles with the greatest impact were mainly published in 2004 and 2005, although the field continues to develop rapidly, and the pace of publication has risen since 2008. As regards the provision of public services through the internet, the most influential articles, rather than focusing on the involvement of new technologies in public administration reforms for service provision, focus more on their impact on users, seeking to explain citizens' perceptions, and considering the factors facilitating acceptance of these services.

Regarding the e-government research in emerging economies, the articles are less cited than those in developed countries and the most cited

articles are those that are the earliest one. These studies focused on organizational transformation of public administrations following the adoption of new technologies to streamline and re-invent their obsolete operations. Similarly, they have addressed how government leaders are using information technology to drive effort both to accelerate decentralized public administration and at the same time to enhance government's ability to oversee key activities.

Meanwhile, the recent studies analyzed the factors that influencing the intention to use e-Government service among citizens and showed how trust, perceived usefulness, perceived image could have a relationship towards intention to use e-government services. Similarly, they showed how online public services are of considerable social and economic value to the citizens because they saved time, money and effort compared with obtaining the services directly from the government office, and also examine the problems and circumstances did not favor the success of e-Government program

Regarding the main journals that published articles on e-Government in emerging countries, it can be seen in Appendix 2 that, in general, there is considerable divergence in the articles published between journals whose editorial offices are located in developing countries and those in developed countries. The former group mainly publish e-government research focused on these countries, while in the latter group, with the exception of *Public Administration and Development* in the area of Public Administration, and *Information Development, Information Technology for Development,* and *Journal of Global Information Technology and Management* in the area of Information Science & Library Science, the studies published focus on e-government in developed countries. These findings indicate that regardless of the subject area addressed by journals, perhaps the essential criterion for acceptance of a research article is that of the geographic area considered.

Only a very few journals – for example, *Transylvanian Review of Administrative Science* (Public Administration), *Journal of Global Information Management* and *Journal of Information Technology* (Information Science & Library Science) – do not present a marked tendency to publish articles on e-government according to the geographic area in which the study is located. This suggests, therefore, that these journals tend to focus less on the content and topics of the article than on the context in which the study was carried out.

In any case, these articles are concentrated in journals in the field of Information Science & Library Science (129 items), in particular, *European Journal of Information Systems, Government Information Quarterly, Information Development, Information Technology for Development, Journal of Global Information Management* and *Journal of Global Information Technology and Management* (see Appendix 2). The journals *CLAD - Reforma y Democracía, Gestión y Políticas Públicas, INNOVAR - Revista de Ciencias Administrativas y Sociales, Public Administration and Development* and *Transylvanian Review of Administrative Science,* all located in developing countries and focusing on Public Administration, published 50 articles on e-government. These findings reveal a marked difference from the Information Science & Library Science journals located in the USA and the UK, which tend to publish articles on e-government regardless of geographic context.

DISCUSSION AND CONCLUSION

Although our findings go further, in general, we agree with Heeks and Bailur (2007) and Yildiz (2007) in that earlier studies have tended to focus on analysing the cases observed and on evaluating the results of e-government initiatives, presenting the results of their analysis of the content of government websites and lists of online services offered by government agencies. In some cases, advice and recommendations have been given on

best practices, but earlier theories were not tested, nor new ones produced, nor any advances made in existing ones. Although the results of such studies may be practical, they are of a merely descriptive nature and do not assist government planners and decision makers in regard to improving plans for e-government (Yildiz, 2007).

In this respect, currently there is a lively debate about the ongoing transformation in the delivering of public sector services (Osborne, 2010). As noted previously in this chapter, e-Government could contribute to enhancing the delivery of public sector services. Nonetheless, this research may have been constrained, to date, and further studies are needed, into these questions and many others, such as incentives for the implementation of e-services, whether public authorities are adopting a suitable model in this respect, the evolution of such services, the need for ongoing improvement and innovation (Osborne & Brown, 2011), whether this implementation represents a transformational change among public sector bodies (Weerakkody et al., 2011), and the possible role of new Web 2.0 tools in improving the distribution of these services.

Regarding communication with stakeholders, e-Government has led to greater electronic democracy (e-participation) and the integration into the community of the political background to governmental decisions (e-decision making), without the need to form part of the public administration or to belong to a political party (Julnes & Johnson, 2011; Chadwick, 2011). In this respect, for citizens to achieve greater integration in public life through the use of online tools, they need to be well informed so that they can form opinions in this respect. For this reason, various studies have examined the use of government websites as a means of information disclosure (Caba et al., 2008). Recent papers on this issue have reflected the need for transparency policies to be established in less developed countries, and for public administrations there to publish technical reports containing financial and budgetary data so that citizens can make informed decisions (Corrêa & Claussen, 2011). In Latin America, recent studies have reflected the importance of the implementation of institutional participation networks, especially those enabling participatory budgeting (Delemaza & Ochseniu, 2010). However, more research is needed to obtain citizens' opinions, especially as to whether the information provided by public sector bodies is relevant, sufficient and understandable.

In this sense, Joia (2004) performed a comprehensive analysis of the implementation of e-government in Brazil, highlighting the barriers that must be overcome and differences between sectors of the population regarding access to new technologies. Cejudo (2008) analysed the changes that have taken place in the Mexican public sector, showing that the administrative reforms undertaken there evolved in a different way from elsewhere, as a result of economic liberalisation and political democratisation. This type of research finding presents new challenges for political leaders, calling on them to make greater efforts.

In view of these considerations, a fruitful area for study would be to analyse the processes by which e-government policies are established in a complex political environment, or to relate the question of e-government more strongly to mainstream research in the field of public administration. The results of future studies could strengthen the connection between e-government and the traditional concerns of public administration. In addition, a model could be proposed incorporating the variables and factors that influence greater civic and political participation, as well as the efforts made by the governments of these countries. Such research contributions are necessary because they enable us to test existing theories and fill in knowledge gaps, and may even highlight assumptions that had not previously been taken into account, but which due to the special circumstances of the context in which the study was developed should be considered.

In brief, research should be aimed at contributing to the development of public administrations in disadvantaged economies. To accomplish this, it is necessary to understand the perceptions and attitudes of public managers and political leaders, as well as the planning and decision-making processes carried out, in order to better understand the complexities involved in introducing innovations in the public sector. In this sense, we agree with Yildiz (2007), for whom researchers should consult policy-makers directly for information on the experience of e-government, as perceptions are an important component of their actions, functions and policy formulation. Furthermore, this information could be of interest with respect to creating efficient mechanisms to evaluate public policies on e-government and to evaluate the organisational and institutional changes that governments must face with the introduction of new technologies. This kind of issue has mainly been addressed in international journals (Appendix 2), although the present article does not directly consider these concerns. In any case, our findings indicate that research on e-government in developing countries should be addressed to journals located in such countries, where the likelihood of their publication is greater.

E-government research could be considered an eclectic field, involving diverse methodologies and disciplines, each contributing specific theories and approaches, but to date the most commonly used methodologies have been of a qualitative nature, perhaps due to researchers' preference to undertake case studies of e-government issues.

The fact that the majority of research in this field is based on the use of qualitative methodologies suggests there is a need to strengthen e-government research with the use of quantitative methods. In this regard, there has been a slight change, and quantitative research tools are now increasingly used. In our opinion, this is a great research opportunity, one expected to become of much future importance with respect to the implementation of new technologies in public administrations, especially in view of its inferential power and because quantitative methods provide more accurate and objective research data (Bailey, 1992).

One research gap in which quantitative methodologies could usefully be applied concerns the need for theoretical studies to be undertaken to better understand the role of new technologies in driving these reforms, and to derive hypotheses with which to test the real usefulness of new technologies in current models of governance. Moreover, few studies are currently being made of the implementation of ICTs in disadvantaged economies. Research is needed to facilitate development in this type of public administration, inquiring into the perceptions and attitudes of public managers about e-government policies, as well as about the planning and decision-taking processes involved, in order to obtain a better understanding of the complexity arising in innovation and reform processes in public administrations (Yildiz, 2007).

In the same way, informational transparency and the analysis of e-Government policies ensure that resources are invested in projects offering the greatest effectiveness and efficiency, thus avoiding the perpetuation of errors committed in previous decisions or by other governments, and maximising returns and minimising the resources invested (a key issue in the current financial crisis affecting all public administrations). To do so, according to Heeks and Bailur (2007), research should be developed to determine what is taking place within the "black box" of electronic administration and to inform about successful experiences elsewhere.

We believe that a useful area for future study could be that of the policy-making processes in e-government projects in a complex political environment, and that the results of such future studies could strengthen the connection between e-government and the traditional concerns of public administration (Yildiz, 2007). This research could be published not only in journals whose publishers are based in developing countries but also by

those in developed countries, thus providing a valuable comparison of the influence and effect of e-government in public administration reforms.

Finally, the essentially empirical approach taken in studies of e-government in recent years has favoured collaborations between researchers from different areas, resulting in the publication of many articles in journals with international impact. There has also been significant input from professionals working in public administrations, who have shared their professional experiences in the case studies analysed by academic researchers.

ACKNOWLEDGMENT

This research was carried out with financial support from the Regional Government of Andalusia (Spain), Department of Innovation, Science and Enterprise (Research Project No. P11-SEJ-7700) and the Spanish National R&D Plan through Research Project ECO2010-20522 (ECON-FEDER) (Ministry of Science and Innovation).

REFERENCES

Alawneh, A., Al-Refai, H., & Batiha, K. (2013). Measuring user satisfaction from e-government services: Lessons from Jordan. *Government Information Quarterly*, *30*(3), 277–288. doi:10.1016/j.giq.2013.03.001

Alcaide Muñoz, L., López Hernández, A. M., & Rodríguez Bolívar, M. P. (2012). La investigación en e-Gobierno referida a economías emergentes: Evolución y tendencia futuras. CLAD. *Reforma y Democracia*, *54*, 95–126.

Andersson, S., & Heywood, P. M. (2009). The politics of perception: use and abuse of transparency international's approach to measuring corruption. *Political Studies*, *57*(4), 746–767. doi:10.1111/j.1467-9248.2008.00758.x

Atkins, S. E. (1988). Subject trends in library and information science research 1975-1984. *Library Trends, 36*(4), 633–658.

Bailey, M. T. (1992). Do physicists use case studies? Thoughts on public administration research. *Public Administration Review, 52*(1), 47–55. doi:10.2307/976545

Bannister, F., & Connolly, R. (2012). Forward to the past: Lessons for the future of e-government from the story so far. *Information Polity, 17*(3-4), 211–226.

Bingham, R. D., & Bowen, W. (1994). Mainstream public administration over time: A topical content analysis of public administration review. *Public Administration Review, 54*(2), 204–208. doi:10.2307/976531

Caba, C., Rodríguez, M. P., & López, A. M. (2008). E-Government process and incentives for online public financial information. *Online Information Review, 32*(3), 379–400. doi:10.1108/14684520810889682

Caba Pérez, M. C., Rodríguez Bolívar, M. P., & López Hernández, A. M. (2010). Transparency and E-government in developing countries. The case of Latin-American municipalities. In *Citizens and E-Government: Evaluating Policy and Management* (pp. 158–183). Hershey, PA: IGI Global. doi:10.4018/978-1-61520-931-6.ch009

Callanan, M. (2005). Institutionalizing Participation and Governance? New Participative Structures in Local Government in Ireland. *Public Administration, 83*(4), 909–929. doi:10.1111/j.0033-3298.2005.00483.x

Cameron, B. D. (2005). Trends in the Usage of ISI Bibliometric Data: Uses, Abuses, and Implications. *Portal: Libraries and the Academy, 5*(1), 105–125. doi:10.1353/pla.2005.0003

Cejudo, G. M. (2008). Explaining change in the Mexican public sector: The limits of New Public Management. *International Review of Administrative Science, 74*(1), 111–127. doi:10.1177/0020852307085737

Chang, Y. W., & Huang, M. H. (2012). A study of the evolution of interdisciplinarity in Library and Information Science: Using three bibliometric methods. *Journal of the American Society for Information Science and Technology, 63*(1), 22–33. doi:10.1002/asi.21649

Cocosila, M., Serenko, A., & Turel, O. (2011). Exploring the management information systems discipline: A scientometric study of ICIS, PACIS, and ASAC. *Scientometrics, 87*(1), 1–16. doi:10.1007/s11192-010-0331-4

Corrêa, I., & Claussen, M. V. (2011). Políticas de transparencia en la administración pública brasileña. *Revista CLAD: Reforma y Democracia, 51*, 129–152.

Delemaza, G., & Ochsenius, C. (2010). Redes de participación institucional y gobernanza democrática local: El caso de los presupuestos participativos en Chile. *Revista CLAD: Reforma y Democracia, 46*, 215–246.

Dunleavy, P., Margetts, H., Bastow, S., & Tinkler, J. (2005). New Public Management is dead – Long live digital-era governance. *Journal of Public Administration: Research and Theory, 16*(3), 467–494. doi:10.1093/jopart/mui057

Edelenbos, J., & Klijn, E. H. (2007). Trust in complex decision-making networks: A theoretical and empirical exploration. *Administration & Society, 39*(1), 25–50. doi:10.1177/0095399706294460

Gao, X., Song, Y., & Zhu, X. (2013). Integration and coordination: Advancing China's fragmented e-government to holistic governance. *Government Information Quarterly*, *30*(2), 173–181. doi:10.1016/j.giq.2012.12.003

Garfield, E. (1972). Citation analysis as a tool in journal evaluation. *Science*, *178*(4060), 471–479. doi:10.1126/science.178.4060.471 PMID:5079701

Gomes de Souza, C., & Azevedo Ferreira, M. (2013). Researchers profile, co-authorship pattern and knowledge organization in information science in Brazil. *Scientometrics*, *95*(2), 673–687. doi:10.1007/s11192-012-0882-7

Gordon, M. D. (1982). Citation Ranking versus Subjective Evaluation in the Determination of Journal Hierarchies in the Social Sciences. *Journal of the American Society for Information Science American Society for Information Science*, *33*(1), 55–57. doi:10.1002/asi.4630330109

Gouscos, D., Kalikakis, M., Legal, M., & Papadopoulou, S. (2007). A general model of performance and quality for one-top e-Government service offerings. *Government Information Quarterly*, *24*(4), 860–885. doi:10.1016/j.giq.2006.07.016

Heeks, R., & Bailur, S. (2007). Analyzing e-government research: Perspectives, philosophies, theories, methods, and practice. *Government Information Quarterly*, *24*(2), 243–265. doi:10.1016/j.giq.2006.06.005

Jaeger, P. T. (2005). Deliberative democracy and the conceptual foundations of electronic government. *Government Information Quarterly*, *22*(4), 702–719. doi:10.1016/j.giq.2006.01.012

Joia, L. A. (2004). Developing government to government enterprises in Brazil: A heuristic model drawn from multiple case studies. *International Journal of Information Management*, *24*(2), 147–166. doi:10.1016/j.ijinfomgt.2003.12.013

Julnes, P., & Johnson, D. (2011). Strengthening efforts to engage the Hispanic community in citizen-driven governance: an assessment of efforts in Utah. *Public Administration Review*, *71*(2), 221–231. doi:10.1111/j.1540-6210.2011.02333.x

Kim, B. J., Kavanaough, A. L., & Hult, K. M. (2011). Civic engagement and internet use in local governance: Hierarchical linear model for understanding the role of local community groups. *Administration & Society*, *43*(7), 807–835. doi:10.1177/0095399711413873

Kromidhan, E. (2012). Strategic e-government development and the role of benchmarking. *Government Information Quarterly*, *29*(4), 573–581. doi:10.1016/j.giq.2012.04.006

Lan, Z., & Anders, K. K. (2000). A Paradigmatic View of Contemporary Public Administration Research: An Empirical Test. *Administration & Society*, *32*(2), 138–165. doi:10.1177/00953990022019380

Lecy, J. D., Mergel, I. A., & Schmitz, H. P. (2013). Networks in public administration: Current scholarship in review. *Public Management Review*. doi: doi:10.1080/14719037.2012.743577

Legge, J. S. Jr, & Devore, J. (1987). Measuring Productivity in U.S. Public Administration and Public Affairs Programs 1981-1985. *Administration & Society*, *19*(2), 147–156. doi:10.1177/009539978701900201

Lio, M. C., Liu, M. C., & Ou, Y. P. (2011). Can the internet reduce corruption? A cross-country study based on a dynamic panel data models. *Government Information Quarterly*, *28*(1), 47–53. doi:10.1016/j.giq.2010.01.005

Löfstedt, U. (2005). E-Government – Assessment of current research and some proposals for future direction. *International Journal of Public Information Systems*, *1*(1), 39–52.

Manoharan, A. (2013). A study of the determinants of county e-Government in the United States. *American Review of Public Administration*, *43*(2), 159–178. doi:10.1177/0275074012437876

Mergel, I. (2013). A framework for interpreting social media interactions in the public sector. *Government Information Quarterly*, *30*(4), 327–334. doi:10.1016/j.giq.2013.05.015

Nord, J. H., & Nord, G. D. (1995). MIS research: Journal status and analysis. *Information & Management*, *29*(1), 29–42. doi:10.1016/0378-7206(95)00010-T

Osborne, S. P. (2010). *The New Public Governance? Emerging perspectives on the theory and practices of public governance.* London: Routledge.

Osborne, S. P., & Brown, L. (2011). Innovation, public policy and public services delivery in the UK: The word that would be king? *Public Administration*, *89*(4), 1335–1350. doi:10.1111/j.1467-9299.2011.01932.x

Park, C. O., & Joo, J. (2010). Control over the Korean Bureaucracy: A review of the NPM civil service reforms under the Roh Moon-Hyun Government. *Review of Public Personnel Administration*, *30*(2), 189–210. doi:10.1177/0734371X09360183

Plümper, T., & Radaelli, C. M. (2004). Publish or perish? Publications and citations of Italian political scientists in international political science journals, 1990-2002. *Journal of European Public Policy*, *11*(6), 1112–1127. doi:10.1080/1350176042000298138

Raadschelders, J. C. N., & Lee, K. H. (2011). Trends in the Study of Public Administration: Empirical and Qualitative Observations from Public Administration Review, 2000-2009. *Public Administration Review*, *71*(1), 19–33. doi:10.1111/j.1540-6210.2010.02303.x

Reddick, C. G. (2011). Customer Relationship Management (CRM) technology and organizational change: Evidence for the bureaucratic and e-Government paradigms. *Government Information Quarterly*, *28*(3), 346–353. doi:10.1016/j.giq.2010.08.005

Rodríguez, M. P., Alcaide, L., & López, A. M. (2010). Trends of e-Government research: Contextualization and research opportunities. *International Journal of Digital Accounting Research*, *10*, 87–111. doi:10.4192/1577-8517-v10_4

Seng, W. M., Jackson, S., & Philip, G. (2010). Cultural issues in developing E-Government in Malaysia. *Behaviour & Information Technology*, *29*(4), 423–432. doi:10.1080/01449290903300931

Susanto, T. D., & Goodwin, R. (2013). User acceptance of SMS-based e-government services: Differences between adopters and non-adopters. *Government Information Quarterly*, *30*(4), 486–497. doi:10.1016/j.giq.2013.05.010

Tseng, Y. H., & Tsay, M. Y. (2013). Journal clustering of library and information science for subfield delineation using the bibliometric analysis toolkit: CATAR. *Scientometric*, *95*(2), 503–528. doi:10.1007/s11192-013-0964-1

United Nations. (2003). *World Public Sector Report 2003: E-Government at the Crossroads.* New York: United Nations.

United Nations. (2012). *United Nations E-Government Survey 2012: E-Government for the People.* New York: United Nations.

Velicu, B. C. (2012). Creating a citizen centric administration through eGovernment in Romania. *Romanian Journal of Political Science*, *12*(2), 103–129.

Vocino, T., & Elliott, R. H. (1982). Journal Prestige in Public Administration: A Research Note. *Administration & Society*, *14*(1), 5–14. doi:10.1177/009539978201400101

Wang, H. J., & Lo, J. (2013). Determinants of citizens' intent to use government websites in Taiwan. *Information Development*, *29*(2), 123–137. doi:10.1177/0266666912453835

Weerakkody, V., Janssen, M., & Dwivedi, Y. K. (2011). Transformational change and business process reengineering (BPR): Lessons from the British and Dutch public sector. *Government Information Quarterly*, *28*(3), 320–328. doi:10.1016/j.giq.2010.07.010

Yildiz, M. (2007). E-government research: Reviewing the literature, limitations, and ways forward. *Government Information Quarterly*, *24*(3), 646–665. doi:10.1016/j.giq.2007.01.002

Yuan, L., Xi, C., & Xiaoyi, W. (2012). Evaluating the readiness of government portal websites in China to adopt contemporary public administration principles. *Government Information Quarterly*, *29*(3), 403–412. doi:10.1016/j.giq.2011.12.009

ADDITIONAL READING

Bélanger, F., & Carter, L. (2012). Digitizing Government Interactions with Constituents: An Historical Review of e-Government Research in Information Systems. *Journal of the Association for Information Systems*, *13*(Special Issue), 363–394.

Bingham, L. D., Nabatchi, T., & O'Leary, R. (2005). The new governance: Practices and processes for stakeholder and citizen participation in the work of government. *Public Administration Review*, *65*(5), 547–558. doi:10.1111/j.1540-6210.2005.00482.x

Grönlund, A., & Horan, T. (2005). Introducing e-gov: History, definitions and issues. *Communications of the Association for Information Systems*, *15*, 39.

Rodríguez Bolívar, M. P., Alcaide Muñoz, L., & López Hernández, A. M. (2012). Studying E-government: Research Methodologies, Data Compilation Techniques and Future Outlook. *Academia. Revista Latinoamericana de Administración*, *51*, 79–95.

Snead, J. T., & Wright, E. (2013). E-government research in the United States. *Government Information Quarterly*. doi: doi:10.1016/j.giq.2013.07.005

KEY TERMS AND DEFINITIONS

Bibliometric Study: The use of statistical methods in the analysis of a body of literature to reveal the historical development of subject fields and patterns of authorship, publication and use.

Digital Divide: This term is used to describe the fact that the world can be divided into people who do and people who do not have access to – and the capability to use – modern information technology, such as the telephone, television, or the Internet. These differences often occur between cities and rural areas, also exists between the educated and the uneducated, between economic classes, and, globally, between the more and less industrially developed nations.

E-Government: The platform through which the government (government line ministries, branches and organs) interacts with its citizens and business entities for the sake of exchange of information, public services and participatory democracy through the use of ICT platforms.

Emerging Economies: These are rapidly growing and volatile economies of certain Asian, African, and Latin American countries. In this chapter, this phrase has been used loosely to include some developing countries which are purely third-world countries.

E-Participation: This terms is related with ICT-supported participation in processes involved in government and governance, hence it is closely related to e-government. E-Participation allow citizens to connect with one another and with their elected representatives, to inform them about the financial position, the performance and the efforts of the government to deliver public services more efficiently, and to raise level of accountability.

Future Trends: E-Government research topics which researchers should analyzed in depth, and it provides the basis for developing research agendas for the future.

Research Methodologies: The set of methods used to analyze the reality for the production of new knowledge.

Appendix 1

Table 1. Citation analysis (developed countries studies vs. developing countries studies)

TOTAL RANKING	TOP DEVELOPED AND DEVELOPING COUNTRIES ARTICLES[1]	TOTAL CITATIONS	AVERAGE CITATIONS PER YEAR	RESEARCH TOPIC	DEVELOPED/ DEVELOPING	RANKING IN DEVELOPED/ DEVELOPING ARTICLES
1	Developing fully functional E-government: A four stage model (Layne and Lee) *Government Information Quarterly* (2001)	377	29.00	Evolution e-Government	DEVELOPED	1
2	The evolution of e-Government among municipalities: Rhetoric or reality) (Moon) *Public Administration Review* (2002)	257	21.42	Evolution e-Government	DEVELOPED	2
3	E-government and the transformation of service delivery and citizen attitudes (West) *Public Administration Review* (2004)	192	19.20	Public services	DEVELOPED	3
4	The utilization of e-Government service: citizen trust, innovation and acceptance factors (Carter and Belanger) *Information Systems Journal* (2005)	177	19.67	Public services	DEVELOPED	4
5	Reinventing local governments and the e-Government initiative (Ho) *Public Administration Review* (2002)	159	13.25	Technological innovation	DEVELOPED	5
7	Linking citizen satisfaction with e-Government and trust in government (Welch et al.) *Journal of Public Administration Research and Theory* (2005)	99	11.00	Public services	DEVELOPED	9
8	Advancing e-Government at the grassroots: Tortoise or hare? (Norris and Moon) *Public Administration Review* (2005)	96	10.67	Technological innovation	DEVELOPED	6
9	Interaction between states and citizens in the age of the internet: "e-government" in the USA, Britain and the European Union (Chadwick) *Governance* (2003)	97	8.82	e-Participation	DEVELOPED	7
11	The new face of government: Citizen-initiated contacts in the era of e-Government (Thomas and Streib) *Journal of Public Administration Research and Theory* (2003)	94	8.55	e-Participation	DEVELOPED	8

continued on following page

Table 1. Continued

TOTAL RANKING	TOP DEVELOPED AND DEVELOPING COUNTRIES ARTICLES[1]	TOTAL CITATIONS	AVERAGE CITATIONS PER YEAR	RESEARCH TOPIC	DEVELOPED/ DEVELOPING	RANKING IN DEVELOPED/ DEVELOPING ARTICLES
13	The effects of e-Government on trust and confidence in government (Tolbert and Mossberger) *Public Administration Review* (2006)	87	10.88	Technological innovation	DEVELOPED	10
14	E-Government evaluation: A framework and case study (Gupta and Jana) *Government Information Quarterly* (2003)	85	7.73	Technological innovation	DEVELOPING	1
34	E-Government strategies in developed and developing countries: An implementation framework and case study (Chen et al., 2008) *Journal of Global Information Management*	48	8.00	Technological innovation	DEVELOPING	2
37	Managing e-transformation in the public sector: an e-Government study of the Inland Revenue Authority of Singapore (IRAS) (Tan and Pan) *European Journal of Information Systems* (2003)	45	4.09	Organizational theory	DEVELOPING	3
55	Managing stakeholder interest in e-Government implementation: Lessons learned from a Singapore e-Government project (Tan) *European Journal of Information Systems* (2005)	28	3.11	Evolution e-Government	DEVELOPING	4
58	E-government in China: Bringing economic development through administrative reform (Man et al.) Government Information Quarterly (2005)	27	3.00	Technological innovation	DEVELOPING	5
60	Factors influencing intention to use e-government services among citizens in Malaysia (Lean et al.) *International Journal of Information Management* (2009)	26	5.20	Public services	DEVELOPING	6
70	Impact and sustainability of e-Government services in developing countries: Lessons learned from Tamil Nadu, India (Kumar and Best) *Information Society* (2006)	23	2.88	Public services	DEVELOPING	7

continued on following page

Table 1. Continued

TOTAL RANKING	TOP DEVELOPED AND DEVELOPING COUNTRIES ARTICLES[1]	TOTAL CITATIONS	AVERAGE CITATIONS PER YEAR	RESEARCH TOPIC	DEVELOPED/ DEVELOPING	RANKING IN DEVELOPED/ DEVELOPING ARTICLES
73	E-Government in developing countries: Experiences from Sub-Sahara Africa (Schuppan) *Government Information Quarterly* (2009)	21	4.20	Technological innovation	DEVELOPING	8
81	Trust and Electronic Government Success: An Empirical Study (Thompson et al.) *Journal of Management Information Systems* (2010)	20	5.00	Technological innovation	DEVELOPING	9
87	Questioning the pace and pathway of e-Government development in Africa: A case study of South Africa's Cape Gateway project (Maumbe et al.) *Government Information Quarterly* (2008)	17	2.83	Evolution e-Government	DEVELOPING	10

Source: Web of Knowledge – "Average citations per year" is the result of dividing the articles' total citations to 2013 by the number of years ranging from the year of publication of articles through 2013.

[1]Bibliometric, scientometric, meta-analysis studies and non-empirical articles were not considered.

Appendix 2

Table 2. Journals publish developed countries studies and developing countries studies

JOURNALS*	EDITORIAL OFFICE	DEVELOPED STUDIES**	DEVELOPING STUDIES**
PUBLIC ADMINISTRATION JOURNALS			
Administration and Society	US	13 – 61.90%	1 – 4.76%
American Review of Public Administration	US	26 – 81.25%	1 – 3.13%
CLAD. Reforma y Democracia	VENEZUELA	8 – 21.05%	17 – 44.74%
Gestión y Políticas Públicas	MEXICO	1 – 16.66%	3 – 50.00%
INNOVAR – Revista de Ciencias Administrativas y Sociales	COLOMBIA	0 – 00.00%	1 – 100%
International Review of Administrative Sciences	ENGLAND	13 – 48.15%	5 – 18.52%
Journal of Comparative Policy Analysis	ENGLAND	2 – 40.0%	2 - 40.00%
Journal of Public Policy	ENGLAND	6 – 85.71%	1 – 14.29%
Lex Localis – Journal of Local Self-Government	SLOVENIA	0 – 00.00%	1 – 100%
Local Government Studies	ENGLAND	13 – 81.25%	1 – 6.25%
Public Administration	ENGLAND	15 – 75.00%	1 – 5.00%
Public Administration and Development	ENGLAND	2 – 13.33%	11 – 73.33%
Transylvanian Review of Administrative Science	ROMANIA	3 – 25.00%	5 – 33.33%
INFORMATION SCIENCE JOURNALS			
European Journal of Information Systems	ENGLAND	10 – 58.82%	7 – 41.18%
Government Information Quarterly	US	166 – 60.36%	44 – 16.00%
Information and Management	NETHERLANDS	11 – 73.33%	3 – 20.00%
Information Development	ENGLAND	1 – 12.50%	6 – 75.00%
Information Technology and Management	US	1 –33.33%	2- 66.67%
Information Technology and People	ENGLAND	6 – 46.15%	6 – 46.15%
Information Technology for Development	ENGLAND	1 – 5.56%	15 – 83.33%
International Journal of Information Management	ENGLAND	14 – 60.87%	6 – 26.09%
Journal of Computer-Mediated Communication	US	9 – 64.29%	3 – 21.43%
Journal of Global Information Management	US	6 – 46.15%	8 – 61.54%
Journal of Global Information Technology and Management	US	1- 16.66%	5 – 83.33%
Journal of Information Science	ENGLAND	4 – 50.00%	2 – 20.00%
Journal of Information Technology	ENGLAND	0 – 00.00%	1 – 100%
Journal of Strategic Information Systems	NETHERLANDS	6 – 75.00%	2 – 25.00%
Journal of the American Society for Information Science and Technology	US	4 – 44.44%	2 – 22.22%
Journal of the Association for Information Systems	US	1 – 25.00%	2 – 50.00%
Malaysian Journal of Library and Information Science	MALAYSIA	0 – 00.00%	1 – 100%
MIS Quarterly	US	1 – 50.00%	1 – 50.00%
Online Information Review	ENGLAND	12 – 85.71%	1 – 7.14%
Scientometrics	HUNGARY	1 – 25.00%	1 – 25.00%
Social Science Computer Review	US	40 – 75.47%	5 – 9.43%
Telecommunication Policy	ENGLAND	9 – 64.29%	2 – 14.29%
The Information Society	US	14 – 53.84%	4 – 15.38%

Source: The authors

*NOTA 1: This table only shows journals that have published articles analyzing the e-Government in developing countries.

Chapter 2
E-Governmentization:
A Panacea for the Democratization of Developing Countries?

JungHo Park
Korea Institute of Public Administration, South Korea

Greg Prombescu
Northern Illinois University, USA

ABSTRACT

The objective of this chapter is to critically evaluate the e-governmentization of administrative processes, which many developing nations have come to enthusiastically espouse. From a theoretical perspective, such a trend is ostensibly positive, as e-government serves to promote transparency and efficient information exchange, which in turn serves to stimulate more equal distributions of power, inside as well as outside the bureaucracy, and perhaps most importantly (efficiently) solicit greater citizen participation. However, such benefits associated with the proliferation of e-government are often contingent upon a host of prerequisite conditions that, often times, developing nations do not meet. Therefore, such enthusiastic attempts by developing nations to e-governmentize administrative processes may be misplaced. As such, the primary thesis of this research is that the e-governmentization of administrative processes are likely to stimulate positive effects only after a certain level of democracy has been achieved. To explore this thesis, this chapter focuses on exploring the evolution and ensuing effects of the proliferation of e-government in South Korea.

INTRODUCTION

The current wave of e-governmentization is not only limited to developed countries, but is instead also affecting many developing and under developed countries, who are drawn to the benefits associated with e-government (Heeks 2003). As the scope of e-government continues to expand from providing public service to communication tools which are critical to the creation and implementation of public policy, e-government is facing a new phase of development (Brewer et al. 2006). To this end, the more e-government is shifting toward a governance platform, the more

DOI: 10.4018/978-1-4666-3691-0.ch002

complicated issues concerning the accessibility and pre-conditions of successful e-government are (Cibbora and Navarra 2005).

The objective of this chapter is to critically evaluate the e-governmentization of administrative processes, which many developing nations have come to enthusiastically espouse. From a theoretical perspective, such a trend is ostensibly positive, as e-government serves to promote transparency and efficient information exchange, which in turn serves to stimulate more equal distributions of power, inside as well as outside the bureaucracy, and perhaps most importantly (efficiently) solicit greater citizen participation (Brewer et al. 2006). However, such benefits associated with the proliferation of e-government are often contingent upon a host of prerequisite conditions that, often times, developing nations do not meet. Therefore, such enthusiastic attempts by developing nations to e-governmentize administrative processes may be misplaced. As such, the primary thesis of this research is that the e-governmentization of administrative processes may serve to stimulate positive effects only after a certain level of democracy has been achieved. To explore this thesis, this chapter will focus on exploring the evolution and ensuing effects of the proliferation of e-government in South Korea, China, and India.

Studying the process of e-govenrmentization in South Korea is particularly relevant for developing nations for two primary reasons. The first is that South Korea may be considered a pioneer in the process of e-governmentization of administrative processes and today is widely considered to have among the most developed e-government infrastructures in the world (United Nations e-government Survey 2012). The second reason the study of e-governmentization in South Korea is relevant for developing countries is that, concurrent to the aggressive e-governmentization of administrative processes that took place throughout the country, South Korea was also in the process of consolidating its young democracy; in other words, South Korea's aggressive adoption of e-government began at a time when democracy in South Korea was underdeveloped, and a developing nation itself. In fact, much of modern South Korean e-government systems can be traced back to the early 1990s, a period when South Korea had just made its transition to democracy, following decades of authoritative rule under a regime of military presidents. Consequently, by obtaining a better understanding of South Korea's experiences throughout its process of e-governmentization, democratization, and development insight may be provided regarding the nature of the relationship that exists between the benefits said to accompany the e-governmentization of administrative processes and levels of democratic development.

This chapter will provide a literature based review of e-government applications in three different contexts. As such, the findings of this research are indicative only, and may be empirically examined in later research. The following section will discuss the rise in popularity of e-government over the past decades, and introduce popular arguments regarding its application. The second section discusses theory that can be used in assessing the extent to which e-government applications may serve to further the development of democracy within a given context. Bearing in mind such arguments, examples of e-government adoption in India and China are discussed. Section three discusses e-government adoption in South Korea. Based upon the findings of this research, this chapter will conclude by proposing some recommendations for developing nations before pursuing the hasty implementation of e-government projects.

BACKGROUND: E-GOVERNMENT AS AN INTERNATIONAL ADMINISTRATIVE BUZZWORD

While definitions of e-government are diverse, a consistent theme found among them is the use of information and communications technology to deliver government information and public services to citizens (Ho 2002, Chadwick and May 2003, Kumar and Best 2006, Brewer et al. 2006, Yildiz 2007). Through the application of information and communications technologies to public sector processes, e-government is said to increase the efficiency with which government provides citizens with information and public services, while at the same time broadening the scope with which citizens are able to interact with their government (Jaeger and Thompson 2003, Brewer et al. 2006). Given the benefits associated with e-government and advances in technology, over the past decades, information and services have continually shifted to online, electronic formats, with such shifts eliciting a great deal of optimism among scholars who viewed such developments as possessing the potential to usher in an era of participatory and responsive governance (Chadwick & May, 2003). Amidst such optimism, the e-governmentization of administrative processes has been portrayed as a gold standard, for all forms of government to embrace (Kumar and Best 2006).

However, while much of the initial discussion concerning e-government has been largely positive, a relatively new and critical vein of literature has emerged, which argues that in spite of the transformative potential of e-government, particularly with regard to relationships between citizens and their government, applications of e-government have instead gone toward improving or reinforcing existing processes (Ho, 2002; Chadwick & May, 2003; Norris & Moon, 2005; Brewer et al., 2006; Im et al. 2013. Accordingly, over the brief, but well documented history of e-government various models of adoption have been laid out, such as those presented by Layne and Lee (2001) or Chadwick and May (2003). While the number of stages may differ between models of adoption, these models share a common perspective that the application of e-government typically evolves from administrative oriented applications of e-government, which focus on enhancing levels of government administrative efficiency, toward more citizen oriented applications of ICT, which solicit greater citizen participation and involvement in government processes. However, a growing body of literature has remarked that the evolution of e-government applications appears to be stalled in the initial administrative oriented phases (Moon 2002, Ho 2002, Chadwick and May 2003, Brewer et al. 2006).

International and Domestic Pressures for E-Government Adoption

Despite a growing body of literature, which acknowledges that applications of e-government remain in an administrative oriented phase (Ho 2002, Brewer et al. 2006, Yildiz 2007, Im et al. 2013), most if not all of the sources within this body of literature do not extend their skepticism to the transformative capacity of e-government with regard to citizen participation. Due to this commonly acknowledged (positive) transformative capacity of e-government, a growing body of domestic, as well as international pressures advocating the adoption of e-government has emerged (Basu 2004, Dada 2006).

At the domestic level, Farooquie (2010) argues that there are four major actors in e-government adoption, those being "lawmakers", "public administrators", "executors", and "citizens". Among these domestic sources of pressure for e-government adoption at the domestic level, certain features of e-government make its adoption particularly attractive to all four categories of actors. These features that are often said to stem from the implementation of e-government systems are; enhanced transparency, greater efficiency and effectiveness, reduced corruption, enhanced citizen participation, and enhanced citizen satisfaction and trust in government (Chadwick & May 2003; Welch et al., 2004; Kumar & Best, 2006; Liou, 2007; Morgeson et al., 2011; Im et al., forthcoming). Keeping in mind the advantages said to stem from the adoption of e-government, for developing nations in particular, the rhetoric advocating the adoption of e-government is likely to be politically attractive to both the ruling and opposition parties[1]. The reason for this is that, from the perspective of the ruling party, e-government adoption can be viewed as a an important factor in supporting a nation's development agenda, whereas for the opposition party e-government adoption can be advocated from the perspective that it serves as a means of targeting (reforming) problematic practices of the ruling party (Yildiz & Kurban, 2011).

At the international level, the adoption of ICT is often advocated by various international organizations and multinational companies for reasons similar to those found at the domestic level. However, unlike the domestic level, many of the international organizations promoting the adoption of e-government often equate the proliferation of this form of administrative tool as associated with better governance (Ruth & Doh, 2007; UN, 2010). For example, the World Bank (2004) has suggested that e-government reforms play a focal role in broad political and economic reforms in developing nations. Complementing this perspective laid out in the report by the World Bank, W'O Okot-Uma (2000), in a report written on behalf of the Commonwealth Secretariat, has argued that, in the pursuit of 'good governance', which he describes as, a "commitment to democratic values, norms, and practices, trusted services, and just and honest business", the implementation of e-government systems is essential, as it provides efficient mechanisms for enhancing service provision capabilities and improving the quality of democracy. The United Nation's E-Government Survey for 2010 echoes these arguments, arguing

that "e-government represents a means of enhancing the capacity of the public sector, together with citizens, to address particular development issues" (UNPAN 2010). Subsequently, many forms of official development aid (ODA) require developing countries to adopt an e-government reform package (Information and Communication Technologies for Development 2008).

International sources of pressure to e-governmentize administrative processes are often related to the (unrealistic) optimistic expectation that, through implementing various forms of e-government, the administrative capacity of a government, or its institutions, will be enhanced. At the domestic level, sources of pressure to e-governmentize possess a different dynamic, as they are likely to be associated with ambitions (or political wills) of various social actors (c.f. Srivastava and Sharma 2010). Furthermore, as previous research has found applications of e-government to often be associated with political objectives of various social actors, it is also important to question the implications of e-governmentization on a nation's democratic trajectory, particularly for developing nations where democratic forms of government and institutions are often less developed, and subsequently more vulnerable to mismanagement (Keefer & Knack, 1997). Indeed, the lofty objectives for e-governmentalization that stem from domestic and international sources of pressure often result in frustration and distrust among citizens of these countries (Kumar and Best 2006). To this end, it is important to critically evaluate the extent to which such gains in governance, said to stem from the application of e-government, are applicable to all governments, developed or developing.

Exploring Perspectives on E-Government

As was mentioned earlier, this book chapter is primarily concerned with addressing the impact of e-government on democratization in developing nations. In this section, we outline relevant theoretical arguments regarding how the ways in which implementation of e-government has been argued to affect the consolidation and growth of democracy in developing nations. In our review of theoretical arguments concerning e-government, we focus upon issues mentioned in the previous section, which are concerned with whether e-government is an appropriate administrative tool for developing and developed nations alike, and the political implications of e-governmentization. We close this section by assessing the validity of theoretical arguments related to the impact of e-governmentization on democratization in a few developing nations.

THEORETICAL PERSPECTIVES

Addressing differing perspectives on government's use of technology over time, Yildiz (2007) observes that, "until the introduction of the Internet and widespread use of personal computers, the main objectives of technology use in government were enhancing the managerial effectiveness of public administrators while increasing government productivity". Sentiments similar to those presented by Yildiz are also present in research conducted by Snellen (2007), who found that the adoption of e-government services by governments was initially heavily influenced by "e-business" templates that were primarily oriented toward enhancing the efficiency, effectiveness, and economy with which information was processed and disseminated, and government services delivered. Taken together, the observations by Yildiz and Snellen lay the foundation for the first of two perspectives concerned with the use of e-government, with the first of these perspectives being e-government as a tool for promoting managerial efficiency.

However, despite the conservative, efficiency oriented use of e-government that is characteristic of internally oriented applications (Ho, 2002; Norris & Moon, 2005; Yildiz, 2007), members of the "Irvine School" assert that while the application of new technologies to existing internal processes is likely to enhance their efficiency, such an internally oriented application of e-government is also likely to result in reinforcing existing status quos, which in turn, leads to exaggerating existing power inequalities and offering the potential to lower levels of transparency and external accountability of the state (Chadwick & May, 2003; Im et al. forthcoming)[2]. The example of the mayor of the autonomous administrative district of Gangnam's application of e-government to the district's bureaucracy for political and power purposes would serve to support the arguments made by the "Irvine School" (Ahn & Bretschneider, 2011).

The second of the two perspectives on e-government is concerned with understanding the implications of e-government on relationships between government and citizens. An important component of this perspective on e-government concerns democracy and citizen participation. E-government, based on its tremendous potential to facilitate the participation of large(r) numbers of citizens in administrative and political processes of the state and its organs is often viewed as an effective means in promoting democracy and institutionalizing associated values and practices in developed and developing nations alike (UN-PAN 2010). Geredimos (2005) explains that the government's use of e-government would trigger a path dependency that would lead toward greater levels of citizen access to government, citizen engagement with government, increased levels of citizen-government deliberation, and subsequently, ultimately lead toward the increased impact of citizens on policy making processes of their government. As such, the argument made by Geredimos is moored in the assumption that through the use of e-government to reach out to larger numbers of citizens, the government's transparency will enhance, as will levels of external accountability (Im et al. forthcoming).

However, scholars have noted that the use of the Internet to promote greater citizen participation in policy making and administrative processes is not without its drawbacks. For example, Kettl (2000) has argued that through the proliferation of the Internet throughout society and the enhanced empowerment of non government actors in society, an environment of hyperpluralism will be cultivated, whereby the state will be forced to compete with increasingly influential non-governmental actors in an attempt to cultivate shared "norms, ideologies, values, and institutions". The nature of this drawback is highlighted by Snellen (2007), who views e-government as a means of shifting from representative forms of democracy toward direct democracy, questions whether such a shift is actually desirable. In his analysis of this question, he highlights two particular potential problems. The first of these problems highlighted by Snellen is that, in the presence of a (more) direct form of democracy, a "single issue approach" would likely result, thereby leading to "incompatible policies both within and between sectors". The second problem highlighted by Snellen, which complements the first potential problem, argues that direct forms of democracy are likely to lead to the oversimplification of complex issues, thereby resulting in the prevalence of short term perspectives throughout government and society, as well as bearing adverse implications on the quality of deliberation regarding public policy. In such a situation, the implication is that, for developing nations, which lack established democracies and political institutions, such threats may be particularly potent, when compared to nations with more developed democracies and political institutions.

From the two (internal and external oriented) perspectives outlined in the preceding paragraphs, there is a clear difference in terms of how the use

of e-government is assessed. The first perspective, which focuses on efficiency, is primarily interested in assessing the implications of e-government proliferation on the internal workings of the organization, whereas the second perspective is primarily interested in assessing how the proliferation of e-government affects the relationships between the state and citizens. Fountain (2001), capturing the dual perspectives on e-government application argues, "policymakers [across the world] view the Internet either as a force to increase the responsiveness of government to its citizens or as a means to further empower the state" (p.3).

The arguments made above with respect to internal and external perspectives on applications of e-government are summarized in the table below. As is illustrated by this table, governments' use of e-government is argued to be highly linked to the political, cultural and institutional contexts it is implemented in; in other words, there is no single trajectory that e-government leads to.

While scholars have acknowledged the utility of e-government in ushering an era of greater citizen participation in government processes, evidence of e-government being used to obtain such ends has generally been scant, with internally oriented applications of e-government being most prominent (Chadwick & May, 2003; Brewer et al., 2006). However, more recently an increasing number of examples of developed and developing nations making use of ICT and e-government to foster greater citizen participation can be found (Holliday & Yep 2005; Ahn & Bretschneider, 2011; Zanello & Maassen, 2011). However, much of this research is also careful to point out that progress in this direction often complements political ambitions of the leaders in charge (Dada 2006, Im et al. 2011), thereby suggesting an interdependency between technology and social systems, highlighted in table 1. Subsequently, the use of e-government as a mechanism for pursuing *better governance* may only be to the extent that doing so allows those in charge to consolidate their position of power vis-à-vis other actors in

Table 1. Internal and external oriented applications of E-government

Internal Management and ICTs	
Ahn & Bretschneider (2011)	Political Control over bureaucracy, increase of accountability and transparency of bureaucrats, case study in South Korea
Thompson & Jones (2008)	The structure of organizations can be more flexible and the form of relationship will be flatter, as such the general structure of public sectors will be like network organizations
Savage (2007)	General public servants (e.g., police officers) and specialists of ICTs have to interact more, while the skills and tasks of current civil servants are changing to those with specialized skills with the newly emerging problems (e.g., cyber space crime).
Fountain (2001)	The change of ICTs does not always lead to the intended outcomes because technology will be embedded in diverse levels of institutional contexts and culture. As such, determinism of technology in explaining anticipated effects is flawed in practice.
Markus & Robey, (1988)	"emergent' perspective in which 'the uses and consequences of information technology emerge unpredictably from complex social interactions" (p.588)
Sahay (1997)	"making clear distinctions between the technical and the social is always problematic, because each has elements of the other embedded within it" (p. 235).
Democracy and ICTs	
Norris (2001)	ICTs may not extend the level of civic participation despite the optimism regarding government use of ICTs. Rather, the existing pattern of participation (e.g., civic engagement) and influences on the political and policy making process may only be reinforced due to the "digital divide"
Smith et al. (2009)	Although the current atmosphere of civic engagement may be similar to Norris' (2001) argument regarding reinforcing effects, as the numerous ways in which ICTs and social networking devices become more developed and used by ordinary citizens, such technologies will enable citizens to participate or communicate their attitude toward public affairs.
Pollitt (2011)	Although it is difficult to determine how ICTs change the relationship of citizens and governments, there are ongoing changes with respect to diverse perspectives: 1) citizens' perspective, 2) governments' perspective, 3) politicians' perspective, and as a whole 4) time and space. In particular, the exchanges between government service providers and citizens shift toward virtual spaces, the time for service provision minimizes due to the ICTs.
Welch (2005)	Online shifts of public services (i.e., government website) can have multifarious effects on trust in government, performance satisfaction, and other aspects, which have been considered as essential for the government reforms.

society, institutions, or political parties. For nations with developed democracies and whose governments possess well functioning institutions, the implications of such political maneuvering may not have significant implications on such nations' democratic trajectories, however, for developing nations the implications are likely to be very different, as they often lack well established political institutions.

Perhaps the best known discussion of politics influencing the adoption of technology such as e-government can be found in Fountain's Building the Virtual State (2001). In this text, she considers the way in which various technologies are

adopted and applied by an organization. Central to her argument is that is the adoption of technology by an organization is highly influenced by that organization's inner workings. Based on the idea that institutional environments influence the adoption of e-government, Fountain develops a "technological enactment framework".

A major component of Fountain's technological enactment framework argues that, due to internal and external sources of influence and pressure on the organization, the application of new technology (e-government) to organizational processes often possesses political characteristics. Hence, the environment in which a new technology is adopted plays a critical role in influencing the way in which the new technology is applied. Hence, while Geredimos's argument has suggested the potential for e-government to serve as a means of fostering democratic values, the technology enactment framework proposed by Fountain assumes an alternative perspective, proposing that e-government can be adopted as a means of enhancing political ambitions of various actors.

E-GOVERNMENT FOR DEVELOPING NATIONS: THE CASES OF CHINA AND INDIA

The Case of E-Government in China

The Chinese government advocates e-governmentization as a means of improving administrative effectiveness, improving administrative process, and enhancing transparency (Ma et al., 2005). Central to the Chinese government's e-governmentization initiatives, which are determined by the leadership of Chinese Communist Party (CCP), is a series of broad "Golden" projects, which intend to establish e-banking networks, as well as an information sharing network between private, public, and international entities.

Moving toward a more systematic approach toward e-governmentization, the Chinese government created the blueprint of the "Government Online Project" in 1999. Following this project, Chinese governments established more specific e-government related goals, which were linked to particular policy agendas and a diverse array of public services. Through the proliferation of this strategy, a particular emphasis was placed upon strengthening the Chinese government's internal capacities in order to better implement e-government programs. Research indicates that this focus on enhancing internal capacities with regard to e-government has been accelerated due

to the nation's increasing prowess in developing and producing a myriad of types of ICTs (Holliday & Yep, 2005; Liu, 2008).

However, in spite of ensuring that the Chinese government itself possesses the internal capacity to pursue e-governmentization, literature on the subject has pointed out that the implementation of e-government in China finds its greatest challenges from the nation's social context. To this extent, the Chinese case is particularly interesting to examine due to its unique social (environmental) conditions, and administrative and political systems, which together raise the question of whether the effects of e-government can lead to the enhanced transparency and accountability as some of the extant theory suggests (Gupta & Jana 2003; Yildiz, 2007).

The administrative tradition of "cadre management", which is prevalent in China, is generally believed to result in a tension between administrative neutrality and loyalty to the political party (Xiaoyun and Im 2009). As such, public servants are likely to be expected to show their loyalty to the CCP as well as their capacity to perform assigned tasks. As such, administrative bureaucrats are said to be "politically committed and heavily involved in political and ideological campaigns and struggles" (Liu, 2008, p.81). This lack of a political administrative dichotomy in the Chinese government is often referred to critically for the reason that it reduces the extent to which the government can be held accountable to Chinese citizens (Xiaoyun and Im 2009). To this extent, the application of e-government services is likely to do nothing other than reinforce existing practices and power configurations, in ways similar to those described by members of the "Irvine School", implying that citizens may continue to be left out of the policy making equation.

Thus, the power structure in China raises the question of whether the e-governmentization offers the potential to promote citizen participation in policy making as the CCP maintains the right to serve as the sole authority in making critical decisions, while public agencies serve to implement such decisions (Liou, 2008). This closed system of decision making and implementation, and the potential of e-government to reinforce this system has led Zhang (2003) to argue that the use of e-government by the CCP serves to "unify the country by tying the center to the provinces and by allowing the government to act across ministerial and industrial demarcation lines" (Zhang, 2002, p.170). Subsequently, while the central government of China attempts to decentralize administrative power and authority to local governments through the use of e-government strategies, the underlying rationale for governance structure is said to be to enhance the centrality of government and the CCP vis-à-vis other actors (Ma et al. 2005). Considerations such as those outlined here have led Ma and colleagues (2005) to present a pessimistic evaluation regarding the effects of e-governmentization on democratization and enhanced citizen participation in China via e-government, claiming that "As a consequence of a deeply centralized and often inefficient administrative management system, China has faced critical problems" (p.24)

As illustrated above, contextual features such as administrative tradition and political system should be considered, as well as the intentions associated with the application of e-government should receive serious consideration when attempting to establish a relationship between e-governmentization and democratic development. As the case of China illustrates, e-government was viewed by the central government as an efficient and effective tool in reinforcing their control vis-à-vis outlying districts by tying them closer to the center, as opposed to granting them more authority or discretion. Accordingly, these results suggest the important role socio political conditions play in the implementation of e-government on their democratic development (Fountain, 2001; Bing, 1992; Tsui, 2005). Moreover, they also illustrate

the way in which extant socio political conditions serve to reinforce themselves through the application of e-government, and thereby buffer government from substantive change (Im et al. forthcoming).

The Case of E-Government in India

The development of e-government in India is said to be in its early stages (Gupta & Jana, 2003; Sristava & Sharma, 2010). However, the Indian government has actively pursued an expansion of its e-government projects through a variety of avenues, with an emphasis placed upon decentralized implementation, and costs expected to exceed $1.5 billion (Sharma, 2010). Today, many experts in the field of e-government have remarked upon the massive scale at which e-government is being applied in India (Haque 2002, Kumar and Best 2006, Farooquie 2010). Haque argues that policy makers in the Indian government justify the massive scale of its e-government projects in an argument that "it costs less, reduces waste, promotes transparency, eliminates corruption, generates possibilities to resolve rural poverty and inequality, and guarantees a better future for citizens"; however, he also contests the validity of such claims (2002, p. 222).

The Indian case of e-government development can be contrasted with both the Korean and Chinese cases because India possesses a federal form of government, which creates two different semi-autonomous levels to which e-government must be applied. To this end, the federal (central) government has primarily served to coordinate e-government policies among the regional governments, as well as coordinating policies between levels of government (Ministry of Communications and Information Technology, Government of India 2011). However given the scale of e-governmentization being undertaken, as well as the fact that India possesses a federal system of government, maintaining a consistent vision has proven to be difficult (Sharma 2010).

Previous literature assessing e-governmentization in developing nations has found that in this category of nations, the task of coordinating e-government projects to fall in line with a coherent long term policy vision is often very difficult, and contributes to the failure of a majority of the e-government projects undertaken in developing nations (Heeks 2003). Research conducted by Kumar and Best (2006) has found that such an argument fits the case of e-governmentization in India very well. In evaluating a program that introduced government service kiosks in the region of Tamil Nadu, India, the authors found that the program initially worked very well, but over time faltered due to a "lack of effective public leadership and sustained commitment". In seeking an explanation as to why commitment to the program dropped among community leaders, the authors found that the implementation of the government service kiosks throughout the region resulted in community level leaders feeling that their authority and legitimacy in their community (and perhaps their income, as well) was being eroded, as these figures were no longer able to use their positions to exert control over "how, when, and to whom the services are provided". To this end, using e-government services to solicit greater citizen participation and involvement, while apparently popular with citizens, turned out to be resisted by existing power configurations at lower levels of government, and subsequently led to the eventual abandonment of the e-government program. However, while the example in Tamil Nadu is certainly an interesting one, it is by no means unique, as additional research has revealed similar findings throughout India, with e-government projects typically being abandoned as policy makers and leaders at different levels of government change (Bhatnagar & Singh, 2010).

Hence, while citizens appear to be receptive to the expansion of participatory applications of e-government, and the Indian government has pledged its commitment and resources toward facilitating this expansion, it appears that a major obstacle to the success of e-government programs in India comes from local leaders, who seek to maintain their status with regard to citizens. Subsequently, the implications of this vein of findings related to the proliferation of e-government in India suggests that the aggressive implementation of e-government applications at the local and regional levels in India may provoke local leaders to attempt to consolidate their power vis-à-vis other social actors, therefore threatening the success of the e-government project, as well as democratic development in the region. To this end, while e-government research was an initial success in terms of increasing the efficiency of internal administrative processes and eliciting citizen participation, ultimately political factors rendered the program unsustainable. Thus, this example presents a different dynamic with respect to what was found in China, as it suggests that, in the event that e-government applications possess objectives of advancing democratic values and enhancing citizen participation, while not offering any incentives to extant elites, e-government reforms will ultimately prove unsustainable.

Mixed Effects: Korean Experiences with E-Government

In 1987, South Korea held its first democratic elections after decades of authoritative military control. Nearly 20 years later, South Korea is now acknowledged as possessing a fully developed democracy (ECI, 2008). Over the course of South Korea's democratic transition, government officials looked to e-governmentization as a means of reducing corruption, enhancing transparency, increasing government's accountability to citizens, and more broadly promoting good governance. As a result of these efforts with respect to e-governmentization, today, South Korea is a nation well known for its highly developed e-government services (Brookings 2008, UNPAN 2010). As much of the construction of South Korea's e-government services occurred at a time when South Korea was in the stages of consolidating its young democracy, the experiences of this nation with e-government are particularly applicable to developing nations who, like South Korea, are coming of age democratically in the age of the Internet. Tables 2 and 3 below provide e-government development index and e-participation index rankings assigned by the United Nations' e-government survey from 2005 to 2010.

The Process of E-Governmentization in South Korea

As is illustrated by the table below, the progression of e-government in South Korea can be categorized into three broad phases, with the beginning of the first phase closely corresponding to South Korea's transition toward democracy in 1987 (Hahm, 2008), and the initiation of the third phase corresponding to international organizations acknowledging South Korea as a fully developed democracy (ECI, 2008). Table 4 below illustrates these three phases.

From table four, the three phases of e-governmentization in South Korea closely suggest that orientation of e-governmentization in South Korea has progressed over time from an internally oriented phase to externally oriented phase, and is therefore similar to the models of e-governmentization suggested by Chadwick and May (2003), or Layne and Lee (2001). In the first phase of e-governmentization in South Korea, a clear emphasis is placed upon using e-government as a method of enhancing administrative efficiency by digitalization of government administrative processes. This internally (efficiency) oriented phase of e-governmentization in South Korea was initiated at a time when South Korea was beginning its democratic transition. It is interesting to note that, despite casting off decades' worth of

Table 2. E-Government development index

Country	2005		2008		2010	
	Score	Rank	Score	Rank	Score	Rank
South Korea	0.8727	5	0.8317	6	0.8785	1
US	0.9062	1	0.8644	4	0.851	2
Canada	0.8425	8	0.8175	7	0.8448	3
UK	0.8777	4	0.7872	10	0.8147	4
Netherlands	0.8021	12	0.8631	5	0.8097	5

Table 3. E-Participation index

Country	2005		2008		2010	
	Score	Rank	Score	Rank	Score	Rank
South Korea	0.8730	4	0.9773	2	1.0000	1
Australia	0.7143	9	0.8864	5	0.9143	2
Spain	0.0794	74	0.3636	34	0.8286	3
New Zealand	0.7937	6	0.7955	6	0.7714	4
UK	1.0000	1	0.4318	25	0.7714	5

Table 4. The evolution of South Korean e-government

Stage	Stage One: E-Government Infra-Development (1987-2002)	Stage Two: Full Fledged Implementation of E-Government (2003-2007)	Stage Three: Further Advancement of E-Government (2008-2012)
Goal	Digitalization of government business processes and the establishment of Information Technology Infrastructure	Expansion of e-government services through digitalization of overall government business processes	Integration of e-government systems for seamless delivery of public services
Key Action	Digitalization of government administrative processes (patent customs, taxes, etc.). Establishment of high speed internet networks. Pursuing e-procurement systems, and initiating the government 4 citizens project.	Expansion and improvement of services for citizens and businesses. Enhanced administrative efficiency and transparency through reform of government work methods. Interoperability among disparate information systems.	Customer-Centric citizen services and enhanced public participation. Intelligent administrative services through digital government networks. Real-time public safety information network. Strengthened e-government infrastructure through enhanced privacy and security.

Source: Korean Ministry of Public Administration and Security 2011

authoritarian rule, e-government policymakers in South Korea did not immediately opt to use ICT as a means of enhancing citizen participation in administrative processes, but rather sought to extend infrastructure that would facilitate the pursuit of this objective in the long term.

The second stage of e-governmentization in South Korea is best thought of as a transition phase, where the initially internally oriented implementation of e-government gradually started to place a greater emphasis upon managing government relationships with citizens. As table four exhibits, the South Korean government considers this stage as "full-fledged implementation of e-government". Subsequently, at this stage, the government began to pursue mechanisms to enhance the extent to which government processes were held accountable to citizens. In order to do so, e-government was used as a means of both disseminating information regarding government processes, as well as soliciting citizen opinions regarding various policies and gathering information concerning citizens' perceptions of government performance. To this end, e-governmentization was used as a means of enhancing citizen participation in only a limited (and perhaps cautious) capacity. This period of e-governmentization and

gradual enhancement of citizen participation can be considered as part of a broader reform agenda that was initiated slightly before the beginning of phase two, which emphasized decentralization and new public management oriented reforms. Finally, the inclusion of greater participatory (externally oriented) mechanisms in e-government in South Korea corresponds to a period when democracy was reaching an advanced stage of development.

The third and current phase of e-government development in South Korea can be considered a predominantly citizen (externally) oriented approach to e-government. In this phase, the government is emphasizing the management of its relationships with citizens, as well as focusing upon means of greater citizen participation in government processes, through the use of e-government and ICT. Based on the proliferation of mobile devices with Internet connectivity, such as smart phones and tablet personal computers, one means of enhancing citizen participation is through reaching out to citizens through such devices, which has led to what some refer to as an era of mobile-government (Rannu, Saksing, & Mahlakov, 2010). Subsequently, greater emphasis is being placed upon enhancing interoperability of different information platforms and ensuring the security of networks responsible for transferring information to and from government in this third phase of e-governmentization pursued by the South Korean government.

Thus, from the South Korean government's approach to e-government adoption, it is clear that an incremental approach was followed. Furthermore, it is interesting to note that the South Korean government persistently exhibited a long term orientation as is suggested by the shifting emphases that can be found with regard to internal and externally oriented applications of e-government. Finally, it appears that the implementation of e-government by the South Korean government was largely related to South Korea's democratic trajectory; as democracy further developed greater participatory mechanisms were included, however there is little evidence that the government immediately pursued participatory applications of e-government or ICT during the early stages of democratization.

Concerning ICT's effect on improving administrative efficiency, Korea experiences reveal largely positive outcomes. For example, the South Korean Procurement Service, which introduced an on-line bidding system, served to enhance transparency and reduce corruption rapidly and efficiently; both enhanced transparency and reduced corruption had been elusive for quite a long time (Im et al. 2007). However the implications of the use of e-government on traditional bureaucratic structures are not clear. Im's (2011) analysis suggests that IT effects on the morphology of government agencies differs according to the core technology used by the agency. Thus, while Im found that IT has increased the ratio of middle managers to subordinates in the Korean Central government, the number of middle managers has not changed radically and in some cases has steadily increased; overall downsizing effects of e-government on the bureaucracy of the central government is not proved. These results may be explained by the rigidity of the Korean government bureaucracy in terms of organizational management style.

Soliciting Citizen Interaction: The Dasan Call Center

A point that has been emphasized throughout the discussion of e-governmentization in this research is that e-government is often used by policy makers to advance political agendas. Furthermore, political applications of e-government are most likely to occur when an external orientation is adopted with regard to the application of e-government, or ICT more generally (c.f. Ahn and Bretschneider 2011). Subsequently, it is likely that, through the South Korean government's gradual introduction of participatory mechanisms in its application of ICT, the government was able to, for the most part, avoid e-government mediated politicking, which offers the potential to negatively affect a developing nation's democratic trajectory. To illustrate the means through which soliciting greater citizen participation can be used for political ends is the Soul Metropolitan Government's (SMG) Dasan Call Center (DCC). These points are elaborated upon below.

The DCC was established toward the end to the second phase of e-governmentization in South Korea, and was created with the intent of enhancing government transparency and accountability to citizens. As a means of doing so, the DCC employed telephone operators who had access to databases, which possessed a variety of non-confidential government information. Furthermore, government officials from various administrative organs of the SMG were established as DCC liaisons, and fielded transferred inquiries that DCC operators were unable to answer, or registered complaints of citizens. To this extent, the DCC served as a means of making government more accountable, while enhancing the government's accountability to citizens.

However, research by Im et al. (forthcoming) has suggested that the DCC, while very popular among citizens as evidenced through its high citizen satisfaction ratings, serves as a tool of the mayor to maintain control over increasingly autonomous local administrative districts in the city. Based on interviews with call center managers, city officials affiliated with the DCC, and an SMG auditor, the authors explain how the call center is used by the mayor's office to gather information regarding the performance of local administrative districts in the city, by collecting citizen complaints about these districts registered via citizens' use of the DCC. However, Im et al. find that while complaints against administrative districts are recorded, complaints against the SMG are disregarded for the purpose of performance evaluation, and that budget allocations made by the SMG to the semi-autonomous local administrative districts would be adjusted according to complaints concerning districts registered through the DCC. Thus, the emerging situation is one where the mayor of the SMG makes use of the DCC to ensure his authority over the local administrative districts in Seoul, despite their increasing autonomy, which ultimately serves to limit the extent to which these administrative districts are held accountable to citizens.

As the example provided by Im et al. (forthcoming) above illustrates, the introduction of participatory mechanisms into government does not immediately imply higher levels of democracy, and instead may actually serve to erode democratic development. Thus, a possible implication here for developing nation, which may be substantiated upon in future empirical research, is that the use of e-government, as well as ICT to promote enhanced citizen participation in government should be gauged according to level of democratic development. While the mayor of the SMG made use of the DCC as a mechanism for consolidating his power over semi-autonomous administrative districts, the argument can be made that the level of democracy present at the time was sufficient to withstand such a power consolidation attempt. In developing nations, which possesses less developed democracies, the likelihood of them possessing well established and influential opposition parties and democratic institutions is low. This

implies that attempts at power consolidation by politicians or various administrative organs may go unchecked.

LESSONS FOR DEVELOPING NATIONS AND CONCLUSION

A consistent theme throughout the case of e-government discussed by this research is that, while e-governmentization offers the potential for enhancing citizen participation in government, this enhanced participation is allowed by existing organizational elites selectively to advance existing agendas, as was the case in China and South Korea, or opposed for the reason that the use of e-government services is perceived by government leaders as a threat to their legitimacy, as was suggested by the Indian case. However, while the use of e-government was assessed in only three nations, what is suggested is that it may be difficult to find instances where e-government was adopted strictly for the sake of enhancing democracy. Rather, what our analysis of three very different cases suggests is that success and failure of e-government projects is often a result of attempts made by leaders at various levels of government attempting to consolidate their authority vis-à-vis other actors in society.

Considering the discussion above, and keeping in mind the relationship between (inevitable) enhancements in technology and increased expectations of citizen participation in government, it is important to acknowledge a few key points, which may be inferred from the arguments made in the previous sections. The first of these points is that an e-government project's chances of success may be bolstered if they possess a political champion who possesses the tenure, resources, and capacity to see the project through to completion. To this end, political leaders must decide upon applications of ICT and e-government that appeal to a broad base of social and political actors. For example, in the first stage of e-government development, South Korea focused almost entirely upon building a large ICT infrastructure throughout the nation, which was something that not only possessed a broad social impact, but was also easily passed from one ruling party to another. By contrast, in the Indian case discussed above, while the e-government applications were seemingly supported by a wide social base, there was insufficient political support.

The second point to bear in mind is that it may be wise for developing nations to view e-government as a means of enhancing levels of participation over the course of time, rather than racing to obtain such a goal in the short term. In doing so democratic values are given time to become more prominent and institutionalized throughout society. As such, citizens, as well as politicians will be given time to acclimatize to increased levels of transparency and external accountability, which are likely to be new concepts in such societies.

The third and final point for nations with developing democracies is that the paradigm of 'the more citizen participation the better democratic development' may require careful consideration in all nations, but particularly in developing nations. While citizen participation is important in the creation of a vibrant democracy, it is worthwhile to consider that many of the developed and stable democracies today were in no immediate hurry to extend e-government promises to expand citizen participation and more direct forms of democracy rapidly, the desirability of such change should also be carefully considered. The point here is not to argue for varying degrees of citizenship based upon access to the Internet, but rather to point out that perhaps it is in the interest of developing nations to focus their resources upon internal applications of e-government first, before moving toward enhancing levels of citizen participation.

ACKNOWLEDGMENT

This work was supported by a grant from the National Research Foundation of Korea (NRF-2011-330-B0195 [I00035]).

REFERENCES

Ahn, M. J., & Bretschneider, S. (2011). Politics of E-Government: E-Government and the Political Control of Bureaucracy. *Public Administration Review*, *71*, 414–424. doi:10.1111/j.1540-6210.2011.02225.x

Basu, S. (2004). E-government and developing countries: An overview. *International Review of Law Computers & Technology*, *18*(1), 109–132. doi:10.1080/13600860410001674779

Bhatnagar, S. C., & Singh, N. (2010). Assessing the Impact of E-Government: A Study of Projects in India e government. *Information Technologies & International Development*, *6*(2), 109–127.

Bhatnagar, S. C., & Singh, N. (2010). Assessing the Impact of E-Government: A Study of Projects in India Information. *Technologies & International Development*, *6*(2), 109–127.

Bing, S. (1992). The Reform of Mainland China's Cadre System—Establishing a Civil Service. *Issues & Studies*, *28*, 23–43.

Brewer, G. A., Neubauer, B. J., & Geiselhart, K. (2006). Designing and Implementing E-Government Systems: Critical Implications for Public Administration and Democracy. *Administration & Society*, *38*(4), 472–499. doi:10.1177/0095399706290638

Chadwick, A., & May, C. (2003). Interaction between States and Citizens in the Age of the Internet: e-Government in the United States, Britain and the European Union Governance. *An International Journal of Policy and Administration, 16*, 271–300. doi:10.1111/1468-0491.00216

Dada, D. (2006). E-readiness for developing countries: Moving the focus from the environment to the users. *The Electronic Journal of Information Systems in Developing Countries, 27*(6), 1–14.

ECI. E.I.U. (2010). The Economist Intelligence Unit's Index of Democracy 2010. *The Economist.*

Fountain, J. (2001). *Building the Virtual State: Information Technology and Institutional Change.* Washington, DC: The Brookings Institute.

Gerodimos, R. (2006). Democracy and the Internet: Access, Engagement and Deliberation. *Systematics. Cybernetics and Informatics, 3*(6), 26–31.

Gupta, M. P., & Jana, D. (2003). E-government evaluation: A framework and case study. *Government Information Quarterly, 20*, 365–387. doi:10.1016/j.giq.2003.08.002

Hahm, C. (2008). South Korea's Miraculous Democracy. *Journal of Democracy, 19*(3), 128–142. doi:10.1353/jod.0.0005

Haque, M. S. (2002). E-governance in India: Its impacts on relations among citizens, politicians and public servants. *International Review of Administrative Sciences, 68*, 231–250. doi:10.1177/0020852302682005

Heeks, R. (2003). *Most egovernment-for-development projects fail: How can risks be reduced?* Retrieved from http://idpm.man.ac.uk/publications/wp/igov/index.shtml

Ho, A. (2002). Reinventing Local Governments and the E-Government Initiative. *Public Administration Review, 62*(4), 434–444. doi:10.1111/0033-3352.00197

Holliday, I., & Yep, R. (2005). E-Government in China. *Public Administration and Development, 25*, 239–249. doi:10.1002/pad.361

Im, T. (2011). Information Technology and Organizational Morphology: The Case of the Korean Central Government. *Public Administration Review, 71*(3), 435–443. doi:10.1111/j.1540-6210.2011.02227.x

Im, T., Porumbescu, G., & Lee, H. (2013). ICT as a buffer to change: A case study of the Seoul Metropolitan Government's Dasan Call Center. *Public Performance Management Review, 36*(3), 436–455. doi:10.2753/PMR1530-9576360303

Im, T., Shin, H. Y., Hong, E. Y., & Jin, Y. G. (2007). IT and Administrative Innovation in Korea. *Korean Journal of Policy Studies, 21*(2), 1–17.

Jaeger, P. T., & Thompson, K. M. (2003). E-government around the world: Lessons, challenges, and future directions. *Government Information Quarterly, 20*, 389–394. doi:10.1016/j.giq.2003.08.001

Kettl, D. F. (2000). The Transformation of Governance: Globalization, Devolution, and the Role of Government. *Public Administration Review, 60*(6), 488–497. doi:10.1111/0033-3352.00112

Knack, S., & Keefer, P. (1997). Does Social Capital Have An Economic Payoff? A Cross-Country Investigation. *The Quarterly Journal of Economics, 112*(4), 1251–1288. doi:10.1162/003355300555475

Kumar, R., & Best, M. (2006). Impact and Sustainability of E-Government Services in Developing Countries: Lessons Learned from Tamil Nadu, India. *The Information Society, 22*, 1–12. doi:10.1080/01972240500388149

Layne, K., & Lee, J. (2001). Developing fully functional E-government: A four stage model. *Government Information Quarterly, 18*, 122–136. doi:10.1016/S0740-624X(01)00066-1

Liou, K. T. (2007). E-Government Development and Chinn's Administrative Reform. *International Journal of Public Administration, 31*, 76–95. doi:10.1080/01900690601052597

Markus, M., & Robey, D. (1988). Information technology and organizational change: Causal structure in theory and research. *Management Science, 34*(5), 583–698. doi:10.1287/mnsc.34.5.583

MOPAS. (2011). *E-government plans for 21st century*. Korean Ministry of Public Administration and Security.

Morgeson, F. V., VanAmburg, D., & Mithas, S. (2011). Misplaced Trust? Exploring the Structure of the E-Government-Citizen Trust Relationship. *Journal of Public Administration: Research and Theory, 21*(2), 257–283. doi:10.1093/jopart/muq006

Norris, D. F., & Moon, M. J. (2005). Advancing E-Government at the Grassroots: Tortoise or Hare? *Public Administration Review, 65*(1), 64–75. doi:10.1111/j.1540-6210.2005.00431.x

Norris, P. (2001). *Digital divide: Civic engagement, information poverty, and the internet worldwide*. Cambridge, UK: Cambridge University Press. doi:10.1017/CBO9781139164887

Pollitt, C. J. (2011). Mainstreaming Technological Change in the Study of Public Administration: A Conceptual Framework. *Public Policy and Administration*. doi:10.1177/0952076710378548

Ruth, S., & Doh, S. (2007). Is E-Government Ready for Prime Time? *IEEE Internet Computing, 11*(2), 80–82. doi:10.1109/MIC.2007.42

Sahay, S. (1997). Implementation of information technology: A space-time perspective. *Organization Studies, 18*(2), 229–260. doi:10.1177/017084069701800203

Savage, S. (2007). *Police Reform: Forces for Change*. Oxford, UK: Oxford University Press.

Smith, A., Schlozman, K., Verba, S., & Brady, H. (2009). The Internet and Civic Engagement. *Pew Internet*. Retrieved from http://www.pewinternet.org

Snellen, I. (2007). E-Government: A Challenge for Public Management. In E. Ferlie, L. E. Lynn, & C. Pollitt (Eds.), *The Oxford handbook of public management*. New York: Oxford University Press.

Thompson, F., & Jones, L. (2008). Reaping the Advantages of Information and Modern Technology: Moving from Bureaucracy to Hyperarchy and Netcentricity. *International Public Management Review, 9*(1), 148–192.

UNPAN (United Nations). (2010). *United Nations e-government survey 2008: From e-government to connected governance*. New York: United Nations.

Welch, E. W., Hinnant, C. C., & Moon, M. J. (2004). Linking citizen satisfaction with e-government and trust in government. *Journal of Public Administration: Research and Theory, 15*, 371–391. doi:10.1093/jopart/mui021

Yang, G. (2003). The Internet and civil society in China: A preliminary assessment. *Journal of Contemporary China, 12*, 453–475. doi:10.1080/10670560305471

Yildiz, M. (2007). E-government research: Reviewing the literature, limitations, and ways forward. *Government Information Quarterly, 24*(3), 646–665. doi:10.1016/j.giq.2007.01.002

Yildiz, M., & Kuban, A. (2011). *Discourses of E-Government: An Inductive Analysis*. Paper presented at the EGPA Conference. New York, NY.

Zhang, J. (2002). Will the government serve the people? The development of Chinese e-government. *New Media & Society, 4,* 163–184. doi:10.1177/14614440222226325

KEY TERMS AND DEFINITIONS

Citizen Participation: Citizens involvement in various government processes.

Democratization: The process of affording citizens greater control over their government.

Developing Nations: Nations that are not included in the OECD list.

E-Government: Online provision of government information and public services.

ICT: Information and communications technology.

Public Administration: Management and delivery of goods and services by administrative organs of the government.

Public Sector Reform: An attempt to improve an administrative process or outcome.

ENDNOTES

[1] Developing nations are often said to possess weaker institutions, which makes them more susceptible to corruption (Lederman et al. 2005). Moreover, developing nations often are found to lack resources that may be used to expand citizens' participation in government processes.

[2] The Irvine School refers to research conducted by Kraemer, King, Kling, Dutton and Danziger who have argued that the application of ICT to administrative processes often serves as a means of reinforcing extant status quos.

Chapter 3
Political and Cultural Issues in Digital Public Administration

Fuat Alican
Central American Scientific Research and Education Center, Costa Rica

ABSTRACT

Political and cultural aspects of digital public undertakings in developing countries are often neglected as more emphasis is placed on the technological components. The mutual impact between political or cultural issues and emerging trends such as cloud computing and social networks exacerbate the problem. This chapter analyzes political and cultural issues which have a significant impact on digital public administration and e-government initiatives in developing countries, also taking into consideration the emerging tendencies and technologies. It combines theory and practice, including studies that demonstrate different political or cultural issues involved in the digital undertakings in these countries, examples from different contexts and nations, and a case study from Turkey. The chapter starts with examples of different political issues, analyzing and summarizing some of the most relevant of these issues, including existing literature related to each subject. It continues with cultural issues. The subsequent section contains a discussion of how political and cultural issues relate to the tendencies of the Information and Communication Technologies (ICTs) sector, and why this context is important for digital initiatives in developing countries, as an initial guide to existing and future challenges. The chapter ends with the case of Turkey, which demonstrates political and cultural issues faced on both national and regional levels, in the context of digital public administration and emerging trends in ICTs.

INTRODUCTION

Almost all countries in the world have taken some steps to digitize their public administration, and have realized e-government initiatives in the recent past, especially in the last decade since the establishment of the Millennium Development Goals of the United Nations (UN). Advanced economies which had the necessary technology, skills, and capital were early adopters, aiming for higher productivity, competitiveness, transparency, and participation. These countries have reached much higher levels of digitization than developing nations. Despite significant efforts

DOI: 10.4018/978-1-4666-3691-0.ch003

in the recent years, including some relatively successful examples, the majority of developing countries still face serious challenges to catch up with their developed counterparts.

Political and cultural issues, neglected in most cases, are among these difficulties, as the above mentioned initiatives have been more technology centered than citizen oriented. When technological design of hard components such as engineering meets soft realities such as politics or culture, the result is almost always the same: partial or total failure.

This chapter aims to explore and address political and cultural challenges developing countries have faced and are expected to confront in digital public administration and e-government initiatives, taking into consideration the emerging tendencies and technologies. It combines theory and practice, building on existing theory on the subject and uses the case study of Turkey, along with other examples, as empirical evidence for these challenges.

POLITICAL ISSUES

One of the current and future challenges in digital public initiatives is politics. Politics, and hence the collective decision making process and structure, influences digital public administration and e-government efforts. The political environment in most of the developing countries is often inadequate for planning, implementing or measuring effectively these initiatives. Political instability, coalition governments, and authoritarian administrations are among the many factors, impeding digital efforts. On the other hand, successful implementation of an e-government design may not improve the human development of a developing nation or make it more democratic, even if it makes the government work more efficiently.

Many research studies argue that e-government nurtures politics through enhanced citizen participation and improved public services, though much remains to be done in this area. Its effects on democracy remain to be seen.

Nonetheless, the political aspect is crucial for the success of e-government initiatives in developing countries. Furuholt and Wahid (2008) argue that the main opportunities for e-government in general, like cost reductions, improved efficiency, and quality of services, will also apply to projects in developing countries, but governments of transitional democracies and developing economies may be driven more by a need to improve openness and citizen opportunities to solidify their legitimacy, and may thus emphasize reforms such as transparency and increased citizen participation.

Hanna (2009) suggests that e-government is essentially a political, not a technical project, which means that managerial and institutional reform must accompany technological change. According to Hanna, e-government is conditioned by the political and institutional context of its application, more than by other concerns such as technical standards and infrastructure. Hanna, therefore, concludes that understanding the political and institutional nature of e-government provides the key to seeking appropriate measures and entry points to realize the transformational potential of information and communication technologies (ICTs) for governance and public service performance.

AL-Shehry (2008) states that the political implications of e-government include many advantages for governors and citizens such as increased citizen participation in political processes, building trust between citizens and their government by improving the government's image, and facilitating democratic stages by voting online. AL-Shehry concludes, after an extensive literature review, that most factors of failure in information systems projects are related to ignoring or not caring about human and organizational issues while a few factors have a technical origin.

A successful e-government initiative includes the political aspect in its design, implementation and follow up, and creates a win-win situation for the government and its citizens, nurturing politics and the political system. The political aspect of digital public undertakings comprises many issues to consider and deal with. The following subsections analyze and summarize some of the most relevant of these issues, including existing literature related to each subject.

ICT as Part of Development Policies

National development plans and other countrywide programs are an increasingly important issue in digital undertakings, while the ICT aspect is gaining clout in national development plans.

ICTs can have a significant impact in the successful implementation of national development plans. They can contribute to all sectors of the economy, making them more productive. This is a crucial reason for ICTs in general and e-government initiatives in particular to be part of national development plans and vice versa.

Heeks, Gao, and Ospina (2010) argue that ICTs were initially ignored by policy while in a few countries they were idolized and seen as the key tool for delivering development, though today best practice is seen as the integration of ICTs into development policies and mainstreaming digital technologies so they become one of many delivery tools.

Though ICTs and digital initiatives should be a part of national development plans, it is convenient for this part to be one of the priorities, particularly considering the increasingly "everywhere" nature of the internet, the Internet of Things, and the convergence among countries, sectors, and

companies. All of these make ICTs and their recent trends much more than a fashion. They can contribute significantly to the sustainable development of emerging nations.

Leadership

Leadership is a key enabler for ICT projects in general. Leaders provide purpose to the rest of the people and actors involved and the proper guidance for them to fulfill that purpose. In many research studies, leadership stands out as the most frequently cited success factor in digital public administration and e-government initiatives.

Heeks, Gao, and Ospina (2010) argue that leadership is the single unifying solution to address the individual challenges for ICT's development contribution; and that ICT policy-making and implementation needs to be backed by strong, stable, and credible leadership with a powerful vision for ICT's development contribution, in order for that contribution to emerge.

Furuholt and Wahid (2008) suggest that in developing countries, especially in societies with a culture of great power-distance, leaders play an important role in deciding to implement e-government, and that strong leadership can ensure long-term commitment of resources and unify different fractions so that they collaborate and support government initiatives.

According to Furuholt and Wahid, success and failure criteria can be grouped into three main categories: management, infrastructure, and human factors. In the management category they include strategic issues, change management, political leadership, institutionalizing, and continuous monitoring and evaluation of projects. Infrastructure embraces ICT infrastructure, legislation, and financial resources; in other words, it includes technological, legal, and financial aspects. Human factors comprise competence and skills, training, and trust. While all three categories involve political issues, the management aspect is the one most directly related to politics.

In most cases, Furuholt and Wahid add, the greatest constraints to e-government are non-technical, in the management category, such as political opposition, deeply ingrained policies and practices, and internal employee resistance. Again, leadership is crucial to overcome these constraints and for governments to implement strategies for sustainable change. Furuholt and Wahid affirm that their literature analysis shows that strong political leadership is one of the most important success criteria for e-government projects in general and in developing countries in particular. This includes the sustainability issue, which involves political, cultural, financial, technological, and environmental factors.

Furuholt and Wahid verify the significance of leadership in e-government projects in the Indonesian case of Sragen, and confirm that strong leadership is important in managing e-government implementations with limited resources, and in generating progress over a period of time. Taking similarities and differences in other districts into account, they believe that this lesson from Sragen may be adopted both by other district governments in Indonesia and even by other developing countries in similar circumstances. According to Furuholt and Wahid, other important lessons to learn from the Sragen case are the involvement of all stakeholders from the beginning, exhaustive training and motivation of human resources, and partnership with external parties. All of these factors require strong leadership.

Hanna (2009) states that while the role of leadership is crucial to success, the majority of e-government initiatives have been managed by mid-level managers and ad hoc committees, with plenty of rhetorical references to the role of new technologies in development, but very little guidance on realizing this potential. According

to Hanna, most political leaders have only a limited understanding of the potential role of new technologies in public sector reform while others see no political incentive in embarking on such a demanding reform process.

Hanna expresses the need to have e-leadership at many political levels, including the executive and legislative branches, with the multifaceted ability and training to understand both the demand and the supply side of ICT. Among the examples given by Hanna, the CIO office in Korea and "transformation teams" in Turkey stand out as efforts to address the leadership issue.

Hanna affirms that decisions about technology are currently left in the hands of technical staffs, with very limited or nonexistent leadership and guidance from the political level, which results in a series of expensive technology acquisition decisions. According to Hanna, lacking standards, ICT governance framework, and top management involvement in setting priorities or enforcing standards typically result in a completely fractured technology platform, rarely driven by the current priorities or future vision of public sector reform.

Hanna suggests a number of measures in order to implement a new e-government vision. First, informed and committed leadership is needed, not only from politicians but also from external actors such as non-governmental organizations (NGOs). Second, incentives for reforms and sustained institutional change are necessary. Hanna stresses the importance to balance investments between quick impact applications and building platforms for wider impact and transformation. Third, a vision, a strategy, a plan, and a budget should be established. Hanna affirms that e-government strategy needs to be embedded in public sector reform strategy (for example, to facilitate decentralization, promote transparency and accountability, extend and improve public services to rural areas and the poor). According to Hanna, once such priorities are set, then ICTs can be integrated with mutually reinforcing measures to change policies, skills processes, investments, and incentives in support of these specific reform objectives.

Hanna suggests that external coalitions for e-government and public sector reforms are needed to complement the efforts of internal change agents and public managers, and adds that several challenges exist on that front: Public servants are often wary of this sort of cooperation; private sector associations defend their interests without contemplating a win-win approach; many of the NGOs are too weak to have an influence in the process; and academic institutions live in a world of their own.

Another key measure is addressing enabling policies at the highest political level in order to create the appropriate environment for a networked society. Hanna states that these include opening markets to competition to improve connectivity; improving opportunities for citizens' access to new technologies; investing in education and training resources to improve the workforce; and addressing infrastructure needs. Many of these policies and enabling conditions cut across sectors and ministries, according to Hanna.

Hanna adds that the image of modernization and the appeal of ICT as a key to the future may also attract political leaders to invest in new technologies to facilitate difficult transformations, converting e-government into a tool not only to redesign processes and substantially increase productivity of the public sector, but also to improve governance and facilitate broad and sustained institutional reforms.

One of the issues mentioned by Hanna is the requirement of a committed team to lead the effort to adopt best practices, which is often difficult, as foreign consultants do not have specific knowledge of the legal, normative, and organizational constraints in the country, while civil servants, their managers and other key stakeholders are often excluded from the initial design, practically guaranteeing their lack of cooperation through the implementation phase.

Private sector participation is another effective measure, according to Hanna, who affirms that in many countries the private sector is ahead of the government in deploying ICT for their own business process transformation and service delivery. Hanna suggests that it is useful to draw on the experience of the private sector in emphasizing the importance of institutional innovations and managerial improvements to realize the productivity potential of ICT investments. He points to experience showing that productivity increases are marginal, compared to the costs involved, when ICT investments are not accompanied by managerial improvements and institutional transformation. Hanna emphasizes that productivity improvements become substantial only when business organizations co-invest in ICT and managerial and institutional innovation.

What Hanna calls "managerial and institutional innovation" can also be translated as "improved processes" as many companies around the globe today, such as Toyota, improve their processes before they implement new technology. This strategy usually lowers technology costs, because when processes improve, and often get simplified, the need for technology decreases. Successful companies continuously improve their people, processes, and technology, in that order.

Hanna acknowledges the difficulty of applying this to the public sector, adding that incentives such as market forces and profit making do not apply to the public sector in the same way. Instead, incentives can exist in the form of public pressure to implement reforms and change in public organizations, while political commitment and an authorizing environment complement public pressure, according to Hanna. Hanna affirms that this pressure can be achieved through enhanced transparency and accountability, which can be provided by ICT.

A number of factors require strong leadership at all levels and by different actors: the vision for ICT's development contribution, ICT policy-making, setting priorities, enforcing standards, long-term commitment of resources, unification of different fractions toward the same purpose, overcoming political opposition and internal resistance, sustainable change, empowerment of the employees to fulfill the purpose, improvement of processes and implementation of new technology. Political leadership is especially important in the case of digital public administration and e-government initiatives.

Citizen Orientation in E-Government

ICTs should be part of development policies and leaders should guide the whole process, but in essence, development is about the people, and ICTs are for the people. This view has recently been gaining more advocates. Citizen orientation is becoming an increasingly important subject in digital public undertakings as the focus of this type of projects shifts from technology to people and from the supply side to the demand side.

Bidyarthi and Srivastava (2008) state that giving stakeholders direct access to government transactions via electronic means removes human intermediaries. With the technical infrastructure in place, according to Bidyarthi and Srivastava, a far more difficult task lies ahead if e-government is to make a significant impact on the interface between citizen and government: The top-down approach of popularizing e-governance needs to be supported by the bottom-up approach where citizens' perspectives play the most important role. This means that, to develop an integrated platform for delivering high-quality e-government services, governments need to pay attention to the services and success factors that are important to their citizens.

Bidyarthi and Srivastava consider "service encounter" a "major opportunity for an organization to make an impression in the minds of its customers as they evaluate service quality" (2008, p. 75). They affirm that these encounters, which

involved personal interactions between frontline employees and customers in the past, have been increasingly mediated by technology.

Bidyarthi and Srivastava give a few crucial tips for e-governance projects to be sustainable for citizens: they must provide cost-effective services, reducing red tape and corruption; a basket of one-stop citizen services should be available under one roof, ranging from registrations to bill payments, and the services should be available uninterruptedly regardless of technology issues; the format should be easily understandable and available in local languages, as language barriers can often lead to the failure of a project; and effective handling of complaints should be built into the system.

Digital public initiatives have the ultimate purpose of improving the life standards of the citizens. Therefore, they should include the citizens' desires, needs and perspectives throughout the project, including its design, implementation and evaluation. This would help improve the lives of the people, facilitate feedback to improve the project, and enhance the democratic system.

Political Aspects in the Failure of E-Government Initiatives

Most ICT projects fail partially or completely. They either cannot obtain the planned results, surpass the budget or are not completed within the deadline. Sometimes all of the above occurs. On other occasions, the project is discontinued before it is completed. There are various reasons behind these failures. One of the key factors is focusing solely on technology while neglecting the more intangible components such as politics or culture.

Digital public undertakings do not escape this reality. Political issues are often among the reasons of failure. Dada (2006, p.1) affirms that "e-government is not merely the computerization of a government system, but a belief in the ability of technology to achieve high levels of improvement in various areas of government, thus transforming the nature of politics and the relations between governments and citizens." This affirmation emphasizes the political nature of e-government initiatives. Dada defines e-government failure as the inability of such a system to achieve predefined goals or other previously anticipated benefits.

Dada quotes Ciborra (2005) who suggests that good governance is not always the outcome of e-government, and that bureaucratic or military administrations will not automatically become more transparent, efficient, and market-like as a result of it. Using a case study of e-government implementation in Jordan as a background, Ciborra suggests that developing countries may not be ready for such a system where citizens are seen as customers. Dada (2006, p.3) deduces that "this would mean that privileged segments of the population may have access to the services more easily, corruption can continue as favoritism and bribery are offered to new intermediaries, and levels of democracy and competition will not be affected." Dada also claims that the notion of e-government on its own is not suited for developing countries to obtain the associated benefits, and that, instead, political and social changes are required alongside the implementation of electronic mediums.

Dada places particular emphasis on two of Ciborra's affirmations. First, an economy will be required to develop to a service delivery state or a minimal state, where failures due to governance breakdown, corruption, rent-seeking, distortions in markets, and the absence of democracy are addressed before e-government can be implemented within it. Second, e-government applications could be used as a technology of control by the West in order to implement a self-regulating and self-monitored system of governance in weak states that may otherwise pose a threat to international security.

At this point, emphasizing the large differences between the design and the reality of e-government applications in developing countries as a signifi-

cant factor in the failure of these applications, Dada highlights the remaining question of whether the technology must be changed by designers to fit the context, or whether norms, structures, mind-sets, and work systems that constitute the context must be changed to fit the technology which is considered to reflect best practice. He suggests that "implementers of e-government must critically assess the situation and the technology at hand, and consider the motivations and the possibility of vested interests of various stakeholders involved in the project" (2006, p. 8). If implementers are aware of the situation, they can create the circumstances where gaps are reduced by social or technical change.

While many studies analyze and determine the factors of failure of both public and private digital initiatives, they are not always clear on the concept of "failure," which makes it more difficult to assess effectively such efforts. Dada admits this limitation and affirms that notions of success and failure are highly subjective. According to Dada, the outcome of something as difficult and complex to achieve as government reform, or higher levels of civic engagement by means of electronic media, may not be felt immediately, and it is easy to overlook positive elements, which often arise as a result of certain perceptions and attitudes.

In summary, at least two conclusions can be drawn from Dada's paper that are relevant to this section and add value to this chapter. First, as a general rule, ICT investments should be accompanied by managerial improvements and institutional transformation in order for the productivity improvements to become substantial, as Hanna (2009) affirms drawing on the experience of the private sector. However, each situation is different, and in the case of public undertakings, implementers of e-government must critically assess the situation and the technology at hand to decide whether social or technical change should come first in reducing the gaps between design and reality. Second, the evaluation and measurement of digital public initiatives must carefully reflect the main purpose, influence desired behaviors accordingly and include different types of variables and indicators, considering both short and long-term effects of the initiatives, and balancing internal and external perspectives, along with financial and operational performance.

E-Politics

While politics influence digital public administration and e-government efforts, the opposite is also true. ICT and digital initiatives play a significant role in the transformation of politics. E-politics has become an important subject both in developed and developing countries.

Finquelievich (2005) lists various innovations of contemporary democracies such as web pages of political parties and parliamentary assemblies, digital access to documentation and to administration of different organisms of public administration, continuous and live transmission of sessions by legislative cameras, electronic two-way communication between citizens and deputies, political forums and virtual groups of discussion and interchange of political information, and e-vote options in referendums and elections. Finquelievich adds that the internet enables its users to have access to a large quantity of information of interest in electronic format and political applications such as agreements signed by the governor; the voting results of the members of parliament; texts of laws; established treaties; transcriptions of the press conferences and platforms of political parties; and other means like online newspapers, magazines, journals, bulletins, newsletters, blogs, and e-mail chains.

Nonetheless, none of these tools by itself guarantees a more just political environment or any significant improvement in the democratic system without the existence of certain elements such as widespread access and usage. Prince (2005) analyzes the use of ICT in political campaigns, the transformation of politics in information society and e-politics. He defines online campaigns as

proselytizing activities developed by parties or candidates of elective posts, with partial, complementary or integral help of the internet, the World Wide Web, and ICT tools. Prince suggests that e-politics cannot exist without the corresponding access of a significant portion of the population to ICT, both quantitatively and qualitatively speaking. He claims that, in any design of new technology, it is important to comprehend not only the current activities and perceptions of their consignees, but also what these will do online in the future, as these factors will define the forms and the contents of political cyber-campaigns.

Prince contemplates important political issues going forward, that will be part of the future challenges of e-government initiatives: Will online political activity favor the concentration of political offer, give more power to the strong media and parties, or, on the contrary, help more marginal stakeholders? Who will take better advantage of this tool, the state and the established order, or the dissidents and anarchists? Or everybody in a dense and profound transformation?

Open-source software is also a part of e-government and e-politics. It is as much a political subject, especially for developing countries, as it is a technological or economic issue. Saroka and Poggi (2005) analyze the use of open-source software as a means to facilitate interoperability, avoid unnecessary purchases, bring flexibility and effectiveness, lower costs, and prescind from the decisions of the supplier to realize corrections or launch a new version. They also warn about the difficulties in implementing such systems like convincing numerous stakeholders, formation of alliances, and coordination of the activities.

Governments and governors in developed and developing countries introduce bills and decrees mandating the use of open-source software in state organizations and e-government. Many developing nations such as Brazil, Venezuela, and Argentina, and their governments, have been advocates of open-source software. Political will and awareness is crucial in the inclusion of open-source software in state affairs and e-government. Open-source, and its relation to e-government, is a subject that deserves a chapter, or a book, on its own. It embraces many fields such as open-source governance and open politics, especially considering the political issues involved in digital public administration. A detailed discussion of open-source software is beyond the purpose of this chapter. Nonetheless, it is important to emphasize that it will increasingly be a part of the political issues in the digital public administration of developing countries.

Local government is another politically relevant issue in e-government. Kaufman (2005) suggests that the local electronic government can and must be more than online information and services. She claims that the interactive potentiality of ICTs enables the development of highly participative mechanics on the virtual front, the substratum of which is derived from the public policies of the real world, and which can be deployed more easily in municipalities and cities than in central governments. According to Kaufman, this is already a fact, where the recipients are transformed into the organizing center of portals. Kaufman's ideas are supported by the fact that in many parts of the world governments first apply pilot projects in local political entities before undertaking a countrywide project. Especially considering the increasing importance of individual cities in the world economy, it is useful to put an emphasis on local governments in digital public initiatives.

E-politics in developing countries is a complex subject, which includes a wide range of issues such as different tools of ICT; access and usage of governments, other institutions, and citizens; open-source; and local governments. A careful consideration of each issue is important for the digital public undertakings to reach their goals and to facilitate the transformation of politics.

Monitoring and Evaluation

Monitoring, evaluation, and performance measurement is an important and often neglected aspect in any ICT project, and particularly in e-government efforts. There are many different forms of neglect and error in such projects and their evaluation: not taking measurements seriously, not dedicating enough time for the establishment of the correct indicators for measurement, measuring a certain part instead of considering the whole picture, not contemplating the ultimate purpose of the project, not including the impact of the measurements on behavior, usage of predetermined international generic models imposed by consulting firms or donor agencies (such as the UN or the World Bank) which often prescribe indicators proved to be useful in developed countries. The last point is an issue worth addressing in the digital public efforts of developing countries in general where donor agencies are involved, as the adaptation of these models can be severely impacted by the political and cultural issues discussed in this chapter.

Hanna (2009) suggests that monitoring of progress and evaluation of the development impact of e-government programs are critical to scaling up innovations and learning from success and failure. According to Hanna, participatory approaches to monitoring and evaluation should be encouraged as they engage clients and users of e-government services in learning, provide continuous feedback for timely adaptation and demand-driven investments, and help citizens apply pressure to realize the benefits of reforms and investments.

Monitoring and evaluation in e-government constitute both a political issue and a technological concern. The significance of the political dimension of digital public administration comes out most forcefully in the light of the errors mentioned above, such as not considering the ultimate purpose and the application of generic models of developed countries to developing nations, not to mention Hanna's suggestions like the evaluation of the development impact, and the use of participatory approaches.

Dialectic between Globalization and the Nation-State

The convergence among countries, sectors of the economy, segments of ICT, companies and individuals, facilitated or enabled by the new trends, products and services of ICT (explained in more detail in the section "Emerging technologies and their relation to politics, culture, and e-government"), creates new concerns, threats and opportunities for all nations. Autonomy is one these issues faced by developing countries. In other words, the paradox of globalization and the nation-state is also among the political concerns involved in digital public undertakings.

Westrup and Al-Jaghoub explore this paradox and argue that "ICT-enabled development needs to be conceptualized within a dialectic process of globalization where, on the one hand, the flows of capital, commodities and information are expanding and accelerating while, on the other, nation-states are essential components in providing the infrastructures for production, regulation and consumption of these flows" (2008, p. 1). Westrup and Al-Jaghoub, in their analysis of Jordan and REACH, this nation's program of ICT-enabled change, conclude that institutions of a developmental network state have to negotiate a series of dilemmas centered on over-autonomy vs. over-embeddedness on the one hand and the capability to sustain and develop through time and space on the other.

Westrup and Al-Jaghoub observe that Jordan, indicative of the difficulties for a post-colonial country in creating a network polity, is shown to be a recent developmental network state, with REACH being paradoxically over-embedded and over-autonomous at the same time. One of the

conclusions of their analysis is that the mediation of glocal processes in REACH shows how important a variety of non-market mechanisms are to the working of ICT-enabled development, and that their absence can help explain early problems, with REACH failing to achieve its targets for ICT foreign direct investment.

Westrup and Al-Jaghoub state that policy initiatives and academic literature argue or presume that the nation-state should play an important role in ICT-enabled development, while a debate remains on what agency a nation-state has and how it may be exercised in a globalizing world. Westrup and Al-Jaghoub discuss what nation-states can do to assist ICT-enabled development in a world where the example of ICTs themselves appears to privilege flows and the global rather than what is in the control of individual states. First, they argue that the role of the state is being rescaled, and, its agency, changing, within a dialectic of globalization in which nation-states are a key component. Second, they focus on a series of dilemmas facing a nation-state engaged in ICT-enabled development that requires the creation of networks of agencies whilst seeking to embed ICT developments in local businesses and communities. Finally, they affirm that this analysis criticizes notions that ICT-enabled development is a distanceless activity in a world of flows where any state can potentially transform its economy through ICT foreign direct investment.

Westrup and Al-Jaghoub use the example of Jordan and REACH, a project that began in 1999 and initially focused on building an ICT industry, to develop these arguments. Jordan is used in this analysis for several reasons: as a small country, many of the processes in ICT-enabled development are easier to delineate; ICT-enabled development has been a central tenet of government policy since 1999, with King Abdullah II being credited as a key instigator for ICT-enabled development and example of political will; and Jordan is seen by the International Monetary Fund (IMF) and the World Bank as an exemplar of a developing country, and provides insights into ICT-enabled development. In short, Westrup and Al-Jaghoub argue that Jordan, a small and relatively success-ful developing country (by IMF and World Bank standards) with few resources, where ICT-enabled development is a central tenet of government policy, is a special case for investigation.

Westrup and Al-Jaghoub conclude that infor-mational capitalism provides the promise of con-nection and inclusion for countries whose previous geographies and histories left them in a limbo of poverty, without showing how global flows can embed in specific territories. Their main finding is that "Jordan shows ICT-enabled development to be enfolded in political, economic and cultural processes" (Westrup and Al-Jaghoub, 2008, p. 27). They suggest that a developmental network state seeks to plan its development strategies, while ICT-enabled development is linked with the creation of new institutional forms, the valorization of the private sphere, and a consequential diminution of the role of the state. Embedded autonomy, as a key feature in preserving the state's ability to plan while engaging business and civil society, is a useful corrective to free-market dogmas of the distanceless and placeless capabilities of ICT on the one hand, and the expectation that develop-ment depends on creating new institutions and institutional change on the other, according to Westrup and Al-Jaghoub.

Westrup and Al-Jaghoub affirm that prescrip-tions for change and placing a bet on the IT sector is a slow process in an unstable region, in which the state cannot afford to relax its control of civil society as the expectations of ICT-enabled development might predict. This pace includes e-government, glocalizing flows of resources, the embedding of these initiatives, and the expected economic and social change. Both the unwilling-ness of the state to cede agency to civil society and the difficulty faced by the civil society to accept new forms of agency expected of them may play a role in the speed of the developments, and a slower rhythm of change enabled by ICTs may

be more likely to embed successfully in Jordan, according to Westrup and Al-Jaghoub.

Westrup and Al-Jaghoub argue that the com-plexity of glocal processes demonstrates how difficult it is to model ICT-enabled development. One of their main findings is that "the experi-ence of Jordan can illustrate the role of the state in seeking to develop ICT industries, but due to the specifics of time and place, these particular experiences cannot be generalized" (Westrup and Al-Jaghoub, 2008, p. 28). This last finding may need interpretation for this chapter. It may be more complete to affirm that it is not recommended to apply the model of Jordan to other countries as each nation has different political, social and economic traits, while lessons drawn from Jordan could be useful in the digital journeys of other developing countries. This affirmation would also be in line with the belief of Furuholt and Wahid (2008) that the lessons from Sragen in their study could be used by other district governments in Indonesia, taking similarities and differences into account in other districts, and even by other developing countries in similar circumstances.

On the other hand, the most relevant conclusion that can be drawn from this study for this section is that digital public initiatives in developing countries include complex political issues such as autonomy. With this subsection, an illustra-tive set of examples of different political issues comes to an end.

CULTURAL ISSUES

Culture is another factor that contributes to the success or failure of any digital public undertak-ing. A wide range of studies, with varying defini-tions of this concept, conclude that culture plays an important role in the ICT adoption process. Moreover, it is a factor that impacts the political system, which in turn influences the technology use in a society. There are different types of im-pact among culture, politics, and technology, as the relationship is not necessarily one way, but rather a dynamic one: the political system can help shape the culture, while technology modifies politics or culture.

Seng, Jackson, and Philip (2010) state that as more and more activities are migrating from physical to virtual media, users and employees have been faced with relentless pressure to use technology, a phenomenon which calls for a greater understanding of the human, social, and cultural issues involved in the acceptance of IT systems by all stakeholders of the organization. Considering the new technological environment of "internet everywhere" and of poorer nations, small and medium-sized enterprises (SMEs), and individuals more empowered and connected than ever, this assertion deserves close attention, in the context of e-efforts of governments in developing countries. The following subsections analyze and summarize some of the most relevant of the cultural issues, including existing literature related to each subject.

Information Culture in Developing Countries

The reciprocal and dynamic relationship between technology and culture, and the social facet of digital public initiatives call for a comprehensive approach, bringing together ICT and the human aspect. This approach, applied to the developing countries, makes information culture a useful starting point to explore the relationship between digital public undertakings and culture, as it encompasses the developmental aspect and the goal to become an information society.

Zheng and Heeks (2008), in an attempt to go beyond the technocentric approach of strategies and perspectives for informatization in many developing countries, conceptualize a more holistic framework for understanding the information society in development. They seek to move not only beyond technocentrism but also beyond the determinisms and other limitations of earlier informational and cultural responses, to a more holistic understanding that is able to combine both arguments for a more information-centric perspective on national development and those for a more sociocultural perspective. Zheng and Heeks build this framework around the idea of an information culture in developing countries, using Giddens' structuration theory as a point of departure, and an exploratory application based around China, with a particular focus on its healthcare sector. They conclude that information culture can be conceived at multiple levels in terms of three interlinked dimensions: information literacy, information openness, and information norms.

Zheng and Heeks highlight the importance of this study to understand how actions can reproduce and reinforce a country's information culture, while it also identifies broader tensions that affect many developing countries: marketization/state-collectivism, globalism/nationalism, technology/manual, and other potential contradictions (some of which are similar to the paradox demonstrated by Westrup and Al-Jaghoub (2008) in the case of Jordan in the subsection "Dialectic between globalization and the nation-state" of the section "Political issues"). They attempt to move to a working definition of information culture: "the general capabilities, views, norms, and rules of behavior, with regard to accessing, understanding, and using information in a social collectivity" (Zheng and Heeks, 2008, p. 8).

Zheng and Heeks state that "the division of information culture into the three dimensions of literacy, openness and norms was seen more as an analytical device than a reflection of experienced structuration, and the interweaving of the dimensions can be seen in the impossibility of neatly compartmentalizing discussion of any one dimension without reference to the others" (2008, p. 17). In their use of China as a case study, they acknowledge the specificities of this country, but also argue that many of the features described in this case are found in many other countries: rapid growth of ICT infrastructure; increasing use of market mechanisms including their use to reform the public sector; increasing imperatives from globalization; lack of information literacy and information-handling skills; widespread information systems failure; rote-learning within the education system; increasing use of new media channels; information asymmetries between citizen and state alongside some signs of change in those asymmetries; cultural norms of relevance to information described in terms such as subjective, personalized, and authoritarian alongside a recognition of the dynamism of culture.

Zheng and Heeks point out that "technology enacts and reproduces or amends information culture, while information culture frames and constrains the use of technology" (2008, p. 17). They argue that visions of an information society need to broaden from that of ICT infrastructure and diffusion to a more holistic vision that also encompasses information culture, which would imply a greater concern with the trajectories of information literacy and information openness, recognition of the way in which information norms impact the economic and social utilization of information, and an interest in social institutions, social practices and social innovation alongside technological innovation.

Zheng and Heeks explain that, in their study, structuration theory is a point of departure rather than complete superstructure for the information culture framework. They claim to have drawn in part on two aspects of Giddens' work that do not appear to receive so much attention in information systems research: "conceptual support for analysis of collectivities, and for analysis of systemic contradictions experienced by members of those collectivities" (Zheng and Heeks, 2008, p. 17). Zheng and Heeks acknowledge that, in order to provide a narrative at national level, their study has necessarily been limited in the extent to which it has engaged with some key aspects of structuration, such as its interpretivism and the duality of structure and agency.

They add that, despite this limitation, "we can understand information culture in developing countries partly through the notion of situated agency that is not determined by structure but is both constrained and enabled by structure and also instantiates that structure in the act of social practice" (Zheng and Heeks, 2008, p. 18). They claim that this must be understood as something that is always present which may be reproduced through social practice but which evolves and may even be cultivated.

Hence, alongside the micro-level basis for the reinforcement of information culture, Zheng and Heeks also find the basis for its dynamism: both the unintended and the reflexively-determined outcomes of individual actions. They discuss the latter in this paper, identifying broader tensions found in China but also in other developing countries (marketization/state-collectivism, globalism/nationalism, technology/manual) that create a reflexive space for agency that, in turn, may incrementally affect information culture. They also identify more specific tensions that may impact individuals, while they interpret the SARS (Severe Acute Respiratory Syndrome) episode "as an occurrence that served to particularly focus and even intensify some of these tensions, thus providing a particular opportunity for change in information culture" (Zheng and Heeks, 2008, p. 18).

Zheng and Heeks conclude that the dynamism of information culture in developing countries can be understood at the level of social collectivities like the nation-state, partly by recognizing the common patterns that can be observed stretching beyond the individual, and by recognizing the different levels at which space for agency can exist. Therefore, Zheng and Heeks see the evolution of China's information culture to be the outcome of social integration (the social practices of individual doctors, health professionals, hospital managers, etc) as well as a result of system integration (the actions of strategically-placed agents with power to affect a collectivity). Hence they believe it remains appropriate to conceive of something called "information culture" at the national level in developing countries even while recognizing its complexity and its dynamism.

The most relevant results, findings, and contributions of this study to consider in digital public undertakings include: a working definition of information culture, combining information-centric and sociocultural perspectives, the dynamic relationship between technology and information culture, the features and contradictions found in developing countries, such as globalism vs. nationalism, and understanding how actions can reproduce and reinforce a country's information culture.

Impact of National Culture on E-Government Readiness

There are many studies which explore the impact of culture on ICT adoption in general and digital public undertakings in particular. Though there are different approaches and methods of exploration on the subject, some of these studies are based on Hofstede's cultural model or use it as a point of departure, as it provides a relatively simple and quantifiable framework.

Kovacic (2005), for example, illustrates how worldwide e-government readiness and its components are related to culture, using Hofstede's model. He sets out to provide a theoretical framework for the impact of national culture on e-government readiness. Kovacic affirms that while most of the other papers in this area focus on an individual indicator of a country's e-readiness (for example, the number of internet hosts per 100 citizens), this one is the first to use a synthetic indicator to measure e-government readiness, with a data set that includes the largest number of countries in comparison to data sets in other papers.

Kovacic states that the concept of culture adopted and used in this paper is based on the works of Hofstede, who defines culture as "a system of collectively held values" (Kovacic, 2005, p.

144). The study uses four largely independent dimensions of differences between national value systems: power distance, individualism vs. collectivism, masculinity vs. femininity, and uncertainty avoidance.

Kovacic states that "the power distance dimension reflects the perception that members of society have about unequal distribution of power in institutions and organizations and the extent to which it is accepted in a society" (2005, p. 147). According to Kovacic, a country with a large power-distance would have a negative attitude toward implementing and using ICTs. Kovacic explains this argument, stating that people in countries where power distance is large accept a hierarchical order in which everybody has a place that needs no further justification, while countries with small power-distance allow upward social mobility of its citizens and their participation in the process of decision making, which could be positive for the implementation of ICTs.

Kovacic further argues that a country with a strong individualistic culture would have a positive attitude toward implementing and using ICTs, as this type of culture would pay more attention to the performance of the individual, where time-management would be important and any technology that could help individuals to perform more efficiently would be highly regarded and quickly accepted.

The third dimension of the study is masculinity/femininity, described as "the achievement orientation in a society" (Kovacic, 2005, p. 147). Kovacic finds a mixed impact on ICTs for this dimension. According to Kovacic, when the preferences in a society are for achievement, assertiveness, and material success, then the country is ranked high on masculinity, while cultures that rank low on masculinity and high on femininity prefer focusing on relationships, caring for the weak, and the quality of life. Kovacic explains that some authors argue that ICTs promote more cooperation at work and better quality of life, which point to high femininity, whereas it could be claimed equally well that in a country with high masculinity there would also be a positive attitude toward implementing ICTs if these technologies improve performance, increase the chance of success, and support competition.

Finally, Kovacic suggests that countries with strong uncertainty-avoidance would be slow in the adoption and use of new ICTs, while nations on the opposite end of this scale would be leaders in implementing new ICTs and willing to take the risk of failure, based on the description of the uncertainty-avoidance dimension: "the degree to which members of a society feel uncomfortable with uncertainty and ambiguity, preferring structured over unstructured situations" (2005, p. 148).

Another important argument of Kovacic is that, though in his conceptualization Hofstede treats national culture as systematically causal, the relationship between organizational cultures and ICTs is not simply causal and either one can cause changes in the other, because technology is part of culture and vice versa. According to Kovacic, "there is a reflexive and dynamic relationship between national culture and ICTs rather than causal" (2005, p. 149).

Kovacic concludes that national cultural indicators have a moderate impact on e-government readiness worldwide, with individualism and power distance being the only significant variables among four cultural dimensions that could be used to explain differences in the level of e-government readiness. The conclusions and findings of Kovacic come with certain reservations as national culture constructs were derived from the Hofstede cultural model, and other cultural models may be necessary to check whether cultural constructs based on alternative theories confirm the impact that national culture has on e-government readiness. According to Kovacic, alternative definitions and indicators of e-government readiness could also prove helpful to see how robust the results in this study are, where e-government readiness is defined as "the aptitude of a government to use ICTs to move its services and activities into

the new environment" (Kovacic, 2005, p. 144), based on the UN's definition: "the generic capacity or aptitude of the public sector to use ICT for encapsulating in public services and deploying to the public, high quality information and effective communication tools that support human development" (UN, 2003, p. 11).

This study demonstrates the impact of culture on e-government readiness worldwide. On the other hand, it is equally significant to note that it is not always a one-way and causal relationship. While it uses Hofstede's cultural model, it is important to highlight its argument that there is a reflexive and dynamic relationship between national culture and ICTs, which has similarities with the affirmation of Zheng and Heeks (2008) that technology enacts and reproduces or amends information culture, while information culture frames and constrains the use of technology. The reciprocal relationship between technology and culture is an important factor to consider in the design, implementation and evaluation of digital public initiatives.

A final note as an addition to the aforementioned reservations, especially with respect to using this study with caution in the context of developing countries, is that it is a worldwide work which comprises a wide range of nations including both developed and developing ones. This global and general picture is complemented in the following subsections where we move toward more regional and specific settings, involving developing countries and their cultures in an increasing and more distinctive manner.

Impact of Cultural Differences on E-Government Adoption in Europe

There has been more emphasis on the supply side of e-government, leaving the demand aspect with little attention, especially in developing countries. Arslan (2009) highlights this focus on the supply side (or government-related issues) such as strategies and policy challenges, technical issues, evaluation of the usability of e-government web-sites, and the neglect on the demand (or citizen's) perspective. He emphasizes that recent studies of the citizen adoption of e-government services suggest that trust, security, and transparency are major issues for e-government adoption, and explores whether cross-national differences in the adoption of e-government in Europe are associated with differences among national cultures as described in Hofstede's model of cultural dimensions.

Arslan mentions various studies with findings that suggest that the cultural factor and the cross-cultural differences, as a source of acceptable norms and behaviors, may influence online expectations, preferences, and experiences of the public attitudes toward ICT adoption in general and e-government adoption in particular. Arslan also quotes a study from the innovation literature, by Herbig and Dunphy (1998), that provides evidence of cross-cultural influence on innovativeness. According to this work, which cites several other studies, societies which provide a suitable environment for innovative ideas are distinguished by higher individualism, willingness to take risks, readiness to accept change, long-term orientation, low power-distance, weak uncertainty-avoidance, openness to new information, frequent travel, positive attitude toward science, high education levels, being early adapters, and religion. Arslan also mentions the findings of Shane (1993), which suggest that rates of innovation, measured as per capita number of trademarks, are mainly influenced by low uncertainty-avoidance, and, to a lesser extent, by weak power-distance and strong individualism.

Arslan chose, among the models that have been developed to analyze cultural differences, Hofstede's model of cultural indexes as the most widely known, despite some criticism, as it provides a general framework for analysis that can be easily applied because it reduces culture and its interactions to quantifiable dimensions. He uses Hofstede's model which consists of four cultural indexes (power distance, uncertainty avoidance,

individualism, and masculinity), and adds, based on a Chinese value survey, a fifth dimension: long versus short-term orientation.

The study realized by Arslan suggests that "culture does play a significant role on e-government adoption for European countries" (2009, p. 12). Nonetheless, Arslan acknowledges that there are other factors to consider such as education level and internet diffusion, and highlights the difficulty of isolating the culture factor from other causes.

This study, which uses Hofstede's cultural model as a point of departure, as in the study of Kovacic (2005), narrows the scope of the exploration of the impact of culture from a worldwide perspective to a regional view for this section. This is especially relevant for the case study covering Turkey at the end of this chapter. The emphasis of Arslan on the demand perspective is also significant within the context of the growing importance of citizen and user participation, and of the empowerment of developing countries, SMEs and individuals.

Cultural Issues in User Experience in E-Government

Europe is a convenient place to study the impact of culture on digital public initiatives as it is a multicultural region which includes developed and developing countries. This heterogeneous characteristic of the continent is also valid for many of the individual nations within the region. Significant differences can exist particularly among the user experiences of the people with different cultural backgrounds within one country, city or local jurisdiction.

Dam, Evers, and Arts (2005) examine the influences of culture on the user experience of local e-government services, testing the hypothesis that people with different cultural backgrounds experience different problems when using e-government applications, in a study that includes participants with the Moroccan, Surinamese and Dutch cultural backgrounds, using a Dutch local e-government site. They conclude that differences in user problems coincide with expectations based on cultural characteristics from the literature, and their findings support the notion that users with different cultural backgrounds experience different user problems.

Dam et al. (2005) divide user experience problems into four categories: concern for detail, browsing behavior, approach to the website, and reaction to usage problems. They affirm that where the Moroccan and Surinamese participants are very concerned with the details of web pages, the Dutch do not put much effort into reading details, erratically clicking on links without concern for error. A consequent finding of the study is that the Moroccans and the Surinamese participants need more time to complete the tasks than the Dutch.

Dam et al. (2005) explain that the browsing behavior of the participants differs considerably: The Dutch and Surinamese participants start browsing in the top left-hand corner, while the Moroccans commence in the top right-hand corner, each therefore missing certain elements of the site in their first glance. One example given by Dam et al. (2005) is that the Dutch and Surinamese participants miss a crucial link to the online form that is situated in the top right-hand corner on certain pages as a result of their browsing behavior, leading to a longer browsing process.

Attitudes with which the website is approached also differ between the participants, according to Dam et al. (2005), the Dutch approach the tasks with nonchalance and confidence, while the Moroccans seem more uncertain. A result of this is that the Dutch users have problems in finding the correct link, as they do not take the time to read details and instructions, while the unconfident Moroccan users consider the long texts cumbersome.

The last category, reaction to usage problems and mistakes, also provides an interesting finding: The Moroccans blame themselves for their problems and often end up in an impasse, resulting in lengthy transactional procedures, while the Dutch

and the Surinamese blame the website and are therefore often hesitant to continue, as a result of their lack of trust in a supposedly flawed system.

Dam et al. (2005) also suggest that the concern for detail of the Moroccan and Surinamese people could be related to their high uncertainty-avoidance, whereas the Dutch culture, known for its low uncertainty-avoidance, only shows caution when legal documents are involved in the tasks.

Dam et al. (2005) claim to have discovered other interesting issues in this study. One of these issues is that the Moroccan language is read from right to left, which is a trait that is reflected in their browsing pattern as these participants scan pages in the same direction. Another suggestion is that the reason behind the Moroccan participants' attention to green and red could be that these are Islamic holy colors.

Another finding of Dam et al. (2005) is that when one considers the manner in which the tasks are carried out on the website, the significant others (variable in which one measures the importance for individuals to perform well in front of others, directing behavior towards the expectations of others) and masculinity variables could be influential. Dam et al. (2005) affirm that Moroccans have high value-scores for these variables, and are therefore prudent and insecure during the process, while the Dutch and Surinamese participants approach the site with more nonchalance and confidence, and complete the task without any notable reaction, possibly as a result of their low significant others value and the high score on femininity. Dam et al. (2005) attribute the open emotional reactions of the Moroccan culture to their affective nature, suggesting that the lack of emotion in the Dutch and Surinamese reactions could be because of their neutral culture.

Dam et al. (2005) further suggest that the fact that Moroccans blame themselves for the mistakes they make could be influenced by their collectivist and high power-distance nature, while the individualist Dutch, who have a low power-distance nature, blame the website. Dam et al. (2005) have a more difficult time explaining the blaming of the website of the Surinamese despite their collectivist culture, concluding that this could be the result of the low power-distance score of the Surinamese.

The low number of participants and cultural backgrounds in this research leads Dam et al. (2005) to recommend being cautious in using or applying their study to other contexts and doing further research with larger and more culturally diverse populations in order to understand with more certainty in what way these differences in cultural background influence behavior and user experience.

Nonetheless, this study is important to highlight the influences of culture on the user experiences of e-government services in a local context within one country. There are many developing countries such as Turkey, India, and China that have regions with important cultural differences among and within themselves that would be useful to contemplate in their national or regional digital public efforts.

Impact of National Culture on E-Government: Developed vs. Developing Country Context

Despite some challenges in common, developing countries face many different issues than the ones experienced by their developed counterparts with respect to digital public undertakings, as the former usually find themselves at earlier stages of e-development. Understanding the similarities and differences in challenges confronted by nations in different stages of development are of particular help in drawing lessons from different contexts.

Ali, Weerakkody, and El-Haddadeh (2009) explore the influence of national culture on e-government implementation and diffusion, conducting a comparative case study in two different countries: the United Kingdom (UK) as a developed country and Sri Lanka as a developing country. Their findings highlight the potential influence of cultural differences on e-government.

Ali et al. (2009) affirm that "although the UK and Sri Lanka show cultural dissimilarity, they share administrative and technological similarities" (2009, p. 2). They take up the following research question: "What is the influence of national culture on e-government implementation and diffusion between two administratively similar, but economically and culturally dissimilar countries?" (Ali et al., 2009, p. 2). Here the authors present a comparison of e-government issues between the West London Borough in the UK and Colombo, Sri Lanka.

First, Ali et al. (2009) find lack of strategy and high level guidance as weaknesses in Sri Lanka, while it was the opposite in the UK, where high-level support and clear strategy were evident. They identify lack of government support as a key issue impeding the progress in Sri Lanka, suggesting that the UK's culture has a long-term orientation whereas Sri Lanka is described as a culture with short-term orientation.

Ali et al. (2009) find the lack of infrastructure in Sri Lanka as a wide technical challenge for e-government, influenced by limitations of the telecommunications system, calling for support from foreign donor agencies or private sector collaboration for further expansion. The situation in Sri Lanka is compared to the issues faced in the British case, where challenges are associated more with procedural issues such as calling tenders and buying the appropriate technology.

Ali et al. (2009) identify the lack of coordination among various e-government-related projects as a key challenge that needs to be addressed in Sri Lanka, as opposed to the UK, where a centralized e-government strategy provides the necessary framework and guidelines for local councils. Ali et al. (2009) attribute this difference to the fact that Sri Lanka's culture is more inclined towards individualism while the UK's culture shows more collectivism.

A common issue found in both cases is the one of paradigm shift or reluctance to change. Ali et al. (2009) find that this challenge applies to both citizens and government officials in Sri Lanka, while in the UK citizens are more neutral towards e-government, suggesting that Sri Lanka's culture is more risk-averse and has higher power-distance than that of the UK.

Language problem is another common issue for the two cultural contexts, though more crucial in Sri Lanka since the majority of the population and government officials operate mainly in Sinhalese or Tamil (the national languages), while most of the new ICT solutions are only available in English. Ali et al. (2009) identify low ICT literacy as another challenge impeding the introduction of the e-government initiative in Sri Lanka. Meanwhile, the study reveals that citizens in West London are more used to face-to-face or telephone contact with their council rather than using web-based e-services, and that many elderly citizens there lack adequate literacy in ICT, suggesting that this is a key challenge not only for Sri Lanka, but also for the UK.

This study demonstrates the influence of cultural differences on e-government implementation and diffusion, comparing nations of different socioeconomic development level. This type of comparisons is especially useful for developing countries which elaborate their digital plans with the current and future states in mind; hence, these studies can help evaluate the challenges at hand, visualize the desired situation and foresee future issues. It may even be more useful for intermediately developed countries that may exhibit characteristics of varying levels of development on different issues. Turkey is a particularly relevant example: As a developing nation aspiring to membership in the European Union (EU), it can use the experiences of its developed counterparts as a benchmark or as best practices, while drawing lessons from other developing countries.

Cultural Factor in E-Government in Developing Countries

There are other studies that explore the impact of culture on digital public undertakings exclusively in developing countries. These studies are important to include in this chapter due to the focus of this book on developing nations.

Seng, Jackson, and Philip (2010) use an anthropological framework based on the Grid and Group Cultural Theory of Mary Douglas to examine cultural barriers and enablers which have impeded or facilitated the implementation of e-government initiatives in Malaysia. They apply the four cultural cosmologies established by this framework to study this issue: hierarchism, egalitarianism, individualism, and fatalism. Seng et al. argue that cultural cosmologies can have both enabling and constraining characteristics and that cultural pluralism in the enabling forms of hierarchism, egalitarianism, and individualism is essential for the successful implementation and operation of e-government services. They illustrate this point through two case studies in Malaysia, one showing constraining characteristics, which impede IT implementation and use, and the other displaying enabling traits, which facilitate IT implementation and use.

Seng et al. highlight three main problems with Hofstede's cultural model: It assumes culture to be static over time; it considers culture to be homogeneous; and it disregards cultural pluralism. They use the Grid and Group Cultural Theory to avoid these difficulties, "grid" referring to the extent to which one's social position is restricted by externally imposed prescriptions, "group" referring to the extent to which the individual's life is absorbed in and sustained by group membership. Seng et al. establish four ways of life by the application of "grid" and "group": fatalism (strong grid, weak group), hierarchism (strong grid, strong group), individualism (weak grid, weak group), egalitarianism (weak grid, strong group). According to Seng et al., fatalism causes an unwillingness to accept IT or new systems, hierarchism favors control, power, and domination, where communication is through formal means, individualism favors autonomy and innovation, where those who take risk and experiment with IT are rewarded with success, and egalitarianism favors fraternity, harmony, and teamwork.

Seng et al. describe various enabling characteristics of hierarchism, egalitarianism, and individualism, while warning against their constraining forms. Hierarchism provides oversight, leadership, reinforcement of vision, allocation of resources, guidance, and clarification of responsibility, while it may also create excessive trust in authority and expertise, restricting innovation and leading to overconfidence in extensive IT solutions. Egalitarianism enables peer-group accountability and provides teamwork, though it may foster internal strife and deadlocks. Individualism promotes creativity and IT innovation, but it may cause a lack of cooperation and individual interests to come before those of the organization.

Seng et al. highlight various limitations of this research, such as being static and disregarding cultural pluralism, the restricted number of local governments studied and interviews conducted, and the single-country setting. Nonetheless, understanding the cultural barriers and enablers which impede or facilitate the implementation of e-government initiatives in a developing nation such as Malaysia is important for this book due to its developing-country context. Deviating from Hofstede's cultural model not only helps avoid some of its relative weaknesses but also brings a different perspective to the cultural issues studied in this section. The diversification provided by the previous subsections and studies that are included in this section complements this study and at least partially mitigates its limitation of the single-country setting and other disadvantages.

Local Governments and Digital Initiatives

The order of this chapter, and of this section, generally proceeds from a global toward a local context, and from more general to more specific settings and issues. In this section on cultural issues, the sequence has been information culture in developing countries, worldwide e-government readiness, the European context, different cultural backgrounds within one country, developed vs. developing country setting, and e-government in one developing country. Most of these subsections, and of the studies included in them, incorporate national or local contexts. The growing importance of cities in analysis, budgets and development plans, coupled with the decentralization efforts in many developing countries, have been a strong motivation to include the local aspect in digital public initiatives. Cultural traits often vary significantly between regions, and sometimes even within one precinct, which makes the local consideration in analyzing the impact of culture on e-undertakings even more interesting and useful.

Nurdin, Stockdale, and Scheepers (2010) explore the role of culture in the adoption of e-government at local government levels. They emphasize that the majority of research in electronic government highlights cultural issues, but they do not identify specific cultural traits influencing e-government adoption and use. Nurdin et al. identify four major cultural traits: involvement, adaptability, mission, and bureaucracy. Based on these cultural traits and other cultural issues surrounding the adoption of e-government, they develop a framework to explore the role of culture in adopting and using e-government systems at local government organizations. Evidence found by Nurdin et al. suggests that the adoption of e-government at local levels is either mandatory or voluntary which is followed by supportive policies from central governments. They finally conclude that "cultural traits contribute to the adoption and use of e-government systems" (Nurdin et al., 2010, p. 79).

Nurdin et al. quote various definitions of culture and organizational culture. Hofstede's "programming of the mind which distinguishes the members of one human group from another" and Sathe's "the set of important understanding that members of a community share in common" are highlighted as definitions for culture. Meanwhile, the study includes Denison's definition of "the underlying values, belief, and principles that serve as a foundation for an organization's management system as well as the set of management practices and behavior that both exemplify and reinforce those basic principles" for organizational culture.

Nurdin et al. affirm that an organization's culture forms the personality of the organization through the socialization process of people in the workplace of the organization, and that it becomes a beneficial asset for an organization if it supports the organization's mission, goals, and strategies, playing an important role in many aspects of the organization.

Nurdin et al. suggest that the adoption of technology in e-government has many similarities to that of an organization, where decisions are made at a senior level and then assimilated into the organization, while the process of adoption may be mandated or voluntary. According to Nurdin et al., in certain contexts, voluntary adoption is more successful, while in another situation mandatory policy may be the only way to induce technology usage because it can encourage the initial behavior to adopt technology.

Nurdin et al. highlight that this concept is not different from the adoption of technology in local government organizations, where the use

of technology is initiated sometimes by central governments, through the setting of certain goals, and sometimes at grassroots levels. An example of the mandatory approach is the UK government's launching a modernization agenda in 1997 to transform local authorities' performance across the UK, followed by the establishment of "e-government targets," that resulted in the implementation of electronic government at local level across the UK.

There are also examples of the voluntary approach. Nurdin et al. mention the US context, where the adoption of e-government at local levels was initiated at grassroots levels in 2000 due to the demand of the citizens, while the E-Government Act, which includes the planning of an e-government strategy and implementation, was launched in 2002. Hence, it is an example to the approach where the efforts were developed on the basis of local government initiatives while in the next step the central government provided guidelines to support better implementation of the initiatives.

Nurdin et al. go on further to suggest that the adoption of e-government can also be mandatory or voluntary in developing countries. They give the case of Hong Kong as an example of successful adoption of an e-government portal by government departments, which was determined by voluntary decision with support from higher level of the government. The Tanzanian case of Integrated Tax Administration as a part of e-government implementation, where adoption of the project was mandatory for all tax regions of the country by 2007, stands out as the example to the first type.

There is a close relationship between central and local governments with respect to e-government. Nurdin et al. explain how e-government infrastructure such as computer networks, communication systems, and shared services typically belongs to various entities at local and central levels, creating a need for cohesiveness and dynamicity in its implementation, which means that both central and local government entities are involved in electronic local government development regardless of whether the initiatives are mandatory or voluntary.

Nurdin et al. affirm that there are many cultural value dimensions or traits mentioned in the literature of culture. They identify four at the level of organizational culture which are relevant to their study (involvement, adaptability, mission, and bureaucracy), and define each concept. According to these definitions, involvement is a subjective psychological state of users that is practiced in forms of participation through behavior and activities. Adaptability is a value of an organization that focuses on external situation demand by developing norms and beliefs that support its capacity to respond to the necessity for change. Mission is a trait that provides purpose to an organization, and also gives direction and identifies goals that enable an organization to act in an acceptable way. Finally, Nurdin et al. state that bureaucratic culture is organizational culture with clear lines of responsibility and authority based on control and power.

Nurdin et al. suggest that the cultural dimensions of an organization are related to both external adaptation and internal integration. In studying the four cultural dimensions and identifying their sub-dimensions, they find that adaptability and mission appear to relate to the dynamics of external adaptation, encouraging organizations to develop their capacity to change in response to external conditions and expectations. Nurdin et al. also affirm that the involvement and bureaucracy dimensions are influenced by internal integration. According to Nurdin et al., high levels of involvement by internal stakeholders in an organization will result in positive integration between the people and the organization's interest, while a bureaucratic culture creates a solid, regulated, structured, and cautious organization.

Finally, Nurdin et al. assert that a government organization's capacity to practice change and flexibility is determined by its culture of adaptability and involvement, while the stability and direction of government organizations are determined by their dimensions of mission and bureaucracy. They conclude that all four cultural dimensions influence the adoption and use of e-government in local government organizations.

One of the conclusions of all the e-government literature studied in this chapter is that there are many actors involved in digital public initiatives such as governments, municipalities, state institutions, non-governmental organizations, private enterprises, and citizens. When all parties are included, each with its own agenda, interest, politics, and culture, the challenges mentioned in this chapter become more complicated. Regional development plans, which are often part of decentralization efforts, exacerbate any prevailing cultural challenge, though this is also a political issue. A political party different than the ruling administration can be in charge of the municipality of a region or city, which may hamper the e-initiative as the opposing party may receive less support than necessary from the ruling one. In another region, the development efforts may differ from the national or other regional efforts due to the differences in culture, language, or socioeconomic development level. For these reasons, it is useful to include different actors, regional concerns, and local aspects in the digital plans, along with political and cultural issues. In the next section, we will discuss how the issues explored so far relate to the tendencies of the ICT sector.

EMERGING TECHNOLOGIES AND THEIR RELATION TO POLITICS, CULTURE, AND E-GOVERNMENT

The recent acceleration and convergence of trends in the ICT sector, such as cloud computing, virtualization, open source, mobile communications, and social networks, create significant opportunities for poorer nations, smaller companies, and individuals all over the world. This environment levels the playing ground for developing countries, and shapes politics and culture, while the opposite is also true: politics and culture influence these trends. This context also creates new threats and risks. Emerging technologies and their relation to politics and culture are crucial for the success of digital public administration efforts.

The 1980s and the 1990s were important decades for the global economy and politics as well as the ICT sector. In this brief period, the Berlin Wall fell; the Soviet Union collapsed; while Russia, India, China, Latin American countries, and other nations opened their economies to the rest of the world. One of the end results of these events was that the number of people that could trade among themselves and do business together practically doubled within a decade.

Technology did not remain behind the (political and economic) globalization process; these two reinforced one another during this period. Microprocessors appeared in the 1970s. Personal computers (PCs) followed. Programs such as Windows popularized the use of the PCs at the end of the 1980s. Computers were no longer the monopoly of rich countries and large enterprises as it became much easier and more economical for poorer countries, smaller firms, and individuals to utilize PCs to digitize their data and automate their processes.

The dissemination of the internet to the general public, the invention of the World Wide Web, and the introduction of the browser took ICT to the masses and connected the world in the 1990s. Now people were able to share the data they were already digitizing, and collaborate with anyone, anywhere, also paving the road for open-source software to become an important part of the ICT world. This period was enriched by the popularization of business methods and tools such as supply chains and outsourcing, facilitated by the above-mentioned political events, as capital was freer to search efficiency and higher returns around the globe. Aided by additional enhancers such as the technological bubble, which helped raise capital for telecommunications firms to lay cables across the world in the second half of the 1990s, and its burst, that made international communications more economical as prices fell when these companies went bankrupt, working from homes, hotels, and vacation houses became possible.

The past decade was marked by mobility as phones became smarter, broadband connectivity a standard, and cloud computing increasingly popular. Social networks completed the picture, mitigating the boring side of ICT, the end result being worldwide connection of people, products, and services. Concepts of interaction and participation replaced those of use and access, with the transition from Web 1.0 to Web 2.0. Now everyone is in touch with everyone, anyone can work from anywhere. Any company or individual can cooperate or compete with anyone, anywhere. Everybody is in the game, 24 hours a day, seven days a week. It is the era of internet everywhere, the Internet of Things.

In this context, developing countries, SMEs, and individuals have more access to ICTs than ever. This is not to say that a digital divide does not exist in different forms such as bandwidth among and within countries, but simply that the production and use of ICT has become more democratic where it is much more feasible for developing countries to concentrate on digital public administration and undertake e-government initiatives.

The mutual reinforcement of the globalization process and the developments in the ICT sector, coupled with the empowerment of developing countries, SMEs, and individuals, create unprecedented opportunities along with significant threats in many subjects such as security and privacy. Every action of every individual on the internet is observed and registered, while physical movements are under similar scrutiny through satellite cameras. State secrets, classified company information, and individual bank accounts are threatened.

Cloud computing, virtualization, social networks, multicore and hybrid processors, mashups, ubiquitous computing, contextual computing, augmented reality, and semantics are among the recent tendencies in the ICT sector, that contribute to the complexity of the technological environment or the convergence of countries, sectors, and people. This conjuncture creates new challenges including the mutual impact between these emerging trends and politics or culture. Understanding this new context and shifting paradigms is a crucial success factor in digital public administration and e-government initiatives.

The empowerment of developing countries, SMEs, and citizens thanks to these recent developments contribute to the creation of a more interactive political environment and a more participative democratic system where warranted. ICT played a role in the election of Barack Obama in 2008 as it facilitated the mobilization of the supporters and the collection of funds during the election campaign. The latest social and political events in North Africa and the Middle East, which resulted in change of governments, promise of reforms, or civil war in different countries, were facilitated by ICT tools, as masses could organize themselves rapidly in order to gather for protests thanks to the internet and social networks.

Politics also impact the course of these tendencies as governments play a role in the creation of the success factors for the use and production of ICT in a way that would contribute to the sustainable development of their countries, through the establishment of the judicial, technological, and educational infrastructure for the development of the emerging technologies. While the role of the government as a facilitator is usually praised, a wide range of governments throughout the world, such as the United States, China, and Saudi Arabia prevent, filter, or limit access in varying degrees and with different sorts of justification such as national security, privacy, or ethics. For example, a tailored version of the internet with a large filter system was set up in Saudi Arabia in the 1990s, due to the concerns of the Saudi authorities about undesired material such as pornography and

because of other political and cultural concerns (AL-Shehry, 2008). Though concepts like neutrality, freedom, and openness find many advocates, consequences of political intervention in ICT in general and in the internet in particular is yet to be seen.

As countries and their people interact more with others thanks to the recent technological advancements, cultures are inevitably impacted. An illustrative example is the use of social networks, such as Facebook or Twitter, which transcend national boundaries. Cultures also influence tendencies. It is not uncommon to see a devout Christian Costa Rican female marrying a coreligionist North American male who she met through an electronic Christian dating service.

The reciprocal impact between the emerging technologies and politics or culture influences digital public administration and e-government initiatives which are becoming more participative and citizen oriented as a result of the paradigm shift. Understanding the recent tendencies will be crucial for the successful implementation of digital public undertakings in developing countries.

A CASE STUDY: EMERGING TURKEY

Turkey is an intermediately developed country that, despite the progress achieved in the more recent past, faces significant political and cultural challenges in its digitization efforts, struggling to keep up with the emerging trends and the paradigm shift at the same time. The final section of this chapter focuses on the Turkish example for political and cultural issues, including international indicators and comparisons such as the competitiveness and readiness indexes of the World Economic Forum (WEF), and the e-government development ranking of the UN.

Turkey is a good example of political and cultural issues faced both on national and regional levels, in the context of digital public administration and the emerging trends in ICT. The e-transformation process, the Information Society Strategy of the State Planning Organization (Devlet Planlama Teşkilatı or DPT in Turkish), and the efforts to apply knowledge-based development models to the southeastern region of Turkey are examples of these difficulties and complexities, as they point to different political and cultural challenges within one single country.

After a decade-long political and economic chaos in the 1990s, where the nation hopped from one crisis to another under the sponsorship of unsuccessful coalition governments, Turkey seems to have come to grips with political and economic reality, evidenced by its recent performance. When many countries including some of the developing ones were taking steps to advance in ICT in general and e-government in particular, Turkey lost the 1990s in this respect, as the country was far from providing the political and economic environment apt for creating success factors on the digital front.

A major economic crisis in 2001 convinced the people and the politicians to apply the necessary measures to lead the country to the twenty-first century. A single-party government ever since, coupled with a favorable global economic conjuncture, guided the economic turnaround in the last decade. The inflation rates, the debt burden, and the budget deficits of the country declined to reasonable levels, while the economy started to grow more rapidly. The positive performance of the economy was matched by social and political reforms, the end result being the initiation of formal negotiations for accession to the EU. These developments also helped improve awareness on the importance of ICT, public and private initiatives proliferated to catch up with the global standards and the emerging trends such as cloud computing and mobility, and digital public administration efforts accelerated.

Despite the initial improvement of its global rankings thanks to these efforts, Turkey has been performing modestly on digital platforms in the past few years in comparison with other countries. The recent advancement of the country on the subject has not been matched by the global comparative figures as its rankings have steadily stalled or worsened while other countries are progressing more rapidly. Reports from the WEF and the UN clearly show this trend, though they should be approached with caution due to the subjective and qualitative nature of the calculation of some of the indicators used in these publications, which sometimes depend on the opinion of the surveyed.

Turkey ranked #61 in both 2009 and 2010 in the Global Competitiveness Index of the WEF (2010). The country's performance is slightly better in the technological readiness pillar of the efficiency enhancers subindex, where it enjoys a ranking of #56.

The Global Information Technology Report of the WEF (2011) offers a deeper look at the technological readiness of countries, using the Networked Readiness Index (NRI), which measures the degree to which countries leverage ICT for enhanced competitiveness. Turkey enjoys the 71st position, down from #69 a year earlier, which is not as promising as the more general competitiveness rankings. Its 64th position in the government readiness subindex shows a better panorama for the government front as opposed to the 93rd and 94th spots of the businesses and individuals, respectively.

On a somewhat more positive note, Turkey occupied the #69 spot in 2010, an improvement from the position of #76 in 2008, in the world e-government development ranking of the UN (2010). Its performance in the form of e-government development index value of 0.4780 is slightly above Western Asia's subregional average of 0.4732 and the world average of 0.4406. It is also important to mention that Turkey is not among the 25 top-ranked developing countries in e-government development, according to the same report.

In state purchases of digital tools, products, and services, price seems to be a more important criterion than quality or the broader picture in general. Unrealistically low budget ceilings, coupled with the difficulty to participate in the state auctions, hamper the consulting process of planning, implementation, or monitoring. Poor compensation packages limit the ICT talent pool within the state.

Political factors stand out among many reasons behind these problems. There is no single ministry in charge of e-initiatives. The ministry of communications, the newly established ministry of science, industry and technology, formerly the ministry of industry and commerce, DPT, and the Scientific and Technological Research Council of Turkey (Türkiye Bilimsel ve Teknolojik Araştırma Kurumu or TÜBİTAK in Turkish) are among a plethora of ministries and other state institutions involved in the e-transformation process of the country.

The absence of leadership and lack of clear political vision demonstrate the degree of awareness on the state or government level about the importance of ICT adoption or e-government, despite the ambitious declarations of the political leaders regarding their commitment to the subject. This can be a serious weakness as leadership is a key enabler for ICT projects, as affirmed by Furuholt and Wahid (2008), and as explained in the subsection "Leadership" of the section "Political issues" of this chapter. Political debt, coupled with subjective shuffling and restaffing of the human resources, exacerbate the problem. It is not uncommon to observe the state as the client, administrator, coordinator, supplier, and evaluator of the same project, often resulting in low efficiency and project failure.

Many governmental services are now offered over the internet by the state portals as part of the e-government efforts in Turkey. The country had a rate of 50% in fully available online basic services in 2007, eight percentage points below the average of EU 27+ (27 member states plus Turkey, Iceland, Switzerland, and Norway), according to a survey prepared by Capgemini (2007), conducted for the European Commission. Sophistication for citizens, as opposed to sophistication for the businesses, and usercentricity are the weaker points of Turkey in this survey, indicating a lagging aspect with respect to the emerging and prevailing concepts of interaction, participation and citizen orientation explained in the previous section "Emerging technologies and their relation to politics, culture, and e-government," and described by Bidyarthi and Srivastava (2008). This information seems to be in line with other estimations for usage rates: Despite a lack of trustworthy data on the subject, independent sources estimate that the usage rates of some of these electronic services have remained low, as the emphasis has been on the supply side neglecting the demand aspect. Some e-services which lacked demand have also been offered through the internet due to different types of political factors.

Turkey's bid to join the EU was one reason; the country had to align its institutions with those of the Union. Mounting pressure from the NGOs, especially those advocating initiatives to promote the ICT sector, was another cause for the rush of the government. Finally, the worldwide frenzy for e-government, making it as much a fashion as a tool for sustainable development, was among the factors behind the excess offer and the indiscriminate nature of the selection of the services. Though all these factors could be considered political, there is a cultural aspect involved in these efforts. Many Turks prefer to go to a physical office to satisfy their bureaucratic needs facing a real person rather than the monitor of a computer. Many like socializing, others have nothing else to do as they may be unemployed or retired. Relatively low ICT literacy rates also contribute to the phenomenon. The 94th position of Turkey in the individual readiness subindex of NRI may be an indication in this regard. Language barriers are sometimes cited as a problem for a part of the population, with different ethnic and linguistic backgrounds, to have access to government services. The last two challenges resonate with the concerns mentioned in the subsection "Impact of national culture on e-government: developed vs. developing country context" of the section "Cultural issues," where Ali, Weerakkody, and El-Haddadeh (2009) reveal language and ICT literacy problems both for Sri Lanka and for the UK.

The partial failure of the Information Society Strategy of the DPT (2006) is a good example for the political issues involved in digital public administration. Alican (2007) states that, constituting the mainstay of the "E-transformation Turkey Project," the Information Society Strategy was expected to improve the global competitiveness of the country in all fields, to help secure a position among developed countries, and to ensure the best possible implementation of the e-transformation project. According to Alican, the implementation stage was planned to run through 2010, with a significant social and economic impact, and a total cost of about TL 2.9 billion (approximately $2 billion), an indicative figure expected to grow as the project unfolded.

Alican (2007) demonstrates that the Information Society Strategy has methodological, theoretical, and practical flaws, both in general, and specifically in relation to the software sector. It is neither necessary nor possible to include all these flaws in the Turkish example for this chapter. Instead, a quick look at the timeframe of this strategy is enough to observe some of the political aspects of these types of projects: The rapid completion of the design of the project, within only six months, was at odds with its size, scope, and importance, and raised questions regarding the effort involved. Again, the government's concern to accelerate the ICT development of the nation to match that of the EU was a factor.

The implementation plan had other time-related problems, as the project was laid out as a five-year undertaking spanning the 2006-2010 period, but less time was available from the beginning, considering that formal adoption took place in July 2006, corresponding to an automatic loss

of six months or 10% of the time allocated for implementation, as explained by Alican (2007). Moreover, a significant portion of total investments scheduled coincided with double (presidential and parliamentary) elections in 2007, which may have hindered target achievement. By the end of 2009, 20% of the planned actions were completed with an average completion rate of 49.65%, according to the DPT (2010). Perhaps even a more important deficiency of the Strategy was that ICT was not properly integrated as part of the development plans and needs of the country, an imperative suggested by Heeks, Gao, and Ospina (2010), who state that today best practice is seen as the integration of ICTs into development policies and mainstreaming digital technologies so they become one of many delivery tools. Most of these weaknesses echo the subsection "Political aspects in the failure of e-government initiatives" of the section "Political issues," and the gap between design and reality.

While the Information Society Strategy demonstrates some of the political and national aspects of digital initiatives, efforts to apply knowledge-based development models to the southeastern region of Turkey run into cultural and regional issues within one country. According to Alican (2010), an imperative step is to include the Kurdish and Arabic languages in these plans, in addition to Turkish, which is the mother tongue of the majority of the country, due to the abundance of Turkish citizens of Kurdish and Arabic origin in the region and also because of the ethnic and cultural structure of the neighboring countries. The Kurdish portion of these plans also points to a political issue as any mention of the Kurdish question, not only in ICT adoption or digital public administration but also in all sorts of social, political, or economic programs, meets with suspicion or resistance by the opposition parties, the Turkish military, and a part of the population, as the country faces and drags along a millennium-long Kurdish problem, including claims of cultural and ethnic discrimination and oppression, turned into a low-density civil war in the form of separatist guerilla warfare in the past three decades.

It is possible to draw further similarities between the case of Turkey and the political and cultural issues, in the context of emerging tendencies, technologies and challenges, illustrated in the first three sections. The section "Cultural issues" of this chapter contains various subsections which can be directly related to the cultural challenges that Turkey confronts in its digital public initiatives. The subsections which include the relation of cultural aspects with e-government in a European context, embracing developed and developing nations, may be of particular use here due to the efforts of Turkey to align its institutions with those of the EU. Additional studies can be carried out to further explore the impact of culture on the digital efforts of Turkey, applying cultural models, cosmologies, dimensions, indexes or categories, and testing hypotheses regarding the success or failure of different initiatives. These are beyond the scope of this chapter.

Nonetheless, various examples from Turkey that are mentioned in this section illustrate clearly the importance and relevance of the political and cultural issues in digital public administration and e-government initiatives in developing countries, which are often considered and treated as a solely technological question.

REFERENCES

AL-Shehry. A. (2008). *Transformation towards e-government in the Kingdom of Saudi Arabia: Technological and organisational perspectives*. (Doctoral dissertation). The School of Computing, CCSR, De Montfort University. Retrieved from https://www.dora.dmu.ac.uk/bitstream/handle/2086/2418/e-thesis%20transformation%20to%20e-government.pdf?sequence=1

Ali, M., Weerakkody, V., & El-Haddadeh, R. (2009). The impact of national culture on e-government implementation: A comparison case study. In *Proceedings of the Fifteenth Americas Conference on Information Systems*. AIS. Retrieved from http://dspace.brunel.ac.uk/bitstream/2438/3660/1/Culture%20and%20eGov_Final.pdf

Alican, F. (2007). Experts without expertise: E-society projects in developing countries – The case of Turkey. *Information Polity*, *12*(4), 255–263.

Alican, F. (2010). Can information technology contribute to social peace? The case of southeastern Turkey. *Information Polity*, *15*(3), 189–198.

Arslan, A. (2009). *Cross-cultural analysis of European e-government adoption* (MPRA Paper No. 20705). Retrieved from http://mpra.ub.uni-muenchen.de/20705/1/MPRA_paper_20705.pdf

Bidyarthi, H. M., & Srivastava, A. K. (2008). Citizen's perspectives of e-governance. In A. Ojha (Ed.), E-Governance in Practice (pp. 69-76). Secunderabad, India: SIGeGOV.

Capgemini. (2007). *The user challenge benchmarking the supply of online public services*. Diegem, Belgium: Author.

Ciborra, C. (2005). Interpreting e-government and development: Efficiency, transparency or governance at a distance? *Information Technology & People*, *18*(3), 260–279. doi:10.1108/09593840510615879

Dada, D. (2006). The failure of e-government in developing countries: A literature review. *The Electronic Journal on Information Systems in Developing Countries*, *26*(7), 1–10.

Dam, N., Evers, V., & Arts, F. A. (2005). Cultural user experience issues in e-government: Designing for a multi-cultural society. In P. V. Besselaar & S. Koizumi (Eds.), *Digital Cities III – Third International Digital Cities Workshop*, (pp. 310-324). Amsterdam, The Netherlands: Springer. doi: 10.1007/11407546_18

Devlet Planlama Teşkilatı (State Planning Organization). (2006). *Bilgi Toplumu Stratejisi (Information Society Strategy). Ratified by the High Planning Council (Decision No. 2006/38) on 11 July 2006 and promulgated in the Official Gazette (No. 26242) on 28 July 2006.* Ankara, Turkey: Author.

Devlet Planlama Teşkilatı (State Planning Organization). (2010). *Bilgi Toplumu Stratejisi Eylem Planı (2006-2010), Değerlendirme Raporu, Rapor No: 5* (Information Society Strategy Action Plan (2006-2010), Evaluation Report, Report No: 5). Ankara, Turkey: Author.

Finquelievich, S. (2005). *E-política y e-gobierno en América Latina.* [E-politics and e-government in Latin America]. Buenos Aires, Argentina: LINKS A.C. Retrieved from http://www.links.org.ar/infoteca/E-Gobierno-y-E-Politica-en-LATAM.pdf

Furuholt, B., & Wahid, F. (2008). E-government challenges and the role of political leadership in Indonesia: The case of Sragen. In *Proceedings of the 41st Hawaii International Conference on System Sciences.* Washington, DC: IEEE Computer Society. doi: 10.1109/HICSS.2008.134

Hanna, N. K. (2009). E-government in developing countries. *Information Policy.* Retrieved from http://www.i-policy.org

Heeks, R., Gao, P., & Ospina, A. (2010). *Delivering coherent ICT policies in developing countries.* Manchester, UK: Centre for Development Informatics, University of Manchester, e-Development Briefing No. 14. Retrieved from http://www.sed.manchester.ac.uk/idpm/research/publications/wp/di/short/CDIBriefing14PolicyCoherence.pdf

Herbig, P., & Dunphy, S. (1998). Culture and innovation. *Cross Cultural Management: An International Journal, 5*(4), 13–21. doi:10.1108/13527609810796844

Kaufman, E. (2005). E-democracia local en la gestión cotidiana de los servicios públicos: Modelo asociativo (público – privado) de gobierno electrónico local. In S. Finquelievich (Ed.), E-política y e-gobierno en América Latina (pp. 130-150). Buenos Aires, Argentina: LINKS A.C.

Kovacic, Z. J. (2005). The impact of national culture on worldwide e-government readiness. *Informing Science Journal, 8,* 143–158.

Nurdin, N., Stockdale, R., & Scheepers, H. (2010). Examining the role of the culture of local government on adoption and use of e-government services. In M. Janssen, W. Lamersdorf, J. Pries-Heje, & M. Rosemann (Eds.), E-government, e-services and global processes (pp. 79-93). Brisbane, Australia: IFIP. doi: 10. 1007/978-3-642-15346-4_7

Prince, A. (2005). Introduciéndonos en y a las campañas políticas online. In S. Finquelievich (Ed.), E-política y e-gobierno en América Latina (pp. 43-54). Buenos Aires, Argentina: LINKS A.C.

Saroka, R., & Poggi, E. (2005). Software de código abierto en la administración pública. In S. Finquelievich (Ed.), E-política y e-gobierno en América Latina (pp. 183-199). Buenos Aires, Argentina: LINKS A.C.

Seng, W. M., Jackson, S., & Philip, G. (2010). Cultural issues in developing e-government in Malaysia. *Behaviour & Information Technology, 29*(4), 423–432. doi:10.1080/01449290903300931

Shane, S. (1993). Cultural influences on national rates of innovation. *Journal of Business Venturing, 8*(1), 59–73. doi:10.1016/0883-9026(93)90011-S

United Nations. (Department of Economic and Social Affairs). (2003). *UN global e-government survey 2003*. New York, NY: Author. Retrieved from http://unpan1.un.org/intradoc/groups/public/documents/un/unpan016066.pdf

United Nations. (Department of Economic and Social Affairs). (2010). *E-government survey 2010: Leveraging e-government at a time of financial and economic crisis*. New York, NY: Author. Retrieved from http://www.unpan.org/egovkb/global_reports/08report.htm

Westrup, C., & Al-Jaghoub, S. (2008). *Nation states, networks of flows and ICT-enabled development: Learning from Jordan*. Manchester, UK: Development Informatics Group, Institute for Development Policy and Management, University of Manchester, Working Paper Series, Paper No. 33. Retrieved from http://www.sed.manchester.ac.uk/idpm/research/publications/wp/di/documents/di_wp33.pdf

World Economic Forum. (2010). *The Global Competitiveness Report 2010-2011*. Geneva, Switzerland: Author.

World Economic Forum. (2011). *The Global Information Technology Report 2010-2011*. Geneva, Switzerland: Author.

Zheng, Y., & Heeks, R. (2008). *Conceptualising information culture in developing countries*. Manchester, UK: Development Informatics Group, Institute for Development Policy and Management, University of Manchester, Working Paper Series, Paper No. 34. Retrieved from http://www.sed.manchester.ac.uk/idpm/research/publications/wp/di/documents/di_wp34.pdf

ADDITIONAL READING

Heeks, R. (2003). *Most egovernment-for-development projects fail: How can risks be reduced?* Manchester, United Kingdom: Development Informatics Group, Institute for Development Policy and Management, University of Manchester, Working Paper Series, Paper No. 14. Retrieved from http://www.sed.manchester.ac.uk/idpm/research/publications/wp/igovernment/documents/igov_wp14.pdf.

Heeks, R. (2009). *The ICT4D 2.0 manifesto: Where next for ICTs and international development?* Manchester, United Kingdom: Development Informatics Group, Institute for Development Policy and Management, University of Manchester, Working Paper Series, Paper No. 42. Retrieved from http://www.sed.manchester.ac.uk/idpm/research/publications/wp/di/documents/di_wp42.pdf.

Heeks, R., & Santos, R. (2009). *Understanding adoption of e-government: principals, agents and institutional dualism*. Manchester, United Kingdom: Development Informatics Group, Institute for Development Policy and Management, University of Manchester, Working Paper Series, Paper No. 19. Retrieved from http://www.sed.manchester.ac.uk/idpm/research/publications/wp/igovernment/documents/iGWkPpr19.pdf.

International Telecommunications Union (ICT Applications and Cybersecurity Division). (2008). *Electronic government for developing countries*. Geneva, Switzerland: Author.

Ministerio de Ciencia y Tecnología de Costa Rica (Ministry of Science and Technology of Costa Rica). (2011). *Plan nacional de ciencia, tecnología e innovación 2011-2014 (National science, technology and innovation plan)*. San José, Costa Rica: Author, April.

Ndou, V. (2004). E-government for developing countries: opportunities and challenges. *The Electronic Journal on Information Systems in Developing Countries (EJISDC), 18(1), 1-24.* Retrieved from http://www.ejisdc.org/ojs2/index.php/ejisdc/article/viewFile/110/110.

Stanforth, C. (2010). *Analysing e-government project failure: comparing factoral, systems and interpretative approaches.* Manchester, United Kingdom: Development Informatics Group, Institute for Development Policy and Management, University of Manchester, Working Paper Series, Paper No. 20. Retrieved from http://www.sed.manchester.ac.uk/idpm/research/publications/wp/igovernment/documents/iGovWkPpr20.pdf.

United Nations. (Economic and Social Council). (2002). *The critical role of public administration and good governance in implementing the United Nations Millenium Declaration: e-government, known applications and enabling environment.* New York, NY: Author, May 13, 2002. Retrieved from http://unpan1.un.org/intradoc/groups/public/documents/un/unpan004391.pdf.

United Nations. (Development Programme). (2010). Human development report. New York, NY: Author.

World Bank. (Center for Democracy and Technology). (2002). *The e-government handbook for developing countries.* Washington, DC: Author, November 2002. Retrieved from http://www.infodev.org/en/Publication.16.html.

KEY TERMS AND DEFINITIONS

Culture: A system of common values, knowledge and memory in a human group that shapes the behavior of its members.

Developing Countries: Countries where the majority of the population has not reached acceptable life standards and human development levels, often measured by criteria such as income, education, health, freedom and safety.

Digital Public Administration: Public administration enabled, facilitated and improved by the use and production of information and communication technologies.

E-Government: The digitization of all state related activities, including the interaction of the government with citizens, private organizations, and state employees and agencies. It refers to the use and production of information and communication technologies to improve the efficiency and effectiveness of the public sector.

Emerging Technologies: Recent technologies, systems and methods that have changed or are expected to modify individual and collective behavior, business models, and paradigms, such as cloud computing, mobile tools, social networks, and virtualization.

Information and Communication Technologies (ICTs): Products, services and systems that help digitize, store, organize, analyze, process, manage, share, and communicate data and information. This refers to the hardware, software, and services segments of information technologies, as well as telecommunications, including the internet and the World Wide Web, recently more as a converging or unified system.

Politics: The collective decision-making process and structure to exercise control over, influence and govern human groups.

Turkey: A transcontinental country, located in Western Asia and Southeastern Europe. Officially the Republic of Turkey, it is one of the largest developing economies in the world.

Chapter 4
Integrated Architecture Framework for E-Government:
A Socio-Technical Assessment of E-Government Policy Documents

Ephias Ruhode
Cape Peninsula University of Technology, South Africa

ABSTRACT

Emerging trends in Information and Communication Technologies (ICTs) in governments around the globe suggest that developing countries should embrace e-government as an enabler of efficient and effective service delivery. The Government of Zimbabwe, which is a case study in this chapter, is acutely aware of the critical role that ICTs play in socio-economic development. This chapter discusses Zimbabwe's e-government policies and programmes and maps them against the e-government architecture framework by Ebrahim and Irani (2005). The e-government architecture framework defines the standards, infrastructure components, applications, technologies, business models, and guidelines for electronic commerce among and between organisations that facilitate the interaction of the government and promote group productivity. The study is theoretically based upon the socio-technical theory, whose view suggests the existence of a technical sub-system and a social sub-system in an organisation. This theory has been adopted in this study to explain the complex relation between the government as an institution and e-government as an artifact. Drawing from the e-government architecture framework and the social-technical theory, an integrated e-government assessment framework is developed to explain the nature of relationships among government, citizens, and technology.

1 INTRODUCTION

The emergence and proliferation of Information and Communication Technologies (ICTs) have made it possible for governments to improve efficiency and effectiveness by relocating services and products from government offices to locations closer to the citizens (Gichoya, 2005). This relates well to an earlier insistence by Tapscott (1995), that ICTs support the "age of network intelligence", reinventing businesses, governments and individuals. ICTs have permeated every layer within

DOI: 10.4018/978-1-4666-3691-0.ch004

governments such that ministries, departments, agencies, bureaus, divisions, units and offices are increasingly being modernised inside the web of multiorganizational, multigovernmental and multisectoral relationships (Goldsmith and Eggers, 2004). Throughout the world, use of ICTs for government reinvention is increasing, though developing countries are still in the early stages of full-scale ICT deployment.

E-government as an artefact is modelled in the e-government architecture framework by Ebrahim and Irani (2005). As generally accepted, e-government is the use of ICTs to support government operations, engage citizens, and provide government services. While this definition captures the essence of e-government, Dawes (2002) unpacks e-government to expose the following four dimensions:

- **E-Services:** The electronic delivery of government information, programs, and services often (but not exclusively) over the Internet.
- **E-Democracy:** The use of electronic communications to increase citizen participation in the public decision-making process.
- **E-Commerce:** The electronic exchange of money for goods and services such as citizens paying taxes and utility bills.
- **E-Management:** The use of information technology to improve the internal management of government.

Analogous to e-commerce, which allows businesses to transact with each other more efficiently (B2B) and brings customers closer to businesses (B2C), e-Government aims to make the interaction between government and citizens (G2C), government and business enterprises (G2B), inter-agency relationships (G2G) and Internal Efficiency and Effectiveness (IEE) more friendly, convenient, transparent, and inexpensive (United States' e-Government Strategy, 2003). The four dimensions of e-government by Dawes (2002)

are captured in the e-government architecture framework by Ebrahim and Irani (2005), which addresses and identifies the standards, infrastructure components, applications, and technologies for e-government. The architecture framework is divided into four layers; access layer, e-government layer, e-business layer, and infrastructure layer.

Zimbabwe has demonstrated knowledge about e-government and its benefits through the formulation of many ICT policies. However, the e-government policy problem is that all policies ignore political and economic dynamics which have a direct bearing on any developmental project. A critical question which is then raised is: *What has the e-government policies achieved towards e-government implementation in Zimbabwe?* Central to this main question is a sub-question: *Do the policies address the peculiarities of social needs of Zimbabweans?*

This chapter seeks to explore and question Zimbabwe's e-government policies which underpin the government's ICT for development discourse. The chapter then presents recommendations that take cognisance of the economic and political pressure Zimbabwe is spooling under. The study is carried out at a time when Zimbabwe is struggling with deep challenges rooted in political and economic tension. Inflation in nine-digit figures, cholera epidemic, HIV/AIDS and dysfunctional social services among other problems, have epitomized the challenges in Zimbabwe. We are conscious of the fact that in the maze of political and economic chaos, e-government initiatives are at the slowest level of development in Zimbabwe. Political pronouncements are made towards modernizing government, but no resources are made available to implement ideas. The findings and recommendations are applicable to other countries, especially in the developing world, that find themselves in situations similar to Zimbabwe.

This chapter is theoretically based upon the socio-technical theory, whose view suggests the existence of a technical sub-system and a social sub-system in organisations. This theory has been adopted in this study to explain the complex relation between the government as an institution and e-government as an artifact. The e-government framework is also described in the context of the theory through an interpretive research paradigm. According to Orlikowski and Baroudi (1991), interpretivism asserts that reality, as well as our knowledge thereof, are social products and hence incapable of being understood independent of the social actors that construct and make sense of that reality.

The chapter is organized as follows: after the introduction which also explains the research problem and the research question, a brief discussion on the theoretical lenses in e-government is presented. In this section, the theoretical underpinnings and the e-government architecture framework are discussed. The following section presents the research method followed by the conceptual framework of the study. The next section is the assessment of Zimbabwe's e-Government policies followed by the discussion. Recommendations are presented in the following section before the chapter ends with a conclusion.

2 THEORETICAL LENS

Much recently, research has seen use of theoretical and philosophical lenses in order to understand the e-government phenomenon. The theories have provided a good framework to position e-government discourses within the field of information systems. Stanforth (2007), through the application of the Actor-Network Theory (ANT) to an e-government application in Sri Lanka, argued that information system innovation is a contingent outcome that is determined not by the properties of the technology but by the result of contested interests of actors linked together in complex networks. Another contemporary theory which has been employed to explain e-government is the Stakeholder theory. This is a contemporary management theory proposed by Freeman (1984) as an integrative framework for the business and society (Schilling, 2000). According to Freeman, organisations exist for the purpose of serving stakeholder interests. A very broad definition of a stakeholder is any group or individual which can affect or is affected by an organization. Scholl (2007) rejects a wholesome application of the stakeholder theory in e-government, but contends that the theory has made a major impact in both the private and public spheres.

Some of the theories within the information systems domain successfully applied to investigate e-government projects and applications are the institutional theory (Yang, 2003) and the structuration theory (Tseng, 2008). Institutional theory holds that social constructs do define the structure and processes of an organization. Yang (2003) argues that "a balance between agent and institution, between strategic choice and institutional constraint should be maintained in analyzing the evolution of e-government as a long-term institutional change".

Structuration is defined as "a social process that involves the reciprocal interaction of human actors and structural features of organizations" (Orlikowski, 1992). To explain the e-government phenomenon using the lens of the structuration theory, structuration can be seen as involving three broad entities: government, technology, and citizens (Heinze and Hu, 2008). Tseng (2008) contends that the impact of ICT environment, institutional properties, and human factors on the effectiveness of e-government information systems (EGIS) is fully mediated by how the public employees use EGIS. This chapter argues the need to discuss equally the role of both technical and non-technical aspects in e-government development initiatives. On this basis, the following sub section presents a discussion of the socio-technical theory.

2.1 Socio-Technical Theory

The term 'Socio-technical' is understood to be a set of theories and concepts that seek to jointly optimize the co-evolution of organizations and technology. According to Bostrom and Heinen (1977), the socio-technical theory holds that a system is made up of two jointly independent, but correlative interacting systems - the social and the technical. Scholars and proponents of the theory assert that organisations are profoundly affected by technological advancement (Appelbaum, 1997) on the one hand and organisational behavior issues on the other. The socio-technical theory, reputed to Emery, Trist and others originated at the Tavistock Institute of Human Relations in London where studies were conducted towards understanding organizational functions. The researchers revealed that improvements in the technical system do not always result in higher productivity or effectiveness if the social system is not supportive. As indicated in Figure 1, the tech-nical sub-system is concerned with the tasks and technology needed to transform inputs to outputs and the social sub-system is concerned with the attributes of people (e.g.. attitudes, skills, values), the relationships among people, reward systems, and authority (Bostrom et al, 1977). Emphasising a complex interweaving of technology and society, Moodley (2007) asserts that "new technology is as much a social product as the shape of society is a technological product".

2.2 E-government Architecture Framework

According to Ebrahim and Irani (2005), the e-government architecture defines the standards, infrastructure components, applications, technolo-gies, business model and guidelines for electronic commerce among and between organisations that facilitates the interaction of the government and promotes group productivity. The architecture framework is composed of four layers as shown

Figure 1. Socio-technical system

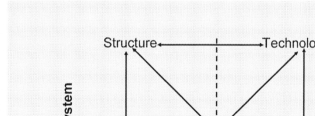

Adapted from Bostrom and Heinen (1977)

in Figure 2. The following is a discussion of the four layers of the framework as well as mapping of the technology developments in Zimbabwe to the framework.

2.2.1 Access Layer

The access layer is divided into two: government users (recipients of government services) and channels (data communication devices). Government users are citizens, business, employees, other governments, and other community members. The access layer involves the channels that government users can access the various government services. According to Ebrahim and Irani (2005), access channels consist of online and offline channels or routes of distribution through which products, services and information are used, accessed and communicated by multiple technologies. For example, web sites accessible from PCs, kiosks, mobile phone (WAP), digital TV, and call and contact centre.

Access Layer and ICTs in Zimbabwe

The Zimbabwe e-Readiness Survey Report (2005) reported that the national tele-density was 2.5 per 100 inhabitants. Tele-density is a metric that is used to broadly estimate the number of telephone lines per 100 individuals. The tele-density of 2.5 people in every 100 shows a huge gap in telephone usage. Most of the telephone infrastructure is located in towns. The Zimbabwe e-Readiness Survey Report (2005) estimated that 90% of the fixed line users were urban or peri-urban based. Even in towns the tele-density varies with a high concentration in the central business district (CBD) and reduced availability in high-density areas. Availability of a telephone line is in many cases a precursor to individuals having a basic Internet access (Ngini *et al*, 2002). The network of communication system in Zimbabwe consists of microwave radio relay links, open wire lines, radio telephone communication stations, fixed wireless local loop installations, mobile cellular networks and optic fibre networks for data transmission. Fixed telephone services and International communications are offered by TelOne, a government-owned company. The company has two international digital gateway exchanges located in the cities of Harare and Gweru and two satellite earth stations. Some of the internal data transmission infrastructure is provided by Powertel (a subsidiary of the government-owned power utility company, the Zimbabwe Electricity Supply Authority (ZESA)), the National Railways of Zimbabwe and a private company, Africom. Zimbabwe has three licensed cellular service providers – one government-owned, NetOne and two private companies, Econet and Telecel. Internet Serrvice Providers (ISPs) are more than 15 but these are concentrated in major cities. Radio and television services are provided by the Zimbabwe Broadcasting Holdings (ZBH), a company wholly owned by the Government of Zimbabwe. Zimbabwe has a critical shortage of electricity, which is one of the main inhibiting factors in rolling out ICTs to the whole country. Internally, Zimbabwe can generate 750megawatts (MW) from Lake Kariba, 920MW from Hwange Power Station and 300MW from other smaller stations at Munyati, Bulawayo and Harare. The domestic power consumption requirement is estimated at more than 2700MW, so the remainder is imported from the Democratic Republic of the Congo (DRC), Zambia, Mozambique and South Africa.

2.2.2 E-Government Layer

According to Ebrahim and Irani (2005), the e-Government layer depicts integration of government services that are made available via a government web portal. Cross-agency web portals can help citizens, business, researchers and other stakeholders to get and share information from one pool. The use of an integrated web-portal is increasingly becoming an important component

Figure 2. E-government architecture framework (Adapted from Ebrahim and Irani (2005))

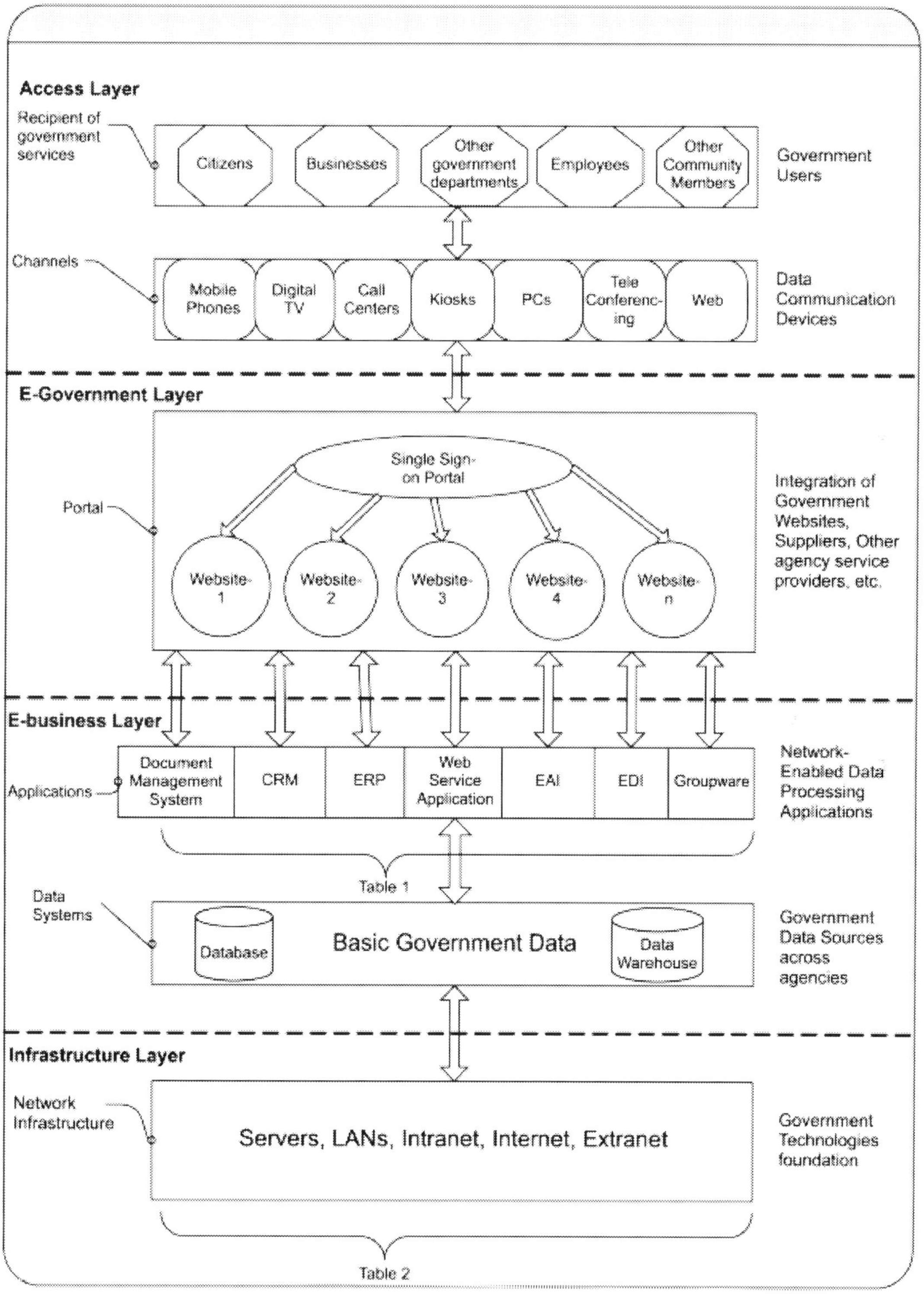

of e-government infrastructure. This layer enables users, through the Internet, intranets and extranets, to enhance public sector wide information access and exchange as well as to maximise the benefits of government-wide acquisition of telecommunications services. The government web portal has a web-based front-end application that allows dispersed sources of information to be linked together, (Ebrahim and Irani, 2005).

E-Government layer in Zimbabwe's E-Government

The Zimbabwe e-Readiness Survey Report (2005) indicates that almost all government departments in Zimbabwe have Internet and e-mail facilities. Government systems are not networked to an extent that links could be established for the whole service. The Zimbabwe e-Readiness Report (2005) asserts that the Zimbabwe Government possesses an immense potential for e-Government through its wide area network (WAN) and application systems such as SAP software, civil service payroll, national registration system and processing pensions. A web site portal called Zimbabwe Government Online, located at http://www.gta.gov.zw has links to all the government ministries and stand-alone departments. Most of the on-line communication available on the portal is G2B and G2C. There is no provision yet for C2G on-line communication.

2.2.3 E-Business Layer

The business layer's primary function is to support business transactions with the government. It also explains use of ICT applications and tools for knowledge and information sharing within and across agencies. Ebrahim and Irani (2005) assert that this layer "practically integrates front-end e-government layer applications, such as online catalogues and transaction interfaces in the government portal with back-end activities such as existing databases and data warehouses".

While ICTs have been harnessed in many governments throughout the world, the European Commission (2003) reported the emergency of 'islands' of government that are frequently unable to interoperate due to fragmentation resulting from uncoordinated efforts at all levels of public administration. The e-Business layer therefore implies that computer systems and applications of different public departments and organisations are being connected to or at least communicating with each other in order to mash the 'islands'. As a result, the transaction from one system can be interchanged with another system (Ebrahim and Irani, 2005). This layer interfaces between front-end and back-end services, which is the thrust of the whole-of-government concept.

E-Business Layer and E-Government in Zimbabwe

According to the European Union's checklist of 20 basic public services that should be provided on line, the Zimbabwe e-Readiness Survey Report (2005) indicates that Zimbabwe is still far from an effective e-government implementation. The list includes income tax declaration, access to social security information, application for passports and driver's licenses, automobile registration, the filing of police reports, requests for birth and marriage certificates, and registration for university classes, to name only a few. Businesses, too, should be able to declare taxes, submit statistical data, deal with the Customs Authority and obtain environmental permits all at the click of a mouse. Table 1 illustrates the services availability in Zimbabwe, (Zimbabwe e-Readiness Survey Report (2005).

2.2.4 Infrastructure Layer

The Infrastructure layer explains the underlying technologies that drive and host e-government applications. According to Ebrahim and Irani (2005), "an e-government IT infrastructure may comprise of a number of technologies with a

Table 1. Checklists for on-line services available to citizens and businesses

Basic Public Services for Citizens	Service Availability in Zimbabwe
Income taxes: declaration, notification of assessment	Paper based
Job search services by labour offices	Advertised electronically but processing is paper Based
Social security contributions	Facility for G2B and B2G transfer of funds is available
Personal documents (passport and driver's license)	Communication with citizen is still paper based but in-house processing is electronically based
Car registration (new, used and imported cars)	State of the art databases exist but interaction with citizenry (G2C interactions) are paper based
Application for building permission	There are electronic databases but G2C interactions are paper based
Declaration to the police (e.g. in case of theft)	Some ICTs such as telephones are used but there are no on-line facilities
Public libraries (availability of catalogues, search tools)	Most academic libraries allow on-line searches. However, public, municipal and the National Free Library do not enable on-line searches
Certificates (birth, marriage): request and delivery	There are electronic databases that store records of births, marriages and deaths but G2C interactions are paper based
Enrolment in higher education / university	Most higher institutions advertise their programmes electronically and allow download of application forms but interaction is paper based
Announcement of moving (change of address)	This is available for C2C communication but there is no central facility for this service (C2G and G2C)
Health related services	None
Social contribution for employees	Electronic transfer to NSSA for large organisations but excludes some SMEs and the informal sector
Corporation tax: declaration, notification	Available
VAT: declaration, notification	Available
Registration of a new company	Not available on-line
Submission of data to statistical offices	Not available on-line
Customs declarations	Not available on-line
Environment-related permits (incl. reporting)	Not available on-line
Public procurement	Paper based

Source: Zimbabwe e-Readiness Survey Report (2005)

network infrastructure at its genesis; including an application server, hardware and operating systems, and data and application development tools". This layer describes the network and associated communication protothols upon which all other applications rely to facilitate integration and data sharing. The network may be a local area network (LAN) or a wide area network (WAN). Operating systems, hardware, application servers all form part of the infrastructure layer.

Zimbabwe's Infrastructure Layer

Inadequate electricity and poor telecommunications infrastructure in Zimbabwe makes it difficult to establish WANs throughout the country. In addition to the problem of limited access technologies to establish WANs, Zimbabwe's major problem lies in low national and international bandwidth capacities. Bandwidth is defined as the amount of data that can pass through a given communication channel per standard amount of time (usually per second). The Zimbabwe e-Readiness Survey Report (2005) gives the national bandwidth between the various point of presence (POP) and the Internet gateway routes as summarised in Table 2.

Table 2 shows that Zimbabwe has inadequate access technologies as POP regions indicated are only the country's major cities. The rest of the country is totally isolated from the digital revolution. The following section explains the research method that was applied to investigate the problem and questions which were presented in Section 1.

3 RESEARCH METHOD

The investigation finds its methodological home in qualitative document study and analysis. According to Henning, et al (2004) through qualitative enquiry, the researcher wants to understand and to explain in argument, by using data from the evidence and literature, what the phenomenon is about. A document study approach is an analysis of any written material which contains information of the phenomenon being studied. Documents are classified under personal and official documents. Personal documents include diaries, autobiographies, personal letters, verbal communications, photographs, video recordings etc. Official documents are more formal and structured and are maintained by large organisations such as governmental institutions. The documents which were studied in this enquiry are government policy documents that are made available in the public domain. All the documents that provided primary data in this study were available at the former ministry of Science and Technology Development offices in Zimbabwe. Some of the policy documents under study are the National ICT Policy Framework (2006), e-Readiness Survey Report (2005) and Science and Technology Policy (2002). This study recognises that there are more recent e-readiness survey results from independent research institutions. However, the e-Readiness Survey Report (2005) is the only e-readiness survey undertaken by the government of Zimbabwe since this study was initiated. Against this backdrop, the same e-readiness report is one of the documents under study. The e-government integrated assessment

Table 2. National capacity

POP REGION	SERVERS	BANDWIDTH
Harare	DNS1, DNS2 Webmail Mail Relay Access Server Terminal Server Radius Server	100Mbps
Bulawayo	Access Server	2 Mbps
Gweru	Access Server	2Mbps
Mutare	Access Server Terminal Server	128 Kbps
Masvingo	Access Server Terminal Server	128Kbps
Kwekwe	Access Server	128Kbps
Victoria Falls	Terminal Server	128Kbps
Chinhoyi	Terminal Server	128Kbps
Kariba	Terminal Server	128Kbps

Source: Zimbabwe e-Readiness Survey Report (2005)

framework, against which the study maps the e-government policy documents, is presented in the next Section 4.

3.1 E-Government Policy Documents

The Government of Zimbabwe, like others in the Southern African Development Community (SADC), is acutely aware of the critical role that science and technology plays in socio-economic development. Among many policies and programmes adopted by the Government of Zimbabwe on promoting technology development, the National Science and Technology Policy was adopted in 2001. In 2002, a department of Science and Technology Development was established, which three years later was transformed into a ministry. What is particularly salient about the ministry of Science and Technology Development (MSTD) is its vision that says "To be a facilitator for a Science and Technology driven economy" and the mission statement, "To strategically coordinate and promote the systematic development and application of Science and Technology in support of national development through effective engagement of public and private sector partners." The following are the e-government policy documents which have been studied in this chapter.

3.1.1 The National ICT Policy Framework (2006)

A National ICT Policy Framework was developed in Zimbabwe in 2006 whose purpose was the requisite guidance and direction to the formulation and implementation of ICT strategies and programmes in and across all sectors of the economy. It was crafted under the following vision: "to transform Zimbabwe into a knowledge-based society by the year 2020", the Mission of which is, "to accelerate the development and application of ICTs in support of sustainable socio-economic growth and development in Zimbabwe". A well defined National ICT Strategy would enable Zimbabwe to

effectively participate in the global market along with other countries that have embraced ICT and the knowledge economy as well as facilitating co-operation and co-ordination of various initiatives by the government, the private sector and other stakeholders in order to optimise the allocation and utilisation of ICT resources (Zimbabwe: National Information & Communication Technology Project, 2004). The National ICT Policy Framework would enable Zimbabwe to coordinate various initiatives in the public and private sectors and of other stakeholders within and outside Zimbabwe in order to optimise the allocation and utilisation of resources in the development and use of ICTs across all sectors of the economy (National ICT Policy Framework, 2006:11). Some of the particular issues that have been addressed by the Policy Framework include the following:

- ICT Policy directions for implementation by each sector. These form the basis for the development of activity programmes and action plans by relevant line ministries and their stakeholders.
- Policy actions to be undertaken to develop the requisite infrastructure like telecommunications, electricity, transport and computer hardware and software in support of ICTs.
- Access to and use of ICTs by special groups such as women, youths, the disabled and the elderly.
- Need to develop and retain globally competitive and high quality human resources in ICTs and related disciplines.
- Leadership and catalytic role of government especially with respect to the development of the political, institutional, economic, legal and security frameworks for ICTs.
- The establishment of a National Information and Communications Technology Authority responsible for ensuring policy coherence across all sectors

of the economy and also to develop legislative instruments on privacy, security, cyber crimes, ethical and moral conduct, encryption, digital signatures, copyrights, intellectual property rights and fair trade practices.

- The need to mobilise adequate resources (human infrastructure, institutional, financial and technological) to effectively implement the ICT Policy.

The objectives of the National ICTs Policy Framework were (i) ensure provision and maintenance of infrastructural facilities necessary for ICT's development, (ii) promotion of systematic, relevant and sustainable development of ICTs, (iii) embark on extensive educational and training programmes to provide adequate supply of qualified ICTs personnel and knowledge workers in all sectors, (iv) establish institutional mechanisms and procedures for determining sectoral application priorities and (v) encourage the development and use of, and ensure equitable access to benefits offered by ICTs across gender, youths, the disabled and the elderly (National ICT Policy Framework, 2006:15).

3.1.2 National E-Readiness Survey Report (2005)

In formulating the National ICT Policy Framework, a prior research called National e-Readiness Survey had been conducted. The Government of Zimbabwe in conjunction with the National Economic Consultative Forum (NECF) and with support from the United Nations Development Programme (UNDP) commissioned an e-Readiness Survey whose purpose was to assess the country's readiness to become a knowledge society. The National e-Readiness Survey indicated that there was a lot of work to be done in terms of preparing Zimbabwe for e-business, for out of a score of 4, the country scored only 1.4 (National e-Readiness Survey, 2005). With specific to e-Government, the following were the findings of the e-Readiness Survey:

- Government possesses an immense potential for e-Government through its wide area network and application systems such as SAP software, civil service payroll, national registration system and pensions processing.
- Most of the online communication is government-to-business and government-to-citizen. There is no provision for citizen-to-government online communication.
- The institutional mechanisms for ICT are not well-defined and coordinated. The application systems are also not integrated.
- There is no integrated government policy framework for the development of e-Government.

The e-Readiness Survey Report had the following findings on e-Governance:

- In spite of the fact that almost all government departments in Zimbabwe have internet and email facilities, there is gross under-utilisation of the existing infrastructure for information dissemination on e-Governance issues.
- E-Governance online content currently covers a small range of topics including parliamentary debates (Hansard), voter education, etc.
- There is no interactive communication for Citizen to Citizen, Government to Citizen and Citizen to Government which are nec-

essary for a people-centred information interchange.

- There is no institutional mechanism to co-ordinate e-Governance at a national level.

3.1.3 Other Policies and Programmes

Many policies and programmes have been established by the Zimbabwe Government over the years, suggesting that there is willingness by the government to adopt ICTs as drivers of the knowledge economy. The Science and Technology Policy (2002), recognises the ICT sector as a key enabler of national development and accordingly directs that Zimbabwe develops a framework to guide its development and use (National ICT Policy Framework, 2006:14). The National Economic Recovery Programme (NERP) (2004 – 2006), was launched by the President of Zimbabwe in 2003. NERP emphasises the need for Zimbabwe to exploit the potential of Science and Technology in general and ICTs in particular in order to leap-frog national economic competitiveness and in the process increase export market penetrability (National ICT Policy Framework, 2006:14). The Nziramasanga Education Commission Report of 1999 recommended the introduction and mainstreaming computer-based teaching and learning in the pedagogy of the Zimbabwe's education system - schools, colleges, universities and other institutions of higher learning (National ICT Policy Framework, 2006:14). The Industrialisation Policy of 2004 recognises and advocates for the development and use of ICTs in the manufacturing sector in general and to under-gird the national export strategy in particular. ICTs are identified as indispensable in effectively marketing industrial products both on the domestic and export markets (National ICT Policy Framework, 2006:14). The Zimbabwe Millennium Development Goals (MDGs) of 2005 recognise the role of ICTs as tools that add value and contributes significantly to the achievement of the MDGs by 2015 (National ICT Policy Framework, 2006:15). World Summit on the Information Society (WSIS) held in Geneva in 2003 and Tunis in 2005 also deserves to be considered because Zimbabwe was fully represented. The main objective of WSIS was to develop and foster a clear statement of political will and take concrete steps to establish the foundations for an Information Society for all.

Drawing from the e-government architecture framework and the social-technical theory, an integrated e-government assessment framework, whish is presented in the next chapter, explains nature of relationships among government, citizens and technology.

4 INTEGRATED E-GOVERNMENT ASSESSMENT FRAMEWORK

The Integrated e-Government Assessment Framework (Figure: 3) draws from the Socio-technical system of Bostrom and Heinen (Figure 1) and the e-Government Architecture Framework of Ebrahim and Irani (Figure 2). The integrated e-government assessment framework takes on similar views as the socio-technical system while fusing the layers of the e-government architecture framework. The social sub-system incorporates three main components which cover aspects required to answer all social questions related to the e-government system. Some of the questions are:

- How can the e-government application support the aims of government, meet the employees' needs, further the aims of management and the general politics and the economy around the government?
- How can e-government meet increasing demands of citizens to access information and services?
- How can e-government promote best practices in dealing with business and other bodies like the non-governmental organisations and other governments?

The technical sub-system is made up of the layers as described in the e-government Architecture Framework of Ebrahim and Irani (Figure: 2). The technical sub-system will be able to answer the following technical questions:

- What is the network configuration and specification of the e-government system?
- What are the government data sources and the network-enabled data processing applications?
- How integrated are the government websites and what is the level of maturity of these websites?
- What are the data communication devices that users employ to access e-government services?

As in e-commerce and other organizational systems, e-Gov is foremost a business system installed and implemented to serve the purpose of an over-arching social imperative. As in any business information system, the technical sub-system exists solely to support the higher business system. Consequently, as shown on Figure 3, the technical sub-system is subordinated to the social sub-system that subsumes the business system.

4.1 Application of the Integrated E-Government Assessment Framework

The framework provides e-Government developers with a mechanism to interrogate and ascertain the extent to which each module of each layer of the technical sub-system supports the superordinate modules in the social sub-system. This essentially requires each technical module to serve one or more modules of the social sub-system. From this, a two-phase assessment procedure of policy documents can be performed:

Phase I: Internal Consistency Check of Sub-Systems

Here, a detailed routine check of the sub-system modules is conducted. The outputs of this exercise are:

1. A detailed specification and description of each module,
2. The functions and purpose of each module,
3. An identification of the modules of the social sub-system supported and serviced by each module of the technical sub-system, along with an explanation of the nature of the support and service provided.

Phase II: Policy Check and Assessment

This follows after Phase I has been completed satisfactorily. In this phase, the policies are fed through both sub-systems, as indicated in Figure 3. In essence, it is here that the policies are interrogated by the modules of each sub-system. The output of this phase is a detailed description of the extent to which the policies cover the layers and modules of each sub-system. Part of this output is also an identification of omissions and gaps in policy formulations, and a specification of the necessary corrective measures to be taken. The overarching aim of this phase is to ensure that policies address both social and technical issues in a comprehensive and correct way.

In some situations, and depending on the specific needs of developers, it may simply be sufficient to limit the output of Phase II to indicating the strength with which the policy addresses the social and technical issues of interest. The output coverage in this case is then "Strong", "Intermediate", "Weak" or "No Coverage" for each policy as illustrated on Table 3. E-government as a socio-technical system is interrelated into net-

Figure 3. Integrated e-Government assessment framework

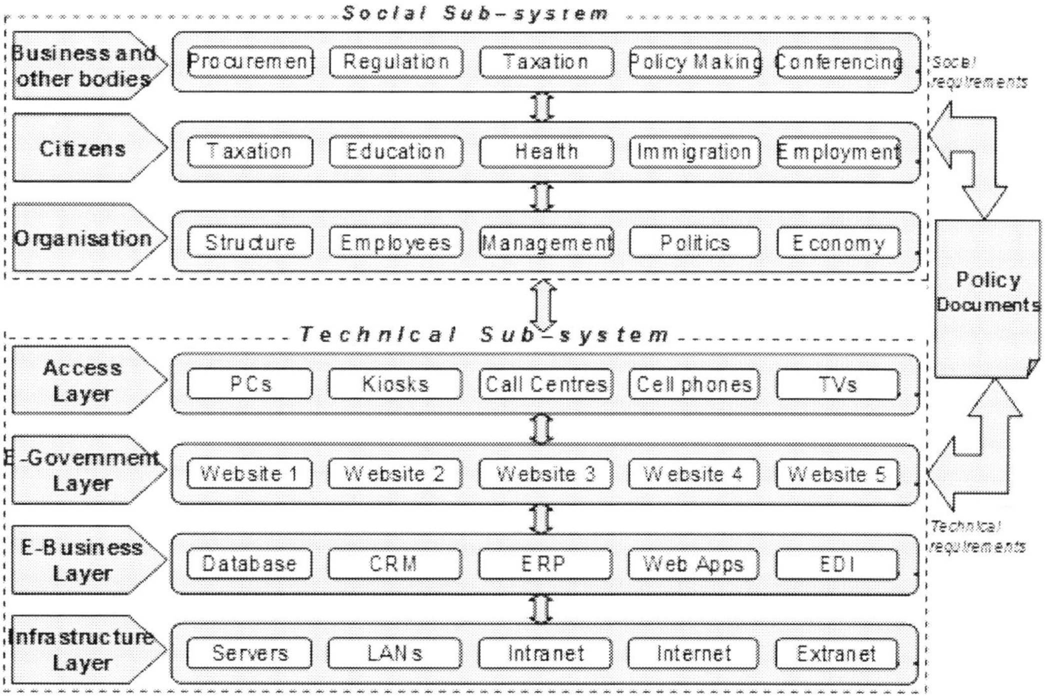

Table 3. Assessment of e-government policy documents

Policy	Brief Description	Assessment (Social/Technical)
National ICT Policy Framework	To provide guidelines for national ICT implementations	1. Intermediate Social 2. Strong Technical
National e-Readiness Survey	To assess the degree of the country's e-Readiness towards becoming an information society	1. Weak Social 2. Strong Technical
Zimbabwe Millennium Developed Goals (MDGs)	A report recognising ICT as a player in meeting UN's MDGs	1. Weak Social 2. Strong Technical
National Economic Recovery Programme (NERP)	Economic Turnaround Strategy using Science and Technology	1. Strong Technical 2. Intermediate Social
Industrialisation Policy	To embrace ICTs in the manufacturing sector to boost export	1. Strong Technical 2. No Social Coverage
Science and Technology Policy	To promote and harness Science and Technology for national development	1.Strong Technical 2. No Social Coverage
Nziramasanga Education Commission Report	Recommended the introduction of ICT teaching and learning in schools	1. Strong Technical 2. Intermediate Social

work of knowledge stakeholders such as humans, machine agents, and artifacts like norms, laws, formal procedures, social and cultural practices (Gatautis, 2010). These stakeholders form the basis of assessment criteria which is presented in

Section 5. Presumably drawing from the socio-technical perspective, Avgerou and Walsham (2000) argue that the "design and implementation of ICT projects in developing countries must be able to address the specific contextual characteristics of the organization, sector, country, and region" (Stanforth, 2007). According to Latour (1993), there should not be a fundamental separation between "technology" and "society", but that a mutually responsive network of interaction develops between these dimensions.

5 ASSESSMENT OF ZIMBABWE'S E-GOVERNMENT POLICIES

This chapter argues that tenets of the socio-technical perspective were ignored in Zimbabwe's e-government debates. Table 3 summarises the assessment of Zimbabwe's e-government policies and documents. The e-government assessment framework (Figure 3), reflects the need for strong socio-technical analysis and design in the development of e-government systems. Table 3 however, shows that all the documents and policies do not take on different views such as organisational, technical, human-oriented, etc.

An output which is rated "strong" points to a policy's thrust being socially or technically-oriented. A phenomenon observed in the assessment outputs is that there is no policy document with a "strong" rating in its social sub-system component. An output which is rated as "weak" depicts very little characteristics of either technical or social aspects. "Intermediate" rating is when an aspect, either social or technical, is addressed in the policy but not sufficiently. "No coverage" rating shows that a policy pays no attention to features of either social or technical sub-systems.

Collectively, the policies fail to show how e-government can be a tool for development in a developing country where basic needs like food and education are beyond reach for many. In Table 3, the national ICT Policy Framework and National e-Readiness Survey are weak in addressing the social component of the assessment framework because they lack a strategy and roadmap on how Zimbabwe would implement e-government under poor economic conditions. The rest of the policies

do not exhibit a social thrust of ICTs except a documentation of how the citizens would benefit out of ICT deployment.

Mhlanga (2007) observes that the e-readiness survey promotes technological determinism at the expense of social constructivism. We subscribe to the view that interplay of the two paradigms should underpin any e-government discourse. An analysis of other policies like the National ICT Policy Framework (2006) and other policies and programmes points to the same phenomenon of technological determinism. Technological determinism is a technology-led theory of social change premised on the view that "particular technical developments, communications technologies or media, or, most broadly, technology in general are the sole or prime antecedent causes of changes in society, and technology is seen as the fundamental condition underlying the pattern of social organization" (Chandler, 1995). We can conclude therefore that the technological deterministic view of ICT diffusion asserts that ICTs are incrementally and fundamentally changing the working, social and personal lives of people. This claim underscores that availing ICTs to a society then becomes a panacea for development. The United Nations World Public Sector Report (UNWPS) (2003), operating on the premise of technological determinism, report that the potential of e-government as a development tool for all citizens hinges upon three prerequisites:

- A minimum threshold level of technological infrastructure;
- Human capital; and
- E-Connectivity.

Simply put, UNWPS claims e-government readiness strategies and programmes will be able to be effective and include all people only if, at the very minimum, all have functional literacy and education, which includes knowledge of computer and Internet use; all are connected to a computer; and all have access to the Internet (UNWPS, 2003).

Yet, to say that society should avail itself of the most modern technologies to solve problems is not a practical reality in Zimbabwe.

Social constructivism on the other hand, is a theory of knowledge that considers how social phenomena develop in particular social contexts. It involves looking at the ways social phenomena are created, institutionalized, and made into tradition by humans. In this rergard, Mhlanga (2007) argues that ICTs should be harnessed for structural poverty reduction as well providing social services. One example is MTN's Mobile Banking in South Africa where ICT-enabled financing instruments have been introduced as intermediation to enhance access to financial services for poverty alleviation in poor communities. This is an example where emerging information society offers a number of opportunities for poor communities to access financial capital to help alleviate poverty and enable them to participate in the mainstream economy. Majority of the black population in South Africa have traditionally been excluded from financial services and the effort to address the specific needs of the disadvantaged poor communities has taken centre stage. Historically, poor rural communities in Zimbabwe (and other developing countries) have been left out in developmental activities since cost of servicing poor communities has been a major barrier. In such instances, the Kenya case, reported by the OECD (2003), is an example of the social constructivism approach where ICT-assisted development was initiated to address critical issues of education, health, and poverty. The report says that the World Food Programme (WFP) in Kenya started looking to ICTs to enhance its work in famine-stricken areas with help and support from Microsoft. WFP developed a handheld device to enable its teams to gather data directly in the field and transmit the data to a central computer using wireless technology. The new system allows faster and more efficient deliveries of relief and food – literally saving lives, and giving new meaning to the term "just in time" delivery. Through such efforts, experience

is proving that information technology can play a vital role in understanding development problems and implementing better solutions (OECD, 2003). All the e-government initiatives in Zimbabwe are silent on such potential of ICTs to play a role as a catalyst for rural development.

The Geneva Action Plan of WSIS (2003) covers commendable ground to bringing both aspects of technological determinism as well as social constructivism. While it was agreed during WSIS (2003) that individual economies would operate within their economic strengths as they attend to these action plans, the Zimbabwe Government did not develop their own action plans to implement the resolutions. What has since been witnessed was the distribution of computers to urban and rural primary and secondary schools by the president without accompanying action plans to operationalise the equipment.

6 DISCUSSION: POLITICAL AND ECONOMIC REALISM

The National ICT Policy Framework (2006) was adopted at a time when Zimbabwe had already been locked in political and economic despair, but the framework or any other ICT policy ignores these complex dynamics. It would have been expected of any policy debate to address a plan of ICT diffusion under such levels of political and economic instability as well as extreme cycles of poverty and diseases. Deployment of ICTs in Zimbabwe is weighed down by inadequate electricity in rural and marginalized areas as well as power cuts in all urban and semi-urban areas. Zimbabwe is currently in a state of economic and political isolation, so it is therefore very difficult to finance any electrification projects due to severe foreign currency shortage. The Rural Electrification Programme whose master plan was approved by cabinet in 1997 and funded by the African Development Bank (ADB) (Mapako & Prasad, 2004) was a noble venture until financial resources ran dry.

Another factor that led to failure of the programme was its political agenda (Mhlanga, 2007) in the political chaos that proceeded by the turn of the century. There was political control on the Rural Electrification Programme which however faced a natural death due to shortage of resources. In the absence of electricity, rolling out ICT resources and programmes was out of the question. Therefore, professionals like teachers, farmers and nurses who are deployed to work in remote areas cannot access e-services like the internet or even basic email despite having elementary literacy to use the services.

While both the e-readiness survey (2005) and the National ICT Policy Framework (2006) strongly emphasise the need to close the digital divide, there is no action plan on executing this agenda. According to Mhlanga (2007), lack of action plans exposes the government to the risk of giving their critics an opportunity to regard these policies as political rhetoric since the mechanisms used in the e-readiness survey and subsequent compilation of the policy framework are a preserve of those in power. The rural electrification programme has since been abandoned by the government, making it impossible to ever consider ICT diffusion in non-electrified and marginalized areas. It follows therefore that while the National ICT Policy Framework (2006) includes references to ICTs in education and the Nziramasanga Education Commission Report (1999) strongly recommending ICT-based education, no meaningful ICT education programmes can be implemented without electricity. Non Governmental Organisations (NGO) initiated ICT education programmes were also unsuccessful due to lack of supporting infrastructures and utilities like electricity in remote areas. The Kubatana Trust of Zimbabwe, which includes an NGO network organisation called the NGO Network Alliance Project (NNAP), was established to strengthen the use of e-mail and Internet among Zimbabwean NGOs and civil society organisations and to provide human rights and civic education. Initially Kubatana had a network of 240 NGOs and community service organisations which were involved in its lobbying and advocacy campaigns. Many of these NGOs were de-registered and banned from operating in Zimbabwe as they were accused by the government of meddling in political affairs. The effectiveness and thrust of Kubatana was then terribly dented and this in turn reduced the impact and success originally envisaged. World Links Zimbabwe which is part of the international network of World Links organisations which historically has been a pioneer in the promotion of education through ICTs opened its doors to Zimbabwe in 1999 but has realized very few of its dreams because of the not very conducive political environment.

7 RECOMMENDATIONS

The earlier discussion on the e-government architecture framework provided an accurate understanding of the variance between Zimbabwe's ICTs status and what needs to be achieved. This section therefore presents recommendations based on the integrated e-Government assessment framework (Figure 3).

7.1 Social Sub-System

The thrust is to factor in government users as they are a component of the social construction of technology. Relevant social groups such as government employees, business, citizens, or other governments assist in establishing technological frames which help towards optimization of e-government systems. Zimbabwe is currently a fragmented society with no trust between government and citizens, government and business, government and non-governmental organisations as well as government and other governments.

Successful EGIS can only be implemented after a comprehensive research of the needs of these stakeholders.

7.2 Technical Sub-System

7.2.1 Access Layer

Access channels have been adversely affected by a variety of factors. It has been mentioned earlier that inadequate electricity is the main hurdle in rolling out ICTs to the whole country. Mobile phone operators require electricity to power their base stations around the country, and so do Internet Service Providers (ISPs) for their Internet and email servers. Basically all ICT-related equipment requires electricity. It is therefore obvious that the Government of Zimbabwe should consider boosting electricity generation before any meaningful discussion on ICT rollout is made. The Zimbabwe e-Readiness Survey Report (2005) makes mention of increasing power generation capacities of plants at Hwange, Kariba and Munyati as well as need to explore other forms of energy generation like solar, wind, biogas and even nuclear energy. Improving power generation and distribution capacity would result in improving the tele-density as phone operators spread wings throughout the country. Making personal computers (PCs) affordable is another possible solution to improving access channels to ICTs. The country's president has been donating computers to schools, which on its own is a positive development. However, establishing community computer centres and kiosks in public places as schools, libraries, district offices, etc with those computers would also be an equally important initiative. The economically struggling government of Zimbabwe can initiate computer assembly projects as in the case of the Madaraka computer project in Kenya. Though the Madaraka project's success is still questionable (Wanjiku, 2008), it is important to understand that the underlying idea when implemented properly, can yield phenomenal results. Secondly the Government of Zimbabwe, like Kenya and Ghana, can also organise to receive used but recyclable computers from developed countries as Japan, the US and European countries for free.

7.2.2 E-Government Layer

A well designed and optimised e-government web portal would provide the basis for integrating different government websites with suppliers and other service providers. A web portal is a tool for better information sharing, coordination and planning among donors and governments. A government web portal, by definition, is a website that constitutes the central access or entry point to all available government information and electronic services. The portal should make available an array of online services including government information publicity, government and citizen interaction, government service for individuals, government service for business, culture services, etc. Basic services that many e-government portals throughout the world are offering, but not yet available in Zimbabwe are: voter registration, ordering birth, death, and marriage certificates, filing state taxes, hunting and fishing licenses, accessing to medical information, etc. The website must be interactive and not static like the current Government of Zimbabwe site. Citizens and the business community must be able to interact with the government through emails, text messages, multimedia, etc. that are facilitated via the government web portal.

7.2.3 E-Business Layer

Replacing closed systems with open enterprise resource planning (ERPs) software, customer relationship management (CRMs) systems and integrated databases will facilitate collaboration of the whole public sector, resulting in improvement of user-focused services as well as internal and external delivery effectiveness. The Zimbabwe government can be spurred by the example of developing countries, such as India, that seem to be "riding the ICT wave" successfully. India and indeed many other countries, has established technology park concept, commonly known as technoparks to promote research and development (R&D) especially in software development. Many developing countries such as Turkey, China, Malaysia, Singapore, Taiwan, Thailand, have sought to emulate these successes and reap the benefits of ICT-led growth for their own economies. Applications that are locally developed in these technoparks are then deployed to various private and public organisations, promoting basic e-services that should be provided online. The Turkish government passed a technology development zones law in 2001 whose thrust was to promote the establishment of technoparks under the guidance and lead of universities. According to this law, companies are encouraged to invest more into R&D and software development through tax incentives and according to this law, any kind of software development activity is considered an R&D activity. Phenomenal expansion of ICT applications (e.g., e-commerce, e- learning and tele-medicine etc.) especially in rural and remote areas in Turkey has been witnessed since then. The government of Zimbabwe can inject minimal capital to initiate open source software development in technoparks in order to save a lot of money currently used on Windows software licensing. Open source platforms which are basically free, come loaded with many valuable free software applications like word processing, spreadsheets, presentations, databases, web servers, email servers, fax servers, call centres, phone billing, internet café billing, hotel reservation, project management, programming tools, educational and scientific software and many others. If the technopark concept on open source development platform is considered by the government of Zimbabwe, a lot of improvement in business layer applications will be realised.

7.2.4 Infrastructure Layer

Putting in place better and modern access technologies can greatly improve national and international bandwidth and optimise performances of LANs, Intranets and the Internet. Allowing multiple gateways will also serve as an assurance that Zimbabwe does not experience network failures. The Zimbabwe Government must wake up to the reality that a sound technological infrastructure is the foundation for a networked society. Broadband technologies such as fibre optics though expensive, are the best way to building a reliable technological infrastructure. Fibre optics allow for broader bandwidth nationally between POPs. International bandwidth can be improved by connecting to the undersea cable that is running around Africa. Zimbabwe can reach this cable via fibre optics at say the Indian Ocean side at Beira. Many countries including South Africa are building network infrastructures whilst drawing bandwidth from the undersea cable.

8 CONCLUSION

Conclusion to the study is presented in three subsections as follows: summary, limitations and related further study.

8.1 Summary

In this chapter, we have presented an e-government architecture framework that underpins a successful e-government implementation. The socio-technical theory was used to explain the complex relation between government as an institution and e-government as an artefact. E-government policies in Zimbabwe were analysed against the conceptual framework drawn from the e-government architecture framework and the socio-technical theory. Due to political and economic challenges obtaining in Zimbabwe, the digital divide has even grown wider as companies are under financial stress that they are unable to make investments into rural and marginalized areas. E-government initiatives have not been successful in Zimbabwe because they have been set up at a time when Zimbabwe is facing political and economic challenges. A set of recommendations based on the integrated e-government assessment framework was then presented in the chapter.

8.2 Limitations

The chapter is limited to studying only the policy documents by the Zimbabwe Government discussed in the article. Other documents that may have been published after the commencement of this study are not considered. Although the study presented in this article is based on Zimbabwe, it is deemed by the authors to be applicable to all other developing countries which find themselves in similar setting as Zimbabwe, especially countries in Sub-Saharan Africa.

8.3 Related Further Studies

We have exposed the status of e-government development in Zimbabwe through analyzing e-government policies and documents. We have also presented recommendations towards improving e-service delivery by the Government of Zimbabwe. Further research is however needed on how the Zimbabwe government can employ ICTs to extend electronic service delivery to citizens particularly under the current economic environment. On the same note, further research will be carried out covering the expanded discussion of the assessment exercises with a more comprehensive and elaborate illustration of the phases identified in section 4.

REFERENCES

Akther, M. S., Onishi, T., & Kidokoro, T. (2007). E-government in a developing: Citizen-centric approach for success. *International Journal of Electronic Governance*, *1*(1), 38–51. doi:10.1504/IJEG.2007.014342

Anderson, G. L., Herr, K., Nihlen, A. S., & Noffke, S. E. (2007). *Studying Your Own School: An Educator's Guide to Practitioner Action Research.* Corwin Press.

Appelbaum, S. H. (1997). Socio-technical systems theory: An intervention strategy for organizational development. *Management Decision*, *35*(6), 452–463. doi:10.1108/00251749710173823

Atkinson, D. R. (2003). *Network Government for the Digital Age.* Washington, DC: Progressive Police Institute.

Avgerou, C., & Walsham, G. (2000). *Information Technology in Context: Studies from the Perspective of Developing Countries.* London: Ashgate.

Bostrom, R. P., & Heinen, S. (1977). MIS problems and failures: A socio-technical perspective, part II: The application of the socio-technical theory. *Management Information Systems Quarterly*, *1*(4), 11–28. doi:10.2307/249019

Canadian International Development Agency. (2007). *Knowledge-Sharing Plan.* Retrieved February 19, 2008, from http://www.acdi-cida.gc.ca/CIDAWEB/acdicida.nsf/En/EMA-218122154-PR4

Chan, O. J. (2005). Enterprise Information Systems Strategy and Planning. *The Journal of American Academy of Business*, *6*(2), 148–153.

Chandler, D. (1995). *Technological or Media Determinism*. Retrieved September 18, 2008 from http://www.aber.ac.uk/media/Documents/tecdet/tecdet.html

Davison, M. R., Wagner, C., & Ma, C. K. L. (2005). From government to e-government: A transition model. *Information Technology & People*, *18*(3), 280–299. doi:10.1108/09593840510615888

Dawes, S. S. (2002). *The Future of E-Government*. Retrieved July 3, 2008, from www.vinnova.se/upload/EPiStorePDF/vr-06-11.pdf

Dul, J., & Hak, T. (2007). *Case Study Methodology in Business Research*. Burlington, MA: Butterworth-Heinemann.

Ebrahim, Z., & Irani, Z. (2005). E-government adoption: Architecture and barriers. *Business Process Management Journal*, *11*(5), 589–611. doi:10.1108/14637150510619902

European Commission. (2003). Linking-up Europe: The importance of interoperability for e-Government services. *European Commission*. Retrieved July 20, 2007, from http://europa.eu.int/ISPO/ida/

Freeman, R. E. (1984). *Strategic Management: A stakeholder approach*. Boston: Pitman.

Gatautis, R. (2010). Creating public value through e-Participation: Wave project. *Economics and Management*, (15), 483-490.

Gichoya, D. (2005). Factors Affecting the Successful Implementation of ICT Projects in Government. *The Electronic. Journal of E-Government*, *3*(4), 175–184.

Haricharan, S. (2005). *Knowledge Management in the South African Public Sector*. Retrieved July 5, 2008 from http://www.ksp.org.za/holonl03.htm

Heeks, R. (2002). *eGovernment in Africa: Promise and Practice* (Working Paper 13). iGovernment.

Heeks, R. (2003). *e-Government Special – Does it Exist in Africa and what can it do?* Retrieved September 30, 2007, from http://www.balancingact-africa.com/news/back/balancing-act93.html#headline

Heinze, N., & Hu, Q. (2005). *e-Government Research: A Review via the Lens of Structuration Theory*. Paper presented at the Ninth Pacific Asia Conference on Information Systems (PACS 2005). Bangkok, Thailand.

Henning, E., Van Rensburg, W., & Smit, B. (2004). *Finding your way in Qualitative Research*. Pretoria, South Africa: Van Schaick.

Ifinedo, P. (2005). Measuring Africa 's e-readiness in the global networked economy: A nine-country data analysis. *International Journal of Education and Development Using ICT*, *1*(1), 1–19.

Kaaya, J. (2004). Implementing e-Government Services in East Africa: Assessing Status Through Content Analysis of Government Websites. *The Electronic. Journal of E-Government*, *1*(2), 39–54.

Kumar, V., Mukerji, B., Butt, I., & Persaud, A. (2007). Factors for Successful e-Government Adoption: A Conceptual Framework. *The Electronic. Journal of E-Government*, *5*(1), 63–76.

Latour, B. (1993). *We Have Never Been Modern*. Cambridge, MA: Harvard University Press.

Layne, K., & Lee, J. (2001). Developing fully functional E-government: A four stage model. *Government Information Quarterly*, *18*(2), 122–136. doi:10.1016/S0740-624X(01)00066-1

Marche, S., & McNiven, J. D. (2003). E-Government and E-Governance: The Future isn't what it used to be. *Canadian Journal of Administrative Sciences*, *20*(1), 74–86. doi:10.1111/j.1936-4490.2003.tb00306.x

Mhlanga, B. (2006). Information and Communication Technologies (ICTs) Policy for change and the Mask for Development: A Critical Analysis of Zimbabwe's e-Readiness Survey Report. *The Electronic Journal on Information Systems in Developing Countries, 28*(1), 1–16.

Moodley, S. (2003). The challenge of e-business for the South African apparel sector. *Technovation, 23*(7), 557–570. doi:10.1016/S0166-4972(02)00002-0

Orlikowski, W. J., & Baroudi, J. J. (1991). Studying Information Technology in Organizations: Research Approaches and Assumptions. *Information Systems Research, 2*(1), 1–28. doi:10.1287/isre.2.1.1

Parajuli, J. (2007). A Content Analysis of Selected Government Web Sites: A Case Study of Nepal. *The Electronic. Journal of E-Government, 5*(1), 87–94.

Ruhode, E., Owei, V., & Maumbe, B. (2008). *Arguing for the Enhancement of Public Service Efficiency and Effectiveness through e-Government: The Case of Zimbabwe.* Paper presented at the IST-Africa 2008 Conference. Windhoek, Namibia.

Schilling, M. A. (2000). Decades ahead of her time: Advancing stakeholder theory through the ideas of Mary Parker Follett. *Journal of Management History, 6*(5), 224–242. doi:10.1108/13552520010348371

Scholl, J. H. (2001). *Applying Stakeholder Theory to E-Government: Benefits and Limits.* Boston: IFIP, Kluwer Academic Publishers.

Seddon, P. B. (2005). Are ERP Systems a Source of Competitive Advantage? *Strategic Change, 14*(5), 283–293. doi:10.1002/jsc.729

Stake, R. E. (1995). *The Art of Case Study Research.* Thousand Oaks, CA: Sage Publications.

Stanforth, C. (2007). Using Actor-Network Theory to Analyze E-Government Implementation in Developing Countries. The Massachusetts Institute of Technology Information Technologies and International Development, 3(3), 35–60.

Tapscott, D. (1995). Leadership Needed in Age of Networked Intelligence. *Boston Business Journal, 11*(24), 15.

Tellis, W. (1997). Introduction to Case Study. *Qualitative Report, 3*(2).

Tseng, T. T. Y. (2008). A study of e-government system effectiveness: Applying structuration theory to context-aware ICT applications in public organisations. *International Journal of Electronic Business, 6*(4), 405–432. doi:10.1504/IJEB.2008.020677

United Nations. (2008). *E-Government Survey Report.* Retrieved June 10, 2008, from unpan1.un.org/intradoc/groups/public/documents/UN/UNPAN028607.pdf

United Nations World Public Sector Report. (2003). *E-Government at the Crossroads.* Author.

Uzoka, F. E., Shemi, A. P., & Seleka, G. G. (2007). Behavioural Influences on E-Commerce Adoption in a Developing Country Context. *The Electronic Journal of Information Systems in Developing Countries, 31*(4), 1–15.

Wanjiku, R. (2008). Still waiting for Madaraka PC. *Computerworld Kenya: The Voice of IT Management.* Retrieved November 2, 2010 from http://www.computerworld.co.ke/articles/2008/09/30/still-waiting-madaraka-pc

Yang, K. (2011). Emergent accountability and structuration theory: Implications. In G. Frederickson, & M. Dubnick (Eds.), *Public Accountability and Its Promises* (pp. 269–281). Armonk, NY: M. E. Sharpe.

KEY TERMS AND DEFINITIONS

Architecture Framework: Establishes a standards, infrastructure components, applications, technologies, business model and guidelines for electronic commerce among and between organisations that facilitates the interaction of the government and promotes group productivity.

Assessment Framework: Assessment criteria for evaluating content and meaning of policy documents.

E-Government: The use by government agencies of information technologies (such as Wide Area Networks, the Internet, and mobile computing) that have the ability to transform relations with citizens, businesses, and other arms of government. These technologies can serve a variety of different ends: better delivery of government services to citizens, improved interactions with business and industry, citizen empowerment through access to information, or more efficient government management. The resulting benefits can be less corruption, increased transparency, greater convenience, revenue growth, and/or cost reductions.

ICTs: Range of electronic tools, which facilitate the operational and strategic management of organisations by enabling them to manage their information, functions and processes as well as to communicate interactively with their stakeholders for achieving their mission and objectives.

Socio-Technical: Describes organizational systems design that recognizes the co-evolution of organisations and technology with respect to people and organisational tools.

Chapter 5

E-Governance as a Paradigm Shift in Public Administration:
Theories, Applications, and Management

Muhammad Muinul Islam
Jahangirnagar University, Bangladesh

Mohammad Ehsan
University of Dhaka, Bangladesh

ABSTRACT

The ICT-blessed e-governance is transforming public administration systems worldwide and forcing a paradigm shift. E-governance renders a new way and style in each and every aspect of public administration. It brings about changes in the structure, functions, and processes of public service delivery, ushering transformation in the system through effectively connecting, engaging, and streamlining the relations among government, businesses, citizens, and other relevant stakeholders. Irrespective of certain obvious limitations and challenges, it not only attempts to ensure economy, efficiency, and effectiveness in service delivery, but also offers unlimited potential for combating corruption and many other bureau-pathologies in public administration. Based on secondary sources, this chapter offers brief theoretical discussions on e-governance, including, among others, its emergence, types of service delivery, and transformation stages.

INTRODUCTION

An effort to claim for a paradigm shift in an academic discipline is daunting. Without a firm-rooted trend, distinguishing characteristics and evidence-based transformation, the claim for a paradigm shift would be futile. How far e-governance has provided and managed a space for a shift in paradigm is still debatable in the academic circle. But the trends and applications are so widespread, inevitable and visible that a modest claim for a paradigm shift is timely and due. The fundamental reasons and clues for such a 'claim' are justified by the transformation that occurred not only in the processes and practices of public administration, policy and management, but also in the structure that shapes it. From a systems approach, the changes are evident in both

DOI: 10.4018/978-1-4666-3691-0.ch005

inputs, throughputs and outputs thus bringing out a holistic transformation in public administration functionaries. No doubt that a system of public administration is all-pervasive and has been ubiquitous since times immemorial. Today, what we understand as the public administration existed even before the birth of modern states. The nature, functions, and mode of public service delivery, however, have gone through radical changes from those earlier times. This chapter offers an extension of public administration paradigms proposed and postulated by Henry (1975) and Golembiewski (1977). It also deals with the basic theoretical backgrounds of e-governance, its types of ICT-driven service delivery and transformation phases.

The birth of public administration as a separate field of study is marked by Wilson's seminal publication in 1887. Since then to the late 1970s, Henry identified five paradigms of public administration. These are: paradigm one: the politics/administration Dichotomy 1900-1926; paradigm two: the principles of administration 1927-1937; paradigm three: public administration as political science 1950-1970; paradigm four: public administration as management 1956-1970; and paradigm five: public administration as public administration, 1970-? Henry did not mention the exact end year of the fifth paradigm as it was still dominant in the intellectual discourse of the discipline of Public Administration. But we can cautiously suggest the finishing line of the fifth paradigm to be the early 90s. Since 2001, a new idea[1] slowly permeated in the theories and practice of public administration forcing a paradigm shift in the discipline. The sixth paradigm, as an extended version of Henry's paradigm, can thus be called as "*Public Administration as New Public Management (NPM), 1991-?*" However, as others suggested, we can also think of another paradigm shift in the discourses of public administration that concurrently exists with the sixth one and is very likely to be a dominant one for years to come. This seventh paradigm can be called "*Public Administration as E-governance[2] 1995-?*" By now, there is widespread agreement among the academicians and practitioners of the role that information and communication technology (ICT) plays in the day to day operations of public administration. ICTs dramatically revolutionized the structure, processes, and radically transformed the way public administration systems work around us (Roy, 2011). E-governance has been ubiquitously adopted and adapted, to various degrees, by the governments of developed, transitional and developing countries.[3] The glaring transformation that public administration so far has undergone through e-governance has been remarkable.

In fact, over the past three and a half decades, information and communication technology has brought changes in the operations of government organizations both in developed and developing countries. This is due to the process of converting information from analog to digital forms. The lifeblood of government is information and the digital revolution has allowed government organizations to store, analyze, and retrieve information more effectively and efficiently. This process has also been strongly affected by changes in telecommunications technology and the convergence of computer and communication technologies. The most striking manifestation of this process of technological change is the advent of Internet or World Wide Web (Bretschneider, 2003).

This reform of government administration and the provision of improved services to citizens have long been acknowledged as a major criterion for development and today's drive towards e-governance in many parts of the world can be considered as a part of this wider developmental goal (Madon, 2004). Throughout the world, governments, businesses and NGOs are working together to adopt e-governance – from Singapore to South Africa, Andhra Pradesh to Washington, or Bangladesh to Malaysia. These are not just experiments in new modes of service delivery. E-governance inevitably also embraces – and is driven by – new models of policy formulation, new forms of citizenship, new patterns of relationship and power, new options for economic development, and the search for new ways to connect people with the political process. As indicated, the rapid adoption of e-governance is facilitated by dynamic technological and telecommunication innovations. In many countries, ICTs are seen as a catalyst for e-governance. "After e-commerce and e-business," as *The Economist* (2000) predicted long ago, the next Internet revolution would be e-government." It is naturally expected that e-governance will ensure transparency, speedy information dissemination and improved service in public administration. In the era of informed citizens, e-governance is also seen as a vehicle for cost-effective and efficient way of public service delivery (Agarwal *et al.* 2003). Furthermore, e-governance is expected to empower the citizens, increase the profit margin of the businesses and enterprises, enhance flexibility in government service delivery, force data digitization and also strengthen the anti-corruption movement (Bhogle, 2008).

Governments around the world with a view to transform their governance structure and processes from traditional to electronic form are putting critical information online, automating once cumbersome processes, and interacting electronically with their citizens. This enthusiasm comes in part from a belief that technology can transform government's often-cited negative image. In many places, citizens view their governments as bloated, wasteful, and unresponsive to their most pressing needs. Mistrust of government is rife among the public and businesses. Civil servants are often seen as profiteers. The spread of information and communication technology brings hope that governments can transform. And, indeed, forward-looking public officials everywhere are using technology to improve their governments (PCIP 2002).

Governments, over the years, have taken multifarious decisions on how best to accommodate ICTs to transform public administration for enhancing the wellbeing of citizens. However, e-government and e-governance mean more than ICTs. Traditional pathways to better governance and government have been transformed through integrating innovation in ICTs, innovation in organizational and business practices, and changes in people's skills and expectations. E-governance is often embraced as facilitating changes in citizen involvement, transforming traditional hierarchical approaches to coordinated network approaches, and breaking down barriers – among the government departments, among layers of government (national, regional, local etc), and between the public and private sectors – to enhance a citizen/customer-focused approach to service delivery. This can bring about improvements in the accountability, transparency, and openness of public institutions. But e-governance also presents new challenges to citizens' trust in governments. Security of digital transactions and communications also needs to be assured; privacy needs to be protected, and citizens need to be able to control their personal data and must be ensured that only selective government officials would have access to it (Dugdale, 2004).

This chapter, which is primarily based on secondary sources, endeavors to shed some lights on the theoretical issues of e-governance. Our effort here remains brief as many authors, by now, have done excellent theoretical discussions on the issue. In so doing, the chapter at the outset presents a brief overview of the notion of e-governance in the intellectual discourse, and how it is conceptualized by academician, practitioners and also by different international agencies. Later on, it focuses on the ways e-governance is transforming the public administration system. The chapter culminates with a brief discussion on the prospects and challenges that e-governance offer in the operational field of public administration.

UNDERSTANDING E-GOVERNANCE: SOME THEORETICAL ISSUES

From Governance to E-Governance

The word 'e-governance' can be viewed at the crossroad of two major shifts - governance and information revolution. The idea of 'governance' has been around for decades. According to concise Oxford Dictionary, the word 'governance' has been developed from a Greek word *'kuberna'* which means to steer. The first classic political science essay on the subject discuss about the concept of 'governability,' which made *rule of law* as the core to development (Johnson 1997).

Clearly 'governance' gets into development discourse around the period of late 1980s. Human Development Report 1991 accepts the fact that freedom and democracy, though not a necessary condition, are entirely consistent with growth and development. 'International development' therefore shifted its focus from *'economic growth'* of the 1950s (UN Development decades) to *'sustainable human development'* that includes concerns for people and nature to be widely accepted by state, market and civil society. The environmental movement considered 'governance' as an urgent issue to deal the development agendas in a holistic manner: to include not only the sector at hand and the obvious stakeholders, but also others affected by them in other areas. It has forced a redefinition of the public interest with nature itself as a recognized stakeholder (Carino).

Intense globalization of market and trade, after the collapse of Soviet Union in 1989, left most countries but to join the World Trade Organization (WTO), which gave concern about the markets being opened to cheaper products and labor forces. This resulted in creation of safety nets and bureaucracies to be involved with regulatory governance mechanism. But at the same time because of trade globalization and networked economy, the countries cannot avoid creating a level playing field with transparent governance mode (Carino). This openness and predictability of government functioning is further echoed at e-governance.

Globalization with the emergence of new information and communication technologies, had a profound impact in the development of the notion of e-governance. ICT replaced two basic elements of productions - 'labor' and 'capital' by 'information' and 'knowledge' for the first time in the last two centuries. Internet created the same break-through as the printing press did in the 15th century. It shapes the ability to communicate, share, distribute, exchange, formalize, use and network information at a speed that is not experienced before. Moore's law[4] pointed out that, the processing power of microchips is doubling every 18 months with a trend of 20-30% decline in quality adjustment prices for computers. This means computers are getting cheaper, powerful and ubiquitous, making the network and automation of services viable to government. Political activism on the other hand, is also using the space with increased number of public interest groups, community or voluntary organizations propagating their demands and activities in the electronic network.

Over the years, the Weberian[5] principles of bureaucratic governance are being replaced with the trends of horizontal, leaner, dynamic and networked governance. Administrative reform and development have experienced TQM[6] in 1980s, and 're-engineering and re-invention' in the 1990s. E-governance reflects this process of re-invention and re-engineering in governance and *'is aimed at adapting administration to the further increasing flow of information: accelerating the process of decision making by optimizing resources, and making the mechanism for decision making self-regulating'* (Baev 2003). This led 'Governance' be defined independently from the 'the act of government' to the practice of getting the consent and cooperation of the governed. The concrete objective of e-governance is to support and simplify governance for all parties - government, citizens, and businesses through online services and other electronic means. In other words, e-governance uses electronic means to support and stimulate good governance (Backus 2001).

However, the core ideas and techniques associated with "putting government online" first emerged in the most technologically advanced Western countries, especially those whose populations were pioneers in the adoption of the Internet in the 1990s. In the United States, the objective of Bill Clinton's administration of "reinventing government" closely followed the managerial path, and the Bush administration had remained on the same track, with an even greater emphasis on cost reduction through efficiency gains. The subsequent regimes follow suit at the volatile time of financial meltdown. In the British case, on the other hand, the managerial use of ICTs emerged as a strong theme in the Labour administration's obsession with "joined-up government" – a phrase that has recently crossed the Atlantic to the U.S. At the level of the European Union, despite greater recognition of the democratic potential of new ICTs, most discussion has centered on issues of efficiency and "service delivery." It was the United States and Britain (along with other countries, notably Canada and Australia) that led the way, both in establishing a basic informational form of Web presence in the mid-1990s and in developing what became known as "e-government" in the late 1990s (Chadwick and May 2003).

As e-governance supports and facilitates good governance for all stakeholders, we need to understand that e-governance is not just about a website or not merely a digitization of service delivery. It certainly stands on a greater definition of engagement and depth of relationship that surrounds both the citizens and the government (Fang 2002).

From among the popular definitions of e-governance, the US 2002 E-Government Act defines it as "the use by the Government of web-based Internet applications and other information technologies, combined with processes that

implement these technologies, to: a) enhance the access to and delivery of Government information and services to the public, other agencies, and other Government entities or b) bring about improvements in Government operations that may include effectiveness, efficiency, service quality, or transformation (U.S. Congress, 2002)." OECD defines e-governance as "the use of ICTs, and particularly the Internet, as a tool to achieve better government (OECD, 2003, 23). The e-governance efforts by the European Union are based on the following definition: "e-government is the use of Information and Communication Technologies in public administrations combined with organizational change and new skills in order to improve public services and democratic processes" (EU, 2004). According to Perry 6, e-governance should be divided, in the first instance, into four distinct areas of activity, namely e-democracy, e-service provision, e-management and e-governance. Although, Perry 6 clarifies, they are distinct, there are important relationships between them. In defining e-governance, he wrote, "by the term 'e-governance', I mean to pick out the activities of *digital support for policy formulation and the scrutiny and oversight of the achievement of policy goals*" (Perry 6, 16).

There is a difference of meaning between e-governance and e-government. Governance is the manner or the process to guide a society to best achieve its goals and interests, while government is the institution or the apparatus to perform that job. This means government is one (of the many) institutions of governance. Interestingly, international bodies define e-governance as per their focuses to frame governance in general. For example, World Bank's concern on governance is exclusively related to the contribution they make to social and economic development by economic and structural liberalization. Therefore to them, e-governance implies the use of ICT channels to change the way citizens and business interact with government to enable citizen's involvement in decision making, increased access to information, more transparency and civil society strengthening (Deane, 2003). Grönlund provides rather a vivid distinction of e-government and e-governance. To him, e-government refers to what is happening within government organizations while e-governance, on the other hand, refers to the whole system involved in managing a society. The system includes activities not only by government organizations but also companies and voluntary organizations, as well as citizens. Moreover, it features the processes and flows of governance, dimensions that are critical to understanding the context of information systems deployment and use (Atkinson, 2003).

Most North American and European nations reach interactive stage of e-governance maturity and it poses increased reflexivity in relationship between administration and citizenry. Being e-government is not the major concern now for these developed nations; rather an effective and timely service to citizen through e-governance is probably one of major goals of these countries. In the words of Marche and McNiven, "it is not just a question of e-government, it is also a question of e-governance". According to them, "e-governance is the provision of routine government information and transactions using electronic means, most notably those using Internet technologies, whether delivered at home, at work, or through public kiosks. E-governance, on the other hand, is a technology-mediated relationship between citizens and their governments from the perspective of potential electronic deliberation over civic communication, over policy evolution, and in democratic expressions of citizen will" (2003, 75).

Bhatnagar observes that the World Bank refers to e-governance as the use of information technologies (such as Wide Area Networks, the Internet, and mobile computing) by the government agencies. In other words, e-governance may be defined as the delivery of government services and information to the public by using electronic means. These technologies enable the government to transform its relations with its other wings, citizens, businesses. Such an exercise leads to better delivery of government services to citizens, improved interactions with business and industry, citizen empowerment through access to information and a more efficient government management. The resulting benefits can be lesser corruption, increased transparency, greater convenience, revenue growth, and/or cost reductions (Bhatnagar, 2001).

UNDP (2003) relates the concept of governance to that of sustainable human development. It views e-governance as a process of "creating public value with the use of modern ICT" where public value is defined as a notion "rooted in people's preferences." Therefore, e-government is justified if it enhances the capacity of public administration to increase the supply of public value – the outcome of a high quality of life. Focusing more on the 'governance' possibilities, UNDP is of the view that e-governance can "equip people for genuine participation in an inclusive political process that can produce well-informed public-consent, the ever more prevalent basis for the legitimacy of governments." The UN's five guiding principles on e-government objectives are: (1) building services around citizens choices; (2) making government and its services more accessible; (3) social inclusion; (4) providing information responsibly; and (5) using IT and human resources effectively and efficiently (UN Survey 2002). The Public Administration (PUMA) Group of the Organization for Economic Cooperation and Development (OECD) focuses on three main components of online and participatory e-governance: "information, active participation and consultation" (Riley 2003).

The Government of India took the basis of SMART for its vision statement on e-governance. This relates to "application of IT to the process of government functioning to bring out *Simple, Moral, Accountable, Responsive* and *Transparent governance* (SMART)." This vision helped India outlining further objectives and strategic initiatives on e-governance. Rogers W'O Okot-Uma of Commonwealth Secretariat in London thinks that, e-governance seeks to realize processes and structures for harnessing the potentialities of information and communication technologies at various levels of government and the public sector and beyond, for the purpose of enhancing good governance.

Brown (2005) proposes a comprehensive definition of e-governance. To him, "a broader view of e-government is that it relates to the entire range of government roles and activities, shaped by and making use of information and communications technologies. A high-level statement of this view is 'knowledge-based government in the knowledge-based economy and society.' More concretely, e-government brings together two elements that have not been naturally joined in the past. One is the environment, within government and in the society at large, created by the use of electronic technologies such as computing, e-mail, the World Wide Web, wireless and other ICTs, combined with management models such as client/citizen centricity and single-window convergence. The other is the basic model of the state and of public administration within that, linking the dynamics of democracy, governance and public management."

Among the four different dimensions of e-government that are based on the functions of government, e-governance is one of the prominent, the others being e-administration, e-services, and e-democracy (Annttiroiko 2008). E-governance in the context of public sector is about managing and steering multi-sectoral stakeholder relations on a non-hierarchical basis with the help of ICTs for the purpose of taking care of the policy, service, and development functions of government. In practical terms, it is about cooperation, networking, and partnership relations between public organizations, corporations, NGOs, civic groups, and active citizens, utilized by public organizations to gather and coordinate effectively both local and external resources to achieve public policy goals (Gronlund, 2007; Finger and Langenberg 2007 cited in Annttiroiko 2008). Despite varia-

tions in definition, it is true that e-governance has enormous potential to ensure that citizens are no longer passive consumers of services offered to them as it also allows them to play a more proactive role in deciding the kind of services they want and the structure through which this service can best be provided.

Actors and Tools in E-Governance Ecology

E-government encompasses a broad spectrum of activities involving improved government operations and services as well as enabling a more cooperative and meaningful relationship with citizens and other non-state actors. E-government initiatives, however, have predominantly focused on changing government operations, structures, and services rather than redefining a new role and set of responsibilities for citizens." Heeks observes that e-governance should be seen to encompass all ICTs, but the key innovation is computer networks – from intranets to the Internet – creating a wide range of new digital connections:

- Connections within government – permitting 'joined-up thinking;'
- Connections between government and NGOs/citizens – strengthening accountability;
- Connections between government and business/citizens – transforming service delivery;
- Connections within and between NGOs – supporting learning and concerted action;
- Connections within and between communities – building social and economic development.

The novelty of using new technologies in governance is that it expands beyond internal government operations to include electronic service delivery to the public and the subsequent interaction between the citizen and the government.

This potential for interactivity can be identified as one of the most important elements in the way e-governance will change the nature of government (Heeks, 2001).

A variety of e-governance tools are in use for harnessing improved services in public management and policy. Perry 6 has identified six basic categories of purposes for using these e-governance tools. An overview of these tools and uses are captured in Table 1:

Types of Service Delivery through E-Governance

The quest to improve service delivery through the use of ICTs in governments typically focuses on four main dimensions. These are:

1. **G2C (Government-to-Citizens):** This focuses primarily on developing user-friendly one-stop centers of service for easy access to high quality government services and information. Citizens-to-Government (C2G) has also emerged as an important stakeholder relationship.
2. **G2B (Government-to-Business):** This aims to facilitate and enhance the capability of business transactions between the government and the private sector by improving communications and connectivity between the two parties. Business-to-Government (B2G) has also emerged as an important stakeholder relationship.
3. **G2G (Government-to-Government):** This is an inter-governmental effort that aims to improve communication and effectiveness of services between federal, state and local governments in the running of day-to-day administration.
4. **Intra-Government:** This aims to leverage ICT to reduce costs and improve the quality of administration and management within government organization (Karim 2003, 192).

The Stages of E-Government Transformation

Gartner (2000) suggests that e-governance matures following four stages in their E-governance Maturity Model (Baum and Maio, 2000). As an addition, we propose 'institutionalization' as the fifth stage of e-governance maturity:

1. Information → Presence.
2. Interaction → Intake processes.
3. Transaction → Complete transactions.
4. Transformation → Integration & change.
5. Institutionalization → Interactive democracy and public outreach.

In the *first stage,* e-governance means being present on the web, providing the public (G2C & G2B) with relevant information. The format of the early government websites is similar to that of a brochure or leaflet. The value to the public is that government information is publicly accessible; processes are described and is more transparent, which improves democracy and service. Internally (G2G), the government can also disseminate static information with electronic means, such as the Internet.

In the *second stage,* the interaction between government and the public (G2C & G2B) is stimulated with various applications. People can ask questions via e-mail, use search engines, and download forms and documents. These ultimately save time. In fact, the complete intake of (simple) applications can be done online 24 hours per day. Normally this would only have been possible at a counter during opening hours. Internally (G2G) government organizations use LANs, intranets and e-mail to communicate and exchange data.

With stage *three,* the complexity of the technology is increasing, but customer (G2C & G2B) value is also higher. Complete transactions can be done without going to an office. Examples of online services are filing income tax, filing property tax,

Table 1. Types of e-governance tools by category of purposes

1	**Generating Understanding**
	• Data systems enabling dictionaries of key terms; • Idea generation tools; • Graphical problem structuring tools (modelling in software procedures); • Mind mapping and representation; • Online consultations; • Multi-user argumentation support tools for generating options, identifying pros and cons and debates; • Use of electronic whiteboards; • RSS feeds; • Blogs for sharing ideas and debates.
2	**Collecting Data or Observations**
	• Search engines; • Digital agents based on neural nets for context sensitive searching; • Sensors; • Communication records and storage systems; • Remote sensing and optimization.
3	**Organizing and Analyzing Data**
	• Spreadsheets and budget systems; • Organizational memory capture and management tools; • Document profiling systems in shared work spaces; • Techniques of MIS software; • Hypermedia geographic information systems (GIS); • Training simulation systems for decision makers; • Formal models.
4	**Supporting Communication and Transactions**
	• E-mail; • Electronic conferencing; • Video-conferencing; • Webinar; • Meeting management tools; • Tools to model and manage conflict; • Argumentation support systems; • Electronic document interchange.
5	**Modelling Decisions and Advising on Possible Consequences**
	• Spreadsheets; • Testing consistency and precision in drafting legislation; • Neural nets; • Modelling systems for problems.
6	**Environments that Provide Integration and Storage**
	• Intranets; • The World Wide Web.

Source: Taken from Perry 6 (2004, pp. 22-23) with slight modification.

extending/renewal of licenses, visa and passports and online voting. State three is made complex because of security and personalization issues. For example, digital (electronic) signatures will be necessary to enable legal transfer of services. On the business side, the government is starting with e-procurement applications. In this stage, internal (G2G) processes have to be redesigned to provide good service. Government needs new laws and legislation to enable paperless transactions.

The *fourth stage* is to reach a stage where all information systems are integrated and the public can get G2C & G2B services at one virtual counter. One single point of contact for all services is the ultimate goal. The complex aspect in reaching this goal is mainly on the internal side, e.g., the necessity to drastically change culture, processes and responsibilities within the government institution (G2G). Government employees in different departments have to work together in a smooth and seamless way. In this stage, cost savings, efficiency and customer satisfaction reach highest possible levels.

The fifth stage is interactive democracy with public outreach and a range of accountability measures. Here, government websites move beyond a service-delivery model to system-wise political transformation. In addition to having integrated and fully executable online services, government sites offer option for website personalization. Through these and other kinds of advanced features, visitors can personalize websites, provide feedback, make comments, and avail themselves of a host of sophisticated features designed to boost democratic responsiveness and leadership accountability (West, 2004).

OPPORTUNITIES OF E-GOVERNANCE

The digital transformation of public administration opens up immense opportunities towards effective realization of policy goals. The age-old problems of bureaucratic red-tapism, slow delivery of services, accountability and corruption can be countered by appropriate tools and strategies provided through ICT-enabled e-governance. The major task of public sector reform today is based on introducing and implementing e-governance projects. Innovative and sustainable application of Internet and ICTs bring good governance among the government, private sector and citizens.

Application of Internet technologies and ICTs in public management helps achieve development goals of the nations. There are great deals of empirical evidences that suggest that e-governance contributed enormously to development goals.

They can do so at both micro and national levels by increasing the effectiveness and reach of development interventions, enhancing good governance and lowering the costs of service delivery. A project study in Italy comments that "e" means efficiency, effectiveness, empowerment, and economic and social development (UNDESA 2002).

Among different benefits of e-governance are reduced transaction costs to better capacity to target groups, increased coverage and quality of service delivery, enhanced response capacity to address issues of poverty and increase in revenue. Besides, e-governance provides increased accountability and transparency, which may greatly reduce the risk of corruption and raise the perception of good government among citizens. Citizens' trust in their government may have an impact on their willingness to invest and to pay taxes and levies for services.

Other benefits include employment creation in the third sector, improvements in the education and health system, providing better government services, and developing increased capacity for the provision of safety and security.

E-governance can offer to reduce functional insularity in public administration often referred to as "silos" or "stove-piping." This means the tendency on the part of bureaucracy not to integrate service provisioning across government departments when responding to citizen's needs. E-governance in this regard provides easy access and opportunities that permit cross-organizational services through internet and other communication technologies. It not only improves services and offer convenience to the users, but is also cost-effective (Marche and McNiven 2003, 75).

THREATS OF E-GOVERNANCE

With its divergent opportunities, e-governance poses different risks and threats. These threats have an impact on both individual and institutional levels. At individual level, threats are posed at liberty and privacy in the ways in which personal information tends to be used and abused by policy makers as they match data from many sources (Rabb, 1997). Others threats include, as cited by Perry 6 (2004, 77-78), erosion of citizen's collective (democratic) influence over governmental decision, loss of control by politicians over the decision making agenda in favor of control by civil servants, loss of civil servants' capability to exercise constraints upon the populism of politicians, the erosion of meaningful relationships among decision makers because of the loss of face-to-face contact (Wilson, 1999), the loss of quality in decision making because the focus on quantitatively measurable dimensions (Power, 1997), the loss of commitment to decisions made on the advice of computer based neural net models and expert system, due to the reduced user control and understanding of the model, and the larger numbers of options generated (Landsbergen *et al.*, 1997), security against hackers and potential forms of tampering, and maintaining the integrity and confidentiality of increasingly precious database etc.

At institutional level, the most striking challenge of e-governance is digital divide within the country as well as among different countries of the world. A study of Chatfield and Alhujran confirm a wide digital divide that remains between the Arab countries and the leading developed countries (2009, 151).

Heeks (2003) made an extensive research on e-governance projects. In his analysis, most e-government projects, both in industrialized and developing countries, fail either totally or partially. There are very little data about rates of success and failure of e-government projects, but some baseline estimates indicate that behind the high-tech glamour of these projects lies a dirty reality – the majority of projects are failures. The reasons for such failures are, as Heeks observed, lack of "e-readiness," and the oversize gaps between project design and on-the-ground reality (known

as "design-reality gaps"), meaning the lack of assessment of needs prior to the implementation of a project.

CONCLUSION

As evident, e-governance facilitates development and offers many benefits to the citizens. It has the potential which made governments around the world to initiate innovative changes in the delivery of public services. The issues of poverty reduction, economic underdevelopment, illiteracy, pervasive corruption can be minimized, if not completely eliminated, through the skillful application of e-governance initiatives. Despite its enormous potential, it is also true that the benefits of e-governance are not duly reaped by the governments, both in developed and developing countries. The main stumbling blocks in the way are basically the political leadership and bureaucratic inertia. Another major concern for global equitable access of e-governance is the 'digital divide'[7] often called as "information black hole." As indicated, e-governance can very positively direct a paradigm shift, from traditional bureaucratic administration to a more responsive, accountable and effective public administration, that many governments around the world are aspiring for a long time.

REFERENCES

Accenture. (2002). *E-government leadership – Realizing the vision*. Retrieved from www.accenture.com/xd/xd.asp?it=enWeb&xd=industries%5Cgovernment%5Cgove_welcome.xml

Agarwal, V., Mittal, M., & Rastogi, L. (2003). *Enabling e-Governance – Integrated citizen relationship management framework – The Indian perspective, India*. Retrieved from http://www.e11online.com/pdf/e11_whitepaper2.pdf

Anderson, K. (1999). Reengineering public sector organizations using information technology. In R. Heeks (Ed.), *Reinventing Government in the Information Age*. London: Routledge.

Atkinson, R. (2003). *Network Government for the Digital Age*. Washington, DC: Progressive Policy Institute.

Backus, M. (2001). *E-governance and developing countries: introduction and examples* (Research Report, No. 3). International Institute for Communication and Development (IICD). Retrieved from editor.iicd.org/files/report3.doc

Baev, V. (2005). Social and Philosophical aspects of E-governance Paradigm Formation for Public Administration. *Razon Y Palabra, 42*.

Baum, C., & Maio, D. (2000). *Gartner's four phases of e-government model*. Gartner's Group.

Bhatnagar, S. C. (1999). *E-government: Opportunities and Challenges*. Ahmadabad, India: Indian Institute of Management.

Bhatnagar, S. C. (2001). *Philippine Customs Reform*. Washington, DC: World Bank.

Bhogle, S. (2008). E-governance. In A.-V. Anttiroiko (Ed.), *Electronic Government: Concepts, Methodologies, Tools and Applications*. Hershey, PA: IGI Global. doi:10.4018/978-1-59904-947-2.ch006

Bretschneider, S. (2003). Information technology, e-government, and institutional change. *Public Administration Review, 63*(6). doi:10.1111/1540-6210.00337

Brown, D. (1999). Information systems for improved performance management: Development approaches in U.S. public agencies. In R. Heeks (Ed.), *Reinventing Government in the Information Age*. London: Routledge.

Brown, D. (2005). Electronic Government and Public Administration. *International Review of Administrative Sciences, 71*(2), 241–254. doi:10.1177/0020852305053883

Cariño, L. V. (2006, January-October). From traditional public administration to governance: Research in NCPAG, 1952-2002. *Philippine Journal of Public Administration*.

Chadwick, A., & Christopher, M. (2003). Interaction between States and Citizens in the Age of Internet: 'E-government' in the United States, Britain and European Union. *Governance: An International Journal of Policy, Administration and Institutions, 16*(2). doi:10.1111/1468-0491.00216

Deane, A. (2003). *Increasing Voice and Transparency Using ICT Tools: E-Government, E-Governance*. Washington, DC: World Bank.

Dugdale, A. (2004). *E-Governance: Democracy in Transition*. National Institute for Governance Report.

Economist. (2000, June 22). A survey of government and the Internet The next revolution. *The Economist*.

Economist. (2000, June 24). The Next Revolution – A survey of government and the internet. *The Economist*, p. 3.

Ehsan, M. (2004). Origin, Ideas and Practice of New Public Management: Lessons for Developing Countries. *Administrative Change, 31*(2), 69–82.

EU. (2004). eGovernment Research in Europe. *European Commission*. Retrieved from http://europa.eu.int/information_society/programmes/egov_rd/text_en.htm

Fang, Z. (2002). E-Government in digital era: Concept, practice, and development. Bangkok, Thailand: School of Public Administration, National Institute of Development Administration (NIDA).

Finger, M., & Langenberg, T. (2007). Electronic governance. In A. V. Anttiroiko, & M. Malkia (Eds.), *Encyclopedia of Digital Government* (Vol. 2). Hershey, PA: Idea Group Reference.

Fountain, J. (2001). *Building the virtual state: Information technology and institutional change.* Washington, DC: Brookings Institution.

Gotembiewsky, R. T. (1977). *Public Administration as a developing discipline, part I: Perspectives on past and present.* New York: Marcel Dekker.

Gronlund, A. (2007). Electronic government. In A. V. Anttiroiko, & M. Malkia (Eds.), *Encyclopedia of Digital Government* (Vol. 2). Hershey, PA: Idea Group Reference.

Heeks, R. (2001). *Reinventing Government in the Information Age.* London: Routledge.

Heeks, R. (2003). *Most eGovernment-for-Development Projects Fail: How Can Risks be Reduced?* (iGovernment Working Paper Series, No 14). Manchester, UK: IDPM, University of Manchester.

Henry, N. (1995). *Public Administration and Public Affairs.* Prentice-Hall, Inc.

Johnson, I. (1997). Redefining the Concept of Governance. Gatineau, Canada: Political and Social Policies Division, Policy Branch, Canadian International Development Agency (CIDA).

Karim, M. R. A. (2003). Technology and improved service delivery: Learning points from the Malyasian experience. *International Review of Administrative Sciences, 69.*

Landsbergen, D., Coursey, D. H., Loveless, S., & Shangraw, R. F. Jr. (1997). Decision quality, confidence and commitment with expert systems: an experimental study. *Journal of Public Administration: Research and Theory, 7*(1), 131–158. doi:10.1093/oxfordjournals.jpart.a024336

Madon, S. (2004). Evaluating the developmental impact of e-governance initiatives: An exploratory framework. *The Electronic Journal on Information Systems in Developing Countries, 20*(5).

Marche, S., & McNiven, J. D. (2003). E-government and E-governance: The future isn't what it used to be. *Canadian Journal of Administrative Sciences, 20*(1), 74. doi:10.1111/j.1936-4490.2003.tb00306.x

Moon, M. J., & Stuart, B. (1997). Can state government actions affect innovation and its diffusion? An Extended Communication Model and Empirical Test. *Technological Forecasting and Social Change, 54*(1), 57–77. doi:10.1016/S0040-1625(96)00121-7

Nye, J. Jr. (1999). Information Technology and Democratic Governance. In E. C. Karmarck, & J. Nye Jr., (Eds.), *Democracy.com? Governance in Networked World.* Hollis, NH: Hollis Publishing Company.

OECD. (2003). *The e-Government Imperative.* Paris: OECD e-Government Studies.

Organization for Economic Co-operation and Development (OECD). (2001). *Understanding the Digital Divide.* Paris: OECD Publications. Retrieved from http://www.oecd.org/dataoecd/38/57/1888451.pdf

Pacific Council on International Policy (PCIP). (2002). *Roadmap for E-government in the Developing World*. Los Angeles, CA: The Working Group on E-Government in the Developing World. Retrieved form http://www.pacificcouncil.org/pdfs/e-gov.paper.f.pdf

Perry 6. (2004). *E-governance – Styles of political judgment in the information age polity*. New York: Palgrave.

Power, M. (1997). *The audit society: Rituals of verification*. Oxford University Press.

Raab, C. (1997). Privacy, information and democracy. In *The governance of cyberspace: Politics, technology and global restructuring*. London: Routledge. doi:10.4324/9780203360408_chapter_10

Riley, T. B., & Riley, C. G. (2003). E-governance to e-democracy - Examining the Evolution. In *International Tracking Survey Report 2003*. Riley Information Services.

Roy, J. (2011). The promise (and pitfalls) of digital transformation. In R. P. Leone, & F. L. K. Ohemeng (Eds.), *Approaching Public Administration: Core Debates and Emerging Issues*. Toronto, Canada: Edmond Montgomery Publications.

UNDESA. (2002). *Plan of Action - e-government for Development*. Government of Italy, Ministry for Innovation and Technologies. Retrieved from www.palermoconference2002.org

U.S. Congress. (2002). *2002 E-Government Act*. US: Author.

West, D. M. (2004). E-government and the Transformation of Service Delivery and Citizen Attitudes. *Public Administration Review, 64*(1). doi:10.1111/j.1540-6210.2004.00343.x

Wilson, F. (1999). Cultural control within the virtual organization. *The Sociological Review, 47*, 672–694. doi:10.1111/1467-954X.00191

KEY TERMS AND DEFINITIONS

Digital Divide: A gap in the opportunity to access, use and maximize benefits, among others, in government information and services within in-country and global settings at different levels due to lack of basic ICT infrastructure.

E-Governance: Innovative and new process of service delivery in the public, private and non-profit sectors aided by information and communication technologies which are presumably faster, efficient and effective.

E-Government Transformation: An evolutionary process of changes in public administration systems transforming traditional systems into digitalized mode of services that matures incrementally through five stages from information to interaction and then to transaction to transformation and finally institutionalization.

E-Government: Application of digital technologies within the system of public administration that turns governmental service processes faster, easily accessible and accountable and makes the government perform better in the delivery of services to citizens replacing traditional mode of operation by the government.

Paradigm Shift: A change over or alteration of *loci* and *foci* of a field of study that endures for a moderately long time and becomes a dominant focus for the scholars of that as well as other allied disciplines.

ENDNOTES

[1] The concept of 'New Public Management (NPM)' is coined by Christopher Hood in 2001 in his famous article *"A public management for all seasons?"* Apart from him, other scholars like Pollitt, Lan and Rosenbloom, Osborne and Gaebler have also worked on the same idea in different names in the early period of 1990s.

2   E-governance as a paradigm shift in the discipline of public administration can be benchmarked in the mid-1990s with the introduction of Internet and web-presence by the government.

3   The dramatic changes occurred due to technological revolution are in the domains of politics (Nye 1999), government institutions (Fountain 2001), performance management (Brown 1999), red tape reduction (Moon and Bretschneider 2002), and re-engineering (Anderson 1999) in the administration.

4   A founder of Intel Corporation, Gordon Moore made his famous observation in 1965, just four years after the first planar integrated circuit was discovered. The press called it "Moore's Law." More information can be found at: http://www.intel.com/research/silicon/mooreslaw.htm

5   Max Weber has given the ideal typical model of Bureaucracy. The Weberian model categorically focuses on two dimensions (i) the structural, relating to the hierarchical arrangement of positions, legal rational basis of authority, with system of compensation, and (ii) the behavioral, relating to the merit based selections of officials with the emphasis on training.

6   For detail of TQM please visit: http://www. google.com/search?hl=en&lr=&oi=defmo re&q=define:TQM

7   Digital divide refers to the gap between individuals, households, businesses and geographic areas at different socio-economic levels with regard to both the opportunities to access information and communication technologies and to their use of the Internet for a wide variety of activities (OECD).

Chapter 6
Realizing E-Government:
Delineating Implementation Challenges and Defining Success

Alexandru V. Roman
California State University – San Bernardino, USA

ABSTRACT

There is a growing recognition among scholars, practitioners, and elected officials that e-government success is not a deterministic outcome of entrepreneurial design or exacting implementation. In fact, constructing cost-efficient and policy effective e-government platforms has proved to be much more challenging than originally expected. In many instances, failed e-government experiments have led to significant financial losses and to increased dissatisfaction levels among citizenry. These latter experiences have nuanced the need for a much more thorough understanding and appreciation for the difficulties faced within the conceptualization and application of e-government platforms in successfully achieving the expected administrative and democratic outcomes. This chapter, by tracing the evolution of e-government both as a concept and as an administrative trend within the transformation of governance, delineates the main challenges in achieving the core goals and the democratic scope of e-governance. It is argued that in e-governance, success is a function of three fundamental vectors – security, functionality, and transformation.

INTRODUCTION

There has always been an intimate relationship between technology and the historical developments within the evolution of humanity. In a number of ways, the two are inseparable. The history of mankind is by and large a story of technological innovations. Typically, technology induced changes take time to motivate genuine transformations and they are rather incremental in character. Some technologies, however, by their very nature, can be sufficiently powerful to re-write the trajectory of economies and societies. Although rarely, on occasions technologies do motivate immediate and dramatic shifts. In the eyes of many (Johnson, 1998; Milakovich, 2012; Nye, 2002) this is exactly the type of impact that Information Communication Technologies (ICTs) can have. Perhaps for the first time since the industrial revolution, a technology can radically and

DOI: 10.4018/978-1-4666-3691-0.ch006

immediately affect not only the world economy but also the very fabric of social matrices. The Internet and all its derivative applications do indeed possess the capacity to be revolutionary in the sense that they can meaningfully recode social structures.

As a technology, the Internet is unlike any other revolutionary technological development of the past, such as the internal combustion engine or electricity. The effects and changes induced by adoption of ICTs are significantly more difficult to trace than it was ever the case with most other technologies. For instance, in the case of an engine, its power and impacts can be examined and controlled fairly easy. Its effective range and exposure is also constrained by the physical limits imposed by its design. This is not the case for ICTs. Due to their amorphous and ambiguous nature they do not lend themselves to precise evaluations nor tracking. This latter fact makes monitoring and forecasting their evolution rather challenging. Furthermore, unlike electricity, ICTs are much more responsive and can be much more easily shaped into political instruments (Fountain, 2001; Milakovich, 2012). Finally, the identity of ICTs and their applications are not necessarily defined by their technical capacities or functionalities but by the scope of their uses. For instance, social media, such as Twitter and Facebook can be used as pure communication tools similar to mobile texting or e-mailing, or they could become the mainframe for organizing and propelling social unrest. When it comes to ICTs it is not necessarily about what they can do as much as it is about how and for what they are used. In this sense, then, ICTs, the Internet in particular, is different in many important ways from previous technologies deemed as revolutionary, not the least being that it can take on an identity of its own and become controversial fairly easily.

Notwithstanding military applications, governments are usually much slower in adopting technology for purposes of governance. Given that in the public sector stakes are high and large scale

failures are becoming exceedingly scrutinized, governments typically prefer to allow others to test a specific technology and work out the bugs before they adopt it on a large scale. Furthermore, similar to most capital projects, technology implementation demands significant financial and time investments. Once a certain platform becomes implemented, its high costs will justify and impose great pressures for it to stick for the long-run. This is further complicated by the fragmented nature of the technology market and the unpredictability of technological innovation. Unlike a highway or a bridge, a digital infrastructure requires permanent learning and change. This, too, imposes costs that can rarely be realistically predicted. Most importantly, however, even the most up to date digital platforms can become obsolete in a matter of months. Yet, despite all these risks and the enormous price tags, governments cannot avoid placing ICTs at the administrative core of governance (Milakovich, 2012). E-government is no longer a choice, it is to some extent a necessity. In fact, there are now enormous pressures both from citizens and from the private sector to operationalize most of governmental services and interactions within ICTs-based frameworks. These pressures motivate governments to embark on costly ICTs projects, often without having sufficiently complete understandings of the nature of the technology or the actual scope of the projects. Administrative and political burdens are so great that doing something is often considered better than doing nothing, even if what is being done is strategically chaotic. Within this context, it becomes critical to develop clear and practical understandings of the challenges of successfully constructing an ICTs-driven governance.

This chapter examines in detail the concepts of e-government and e-governance. It provides an overview of the latest developments and trends both in e-government research and practice. The primary focus is placed on defining success. What does success mean within the context of e-governance? Why are some projects successful while others not? What are the main challenges in achieving success? What can the history of e-government tell us about its nature and can it help us predict and prepare for future success? These are just a few of the questions that this chapter explores and addresses. Drawing on the answers to these questions, it is argued that e-government success is a function of three interdependent vectors – security, functionality and transformation. E-government cannot and should not be thought of as a one dimensional technological project. Success of e-government cannot be guaranteed by the mere successful implementation of a given platform. E-government success is much more than that.

DEFINITIONS AND CONCEPTUALIZATIONS

Conceptualizing E-Government and E-Governance

Before a clear understanding of the challenges faced in e-government implementation can be delineated it is imperative to develop a working definition of what e-government and e-governance "are." While at first glance this might appear as a trivial task, this is far from being the case. Depending on what is being emphasized - a function, a philosophical preconception or an ideological image, e-government might be defined rather differently (Torres, Pina, & Royo, 2005; Stahl, 2005; Dawes, 2008; Hardy & Williams, 2011; Gil-Garcia, 2012). Each definition carries its fair share of assumptions, biases and normative preconceptions.

As new possibilities are considered and myths are being debunked, the concept of e-government, subsequently its definition, remains very much fluent and ambiguous and is continuously evolving (Moon, 2002; Norris & Moon, 2005; Stanimirovic & Vintar, 2013). E-government, according to the Commission of European Communities, is "the

use of information and communication technologies (ICT) in public administrations combined with organisational changes and new skills. The objective is to improve public services, democratic processes and public policies." Others have defined e-government as "the electronic provision of information and services by government 24 hours per day, seven days per week" (Norris & Moon, 2005, p. 64). Finally, e-government can be defined as "myriad tools and applications from fax machines and mainframe computing to social media and open government strategies…[it] does not refer to technological artifacts only, but also to the social and organizational aspects and elements around those artifacts…a socio-technical phenomenon" (Gil-Garcia, 2012, pp. 2-3). On the one hand, it has been suggested that the concept of e-government is revolutionary and represents a significant and original development within the context of the evolution of governance; on the other hand, it has been asserted that e-government is nothing more than a catchy label for an old phenomenon - the use of IT in government (Gil-Garcia, 2012). In the same vein, some scholars make it a point to emphasize that e-government is noticeably different from the mere use of IT by government; IT in government refers to inward applications while e-government is the outward applications of IT (Moon, Lee, & Roh, 2014; Norris, 2010).

Whatever the case might be, it is clear, however, that e-government is not something that can be captured by a single term; it is "an evolving and diverse collection of practices." (Carrizales, 2008, p. 24). That is perhaps the main reason why scholars (Dawes, 2008; Fountain, 2001; Maureen Brown, 2007; Moon, 2002; Roman, 2013; Roman & Miller, 2013; West, 2005) prefer to broadly define e-government as *the use of ICTs by government for purpose of governance*. Along similar lines, e-governance (or digital governance) is typically defined as "a set of technology-mediated processes that are changing both the delivery of public services and the broader interactions between citizens and government" (Torres et al., 2005, p. 534). Digital governance, according to Milakovich (2012, p. 9), is "a broader umbrella term referring to the networked extension of ICT relationships to include faster access to the Web, mobile service delivery, networking, teleconferencing and multi-channel information technologies to accomplish higher-level two-way transactions." Taken together, then, e-governance could be thought of as *the art of governance within which the role of ICTs is emphasized*.

While there are a number of fundamental disagreements among scholars when it comes to conceptualizing e-government, two of them stand out. One terminological debate deals with the relationship between e-government and e-governance. Some (Calista & Melitsky, 2007; D'agostino et al., 2011) see e-government and e-governance as two rather distinct concepts. E-government is associated mainly with the technical aspects of the use of ICTs in governance while e-governance emphasizes democratic aspects such as collaboration and citizens' participation in governance through the means of technology (Abramson & Morin, 2003; D'agostino et al., 2011). Others choose not to distinguish between the two. The second conceptual debate revolves around e-governance and e-democracy. A number scholars (Backus, 2001; Lee, Chang, & Berry, 2011; Lenihan, 2005) prefer the latter to the former when referring to participation inducing efforts within the context of administrative shifts towards e-government. They find that e-democracy, both as a concept and as a term, does a better job of capturing concerns for democratic prerogatives. In this sense, unlike e-governance, e-democracy provides added conceptual value in the discussions of e-government. Although, it is probably unrealistic to expect these definitional debates to end anytime soon, the perspective suggested by Carrizales (2008) does offer a convenient escape route. According to Carrizales (2008) e-government has four core functional roles: e-

democracy/e-participation (Ahn & Bretschneider, 2011; Dawes, 2008; United Nations 2003, 2010), e-services, e-partnering and e-organization/e-administration. Following this line of argument, then, e-government and e-governance defer in meaning only as much or as little as government and governance does.

Theoretical Perspectives

As a field of study, e-government research is a relatively young. Like any developing field it is struggling to gain legitimacy and significance. The concept of e-government is evolving both within practice and within theory. Its evolution "appears to be rapid and diffuse, truly a moving target" (Norris & Moon, 2005, p. 65). Although, at the moment, we can hardly speak of e-government as an established field or of an "e-government theory," e-government scholars have been rather productive in terms of generating practical knowledge and moving the field forward (Moon et al., 2014; Scholl, 2009).

A lack of established theoretical perspectives is currently perhaps the main barrier in the progression of the field (Stanimirovic & Vintar, 2013). Given that there is "nothing more practical than a good theory" (Lewin, 1952, p. 169), until scholars develop original lenses it becomes difficult to envision e-government developing into a full-fledged discipline. At least at the moment, e-government research has to draw heavily from other disciplines; many of which have a weak theoretical standings themselves, hence, proving more questions than answers. E-government research has been described as "as the offspring of information systems and public administration, it is the child of two parents that are themselves perceived as intellectual weaklings—accused at times of philosophical, theoretical, methodological, and practical shortcomings—and shows all signs of having inherited the expected 'genetic' profile" (Heeks & Bailur, 2007, p. 261).

Until it does develop its own theories, however, there are a number of frameworks that e-government research can rely on. The Structuration Model of Technology, (SMT, Orlikowski, 1992, 2000) although not developed with e-government in mind, provides a rather adequate theoretical framework within which e-government research can be conceptualized. SMT, drawing on Gidens (1976, 1979, 1984), identifies technology as having both an objective character and a subjective, socially constructed, identity. As such, technological outcomes are simultaneously deterministic and unpredictable. The latter is primarily due to technological outcomes being the results of human action. Given that there is much more to e-government than the Internet and given that e-government as a direction of action is concurrently partially deterministic and socially constructed, SMT appears to be particularly well fit to guide scholarly research in the area. Due to its intrinsic flexibility SMT is able to deal with relatively high levels of conceptual ambiguity and it is well suited for conceptualizing e-government research and practice in developing countries (Mota & Filho, 2011). Following a similar line of argument, theories of policy learning and policy diffusion can be quite insightful and do lend themselves easily to applications within e-government research. Lee, Chang and Berry's (2011) study of e-democracy diffusion is a case in point.

Another avenue for theoretical structures can be located within theories of technology diffusion and innovation. Numerous scholars have used them to examine associations between information technology (IT) adoption and organizations. Scholars have studied the link between IT adoption and organization size (see Brudney & Selden, 1995; Holden, Norris, & Fletcher, 2003; Moon, 2002; Norris & Kraemer, 1996; Thorp, 1998); between organizational structure and the probability of implementing technology (see Norris & Kraemer, 1996; Norris & Moon, 2005); and between organizational culture, processes or outcomes and IT (see Danziger, 1979; Garson, 2003; Heintze &

Bretschneider, 2000;Lee & Perry, 2002; Norris & Kraemer, 1996; Moon & Bretschneider, 2002; Norris, 2003; Peled, 2001).

IT and organizational behavior theories provide an additional rich source of theoretical frameworks that can be rather useful for e-government researchers. These theories are well suited for constructing empirical analyses. Of particular interest are the theory of reasoned action (TAR, see Davis, Bagozzi, & Warshaw, 1989), theory of planned behavior (TPB, see Harrison, Mykytyn, & Riemenschneider, 1997), technology acceptance models (TAMs, see Venkatesh & Davis, 2000), motivational model (MM, see Venkatesh & Speier, 1999), model of PC utilization (MPCU, see Thompson, Higgins, & Howell, 1991), innovation diffusion theory (IDT, see Plouffe, Hulland, & Vandenbosch, 2001) and social cognitive theory (SCT, see Compeau, Higgins, & Huff, 1999). Any of the abovementioned theories are adequate and can be used to guide an agenda of systematic empirical research in e-government.

TRACING THE HISTORY OF E-GOVERNMENT

As it is the case with many other things, there is much that the history of e-government, of the Internet in particular, can tell us about its current nature. Contextually placing e-government within the historic use of technology for governance purposes goes a long way in terms explaining its core characteristics and the narratives that guide it (Gil-Garcia, 2012; Heeks & Bailur, 2007), but also in terms of delineating and understanding the challenges that it faces. Historically, governments have always had a deep appreciation for the importance of technology in constructing and conducting effective governance. There is much that a perspective not accounting for the latter would miss. Simply put, e-government cannot be satisfactorily understood outside of its history.

The history of the Internet can be traced back to the Advanced Research Projects Agency (ARPA) established in 1958. ARPA, whose name was later changed to Defense Advanced Research Projects Agency (DARPA), constituted a set of defense related projects within academia, government and the military industry. It represented a reaction to the launch of Sputnik by the Soviet Union and it had the mission to develop new generations of technologies. Part of the original mission of ARPA, then DARPA, was to advance technologies that could have applications beyond military purposes and had the potential to have high levels of positive spillovers (DARPA, 2014).

The Advanced Research Projects Agency Network (ARPANET), the packet switching network used by ARPA members for communication purposes, set the technical and logical framework for the eventual development of the Internet. Soon after its introduction, the technology quickly dispersed through governments, corporations and academic institutions. Given the technology's ability to provide members with instant and simultaneous access to information, even when geographically dispersed, made it very popular among the users. With a growing number of users, who found new and original ways to use it, the technology kept constantly evolving. Yet, ARPANET did not transform into the Internet, as we currently know it, until 1993. It fully transitioned to the Internet when a group of University of Illinois students developed Mosaic, the Web's first graphical browser (Hindman, 2009). This seemingly harmless development made an otherwise dull information exchange network cool, easy to learn and use. The improved friendliness of the interface motivated an extraordinary, in countless ways unprecedented, growth throughout the 1990s.

With the removal of the last regulatory restrictions in the mid-1990s the Internet became a truly global medium of communication and information sharing. Nye (2002) has argued that the exponential growth of the technology was fueled by three important contextual forces. First, the world, especially after the end of the Cold War, was characterized by growing globalization trends. With an increasingly interdependent world economy there was a significant need for a communication platform to support it. Second, the Internet, being fun and easy to use, provided access to new customers and markets. All of the sudden, things that have previously been constrained to brick-and-mortar provision, such as education, became highly marketable. Finally, the sharp decrease in the prices of computers minimized accessibility barriers and made the Internet a critical communication tool both locally and globally. To a certain extent, within a decade the Internet was transformed from something fun into something that could fundamentally re-shape people's lives.

At the same time that the Internet was redefining global communications and markets the administrative narratives of many developed countries were being captured by New Public Management (NPM) perspectives. By and large, NPM was driven by public choice interpretations and individualism, which made public values a peripheral consideration (Bozeman, 2007). NPM was both a reaction and a driver behind the economic developments of the 1980s-1990s. For many traditionally powerful economies, such as the United States and Great Britain, this period represented a rather rude awakening to the fact that their economic structures were no longer competitive. This required leaders, such Margaret Thatcher in United Kingdom and Ronald Reagan in United States, to make difficult economic and social choices. One convenient way in which these socially unpopular solutions became possible to implement was by framing the blame for the economic condition on government. In fact, Ronald Reagan, a republican, constructed a whole campaign around the idea that "government is the problem," while Bill Clinton, a democrat, deemed bureaucracies as "bad systems" that suffocated "good people" (Cooper, 2009).

Although by the early 1990s, in grand part due to the end of the Cold War, the tides of the global economy started to change, the narrative that government was "wasteful, unresponsive, inefficient and too big" became well entrenched through most of the developed world and at all levels of government. Driven by the enthusiastic belief in the almost limitless possibilities offered by the evolving ICTs, transforming governance by means of technology appeared both real and achievable. It is specifically within this environment that the idea and the subsequent discourses of e-government were constructed.

The concept of "electronic government" was delineated in 1993 within the language of National Performance Review (NPR) report (Dawes, 2008; Heeks & Bailur, 2007; Lenk & Traunmüller, 2002). The NPR, later renamed The National Partnership for Reinventing Government, was an inter-agency task force established under Bill Clinton with the ambitious scope of using ICTs to dramatically transform how the federal administration operated. ICTs provided, at least in theory, the ability to do more with less. NPR suggested that e-government would manage to simultaneously achieve two, what otherwise might appear mutually exclusive, scopes – increase the quality of government services while shrinking the size of government. Indeed, the early 1990s presented themselves as a perfect storm. On the one hand, the criticism, mostly unwarranted, of public administration practices was at an all-time high and there was a genuine belief that government needed to be dramatically reformed. On the other hand, the euphoria associated with the end of the Cold War, the improving global economy and the apparently unbounded possibilities of the Internet made even some of the more outrages scenarios and expectations appear plausible.

Yet, while on the face of it NPR sought to transform the very nature of governance, in particular in terms of its democratic characteristics, in practice this was far from being the case. A closer examination of NPR's language and strategic approach reveals that the suggested reforms were mainly instrumental in nature. While, responsiveness, responsibility, entrepreneurship and accountability were powerful buzz words thrown around the bulk of the reform targeted efficiency and cost reduction (Fountain, 2001). Contrary to what some of e-government's original sponsors and supporters might have initially suggested, e-government was neither common sense nor a panacea for all shortfalls of administration within a democracy. As the latter decade made clear, the overzealous promises and expectations were a byproduct of partisan political promises, optimistic scholars and a heavy private side push (Gil-Garcia,2012; Heeks & Bailur, 2007). The reinventing government movement, while radical in its promises, turned out to be rather incremental in character.

E-GOVERNANCE: EXPLAINING THE GAP BETWEEN EXPECTATIONS AND THE CHALLENGES OF PRACTICE

The Grand Promises of Conceptualization

In its conceptualization, e-government was routinely associated with a great number of positive outcomes (Schelin, 2003). Originally, it was even suggested that the Internet was so powerful and innovative that it could revolutionize democracy itself (Johnson, 1998). Inspired by the Internet's successful applications in the private sector in terms of communication and e-commerce many expected similar quick and dramatic changes when it came to the provision of public services. Interestingly, the initial demand for e-government was mainly a function of a supply side push. In its early stages of conceptualization e-government was informed and constructed based on private sector e-commerce practices and attempted to imitate the apparent efficiency of the private sector (Moon, 2002).

Today, practitioners and scholars alike continue to suggest that redefining and reconstructing governance mechanisms around ICTs could lead to an increasingly responsible, accountable, responsive, efficient, transparent and effective government (see Bekkers & Homburg, 2007; Bertot, Jaeger, & Grimes, 2010; Brainard & McNutt, 2010; Dunleavy, Margetts, Bastow, & Tinkler, 2006; Hanberger, 2003; Korac-Kakabadse & Korac-Kakabadse, 1999). E-government sponsors often link its adoption with the possibility of achieving significant cost savings and improved quality of services. Enhanced political oversight of administrative actions is another significant expectation associated with e-government (Ahn & Bretschneider, 2011). Most importantly, however, e-government is regularly linked with the capacity to provide a more democratic governance by increasing system responsiveness (Halvorsen, 2003) and to stimulate increased levels of participation among citizens (see Ahn & Bretschneider, 2011; Brewer, Neubauer, & Geiselhart, 2006; Dawes, 2008; Halvorsen, 2003; OECD, 2003; Stanley & Weare, 2004; Watson & Mundy, 2001).

It is believed that effective and responsive public provision of public services can no longer be designed or envisioned outside of e-government platforms (Bekkers & Homburg, 2007; Dunleavy et al., 2006; Hanberger, 2003; Milakovich, 2012; West, 2004). To a large extent, the use of ICTs for administration is being perceived as common sense. Within the scope of e-governance, technologies such as geographic information systems (GISs), can be transformed from mere mapping instruments into means of empowering marginalized social groups (Craig, Harris, & Weiner, 2002; Gessa, 2008; Ghose, 2001; Haque, 2001; Sieber, 2000). Indeed, when taken together, in theory, the possibilities of e-government and its benefits appeared and continue to appear unbounded.

The Challenges and Realities of Implementation

The experiences of some of the leaders in e-government implementation such Singapore, Norway, United Arab Emirates, Saudi Arabia (Accenture, 2014), the Netherlands, United Kingdom, Denmark, United States (Milakovich, 2012, United Nations, 2012a) and South Korea (Accenture, 2014; Im, 2011; Im, Shin, & Jin, 2007; United Nations, 2012a) suggest that indeed many of the promises associated with e-government can become reality. Yet, a closer examination reveals that behind every success story there are a number of failed costly experiments. Thus far, e-government, as realized in practice, has been rather disappointing (Stanimirovic & Vintar, 2013). Particular difficult and fraught with challenges has been the implementation of e-government platforms within developing countries (Elkadi, 2013). While there have been a few successes, most of the e-government systems have been partial or total failures (Heeks, 2002).

There is a significant gap between the optimistic politically endorsed e-government narratives and the challenges and realities of its implementation (Bekkers & Homburg, 2007; Coursey & Norris, 2008; Edmiston, 2003; Roman, 2013; West, 2004, 2005). While elected officials and top administrators enjoy to advertise and embrace the benefits of e-government, they are often less willing to admit to or acknowledge the numerous challenges of implementation. Of particular interest in this case is the fact that the recent shift towards e-governance has exposed a number of important negative effects associated with rushed e-government adoptions. Many of these issues have yet to be properly understood, formulated or addressed.

In aggregate and when judged on the backdrop of the original expectations, the adoption of e-government has had a somewhat modest impact on governance. E-government induced changes have been incremental in nature, which represents a far cry from the transformational shifts with which it was originally associated (West, 2005). Some have argued that, at least in the short run, e-government might be unsuccessful in terms of meaningfully redefining extant governance structures (Torres et al., 2005). E-government has also failed to significantly impact democratic behaviors, as research shows that elites still dictate and control the political debates in cyberspace (Hindman, 2009). Moreover, it has been suggested that the emphasized use of ICTs can have negative effects on governance by centralizing access (Hindman, 2009; Yoon, 1996), enforcing existent divides and power structures (Bellamy, 2000; Nam, 2011; Stallman, 1995), encouraging faction perspectives (Hanberger, 2003; Rethemeyer, 2006), decreasing accountability (Romzek & Johnston, 2005) and motivating undemocratic behaviors (Breen, 1999). Many scholars and practitioners routinely raise concerns about e-government and remain cautious in sponsoring or advocating its untested benefits and advantages.

Perhaps the most disappointing fact about e-government implementation is its failure to meaningfully improve citizens' participation in matters of governance. There is little to suggest that e-government platforms have been designed with the genuine intention of incentivizing citizens' involvement in policymaking and governance (Roman & Miller, 2013). Most of the government-citizens Internet interactions are one directional and are primarily concerned with information or service provisions (Brainard & McNutt, 2010; Coursey & Norris, 2008; Edmiston 2003; Koh, Prybutok, & Zhang, 2008; Moon, 2002; Roman & Miller, 2013). It is still unclear who the most active e-government users are and what are their true intentions (Brainard, 2003, McCall, 2003; Schlossberg & Shufold, 2005). Are they ordinary citizens or do they represent and lobby for a well-organized interest? The "heaviest users" and those who the benefit the most from e-government are not necessarily representative in terms of their needs and goals of the broader "public interest" (Garson, 2004). A case in point is the experience in United States with e-rulemaking at the federal level. A number of initiatives, such as Clinton's NPR, Bush's E-government Strategy and Obama's Executive Order 13563, have attempted to increase citizens' participation in rulemaking through e-rulemaking. All these efforts, however, rather than increasing meaningful participation have only imposed higher administrative demands on agencies (Benjamin, 2006). In reality, e-rulemaking has made it easier for organized powerful interests to influence public policy (Kerwin & Furlong, 2011) and it can be considered a success only in the eyes of the over-optimists (Muhlberger, Stromer-Galley, & Webb, 2011).

To date, the patterns in e-government usages and demands do not reflect a shift towards more democratic governance. Well-funded interests have been able to shape the nature of e-government and its narratives within the desired paths. The impacts of social media too have been somewhat discouraging. For instance, Facebook once offered a great deal of promise in terms of its ability to create the interactive environment needed to stimulate e-governance. Yet, by latest accounts, due to its marketization as a medium of communication, governments are faced with the need to search for "an exit strategy" (Belt, 2014). Facebook, as a vehicle of interaction, can no longer provide a trusted guarantee that the messages posted online will reach "ordinary" citizens. The old questions regarding who is listening to the messages and whose are the loudest voices heard within the Facebook space remain without a satisfactory answer.

A heavy reliance of ICTs, according to Bovens and Zouridis (2002), can lead to a decrease in responsiveness on the part of public administrators and might undermine the constitutional legitimacy of governance. Scholars (Elwood, 2008; Harris & Weiner, 1998) have also suggested that information gathered through e-government platforms, for instance GISs or Twitter, can become powerful tools that could be used to marginalize certain underrepresented social groups. Others (Norris & Moon, 2005; Torres et al., 2005) have questioned whether e-government platforms, at least in the short run, can lead to increased revenue production, reduction in staff, lower administrative costs and increased internal and external customer satisfaction. If fact, in a number of instances e-government implementation has motivated significant levels of dissatisfaction among citizenry (Accenture, 2014; Cohen, 2006) and among public servants, whose workloads have increased as a result of the adoption (Norris & Moon, 2005). The digital divide remains another serious issue (Norris, 2001; West, 2004) that has yet to be properly addressed.

Something that routinely gets lost within the e-government discourse is the real cost of developing and implementing e-government projects. ICT projects, in general, are known for their high failure rates (Berlin, Raz, Glezer, & Zviran, 2009). By some estimates (Goldfinch, 2007) approximately 30% of all ICT projects fail. According to Dunleavy et al. (2006), "high scrap rates" are rather characteristic for IT implementation. What is even more concerning is that the benefits of implemented e-government platforms are often much lower than and do not justify the high costs that came with their designs, implementations and operations (Norris & Moon, 2005). Furthermore, even when highly technical platforms do become operational, they rarely manage to motive more participation in governance by citizens (OECD 2003, 2009).

If one examines e-government implementation of recent years one will be able to discover numerous examples of disappointments and failures. No country, developed or developing, nor level of government appear to have the blueprint for a challenge-free implementation. The enactment of the Patient Protection and Affordable Care Act (ACA) in United States represents one very telling experience. The Act, also known as Obamacare,

signed into law on March 23rd 2010, intended to reform the American healthcare system, in particular the market for health insurance. The ACA set to increase the access and the quality of health insurance while decreasing costs by expanding the pool of those insured (GPO, 2010). At the core of the reform lied the establishment of state-based marketplace exchanges. They were expected to become fully operational by October 2013.

The ACA was undoubtedly highly political. Its constitutionality has been challenged and its opponents heavily lobbied against it. One thing that was drowned within the heated debate surrounding ACA was the fact that this represented a very challenging IT undertaking. Neither the design nor the operation of such exchanges was a trivial task by any means. This latter fact was, however, routinely overlooked given the assumed "infallibility aura" often attributed to ICTs. For the most part it was believed that although complicated this was something more than doable within the context of the latest IT developments. After all, how difficult can it be to design and run a website? The folly of these unfounded expectations was quickly exposed as soon as individuals attempted to sign up for the healthcare plans. With few exceptions, most marketplace websites were neither operational nor had the design needed to face the actual levels of demand (Cohen, 2013; Morgan & Cornwell, 2013). The healthcare exchanges turned out to be more than just a website, as their operationalization was as much about technical aspects as it was about public policy. While eventually most of the issues were solved, the unrealistic expectations have motivated a lot of dissatisfaction and costs to both state and federal governments. This experience has also further confirmed that it is erroneous to take the successful implementation of an e-government platform as a given. An e-government project is for a number of reasons, in particular due to their political nature, more than just another IT project.

In another case, in 2005 the state of Texas, by legislative mandate, contracted IBM to improve the informational platforms for 28 state agencies. The project's initial cost was estimated at $863 million and was envisioned to be completed within seven years. By December 2009, however, only approximately 12% of the contracted work was completed at a cost of $758 million (Alexander, 2012). In March of 2012, after reaching a settlement with IBM, Texas contracted Xerox (6 years – $54 million) and Capgemini (6 years – $127 million) to attempt to salvage the project. Along similar lines in 2011, Virginia's state department of motor vehicles had to scrape an upgrade to its data system and start anew after spending $28 million on a project that started in 2005 with an original estimated cost of $32.5 million.

Although, the examples of failed IT projects speak volumes of the high risks and costs of any large scale e-government efforts, there is another lesson to be learned here. What these cases make clear is the fact that e-government is much more than simple IT implementation and technology is not fully deterministic by nature and does not guarantee positive outcomes at implementation. E-government initiatives, do not exists, hence cannot be constructed without appropriate considerations for policy and politics. The life cycles for e-government platforms offer many opportunities for things to "go wrong." As it has been argued by Milakovich (2012) the success of e-government is as much a function of politics as it is one of technological knowhow, with the former often playing a much more critical role than the latter.

Why Did Many of the Original Expectations Fail to Lead to Transformation?

Although, it is evident that thus far e-government, both in the developed and developing countries, has failed to progress into the governance transformation mechanism that many expected it to become, the motives behind it not doing so are less obvious. Taken together, there are at least four major reasons why current e-government initia-

tives are only modest versions of the e-government promises made within political discourse. The most significant motive can be located at the very core of e-government as a concept. Globally, e-government adoption was routinely couched within NPM perspectives (Dunleavy et al., 2006; Milakovich, 2012; Osborne, 2006; Torres et al., 2005). Given the latter, e-government, although in narrative sought to lead to transformation, in practice and by conceptual design, addressed functionality and process flows (Fountain, 2001). Furthermore, although e-participation and e-democracy are nice catchwords and are rather appealing in theory, politically, they might be perceived as risky, hence might lead some to marginalize these aspects of e-government (Roman & Miller, 2013; Scott, 2006; Vigoda, 2002; West, 2005). In addition, e-government regulation goes beyond existing norms and laws, it can be located within the implicit design selections and software codes that dictate the choices that the end users have (Lessig, 1999). In this sense, then, given its design and the underlying philosophies guiding it, it is not realistic to expect that e-government would lead to dramatic shifts in the nature of governance. Its technical design can fairly easily become prohibitive of genuine transformation.

Second, e-government expectations and promises were not supported by adequate financial and budgetary allocations. The majority of e-government investments have been undertaken within a "cost-cutting" strategy rather a "governance improving" one. Such investments often turn out to be more about efficiency than about democracy, and more often than not these "investments" don't amount to higher budgetary allocations, but rather to asking public agencies to do more with less. Political leaders and reform entrepreneurs are often inclined to exaggerate efficiency gains and cost savings associated with IT projects. On many occasions there is little appreciation for the true costs or scale of the necessary investments needed to reach "transformation." Some can become so enamored with the promise of IT salvation that they might expect e-government projects to pay for themselves. Currently, according to Torres et al. (2005, p. 546), "e-democracy is little more than a promise not included in the budget…"

Third, given that e-government means different things to different people, it causes great levels ambiguity. This, however, results in the fact that e-government implementation is fraught with contradictory demands, expectations and visions. Research, too, is negatively impacted by a lack of cohesive agreement regarding the nature of e-government. The lack of original and established theoretical frameworks is a central challenge both for e-government theory and practice (Heeks & Bailur, 2007).

Finally, e-government implementation is highly technical and costly (Milakovich, 2012). For a number of local governments as well as developing countries the cost of "good" e-government can be rather prohibitive. They might also lack the "knowhow" when it comes to effective implementation. Based on survey data from International City/County Management Association (ICMA), Norris and Moon (2005) have identified - (1) lack of trained staff, (2) lack of financial resources, (3) security concerns, (4) lack of expertise, and (5) privacy issues – as the top five challenges within e-government implementation. Other factors, such as online fees, outdated technology and lack of support from elected officials, were also suggested as being critical barriers.

In summary, then, the initial overly enthusiastic drive for e-government initiatives can be traced to what was perceived in 1990s to be a lack of performance by government, specifically due to its reliance on traditional hierarchical structures (Carrizales, 2008). Globally, political discourse became driven by NPM imageries and it was believed that there was an imminent need for drastic changes. Such changes, many suggested, were not only necessary, but given the technological progress, were also quite feasible and simple. ICTs did indeed seamlessly fill the role of a "simple solution" to a complex problem. E-government's

benefits were expected to be immediate and with limited expense of public funds. It came with the promise of major transformations and the idea was popular and widely accepted by citizens, legislators and scholars. In its original conceptualization e-government was perceived as a politics free issue and it promised to translate the supposed private sector efficiency into public administration. Whilst, surely there is always a place for business perspectives and e-commerce within the context of e-government, to transpose private sector habits directly into public sector operations, however, is to fail to realize the subtle, yet fundamental, differences between private and public governance. The latter has proven to be perhaps the most significant oversight that has led many e-government projects to fail to reach the expectations built within their designs. This is in no way trivial, a flawed and poorly operating e-government platform is rarely, if ever, an improvement over the brick-and-mortar administration.

CRITICAL FACTORS IN E-GOVERNMENT SUCCESS

There are a number of factors on which e-government realization is hinged. Success in e-government is neither a function of one single variable nor a deterministic outcome of system design. In order for e-government to deliver on its original promises it needs to fulfill expectations along three broad dimensions: security, functionality and transformation. Serious oversights or implementation failures along any of the three dimensions is most likely to lead to large scale disappointments. If citizens do not feel secure about their privacy or about interacting with government they will not become the expected force within e-governance. Similarly, if e-government platforms fail to deliver along functional and technical lines they will turn into unpopular artifacts of grand projects. Finally, if the use of ICTs in governance do not lead to its eventual transformation, then the scholars who have argued that e-government is just a catchy label for an old dynamic might be correct. E-government devoid of transformation is certainly nothing more than IT in government.

Security

According to the United States Computer Emergency Readiness Team in 2012 there were a total of 153,043 (107,655 in 2011) known cyberattacks across all levels of government (OMB, 2013). In 2012, the federal government was targeted 48,842 times (43,889 in 2011) (OMB, 2013). The security threats in cyberspace are constantly evolving. Unlike the security concerns characteristic for brick-and-mortar administrations, within the context of e-government, threats are not geographically constrained and their nature is significantly different. Addressing them might require entirely new perspectives and approaches. It also might call for different types of expertise and operational strategies. The security of the digital environment in terms of citizen privacy, loss of financial assets, developing trust and ethical behavior, has been delineated by scholars as a fundamental factor in the success of e-government (see Carter & McBride, 2010; Karokola, Yngström, & Kowalski, 2012; Moon et al., 2013; Mullen & Horner, 2004; Roman, 2013). If e-government platforms fail to convince that the interaction with government is secure, citizens will most likely seek to minimize their exposures or refuse to use e-government functions altogether. Moreover, a system, as a result of constant cyber-attacks, can quickly degrade to the point where it loses most of its operational capacity. This latter fact defies the reasoning of the implementing the system in the first place.

When it comes to e-government security it becomes crucial to realize that traditional approaches to security might no longer be adequate. Historically, cyber security was philosophically constructed on the traditional secure-perimeter-type defenses; such an approach, however, has been shown to be quite ineffective in dealing with emerging cyber security threats (Jackson, 2012). E-government, due to its complexity and high stakes, demands considerably different and innovative approaches to security (Hwang, Li, Shen, & Chu, 2004; Zhou & Hu, 2008). To some extent, it is no longer realistic to expect to develop a completely secure digital environment; security failures might become a "normal" part of e-government operations (Cichonski, Millar, Grance, & Scarfone, 2012). Such considerations, and a realistic estimations of consequences, have to be built into the design of e-government platforms. Although security standards such as ISO 27002 can develop into a useful starting point for all e-government initiatives, such standards are not sufficient on their own (Karokola et al., 2012). The success of e-government security should probably be evaluated not by the successes in managing damages, but by the ability to foresee, prevent, adapt and activate under unpredictable and ambiguous environments.

A particular serious issue, whose implications we have yet to fully grasp, is the distortionary effect in terms of accountability that e-government, technology in general, has on public administration and the individuals who operate within it. Scholars (Roman & Miller, 2013; Romzek & Johnston, 2005) have suggested that an increased reliance on ICTs could lead to decreased accountability on the part of public administrators. With less face-to-face interaction with citizens public administrators could become inclined to avoid responsibility for failures, to take ownership of projects or to act entrepreneurially. Furthermore, given the complexity of e-government, it is becoming increasingly difficult to identify who should be held accountable for security breakdowns? Is it the developers, the administrators, the agency or government at large? What about citizens? What is their role? These are just a few of many questions that will have to be addressed.

In United States during the presidency of George W. Bush, local and state governments, within the context of public-private partnerships, were expected to take the lead on implementing e-government. This has led to the fact that the private sector ended up controlling the majority of cyber resources (Harknett & Stever, 2011). Accountability became diffuse and difficult to enforce. President's Barack Obama's Cyberspace Policy Review (Executive Office of the President, 2009) was supposed to address these shortcomings by implementing a top-down approach. Yet, thus far the changes have been rather disappointing (GAO, 2010a, 2010b; Harknett & Stever, 2011). The United States Government Accountability Office has identified that the majority of federal agencies face numerous challenges in managing cybersecurity (GAO, 2011). By some accounts, United States is relatively less prepared to face the increasingly complex security concerns within cyberspace (Grauman, 2012). Security, according to some, is rarely delineated as a top priority for many e-government initiatives and is not seriously considered until the later stages of implementation (Bishop, 2006; McGraw, 2005).

Functionality

Functionality has been the main driver behind e-government conceptualization. From the start, it was expected that e-government would provide the environment within which it would become possible to offer improved public services at lower costs. It is this specific ability that made e-government so attractive, as an idea, to management, citizens and governments (Milakovich, 2012). Given that governments and bureaucracies emphasize service delivery within e-government first and everything else second (Stahl, 2005), functionality is perhaps the most visible dimension for judging e-government success. If e-government platforms fail in terms of delivering and improving public service, there is little hope that e-government can be realized as originally envisioned.

The advantage of functionality being the etalon of success is the fact that it lends itself relatively easier (when compared to security and transformation) to measurement and performance evaluation. The literature already provides manifold evaluation techniques, such as cost benefit analysis or usage metrics, that could be used as evaluation criteria. For instance, indexes such the ones proposed by West (2004, 2005), Holzer and Kim (2003), Carrizales et al. (2006), D'agostino et al. (2011) are well developed and can be easily deployed for comparing and examining the performance of Websites across a large spectrum of interests. Similar progress has been made in terms of providing evaluation frameworks for e-government projects and policies. WiBe 4.0 (Rothig, 2010) and MAREVA (ADAE, 2007) represent two very good examples in this sense. Countries and global nongovernmental organizations (NGOs) have also developed a number of benchmarking measurements. Those developed by Capgemini (2011), United Nations (2012b), Accenture (2009, 2014) and International Telecommunication Union (2012) seem to be among the most widely used ones. Although these indicators do not provide a clear or comprehensive evaluation base, even when taken together, they still offer a solid foundation on which functionality could be evaluated. The same thing cannot be said about security or transformation. They are much more difficult to gauge. The disadvantage of placing functionality at the forefront of e-government realization is, however, significant as well. If functionality is used as the main dimension along which e-government success is judged – there is a real danger that e-government will fail to meaningfully move beyond IT for government.

At this point it is important to note that the availability of evaluation tools should not mislead one into believing that evaluating functionality of e-government is by any means easy. The main difficulty is associated with the fact that most of these analytic tools have efficiency built in as their core value. While efficiency is to be sure an important consideration for e-government, it is not necessary the central one. The realization of e-governance does not call for efficiency alone, it also demands quality. The latter, however, is difficult to evaluate and often subjective in nature.

Transformation

This represents the most elusive and critical factor within e-government realization. Transformation, which can be understood as an "epochal break-through" (Volti, 2006) or as the Oxford online dictionary defines it – "a marked change in form, nature or appearance," is what was supposed to set e government apart from mere technological applications for administrative purposes. Government has historically relied on technology and will surely continue to do so. Since e-government was envisioned to be much more than technology, it will be truly realized only if it manages to inspire a meaningful change in the form, nature and appearance of governance. Otherwise, e-government runs the danger of being remembered by history as nothing more than a passing managerial fad.

The difficulty of achieving transformation is directly linked with the very nature of e-government. Given its NPM roots and being driven by an e-commerce paradigm (Stahl, 2005) e-government, within its technical design, is not envisioned to be transformative. Even if a significant change in the nature of governance should be eventually inspired by e-government, the transformation would most likely be the result of an incremental process rather than a onetime event (West, 2005). Paradoxically, the critical variable in achieving transformation of e-government can be located within the end users. Unless citizens "buy into" e-government, it will most likely fail in its efforts to transform governance. Although, e-government has the capacity to significantly change in form governance, if it is not used accordingly it will not succeed in this scope. For instance, while in theory e-government platforms can increase transparency and reduce corruption, in practice, they can become the very mechanisms used by corrupt administrators to pursue their interests.

"User failure" is a much more common reason for unsuccessful e-government implementation, especially in developing countries, than we are comfortable to admit (see Abdelsalam, Reddick, Elkadi, & Gama, 2012; Elkadi, 2013; Roman, 2013b). The values and habits of managers and street level public administrators, too, play a critical role and can make the difference between failure and success (Abdelsalam et al., 2012; McCue & Roman, 2012; Reddick, Abdelsalam, & Elkadi, 2011; Roman, 2013c).

Transformation is also the most difficult to evaluate amongst the three dimensions. Its subjective and qualitative nature make scale explorations rather challenging. One would need access to panel data. The latter, however, is rather difficult to collect and is rarely standardized in terms of its definitions. In addition to the typical difficulties associated with evaluation efforts, many of the leading elevation frameworks are country specific or are too difficult to apply to developing countries which lack sophisticated data tracking systems (Stanimirovic & Vintar, 2013). The scholarly literature also currently fails to provide a widely accepted and agreed upon evaluation model. Functionality success is most of the time used as a proxy for transformation. This is obviously non-sufficient and remains an area on which both scholars and practitioners should focus in the future.

FUTURE RESEARCH DIRECTIONS

In recent years there has been significant progress in e-government research. There are many areas, such as maturity models and benchmarks, which are quite well developed within the literature and have progressed significantly in the past decade. There is, however, much that still has to be done. Most areas, for instance, are still characterized by rather incongruent research agendas and theoretical approaches. Little is known about the factors that lead to successful e-government realization. Within this context a particular interest is e-government policy. For instance, are legislative mandates effective in conditioning e-government success? Is e-government driven by the supply side or by the demand side?

Transformation, is another area that is seriously underexplored. Due to methodological and conceptual difficulties in operationalizing "transformation" many scholars prefer to avoid such research. However, as it was suggested in the previous section, e-government success is hinged on delivering on the original transformation promises. Future research should investigate the degree to which e-government has indeed impacted, if at all, the nature of governance. Have there been any shifts in the pattern and quality of citizen interaction with government? Has e-government led to a more democratic governance? Has the nature of current governance meaningfully changed as a result of e-government?

CONCLUSION

This chapter set to identify the main challenges that are faced by governments within their efforts to realize e-government. It also sought to delineate the critical dimensions in achieving e-government success. The latter is by and large a function of three major factors – security, functionality and transformation. Failures along any of these dimensions will most likely lead to failure in e-government. Functionality is the dimension that is the most often emphasized within the design of e-government projects. Security, typically does not become a major consideration until the later stages of implementation. Meanwhile, transformation is seldom explicitly considered and is more often than not unwarrantedly expected to be a deterministic outcome of technology adoption.

REFERENCES

Abdelsalam, H. M., Reddick, C. G., ElKadi, H. A., & Gama, S. (2012). Factors affecting perceived effectiveness of local e-government in Egypt. *International Journal of Information Communication Technologies and Human Development, 4*(1), 24–38. doi:10.4018/jicthd.2012010102

Abramson, M. A., & Morin, T. L. (2003). E-government: A progress report. In *E-government 2003*. New York: Rowman & Littlefield Publishers, Inc.

Accenture. (2009). *From e-government to e-governance: Using new technologies to strengthen relationships with citizens*. Dublin, Ireland: Institute for Health and Public Service Value.

Accenture. (2014). *Digital government pathways to delivering public services for the future: A comparative study of digital government performance across 10 countries*. Retrieved from http://nstore. accenture.com/acn_com/Accenture-Digital-Government-Pathways-to-Delivering-Public-Services-for-the-Future.pdf

Ahn, M. J., & Bretschneider, S. (2011). Politics of e-government: E-government and the political control of bureaucracy. *Public Administration Review, 71*(3), 414–424. doi:10.1111/j.1540-6210.2011.02225.x

Alexander, K. (2012). 2 Firms to replace IBM on Texas' data consolidation effort. *American-Statesman*. Retrieved from http://www.statesman.com/news/texas-politics/2-firms-to-replace-ibm-on-texas-data-2233786.html

Backus, M. (2001). *E-governance and developing countries: Introduction and examples*. Retrieved from http://www.iicd.org/articles/IICDnews.import1857

Bekkers, V., & Homburg, V. (2007). The myths of e-government: Looking beyond the assumptions of new and better government. *The Information Society*, *23*(5), 373–382. doi:10.1080/01972240701572913

Bellamy, C. (2000). The politics of public information systems. In G. D. Garson (Ed.), *Handbook of public information systems* (pp. 85–98). New York, NY: Marcel Dekker.

Belt, D. (2014). We need an exit strategy for Facebook. *GovLoop*. Retrieved from http://www.govloop.com/profiles/blogs/we-need-an-exit-strategy-for-facebook?elq=4032ae94bb34426b8c0b2cf075679922&elqCampaignId=4352

Benjamin, S. M. (2006). Evaluating e-rulemaking: Public participation and political institutions. *Duke Law Journal*, *55*(5), 893–941.

Berlin, S., Raz, T., Glezer, C., & Zviran, M. (2009). Comparison of estimation methods of cost and duration in IT projects. *Information and Software Technology*, *51*(4), 738–748. doi:10.1016/j.infsof.2008.09.007

Bertot, J. C., Jaeger, P. T., & Grimes, J. M. (2010). Using ICTs to create a culture of transparency: E-government and social media as openness and anti-corruption tools for societies. *Government Information Quarterly*, *27*(3), 264–271. doi:10.1016/j.giq.2010.03.001

Bishop, M. (2006). *Computer security – Arts and science*. Reading, MA: Addison-Wesley.

Bovens, M., & Zouridis, S. (2002). From street-level to system-level bureaucracies: How information and communication technology is transforming administrative discretion and constitutional control. *Public Administration Review*, *62*(2), 174–184. doi:10.1111/0033-3352.00168

Bozeman, B. (2007). *Public values and public interest: Counterbalancing economic individualism*. Washington, DC: George Washington Press.

Brainard, L. (2003). Citizen organizing in cyberspace. *American Review of Public Administration*, *33*(4), 384–406. doi:10.1177/0275074003257430

Brainard, L., & McNutt, J. (2010). Virtual government-citizen relations: Informational, transactional, or collaborative? *Administration & Society*, *42*(7), 836–858. doi:10.1177/0095399710386308

Breen, M. (1999). Counterrevolution in the infrastructure – A cultural study of technscientific impoverishment. In *Ethics and electronic information in the 21st century* (pp. 29–45). West Lafayette, IN: Purdue University Press.

Brewer, G. A., Neubauer, B. J., & Geiselhart, K. (2006). Designing and implementing e-government systems. *Administration & Society*, *38*(4), 472–499. doi:10.1177/0095399706290638

Brudney, J., & Selden, S. (1995). The adoption of innovation by smaller local governments: The case of computer technology. *American Review of Public Administration*, *25*(1), 71–86. doi:10.1177/027507409502500105

Calista, D., & Melitski, J. (2007). E-government and e-governance: Converging constructs of public sector information and communications technologies. *Public Administration Quarterly*, *31*(1), 87-99, 101-120.

Capgemini & IDC. (2011). *E-government benchmarking in 2011*. Brussels: European Commission, Directorate General for Information Society and Media.

Carrizales, T. (2008). Functions of e-government: A study of municipal practices. *State and Local Government Review*, *40*(1), 12–26. doi:10.1177/0160323X0804000102

Carrizales, T., Holzer, M., Seang-Tae, K., & Chan-Gon, K. (2006). Digital governance worldwide: A longitudinal assessment of municipal websites. *International Journal of Electronic Government Research*, *2*(4), 1–23. doi:10.4018/jegr.2006100101

Carter, L., & McBride, A. (2010). Information privacy concerns and e-government: A research agenda. *Transforming Government: People. Process and Policy*, *4*(1), 10–13.

Cichonski, P., Millar, T., Grance, T., & Scarfone, K. (2012). Computer security incident handling guide. *NIST Special Publication*, *800*, 61.

Coglianese, C. (2004). E-rulemaking: Information technology and the regulatory process. *Administrative Law Review*, *56*, 353–402.

Cohen, J. E. (2006). Citizen satisfaction with contacting government on the internet. *Information Polity*, *11*(1), 51–65.

Cohen, T. (2013). Rough Obamacare rollout: 4 reasons why. *CNN*. Retrieved from http://www.cnn.com/2013/10/22/politics/obamacare-website-four-reasons

Compeau, D. R., Higgins, C. A., & Huff, S. (1999). Social cognitive theory and individual reactions to computing technology: A longitudinal study. *Management Information Systems Quarterly*, *23*(2), 145–158. doi:10.2307/249749

Cooper, P. J. (2009). *The war against regulation from Jimmy Carter to George W. Bush*. Lawrence, KS: University Press of Kansas.

Coursey, D., & Norris, D. F. (2008). Models of e-government: Are they correct? An empirical assessment. *Public Administration Review*, *68*(3), 523–536. doi:10.1111/j.1540-6210.2008.00888.x

Craig, W. J., Harris, T. M., & Weiner, D. (Eds.). (2002). *Community participation and geographic information systems*. London: Taylor & Francis.

D'agostino, M., Schwester, R., Carrizales, T., & Melitski, J. (2011). A study of e-government and e-governance: An empirical examination of municipal websites. *Public Administration Quarterly*, *35*(1), 3–25.

Danziger, J. N. (1979). Technology and productivity: A contingency analysis of computers in local governments. *Administration & Society*, *11*(2), 144–171. doi:10.1177/009539977901100202

Davis, F. D., Bagozzi, R. P., & Warshaw, P. R. (1989). User acceptance of computer technology: A comparison of two theoretical models. *Management Science*, *35*(8), 952–1002. doi:10.1287/mnsc.35.8.982

Dawes, S. S. (2008). The evolution and continuing challenges of e-governance. *Public Administration Review*, *68*, S86–S102. doi:10.1111/j.1540-6210.2008.00981.x

Defense Advanced Research Projects Agency (DARPA). (2014). *History*. Retrieved from http://www.darpa.mil/About/History/History.aspx

Dunleavy, P., Margetts, H., Bastow, S., & Tinkler, J. (2005). New public management is dead -Long live digital-era governance. *Journal of Public Administration: Research and Theory*, *16*(3), 467–494. doi:10.1093/jopart/mui057

Edmiston, K. (2003). State and local e-government: Prospects and challenges. *American Review of Public Administration*, *33*(1), 20–45. doi:10.1177/0275074002250255

Elkadi, H. (2013). Success and failure factors for e-government projects: A case from Egypt. *Egyptian Informatics Journal*, *14*(2), 165–173. doi:10.1016/j.eij.2013.06.002

Elwood, S. (2008). Grassroots groups as stakeholders in spatial data infrastructures: Challenges and opportunities for local data development and sharing. *International Journal of Geographical Information Science*, *22*(1), 71–90. doi:10.1080/13658810701348971

Executive Office of the President. (2009). *Cyberspace policy review: Assuring a trusted and resilient information and communication infrastructu*re. Retrieved from http://www.whitehouse.gov/assets/documents/Cyberspace_Policy_Review_final.pdf

Fountain, J. E. (2001). *Building the virtual state: Information technology and institutional change.* Washington, DC: Brookings Institution Press.

Garson, D. G. (2003). Toward and information technology research agenda for public administration. In *Public information technology: Policy and management issues* (pp. 331–357). Hershey, PA: Idea Group Publishers.

Garson, D. G. (2008). The promise of digital government. In *Digital government: Principles and best practices* (pp. 2–15). Hershey, PA: Idea Group Publishing.

Ghose, R. (2001). Use of information technology for community empowerment: Transforming geographic information systems into community information systems. *Transactions in GIS, 5*(2), 141–163. doi:10.1111/1467-9671.00073

Giddens, A. (1976). *New rules of sociological method.* New York: Basic Books.

Giddens, A. (1979). *Central problems of social theory: Action, structure and contradiction in social analysis.* Berkeley, CA: University of California Press.

Giddens, A. (1984). *The constitution of society: Outline of the theory of structure.* Berkeley, CA: University of California Press.

Gil-Garcia, R. J. (2012). *Enacting electronic government success: An integrative study of government-wide websites, organizational capabilities, and institutions.* New York, NY: Springer. doi:10.1007/978-1-4614-2015-6

Government Accountability Office. (2010a). *Cybersecurity: Progress made but challenges remain in defining and coordinating the comprehensive national initiative.* Washington, DC: U.S. Government Printing Office.

Government Accountability Office. (2010b). *Cyberspace policy: Executive branch is making progress implementing 2009 policy review recommendations, but sustained leadership is needed.* Washington, DC: U.S. Government Printing Office.

Government Accountability Office. (2011). *Cybersecurity human capital: Initiatives need better planning and coordination.* Retrieved from http://www.gao.gov/assets/590/586494.pdf

Government Printing Office. (2010). *The patient protection and affordable healthcare act.* Retrieved from http://www.gpo.gov/fdsys/pkg/PLAW-111publ148/pdf/PLAW-111publ148.pdf

Grauman, B. (2012). *Cyber-security: The vexed question of global rules: An independent report on cyber preparedness around the world.* Retrieved from http://www.mcafee.com/us/resources/reports/rp-sda-cyber-security.pdf?cid=WBB048

Halvorsen, K. (2003). Assessing the effects of public participation. *Public Administration Review, 63*(5), 535–543. doi:10.1111/1540-6210.00317

Hanberger, A. (2003). Democratic implications of public organizations. *Public Organization Review, 3*(1), 29–54. doi:10.1023/A:1023095927266

Haque, A. (2001). GIS, public service, and the issue of democratic governance. *Public Administration Review, 61*(3), 259–265. doi:10.1111/0033-3352.00028

Hardy, C. A., & Williams, S. P. (2011). Assembling e-government research designs: A transdisciplinary view and interactive approach. *Public Administration Review, 71*(3), 405–413. doi:10.1111/j.1540-6210.2011.02361.x

Harknett, R. J., & Stever, J. A. (2011). The new policy world of cybersecurity. *Public Administration Review, 71*(3), 455–460. doi:10.1111/j.1540-6210.2011.02366.x

Harris, T. M., & Weiner, D. (1998). Empowerment, marginalization and community-integrated GIS. *Cartography and Geographic Information Science, 25*(2), 67–76. doi:10.1559/152304098782594580

Harrison, D. A., Mykytyn, P. P., & Riemenschneider, C. K. (1997). Executive decision about adoption of information technology in small business: Theory and empirical tests. *Information Systems Research, 8*(2), 171–195. doi:10.1287/isre.8.2.171

Heeks, R. (2002). Information systems and developing countries: Failure, success, and local improvisations. *The Information Society, 18*(2), 101–112. doi:10.1080/01972240290075039

Heeks, R., & Bailur, S. (2007). Analyzing e-government research: Perspectives, philosophies, theories, methods, and practice. *Government Information Quarterly, 24*(2), 243–265. doi:10.1016/j.giq.2006.06.005

Heintze, T., & Bretschneider, S. (2000). Information technology and restructuring in public organizations: Does adoption of information technology affect organizational structures, communications, and decision making? *Journal of Public Administration: Research and Theory, 10*(4), 801–830. doi:10.1093/oxfordjournals.jpart.a024292

Hindman, M. (2009). *The myth of digital democracy*. Princeton, NJ: Princeton University Press.

Holden, S. H., Norris, D. F., & Fletcher, P. D. (2003). Electronic government at the local level: Progress to date and future issues. *Public Performance and Management Review, 26*(3), 1–20.

Holzer, M., & Kim, S. (2003). *Digital governance in municipalities worldwide: An assessment of municipal we sites throughout the world*. Newark, NJ: The E-Governance Institute/National Center for Public Productivity. Retrieved from http://unpan1.un.org/intradoc/groups/public/documents/aspa/unpan012905.pdf

Hwang, M., Li, C., Shen, J., & Chu, Y. (2004). Challenges in e-government and security of information. *Information & Security, 15*(1), 9–20.

Im, T. (2011). Information technology and organizational morphology: The case of the Korean central government. *Public Administration Review, 71*(3), 435–443. doi:10.1111/j.1540-6210.2011.02227.x

Im, T., Shin, H. Y., & Jin, Y. (2007). IT and administrative innovation in Korea: How does IT affect organizational performance? *Korean Journal of Policy Studies, 21*(2), 1–17.

International Telecommunication Union. (2012). *Measuring the information society 2012*. Geneva: International Telecommunication Union.

Jackson, W. (2012). Could you continue to operate under cyberattack? *Government Computer News*. Retrieved from http://gcn.com/Articles/2012/02/27/Cybereye-operating-while-under-attack.aspx?Page=2

Johnson, S. (1998). The internet changes everything: Revolutionizing public participation and access to government information through the internet. *Administrative Law Review, 50*(2), 277–337.

Karokola, G., Yngström, L., & Kowalski, S. (2012). Secure e-government services: A comparative analysis of e-government maturity models for the developing regions–The need for security services. *International Journal of Electronic Government Research, 8*(1), 1–25. doi:10.4018/jegr.2012010101

Kerwin, C. M., & Furlong, S. R. (2011). *Rulemaking: How government agencies write law and make policy* (4th ed.). Washington, DC: CQ Press.

Koh, C. E., Prybutok, V. R., & Zhang, X. (2008). Measuring e-government readiness. *Information & Management, 45*(8), 540–546. doi:10.1016/j.im.2008.08.005

Korac-Kakabadse, A., & Korac-Kakabadse, N. (1999). Information technology's impact on the quality of democracy: Reinventing the democracy vessel. In *Reinventing government in the information age: International practice in IT-enabled public sector reform* (pp. 211–228). London: Routledge.

Lee, C. P., Chang, K., & Stokes Berry, F. S. (2011). Testing the development and diffusion of e-government and e-democracy: A global perspective. *Public Administration Review, 71*(3), 444–454. doi:10.1111/j.1540-6210.2011.02228.x

Lee, G., & Perry, J. L. (2002). Are computers boosting productivity? A test of the paradox in state governments. *Journal of Public Administration: Research and Theory, 12*(1), 77–102. doi:10.1093/oxfordjournals.jpart.a003525

Lenihan, D. G. (2005). Realigning governance: From e-government to e-democracy. In *Practicing e-government: A global perspective* (pp. 250–288). Hershey, PA: Idea Group. doi:10.4018/978-1-59140-637-2.ch012

Lenk, K., & Traunmüller, R. (2002). Electronic government: Where are we heading? In R. Lenk & B. Traunmüller (Eds.), *Electronic Government: First International Conference, EGOV 2002* (pp. 173–199). New York: Springer.

Lessig, L. (1999). *Code and other laws of cyberspace*. New York: Basic Books.

Lewin, K. (1952). *Field theory in social science: Selected theoretical papers by Kurt Lewin*. London: Tavistock.

Margolis, M., & Resnick, D. (2000). *Politics as usual: The cyberspace revolution*. Thousand Oaks, CA: Sage Publications.

McCall, M. K. (2003). Seeking good governance in participatory-GIS: A review of processes and governance dimensions in applying GIS to participatory spatial planning. *Habitat International, 27*(4), 549–573. doi:10.1016/S0197-3975(03)00005-5

McCue, C., & Roman, A. V. (2013). E-procurement: Myth or reality? *Journal of Public Procurement, 12*(2), 221–248.

McGraw, G. (2005). *Software security*. Reading, MA: Addison-Wesley.

Milakovich, M. E. (2012). *Digital governance: New technologies for improving public service and participation*. New York, NY: Routledge.

Moon, J. M. (2002). The evolution of e-government among municipalities: Rhetoric or reality? *Public Administration Review, 62*(4), 424–433. doi:10.1111/0033-3352.00196

Moon, J. M., & Bretschneider, S. (2002). Does perception of red tape constrain IT innovativeness in organizations: Unexpected results from simultaneous equation model and implications. *Journal of Public Administration: Research and Theory, 12*(2), 273–292. doi:10.1093/oxfordjournals.jpart.a003532

Moon, M. J., Lee, J., & Roh, C. Y. (2014). The evolution of internal IT applications and e-government studies in public administration: Research themes and methods. *Administration & Society, 46*(1), 3–36. doi:10.1177/0095399712459723

Morgan, D., & Cornwell, S. (2011). Contractors describe scant pre-launch testing of U.S. healthcare site. *Reuters*. Retrieved from http://www.reuters.com/article/2013/10/25/us-usa-healthcare-idUS-BRE99M0VD20131025

Mota, F. P. B., & Filho, J. R. (2011). Public e-procurement and the duality of technology: A comparative study in the context of Brazil and of the state of Paraiba. *Journal of Information Systems and Technology Management*, 8(2), 315–330. doi:10.4301/S1807-17752011000200003

Muhlberger, P., Stromer-Galley, J., & Webb, N. (2011). Public policy and obstacles to virtual agora: Insights from the deliberative e-rulemaking project. *Information Polity*, 16, 197–214.

Mullen, H., & Horner, D. S. (2004). Ethical problems for e-government: An evaluative framework. *Electronic Journal of E-Government*, 2(3), 187–196.

Nam, T. (2011). Whose e-democracy? The democratic divide in American electoral campaigns. *Information Polity*, 16(201), 131–150.

Norris, D. F. (2003). Leading edge information technologies and American local governments. In *Public information technology: Policy and management issues* (pp. 139–169). Hershey, PA: Idea Group Publishers.

Norris, D. F. (2010). E-government 2020: Plus ça change, plus c'est la meme chose. *Public Administration Review*, 70, s180–s181. doi:10.1111/j.1540-6210.2010.02269.x

Norris, D. F., & Kraemer, K. L. (1996). Mainframe and PC computing in American cities: Myths and realities. *Public Administration Review*, 56(6), 568–576. doi:10.2307/977255

Norris, D. F., & Moon, M. J. (2005). Advancing e-government at the grassroots: Tortoise or hare? *Public Administration Review*, 65(1), 64–75. doi:10.1111/j.1540-6210.2005.00431.x

Norris, P. (2001). *Digital divide: Civic engagement, information poverty, and the Internet worldwide*. Cambridge University Press. doi:10.1017/CBO9781139164887

Nye, J. S. (2002). Information technology and democratic governance. In E. C Kamarck, E. C., & J. S. Nye (Eds.), Governance.com: Democracy in the information age (pp. 1-16). Washington, DC: Brookings Institution Press.

Office of Management and Budget. (2013). *Fiscal year 2012: Report to congress on the implementation of the federal information security management act of 2002*. Retrieved from http://www.whitehouse.gov/sites/default/files/omb/assets/egov_docs/fy12_fisma_0.pdf

Organisation for Economic Co-Operation and Development. (2003). *Promise and problems of e-democracy – Challenges of online citizen engagement*. Paris: OECD.

Organisation for Economic Co-Operation and Development. (2009). *Rethinking e-government services: User-centred approaches*. Paris: OECD Publishing.

Orlikowski, W. J. (1992). The duality of technology: Rethinking the concept of technology in organizations. *Organization Science*, 3(3), 398–427. doi:10.1287/orsc.3.3.398

Orlikowski, W. J. (2000). Using technology and constituting structures: A practice lens for studying technology in organizations. *Organization Science*, 11(4), 404–428. doi:10.1287/orsc.11.4.404.14600

Osborne, S. (2006). The new public governance. *Public Management Review*, 8(3), 377–387. doi:10.1080/14719030600853022

Peled, A. (2001). Do computers cut red tape? *American Review of Public Administration*, 31(4), 414–435. doi:10.1177/02750740122065027

Plouffe, C. R., Hulland, J. S., & Vandenbosch, M. (2001). Research report: Richness versus parsimony in modeling technology adoption decisions – Understanding merchant adoption of smart card-based payment system. *Information Systems Research, 12*(2), 208–222. doi:10.1287/isre.12.2.208.9697

pour le Développement de l'Administration Electronique, A. (ADAE). (2007). *MAREVA methodology guide: Analysis of the value of ADELE projects.* Dubai, UAE: Fourth High Level Seminar on Measuring and Evaluating E-government.

Reddick, C. G., Abdelsalam, H. M., & Elkadi, H. (2011). The influence of e-government on administrative discretion: The case of local governments in Egypt. *Public Administration and Development, 31*(5), 390–407. doi:10.1002/pad.615

Rethemeyer, K. R. (2006). Policymaking in the age of internet: Is the internet tending to make policy networks more or less inclusive? *Journal of Public Administration: Research and Theory, 17*(2), 259–284. doi:10.1093/jopart/mul001

Roman, A. V. (2013a). Framing the questions of e-government ethics: An organizational perspective. *American Review of Public Administration.* doi:10.1177/0275074013485809

Roman, A. V. (2013b). Public policy and financial management through e-procurement: A practice oriented normative model for maximizing transformative impacts. *Journal of Public Procurement, 13*(3), 337–363.

Roman, A. V. (2013c). The mental revolution of public procurement specialists: Achieving transformative impacts within the context of e-procurement. In N. Pomazalová (Ed.), *Public sector transformation processes and Internet public procurement: Decision support systems* (pp. 1–16).

Roman, A.V., & Miller, H. (2013). New questions for e-government: Efficiency but not (yet?) democracy. *International Journal of Electronic Government Research, 9*(1), 65-81. doi: 10.4018/jegr.2013010104

Romzek, B. S., & Johnston, J. M. (2005). State social services contracting: Exploring the determinants of effective contract accountability. *Public Administration Review, 65*(4), 436–449. doi:10.1111/j.1540-6210.2005.00470.x

Rothig, P. (2010). *WiBe 4.0 methodology: Economic efficiency assessments in particular with regard to the use of information & communication technology.* Berlin: Federal Ministry of the Interior.

Schelin, S. H. (2003). E-Government: An overview. In G. D. Garson (Ed.), *Public information technology: Policy and management issues* (pp. 120–137). Hershey, PA: Idea Group Publishing.

Scholl, H. J. (2009). Profiling the EG research community and its core. In M. A. Wimmer, H. J. Scholl, M. Janssen, & R. Traunmüller (Eds.), *Electronic government: 8th international conference, EGOV 2009* (pp. 1-12). Berlin: Springer-Verlag.

Scott, J. (2006). E the people: Do U.S. municipal government web sites support public involvement? *Public Administration Review, 66*(3), 341–353. doi:10.1111/j.1540-6210.2006.00593.x

Sherfinski, D. (2012). Virginia ditchedDMV customer service overhaul after spending $28M. *The Washington Times.* Retrieved from http://www.washingtontimes.com/news/2012/apr/3/virginia-ditched-dmv-customer-service-overhaul-aft/?page=1

Sieber, R. E. (2000). Conforming (to) the opposition: The social construction of geographical information systems in social movements. *International Journal of Geographical Information Science*, *14*(8), 775–793. doi:10.1080/136588100750022787

Stahl, C. B. (2005). The ethical problem of framing e-government in terms of e-commerce. *The Electronic Journal of E-Government*, *3*(2), 77–86.

Stallman, R. (1995). Are computer property rights absolute? In *Computers, ethics & social values* (pp. 115–119). Upper Saddle River, NJ: Prentice Hall.

Stanimirovic, D., & Vintar, M. (2013). Conceptualization of an integrated indicator model for the evaluation of e-government policies. *Electronic. Journal of E-Government*, *11*(2), 293–307.

Stanley, W. J., & Weare, C. (2004). The effects of Internet use on political participation. *Administration & Society*, *36*(5), 503–527. doi:10.1177/0095399704268503

Thompson, R. L., Higgins, C. A., & Howell, J. M. (1991). Personal computing: Toward a conceptual model of utilization. *Management Information Systems Quarterly*, *15*(1), 125–143. doi:10.2307/249443

Thorp, J. (1998). *The information paradox: Realizing the business benefits of information technology*. Toronto, Canada: McGraw Hill Ryerson.

Torres, L., Pina, V., & Royo, S. (2005). E-government ant the transformation of public administration in EU countries: Beyond NPM or just a second wave of reforms? *Online Information Review*, *29*(5), 531–553. doi:10.1108/14684520510628918

Unisys. (2012). *United States security index*. Retrieved from http://www.unisyssecurityindex.com/usi/us

United Nations. (2010). *E-government survey 2010: Leveraging e-government at a time of financial and economic crisis*. New York: United Nations.

United Nations. (2012a). *UN public administration programme: Data center*. Retrieved from http://unpan3.un.org/egovkb/datacenter/countryview.aspx

United Nations. (2012b). *United Nations e-government survey 2012: E-government for the people*. New York: The United Nations Department of Economic and Social Affairs.

Vekatesh, V., & Davis, F.D. (n.d.). A theoretical extension of the technology acceptance model: Four longitudinal field studies. *Management Science*, *45*(2), 186-204.

Vekatesh, V., & Speier, C. (1999). Computer technology training in the workplace: A longitudinal investigation of the effect of the mood. *Organizational Behavior and Human Decision Processes*, *79*(1), 1–28. doi:10.1006/obhd.1999.2837 PMID:10388607

Vigoda, E. (2002). From responsiveness to collaboration: Governance, citizens, and the next generation of public administration. *Public Administration Review*, *62*(5), 527–540. doi:10.1111/1540-6210.00235

Watson, R., & Mundy, B. (2001). A strategic perspective of electronic democracy. *Communications of the ACM*, *44*(1), 27–30. doi:10.1145/357489.357499

West, D. M. (2004). E-government and the transformation of service delivery and citizen attitudes. *Public Administration Review*, *64*(1), 15–27. doi:10.1111/j.1540-6210.2004.00343.x

West, D. M. (2005). *Digital government: Technology and public sector performance*. Princeton, NJ: Princeton University Press.

Yoon, S. H. (1996). Power online: A poststructuralist perspective on computer-mediated communication. In C. Ess (Ed.), *Philosophical perspectives on computer-mediated communication* (pp. 171–196). Albany, NY: State University of New York Press.

Zhou, Z., & Hu, C. (2008). Study on the e-government security risk management. *International Journal of Computer Science and Network Security, 8*(5), 208–213.

ADDITIONAL READING

Al-Hakim, L. (Ed.). (2007). *Global e-government: Theory, applications and benchmarking.* Hershey, PA: Idea Publishing Group.

Barlow, A. (2007a). *Blogging America: The new public sphere.* New York, NY: Praeger.

Barlow, A. (2007b). *The rise of the blogosphere.* New York, NY: Praeger.

Bimber, B. (2003). *Information and American democracy: Technology in the evolution of political power.* New York, NY: Cambridge University Press. doi:10.1017/CBO9780511615573

Borins, S. (2010). Strategic planning from Robert McNamara to gov 2.0. *Public Administration Review, 70*(1), s220–s221. doi:10.1111/j.1540-6210.2010.02278.x.

Chen, Y., & Thurmaier, L. (2008). Advancing e-government: Financing challenges and opportunities: New perspectives on e-government. *Public Administration Review, 68*(3), 537–548. doi:10.1111/j.1540-6210.2008.00889.x

Chesbrough, H. W. (2003). *Open innovation: The new imperative for creating and profiting from technology.* Boston: Harvard Business School Press.

Ciborra, C. (2002). *The labyrinths of information: Challenging the wisdom of systems.* Oxford, UK: Oxford University Press.

Eggers, W. (2005). *Government 2.0: Using technology to improve education, cut red tape, reduce gridlock, and enhance democracy.* Lanham, MD: Rowman & Littlefield Publishers.

Feld, L., & Wilcox, N. (2008). *Netroots rising: How a citizen army of bloggers and online activists is changing American politics.* New York, NY: Praeger.

Fountain, J. E. (n.d.). *Bureaucratic reform and e-government in the United States: An institutional perspective.* Retrieved from http://www.umass.edu/digitalcenter/research/working_papers/07_006FountainBureauReform.pdf

Garson, D. G. (2006). *Public information technology and e-governance: Managing the virtual state.* Sudbury, MA: Jones and Bartlett.

Heeks, R. (2006). *Implementing and managing e-government.* London, UK: Sage Publications.

Hendricks, J., & Denton, R. E. (2010). *Communicator-in-chief: How Barack Obama used new media technology to with the White House.* New York, NY: Lexington Books.

Homberg, V. (2008). *Understanding e-government: Information systems in public administration.* London, UK: Routledge.

Hong, E. K. (2009). Information technology strategic planning. *IT Professional, 11*(6), 8–15. doi:10.1109/MITP.2009.126

Jaeger, P. T. (2005). Deliberative democracy and the conceptual foundations of electronic government. *Government Information Quarterly, 22*(4), 702–719. doi:10.1016/j.giq.2006.01.012

Keren, M. (2006). *Blogosphere: The new political arena.* Lanham, MD: Lexington Books.

Noveck, B. (2009). *Wiki-government: How open-source technology can make government decision-making more expert and more democratic.* Washington, DC: Brookings Institution Press.

Rocheleau, B. (2007). *Case studies on digital government.* Hershey, PA: Idea Group Publishing. doi:10.4018/978-1-59904-177-3

Thomas, G., & Fernández, W. (2008). Success in IT projects: A matter of definition? *International Journal of Project Management, 26*(7), 733–742. doi:10.1016/j.ijproman.2008.06.003

Thomson, J. D. (2009). Remodelled and restyled e-procurement – New power relationships down under. *Electronic Journal of E-Government, 7*(2), 183–194.

Tolber, C. J., Mossberger, K., & McNeal, R. (2008). Institutions, policy innovation, and e-government in the American states. *Public Administration Review, 68*(3), 549–563. doi:10.1111/j.1540-6210.2008.00890.x.

Wang, P. (2010). Chasing the hottest IT: Effects of information technology fashion on organizations. *Management Information Systems Quarterly, 34*(1), 63–85.

Warschauer, M. (2003). *Technology and social inclusion: Rethinking the digital divide.* Cambridge, MA: MIT Press.

Weissenberger-Eibl, M. A., & Teufel, B. (2011). Organizational politics in new product development project selection: A review of the current literature. *European Journal of Innovation Management, 14*(1), 51–73. doi:10.1108/14601061111104698

Wenjing, L. (2011). Government information sharing: principles, practice, and problems – An international perspective. *Government Information Quarterly, 28*(3), 363–373. doi:10.1016/j.giq.2010.10.003.

KEY TERMS AND DEFINITIONS

Deterministic: A guaranteed outcome based on a given state of preexisting conditions.

E-Democracy: The use of ICTs for support of democratic constructs.

E-Governance: Governance that fundamentally relies on ICTs.

E-Government: The use of ICTs for purposes of governance.

E-Participation: Citizens' involvement in governance through the means of ICTs.

Information Communication Technologies (ICTs): Storage and communication technologies used for information collection, storage, transmission, processing, and decision-making.

National Performance Review (NPR): An interagency task force established in 1993 under Bill Clinton with the American federal government.

New Public Management (NPM): A broad body of perspectives on government reform driven by the idea that market oriented techniques should be applied to the public sector.

Transformation: A substantial change in pattern, condition, or nature.

Chapter 7

Design of a Triple Helix Strategy for Developing Nations Based on E-Government and Entrepreneurship:
An Application to Ecuador

José Manuel Saiz Alvarez
Nebrija University, Spain & Catholic University of Santiago de Guayaquil, Ecuador

Rubén González Crespo
Universidad Internacional de La Rioja, Spain

ABSTRACT

The arrival of Rafael Correa in Ecuador is leading to a structural transformation of the Ecuadorian economy and society with the arrival of e-Government and the introduction of the digital economy in the country. The objective of this chapter is to design a strategy based on entrepreneurship, e-Government, and higher education for creating a digital society in Ecuador (the triple helix strategy). To achieve it, the authors analyse the Ecuadorian's National Plan for Good Living 2013-2017 linked to higher education reforms and the influence of the European-based e-Government policies in Ecuador. The authors finish with some perspectives and the foreseeable impact of a digital society in this developing nation.

INTRODUCTION

After coming to power on January 15, 2007, the government of Rafael Correa has begun to digitally change Ecuador, as well as the whole Ecuadorian macroeconomic structure, resulting into the achievement of a stronger relationship between citizens and digital public administration. A first result of this digital modernization has been reflected at the end of February 2014 with the publication of the election results just an hour after the polls closed in Santo Domingo de los Tsáchilas through the use of Smartmatic-based electronic voting system (AA.VV., 2014).

DOI: 10.4018/978-1-4666-3691-0.ch007

As this type of digital voting is secured and fast, avoiding corruption practices, it will be used nationwide in the next general election to be held in 2017, according to the article 89, first paragraph, of the Organic Law on Elections and Political Organizations of the Republic of Ecuador, Code of Democracy.

One of the keys to achieve a digital economy is by reforming and impulsing higher education, focusing efforts on technical and business oriented studies. In this sense, Ecuador has approved on October 12, 2010 the Organic Law on Higher Education (LOES, from the Spanish, *Ley Orgánica de Educación Superior*) linked to the 2007-2010 National Development Plan (NDP) for the Public Sector, with the objective to reallocate the best human resources towards the highest-ranked Ecuadorian private and public higher education institutions using a system of accreditation deeply inspired by the currently used in the European Higher Education Space (EEES).

Although Ecuador is now quite far away from having "smart cities" characterized by offering advanced and innovative digital services to citizens (Piro et al, 2014), the nation is heading towards this goal. The objective of this chapter is to analyse the importance of entrepreneurship and higher education in achieving a digital society in Ecuador. To cope with this goal we will study the importance of improving higher education in Ecuador and its relation with R&D and entrepreneurship. Applied these ideas to the Ecuadorian's National Plan for Good Living, 2013-2017, we will be able to design a triple helix strategy for developing nations. We finally draw some conclusions.

HIGHER EDUCATION, R&D AND ENTREPRENEURSHIP IN THE NATIONAL PLAN FOR GOOD LIVING, 2013-2017

Education reform in Ecuador by the Correa government began in 2009 through the General Unified High School where technical subjects are promoted and those related to business administration. As a result, it has been introducing new technologies in education, also including university education, so the Correa's government has closed in April 2012 the fourteen universities with lower educational and research quality in the country.

To achieve greater quality in higher education, the government has increased the amount spent on education up to 6% of the Gross Domestic Product (GDP), and it has introduced free education in primary education, to prevent illiteracy, along with courses on health and nutrition for the most economically disadvantaged population. All this combined with the training of teachers, and the increase of investment in R&D and innovation, will permit Ecuador to digitalize its economy.

It is intended in the same way to give a response to the need to eliminate the digital gap and to help to digital literacy in all population. The gap in technological development among those nations more visionary and the rest has begun to be consolidated, although this digitalization process goes very slowly but inexorably (Cáceres, 2004). Internet is a technological infrastructure for short life; however, the speed of its development in some nations has led to extend its application beyond the computers and spaces associated with them. This solution will help increasing the use of the technologies associated with Internet.

In fact, enhancing the application of Information and Communication Technologies (ICT) to the education and training systems in Ecuador will contribute to foster economic growth while reducing social differences in terms of poverty, education, and technical skills development in the nation. Increasing use of advanced digital services by the public will force regional, local and national authorities to develop the technological capabilities of the ICT sector, facilitating the development of an effective e-Government, joining a content service capability, service delivery capability and on-demand capability (Hu, Lin &

Pan, 2013) to permit Ecuador to follow the path towards offering better services to their citizens.

This strategy has been reinforced in the National Plan for Good Living, 2013-2017. This Plan, approved in the 24 June 2013 session by Resolution No. CNP-002-2013, was prepared under the leadership of the National Secretariat of Planning and Development (Senplades), as the Technical Secretariat of the National Decentralized Participatory Planning System, pursuant to the General Public Planning and Finance Code, and submitted by President Rafael Correa for the revision and approval of the National Planning Council. The National Plan for Good Living is divided into 12 objectives including social, economic, educational, and technological aspects to be achieved. So, the objective 11 is focused on ensuring the sovereignty and efficiency of the strategic sectors for industrial and technological transformation policies. In this sense, the Montecristi Constitution defines strategic sectors as those that, because of their transcendence and magnitude, have a decisive economic, social, political or environmental influence on the country, and are oriented toward full development of citizens' rights and general public interest. Strategic sectors are those involving the use of non-renewable natural resources, such as hydrocarbons and mining, and renewable natural resources such as water, biodiversity and genetic heritage. Other strategic sectors are energy in all forms, telecommunications and the broadcasting spectrum. The Constitution states that "the State reserves the right to administer, regulate, oversee and manage strategic sectors, pursuant to principles of environmental sustainability, precaution, prevention and efficiency" (Article 313) having into mind the e-Government and entrepreneurship practices.

In Correa's 2013-2017 Government program states that Ecuador must manage its strategic resources within the framework of international insertion, so the current technological cycle based on automation, robotics and microelectronics can contribute to an overall increase in well-being for its inhabitants. This fact will constitute the arrival of a digital society in Ecuador characterized by joining R&D, education and entrepreneurship. This combination will contribute to deeply change the social and economic structures in the country, and this will be achieved by an array of policies for import substitution, as stated by the seminal works of Singer (1950) and Prebisch (1962), due to the combination of technology transfer, specialization, and first-order competitive advantages acquisition (Porter, 1991), while industrializing for export, redistributing wealth and implementing industries to produce intermediate and final goods, within national territory.

As a result, the productive and industrial structures will be transformed, democratizing access to telecommunications services, strategically managing water and the sea for production and research, and promoting the chemical, pharmaceutical and foods industry. To achieve this digital economy in Ecuador, five policies must be put into action: (1) to restructure the energy matrix under criteria of transforming the productive structure, inclusion, quality, energy sovereignty and sustainability, increasing the share of renewable energy; (2) to industrialize mining activity as the basis of the transformation of the productive structure, in the framework of strategic, sustainable, efficient, sovereign, socially just and environmentally sustainable governance; (3) to democratize public telecommunications service provision and ICT, including radio and television broadcasting and the radioelectric spectrum, enhancing universal usage and access; (4) to manage water resources, under a constitutional framework of sustainable, participatory management of watersheds and marine spaces, and (5) to promote the chemical, pharmaceutical and foods industry, through sovereign, strategic, sustainable use of biodiversity (Senplades, 2013, p. 83). These policies are aimed to achieve the following objectives: (1) to achieve 60.0% renewable installed power; (2) to attain 76.0% secondary energy sufficiency; (3) to increase the installed capacity for electrical generation to 8741 MW; (4) to identify mineral resource availability in 100.0% of the nation's territory; (5) to accomplish a rate of digitization of 41.7; (6) to reach a rate of e-government of 0.55; (7) to reduce digital illiteracy to 17.9%, and (8) to increase the percentage of people using ICT to 50.0%.

One of the fundamental aspects of the digitalization of land is given by the usability of it. In this sense, and applied to the Chilean case, Garrido, Lavin & Peña (2014) propose a model for measuring the usability of existing public services in Latin America. Good usability in the use of services with reduced operating costs leads to the creation based on Fuzzy Cognitive Maps (Irani et al, 2014), expert systems that lead to optimal use of scarce resources by definition.

Close with usability, e-government practices contribute to reduce corruption, although according to Krishnan, Teo & Lim (2013), it does not affect to economic prosperity and environmental degradation, as these variables are affected by economic policy and social and consumer behaviour. What is important is the social influence through social feedback and public participation in decision-making processes, as in the web "regulations.org" (Bryer, 2013).

THE INFLUENCE OF THE EUROPEAN-BASED E-ADMINISTRATION IN ECUADOR

As shown by Cerrillo (2008), the e-Administration, defined as the union of all electronic mechanisms that allow the provision of public services in the Administration, to the citizens and businesses, is formed by the conjunction of (1) e-Government, as a form of relationship between citizens and public administration using ICT; and (2) e-Democracy, as a way of allowing the participation of citizens in political life, either directly or through their representatives. Both forms of e-Administration are recently present in Ecuador, although with some limitations in rural areas, given the previous need to develop ICT in these areas.

Figure 1. The triple helix strategy for developing nations

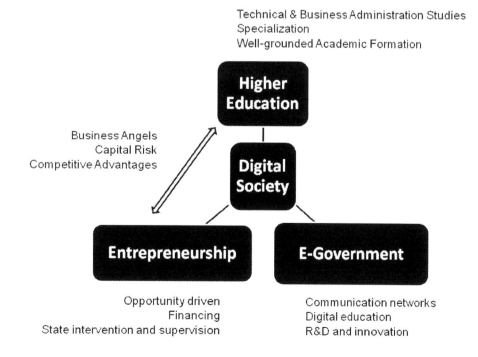

In fact, the e-Government is an opportunity to advance to a "better government" of public administration, where technology is a means and not an end in itself. The way to provide the services is transformed, and this requires coordination between departments and the most important thing a cultural change in the public officials (González et al, 2013).

Due to the strong European influence on Rafael Correa's Government in terms of digital and economic policy, mainly in education and social issues, Ecuador is recently imitating the digital path established by the European Council held in Lisbon in June 15-16, 2000 to make Europe the most competitive economy worldwide based on R&D and innovation (Torrejón, 2005) due to the adoption of the Plan of Action e-Europe 2002 with three clear objectives: (1) to get an intranet quickly and cheaply; (2) to invest in people and training, and (3) To stimulate the use of the Internet. Goals strengthened in the Lisbon Agenda 2004 and the Plan of Action e-Europe 2005 with the use of (1) on-line public services, specifically with the development of advanced electronic Administrations interconnected with broadband networks, education services on-line, and on-line health services; (2) dynamic environments that favours e-business, mainly Business-To-Consumer (B2C), Business-To-Business (B2B), and Business-To-Government (B2G) practices; (3) greater availability to broadband access at competitive prices, and (4) digital infrastructures for secure communications. Given these successful European digital experience, Ecuador has fostered private-public network industries, foreign human capital attraction, entrepreneurship, university education, social inclusion policies, and sustainable development practices. As a result, the Ecuadorian Administration has digitally established 20 basic public services to citizens, including the issue of personal documents (birth and marriage certificates, notification of changes of address and personal data, registration of private vehicles,

and individual health-related services), education (registration in institutions of higher education, and access to libraries' catalogues), employment (job search services, statement of income, and public requests), national security (statements to the police, request and authorizations of customs duties), business (social contribution to employees, registration of new companies, declaration and notification of the Value Added Tax, and public services for companies), and public sector (statements from customs duties, and sending data to statistical offices)(González et al, 2013).

In order to accelerate changes towards a deeper digital implementation in Ecuador, it is required a cultural change in a large part of the Ecuadorian population, mainly among the 55 cultural groups existing in rural Ecuador, whose rights have been protected in the article 1, third paragraph, of the Constitution of Ecuador as all indigenous languages (Achuar, Awa, Chachi, Cofán, Epera, Huaorani, Kichwa, Secoya, Shuar, Siona, Tsáchila and Zápara) are co-official with Spanish. The cultural integration of these nationalities will be stronger when there will be a real universal access to the Internet, with the development of a comprehensive strategy that integrates these communities into the digital world through education and free public services in remote areas only. As a result, it becomes necessary to develop a horizontal strategy comprising education, R&D, entrepreneurship and the development of family businesses that must be supervised and financially aided by the public administration with the development of a "back office" if needed.

Finally, in order to promote ICT-based changes in Ecuadorian industrial sectors by strengthening digital contents, firms must extend the culture of safety among the citizens and businesses, improve the capacity and the extension of telecommunications networks, promote innovative processes in ICT, extend the ICT in the health and social welfare, and apply the use of ICT solutions for business in the company.

CONCLUSION AND FUTURE WORK

The e-government strategies are a reality in several countries around the world, but it must be improved both in countries with depth expertise in this knowledge area and in countries which are booming like Ecuador. The future of e-government is increasing coherency and integration of the public sector through innovation and change (Díaz-Piraquive, 2014). The public sectors in many countries are quickly becoming more coherent and integrated by eliminating redundancies and ensuring the sharing of resources where possible will dominate the e-government agenda towards 2020. This requires an unprecedented change of mind-sets and traditional silo-thinking towards ownership of the public sector as a whole by each civil servant (Piedra-Calderón, González & Rainer, 2013).

The arrival of a digital economy in Ecuador will allow citizens to control the Ecuadorian public sector, as this economy is focused on users benefitting from public sector activities while diminishing silo-thinking and increasing civil service providers' awareness of user needs and demands. Although Ecuador is far away from Korea, as it has pioneered this process, and is the current world leader in commissioning and implementing e-Government (O'Donnell & Turner, 2013), e-Government will enable Ecuador to hand-over major parts of public sector development and operations to users directly, since competencies and skills of society at large are improving and affecting an increasing number of people. Collaborative involvement of users in service design and operation could allow them to build their own set of public services adapted to their personal needs at different stages of their lives.

Finally, globalization is affecting all countries' public sectors. Regional cross-border seamless services are increasingly apparent. This extra pressure for international collaboration and co-operation leads to increased global integration. International collaboration is already underway in the European Union, and continues to increase, especially among Latin American countries and Spain, making both shared e-government services, such as cross-border electronic identification systems and health care, a real possibility to be achieved, especially in these developing nations.

REFERENCES

AA.VV. (2014, February 25). Smartmatic permite resultados electorales en tiempo récord en Ecuador. *IT/Users Magazine*. Retrieved March 11, 2014 from http://itusersmagazine.com/category/e-government/

Bryer, T. A. (2013). Public participation in regulatory decision-making: Cases from Regulations.org. *Public Performance & Management Review*, *37*(2), 263–279. doi:10.2753/PMR1530-9576370204

Cáceres, S. (2004). *Observatorio de la Sociedad de la Información: Un mundo de brechas y puentes digitales*. Retrieved Feb. 5, 2014 from http://fundacionorange.es/areas/28_observatorio/pdfs/DEF_20.pdf

Cerrillo, A. (2008). e-Administración. Barcelona, Spain: UOC.

Díaz Piraquive, F. N. et al. (2014). ICT as a Means of Generating Knowledge for Project Management. In *Proceedings in Complexity* (pp. 617–629). Springer. doi:10.1007/978-94-007-7287-8_50

Garrido, M., Lavin, C., & Peña, N. R. (2014). Detecting Usability Problems and Offering Lines of Solutions: An Instrument' Proposal for Measuring Usability in Online Services. *IEEE Latin America Transactions*, *12*(1), 9–16. doi:10.1109/TLA.2014.6716486

González, R. et al. (2013). Design of an Open Platform for Collective Voting through EDNI on the Internet. In *E-Procurement Management for Successful Electronic Government Systems*. Hershey, PA: IGI Global.

Hu, G., Lin, H., & Pan, W. (2013). Conceptualizing and Examining E-Government Service Capability: A Review and Empirical Study. *Journal of the American Society for Information Science and Technology, 64*(11), 2379–2395. doi:10.1002/asi.22921

Irani, Z. et al. (2014). Visualising a knowledge mapping of information systems investment evaluation. *Expert Systems with Applications, 41*(1), 105–125. doi:10.1016/j.eswa.2013.07.015

Piedra-Calderón, J. C., González, R., & Rainer, J. J. (2013). IT Projects & Their Specific Elements. *La Pensee, 75*(12).

Piro, G. et al. (2014). Information centric services in Smart Cities. *Journal of Systems and Software, 88*, 169–188. doi:10.1016/j.jss.2013.10.029

Porter, M. (1991). *La Ventaja Competitiva de las Naciones*. Barcelona, Spain: Plaza & Janés.

Prebisch, R. (1962). The Economic Development of Latin America and its Principal Problems. *Economic Bulletin for Latin America, 7*(1), 1–22.

Ray, R., & Kozameh, S. (2012). La economía de Ecuador desde 2007. Washington, DC: Centre for Economic and Policy Research (CEPR).

Senplades. (2013). *National Development Plan/National Plan for Good Living, 2013-2017*. Quito.

Singer, H. W. (1950). U.S. Foreign Investment in Underdeveloped Areas: The Distribution of Gains between Investing and Borrowing Countries. *The American Economic Review, 40*, 473–485.

Torrejón, A. (2005). *Observatorio de la Sociedad de la Información: Algunas reflexiones sobre las ciudades del siglo XXI*. Retrieved Feb. 5, 2014 from http://fundacionorange.es/areas/28_observatorio/pdfs/DEF_26.pdf

KEY TERMS AND DEFINITIONS

Digital Economy: Characterized by joining R&D and innovation, education and entrepreneurship, the inclusion of the digital economy in Ecuador will be defined by five policies to reshape the economic structure as a whole to include ICT benefitting, the public and private sectors, mainly consumers.

E-Administration: The union of all electronic mechanisms that allow the provision of public services by the Public Administration, it is formed by the conjunction of e-Government and e-Democracy. Both forms of e-Administration are recently present in Ecuador, although with some limitations in rural areas.

E-Europe Action Plan: Launched in 2000, e-Europe seeks to ensure that the European Union realizes the full potential of the information society to drive growth through improved productivity and competitiveness. To do this, e-Europe focuses on the widespread availability of secure broadband services and on action to promote greater digital use, strategy also followed now by the Ecuadorian Administration in 20 basic public services to citizens.

Fuzzy Cognitive Maps: Fuzzy-graph structures for representing causal reasoning. Their fuzziness allows hazy degrees of casualty between concepts, while their graphic structure allows systematic causal propagation. Born in the engineering field, they are increasingly used in economic planning.

Plan for Good Living: Approved on June 24, 2013 by the Correa's Government, this Plan is formed by an ambitious political strategy made of twelve social, economic, educational, and technological objectives to be developed and reached for the period 2013-2017 in Ecuador.

Smart Cities: A: set of policies put into action to improve urban life through more sustainable and digital integrated solutions for firms and citizens, in terms of applied innovations, better planning, higher energy efficiency, better transport solutions, and intelligent use of ICT.

The Montecristi Constitution: Written between November 30, 2007 and July 24, 2008, by the National Constituent Assembly in Montecristi, this is the Constitution now in force in Ecuador since October 20, 2008.

Chapter 8
Not Just Videogames:
Gamification and its Potential Application to Public Services

Alberto Asquer
University of London, UK

ABSTRACT

The aim of this chapter is to discuss how the emerging process of gamification can impact the production of public services. Gamification is a relatively recent phenomenon that relates, in broad terms, to the introduction to game elements in non-game contexts. After reviewing the concept, design principles and techniques, and effects of gamification, the chapter discusses the extent to which gamification may affect the production and delivery of public services. The conclusions discuss the possible role of gamification in reshaping the identity and role of citizens and their relationship with public authorities.

1. INTRODUCTION

The aim of this chapter is to discuss how the emerging process of gamification can impact on the production of public services. Gamification is a relatively recent phenomenon that relates, in broad terms, to the introduction of game elements in non-game contexts. Examples of gamification include Nike+, a social running game-like service that is intended to encourage runners to compete and to provide them motivation to attain fitness goals, and Fold.it, a collaborative game-like online program for discovering how proteins fold. At first sight, gamification may seem confined to small niches of web-based applications that mostly ap-

peal to computer geeks or video-gamers. There are, however, some indications that gamification may extend to various aspects of everyday's life, including business services, education, and health.

As a social phenomenon, gamification has been little researched so far. Some works have been done on the very description and definition of what gamification is (Deterding et al., 2012; Hamari, 2013; Huotari and Hamari, 2012; Xu, 2011). Other studies highlighted the features of effective design and implementation of gamification mechanisms (Donovan, 2012; Easley et al., 2013; Groh, 2012; Hamari and Eranti, 2011; Nicholson, 2012; Paharia, 2012; Wang and Sun, 2011; Werbach and Hunter, 2012). Other research, finally, has been

DOI: 10.4018/978-1-4666-3691-0.ch008

done on the motivational and behavioral effects of gamification (Groh, 2012; Hamari et al., 2014; Oprescu et al., 2014). Yet, most of the scholarly literature primarily focused on gamification in the business sector, and its possible applications in the public one have been relatively ignored so far. Gamification may have relevant implications on the conduct of public administration and in e-government policies, however. As a system designed to affect human motivation and behavior, gamification may be relevant in the repertoire of the tools of government (Hood, 1983), i.e., of the devices and mechanisms that are installed and exploited with the aim of orienting the conduct of individuals and private sector organizations. As such, gamification poses interesting issues about whether it can help guiding the behavior of citizens towards socially desirable aims (e.g., greater care for health, for education, and for the environment). In addition, it also poses concerns about the extent to which public authorities may increase their capacity to influence citizens' psychology and behavior in a manipulative way. If gamification will ever become a component part of public authorities' instruments to affect individuals, then research should start paying attention to how gamification of the public sector can work and to what effects.

This chapter will review, first, works that have been done on what gamification is. Third section will provide an account of the principles for the design of gamification, of the core elements of gamification, and of the mechanisms of effective gamified systems. Fourth section will discuss the motivational and behavioral effects of gamification. Section five will tackle the issue of how gamification could affect the production and delivery of public services. Finally, section six will draw the conclusions, including critically assessing the implications of turning citizens to 'gamers' of re-designed public services and public policy processes.

2. WHAT IS GAMIFICATION?

The term "gamification" was rarely used until 2010, when it gained attention as a way to generally address the growing relevance of game-like components in various kinds of human and computer-human interactions. By that time, a growing number of individuals in the world had come to experience digital technologies (or Information and Communication Technologies, ICT) as a common aspect of their daily life. A large part of them, moreover, had come to consider digital entertainment - especially video-games - as a familiar way to amuse themselves. The social trend was described as a "ludification of culture" (Raessens, 2006), that related to the increased relevance of video-games as cultural medium along other traditional forms such as literature, movies, and television. In relation to this, a growing number of individuals started to take the presence of games or game-like experiences as an ordinary feature of their experiences, especially when dealing with the Internet.

In essence, gamification refers to the intended addition of a game layer to an existing activity with the aim of inducing desired motivational and possibly behavioral effects. Gamification may take place in various means, but they all generally consist of introducing some game design, element, and mechanism principles so that the individual experiences the activity as having game-like features. For example, the individual may be required to do something at a particular time or place; or they may enjoy the possibility to affect the actions of other individuals; or they may be required to attain a sequence of goals, that are typically ordered at higher levels of complexity and difficulty; or they may be expected to coordinate with other individuals in order to solve a challenge; or they may experience a combination of these (and possibly other) features (Xu, 2011). Gamification takes place when the individuals experience such game-like features as a game, and therefore strive to participate and succeed in accomplishing the game because of the very satisfaction of winning the game.

Early instances of gamification arose within the digital mobile technology trend (Xu, 2011). They include FourSquare, a location-based game-like service that requires players to check-in to locations for earning points, badges, and rewards. The game, that attracted more than 10 million customers, primarily aimed at stimulating consumers to visit again a location, such as a restaurant or a pub, and to become a loyal customer. Rewards included intangible acknowledgements, such as becoming the "mayor" of a location, and more tangible ones, such as converting badges earned into real products. Another early instance of gamification is Farmville, a virtual shopping environment where consumers grow farming products and sell or exchange them in markets. The game essentially aimed to induce customers to eventually pay for playing the game above a certain level: early progress in Farmville was relatively plain and straightforward, while customers who wanted to advance to further stages could not do it without spending money for acquiring virtual goods.

At the present, gamification has extended, in various forms, to a plethora of digital services and online activities. Instances include gamified experience of listening to music (e.g., Last. fm), watching TV (e.g., GetGlue), doing fitness (e.g., Fitocracy), and contributing to scientific research (e.g., Fold.it) (Hamari et al., 2014; Groh, 2012). Gamification has been applied to learning (including distance learning based on online systems) with apparent positive effects on some cognitive performance (Domínguez et al., 2013), retention rates, and collaboration (Lawley, 2012). The range of possible applications of gamification, however, has not been fully explored yet. For some authors, they include various forms of customer engagement, employee performance, training and education, innovation management, personal development, sustainability, health and

wellness (Burke 2013), user retention (Hamari and Järvinen, 2011), and greener energy consumption (see, e.g., McGonical 2011).

Gamification has been defined in many different ways so far. In a much quoted definition, Deterding et al. (2011) understand it as "the use of game design elements in non-game contexts", especially for the sake of improving user experience and user engagement. Huotari and Hamari (2012), instead, define it as "a process of providing affordances for gameful experiences which support the customers' overall value creation". Other definitions include gamification as a "service packing where a core service is enhanced by a rule-based service system that provides feedback and interaction mechanism to the user with an aim to facilitate and support the users' overall value creation" (Huotari and Hamari, 2012), a system "where you use game elements to try and get people do stuff they don't want to do" (Brian Reynolds, quoted in Xu, 2011), "a problem solving situation that you enter into because you want to" (Jesse Schell, quoted in Xu, 2011), "a process of enhancing services with (motivational) affordances in order to invoke gameful experiences and further behavioral outcomes" (Hamari, 2013), a system to "apply game mechanics in everyday applications and situations to boost engagement, fun and good behaviors" (Llagostera, 2012), and "the use of game mechanics and experience design to digitally engage and motivate people to achieve their goals" (Burke, 2014).

Setting minor differences aside, the definitions of gamification tend to highlight that the term should be understood as a process or system that makes individuals enjoy a game experience albeit outside the context of an explicit game interaction (or, as Huizinga put it, the "magic circle" of the game). A "game" is conceived here as "an immersive, voluntary and enjoyable activity in which a challenging goal is pursued according to agreed-upon rules" (Kinzie and Joseph, 2008; Sung and Hwang, 2013). In gamification, individuals are aware that they are exposed to stimuli that invite to the attainment of challenging goals and in accordance to clearly specified rules, and they typically experience this on voluntary basis and as an enjoyable occurrence. However, in gamification experience the individuals may not sense to draw any clear-cut boundaries between the game and the other activities they are involved with. Indeed, it is the very purpose of gamification the one of providing game-like stimuli to individual psychology and behavior while being concerned that attitudes and behavior of individuals are appropriately modified when they deal with the non-game part of of the context.

Gamification bears some similarities to other forms of "playful" systems that are intended to affect individual psychology and behavior (Hatari et al., 2014). So-called "games with a purpose", for example, are designed as systems that call individuals to collaborate in performing a task that requires skills that humans possess better than computers (e.g., image recognition). So-called "serious games", instead, aim to teach or to train individuals to carry out particular performances, possibly with the inclusion of game-like enjoyable features (although they are not mainly intended to entertain). Other systems, instead, can build on so-called "persuasive technologies", that relate to interactive computer systems that are designed to change the attitude and/or behavior of individual users (Fogg, 2002, 2003, 2009; Oinas-Kukkonen and Harjumaa, 2009). With respect to these systems, however, gamification typically provides a more explicit "game structure" interaction, primarily aims to affect motivation rather than attitudes or behavior directly, and generally builds on existing activity systems rather than constructing a brand new interaction system. As such, gamification is also different from plain economic incentives or various forms of loyalty programs (e.g., stamp collections) that have been long adopted in business practices.

The interest towards gamification has been largely fueled, so far, by pragmatic business concerns. Gamification is generally regarded as a scheme that can make customers enjoy the participation to a business service, with the effect of making customers more loyal, increase customer retention rate and possibly stimulate word-of-mouth and network effects (Herzig et al., 2012). Recently, gamification has been also considered as a way to enhance the engagement of employees in the workplace, with the effect of making them more motivated, improve organizational commitment, and boost job performance. The so-called "gamification-of-work" movement (Nelson, 2012) precisely holds that productivity at work can be increased if workers are subjected to the competitive pressure to outperform other workers (either individually or in teams) in games organized on work-related matters. In essence, the movement (and related managerial doctrine) aims to exploit some of the motivating power that game mechanics have (Nelson, 2012) in order to elicit employees' efforts without additional monetary incentives, or to stimulate additional efforts but those that can be extracted on the basis of monetary incentives alone.

Gamification is unlikely to attain the desired motivational and behavioral effects, however, if it is not properly done. An effective implementation of gamification of any activity does not consist of adding a "layer" of game-like elements, such as goals, rules, points, badges, leader-boards, and so on, if they do not provide, on the whole, the sense of "playing a game" to the individuals. Individuals rather believe that they are engaged in a game if they attribute such meaning to the interactions that they are exposed to. The gamified system, therefore, should provide individuals with appropriate cues that they face challenges and that they have the option to make meaningful choices (Detering et al., 2012). As McGonigal put it, effective gamification provides a meaningful experience that forms a type of intrinsic reward in itself, because "… we want to belong to and contribute to something that has lasting significance beyond our own individual lives" (McGonigal, 2011: 50; Mekler et al., 2013).

3. DESIGN AND ELEMENTS OF GAMIFIED SYSTEMS

The process of gamification - that is, the introduction of game-like features into an existing activity - entails the design of a game system and the introduction of game elements. Writings on gamification are especially attentive to distinguish between these components (Werbach and Hunter, 2012). While game elements (such as points, badges, leader-boards, and so on) are the most evident feature of a gamified activity, the actual performance of a gamification process (that is, the effects that gamification exerts on the carrying out of the existing activity) largely depends on an effective design. In other words, the introduction of game elements may not, by itself, result in any substantive change on the way an existing activity is performed - actually, it can even make it worse if individuals sense that the existing activity is contaminated by alien game-like components and that the intention of the clumsy gamification intervention is the one to manipulate their conduct.

At the core of the design of a gamified activity should be placed an understanding of the psychology of the gamer, i.e., what motivates gamers to play (Rigby and Ryan, 2011). An influential explanation for gamers' motivation is the "flow theory" of Czikszentmihalyi (2008), who argued that playing stimulates a state of happiness (the "flow") that originates from particular conditions and characteristics of the game experience. Conditions include the presence of clear tasks, feedback, adequate concentration and focus, and attainable balanced goal. Characteristics of the game experience include a sense of control, a diminished sense of self, and an altered sense of time - although the gamer may not be fully aware of them. Such state of "flow" is especially attained when the gamer is challenged to achieve goals that are adequate with respect to their level of skills. If the goals are set at a level that the gamer cannot achieve with the present level of skills, then the gamer experiences frustration and anxiety; if

the goals are too easy to attain, instead, then the gamer feels bored and loses interest.

Bartle (2004) provided another theory of gamer motivation that distinguished among four types of gamer personalities. So-called "achievers" are individuals who are driven by in-game goals, usually some form of points gathering. "Explorers" are driven to find out as much as they can about the game environment, including mapping its geography and understanding the game mechanics. "Socializers" use the game environment to converse and role-play with their fellow gamers. "Killers" use the game environment to cause distress on other players, and gain satisfaction from inflicting anxiety and pain on others. According to this theory, sources of gamer motivation depend on the type of personality profile of the gamers.

Fogg (2002, 2003, 2009) argued that gamer behavior is rather dependent on three elements. First, the motivation of the gamer to desperately want to perform the behavior. Second, the ability that the gamer has to carry out the behavior, that should be mastered through gamer's skills. Finally, the presence of a trigger that stimulates the behavior, in the form of a cue, a reminder, a request, or a call to action. In order to explain the actual behavior of gamers, we should be attentive as to whether motivation, ability and trigger converge at the same moment.

Ryan and Deci (2000) explained individuals' desire to play on the basis of innate psychological needs. According to this theory, intrinsic motivation to play originates from a genuine interest and from a sense of freedom, i.e., lack of imposition on individual conduct. When playing games, individuals fulfill three basic needs, namely, autonomy, competence and relatedness. Autonomy refers to the sense of will when performing a task, that is carried out for personal interest. Competence relates to the desire of individuals to tackle challenges and to feel competent and efficient when resolving them. Relatedness happens when a person feels connected to others, in such a way to convey a sense of security. Pink (2009) proposed a similar argument where motivation to play games is related to sources of personal satisfaction, in the form of autonomy (the desire of individuals to control their own lives and how they do their jobs), mastery (the desire to achieve personal satisfaction through challenges that fit the capabilities of individuals) and purpose (the sense of consistency of intrinsic needs as a way to attain personal fulfillment).

Other works on gamer motivation have focused on the relationship between internal and external sources of motivation. Deci et al. (2001), for example, showed that all forms of external rewards have the effect of reducing internal motivation. Nicholson (2012) argued that external sources of motivation in gamification - such as the kind of virtual rewards provided by games in the forms of points, badges, leader-boards, and so on) - may have detrimental effects on any source of internal motivation that individuals may feel towards the activity that is gamified. Zichermann and Cunningham, (2011), instead, held that the external rewards associated to gamification can support and strengthen internal sources of motivation, although once external rewards are introduced than individuals strongly expect the external rewards system to keep operating and therefore the subsequent withdrawal of external rewards may have detrimental effects on motivation.

Deterding (2011) argued that gamer motivation may be related to "situated motivational affordance". Drawing from theories of human-computer interaction, the explanation holds that a gamer is motivated by a feature of the gamified system when they experience a match between the feature and the background of the individual. If a feature of the gamified system is related to other forms of meaningful reward provided by the organizational context, for example, then the gamified system exerts greater motivational influence on the individual than "just" the provision of extemporal virtual rewards. Accordingly, the design of a gamification process should take into consideration the "underlying" system of activities that should be gamified. The activities that are gamified should have already some intrinsic value for the individuals, that is, individuals should have a rationale for being engaged with the activities already. Merely putting points, badges, and other virtual forms of extrinsic rewards cannot induce individuals to do activities that they do not want or care to do (Paharia, 2012).

Gamification design provides the system that stimulates the mechanisms of motivation. Virtual forms of extrinsic rewards - or game elements - are the most apparent manifestation of a gamified system. Game elements, however, only are relevant insofar as they interact with each other and with the context of the gamified activities. Points, badges, leader-boards, etc., jointly contribute to the formation of the game experience; in addition, the context of the activities provides the individual of the meaning for why they should care or wish to be engaged in the game. Game elements alone are insufficient to stimulate motivation to play, i.e., individuals typically do not care of collecting points or other forms of virtual reward for their own sake. The meaningful context is insufficient to generate any game experience, i.e., generally there is no "fun" feature in the activities that we wish to gamify.

When gamification is appropriately done, then it can unleash powerful psychological and social processes that induce motivation and possibly behavioral change. One of such processes is learning (Donovan, 2012). In gamification, games are often designed in such a way as to elicit gamers' acquisition of new knowledge and skills that are required to solve problems and tackle virtual challenges. Gamification, in this respect, can heavily draw from major constructivist approaches to learning. Based on Piaget's work (1960), for example, games can stimulate the progressive adaptation of cognitive structures to the inflow and accommodation of novel information and experiences. Also drawing from social constructivist approaches such as Vygotsky's (1978), game design can create virtual environments where individuals interact with each other - in the roles of co-workers, instructors, etc., - and mutually assist learning.

Other psychological and social processes that come into play into gaming experience include recognition, network externalities, social comparison, and goal-oriented behavior (Hamari, 2013). Recognition relates to the influence that perception of others' beliefs about an individual affects individual motivation and behavior. Others' beliefs include expectations about an individual's conduct (Aizen, 1991; Fishbein and Aizen, 1975). Individuals, therefore, tend to adjust their behavior in order to fulfill what they believe are others' expectations about their behavior. In addition, recognition is mutually shared between individuals, with the effect that observation of others' conduct can feed back into reinforcing one's beliefs about others' expectations about their own behavior. Network externalities also relate to the influence of other gamers, in the sense that one's conduct is affected by the number of other gamers (Katz and Shapiro, 1985; Lin and Bhattacherjee, 2008). Social comparison (Festinger, 1954) relates to individuals' inclination to compare their status - including the endowment of virtual forms of rewards, such as points, badges, etc. - with those of other players, and to benchmark themselves - including the use of leader-boards. Social comparison is also associated with social proof theory (Cialdini, 2001a, 2001b; Goldstein et al., 2008), that helps explaining individual behavior on the basis of confirmatory cues that originate from the conduct of others. Finally, goal-oriented behavior relates to individuals' inclination to exert effort to attain predetermined objectives, that originates from the fulfillment of performance expectations, satisfaction from self-efficacy, and gratification from increased level of target. Goal-oriented behavior is strengthened if individuals are provided

immediate feedback and the goals are related to context conditions.

Sometimes, the psychological and social processes stimulated by the gamified system may be strengthened by the introduction of avatars for the gamers. Within computing, avatars refer to the graphical representation of a user, or a user alter ego or character. Apart from providing a form of conveying the identity of a user in pictorial form, avatars also bear important motivational and behavioral effects. Avatars may induce gamers to orient their conduct along the identity and expected codes followed by the avatar and, to some extent, gamers may transfer the learned conduct to non-game contexts (Hershfield et al., 2011; Yee et al., 2009). Avatars may be also socially relevant because they convey "model roles" within the economy of the game that gamers may believe worthy to follow (Fox and Bailenson, 2009).

While gamification design relates to the whole system architecture, game elements refer to the particular game-like features that a gamified system contains. Game elements especially refer to various forms of virtual rewards, such as points and badges. Points provide a numerical score for various kinds of performance attained while playing the game. Badges, instead, provide a recognition of some particular achievement that the gamer accomplished. Badges have been widely researched for their apparent ability to guide the behavior of the gamer, especially because they are typically earned when the player fulfills clear and specific requirements. Badges function as "guidance mechanism" (Montola et al., 2009; Jakobsson, 2011; Hamari and Eranti, 2011) because they indicate the gamer what they should do. They also help gamers to differentiate their way of playing depending of their interests or inclination, they may be functional to the indoctrination of individuals, they provide information about past achievements of gamers and their skills, they elicit motivation as status symbol, and they may facilitate group formation and cohesion (Antin and Churchill, 2011). The role of badges in games is so pivotal that the same badge design has become a research issue by itself (Easley and Ghosh, 2013).

Badges are among the most "immediate" forms of gamification of an existing activity. To some extent, indeed, badges have long been a component part of marketing tools, in the form of loyalty stamps that customers collect in relation to attaining some achievements like shopping for a certain amount of money or in particular time or place, or winning a company lottery (Hamari and Eranti, 2011; Hamari and Järvinen, 2011, Huotari and Hamari, 2011). Gamification through badges may result in effects such as greater user engagement, customer retention, and network effects. Badges may be especially functional to stimulating gamers' attention towards achievements, that is, optional sub-goals within the overall game system (Montola et al., 2009; Hamari and Eranti, 2011). Achievements are separated from the fundamental objectives that the gamer should attain, in the sense that the lack of achievements should not preclude a gamer to succeed in the game. However, gamers may become interested in attaining achievements and, relatedly, to collect badges in the same way as they care about the overall game objectives. Rather than secondary reward systems, therefore, badges earned from achievements could be understood as games on their own nested within the overall game system (Jakobsson, 2011).

4. PUTTING GAMIFICATION INTO PRACTICE

Does gamification work to affect motivation and behavior of individuals? This question is fundamental if gamification is to be seriously considered as an approach to enhance the perceived value of services and attain desired business objectives. Theories from psychology and sociology suggest that gamification needs to be properly designed and implemented if it is to have any effect on human motivation and behavior. Yet, additional evidence is needed to assess whether the introduction of a game-like experience - properly done - bears any relevance for the marketing and delivering of services. Also because of the novelty of gamification, however, there have been relatively few studies on its effects and effectiveness so far.

Hamari et al. (2014) provide one of early reviews of scholarly works on gamification effects. Building on the findings of (quantitative and qualitative) 24 empirical studies, they aimed to assess whether gamification has any effects on motivation, engagement, and behavior. They concluded that the majority of reviewed works suggest that gamification produces positive effects and beneficial results to the activities that are gamified. They also notices, however, that some studies suggest that the effects of gamification may be limited to the short term only, especially in relation to the novelty effect on the activity that is gamified. The introduction of game-like features, moreover, tends to raise up expectations of users, with the effect that the removal of gamification may have negative effects on individuals' motivation and behavior.

Most of the reviewed studies on gamification effects focused on the education sector. The gamification of education has long been an important area of research within pedagogy and cognitive psychology disciplines and practices. The introduction of game-like features in education (e.g., a system of virtual rewards attached to completion of learning tasks or the successful accomplishment of learning objectives) has been experimented, for example, both in K-12 as well in university level courses (including various forms of "edutainment"). Generally the studies reviewed by Hamari et al. (2014) concluded that the gamification of education results in positive effects in terms of motivation, engagement, and some cognitive achievements.

Scholarly works done on gamification effects, however, still present some limitations. In part, studies tend to be descriptive in nature and they lack any hypothesis testing. The evidence is generally collected from the perception of the individuals, rather than from measures of the actual behavior. The range of sectors where gamification has been applied is rather limited, and the effects of gamification on business marketing has been relatively little researched so far. In addition, the reviewed studies suggest that features of the context and of the individual users should be also taken into account to explain whether gamification works and how.

Although evidence on the effects and effectiveness of gamification are still modest, there is no shortage of works that argue that game-like features should be included in business activities and that provide advice about how gamification should be done. Works done on the introduction of "fun" elements in business processes originate since the 1990's (Deal and Key, 1998; Hemsath and Yerkes, 1997), and boomed during the 2000's (Lundin et al., 2000; Gregerman, 2000; Greenwich, 2001; Fluegge, 2008; Fleming, 2009; Andersen, 2009; Reeves and Read, 2009). Original curiosity towards the diffusion and benefits of game-like features in marketing activities gradually extended towards other areas, including the gamification of education and of the workplace.

Oprescu et al. (2014) provide an additional review of research works on gamification that results in the formulation of ten principles of gamification specifically focused on the workplace. They argued that gamification is effectively introduced by placing the user at the centre of the experience, by introducing game-like features based on sound psychological and behavioral theories, by focusing on knowledge acquisition, skill development, motivational outcomes and behavioral change objectives, by introducing a justifiable and predictable return on users' investment, by focusing on "Generation Y" individuals (that are generally understood as those who were born in the period about 1980-2000, and who constitute the fastest growing segment of the workforce), by including humor, play and fun elements as part of the work process, by balancing competition and collaboration to transform existing work processes, by focusing on personal and organizational well-being, by stimulating collaborative research efforts, and by valuing knowledge both as an outcome and feedback.

In Oprescu et al.'s (2014) view, the gamification of the workplace can become an important feature of future internal business processes with beneficial effects on recruitment and retention of a productive and healthy workforce. They argue that contemporary organizations are afflicted by issues of high stress (Perryer et al., 2012), erosion of social capital (Zhu et al., 2013), and reduced loyalty and rapid change in workforce composition (Dorling and McCaffery, 2012), and that gamification may effectively address them by increasing wellbeing at both the organizational and individual levels. Instances of the use of game-like features in the workplace include training (e.g., in the military), selection (e.g., problem based interviewing), continuous professional development (e.g., targeted courses for health professions), and personal healthy life style.

In one of the few field experiments of gamification, Mollick and Rothbard (2013) examined whether managerially-imposed games affect workers' performance. They found that consent of the employees plays an important role to increase the positive influence of games in work processes. When there is no consent, instead, both employees' attitudes and performance are diminished. These findings are consistent with a research tradition that noted the importance of games and game playing at work (Burawoy, 1979; Roy, 1952; 1959; Sherman, 2007). In effect, games have often arisen in the workplace from the initiative of the same employees, who search for ways to alleviate the fatigue of work efforts and the monotony of tasks. At present, however, organizations can leverage on the opportunities offered from digital technologies (and, relatedly, from the shift from paperwork to digitally-based work processes) for providing employees with game-like experiences inserted within the ICT systems that they routinely use at work.

The gamification of work processes is, of course, an "imposition" of managers on the employees. Game-like features are added on the top of business processes as a way to stimulate workers' motivation and induce desired behavioral effects, especially in terms of higher productivity, creativity, satisfaction and collaboration (Fineman, 2006; Fleming and Sturdy, 2010). The kind of "spontaneous" play that workers may experience, therefore, is displaced by devices intended to boost employees' morale for organizational goals. "Gamification of work", therefore, results in a paradox of "mandatory fun" where a purposeful managerial scheme is intended to stimulate greater contribution of employees to the attainment of organizational goals out of gaming activities that would be rather supposed to offer workers circumscribed areas of relief from organizational pressures. In addition, employees would be expected to believe that their gaming activity is not hierarchically directed, else the sense of imposition - and, arguably, the possibility that employees do not consent to be entertained in such a way - would undermine the effectiveness of the gamified activities (Burawoy, 1979).

"Gamification of work" does not entail that the underlying activity being gamified becomes more interesting or challenging or fun because of the inclusion of game-like elements. Indeed, the relationship between employees and the work activities remain unchanged. On the top of work activities, however, gamification places a "layer" of game experience that supplements the employees with other sources of motivation and rationales for behavioral change (Bruckman, 1999, conveyed the idea with the expression of "chocolate covered broccoli"). While individuals may enjoy playing games, they do not necessarily enjoy the work activities by themselves.

5. GAMIFYING THE PRODUCTION OF PUBLIC SERVICES

Does gamification bear any relevance to the public sector? Could the principles and techniques of gamification be effectively applied to stimulate greater engagement of public sector workers, improve the delivery of public services, and making citizens more satisfied with e-government policies? How desirable would a "gamified" public service be? These questions may shed some unusual light onto the ways in which we commonly conceive the role and working of the public sector. Traditionally, public administration has been long related to the application of principles such as compliance with the law, impartiality and equal access to services, and adherence to strict public service ethics and canons of conduct. Gamification does not, by itself, contradict any of these principles, but arguably the image of a civil servant playing games at work or the one of a citizen striving to score points in a governmental web-based services may be at odds with the roles that we usually attach to public service delivery system.

Yet, the role and tools of the public sector necessarily change over time, especially along a process of adaptation to novel technologies and features of the society and culture. During the last decade, for example, the diffusion of mobile Internet devices (e.g., smart phones) led to a growing interest towards the possibility to provide e-government information and deliver public services to users "wherever and whenever" they wish. Provided that a country possesses the adequate infrastructure, the provision of public services on the basis of digital technologies constitute one of the "new frontiers" of the public sector. The Internet, in particular, has come to mediate the relationship between public sector organizations and clients or citizens, businesses, and other public sector bodies. If certain societal and cultural trends that underpin the rise and possibly the diffusion of gamification are to hold, then it may be possible that also public services - especially, those delivered through digital media - may well come to incorporate game-like features in part of their activities.

The use of games, of course, is not completely alien to governmental policies. Herodotus told that, during the kingdom of Atys, the Lydians used to fast and entertain themselves by playing games every other day during a period of famine. Juvenal decried the recourse to *panem et circenses* (bread and circuses) as a way to provide easy sources of satisfaction to people, distract the population from more serious matters, and rise up to power. In modern days, lotteries and various forms of gambling are permitted or organized by public authorities, often in conjunction to fiscal objectives. Gamification of public services, however, would fundamentally differ from the set up of games by public authorities or concessionaires.

What kind of public sector activities may be more susceptible to gamification? Drawing from the range of experiences conducted so far, various kind of public services may be open to the inclusion of game-like features. Education, for example, has been already subjected to some forms of experimentation that was primarily concerned with enhancing the motivation of pupils to learn. Other areas where some amount of behavioral change from the side of clients or citizens is desirable, moreover, are likely gamification targets. Gamified activities, for example, may stimulate greater inclination to take care of the environment, or of one's health, or of the needs of weaker individuals. To some extent, early instances of application of gamification already showed some encouraging results, e.g., the Volkswagen-sponsored "Piano Staircase" and the "Bottle Bank Arcade" installed in Sweden illustrate how gamified activities may induce individuals to do more physical exercise and to collect and sort garbage in parks (Werbach and Hunter, 2012). We lack, however, a framework for arguing how gamification can be used to affect individuals' motivations and behavior in such a way as to contribute to the greater attainment of public goals.

It is argued, here, that the scholarly work done on the area of "co-production of public services" provides a frame of reference for thinking how gamification can be introduced in the public sector. Scholarly interest towards the co-production of public services (generally understood as "the mix of activities that both public service agents and citizens contribute to the provision of public services"; Parks et al., 1981; Ostrom, 1996) increased substantively during the last decades. Public service co-production is related to citizens' contribution to the execution of public programs, such as those on community safety (Marschall, 2004), childcare (Pestoff, 2006), social housing (Bovaird and Löffler, 2007; Needham, 2007) and unemployment (Alford, 2009), on a regular and fundamentally voluntaristic basis. Several works have addressed issues related to the factors that induce clients to co-produce public services and that affect efficiency and effectiveness of co-production efforts (Alford, 2000, 2002, 2009; Bovaird, 2007; Bovaird and Löffler, 2003; Brandsen and Pestoff, 2006; Fung, 2004; Osborne, 2010; Pestoff, 2012; Pestoff et al., 2012; Verschuere et al., 2012).

The willingness of citizens to co-produce has been primarily related the presence of a voluntaristic "animating spirit" (Alford, 1998, 2009: Flynn, 2012; Hood et al., 1996). In addition, the co-production of public services can be triggered by diverse factors, including extrinsic rewards, intrinsic rewards, sociality, and normative commitment (Alford, 2002, 2009; Rosentraub and Sharp, 1981; Wilson, 1973; Clark and Wilson, 1961). Clients co-produce because they receive immediate material gratification (or avoid tangible sanctions), gain benefit from the expression of self-determination, enjoy the possibility to demonstrate their competence, appreciate the sense of group membership and identification, or contribute affirming moral and social values (Alford, 2009; Blau, 1964; Ekeh, 1974; Deci, 1975). Motivation to co-produce is also affected by circumstances such as ease of involvement and perceived salience or importance of the service provided (Pestoff, 2012; Alford, 2009).

Existing theory of public service co-production largely builds on the service management paradigm, which highlights that the acts of production and consumption of services are necessarily intertwined (Normann, 2002; Löffler et al., 2008). Clients' participation to the production of services is an inherent part of their consumption experience (Osborne, 2010). As services are intangible and cannot be stored, moreover, production and consumption take place simultaneously. These features of the joint production and consumption of services bear important consequences for the management of client-provider relationship, as it has been widely discussed especially in the business and marketing literatures (Bendapudi and Leone, 2003; Wikström, 1996; Lusch and Vargo, 2006a, 2006b; Pralahad and Ramaswamy, 2004; Vargo and Lusch, 2004; Burger-Helmchen and Cohendet, 2011; Hienerth et al. 2011), and for the research agenda on co-production of public services, in particular.

It is argued here that gamification holds a promising role in the stimulation of citizens' interest and efforts to co-produce public services. Co-production of public services is generally oriented to the provision of services that citizens value and care about, such as health care, social care, welfare, environmental preservation and protection of private property. As such, citizens should already hold some amount of motivation to the co-production of public services. It has been noted that, despite the presence of such motivation, citizens' participation (especially repeated participation over time) may be hard to attain because of various sources of distraction to commit in co-production efforts. The presence of

a modicum of motivation, however, satisfies an essential requisite for gamification to potentially result in the desired behavioral change.

Gamification can potentially provide a "game layer" to the public service co-production experience that could effectively induce citizens to exert the co-production efforts. As discussed in the previous sessions, the gamification of a co-produced public service process entails the design of a game system that provides individuals adequate stimuli - in such terms of challenging goals and learning opportunities, for example - to participate to the game. A digital support, for example, could provide various kinds of virtual rewards - such as points, badges, and leader-boards - that are earned when individuals perform tasks that are functional to the co-production of the public service under consideration (either for the personal benefit or for the one of the community at large).

There is no shortage of public services that are co-produced by citizens (or, more precisely, by clients or users) and that could benefit, in principle, from a gamification process. For example, gamification may be functional to the co-production of services such as monitoring cleanness in public transport, sharing information among users, and participation to public consultation forums - all activities that, despite being potentially relevant to produce public value, may typically suffer from relatively low participation rates. Digital technologies could provide the technological basis needed to track individual activities, also through mobile applications. Gamified systems of virtual rewards may instill sources of self-satisfaction with the activities performed, of recognition within the community, and of sustained behavioral change.

Not all public services, however, may be so easily subjected to gamification, especially for ethical or cultural reasons. For example, health screening (or health check) is a public service that typically requires some amount of participation from the side of the citizen, who should at least devote some time to visit the health centre providing the check (that is typically done for free). Despite the importance of the service for timely detecting and combating illnesses and health problems, participation rates among populations is not fully satisfactory yet (e.g., in the UK, NHS, 2011). Various measures to elicit more efforts of clients to do the health checks have been introduced or are planned, such as monetary incentives to health providers and patient navigators. Gamification of health screening, however, may be irrelevant or backfire, provided that the service under consideration entails such sensitive results as to inform the clients of their health problems.

6. CONCLUSION: FROM CITIZENS TO CONSUMERS... TO GAMERS?

Gamification is an emerging phenomenon that has been spotted in various business and social areas. While gamification is not necessarily implemented with the support of digital technologies, the diffusion of consumer electronics and mobile devices opened up plenty of opportunities for introducing game-like features to various activities. As more and more companies realize that games have important motivational and behavioral effects, an increased number of services may be gamified with the aim of increasing customer satisfaction, retention, and loyalty. Not surprisingly, there has been a growing interest towards gamification especially from the side of marketing agencies, and expectations is that gamification is on the rise (Burke, 2013, 2014).

Gamification has also stimulated various critiques about the methodological foundations, the practices, and the discourse of the approach. Deterding (2011) highlighted that much of gamification seems primarily concerned with the design of game mechanisms while being relatively little attentive to the "playfulness" of the gaming experience. Hamari and Eranti (2011) argued that excessive focus on extrinsic rewards (such as points, badges, etc.) results in detrimental effects to intrinsic motivation, creativity and performance, especially in the long run. Robertson (2010) condemned "pointsification" as the superficial tendency to add game-like features to activities without deeply understanding individuals' drivers to play a game.

The rise of gamification within business management and consulting circles has been exactly criticized because of the desultory attention on sound game design principles. Bogost (2011), for example, commented that "[…] Gamification is marketing bullshit, invented by consultants as a means to capture the wild, coveted beast that is videogames and to domesticate it for use in the grey, hopeless wasteland of big business, where bullshit already reigns anyway. […] The rhetorical power of the word "gamification" is enormous, and it does precisely what the bullshitters want: it takes games—a mysterious, magical, powerful medium that has captured the attention of millions of people—and it makes them accessible in the context of contemporary business". Provocatively, he proposed to substitute the term gamification with "exploitationware", that would better capture gamifiers' real intentions to capitalize on a cultural moment for the sake of attaining short-term gains.

When gamification is properly designed and implemented, however, it seems to hold the key to relevant effects on individual and organizational conducts. The gamification of an activity is akin to the introduction of a "persuasive technology", that is, of "an interactive product designed to change attitudes or behaviors or both by making a desired outcome easier to achieve" (Fogg, 2003: 32). Gamified activities can guide individuals conducts to follow a step-by-step process ("tunneling") that prescribes a very specific course of action and they can track individual actions and performance and feedback this information to the same users (in a "self-monitoring" style) and to others, with the effect that individuals are therefore subjected to a system of "surveillance" and social pressures. Points, badges, and other forms of extrinsic rewards contribute to the working of the persuasion "machinery" of gamification.

The central concern of this chapter has been with the question as to whether gamification can potential affect public services. A possible answer is to dismiss the scenario on the basis that the public sector is just "too serious" to incorporate any game-like feature in its organizational processes, and that gamification will remain a marketing fad that will modestly affect the most superficial and ephemeral aspects of business service delivery. Another possible answer, however, is that - as other managerial doctrines and practices in the past - gamification may find its way, to some extent at least, into the production and delivery of public services. Indeed, early experimentations with gamification in public spaces show that game-like features may have a positive effects on individual conducts. With some speculation, we could even figure out that gamified activities may result in desirable effects on individuals' effort to co-produce public services.

The prospect of gamifying part of public sector activities also poses some political and cultural issues. How desirable is to try and instill a sense of playfulness in the relationship between citizens and public service providers - and, relatedly, public authorities? What would it mean to suggest citizens to cast themselves - albeit on occasional basis - in the role of gamers, within a context of a gaming experience designed and offered by public authorities? Would gamification serve as yet another form of discipline, or would it foster further cynicism towards public authorities in the eyes of disillusioned citizens? During the last decades, the public sector has been variously affected by the rise of neo-liberal and managerialist ideas (e.g., the New Public Management doctrine; Hood, 1991; Barzelay, 2001) that entailed, among other effects, the emergence of a discourse around the construction of the citizens as the "consumer" of public services. The gamification of public services could introduce novel ways to characterize the citizens, that could also affect their identity and role within their relationship with public authorities.

REFERENCES

Ajzen, I. (1991). The theory of planned behavior. *Organizational Behavior and Human Decision Processes*, *50*(2), 179–211. doi:10.1016/0749-5978(91)90020-T

Alford, J. (1998). A Public Management Road Less Traveled: Clients as Co-producers of Public Services. *Australian Journal of Public Administration*, *57*(4), 128–137. doi:10.1111/j.1467-8500.1998.tb01568.x

Alford, J. (2000). Why Do Public-Sector Clients Coproduce? Toward a Contingency Theory. *Administration & Society*, *34*(1), 32–56. doi:10.1177/0095399702034001004

Alford, J. (2002). Defining the Client in the Public Sector: A Social-Exchange Perspective. *Public Administration Review*, *62*(3), 337–346. doi:10.1111/1540-6210.00183

Alford, J. (2009). *Engaging Public Sector Clients: From Service Delivery to Co-production*. New York: Palgrave Macmillan. doi:10.1057/9780230235816

Andersen, N. A. (2009). *Power at Play: The Relationships between Play, Work and Governance*. Palgrave Macmillan. doi:10.1057/9780230239296

Antin, J., & Churchill. (2011). *Badges in Social Media: A Social Psychological Perspective*. Paper presented at the Gamification Workshop, CHI2011. New York, NY.

Bartle, R. (2004). *Designing virtual worlds*. Indianapolis, IN: New Riders Publishing.

Barzelay, M. (2001). *The New Public Management: Improving Research and Policy Dialogue*. New York: Sage.

Bendapudi, N., & Leone. (2003). Psychological Implications of Customer Participation in Co-Production. *Journal of Marketing*, *67*(1), 14–28. doi:10.1509/jmkg.67.1.14.18592

Blau, P. M. (1964). *Exchange and power in social life*. New York: John Wiley.

Bogost, I. (2011). *Gamification is Bullshit: My position statement at the Wharton Gamification Symposium*. Retrieved from http://www.bogost.com/blog/gamification_is_bullshit.shtml

Bovaird, T., & Löffler. (2003). Evaluating the Quality of Public Governance: Indicators, Models and Methodologies. *International Review of Administrative Sciences*, *69*(3), 313–328. doi:10.1177/0020852303693002

Bovaird, T. (2007). Beyond Engagement and Participation – User and Community Co-production of Public Services. *Public Administration Review*, *67*(5), 846–860. doi:10.1111/j.1540-6210.2007.00773.x

Bovaird, T., & Löffler. (2007). Assessing the Quality of Local Governance: A Case Study of Public Services. *Public Money & Management*, *27*(4), 293–300. doi:10.1111/j.1467-9302.2007.00597.x

Brandsen, T., & Pestoff. (2006). Co-production, the Third Sector and the Delivery of Public Services: An Introduction. *Public Management Review*, *8*(4), 493–501. doi:10.1080/14719030601022874

Bruckman, A. (1999). *Can Educational Be Fun?* Paper presented at the Game Developer Conference. San Jose, CA.

Burawoy, M. (1979). *Manufacturing consent: Changes in the labor process under monopoly capitalism*. Chicago, IL: University of Chicago Press.

Burger-Helmchen, T., & Cohendet. (2011). User Communities and Social Software in the Video Game Industry. *Long Range Planning*, *44*, 317–343. doi:10.1016/j.lrp.2011.09.003

Burke, B. (2013, January 21). The Gamification of Business. *Forbes*.

Burke, B. (2014, April 4). Gartner Redefines Gamification. *Gartner*.

Cialdini, R. (2001). Harnessing the science of persuasion. *Harvard Business Review*, *79*(9), 72–79.

Cialdini, R. (2001). *Influence: Science and Practice* (4th ed.). Allyn & Bacon.

Clark, P. B., & Wilson. (1961). Incentive Systems: A Theory of Organizations. *Administrative Science Quarterly*, *6*, 129–166. doi:10.2307/2390752

Csikszentmihlyi, M. (2008). *Flow: The Psychology of Optimal Experience*. Harper Collins.

Deal & Key. (1998). *Corporate Celebration: Play, Purpose, and Profit at Work*. Berrett-Koehler.

Deci, E. L. (1975). *Intrinsic Motivation*. New York: Plenum. doi:10.1007/978-1-4613-4446-9

Deterding, S. Dixon, Khaled, & Nacke. (2011). *Gamification: Toward a Definition* Paper presented at the CHI 2011 Gamification Workshop. New York, NY.

Deterding, S. O'Hara, Sicart, Dixon, & Nacke. (2011). *Using Game Design Elements in Non-Gaming Contexts*. Paper presented at the CHI 2011 Gamification Workshop. New York, NY.

Deterding, S. (2012, July-August). Gamification: Designing for Motivation. *Forum: Social Mediator*, 14-17.

Deterding. (2011). *From game design elements to gamefulness: Defining gamification*. MindTrek.

Domínguez, A., Saenz-de-Navarrete, de-Marcos, Fernández-Sanz, Pagés, & Martínez-Herráiz. (2013). Gamifying Learning Experiences: Practical Implications and Outcomes. *Computers & Education*, *63*, 380–392. doi:10.1016/j.compedu.2012.12.020

Donovan, L. (2012). *The Use of Serious Games in the Corporate Sector: A State of the Art Report.* Dublin, Ireland: Learnovate Centre.

Dorling, A., & McCaffery, F. (2012). The Gamification of SPICE. In *Software Process Improvement and Capability Determination* (pp. 295–301). Academic Press. doi:10.1007/978-3-642-30439-2_35

Easley, D., & Ghosh. (2013). *Incentives, Gamification, and Game Theory: An Economic Approach to Badge Design.* Paper presented at EC'13. Philadelphia, PA.

Ekeh, P. P. (1974). *Social Exchange Theory: The Two Traditions.* London: Heinemann.

Festinger, L. (1954). A theory of social comparison processes. *Human Relations, 7*(2), 117–140. doi:10.1177/001872675400700202

Fineman, S. (2006). On Being Positive: Concerns and Counterpoints. *Academy of Management Review, 31*, 270–291. doi:10.5465/AMR.2006.20208680

Fishbein, M., & Ajzen. (1975). *Belief, attitude, intention, and behavior: An introduction to the theory and research.* Reading, MA: Addison-Wesley.

Fleming & Sturdy. (2011). 'Being yourself' in the electronic sweatshop: New forms of normative control. *Human Relations, 64*(2), 177–200. doi:10.1177/0018726710375481

Fleming. (2009). *Authenticity and the Cultural Politics of Work: New Forms of Informal Control.* Oxford University Press.

Fluegge. (2008). *Who Put the Fun in Functional? Fun at Work and its Effects on Job Performance.* (PhD thesis). University of Florida.

Flynn, N. (2012). *Public Sector Management.* London: SAGE.

Fogg, B. J. (2002). *Persuasive technology: Using computers to change what we think and do.* Ubiquity.

Fogg, B. J. (2009). *A behavior model for persuasive design.* Paper presented at Persuasive 2009, 4th International Conference on Persuasive Technology. Claremont, CA.

Fogg. (2003). *Persuasive Technology: Using Computers to Change What We Think and Do.* Morgan Kaufmann.

Fox, J., & Bailenson, J. N. (2009). Virtual self-modelling: The effects of vicarious reinforcement and identification on exercise behaviours. *Media Psychology, 12*, 1–25. doi:10.1080/15213260802669474

Fung, A. (2004). *Empowered Participation: Reinventing Urban Democracy.* Princeton, NJ: Princeton University Press.

Goldstein, N., Cialdini, R., & Griskevicius, V. (2008). A room with a viewpoint: using social norms to motivate environmental conservation in hotels. *The Journal of Consumer Research, 35*(3), 472–482. doi:10.1086/586910

Greenwich. (2001). *Fun and Gains: Motivate and Energize Staff with Workplace Games, Contests and Activities.* McGraw-Hill.

Gregerman. (2000). *Lessons from the Sandbox: Using the 13 Gifts of Childhood To Rediscover the Keys to Business Success.* McGraw-Hill.

Groh, F. (2012). Gamification: State of the Art, Definition and Utilization. In *Proceedings of the 4th Seminar on Research Trends in Media Informatics Institute of Media Informatics.* Ulm University.

Hamari, J. (2013). Transforming Homo Economicus into Homo Ludens: A Field Experiment on Gamification in a Utilitarian Peer-to-Peer Trading Service. *Electronic Commerce Research and Applications*, *12*, 236–245. doi:10.1016/j.elerap.2013.01.004

Hamari, J., & Järvinen, A. (2011). Building customer relationship through game mechanics in social games. In M. Cruz-Cunha, V. Carvalho, & P. Tavares (Eds.), *Business, Technological and Social Dimensions of Computer Games: Multidisciplinary Developments*. Hershey, PA: IGI Global. doi:10.4018/978-1-60960-567-4.ch021

Hamari, J., Koivisto, J., & Sarsa, H. (2014). Does Gamification Work? A Literature Review of Empirical Studies on Gamification. In *Proceedings of the 47th Hawaii International Conference on System Sciences*. IEEE.

Hamari & Eranti. (2011). Framework for designing and evaluating game achievements. In *Think Design Play: The fifth international conference of the Digital Research Association* (DIGRA). Hilversum, The Netherlands: DiGRA/Utrecht School of the Arts.

Hemsath & Yerkes. (1997). *301 Ways to Have Fun at Work*. Berrett-Koehler.

Hershfield, H. E., Goldstein, D. G., Sharpe, W. F., Fox, J., Yeykelis, L., Carstenson, L., & Bailenson, J. N. (2011). Increasing Saving Behavior Through Age-Progressed Renderings of the Future Self. *JMR, Journal of Marketing Research*, *48*, 23–37. doi:10.1509/jmkr.48.SPL.S23 PMID:24634544

Herzig, P. Ameling, & Schill. (2012). A Generic Platform for Enterprise Gamification. In *Proceedings of Joint Working Conference on Software Architecture & 6th European Conference on Software Architecture* (pp. 219-223). Academic Press.

Hienerth, C., Keinz, & Lettl. (2011). Exploring the Nature and Implementation Process of User-Centric Business Models. *Long Range Planning*, *44*, 344–374. doi:10.1016/j.lrp.2011.09.009

Hood, C. (1983). The Tools of Government. London: Basingstoke.

Hood, C. (1991). A Public Management for All Seasons. *Public Administration*, *69*, 3–19. doi:10.1111/j.1467-9299.1991.tb00779.x

Hood, C., Peters, & Wollmann. (1996). Sixteen Ways to Consumerize Public Services: Pick 'n Mix or Painful Trade-offs? *Public Money & Management*, *16*, 43–50. doi:10.1080/09540969609387944

Human Organization. (1959). Banana Time: Job Satisfaction and Informal Interaction. *Human Organization*, *18*, 158–168.

Huotari, K., & Hamari, J. (2012). Defining gamification: a service marketing perspective. In *Proceedings of the 16th International Academic MindTrek Conference*. Tampere, Finland: ACM Press.

Huotari & Hamari. (2011). *Gamification from the perspective of service marketing*. Paper presented at CHI 2011. New York, NY.

Jakobsson, M. (2011). The achievement machine: Understanding Xbox 360 achievements in gaming practices. *Game Studies*, *11*, 1.

Katz, M. L., & Shapiro, C. (1985). Network externalities, competition, and compatibility. *The American Economic Review*, *75*(3), 424–440.

Kinzie, M. B., & Joseph, D. R. D. (2008). Gender differences in game activity preferences of middle school children: Implications for educational game design. *Educational Technology Research and Development*, *56*, 643–663. doi:10.1007/s11423-007-9076-z

Lawley, E. (2012, July-August). Games as an Alternate Lens for Design. *Social Mediator*, 16-17.

Lin, C.-P., & Bhattacherjee, A. (2008). Elucidating individual intention to use interactive information technologies: The role of network externalities. *International Journal of Electronic Commerce*, *13*(1), 85–108. doi:10.2753/JEC1086-4415130103

Llagostera, E. (2012). On Gamification and Persuasion. In *Proceedings of SBGames 2012*. XISBGames.

Löffler, E. Parrado, Bovaird, & Van Ryzin. (2008). If you want to go fast, walk alone: If you want to go far, walk together: Citizens and the co-production of public services. Paris: Ministry of Budget, Public Finance and Public Services.

Lundin, Paul, & Christensen. (2000). *Fish! A Remark-able Way to Boost Morale and Improve Results*. Hyperion Books.

Lusch, R. F., & Vargo. (2006a). Service Dominant Logic: Reactions, Reflections and Refinements. *Marketing Theory*, *6*, 281–288. doi:10.1177/1470593106066781

Lusch, R. F., & Vargo. (2006b). *The Service-dominant Logic of Marketing: Dialog, Debate, and Directions*. New York: M. S. Sharpe.

Marschall, M. J. (2004). Citizen Participation in the Neighbourhood Context: A New Look at the Co-production of Local Public Goods. *Political Research Quarterly*, *57*(2), 231–244. doi:10.1177/106591290405700205

McGonigal, J. (2011). *Reality is Broken: Why Games Make Us Better and How They Can Change the World*. Penguin Press.

Mekler, E. Bruhlmann, Opwis, & Tuch. (2013). Disassembling Gamification: The Effects of Points and Meaning on User Motivation and Performance. In *Proceedings of CHI 2013: Changing Perspectives*, (pp. 1137-1142). Paris, France: ACM.

Mollick, E. & Rothbard. (2013). *Mandatory Fun: Gamification and the Impact of Games at Work* (The Wharton School Research Paper Series). http://dx.doi.org/10.2139/ssrn.2277103

Montola, Nummenmaa, Lucero, Boberg, & Korhonen. (2009). Applying game achievement systems to enhance user experience in a photo sharing service. In *Proceedings of the 13th International MindTrek Conference: Everyday Life in the Ubiquitous Era*. New York, NY: ACM.

Needham, C. (2007). Realising the Potential of Co-production: Negotiating improvements in public services. *Social Policy and Society*, *7*(2), 221–231.

Nelson, M. J. (2012). Soviet and American Precursors to the Gamification of Work. In *Proceedings of MindTrek 2012*. Tampere, Finland: ACM. doi:10.1145/2393132.2393138

NHS. (2011). *Breast Screening Programme Annual Review*. London: NHS.

Nicholson, S. (2012). A User-Centered Theoretical Framework for Meaningful Gamification. Paper Presented at Games+Learning+Society 8.0. Madison, WI.

Normann, R. (2002). *Services Management*. Chichester, UK: John Wiley & Sons.

Oinas-Kukkonen, H., & Harjumaa, M. (2009). Persuasive systems design: Key issues, process model, and system features. *Communications of the Association for Information Systems*, *24*(1), 28.

Oprescu, F., Jones, C., & Katsikitis, M. (2014). From games to gamified workplaces: From games to gamified workplaces. *Psychology (Savannah, Ga.)*, *5*(14).

Osborne, S. P. (Ed.). (2010). *The New Public Governance? Emerging Perspectives on the Theory and Practice of Public Governance*. London: Routledge.

Ostrom, E. (1996). Crossing the Great Divide: Co-production, Synergy and Development. *World Development*, *24*(6), 1073–1087. doi:10.1016/0305-750X(96)00023-X

Paharia, R. (2012, July-August). Gamification Means Amplifying Intrinsic Value. *Social Mediator*, 17.

Parks, R. B., Baker, Kiser, Oakerson, Ostrom, Ostrom, … Wilson. (1981). Consumers as Co-producers of Public Services: Some Economic and Institutional Considerations. *Policy Studies Journal: the Journal of the Policy Studies Organization*, *9*(7), 1001–1011. doi:10.1111/j.1541-0072.1981.tb01208.x

Perryer, C., Scott-Ladd, B., & Leighton, C. (2012). Gamification: Implications for workplace intrinsic motivation in the 21st century. *AFBE Journal*, 371-381.

Pestoff, V. (2006). Citizens and Co-Production of Welfare Services: Childcare in Eight European Countries. *Public Management Review*, *8*(4), 503–519. doi:10.1080/14719030601022882

Pestoff, V. (2012). Co-production and Third Sector Social Services in Europe—Some Crucial Conceptual Issues. In *New Public Governance, the Third Sector and Co-production* (pp. 13–34). London: Routledge.

Pestoff, V. Brandsen, & Verschuere (Eds.). (2012). New Public Governance, the Third Sector and Co-production. London: Routledge.

Piaget, J. (1960). General Problems of the Psychological Development of the Child. In *Discussion on Child Development* [). New York: International Universities Press.]. *Proceedings of the World Health Organization Study Group on Psychological Development of the Child*, *4*, 3–27.

Pink. (2009). *Drive: The surprising truth about what motivates us*. Riverhead Books.

Pralahad, C. K., & Ramaswamy. (2004). *The Future of Competition: Co-creating Unique Value with Customers*. Boston: Harvard Business School Press.

Raessens, J. (2006). Playful Identities, or the Ludification of Culture. *Games and Culture*, *1*(1), 52–57. doi:10.1177/1555412005281779

Reeves, B., & Read. (2009). *Total Engagement: Using Games and Virtual Worlds to Change the Way People Work and Business Compete*. Harvard Business School Press.

Rigby, S., & Ryan. (2011). *Glued to Games: How Video Games Draw Us In and Hold Us Spellbound*. Praeger.

Rosentraub, M. S., & Sharp. (1981). Consumers as Producers of Social Services: Coproduction and the Level of Social Services. *Southern Review of Public Administration*, *4*, 502–539.

Roy, D. (1952). Quota restriction and goldbricking in a machine shop. *American Journal of Sociology*, *57*, 427–442. doi:10.1086/221011

Ryan, R. M., & Deci. (2000). Self-determination theory and the facilitation of intrinsic motivation, social development, and well-being. *The American Psychologist*, *55*, 68–78. doi:10.1037/0003-066X.55.1.68 PMID:11392867

Sherman, R. (2007). *Class Acts: Service and Inequality in Luxury Hotels*. University of California Press.

Sung, H-Y., & Hwang. (2013). A Collaborative Game-Based Learning Approach to Improving Students' Learning Performance in Science Courses. *Computers & Education*, *63*, 43–51. doi:10.1016/j.compedu.2012.11.019

Vargo, S. L., & Lusch. (2004). Evolving to a New Dominant Logic for Marketing. *Journal of Marketing*, *68*, 1–17. doi:10.1509/jmkg.68.1.1.24036

Verschuere, B., Brandsen, & Pestoff. (2012). Co-production: The State of the Art in Research and the Future Agenda. *Voluntas: International Journal of Voluntary and Nonprofit Organizations*, 1-19.

Vygotsky, L. S. (1978). *Mind in society: The development of higher psychological processes.* Cambridge, MA: Harvard University Press.

Wang, H., & Sun. (2011). Game reward systems: Gaming experiences and social meanings. In C. Marinka, K. Helen, & W. Annika (Eds.), *Proceedings of the DiGRA 2011 Conference: Think design play.* DiGRA.

Werbach, K., & Hunter. (2012). *For the Win: How Game Thinking Can Revolutionize Your Business.* Philadelphia, PA: Wharton Digital Press.

Wikström, S. (1996). The Customer as Co-producer. *European Journal of Marketing*, *30*(4), 6–19. doi:10.1108/03090569610118803

Wilson, J. Q. (1973). *Political Organizations.* New York: Basic Books.

Xu, Y. (2011). *Literature Review on Web Application Gamification and Analytics* (CSDL Technical Report 11-05). CSDL.

Yee, N., Bailenson, & Ducheneaut. (2009). The Proteus effect: Implications of transformed digital self-representation on online and offline behavior. *Communication Research*, *36*(2), 285–312. doi:10.1177/0093650208330254

Zhu, M., Huang, & Contractor. (2013). Motivations for self-assembling into project teams. *Social Networks*, *35*(2), 251–264. doi:10.1016/j.socnet.2013.03.001

Zichermann, G., & Cunningham. (2011). *Gamification by Design: Implementing Game Mechanics in Web and Mobile Apps.* Sebastopol, CA: O'Reilly Media.

Chapter 9
The Use of Social Network Sites to Market E-Government to Citizens

María de Miguel Molina
Universitat Politècnica de València, Spain

Carlos Ripoll Soler
Universitat Politècnica de València, Spain

ABSTRACT

In this chapter, the authors explore the different literature that analyses the application of Social Network Sites (SNSs) in e-government to help government managers to improve citizens' communication and participation. The use of Web 2.0 tools is perceived as a new way of communication not only in the political arena but also on the government level to improve civic engagement, to coproduce public services, and to increase service personalization. Citizens still like traditional communication tools, and it is important not to overload them through SNSs. The authors show possible new trends for future analysis on the application of SNSs.

INTRODUCTION

The majority of governments today are using Social Networking Sites (SNSs) as a way to improve their relations with citizens. However, scholarship has paid more attention to the application of SNSs on the political than on the public administration level.

It is important for politicians to have an online presence (Jungherr, 2012); nevertheless, while electoral web campaigns are keen to adopt Web 2.0 technology, they sometimes lack a good design, which leads to limited interactivity (Lee, 2014).

For example, Vergeer, Hermans, & Sams (2013) showed that many candidates use SNS reluctantly and predominantly for electoral campaigning and only occasionally for continuous campaigning. That is, candidates normally use SNSs only for electoral purposes in the short/medium term but do not take all the possible profit of SNSs for the long term. Although the first degree networks of the candidates are frequently relatively small and

DOI: 10.4018/978-1-4666-3691-0.ch009

unconnected, these authors have observed that their second degree networks are quite extensive. This is an opportunity to be covered.

Moreover, the use of SNSs in the public administration environment has many facets to be explored. New trends such as geo-localization services, coproduction of public services, and civic engagement using SNSs need deeper attention.

BACKGROUND

Governance networks are those groups or networks of constant relationships between governments and civil society (business, associations, NGOs, and so on) that are mutually implicated in certain public policies. However, in the field of e-government, as a way to deliver information and services by the government through the Internet or other digital means, SNSs can play many different roles in the political process (De-Miguel-Molina & Ripoll-Soler, 2012). For example, SNSs can have different implications on Open Government (Nam, 2012). Those who value transactions with e-government have a positive attitude regarding Open Government and Government 2.0. On the other side, the use of SNSs contributes to positive attitudes towards Government 2.0 and general trust in the government.

Broadly speaking, SNSs could be a complementary communication tool for e-government, where citizens not only receive information but also can collaborate on generating it.

Web 2.0 Definition

If we define Web 2.0 as the online service generation based on networks that allow users to contribute to online contents as co-developers, the key of SNSs would be that they allow users to generate public profiles that collect personal data and information in order to provide tools with which others can interact, related to that published profile (AGPD & INTECO, 2009). In other terms, an SNS is a community of users who establish personal or professional relationships and who share knowledge and experiences. They are normally housed on open websites that are constantly under construction and that involve a group of people with common needs and interests coming together to exchange and strengthen their resources (ONTSI, 2009).

Acquisti and Gross (2006) defined, at a very basic level, an online social network as "an Internet community where individuals interact, often through profiles that (re)present their public persona (and their networks of connections) to others." Moreover, Boyd and Ellison (2008) put forth that SNSs are "web-based services that allow individuals to (1) construct a public or semi-public profile within a bounded system, (2) articulate a list of other users with whom they share a connection, and (3) view and traverse their list of connections and those made by others within the system."

For SNS businesses, the revenues come from all the users' information that allow advertisers to personalize efforts. After joining an SNS, an individual answers a series of questions. The profile is generated using the answers to these questions, and most SNSs also encourage users to upload a profile photo or add multimedia content (Boyd & Ellison, 2008). We could then separate SNS contents into two categories: those related to relationships (friendship, photos, and message exchanges) and those related to entertainment and information (participation and opinion) (Campos, 2008).

Facebook and Twitter are two of the most relevant SNSs. Ellison, Steinfield, & Lampe reviewed in 2007 the evolution of Facebook from its creation in 2004. But seven years later, in January 2014, Facebook has reported over 1 billion registered users. The site includes the possibility of creating groups, even by institutions. For example, a city council can create its own group and interact with its citizens in a different way than just providing a website. Facebook also allows an advertisement system that can deliver messages to very specific target groups. Facebook also allows users to create complete profiles. In fact, it is the SNS with the most retrieved information from its users (Stutzman, 2006). But Facebook users' behaviour has changed from 2006 to 2012. Although users have decreased the amount of personal data in their public profiles, at the same time they have increased the amount and scope of personal information that they reveal privately to other connected profiles, and thereby also to the "silent listeners" on the network: Facebook itself, third-party apps, and (indirectly) advertisers (Stutzman, Gross, & Acquisti, 2012).

Twitter is another SNS, this one based on micro-blogging to connect with friends, family, or co-workers. Its main characteristic is that users can instantly deliver messages (up to 140 characters) to other users who are willing to receive the message. According to Lenhart and Fox (2009), 19% of Internet users actively participate in Twitter. Zhao and Rosson (2009) also classified Twitter as a micro-blog that provides a communication channel for people to broadcast information that they likely would not share through other existing channels (e.g., email, phone, IM, or weblogs). Micro-blogging has become popular quite quickly, raising its potential for serving as a new informal communication medium at work, providing a variety of impacts on collaborative work (e.g., enhancing information sharing, building common ground, and sustaining a feeling of connectedness among colleagues). Users declare the people they are interested in following and then they receive notifications when someone they follow has posted a new message.

However we cannot think of citizens just as individual consumers as in a private organization (transactional relationships) but as social citizens in a network relationship (Osborne, McLaughlin, & Chew, 2010). Maybe some public services can operate in a market sector, but the same cannot be said for all public services. Moreover traditional marketing cannot be sufficient for a governance model, where the concept of relationship market-

ing arises for studying three levels of marketing activity: micro (organisation-consumer), macro (organisation-organization), and meso (organisation-society) (Osborne et al., 2010). We think these different marketing perspectives are not separate. We can take into account various stakeholders when offering a new service; however, we might need different marketing strategies to reach them. A government needs to properly understand its citizens' characteristics, along with other factors that generate satisfaction, before it can develop an effective e-government adoption strategy (Kumar, Mukerji, Butt, & Persaud, 2007).

In this sense, SNSs open a wider perspective where citizens can have a deeper participation if the government uses an appropriate Citizen Relation Management (CRM) tool. Utilizing Web 2.0-based tools, citizens can participate both in the processes of creating and crafting web-based content and in enhancing the service design (Hui & Hayllar, 2010).

That is, SNSs could serve a double purpose in e-government by

- Providing a better understanding of citizens' needs through data processing.
- Allowing for direct interaction with citizens by means of immediate interaction or by including ads.

HOW MARKETING HAS CHANGED AND REACHED A 3.0 APPROACH

Marketing concepts have evolved through time as we can see in Table 1. They seek more and more to personalise messages and to create as much value as possible, even with the participation of consumers/citizens:

But many governments currently only have a presence on the Internet that is mainly based on websites that perform one-way communication from government to citizen or what Reddick (2005) calls "the supply-side perspective." On

Table 1. Evolution of marketing concept. Author's own adapted from Kotler and Kartajaya (2011).

Evolution	Concepts	Marketing 1.0	Marketing 2.0	Marketing 3.0
Years 50-60	Objective	Product	Consumer	Values for society
Years 70-90	Base	Development (marketing mix)	Differentiation, positioning (strategy, special marketing, e-marketing)	Values, value creation (RSC, co-creation, social networks)
XXI century	Interactions	Transactions	Relations	Collaboration

the opposite end, we have the demand-side perspective that considers the actual requirements of information coming from citizens. These actual demands should be transformed into customized content to better reach citizens.

Governments usually adapt business-oriented communication solutions to their own necessities. In this sense, Kotler and Lee (2006) proposed a list of several categories that governments can use to establish communication channels with their citizens. Moreover each category could be divided into offline and online tools (See Table 2).

Leskovec, Adamic, & Huberman (2006) detected that "consumers [have shown] an increasing resistance to traditional forms of advertising such as TV or newspaper ads." This fact has forced organizations to find alternative communication strategies from traditional marketing. Thus online marketing has become an alternative where the use of viral marketing has also been tried successfully. Combining the "offline world" with the "online world" is one of the key elements that governments should consider in establishing better communication with citizens. Traditional approaches should not be completely discarded (Teerling & Pieterson, 2009), but an intelligent movement towards online alternatives as mutually reinforcing elements with offline approaches will benefit in the short term. The offline world is there, and we mainly know its rules, but the online world is becoming central to every aspect of our existence and has a lot of potential to take advantage of.

Kleinberg (2008) stated that "the past decade has witnessed a coming-together of the technological networks that connect computers on the Internet and the social networks that have linked humans for millennia." Those networks are capturing our different styles of communication and remaining governed by our principles of human social interactions. Communication and interaction are a main aspect of the nature of human beings. Thanks to online tools, those principles can now be observed, measured, and quantified at amazing levels never seen before. The data generated by a single online social network can easily help to give an accurate profile of every individual.

A new approach that promotes citizens' active participation has been needed for a long time. Citizens should evolve from service consumers to service "prosumers," leveraging their role to an active participation. Bruns (2009) defined the "prosumer" in the mass media age as a particularly well-informed, and therefore both particularly critical and particularly active, consumer. Tapscott and Williams (2006) declared that "in the new prosumer-centric paradigm, customers want a genuine role in designing the products of the future." The same can be applied to e-government where citizens are willing to have an active role beyond their punctual participation in any elections. For e-government is an important departure point to involve citizens on designing services offered adapted to their actual needs.

Due to the high interrelation between offline and online world, establishing new digital mar-

Table 2. Traditional marketing vs. online marketing. Author's own adapted from Kotler and Lee (2006).

Category	Offline	Online
Advertising	Television, radio, newspapers, magazines, ads on backs of tickets and receipts, ads at theatres using still shots and videos, billboards, bus boards, bus shelter displays, subways, taxis, vinyl wrap cars and buses, sports events, kiosks, restroom stalls, airport billboard and signage.	Internet, Adsense, Adwords, search engine marketing, online newspapers, online magazines, ipTV, ads on mobile applications
Public relations	Stories on television and radio, articles in newspapers and magazines, videos.	Blogging, articles in online newspapers and magazines, YouTube videos, podcasts, Internet radio
Special events	Community meetings, demonstrations/ exhibits, fairs and tours, face-to-face meetings from online communities.	
Direct marketing	Postal mail, telemarketing, catalogues	Newsletters, customized emails, RSS feeds
Printed materials	Forms, brochures, newsletters, flyers, calendars, posters, envelope messages, booklets, and static stickers.	
Special promotional items	Clothing: t-shirts, baseball hats, diapers, bibs; temporary-natured items: coffee sleeves, bar coasters and napkins, buttons, temporary tattoos, balloons, stickers, fortune cookies; functional items: key chains, flashlights, refrigerator magnets, water bottles, litterbags, pens and pencils, bookmarks, book covers, notepads, tote bags, mascots, cell phone cases.	Online discounts, free trial periods
Signage and displays	Road signs, signs and posters on government property or property regulated by the government.	
Personal communication channels	Face-to-face meetings and presentations, workshops, seminars, training sessions, word of mouth.	Word of web, blogs, chats, forums, Twitter
Popular media	public art, songs, scripts in movies, television and radio programs, comic books and comic strips, playing cards and other games.	

keting channels will help to better understand what and why people do things. Those channels are based on the success of the Web 2.0. For e-government, the main advantage is that those channels foster an effective communication with citizens. Additionally, Osimo (2008) remarked key benefits of using Web 2.0 tools on e-government (See Table 3).

But governments should not forget that these communication tools are better used as unobtru-sive marketing channels to increase government e-service usage, without negatively affecting citizens' current level of satisfaction with service delivery (Teerling & Pieterson, 2009).

SNS and Government: New Trends

Although the studies that provided results are still scarce, we have found some new trends in the analysis of governments' SNS usage.

Table 3. Benefits and applications of Web 2.0 tools to e-government. Author's own adapted from Osimo (2008).

Benefits	Examples (UK)
Simple and user-oriented	TheStraightChoice.org allows a user to follow citizenship participation on general elections
Transparent and accountable	The service writetothem.org allows one to contact different stakeholders
Participative and inclusive	Fixmystreet.org allows users to report, view, or discuss local problems
Joined up and networked	Pledgebank.com helps users get things done, especially those that require several people

From a political point of view, SNSs can serve as tools for increasing civic engagement (Macnamara, Sakinofsky, & Beattie 2012). They can help encourage disengaged citizens and youth to engage or re-engage in democratic participation on an ongoing basis.

Moreover, SNSs can be used for public service coproduction (Wigand, 2012). While user coproduction focuses on the relationship between government agencies and individual users, networked coproduction puts the emphasis on the relationship between government and communities of citizens (both users and non-users of the specific service provided) (Meijer, 2011).

Finally, while SNSs can be used in general, they can also be joined with other tools to improve public service value. In this sense, Ganapati (2011) has studied the use of Public Participation Geographic Information Systems (PPGISs) for improving traffic and transit, volunteered geographic information, and customer relationship management. However, limited use of PPGISs for higher levels of participation, such as decision making, has been found, and barriers to using them seem less technological and more institutional.

Concretely, Ganapati (2011) highlighted how PPGISs have enabled local governments to tap into Web services such as Google Maps to provide traffic and transit information. Google Transit is the prime example of such use. Moreover, local agencies can tap into local knowledge to enhance participation for various purposes. PPGISs have been used in customer relationship management (CRM), for example, to help citizens report local problems online, which reports are then routed to the appropriate departments to address.

However, these represent uses in lower levels of public participation and few local governments have used PPGISs in decision-making processes. As e-government scholars have argued (De-Miguel-Molina, 2009), technology adoption is shaped within an organizational and institutional context. Hence, the possibilities of PPGISs will need to be examined within the context in which public participation is elicited.

As Mergel and Schweik (2012) pointed out, although SNSs let information flow within government, across government agencies, and between the government and the public, they are often highly restricted through regulations and specific reporting structures. For this reason, some transformative organizational, technological, and informational challenges will also be necessary ahead, which might lead to resistance to that change.

Some scholars are analysing the trend of citizens' participation through SNS, and we think these studies are often more focused on a political rather than on a managerial and marketing perspective. As we underlined (De-Miguel-Molina & Ripoll-Soler, 2012), many governments will still need realistic marketing plans with a previous network analysis to know their citizens and their necessities. Without this point of view, they would have difficulty reaching effectiveness and efficiency in the delivery of public services through e-government and, moreover, to increase participation through SNSs as tools for new e-governance.

On the other hand, the use of Web 2.0 communication tools is still very recent, so future research will be necessary to measure the efficacy and efficiency of those tools in real cases. These studies could also allow us to compare the use of e-government in different countries and, moreover, the use of it in a country's different administration levels. The first issue will be especially interesting while comparing developed and less-developed countries or democratic and non-democratic countries.

We think that many perspectives in the study of e-government, apart from ours, focused on marketing to citizens, will increase in the future years, and it will be necessary to develop multidisciplinary analyses to enrich the examination of it.

CONCLUSION

We have provided a marketing point of view to the interesting publication on "Digital Public Administration and E-Government in Developing Nations: Policy and Practice," and we have proposed that governments use Web 2.0 communication tools in order to increase citizen participation. But, first of all, governments at any administrative level have to notice that "the success of e-Government efforts" as Kumar et al. (2007) pointed out," depends, to a great extent, on how well the targeted users for such services, citizens in general, make use of them."

As we suggested, social network sites are online tools that can enrich the communication between governments and their citizens and, if possible, their participation in order to reach a "governance" status that, at present, seems to be the goal of many governments.

As we have explained, Web 2.0 could give governments new ways of interaction with citizens to increase their citizens' participation. Additionally, they give us the opportunity to collect very useful reports on website use. However, these facts do not lead to forgetting the traditional tools but to a mixing of the offline and online worlds to cover a wider range of citizens. Moreover, we should notice that e-government is developed in the online world so that its users can be easily reached through those Web 2.0 tools if we apply search engine optimization.

Furthermore, SNSs as a new way to communicate with citizens will need more analysis in the future to see if they have contributed to the governments' objectives. At this point, web analytics can be a powerful source of information to use by governments to assess their management decisions in e-government.

Beyond the benefits that a higher interaction with citizens can have, governments should also consider that these tools are used to define a new kind of society, a Network Society (Castells, 2009), in which new forms of self-organizational processes appear. In this context governments "fear to lose the control of information and communication in which power has always been rooted" (Castells, 2005), so a new way wave of democratization of communication should always be considered when defining Web 2.0 strategies.

If we would like to reach all our citizens, we should take into account digital literacy, which takes into account the groups of people who do not have access to the online world or who are not prepared to use it. Therefore governments will need, at the same time, to improve policies to help these citizens.

REFERENCES

Acquisti, A., & Gross, R. (2006). Imagined communities: Awareness, information sharing, and privacy on the Facebook. In P. Golle & G. Danezis (Eds.), *Proceedings of 6th Workshop on Privacy Enhancing Technologies* (pp. 36–58). Cambridge, UK: Robinson College.

AGPD (Spanish Data Protection Agency) and INTECO. (2009). *Study on data privacy and security in the Social Networks*. Retrieved from https://www.agpd.es/portalweb/canaldocumentacion/publicaciones/common/Estudios/estudio_inteco_aped_120209_redes_sociales.pdf

Boyd, D., & Ellison, N. (2008). Social Network Sites: Definition, History and Scholarship. *Journal of Computer-Mediated Communication, 13*(1), 210–230. doi:10.1111/j.1083-6101.2007.00393.x

Bruns, A. (2009). From Prosumer to Produser: Understanding User-Led Content Creation. In *Proceedings of Transforming Audiences 2009*. London: Academic Press.

Campos Freire, F. (2008). Las redes sociales trastocan los modelos de los medios de comunicación tradicionales. *Revista Latina de Comunicación Social, 63*(2), 287–293.

Castells, M. (2005). The Network Society: From Knowledge to Policy. In *The Network Society: From Knowledge to Policy* (pp. 3–22). Washington, DC: Center for Transatlantic Relations.

Castells, M. (2009). *The rise of the network society: The information age*. Chichester, UK: Wiley-Blackwell. doi:10.1002/9781444319514

De-Miguel-Molina, M. (2009). E-Government in Spain: An Analysis of the Right to Quality E-Government. *International Journal of Public Administration, 33*(1), 1–10. doi:10.1080/01900690903178454

De-Miguel-Molina, M., & Ripoll-Soler, C. (2012). Marketing e-government to citizens. In *From Government to E-Governance: Public Administration in the Digital Age* (pp. 75–92). Hershey, PA: IGI Global. doi:10.4018/978-1-4666-1909-8.ch006

Ellison, N., Steinfield, C., & Lampe, C. (2007). The Benefits of Facebook Friends: Social Capital and College Students' Use of Online Social Network Sites. *Journal of Computer-Mediated Communication, 12*(4), 1143–1168. doi:10.1111/j.1083-6101.2007.00367.x

Ganapati, S. (2011). Uses of Public Participation Geographic Information Systems Applications in E-Government. *Public Administration Review, 71*, 425–434. doi:10.1111/j.1540-6210.2011.02226.x

Hui, G., & Hayllar, M. R. (2010). Creating Public Value in E-Government: A Public-Private-Citizen Collaboration Framework in Web 2.0. *Australian Journal of Public Administration, 69*, 120–131. doi:10.1111/j.1467-8500.2009.00662.x

Jungherr, A. (2012). Online Campaigning in Germany: The CDU Online Campaign for the General Election 2009 in Germany. *German Politics, 21*, 317–340. doi:10.1080/09644008.2012.716043

Kleinberg, J. (2008). The Convergence of Social and Technological Networks. *Communications of the ACM, 51*(11), 66–72. doi:10.1145/1400214.1400232

Kotler, P., & Kartajaya, S. (2011). *Marketing 3.0*. Madrid: LID.

Kotler, P., & Lee, N. (2006). *Marketing in the public sector*. Upper Saddle River, NJ: Wharton School Publishing.

Kumar, V., Mukerji, B., Butt, I., & Persaud, A. (2007). Factors for Successful e-Government Adoption: A Conceptual Framework. *The Electronic. Journal of E-Government, 5*(1), 63–76.

Lee, B. (2014). Window Dressing 2.0: Constituency-Level Web Campaigns in the 2010 UK General Election. *Politics, 34*, 45–57. doi:10.1111/1467-9256.12029

Lenhart, A., & Fox, S. (2009). *Twitter and status updating*. Washington, DC: Pew Internet & American Life Project.

Leskovec, J., Adamic, L., & Huberman, B. (2006). The Dynamics of Viral Marketing. In *Proceedings of the 7th ACM Conf. on Electronic Commerce* (pp. 228-237). ACM.

Macnamara, J., Sakinofsky, P., & Beattie, J. (2012). E-electoral Engagement: How Governments Use Social Media to Engage Voters. *Australian Journal of Political Science*, *47*, 623–639. doi:10.1080/1 0361146.2012.731491

Meijer, A. J. (2011). Networked Coproduction of Public Services in Virtual Communities: From a Government-Centric to a Community Approach to Public Service Support. *Public Administration Review*, *71*, 598–607. doi:10.1111/j.1540-6210.2011.02391.x

Mergel, I. A., & Schweik, M. (2012). The Paradox of the Interactive Web in the U.S. Public Sector. In E. Downey, & M. A. Jones (Eds.), *Public Service, Governance and Web 2.0 Technologies: Future Trends in Social Media* (pp. 266–289). Hershey, PA: IGI Global. doi:10.4018/978-1-4666-0071-3.ch017

Nam, T. (2012). Citizens' attitudes toward Open Government and Government 2.0. *International Review of Administrative Sciences*, *78*, 346–368. doi:10.1177/0020852312438783

ONTSI (Spanish Telecommunications and Information Society Observatory). (2009). *White Paper on Digital Contents in Spain 2008*. Retrieved from http://observatorio.red.es/contenidos-digitales/articles/id/2662/libro-blanco-los-contenidos-digitales-espana-2008.html

Osborne, S. P., McLaughlin, K., & Chew, C. (2010). Relationship Marketing, relational capital and the governance of public services delivery. In S. P. Osborne (Ed.), *The New Public Governance?* (pp. 185–199). New York: Routledge.

Osimo, D. (2008). *Web 2.0 in government: Why and how? (JRC Scientific and Technical Reports)*. European Commission.

Reddick, C. (2005). Citizen interaction with e-government: From the streets to servers? *Government Information Quarterly*, *22*, 38–57. doi:10.1016/j.giq.2004.10.003

Stutzman, F. (2006). An Evaluation of Identity-Sharing Behavior in Social Network Communities. In *Proceedings of the 2006 iDMA and IMS Code Conference*. International Digital and Media Arts Journal.

Stutzman, F., Gross, R., & Acquisti, A. (2012). Silent Listeners: The Evolution of Privacy and Disclosure on Facebook. *Journal of Privacy and Confidentiality*, *4*(2), 7–41.

Tapscott, D., & Williams, D. (2006). *Wikinomics: How mass collaboration changes everything*. New York: Portfolio, Penguin.

Teerling, M. L., & Pieterson, W. (2010). Multi-channel marketing: An experiment on guiding citizens to the electronic channels. *Government Information Quarterly*, *27*, 98–107. doi:10.1016/j.giq.2009.08.003

Vergeer, M., Hermans, L., & Sams, S. (2013). Online social networks and micro-blogging in political campaigning: The exploration of a new campaign tool and a new campaign style. *Party Politics*, *19*, 477–501. doi:10.1177/1354068811407580

Wigand, D. L. (2012). Communication and Collaboration in a Web 2.0 World. In E. Downey, & M. A. Jones (Eds.), *Public Service, Governance and Web 2.0 Technologies: Future Trends in Social Media* (pp. 1–18). Hershey, PA: IGI Global. doi:10.4018/978-1-4666-0071-3.ch001

Zaho, D., & Rosson, M. (2009). How and Why People Twitter: The Role that Microblogging Plays in Informal Communication at Work. In *Proceedings of the ACM International Conference on Supporting Groupworth* (pp. 243-252). New York: ACM Press.

KEY TERMS AND DEFINITIONS

E-Government: Delivery of information and services by the Government through the Internet or other digital means.

Governance Networks: Those groups or networks of constant relationships between Governments and civil society (business, associations, NGOs and so on) that are mutually implicated in certain public policies.

Micro-Blog: Communication tool to broadcast information immediately through a SNS.

Search Engine Optimization (SEO): Managing an organization website in order to make it easily classified and located by search engines.

Social Network Sites (SNS): Online services that allow users to generate a public profile which collect personal data and information in order to provide tools to interact with other users related to that published profile.

Web 2.0: From many different definitions, for our goal, we could define it as the new online services generation based on networks that allow users to contribute to online contents as co-developers.

Section 2

Evidence:
Case Studies and Issues of E−Government in Practice and Reality

Chapter 10
Articulating Wider Smartphone Emerging Security Issues in the Case of M–Government in Turkey

Ronan de Kervenoael
Sabanci University, Turkey & Aston Business School, UK

Vasileios Yfantis
Ionian University, Greece

ABSTRACT

For the last several years, mobile devices and platform security threats, including wireless networking technology, have been top security issues. A departure has occurred from automatic anti-virus software based on traditional PC defense: risk management (authentication and encryption), compliance, and disaster recovery following polymorphic viruses and malware as the primary activities within many organizations and government services alike. This chapter covers research in Turkey as a reflection of the current market – e-government started officially in 2008. This situation in an emerging country presents the current situation and resistances encountered while engaging with mobile and e-government interfaces. The authors contend that research is needed to understand more precisely security threats and most of all potential solutions for sustainable future intention to use m-government services. Finally, beyond m-government initiatives' success or failure, the mechanisms related to public administration mobile technical capacity building and security issues are discussed.

ICT IN PUBLIC ADMINISTRATION

Given the increasingly multi-level nature of service-driven digital economies, management innovation in public sector, understood as new practices and processes intended to further public administration's goals, requires examining the critical role of mobile technologies towards improving IT and people congruence in the delivery of government digital strategy. The issue of Information Communication Technology (ICT thereafter) has become fundamental in debates concerning the

DOI: 10.4018/978-1-4666-3691-0.ch010

future role and shape of governments (Kushchu, 2007; Kushchu & Kuscu, 2003; Avgerou, 2000; Garson, 2006a; Jorgensen & Klay, 2007; West, 2007) and in particular aspects regarding security are now topping the agenda. Cyber threats, security breaches, hacking are regular headlines in the media and an increasingly acute issue on mobile platforms. As mobility becomes more pervasive, these words have become engrained in our work/life culture. Governments across the globe, but particularly in the emerging market need to grapple with how to build both secure and mobile-enabled infrastructures. While mobile technology has become pervasive in emerging markets, security breach is also becoming a concern that is slowing or preventing citizens' engagement. As such, Turkey, like many other emerging markets, has had a mixed success history with large ICT projects and security in particular. Empirically, many studies have shown the importance of ICT in public administration activities ranging from: overall digital strategies (Kahraman et al., 2007; Ferguson, 2001), impact of e-culture on governments (Hazlett & Hill, 2003), m-government policy issues (Yildiz, 2007; Lam, 2005), service architecture (Sharma & Gupta, 2004; Abramowicz et al., 2006), e-governance (Saxena, 2005; Stahl, 2005; Holliday & Kwok, 2004) to a range of e-government models (Heeks, 2002). While most studies recognize the positive effects of technological development on government service delivery, some also point out traditional concerns regarding, the equity of provision across the entire population and different understanding of the role of the state in society, conflict with the legal system (Moe, 1994) and with anticipation capabilities towards providing services that are needed current and future (Reddick, 2005; Millard, 2006). Yet very few are currently analyzing and discussing the specific issue of security threats (Kurbanoglu, 2004).

In the USA (2014), Cisco and Mobile Work Exchange released findings from a self-assessment tool that highlight some interesting statistics.

- On mobile devices, 31 percent use a public Wi-Fi connection and 25 percent do not set passwords.
- 6 percent of government employees who use a mobile device for work say they have lost or misplaced their phone.
- Despite the Federal Digital Government Strategy, more than one in four government employees have not received mobile security training from their agencies.
- Only 53 percent of government agencies require employees to register their mobile devices with the IT department v.

In spite of the above facts, many analyses of m-government point towards the fact that in practice very little is done both at the government and more importantly at individual citizen level to inform, provide solutions, and remedy the increasing security threat issues. Yet, understanding the nature of the threats associated with e-mobility and the methods to limit exposure to mobile cyber crime has become paramount to any m-government strategy. This, together with a shift in consumer lifestyle towards mobile ICTs, underlined the need to re-consider the meanings of mobility, m-government and m-security in the context of emerging markets and in particular Turkey. Amid this nascent research agenda, in this chapter, we identify three on-going gaps in the literature.

- Firstly, we unpack the understanding of mobility by citizens in emerging markets in view if increasing security threats.
- Secondly, most research tends to remain at a macro - country level rather than investigating everyday expectations faced by citizens and civil servants regarding the meaning of security threats.
- Thirdly, despite some exceptions in the literature, the impact of security on m-technologies in public administration's ICT is not widely considered by researchers.

This chapter reviews the post-launch e-government strategies from 2008-2014, challenges and opportunities of m-government, considering a citizens' perspective as well as public administration organizations' applications through a qualitative analysis of the media (TV, Radio, Press) in Turkey (De kervenoael et al, 2010). This work then considers how macro-opportunities and mobile technology expectations are shaping the nascent provision of m-government security. In so doing, the chapter aims to intensify the understanding of mobility and public administration market driven initiatives in emerging markets and the potential supporting role for m-technologies despite increasing security threats.

MOBILITY AND MOBILE PHONES PENETRATION

The migration of populations between places, is a phenomenon which raises the question of how people will access their communication resources from any place and time. Communication acts as a medium of transferring knowledge and improving the status of the information society. The adjustment of communication practices and behaviours is, furthermore, a complicated situation as a wide variety of behavior exists in different segments in the population. While Smartphone usage is nearly ubiquitous in Turkey, mobile phone and mobile internet usage are taking far greater roles in digital activity among consumers of all ages—and uptake is poised for further growth. Gen X internet users are avid consumers of online content. They typically use social networking sites and video sites via mobile devices. Millennials take online activity up a notch with increased intensity and frequency of usage. Native Internet generation is expected to be fully fluent on multiple platform and devices. In Turkey the Fathit education project, initiated in 2010, will offer tablet computers to students and smart boards technologies will be deployed in all classrooms (TodayZaman, 2014).

One key issue is the standadisation and spread in the the changing environment of the appropriate technologies in order to minimize the barriers and increase engagement. For example certain areas of Istanbul now possess free Wifi access (Huriyetdaily, 2014).

Regarding users, four traditional definitions of mobility are often analysed, (i) A traditional perspective is based around the debate of citizen inclusion and exclusion in public life. Recurring sub-themes of these studies are linked to the governance debate (Heeks, 2001), voice of the civil society, transparency and democracy arguments; (ii) A subsequent view of mobility is often centered around geographical mobility ranging from (a) Inter-jurisdictional mobility reflecting civil servants' varieties of occupational groups' abilities to grow in their careers in different locations; to (b) The relative alignment of service provision, skills and technological intensity; and (c) citizens to access equal competences and service provision. (iii) A further issue relates to m-government as conducive regardless of its success or failure to overall ICT capability building; finally mobility also reflects (iv) lifestyle mobility whereas m-government is necessary to maximize government utility within overall society consumptions. M-government ought to be perceived as "leading the trend towards a ubiquitous and pervasive living environment enabling individuals and organizations to communicate and perform specific tasks anytime and anywhere" (Kushchu et al., 2007 p.135).

Regarding technologies, four basic concepts of mobility are traditionally reviewed in the literature including (i) device mobility, (ii) user mobility, (iii) service mobility, and (iv) session mobility i.e. real time decision. Device mobility deals with the continued access to services while being spatially mobile, that is, moving from one physical location to another. User mobility presents the location-and device independent service access. The mobile phone network, which is utilizing the subscriber identification module (SIM) as a means of user identification in the network is a common example. Service mobility refers to the service delivery regardless of device or user specific settings. Civil servants outside their official setting deliver on the go services. For example, during a visit at home by social services, the individual citizen record is updated as in situ . Finally, session mobility describes the capability of starting, pausing and resuming a user session while switching between devices and/or services in real time.

In other words, mobility commands control over economic resources such as the ability to access greater sources of money and accumulate assets. In turn, mobility enhances cultural social capital by allowing individual to reach a wider group membership, relationships, and networks of influence. Furthermore, mobility is shaping cultural capital towards a post modern society based on global knowledge. Mobility needs to be considered within a dynamic continuum, whereby individual citizens regularly reassess their specific mobility constraints within the given context. Absolute vs relative mobility provides a true reflection in-situs of users practices. Indeed, in emerging market situation, it is important to remember that other macro-societal factors such as gender, race, ethic, and culture create de-facto boundaries for mobility and access to e-government (De Kervenoael et al., 2010).

The complexity of the mobility issue has triggered the invention of new tools for the establishment of communication between people. The most important technological artifact in emerging market condition worldwide has been the rapid penetration of mobile phone and in particular Smartphone. Mobile cellular subscriptions are growing at exponential rate. See Tables 1 and 2 (ITU, 2013):

The future predictions for the mobile communications are positive: Ericsson predicts that in 2019 there will be 9.4 billion mobile subscriptions in the world and 60 percent of them, about 5.6 billion, will be related to a Smartphone (Fitchard, 2013; Heggestuen, 2013). At the end of 2013, the Smartphone penetration have raised from 5% of the global population in 2009, to 22% in 2013. On average, every nine people on earth now own at least one mobile phone.

Table 1. Mobile-cellular subscriptions

	Millions								
	2005	2006	2007	2008	2009	2010	2011	2012	2013
Developed	992	1.127	1.243	1.325	1.383	1.418	1.475	1.538	1.600
Developing	1.213	1.618	2.125	2.705	3.257	3.901	4.487	4.872	5.235
World	2.205	2.745	3.368	4.030	4.640	5.320	5.962	6.411	6.835

Table 2. Active mobile-broadband subscriptions

	Millions								
	2005	2006	2007	2008	2009	2010	2011	2012	2013
Developed	N/A	N/A	225	336	450	529	683	788	934
Developing	N/A	N/A	43	86	165	249	472	768	1.162
World	N/A	N/A	268	422	615	778	1.155	1.556	2.096

FROM E TO M-GOVERNMENT: TURKEY

In order to establish a better understanding of mobility and technology in public administration, we summarily present the specific situation of Turkey. Table 3 presents a summary of the basic levels of m-government. Table 4 then shows that while not last, Turkey is finding it difficult to keep up with the pace of e-government worldwide. Table 5 presents an overview and ranking aginst other of the different service stages. While Table 6 shows World e-Government Development Rankings over the last few years with a clear indication that Turkey is descending in the ranking.

Seven highly abstract topics are prioritized by the Turkish government (Resmi Gazete, 2006): (i) Social transition towards "equal ICT opportunities for all" which involves enabling citizens to effectively use ICT in their daily lives as well as businesses in order to increase social and economic benefits, (ii) Penetration of ICT to all enterprises through "competitive advantage for all" which supports SME's to own computers and have Internet access; hence, enabling the emergence of e-commerce, (iii) Citizen focused government services "provision of high quality public services" with the purpose of improving quality of services provided by government through the utilization of ICT (i.e., receipt date of legal documents, information process levels, request for additional immediate actions and documents) especially in services where demand is high, (iv) Modernization in public administration by "ICT supported reforms in public administration", which constitutes a reform for the entrenched deterministic view of civil services. Moreover, formation of e-government via support of ICT that prioritizes productivity and citizen satisfaction in a compatible fashion with the environment in Turkey is the ultimate goal sought. By prioritizing (v) a globally competitive IT Industry, government aims to support R&D in the IT sector and to enhance its international competitiveness. Yet a larger context needs to be constructed for the ICT and understood from that perspective. Another priority set by the government is the (vi) Competitive, diffused and cheap communication infrastructure and services through "high quality, and cheap wideband access for all". This initiative aims to track the usefulness and impact of the broader social context on e-government opportunities (i.e., pricing, private access). By promoting better infrastructure in telecommunications it's aimed to offer high speed and reliable Internet access to citizens as well as organizations and public agencies. (vii) Improving R&D and innovativeness by "new products and services in response to demand in global markets".

The operationalised result was the launch of the e-Government Gateway platform late 2008 as a one stop portal (TURKSAT, 2008). The E-Government Gateway initiative is described as the provision of all e-government applications through a single portal (Kumas, 2007; Sungu et al., 2008). "Once the e-gateway or the portal is created, the service will be extended to include other communication devices like cell phones and pocket PCs, and users can access the system with

Table 3. Basic models for e-government

Type	Description	Coverage
mG2C	Citizens (Communication between Govt. Organization and common people)	Individual
mG2E	For Employees (Interaction among Govt. and its employees)	Individual
mG2B	Business Community (Explaining the governmental policies to Business)	Organizational
mG2G	Inter-Governmental operations (Referring inter-departmental communications and interactions)	Organizational

(Source: http://www.idosi.org/wasj/wasj28(efmo)13/10.pdf)

Table 4. E-Government development in Western Asia

Country	E-Government Development Index Value		World E-Government Development Ranking	
	2010	2008	2010	2008
Bahrain	0.7363	0.5723	13	42
Israel	0.6552	0.7393	26	17
Cyprus	0.5705	0.6019	42	35
United Arab Emirates	0.5349	0.6301	49	32
Kuwait	0.5290	0.5202	50	57
Jordan	0.5278	0.5480	51	50
Saudi Arabia	0.5142	0.4935	58	70
Qatar	0.4928	0.5314	62	53
Turkey	0.4780	0.4834	69	76
Oman	0.4576	0.4691	82	84
Azerbaijan	0.4571	0.4609	83	89
Lebanon	0.4388	0.4840	93	74
Georgia	0.4248	0.4598	100	90
Armenia	0.4025	0.4182	110	103
Syrian Arab Republic	0.3103	0.3614	133	119
Iraq	0.2996	0.2690	136	151
Yemen	0.2154	0.2142	164	164
Sub-regional average	0.4732	0.4857		
World average	0.4406	0.4514		

(Source: http://unpan1.un.org/intradoc/groups/public/documents/un-dpadm/unpan038848.pdf, p 71)

smart cards or imprinted digital certificates for a secure transaction" (TURKSAT, 2008). The e-Government Gateway initiative is leading Turkey's efforts towards the modernization of the public administration and citizen centric government. In effect, the gateway portal provides a single government brand and consistency in services.

Regarding recent evolutions, starting with ICT, Turkey over the last decade has evidenced considerable progress at least in metropolitan areas. Internet usage is on the rise: on average, in 2013, 49.1 percent of households have access to the Internet at home -- up from 47.2 percent in 2012. The percentage of households with access to the Internet is 57.4 percent in urban areas and 29.1 percent in rural areas. İstanbul (63.3 percent),

West Marmara (58.8 percent), East Marmara (56.8 percent) and West Anatolia (52.4 percent) are above the average in Turkey. Turkish Internet users are very active on the net: 91.6 percent of all users are on the Internet almost every day or at least once a week. Turks like to shop online: 24.1 percent of Internet users bought goods or services over the Internet -- higher that 21.8 percent in the previous year. More importantly, Tukish citizens are getting mobile: 41.1 percent of Internet users aged 16-74 use mobile or smart phones to access the Internet and broadband Internet is popular: 46.5 percent of households have a broadband Internet connection.

Regarding the main activities in 2013: The Internet has become a serious threat to traditional

Table 5. Online service levels in selected developing countries

Rank	Country	Emerging Information Services (Stage 1)		Enhanced Information Services (Stage 2)		Transactional Services (Stage 3)		Connected Services		Total	
		Points	Score (%)	Points	Score (%)	Points	Score (%)	Points	Score (%)	Points	Score (%)
30	Tunisia	52	76	40	34	50	30	10	20	152	38
32	Uruguay	51	75	43	37	36	21	21	42	151	37
36	Kuwait	41	60	39	34	58	34	7	14	145	36
39	Mexico	45	66	52	42	26	15	16	32	139	34
40	El Salvador	48	71	30	26	46	27	10	10	134	33
44	Argentina	53	78	42	36	22	13	13	26	130	32
45	Peru	53	78	37	32	26	15	13	26	129	32
49	Philippines	48	71	25	22	35	21	16	32	124	31
53	Uzbekistan	52	76	39	34	18	11	10	20	119	30
54	Cyprus	44	65	39	34	19	11	15	30	117	29
55	Brazil	53	78	34	29	10	6	19	38	116	29
55	China	54	79	40	34	4	2	18	36	116	29
55	India	45	66	41	35	22	13	8	16	116	29
55	Oman	47	69	33	28	26	15	10	20	116	29
59	Dominican Republic	46	68	30	26	24	14	15	30	125	29
62	**Turkey**	57	84	29	25	9	5	14	28	109	27
62	Ukraine	55	81	31	27	7	4	16	32	109	27
65	Trinidad and Tobago	50	74	39	34	12	7	6	12	107	27
67	Thailand	50	74	31	27	15	9	9	18	105	26
68	Russian Federation	49	72	28	24	15	9	12	24	104	26

(Source: http://unpan1.un.org/intradoc/groups/public/documents/un-dpadm/unpan038848.pdf, p 81)

media; online readership is on the rise: 75.6 percent of Internet users read or download online news, newspapers or news magazines. Turkey's digitally native population is on the rise: Turkish children generally start to use computers at the age of 8, the Internet at the age of 9 and mobile phones at an average age of 10. Turkey's youth is active on the Internet: 45.6 percent of children use the Internet almost every day. Ownership of technological artefacts is also on the rise with 24.4 percent of children aged 6-15 have personal computers, while 13.3 percent have mobile phones and 2.9 percent have game consoles. Children's use of the Internet for education and entertainment is also strongly accelerating especially among children aged 6-15 with a percentage of 84.8 for homework, followed by gaming (79.5 percent), searching for information (56.7 percent) and joining social networks (53.5 percent). 35 million Turkish people are using Facebook, and 9 million are using Twitter. It is the second country in Europe that talks the most on the phone.

For twelve months (April 2011-March 2012) 45,1% of Internet users interacted with public

Table 6. World e-government development rankings

Country	World E-Government Development Rankings		
	2008	2010	2012
Bahrain	42	13	36
Israel	17	26	16
Cyprus	35	42	45
United Arab Emirates	32	49	28
Kuwait	57	50	63
Jordan	50	51	98
Saudi Arabia	70	58	41
Qatar	53	62	48
Turkey	**76**	**69**	**80**
Oman	84	82	64
Azerbaijan	89	83	96
Lebanon	74	93	87
Georgia	90	100	72
Armenia	103	110	94
Syrian Arab Republic	119	133	128
Iraq	151	136	137
Yemen	164	164	167

(Source: E-Government development ranking, UNPAN.)

authorities over the Internet for private purposes. This proportion was 38,9 per cent for the period of April 2010-March 2011. Obtaining information from public authorities' web sites was in the first rank with 42,9 per cent. McKinsey's Turkey (2012) reported that the Internet's contribution to the Turkish economy was still low. Internet's contribution of to the GDP was only 0.9 percent while in a developed country such as Sweden, the Internet contributes 6.3 percent of the GDP, and the world average is 3.4 percent. Still, whilst Turkey is growing by 4%, the ICT sector grows by 8-9%. ICT is fundamental to Prime Minister Erdoğan's 2023 vision and there are several ambitious goals for ICT, including 50% of the ICT sector being supplied by domestic sources as well as ICT contributing to 8% of Turkey's GDP. Again and more importantly, according to the McKinsey research, one of the important reasons why the

Turkish consumer is not kindly disposed toward e-commerce is "distrust." However, regarding the future, in Turkey's Internet Economy Report, it is reported that the Internet share of the economy is to grow 19% until 2017 (Internet Economy Report prepared in partnership of Google and Boston Consulting Group,2013). According to the report, private sector investments contributed 7 billion Liras to Internet GDP wile government spending amounted to 1.6 billion Liras. In Turkey, all telecommunications activities are regulated by the Ministry of Transportation and the Information Technologies and Communications Authority. Five main initiatives-- Mobile Electronic System Integration, Traffic Information System, Mobile information Project (Ministry of education), G2G applications (mobile intranet for ministry personnel) and the National Judicial Network (Court system integration) have lead the nascent model

(Cilingir and Kushchu, 2004; Kuran, 2005). According to the latest development plan (2006-2010) of the Turkish government, digital-government is presented in line with international understanding as a new tool that allows the development of an efficient administration, responsive to the needs of the new knowledge economy by aiming to provide better public services. Turkey as a candidate for EU membership has adopted and integrated the existing 20 e-government applications that the EU prioritizes for its members and candidates, which are described in the e-Europe 2005 Action Plan (e-EAP, 2005; Eurostat, 2007). Still, some limitations and obstacles regarding the various e-government initiatives are emerging. These limitations prevent citizens from receiving effective e-government services and restrict its efficient use both by the citizens and public agencies. First, in 2013, Turkey ranks second after China in demands to ban Internet content, according to a new report by the Economic Policy Research Foundation of Turkey (TEPAV), amid a controversial new Internet law increasing restrictions and the government's power over the Internet. The Telecommunications Communications Presidency (TİB), is also allowed to block access to websites without a court order if the site is deemed to violate privacy or has "insulting" content. Second, Internet subscription prices offered in Turkey have been found to be at the higher hand of the scale and more expensive than many OECD countries for different Internet speed (Huriyet daily, 2013). In Turkey, the average subscription price for high-speed internet reaches $621 per year, while in the closest follower, Luxemburg, the price of high-speed Internet subscription is only $112, according to the research titled "How Is Internet Usage Changing in Turkey? An Assessment of Internet Users.

Turkey's mobile market is one of the largest in the region due to its sizeable population. Strong infrastructure-based competition exists between three mobile network operators that have built GSM/HSPA networks. 3G/HSPA is being used to underpin take up of mobile broadband services, which has overtaken ADSL as Turkey's most popular broadband access method. Turkey is also one of the most advanced markets in the region together with Israel, where mobile broadband networks account for 63% of total mobile connections (as of Q2 2013), Turkey (59%), United Arab Emirates (55%) and Saudi Arabia (54%). In contrast, the average for Southern Europe stands at just 45%, while Western Europe has about half its connections on mobile broadband networks and in Northern Europe around three in five connections are mobile broadband.

All three operators in Turkey benefitted from significant data revenue growth in the year to

Table 7. Benchmarking areas, indicators and scales

Benchmarking Area	Indicator(s)	Scale
20 basic e-Government services	• Full online availability of 20 basic e-Government services. • Sophistication level of 20 basic e-Government services.	1-100
User experience on 20 basic e-Government services	• Level of average user experience on all services. • Level of average user experience on national portal.	1-100
E-Procurement	• E-Procurement availability for the pre-award phase. • Level of e-Procurement visibility.	1-100
Life events	• Maturity level of business life events (Starting up a business is used as an example). • Maturity level of citizen life events (Losing and finding a job is used as an example).	1-100
Availability and use of key enablers	Number of key enablers including organizational and technical frameworks.	N/A

Q1 2013. Turkcell has been particularly active in marketing data services, with its own-branded range of low-priced smartphones (the "T" series) contributing to a smartphone penetration of 22% at the end of Q1 – some 6.9 million devices. The operator has recently introduced a Turkcell-branded tablet, and is also offering innovative speed-based and shared data plans to further boost data consumption. Subsequently, Turkcell's data revenue was up some 65% year-on-year to reach $778 million in FY2012-13. Rival Avea (Turk Telecom) is pursuing a similar strategy. On its Q1 2013 according to Chief Marketing Officer Dehsan Erturk "…mobile data revenue is the backbone of our revenue growth. Data revenue now constitutes 14% of total service revenues with a (traffic) growth of 55% on year-over-year basis thanks to smartphone campaigns and unique internet packages, addressing different customer segment user, various device types and data bundles." As a result Avea has the highest level of smartphone penetration in the country with 27% in Q1 2013. On the back of this, data revenue increased by some 79% annually to hit $348 million in FY2012-13. There are currently three mobile communications operators in Turkey. With respect to revenues, market share of Turkcell is 48,72% while market shares of Vodafone and Avea are 30,15% and 21,13%, respectively.

ARTICULATING WIDER SMARTPHONE EMERGING SECURITY ISSUES

Following the Arab sping revolution, the war in Syria, social media and mobile devices are seen as the new fromtiers in preserving free speech

Table 8. Number of Internet subscriptions

	2012 Q2	2013 Q1	2013 Q2	Quaterly Growth Rate (2013 Q1 – 2013 Q2)	Annual Growth Rate (2012 Q2 – 2013 Q2)
xDSL	6.632.661	6.678.907	6.644.571	-0,5%	0,2%
Mobile Internet from Computer	1.582.984	1.727.861	1.746.814	1,1%	10,3%
Mobile Internet from Mobile Handset	15.908.739	19.041.609	20.038.053	5,2%	26,0%
Cable Internet	485.531	501.201	491.852	-1,9%	1,3%
Fiber	469.668	741.675	860.871	16,1%	83,3%
Other	140.299	137.366	126.824	-7,7%	-9.6%
TOTAL	25.219.882	28.828.619	29.908.985	3,7%	18,6%

(Source: http://eng.btk.gov.tr/kutuphane_ve_veribankasi/pazar_verileri/2013_Q2_ECM_MarketData.pdf)

Table 9. Data on 3G subscribers

	2013 Q1	2013 Q2
3G Subscribers	43.874.972	45.341.769
Mobile Internet from Computer	1.727.861	1.746.814
Mobile Internet from Mobile Handset	19.041.609	20.038.053
Mobile Internet Usage, TByte	27.710	31.297

(Source: http://eng.btk.gov.tr/kutuphane_ve_veribankasi/pazar_verileri/2013_Q2_ECM_MarketData.pdf)

Table 10. ISP market shares based on subscribers

ISP Market Shares Based on the Number of Subscribers, 2013 Q2	
Operator	%
TTNet	80,62
Superonline	10,14
Dogan TV Digital	4,49
Milenicom	1,51
Vodafone Net	1,48
Turknet	0,96
Metronet	0,47
Isnet	0,06
Eser	0,05
Himnet	0,04
Other	0,18

(Source: http://eng.btk.gov.tr/kutuphane_ve_veribankasi/ pazar_verileri/2013_Q2_ECM_MarketData.pdf)

and information objectivity beyond the reach of governments' manipulation and censure. Edward Snowden, Wikkileaks, hacker anonymous are part of a long list of activists using mobile technologies to reveal information often closely guarded by government. They are replacing more traditional forms of activism such as Amnesty International or Greenpeace perceived as institutionalized; i.e., part of the system. Attacks vary, ranging from the uploading of state secrets, industrial espionage, credit cards frauds, password, social security numbers, exams results to corruption scandals. Beyond the ethical and moral dilemma about revealing information that may or may not put life at risk, security remain central to any functioning government and organization. Figure 1 categorizes Cyber crime in Turkey in 2010.

Turkey is part if the European Cyber Crime convention since 2010. Yet, the motivation of the convention is not to protect freedom of expression or intellectual rights as the Council of Europe's Convention on Cybercrime mainly identifies crimes over child porn and intellectual properties.

At the same time, however, Turkey has a wider range of crime descriptions beyond the scope of the convention. For instance Turkey cannot ban the Playboy website according to the description of the convention since it did not list obscenity as a crime, however, Turkey has a clear "obscenity law." There is also serious legislative problem on Internet crimes in Turkey as the telecommunications Directorate, or TİB, can ban a website without a court order. TİB now allows government officials to block sites they deem violate personal privacy and forces Internet companies to retain the data — such as emails and search histories — accumulated by their customers for two years, which some here worry could be used by the authorities to start criminal investigations (NyTimes, 2014). In March, 2014, Turkey started an espionage investigation after a discussion between top officials on potential military action in Syria was leaked on YouTube (Reuters, 2014).The case of Twitter partial closure in 2014 clearly indicates that the government takes seriously social media leaks of government information. Other examples reflect the gravity of the threat: In 2013, hackers claim to have breached the systems of Turkey's Ministry of Finance, leaking an archive containing files including data on income and expenses reports from Turkey's Ministry of Finance for the period between 2006 and 2010. The leaked data consists of city names, district names, units, account names and amounts. Each of the file contains thousands and even tens of thousands of records. In June 2013, hackers claimed to have breached the systems of Turkey's Ministry of Interior, the Prime Ministry's website, and other government sites as a way to protest against new Internet filters. Government control is not new, however; in 2007, a law was passed that allowed the courts to block

Figure 1. Cyber crime arrest-2010

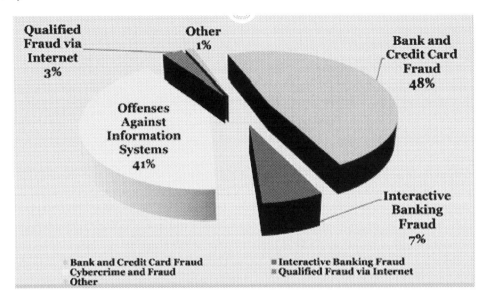

websites containing pornography, along with sites that encouraged gambling, and those insulting the founder of modern Turkey, Mustafa Kemal Ataturk. YouTube, for instance, was blocked entirely for about 18 months (Sofpedia, 2011).

Security in m-government is also related to the technology that is being used for m-government. The more the citizens know how to use the technology, the more the system will be secure because the users will be aware of the risks in using the m-services. However the technology awareness from the user's side, requires that the user will adopt the mobile technology adoption in general . Technology adoption is a crucial element in the implementation of m-government and has been discussed in the world of academia.

This chapter is nested in the traditional Unified Theory of Acceptance and Use of Technology (UTAUT) model that integrates a series of traditional technology acceptance models (Venkatesh et al, 2003). These include: the theory of reasoned action (Davis et al. 1989), the technology acceptance model (Davis, 1989), the motivational model (Davis et al., 1992), the theory of planned

behaviour (Ajzen, 1991), Taylor and Todd (1995) framework that combine TAM and TPB, Thompson et al., (1991) Personal Computing utilization model, the innovation diffusion theory (Rogers, 2003), and the social cognitive theory (Compeau and Higgins, 1995; 1999). Yet lately, the issue of security has casted a shadow on the sustainability of UTAUT in practice.

UTAUT is a model that has been associated with e-government in the past and several scholars used it as a tool to predict the user's intention regarding e-government. Mahmood (2013) discussed the influence of the UTAUT constructs on the citizen's behavioral intention to use m-government services in the country of Jordan. Janssen (2011) along with other researchers used UTAUT as a medium in order to research the e-government adoption in Saudi Arabia. Carter, Schaupp and Evans (2008) used UTAUT to explore the adoption of e-govenment services and especially the adoption of electronic tax filing. AlAwadhi and Morris (2008) used the UTAUT theory in order to research the adoption of e-government services in Kuwait.

One of the four key constructs in the UTAUT mode is the facilitating conditions. This construct describes the degree to which a person believes that several organizational and technical conditions exist in order to support the use of a system. In our case, when the citizens transact with the government through mobile devices, they expect the appropriate technical and organizational conditions that support the use of a mobile system. Facilitating conditions could thus be renamed as mobility in UTAUT. Measurement of mobility will probably be implemented by using as indexes the four important concepts of mobility mentioned in our research:

1. Device Mobility.
2. User Mobility.
3. Service Mobility.
4. Session Mobility.

The inclusion of mobility in UTAUT along the types of mobility are depictured in Figure 2.

While UTAUT describes the potential technology adoption by the citizens, the theory's components do not take into account the issue of security.

According to Hanna (2010) the major policy concerns in e-government and m-govenrment are interopability, privacy, information quality and security. Andersen (2013) points out that the public sector depends highly on the security and data privacy. Andersen states that several problems with the data security in m-government relate to the standards of the network provider. Moreover, an additional problem in m-government is that mobile devices could be used both for private reasons and interactions with the government. In terms of the importance of security, an improved version of the UTAUT model should include security as a factor that influences the behavioral intention for m-government. Figure 3 shows the suggested version of UTAUT including security.

The scope of the current work is beyond the application of a research model and the suggested model will be discussed in a future scientific effort. One of the new constructs explored in our next section is the problem of security.

While most analysts agree that smartphones have outnumbered PCs with a turning point around mid-2013, new behaviour and hence new treats are appearing within the ecosystem. Yet,

Figure 2. The unified theory of acceptance and use of technology model

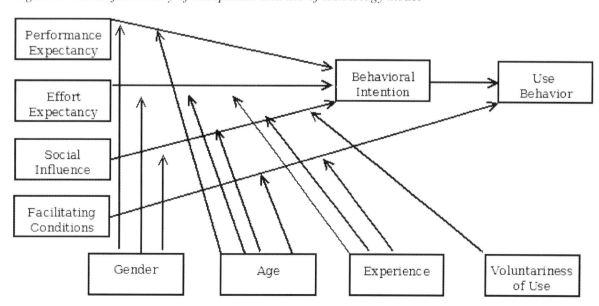

it is rarely addressed in e-government planning, especially in emerging market conditions where others issues such as interoperability may be more of a priority. Wider research in Information Communication Technology (ICT) has confirmed that interoperability is concerned primarily with technical factors such as data semantics and process standardization (e.g. computer readable format, specific type of unit) as well strategic issues including legal, political, and social aspects (e.g. what to do with the data they receive in the exchange) (Ford et al, 2007). Interoperability is often portrayed as: 'the ability of disparate and diverse organizations to interact towards mutually beneficial and agreed common goals, involving the sharing of information and knowledge between the organizations via the business processes they support, by means of the exchange of data between their respective information and communication technology (ICT) systems' (European Communities 2008, p. 5). Interoperability provides many benefits in the long term, including improved efficiency (data exchange), transparency (audit login, monitoring), accountability (activity level), and access, as well as coordination of services at lower costs.

Figure 3. UTAUT with mobility

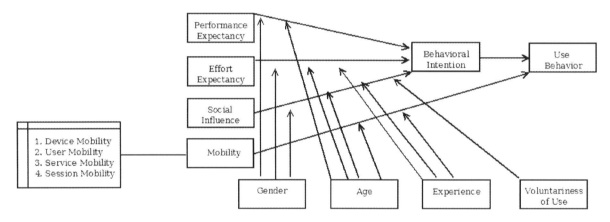

Figure 4. UTAUT with mobility and security

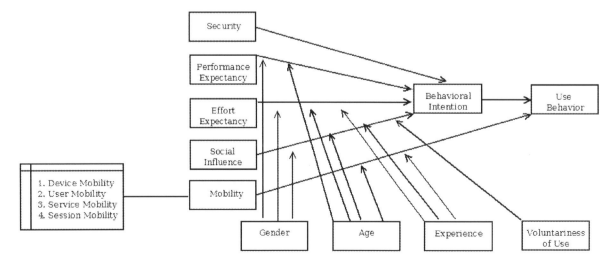

It is then relevant to review and assess the most common smartphone security risks both from an m-government back end operational perspective and from a citizen, user in practice standpoint. First we underline here that the (level of) risk is often a personal subjective appreciation. Questions such as: "How much risk is involved in adopting a technology?" or "Does a high Technology Readiness Levels correspond to a low risk in the investment for that technology?" need to be addressed. As such, risk is part of everybody's daily life, part of the decisions we make. The subjective character of risk not only makes it hard to classify but also its diversity. As a multifaceted concept, risk management can be defined as:

- An organised process to identify what can go wrong, to quantify and assess associated risks, and to implement/control over the appropriate approach for preventing or handling each risk identified (What is " Risk", Hall, D.C., Risk Management Working group INCOSE,2002).

- The systematic and iterative optimisation of the project resources, performed according to the established project risk management policy, which describes the organisation's attitude towards risks (pace Project Management; Risk Assessment, ESA/ESTEC,ECSS standard ECSS-M-00-03A,2000).

- The identification, analysis, prioritization, mitigation planning, and monitoring and control "of events which have a potential of causing unwanted change" (The Relationship of Technology Change Management to Risk Management, Mosier, S.P., Guenterberg, S.A. and Rphael, R.R., Proceedings INCOSE International Symposium 2000,2000.

Regarding Smartphone technologies, risk is often measured on a non-linear scale. The levels are intended to convey relative risk in relation to others, rather than absolute probability or impact level. Taken together, Smartphone security risk is defined as the product of the likelihood and the impact of a threat against the information assets within or distributed to third parties automatically by the technological artefact (GPS, Bluetooth) without conscious decisions by the owner/user. Threats often exploit one or more vulnerabilities. The likelihood of a threat is determined by the number of underlying vulnerabilities, the relative ease with which they can be exploited and the attractiveness for an attacker. Threats are often ranked relative to impact or potential impact on: (a)Personal data; (b) Corporate intellectual property; (c) Classified (non- Public) information; (d) Financialy relevant data; (e) Device and service availability and functionality; (f) Personal and political reputation now and in the future (see Figure 1).

Furthermore, from a strategic management standpoint other aspects ought to be considered including: (a) Insider theft of information, whereby willingly or unwillingly civisl servant may leak data to third parties or the Internet in general; (b) Additional wireless attack vectors as many users are late or not running patches to conteract security holes as they are identified, in the interim period, users remain at risk. Earlier this year, security researchers discovered a serious Android exploit: "The exploit is capable of reading and writing files from an Android's SD card or system partition as well as uploading user data over the internet." Wireless devices generally have at least three different wireless access opportunities: 1) Cellular; 2) Wi-Fi; 3) BlueTooth. Any door can be opened by a person who is determined enough to do so; (c) Loss of sensitive data, Smartphones are easy to lose and easy to steal. As people use these devices more as business tools, or in our case with e-government function the risk of accidental exposure of sensitive information rises significantly. Even the simple act of synchronizing email with a smartphone increases the risk that data will make its way into the wrong hands. Good corporate policy and tools to compartmentalize sensitive information should be considered as safeguards against this all-too-common threat; (d) Inability to appropriately control personal devices by using one device for work related issues. The issue of how to dispose of a handset and the end of the lifecycle also becomes relevant, for example, should a state service be allowed to simply wipe a person's personal device remotely if it is believed that to be compromised, that person has left an/the organization, or the device has been lost or stolen?

Other simple actions arc also ignored by most users including, screen lock with appropriate level of password security (foolproof), enabling or disabling remote locate, lock and wipe, backup or sync of data on a regular basis, applying operating system update as a regular maintenance process, turning off x Bluetooth discovery mode, keeping

one device in Jail rather than open to third parties and probably avoiding the temptation of free Wi-Fi Hotspots.

Education and learning also play a role in the development of new behaviour as few users recognise for example that shopping online with an Internet browser instead of a shopping app is less secure. Unlike browsers, dedicated shopping apps are designed to ward off phishing and other kinds of scams. (Before you download it, just make sure it's really their official app!). Others tend to remain logged into banking, PayPal, eBay, and other sensitive apps. Never, for example, click the box asking the app to save your user ID or password. We all tend to value convenience over security. Furthermore, any user should ask themselves about the type of data they are storing on their Smartphone. Many people store passwords,

Table 11. The top ten information security risks for smartphone users

	Title	Risk	Description
1	Data leakage resulting from device loss or theft	High	The smartphone is stolen or lost and its memory or removable media are unprotected, allowing an attacker access to the data stored on it.
2	Unintentional disclosure of data	High	The smartphone user unintentionally discloses data on the smartphone.
3	Attacks on decommissioned smartphones	High	The smartphone is decommissioned improperly allowing an attacker access to the data on the device.
4	Phishing attacks	Medium	An attacker collects user credentials (such as passwords and credit card numbers) by means of fake apps or (SMS, email) messages that seem genuine.
5	Spyware attacks	Medium	The smartphone has spyware installed, allowing an attacker to access or infer personal data. Spyware covers untargeted collection of personal information as opposed to targeted surveillance.
6	Network Spoofing Attacks	Medium	An attacker deploys a rogue network access point (WiFi or GSM) and users connect to it. The attacker subsequently intercepts (or tampers with) the user communication to carry out further attacks such as phishing.
7	Surveillance attacks	Medium	An attacker keeps a specific user under surveillance through the target user's smartphone.
8	Diallerware attacks	Medium	An attacker steals money from the user by means of malware that makes hidden use of premium SMS services or numbers.
9	Financial malware attacks	Medium	The smartphone is infected with malware specifically designed for stealing credit card numbers, online banking credentials or subverting online banking or ecommerce transactions.
10	Network congestion	Low	Network resource overload due to smartphone usage leading to network unavailability for the end-user.

(Source: http://www.enisa.europa.eu/activities/Resilience-and-CIIP/critical-applications/smartphone-security-1/top-ten-risks, accessed 20 March 2014.)

pins, Social Security numbers, credit card or bank account information on smartphones. It may be a document created expressly for this purpose or an email they themselves send from their computers. Another easy mistake relates to not clearing browser's history.

On mobile devices and platforms, application-aware Firewalls are becoming more common. They represent a split between basic port filtering and granular App controls. As such, it is important to reflect on what is coming next. In that sense, "app-aware" firewall, taken as a firewall that looks at traffic with an awareness of which applications are involved during the entire websurfing event in real time, are becoming central to mobile protection. However, because of their greater complexity in dealing with polymorphic malware, virus and privacy issues and the higher demands they make on processing power, these firewalls can be tricky to deploy with lower end devices and slow connection.

STRUCTURAL UNCERTAINTIES IN TURKEY

As described above, the suggested UTAUT model could be used for the measurement of the country's m-readiness to adopt m-government. Further exploration of the model may reveal the importance of security as a concept in its own right that require further investigation. According to the current status of UTAUT, the following 3 propositions could be stated:

Proposition 1: Digital divide influences the potential m-government use.

Proposition 2: Mobility influences the use behavior towards m-government adoption.

Proposition 3: Security influences the behavioral intention towards the m-government adoption.

The digital divide is a phenomenon that is related with the user's limited access to the technology. Digital divided populations are usually technophobic and do not expect to use technology because they are afraid of its influence to their daily life. On the other hand, populations that are open minded tend to trust the new tools such as an innovative technology. In this case, if people become more technologically literate then there are possibilities to interact with the government through the use of the mobile devices. Device mobility, user mobility, service mobility and session mobility are the suggested types of mobility that the mobility factor consists of. The device mobility is a concept that could affect the use behavior because for instance the size of the Smartphone's screen will affect the intention of the user regarding the place of use. M-government may by considered a modern and innovative way of transacting with the government but unless it is a secure way, it cannot be adopted as a behavioral mode for the m-government. Especially, regading the issues surround m-transactions when m-government becom etrully interactive.

Furthermore, disruptive relationships can easily influence other stakeholders which in turn undermine confidence in the m-government strategy. This view is also consistent with earlier research which emphasised the critical importance of relationship building measures, particularly where substantial financial resources are required to fund change (De Marez et al., 2007). Following Coleman (1990) and Fukuyama (1995) trust needs to be seen in a dynamic situation whereas stakeholders have to be voluntarily ready to trust 'others', commit resources and accept delays in evaluating outcomes, if any engagement is to take place. Trust is often based on cognitive common sense and social elements (hedonic attributes), conventional views of the retail world (utilitarian/functional features), routines, conative personal perspective (e.g. risk averse-lover, level of optimism, access) and an emotional catalyser (Koehn, 2003). In our context of ICT, trust is also understood as a 'measure of belief in the benevolence and competence of the other party' (Mayer, Davis, and Schoorman, 1995 p. 722) and as 'moral and not directly observable' (Fukuyama, 1995). In addition, in the e-environment context Miyazaki and Fernandez's research (2001) have shown that security of personal and financial information was the most predictive concern regarding the e-purchase rate, whilst privacy issues and potential fraudulent behaviour by e-actors were key concerns for many users.

Proposition 4: The likelihood of successful implementation of m-government will be enhanced where participants develop trust through global security standards associated with the appropriate expected protection from the legal framework.

Another related idea that is helpful for understanding the way that m-government strategies are constructed is that of concept of logic (Thornton, 2002; 2004), which refers to the broad cultural beliefs and rules that structure cognition and fundamentally shape decision-making and action in a field. This work suggests that multiple kinds of historically rooted belief systems provide the basis for ongoing conflict and change (Fiss and Zajac, 2004). Therefore m-government security technologies can serve to function as boundary objects crossing traditions, norms, rules, and routines, through which change must pervade (Whittington, 2003). Establishing what constitutes a boundary object and how it is used in practice across m-government layers and stakeholders will help align or disrupt the logic. This also suggests that a disparity in views will exist between how stakeholders perceive the risks associated with security threats and how they respond.

Proposition 5: Competing logics of m-government security solutions will shape variations in the strategic practices of stakeholders.

Proposition 6: When competing logics in m-government security solutions exist along the service chain, stakeholders are more predisposed to resistance to change.

The development of critical mass of services and all government services start to use m-government facilities seem to be at the root of positive engagement and core to developing strongly applied security measures understood by all. The growth and increasing saturation regarding everyday ICT products used by firms, including mobile phones, PDAs, laptops, security passes and also wristwatches (e.g. Mobil's "Speedpass"), will need to be able to demonstrate a minimum level of security standards

Proposition 7: The growth of m-government security solutions will be enhanced when traditional e-government systems are less likely to meet the needs of stakeholders in the marketplace, only if mobile devices manufacturers (software and hardware) can demonstrate appropriate security standards.

Proposition 8: When m-government security solutions is more widespread, stakeholders will become more aware of security threat and predisposed to creativity and broader learning attitudes to security solutions.

While new organizational, procedural and technological standards have been solidified via the e-government gateway platform, most of the beneficial influences that ought to increase e-government success seem, in Turkey and many emerging markets, to be at the same time mirrored by structural uncertainties. The following sub-sections summersises mobile security uncertainties in detail including: *(i) the supplies of technologies within public administration, maintenance, training and development, (ii) The legislative framework, (iii) data handling procedures and protection, (iv) application problems, (v) corrective action and updating of the system, (vi) open, participative and interactive communication and (vii) leadership capabilities.*

1. The supplies of technologies within public administration, maintenance, training and development.

First and foremost, the *supplies of technologies within public administration, maintenance, training* and at a later stage appropriate leverage and control to encourage the development of tailored services at local level have been outlined as structural weaknesses. It is safe to stress that there appear to be few signs that the Turkish government is moving quickly towards more sustainable structures despite an increase in pressure from both internal demands by citizens and many civil servants and externally by the European Union. A lack of forward thinking and ambition is evidenced in a report by the EU regarding Turkey 'i2010 initiative' that only highlights the related activities and projects already put forward in "Information Society Strategy 2006-2010" (State Planning Organization, 2006a), and its annexed "Action Plan 2006-2010" (State Planning Organization, 2006b) but not yet implemented. The usual macro themes are present without providing substantial details –especially financial resources and training- needed in practice for application at x local level. These include: (i) modernization in public administration organization and functioning; (ii) effective, fast, easy-to-access and efficient public service delivery to citizens and businesses; (iii) reducing the digital divide; (iv) increasing employment and productivity and (v) ensuring effective and widespread use of ICT by businesses to create a higher value added. Effective implementation of these strategies is indeed, expected to facilitate Turkey's accession to the EU, and to provide advantages for Turkey in terms of reaching the goals set forth in the Lisbon Strategy (Çayhan, 2008).

2. The legislative framework.

On the one hand, the importance of the *legislative framework* in place was initially underestimated. E-communication and e-applications can only be enacted by the various public administration services only if a strong, valid and legally accepted legislative regulatory framework is in place. While the Law Pertaining to Rights for Information Access was elaborated in 2004 as an important step allowing the creation of a base for future e-government activities (Yeloğlu and Sağsan, 2009), in practice the technology as well as the practical details were never ratified. This omission is highlighted in the non resolved issue regarding the use of e-signature. Subsequently a set of standards for the signature/verification softwares were put in place and strictly defined in the 5070 law regarding electronic signature, only to realize that there were no legal institutions controlling these standards or their use in practice. Indeed, at the launch of the e-government platform in December 2008, it was discovered that most of the transactions and applications through the public agencies such as of justice, health, and finance were legally considered as invalid. The effect was felt within not only the public but also the private administration from a legal perspective. All Internet banking services such as bill payments, fund investments, EFT or money order that require identity information and signature if challenged in court were considered invalid as well because of lack of e-signature recognition within the law. (Anonymous, 2007; Yildirim, 2010). In addition, beyond legal issues, real life problems emerged. As a example, data started to be collected in 2008 for e-ID. Problem of collecting fingerprint data emerged in rural areas in the inability of residents of rural areas to provide fingerprints because of the likelihood of calluses on their fingers. An alternative method named "vein geometry" is available but dramatically increases the system complexity and risk of failure— without analysing the scale of the problem of reaching 70 million people (Canturk, 2010). Cost issues for an already strained budget were also clear.

3.   Data handling procedures and protection.

On the other hand, cultural issues emerged when x data are finally in the system. The key issues *of data handling procedures and protection* surface. In Turkey, the law pertaining to the protection of personal data is still awaiting parliament acceptance (2 years after the official launch of the e-government platform) and regular media coverage the sellling of personal data (alive and dead) over x Internet are current. (Anonymous, 2009a). The immediate results are an obvious lack of trust by the general population. The problem has reached such an extent that the most important issue in the use of e-government transactions today is informing citizens about security and the action taken to strengthen data protection both legally and in practice at local level (Moral, 2009). The Ministry of Transportation stated that in order to change 80 years of traditions, there is the need for a mental and cultural transformation. Only then did they draw up a bill to attempt to capture more than 30 changes required in x legislative aspects (Anonymous, 2010a).

CONCLUSION AND DISCUSSIONS

Never before have citizens used technologies to such an extend to communicate with government. The accessibility of information, stories, videos, audio file and photos on any issue have become highly visible. As such, security is becoming a key variable in the m-government equation especially in emerging market where corruption and political uncertainties are stronger. Government that are used to control traditional media have to content with a whole new set of security threat in the virtual world. State strong filtering systems can relatively easily block the main access to any website, but often sees this basic gate ignored by more advanced techno wizards i.e. the young generations. Furtheremore information blocked or deleted will often remain available outside a country Internet space. In Turkey in 2014, an 11-member government commission is all what is needed to ban a list of more than 138 search terms deemed "harmful." Internet freedom advocates criticized the group's composition, as it was composed exclusively of officials from the ministries of information and family, and did not include any independent experts (Law no. 5651, entitled "Regulation of Publications on the Internet and Suppression of Crimes Committed by means of Such Publication). Among the banned search words are the English terms "porno," "sex," "adult," "fetish," "escort," "mature" and "gay," as well as the Turkish words for "naked," "hot," "sister-in-law," "mother-in-law," "stepmother" and "incest." (Law No. 4982 on the Right to Information). Other words are are part of everyday life, e.g. the words Adrianne, Animal, Hayvan ('Animal'), Beat, Buyutucu ('enlarger'), Citir ('crispy'), Etek ('skirt'), Fire, Girl, Ateşli ('passionate'), Frikik ('freekick'), Free, Gizli ('confidential'), Haydar, Hikaye, Homemade, Hot, İtiraf ('confession'), Liseli ('high school student'), Nefes ('breath'), Nubile, Partner, Pic, Sarisin ('blond'), Sisman ('overweight'), Teen, Yasak ('forbidden'), Yerli ('local'), Yetiskin ('adult') etc.

Turkey's international reputation as a democracy is also suffering as in internet censorship is visible in all international report on free speech, web indexes, and press freedom. In November 2013, the Web Index Report prepared by the World Wide Web Foundation ranked Turkey as 58th out of 81 countries in terms of indicators based on universal access, freedom and openness, relevant content, and empowerment. In the same report, Turkey appears to champion censoring politically sensitive content together with Russia, China and Saudi Arabia. According to the European Union's report on Turkey's Progress in Access to the Union, 32 thousand websites are estimated to have been censored for various reasons. In addition to that, in 2012, the European Court of Human Rights found Turkey guilty in terms of impeding the exercise of free speech on the internet, due to the very same Law 5651.

In summary, The President of Telecommunication Directorate (TIB) is entitled to remove whichever website is demmed contrary to the law.

- TIB is entitled to block access to websites within four hours without a court order.
- Anyone with a claim that a website intrudes into their personal life can demand a website's ban through a petition submitted to TIB without any court order.
- Websites can be shut down by either blocking IP addresses or URL's. Therefore unlike before, only the contentious pages can be shut down instead of the entire website as was the case in the Youtube ban. However that also means, changing DNS settings will not work in accessing the content.

Further exploration of the topic should take into account strategies related to the management of change. When people deal with a new change, they usually pass through a series of emotional stages until acceptance. The familiarity with the new situation could be reached by using the mobile phone as a mediun for gamification because games are always an entertaining challenge for those who deal with complex problems.

The main challenge for the m-government initiative in Turkey remains the accommodation of heterogeneity in its citizens and among civil service layers. Technical and social capabilities need to be integrated within a system that accommodate a wide range of individual context and time specific needs and preferences. Personalized evolvable experiences are a goal as product and services respond to new demands. A call is made here for future research to include the concept of co-creation and co-production of services through m-government technology platforms. Further questions do remain, including the following:

- How can citizen and civil servant centered design be employed to increase trust in m-Government security measures?
- How can citizen-centered m-Government services accommodate the different understanding of the government roles?
- Are there best m-Government practices and modular strategies emerging that ought to be shared among the various state layers?

Finally, according to David Gorodyansky, CEO and founder of AnchorFree, said: "Technology is the great leveller: it has given people worldwide a voice that was previously unobtainable or ignored. With this increased power of the individual, governments have attempted to crack down on internet democracy. Yet, for every new way a government tries to stifle its citizens' voices, people will find tools that will grant them freedom of speech. The incredible uptake of HotSpot Shield in Turkey displays peoples' desire to communicate and the transformative power of technology (Wire, 2014).

REFERENCES

Abaday, A. (2010). E-devlet'le memur işsiz mi kalacak? *Ntvmsnbc*. Retricved March 21 from http://www.ntvmsnbc.com/id/25072060/

Abramowicz, W., Bassara, A., Filipowska, A., Wisniewski, M., & Zebrowski, P. (2006). Mobility implications for m-government platform design. *Cybernetics and Systems: An International Journal, 37*(2-3), 119–135. doi:10.1080/01969720500428255

Akman, I., Yazici, A., & Arifoglu, A. (2002). *E-government: Turkey profile*. Paper presented at the Second International European Conference on e-Government. Oxford, UK.

AlAwadhi, S., & Morris, A. (2008). The Use of the UTAUT Model in the Adoption of E-Government Services in Kuwait. In *Proceeding of the 41st Hawaii International International Conference on Systems Science* (HICSS-41 2008). Waikoloa, HI: IEEE Computer Society.

Andersen, K., Francesconi, E., Grönlund, A., & Engers, T. (2011). Electronic Government and the Information Systems Perspective. In *Proceeding of the Second International Conference, EGOVIS 2011*. New York, NY: Springer.

Anka. (2006). E-Devlet Projesi MERNIS coktu. *E-memleketim*. Retrieved December 10, 2010 from http://www.ememleketim.com/haberler/haber.asp?hbr=247

Anonymous. (2007). İnternet bankacılığı işlemleri hukuki açıdan geçersiz. *Hürriyet*. Retrieved December 10, 2010 from http://hurarsiv.hurriyet.com.tr/goster/haber.aspx?id=5894815&tarih=2007-02-05

Anonymous. (2009a). Uluslar Tek eDevlet Aginda. *Yeni Safak*. Retrieved December 10, 2010 from http://www.edevletmerkezi.org/sitetr/basinda_edem/haber5.html

Anonymous. (2009b). E-devlet modül eğitim ödülü verildi. *Siirtliler.net*. Retrieved November 24, 2011 from http://www.siirtliler.net/goster.asp?nereye=yazioku&ID=125&Siirt_haberleri

Anonymous. (2010a). E-devlette yasanan zorluklar ortadan kalkiyor. *MDevlet*. Retrieved December 10, 2010 from http://www.mdevlet.org/2010/01/e-devlette-yasanan-zorluklar-ortadan-kalkiyor/

Anonymous. (2010b). Emekli Adayina e-Devlet Surprizi. *Gazeteport*. Retrieved December 10, 2010 from http://www.gazeteport.com.tr/EKONOMI/NEWS/GP_803120

Anonymous. (2010c). Sigorta bilgilerini öğrenmek için şifre şartı geldi, çalışanlar mağdur oldu. *Saglik Aktuel*. Retrieved December 10, 2010 from http://www.saglikaktuel.com/habcr/sigorta-bilgilerini-ogrenmek-icin-sifre-sarti-geldi,-calisanlar-magdur-oldu-13905.htm

Anonymous. (2010d). SGK İle İlgili Kişisel Bilgilere 1 Kasım'dan beri ulaşılamıyor. *ShowHaber*. Retrieved December 10, 2010 from http://www.showhaber.com/sgk-ile-ilgili-kisisel-bilgilere-1-kasimdan-beri-ulasilamiyor-365126.htm

Anonymous. (2010e). E-devlet de çökertildi! *BHaber*. Retrieved December 10, 2010 from http://bhaber.net/haber/11116-e-devlet-de-kertildi.html

Anonymous. (2010f). İçişleri Bakanlığı 11 İlde E-İmza Uygulaması Başlattı. *ShowHaber*. Retrieved December 10, 2010 from http://www.showhaber.com/icisleri-bakanligi-11-ilde-e-imza-uygulamasi-baslatti-333521.htm

Anonymous. (2010g). E-devlete geçiş:Bazı sorunlar ve çözüm önerileri. *Bir iyilik*. Retrieved December 11, 2010 from http://www.biriyilik.com/odevler-kaynaklar/iktisat-isletme-ve-ekonomi/e-devlete-gecis-bazi-sorunlar-ve-cozum-onerileri-31741.html

Anonymous. (2010h). Şanlıurfa Türkiye'ye örnek oldu. *Şanlıurfa.com*. Retrieved December 11, 2010 from http://www.sanliurfa.com/news_detail.php?id=17030

Anonymous. (2010i).Teknoloji hayal gücüyle besleniyor. *Koç Sistem.* Retrieved December 10, 2010 from http://www.kocsistem.com.tr/tr/rop14.aspx

Anonymous. (2011). *Testimony.* Retrieved April 5, 2011 from http://democrats.energycommerce.house.gov/sites/default/files/image_uploads/Testimony_05.04.11 _Spafford.pdf.

Anonymous. (2014). *Complexity metrics.* Retrieved April 12, 2014 from http://www.aivosto.com/project/help/pm-complexity.html

Arango, T., & Yeginsu, C. (2014). *Amid Flow of Leaks, Turkey Moves to Crimp Internet.* Retrieved April 12, 2014 from http://www.nytimes.com/2014/02/07/world/europe/amid-flow-of-leaks-turkey-moves-to-crimp-internet.html?_r=0

Avgerou, C. (2000). Recognising alternative rationalities in the deployment of information systems. *The Electronic Journal on Information Systems in Developing Countries, 3*(7), 1–15.

Aviv, A., Gibson, K., Mossop, E., Blaze, M., & Smith, J. (2010). *Smudge Attacks on Smartphone Touch Screens.* Retrieved April 12, 2014 from https://www.usenix.org/legacy/event/woot10/tech/full_papers/Aviv.pdf

Balcı, A., & Medeni, T. (2010). E-Government Gateway Development in Turkey: Some Challenges and Future Directions for Citizen Focus. In E. Downey, C. D. Ekstrom, & M. A. Jones (Eds.), *E-Government Website Development: Future Trends and Strategic Models.* Hershey, PA: IGI Global. doi:10.4018/978-1-61692-018-0.ch010

Bertucci, G. (2008). *UN e-Government Survey: From e-Government to Connected Governance.* New York: United Nations, Division for Public Administration and Development Management.

Blackberry. (2011). *Blackberry developers documents.* Retrieved April 12, 2014 from http://www.blackberry.com/developers/docs/7.0.0api/net/rim/device/api/io/nfc/se/SecureElemen.html

Canturk, S. (2010). E-kimlik Kartlarina Ayar. *Sabah.* Retrieved December 10, 2010 from http://www.sabah.com.tr/Gundem/2010/10/16/ekimlik_kartlarina_nasirli_parmak_ayari

Carter, L., Schaupp, L. C., & Evans, A. (2008). *Antecedents of e-File adoption: The US Perspective.* Retrieved April 20, 2009 from://ieeexplore.ieee.org/stamp/stamp.jsp?arnumber=04438920

Çayhan, B. E. (2008). Implementing e-government in Turkey: A comparison of online public service delivery in Turkey and the European Union. *The Electronic Journal on Information Systems in Developing Countries, 35*(8), 1–11.

Cilingir, D., & Kushchu, I. (2004). E-government and m-government: Concurrent leaps by Turkey. In D. Remenyi (Ed.), *Proceedings of European Conference on E-Government (ECEG),* (pp. 813-821). Reading, UK: Academic Conferences International.

Cisco. (2014). *Cisco 2014 Annual Security Report.* Retrieved April 12, 2014 from http://www.cisco.com/web/offers/lp/2014-annual-security-report/index.html

Cloud Computing: Benefits, Risks and Recommendations for information security. (2009). Retrieved April 12, 2014 from http://www.enisa.europa.eu/act/rm/files/deliverables/cloud-computing-risk-assessment

Coleman, J. S. (1990). *Foundations of Social Theory.* Cambridge, MA: Belknap Press of Harvard University Press.

De Kervenoael, R., Palmer, M., & Cakici, M. (2010). Exploring civil servant resistance to m-government: A story of transition and opportunities Turkey. In A. A. El-Masry, & A. G. Abdel-Wahab (Eds.), *Mobile Information Communication Technologies Adoption in Developing Countries: Effects and Implications* (pp. 134–160). Hershey, PA: IGI Global. doi:10.4018/978-1-61692-818-6.ch010

De Marez, L., Vyncke, P., Berte, K., Schuurman, D., & De Moor, K. (2007). Adopter segments, adoption determinants and mobile marketing. *Journal of Targeting. Measurement & Analysis for Marketing, 16*(1), 78–95. doi:10.1057/palgrave. jt.5750057

Dedeoglu, A. O. (2004). The symbolic use of mobile telephone among Turkish consumers. *Journal of Euromarketing, 13*(2-3), 143–162. doi:10.1300/J037v13n02_08

Dotson, K. (2011). *Turkey Hit by Further Anonymous Hacks and Data Leaks*. Retrieved April 12, 2014 from http://siliconangle.com/blog/2011/07/08/turkey-hit-by-further-anonymous-hacks-and-data-leaks/

e-EAP (e-Europe Action Plan). (2005). Retrieved December 10, 2010 from http://ec.europa.eu/information_society/eeurope/2002/news_library/documents/eeurope2005/eeurope2005_en.pdf

ENISA. (2014). *Top Ten Smartphone Risks*. Retrieved 12 April, 2014 from http://www.enisa.europa.eu/act/application-security/smartphone-security-1/top-ten-risks

European Union. (2012). *EU Data Protection Directive 95/46/EC*. Retrieved April 12, 2014 from http://eur-lex.europa.eu/LexUriServ/LexUriServ.do?uri=CELEX:31995L0046:en:HTML

Eurostat. (2007). *E-government on-line availability*. Retrieved April 12, 2014 from http://epp.eurostat.ec.europa.eu/statistics_explained/index.php/E-government_statistics

Evci, C., Ciliz, K., Anarim, E., & Sankur, B. (2004). *Wireless networks in Turkey: A jewel in the crowd*. Alcatel Telecommunications Review.

Ferguson, M. (2001). e-Government- A strategic Framework for public services in the information age. London: Society of IT Management.

Fiss, P. C., & Zajac, E. J. (2004). The diffusion of ideas over contested terrain: The (non) adoption of shareholder value among German firms. *Adminstration Science Quarterly, 49*, 501–534.

Fitchard, K. (2013). *Ericsson: Global smartphone penetration will reach 60% in 2019*. Retrieved March 31, 2014 from http://gigaom.com/2013/11/11/ericsson-global-smartphone-penetration-will-reach-60-in-2019/

Fukuyama, F. (1995). *Trust: The Social Virtues and the Creation of Prosperity*. New York, NY: Free Press.

Garson, G. D. (2006a). *Public Information Technology and E-governance: Managing the Virtual State*. Sudbury, MA: Jones and Bartlett.

Ghyasi, A. F., & Kushchu, I. (2004). *Uses of mobile government in developing countries, unpublished*. Mobile Government Lab.

Google. (2012). *ClientLogin for Installed Applications*. Retrieved April 12, 2014 from http://code.google.com/apis/accounts/docs/AuthForInstalledApps.html

Google. (2013). *Google Wallet Security*. Retrieved April 12, 2013 from http://www.google.com/wallet/how-it-works-security.htm

Google. (2014). *Google Seek For Android*. Retrieved April 12, 2014, from http://code.google.com/p/seek-for-android/

Gubbins, M. (2004). Global IT spending by sector. *Computing, 8*, 28.

Gülaçtı, E. (2009). *Elektronik İmza ve Güvenlik*. Tubitak, Uekae.

Hanna, N. (2010). *Transforming Government and Building the Information Society: Challenges and Opportunities for the Developing World*. New York, NY: Springer.

Hazlett, S. A., & Hill, F. (2003). E-government: The realities of using IT to transform the public sector. *Managing Service Quality, 13*(6), 445–452. doi:10.1108/09604520310506504

Heeks, R. (2002). *Failure, Success and Improvisation of Information Systems Projects in Developing Countries. Institute for Development Policy and Management (IDPM)*. University of Manchester.

Heggestuen, J. (2013). *One In Every 5 People In The World Own A Smartphone, One In Every 17 Own A Tablet*. Retrieved March 31, 2014, from http://www.businessinsider.com/smartphone-and-tablet-penetration-2013-10

Holliday, I., & Kwok, R. C. V. (2004). Governance in the information age: Building e-government in Hong Kong. *New Media & Society, 6*(4), 549–570. doi:10.1177/146144804044334

Humeyra, P. (2014). *Turkey begins espionage investigation after Syria leak*. Retreved April 12, 2014 from http://www.reuters.com/article/2014/03/29/us-turkey-election-idUS-BREA2R12X20140329

Hurriet Daily News. (2013). *Istanbul's Kadıköy offers free Wi-Fi on streets*. Retrieved from http://www.hurriyetdailynews.com/istanbuls-kadikoy-offers-free-wi-fi-on-streets.aspx?pageID=238&nID=55204&NewsCatID=341

Hurriet Daily News. (2014). *Turkey ranks second in Internet censors: Report*. Retrieved from http://www.hurriyetdailynews.com/turkey-ranks-second-in-internet-censors-report.aspx?pageID=238&nID=62219&NewsCatID=339

ICTA. (2013). *Electronic Communications Market in Turkey*. Retrieved April 12, 2014 from http://eng.btk.gov.tr/kutuphane_ve_veribankasi/pazar_verileri/2013_Q2_ECM_MarketData.pdf

IETF. (2012). Retrieved April 12, 2014 from http://tools.ietf.org/html/draft-ietf-websec-strict-transport-sec-02

Intelligence, G. S. M. A. (2014). *Mobile data usage on the rise in the Middle East*. Retrieved April 12, 2014 from https://gsmaintelligence.com/analysis/2013/07/mobile-data-usage-on-the-rise-in-the-middle-east/393/

ITU. (2013). *Key ICT indicators for developed and developing countries and the world*. Retrieved April 6, 2014 from http://www.itu.int/en/ITU-D/Statistics/Documents/statistics/2013/ITU_Key_2005-2013_ICT_data.xls

Janssen, M., Scholl, H., Wimmer, M., & Hua Tan, Y. (2011). *Electronic Government: 10th International Conference*. New York, NY: Springer.

Jorgensen, D. J., & Klay, E. W. (2007). Technology-driven change and public administration: Establishing essential normative principles. *International Journal of Public Administration, 30*, 289–305. doi:10.1080/01900690601117770

Kahraman, C., Demirel Cetin, N., & Demirel, T. (2007). Prioritization of e-government strategies using a SWOT-AHP analysis: The case of Turkey. *European Journal of Information Systems, 16*, 284–298. doi:10.1057/palgrave.ejis.3000679

Koehn, D. (2003). The nature of and conditions for online trust. *Journal of Business Ethics, 43*, 3–19. doi:10.1023/A:1022950813386

Kumas, E. (2007). E-devlet kapısı ve risk değerlendirme metodolojisi. *Turkiye'de Internet Konferansi, 12*.

Kuran, N. H. (2005). *Türkiye icin E-devlet modeli.* Istanbul, Turkey: Bilgi Universitesi Yayınları.

Kurbanoglu, S. (2004). An overview of information literacy studies in Turkey. *The International Information & Library Review*, *36*(1), 23–27. doi:10.1016/j.iilr.2003.07.001

Kushchu, I. (2007). *Mobile Government: An Emerging Direction in E-Government.* Hershey, PA: IGI Publishing. doi:10.4018/978-1-59140-884-0

Kushchu, I., & Kuscu, H. (2003). From e-government to m-government: Facing the inevitable. In *Proceeding of European Conference on E-Government* (ECEG), (pp.253-260). Reading, UK: Academic Conferences International.

Lam, W. (2005). Barriers to e-government integration. *The Journal of Enterprise Information Management*, *18*(5), 511–530. doi:10.1108/17410390510623981

Lusch, R. F., & Vargo, S. L. (2006). Service dominant logic reactions, reflections and refinements. *Marketing Theory*, *6*(3), 281–288. doi:10.1177/1470593106066781

Mahmood, Z. (2013). *E-Government Implementation and Practice in Developing Countries.* Hershey, PA: IGI Global. doi:10.4018/978-1-4666-4090-0

Mao, E., Srite, M., Thatcher, J. B., & Yaprak, O. (2005). A research model for mobile phone service behaviors: Empirical validation in the U.S. & Turkey. *Journal of Global Information Technology Management*, *8*(4), 7–29.

Mayer, R. C. Davis, & Schoorman, F.D. (1995). An integrative model of organizational trust. Academy of Management Review, 20, 709-734.

Meshur, H. F. A. (2007). *Information and Communication Technologies (ICT) and the Changing Nature of Work: Anytime, Anyplace, Anywhere.* Selcuk University.

Millard, J. (2006). User attitudes to e-government citizen services in Europe. *International Journal of Electronic Government Research*, *2*(2), 49–58. doi:10.4018/jegr.2006040103

Moe, R. (1994). The "Reinventing Government" Exercise: Misinterpreting the Problem, Misjudging the Consequences. *Public Administration Review*, *54*(2), 111–122. doi:10.2307/976519

Moral, C. (2009). Türkiye Bölgede Lider Olmaya Aday. *BThaber.* Retreived December 10, 2010 from http://www.bthaber.com.tr/haber.phtml?yazi_id=705000782

Naralan, A. (2008). Türkiye'de E-Devlet Güçlükleri. *EKEV Akademi Dergisi*, *12*(37), 27–40.

Ng, K. (2010). Turkey's GCIO reveals success of citizen ID. *Asia Pacific FutureGov.* Retrieved December 10, 2010 from http://www.futuregov.asia/articles/2010/mar/02/Turkey-GCIO-reveals-success-citizen-ID/

NIST Computer Security. (2009). Retrieved December 10, 2009 from http://csrc.nist.gov/publications/nistpubs/800-57/sp800-57_PART3_key-management_Dec2009.pdf

Odabaş, Ç. (2005). Stratejik Yönetim ve E-Devlet. *Sayıştay Dergisi*, *55*, 83–94.

OWASP. (2014a). *Cloud Top 10.* Retreved April 12, 2014 from https://www.owasp.org/index.php/Category:OWASP_Cloud_%E2%80%90_10_Project

OWASP. (2014b). *Top 10 mobile risks.* Retrieved 12 April, 2014 from https://www.owasp.org/index.php/OWASP_Mobile_Security_Project#tab=Top_Ten_Mobile_Risks

OWASP. (2014c). *Web Services.* Retrieved April 12, 2014 from https://www.owasp.org/index.php/Web_Services

Ozcan, Y. Z., & Kocak, A. (2003). Research note: A need or a status symbol? Use of cellular telephones in Turkey. *European Journal of Communication, 18*(2), 241–254. doi:10.1177/0267323103018002004

Payne, A. F., Storbacka, K., & Frow, P. (2008). Managing the co-creation of value. *Journal of the Academy of Marketing Science, 36*(1), 83–96. doi:10.1007/s11747-007-0070-0

Port Turkey. (2013). *Internet economy of Turkey to grow 19% until 2017*. Retrieved April 12, 2014 from http://www.portturkey.com/internet/5097-internet-economy-of-turkey-to-grow-19-until-2017

Reddick, C. G. (2005). Citizen interaction with e-government: From the streets to servers? *Government Information Quarterly, 22*, 38–57. doi:10.1016/j.giq.2004.10.003

ResmiGazete. (2006). Yüksek Planlama Kururu Kararı. *Elektronik Resmi Gazete, 26242*.

Sahin, A., Temizel, H., & Temizel, M. (2010). Türkiye'de demokrasiden e-demokrasiye geçiş süreci ve karşılaşılan sorunlar. *E-demokrasi*. Retrieved December 11, 2010 from http://www.e-demokrasi.org/index.php?option=com_content&view=article&id=31:tuerkiyede-demokrasiden-e-demokrasiye-geci-suereci-ve-karlalan-sorunlar&catid=7:makaleler&Itemid=21

Saxena, K. B. C. (2005). Towards excellence in e-governance. *International Journal of Public Sector Management, 18*(6), 498–513. doi:10.1108/09513550510616733

Schweitzer, D., Boleng, J., Hughes, C., & Murphy, L. (2009). *Visualizing Keyboard Pattern Passwords*. Retrieved April 12, 2014 from cs.wheatoncollege.edu/~mgousie/comp401/amos.pdf

Sharma, S. K., & Gupta, J. N. D. (2004). Web services architecture for m-government: Issues and challenges. *Electronic Government, 1*(4), 462–474. doi:10.1504/EG.2004.005921

Softpedia. (2013). *Hackers Claim to Have Breached Turkey's Ministry of Finance, Data Leaked*. Retrieved April 12, 2014 from http://news.softpedia.com/news/Hackers-Claim-to-Have-Breached-Turkey-s-Ministry-of-Finance-Data-Leaked-364642.shtml

SSLSNIFF. (2014). Retrieved April 12, 2014 from http://tools.ietf.org/html/draft-ietf-websec-strict-transport-sec-02

Stahl, B. C. (2005). The ethical problem of framing e-government in terms of e-commerce. *The Electronic. Journal of E-Government, 3*(2), 77–86.

State Planning Organization. (2006a). *Information Society Strategy (2006-2010)*. Retrieved December 10, 2010 from http://www.bilgitoplumu.gov.tr/eng/docs/Information_Society_Strategy.pdf

State Planning Organization. (2006b). *Information Society Strategy (2006-2010) Action Plan*. Retrieved December, 2010 from http://www.bilgitoplumu.gov.tr/eng/docs/Action_Plan.pdf

Sungu, E., Sungu, H., & Bayrakci, M. (2008). *E-inclusion: Providing services towards an information society for all*. Paper presented at the 8th International Educational Technology Conference. New York, NY.

Taşçı, B. (2010). Aradiginiz e-Devlet'e ulasilamiyor. *HTEKONOMI*. Retrieved October 12, 2010 from http://ekonomi.haberturk.com/teknoloji/haber/541303-aradiginiz-e-devlete-ulasilamiyor

Thornton, P. H. (2002). The rise of the corporation in a craft industry: Conflict and conformity in institutional logics. *Academy of Management Journal, 45*, 81–101. doi:10.2307/3069286

Thornton, P. H. (2004). *Markets from culture: Institutional logics and organizational decisions in high education publishing.* Standford, CA: Stanford University Press.

Todays Zaman. (2014). *FATİH project distributes tablet PCs.* Retrieved April 12, 2014 from http://www.todayszaman.com/news-339699-fatih-project-distributes-tablet-pcs.html

Torenli, N. (2006). The 'other' faces of digital exclusion: ICT gender divides in the broader community. *European Journal of Communication, 21*(4), 435–455. doi:10.1177/0267323106070010

TSI. (2008). *ICT Usage Survey on Households.* Turkish Standards Institute.

TUIK. (2007). *ICT usage survey on households and individuals.* Ankara, Turkey: Turkish Statistical Institute.

TUIK. (2008). *ICT usage survey on households and individuals.* Ankara, Turkey: Turkish Statistical Institute.

TURKSAT. (2008). Retrieved December 10, 2010 from http://www.turksat.com.tr/english/index.php/e-Government-/e-Government-Gateway-Project/What-is-e-Government-Gateway-Project.html

TURKSTAT. (2012). *Information and communication technology (ICT) usage survey on households and individuals.* Retrieved April 12, 2014 from http://www.turkstat.gov.tr/PreHaber-Bultenleri.do?id=10880

TUSIAD. (2010). *Türkiye İçin E-devlet Yönetim Modeline Doğru: Mevcut Durum Değerlendirmesi ve Öneriler, Report.* Author.

Uçkan, Ö. (2003). *E-devlet,-demokrasi ve e-yönetişim modeli:Bir ilkesel öncelik olarak bilgiye erişim özgürlüğü.* Retrieved December 11, 2010 from http://www.stradigma.com/turkce/haziran2003/print_09.html

University, U. L. M. (2014a). *Google's Client-Login implementation.* Retrieved April 12, 2014 from http://www.uni-ulm.de/in/mi/mitarbeiter/koenings/catching-authtokens.html

University, U. L. M. (2014b). *Google vulnerability of Client Login account credentials on unprotected.* Retrieved April 12, 2014 from http://www.uni-ulm.de/in/mi/mitarbeiter/koenings/catching-authtokens.html

Ustun, A., Yazici, A., Akman, I., & Arifoglu, A. (2008). *Mobile government in Turkey: Investigating drivers and barriers.* Paper presented at the European Conferences on e-Government (ECEG). Lausanne, Switzerland.

Warschauer, M. (2004). *Technology and Social Inclusion: Rethinking the Digital Divide.* Cambridge, MA: The MIT Press.

West, D. M. (2007). *Global E-Government.* Providence, RI: Brown University.

Whittington, R. (2003). The work of strategizing and organizing: For a practice perspective. *Strategic Organization, 1*(1), 117–125. doi:10.1177/1476127003001001221

Wire. (2014). Retrieved from http://www.wired.co.uk/news/archive/2014-03/27/turkey-youtube-ban

Wolcott, P., & Cagiltay, K. (2001). Telecommunications, liberalization and the growth of the internet in Turkey. *The Information Society, 17*(2), 133–141. doi:10.1080/019722401750175685

Yeloğlu, H. O., & Sağsan, M. (2009). The diffusion of e-government innovations in Turkey: A conceptual framework. *Journal of US-China Public Administration, 6*(7), 17–23.

Yildirim, M. (2010). Yanlışlığı düzeltmek gerek. *EGA.* Retrieved December 10, 2010 from www.ega.com.tr/haber_detay.php?haber_id=48

Yildiz, M. (2007). The state of mobile government in Turkey: Overview, policy issues, and future prospects. In I. Kushchu (Ed.), *Mobile Government: An Emerging Direction in E-Government.* Hershey, PA: IGI Publishing. doi:10.4018/978-1-59140-884-0.ch013

Yucel, I. H. (2006). *Türkiye'de Bilim Teknoloji Politikalari ve İktisadi Gelişmenin Yönü. Sosyal Sektörler ve Koordinasyon Genel Müdürlüğü.* Devlet Planlama Teşkilatı.

KEY TERMS AND DEFINITIONS

Cellular Phone: A device that operates as a medium for communication while the user moves from one geographic area to the other.

Digital Divide: A phenomenon that is related to the user's limited access to the technology.

Digital Divided Populations: Technophobic populations that do not expect to use technology because they are afraid of its influence to their daily life.

E-Government: The digital transaction between the government and the citizens or the government and other governments.

Government Services: The public services that are offered by the government to the citizens.

M-Government: The transaction between the government and the citizens or between the government and other governments through the use of mobile devices.

Mobile Communication: A medium of transferring knowledge and improving the status of the information society.

Practice: The method which aims to standardize the way of acting in specific processes.

Chapter 11

A Road Far Too Long?
E-Government and the State of Service Delivery in Bangladesh

Noore Alam Siddiquee
Flinders University, Australia

Md Gofran Faroqi
Flinders University, Australia

ABSTRACT

This chapter reviews the state of e-government development and associated changes to service delivery in Bangladesh. Using the "stage model" as a frame of reference, the authors show the progresses Bangladesh has made in terms of informational, interactive, transactional, and integrated services. They argue that although Bangladesh's overall progress is still modest for it allows only limited advanced levels of services, there are encouraging trends underway. In its conclusion, the chapter highlights some of the impediments and challenges that hamper e-government initiatives undermining their potentials and benefits in the country.

INTRODUCTION

While public sector reform is nothing new, the advent of information and communication technology (ICT) has marked the beginning of a new phase of reform which promises to bring about radical improvements in governmental operations and services. Widely known as e-government, the new reform has acquired a global character with both developed and developing countries embracing it. At its simplest, it entails the application of ICT in the public sector. While there are various interpretations of e-government in this chapter we use the term to mean the governmental system that delivers public services by using ITC as a tool. It is more than mere presence of governmental websites on the Internet; it involves the transaction and information exchange between government, citizens and businesses with the help of ICT. Though it seeks to enhance the efficiency of government, at the heart of e-government is the desire to increase the availability of governmental information and services by making them accessible to citizens and other users at all

DOI: 10.4018/978-1-4666-3691-0.ch011

times. Bekkers captures it all when he says that e-government is the 'use of ICT to design new or redesign existing information, communication and transaction relationships between governments and citizens, companies and non-governmental organisations as well as between different government organisations and layers in order to achieve specific goals" (Bekkers, 2013: 253). Relevant goals, according to him, include the improvement of the access to government, the enhancement of the quality and efficiency of public service delivery processes, the improvement of internal and external efficiency, the support of public and political accountability, the support of the political participation of citizens and the strengthening of inter-organisational cooperation. Indeed, these are some of the areas where e-government can deliver significant benefits.

Not surprisingly, e-government has enjoyed massive popularity fuelled by the belief that it can enhance service delivery and produce significant improvements in various domains. A UN report asserts that e-government can result in better delivery of services to citizens, improved interactions with businesses and industry, citizen's empowerment through greater access to information and/or efficient governmental management (UN, 2003). It is also believed to be associated with a range of other values. Foremost among them are savings in time and efforts, operational efficiency, convenience and user-friendliness. It is seen as a mechanism that can transform the outmoded bureaucracy, give citizens and businesses greater access to governmental services at the same time help reduce paperwork, and eventually save governmental resources (Backus, 2001, Lam, 2005). Online availability of services also means that the users will benefit from 24x7x365 access to government information and services. Apart from economic and administrative benefits as above, e-government is desirable for it fosters good governance in the society: it does so by promoting transparency in governmental operations, help-

ing combat corruption, improving governmental accountability and responsiveness (West, 2004).

However, the benefits of e-government can hardly be taken for granted: the extent to which such merits translate into reality depends largely on the state of e-government development – a phenomenon explained by a number of theories and models. One of the most popular among them is the maturity/stage model which postulates that countries go through a number of stages in their e-journey before they are able to transform service delivery systems and deliver the benefits, as noted. The United Nations model (UN, 2008) suggests that as countries move towards maturity they pass through several thresholds in terms of information development, content delivery, business re-engineering and so on. This model involves five stages: *emerging presence* (development of websites with some basic information), *enhanced presence* (websites with greater information and download option), *interactive stage* (further development with interactive features), *transactional stage* (provision of complete and two-way transactions) and finally the *connected stage* (complete integration of service delivery and the institutions offering them). These stages are used to benchmark the UN member states based on their ability to deliver online services to citizens and other stakeholders[1]. Likewise, Moon's model suggests that e-government development entails five basic stages: information, communication, transaction, integration and participation. Each of these stages is characterized by a different level of sophistication and interface with citizens and others. Stage 1 is the most basic - featuring one-way information dissemination and stage 5 is the most sophisticated level which allows variety of political participation including online voting, opinion polls and consultation (see Moon, 2002). However, it must be noted that while each stage is distinct, different stages can occur simultaneously (Herman & Cullen, 2006). Also, it is relevant to note that along the way there are formidable barriers and obstacles that thwart a country's transition from one stage to the other thus affecting developmental impacts and benefits.

Drawing on these models above in this chapter we review the experience of a South Asian country - Bangladesh in the realm of e-government. The primary aim of the chapter is to show how and to what extent Bangladesh has progressed in terms of informational, interactive, transactional and integrated services[2]. It also seeks to present recent initiatives towards making e-services available at the grassroots level. The chapter is based on information available in secondary sources and primary data collected from district and union levels[3]. It is organized as follows. Following the introduction, it sets out with the trajectory of e-government in Bangladesh highlighting the policy framework and institutional arrangements for the purpose. Section two outlines the current state of e-government and levels of informational, interactional, transactional and integrated services currently available. Section three focuses on the development of Union Information & Service Centres (UISCs) and District E-Service Centres (DESCs) – the two most recent schemes intended to reach governmental services to the doorsteps of the rural communities. Finally, in its conclusion the chapter highlights some of the current impediments and challenges that hamper the speedy implementation of e-government and broadening the scope of online services.

E-Government in Bangladesh: The Institutional and Policy Environment

Although emphasis to modernize public administration with the help of science and technology was put as early as in 1972 immediately after the birth of Bangladesh the actual process in this regard did not begin until the mid-1990s. After a prolonged period of confusion and inaction, it was the *Awami League* government during its second term in office (1996-2001) that took concrete steps towards adoption of ICT in the public sector. It agreed to connect the country with Information Super Highway, designated the ICT as a thrust sector, waived taxes on computers and computer accessories and formed a Task Force with the Prime Minister as its head. All this marked the beginning of Bangladesh's journey towards e-government.

Following the political change in 2001 the new government continued with the implementation of e-government as suggested by Public Administration Reform Commission, 2000. It also outlined a framework of strategies and actions in this regard. The formulation of the National ICT Policy, 2002 was among the most significant developments during 2001-2005 periods. The policy outlined the visions of e-government with the objective of improving the quality of services to the citizens. Among others, the policy envisaged the establishment of telecommunication infrastructure nationwide, connecting to submarine fibre optic cable networks, extending internet facility to rural areas, establishing cyber kiosks in post offices, union and *upazila* (sub-district) complexes, setting up an internet exchange and increasing the bandwidth capacity and availability. It also emphasised the spread of ICT in governmental agencies across the country including ministries, divisions, departments, autonomous bodies and all district and *upazila* headquarters and *Union Parishad* offices (GOB, 2002). Subsequent changes and modifications to the ICT policy identified action plans, the actors, expected deliverables and benefits and goals for short, medium and long-term development. The revised ICT Policy announced in 2009 started from a singular national vision of enhancing social equity through the use of ICT; it outlined specific objectives, strategic themes and action plans for realizing the visions into reality. The policy envisaged expanding the use of ICT with the ultimate aim of instituting an accountable, transparent and responsive government. ICT is seen as a driving force supportive of the national goal of becoming a middle-income country within 10 years and joining the ranks of developed countries within 30 years (GOB, 2009; Siddiquee & Faroqi, 2013).

Since the implementation of ICT policy required a legal framework as well as management structures the government introduced relevant legislation and institutional mechanisms. The ICT Act passed in 2006 aims to prevent crimes related to computer fraud, hacking, damaging programmes and data and launching computer viruses. The ICT (Electronic Transactions) Act, 2006 was designed to facilitate e-commerce by safeguarding the online transactions. It is also intended to foster electronic filing in government agencies and ensure efficient delivery of electronic records. The Official Internet Connection and Usage Policy 2004 outlines the framework for the use of internet facilities in government offices and determines its management and financial aspects, such as 'entitlement', 'approval procedures', and 'cost limits' (Hoque, 2006). Meanwhile the current *Awami League* government has articulated the vision of 'Digital Bangladesh' making it a part of the nation's development strategy. Conceived and implemented under the UNDP funded Access to Information (A2I) program Digital Bangladesh represents the cornerstone of e-government in Bangladesh. Digital Bangladesh agenda includes a digitized government, ICT enabled services, nationwide internet connectivity and high tech-parks for business and IT trained professionals (A2I, 2008). It also aims at developing human resources ready for the 21st century, connecting citizens in ways most meaningful to them, bringing services to the doorsteps of the citizens' and making the private sector and market more productive and competitive through the use of ICTs (GOB, 2009). A number of policy measures introduced since then including the ICT Policy 2009, ICT Act 2009[4], Right to Information Act 2009, various local government acts have laid the foundation for making Digital Bangladesh a reality (Siddiquee, 2013).

Efforts have also been made to create and strengthen the management structure for the implementation of e-government. The structure involves a number of organisations with the Information & Communication Technology Division of the Ministry of Posts, Telecommunications & Information Technology (MoPTIT) in the leading position. It has been assigned the responsibility for the development and promotion of the ICT sector. The Prime Minister's Office (PMO) plays the central role on policy matters related to e-government. The E-government Cell established within the PMO provides directives and guidelines for the implementation of e-government programs including oversight and coordination of the implementation of such initiatives. The National ICT Task Force (NTF) chaired by the Prime Minister is responsible for mainstreaming ICT throughout the public sector. Renamed recently as the Digital Bangladesh Task Force (DBTF) it is represented by stakeholders from the government, the private sector and the civil society and responsible for monitoring milestones in the implementation of Digital Bangladesh agenda and advising the government on policy matters and means of achieving goals. A number of government ministries have also been given significant roles to play. The MoPTIT is responsible for the development of infrastructure and human resources for successful application of ICT in the society. It also formulates ICT policies and oversees the implementation of such policies. The Bangladesh Telecommunications Regulatory Commission (BTRC), an autonomous body under the ministry, regulates the telecommunication providers - both fixed and mobile lines. It also oversees the licensing for the VSAT operators and Internet Service Providers (ISPs), the development of digitization schemes, regulation of tariffs and setting of standards (BTRC, 2009). The Ministry of Finance plays an important role by incorporating the development and strategies of e-government in annual budgets and allocating resources for the purpose. Apart from the government agencies a number of private organisations e.g. the Bangladesh Computer Council (BCC), the Bangladesh Computer Samity (BCS), the Bangladesh Internet Service Providers (ISP) Association, and the Bangladesh Association for Software and Information Services (BASIS) have important roles in e-government. Among others, they advocate for broadening of e-government, render expert services on ICT, lobby for ICT policy decisions/laws and provide training for human resources development.

E-Government and Transformation of Service Delivery: Developments and Trends

Since mid-1990s Bangladesh has witnessed variety of efforts toward the goals of e-government. The early initiatives focused on the development of ICT infrastructure and automation of existing governmental processes seeking to enhance efficiency in service provision. With the launch of the A2I program e-government initiatives received further boost which saw a shift in focus from institution-building to delivery of services at various levels. While the drive for infrastructure development still continues in view of the nation's overall poor infrastructure situation, since 2010 the provision of integrated services has become a core objective of e-government. Under the Digital Bangladesh agenda, emphasis is placed on fostering integration and expanding scopes for transactional services (IGS, 2009). Numerous programs and projects implemented since the early years have led to significant changes to the way government operates and delivers important services to the citizens and other users. This section outlines the development of e-government with a specific focus on informational, interactive, transactional and integrated services.

Informational Services

Bangladesh has recorded commendable progress in respect of informational service and/or online presence of the government. The latest UN Survey shows that Bangladesh is among the developing countries that have fully utilized online presence although progress in other areas is not equally impressive (United Nations 2012). All offices of the government from the *Union Parishad* to the central secretariat have websites containing information about the office, the organisational hierarchy, services provided, achievements, relevant policies and contact address, among others. The national web portal of Bangladesh (www.bangladesh.gov.bd) serves as an access point for information and contact details of various government agencies and departments. This site also contains the web addresses of the President's Office, the Prime Minister's Office, the Council of Ministers, the Parliament, the Judiciary, statutory bodies, 41 ministries and divisions apart from information about citizen services, business services, various circulars and gazettes. It also displays important events and information related to education, disaster management, passport, income tax and market prices. It also contains information on process of starting a business, foreign direct investment, weather and climate, tourism and national statistics, government forms, postal services, stock exchanges, and currency rate (NWPB, 2014). Majority of the governmental websites contain various information or charter of services offered without giving the users an opportunity to interact or complete transaction (BEI, 2010). In fact, 78% of offices do not use any customized software to provide required services to their customers.

An important feature of e-government and informational services is the development of *e-tothyakosh* (electronic information cell) available at www.infokosh.bangladesh.gov.bd. This information hub is user friendly and can be understood by all classes of users as it encompasses a host of options such as text document, audio, video, animation and picture. Though all forms of information provision have not been equally developed, text document being the dominant, still *e-tothyakosh* pulls together huge information from various public and private institutions on agriculture, education, health, literature and culture, law and human rights, citizen services, tourism, non-agriculture enterprise, environment and disaster management, science & information and communication technology, commerce and industry, labor and employment, etc. For instance, the website guides users how to apply for land copy, passport, TIN registration, how to obtain the national identity card or amend it, set up a small business, prevent women and children from repression, use technology, fertilizer and pesticides in agriculture, treat minor ailments and get examination results or registration/admission (GOB, 2014). With some interactive features this website allows anyone to contact with the authority to post any information or comment on existing ones by providing e-mail ID. Citizens can also access some of these pre-recorded information, especially how to receive services from the local government bodies- the city corporations, thorough interactive voice response (IVR) using the mobile phone on 24/7 basis.

Interactive Services

Government web sites with interactive features are surging. Though in the UN survey Bangladesh has scored 60% in terms of utilisation interactive services, a great majority of this genre only allows one-way interaction. The one way interaction enables citizens to access government websites and download forms without any authentication. Various governmental forms are available through 'Bangladesh Government Digitized Forms -e-Citizen Services Application' linked to www.forms.gov.bd. A total of 65 different kinds of service forms of various public entities including forms for birth and death registration, driving license, vehicle registration, citizenship certificate, family pension, passport and immigration, income tax return are available. Also available in the website are no objection certificate (NOC), visa application form, utility bills form, telephone connection

forms, TIN application. Without providing any identification anyone can download these forms. The same goes with e-books developed by the Ministry of Education and the National Curriculum and Textbook Board (NCTB). All primary and secondary school and *Madrasah* textbooks as well all books of Technical Education Board (TEB) are available online and anyone can download these books without giving any identity (NCTB, 2014).

Bangladesh has also made considerable inroads in terms of two-way interactive services both for citizens and businesses. Major interactive services for citizens are e-taxation, online request to the Police, admission/ registration and result check, health and agriculture consultation, passport and land copy application, VISA check, etc. The e-taxation website hosted by National Board of Revenue (NBR) allows both individual and corporate bodies online tax calculation and submission of Income Tax Return (NBR, 2014). There is an online service for the Citizen Help Request (CHR) mostly for non-urgent cases to the Dhaka Metropolitan Police (DMP, 2014). A horde of educational services are interactive that can be accessed through mobile SMS or online. Online/SMS admission and registration, for instance, is a very popular interactive service offered by majority of educational institutions. Some of them even allow financial transactions with the help of mobile operators or credit cards. For instance, payment of admission fees in universities like Bangladesh University of Engineering & Technology (BUET) and Shahjalal University of Science and Technology can be made using mobile phone (Bhuiyan, 2011).

Almost all secondary educational institutions have to register their students for public exams online with the respective education boards. The Directorate of Secondary and Higher Education allows teachers to apply online for MPO/Subject/ Index/Designation correction or for Selection Grade/Time Scale. Non-government teachers can also apply online for welfare assistance as well as to Employee Retirement Benefit Board for retirement benefits. Non-government Teachers' Registration and Certification Authority (NTRCA) under the Ministry of Education provides teacher's registration online. Result check through SMS has become an easy and extremely popular method across Bangladesh. In 2013, between January and June 63 million results of public examinations were delivered through online and 38 million over SMS (MoE, 2014) .

The Ministry of Agriculture has introduced some interactive services for the farmers including mobile phone advice on agriculture, and local market prices (MoA, 2014).The Ministry of Health offers mobile phone health service by making the mobile numbers of doctors working in the local upazila/ district available in its website, mobile advice for pregnant mothers, telemedicine through UISCs and community clinics (MoH, 2014). The Department of Immigration and Passports allows online application for machine readable passport (MRP) in which the clients can register and submit the initial application. The electronic system then sorts those applications out before advising the applicant to visit the passport office of his/her local area with necessary documents (DIP, 2014). Similarly people can make initial application for land copy online using the websites of their respective Deputy Commissioner's Office. Online visa checking hosted by Bureau of Manpower, Employment and Training (BMET) ensures the verification of authenticity of visa to those seeking jobs overseas and protects them from forgery and deceit (BMET, 2014). Bangladesh Public Service Commission (BPSC) has made all its examination registration and result checks available online. Applications for civil service examination, departmental or senior scale examination for government officers can be executed online. The results can also be known through online checking (BPSC, 2014). Other interactive e-government services include Online Hajj Information Management System that can also be accessed through mobile phone, as with early warning of disaster by the Ministry of Disaster Management and Relief.

Like services for common citizens, a bunch of interactive services are also available for businesses. These include corporate tax, public procurement and electronic banking. Corporate tax can be assessed and calculated using the online tool provided by the National Board of Revenue (NBR) and submitted online. The e-procurement which was initially piloted in 16 procuring entities under four major agencies is now being rolled out to 291 entities. It would be gradually expanded to other sectoral agencies of the government stretching up to districts and *upazila* levels. The e-procurement system enables the tenderers to interact with PEs in registration by giving their credentials, documents and submitting bids and work plans online. The e-contract management system (e-CMS) emboldens the PEs to rate vendor, monitor progress, perform quality checks, and generate bills, among others. This system has improved transparency and accountability in the procurement system of many of the government agencies (CPTU, 2014). Perhaps the biggest provider of online interactive services to business is the central bank of the country that delivers services to its primary clients- the banks and financial institutions. The Bangladesh Bank's online Credit Information Bureau (CIB) supports banks and financial institutions' access to credit information of potential and current borrowers and avoid risks as well as allow them to furnish any new credit information. E-tendering system in the Bank permits bidders from local and international market to participate in Bank's procurement process. A range of other online services such as e-returns, online recruitment system, LC monitoring system, online import management system (Bangladesh Bank, 2014) indicate the progress made in this regard.

While these services are interactive in nature, they are marked by the absence of a significant part of interaction - the financial payment. Though people/businesses can upload applications or submit online, still they need to visit those providers to make financial transactions or to validate their online application, both of which can be avoided through complete application of e-transaction. Bangladesh's progress in transactional services is hampered by inadequate development of online payment system and the absence of legal framework for e-payment and digital signature.

Transactional Services

Bangladesh has made limited progress in the area of transactional services. Currently, some banks are facilitating online transactions with debit and credit cards to purchase commodities from trading outlets alongside VISA/ Master cards. But such payment system has remained confined mostly to private companies with limited application in the government. Some utility providers permit online transactions. The utility providers such as Power Development Board (PDB), Dhaka Electricity Supply Authority (DESA), Water and Sewerage Authority (WASA), Titas Gas, Bangladesh Telegraph and Telephone Board (BTTB) have all made contracts with different banks for their bills to be paid electronically using internet banking, ATMs, Ready Cash Card, Q-Cash Card, POS and other channels. However, these efforts are only limited to cities thus providing services to the urban population. Utility bills of some providers can also be paid through mobile phone (UNDP, 2006, p. 4).

Major banks in Bangladesh, especially the private ones have introduced online banking and e-commerce for their clients. Clients are allowed to manage their accounts online and transfer money from one account to another within the same bank or other banks that have such arrangement with the client's bank, download statements and see transaction history, etc. Partnered with mobile operators three private banks, namely the Dutch-Bangla Bank, the Trust Bank and the BRAC bank have introduced inward remittance transfer facility in their outlets at grass root levels, popularly known as *mobile banking.* Mobile banking has the potential to bank nearly 87% of unbanked people (those who do not have bank accounts - especially

millions of poor). Anyone can open an account with any of these providers using his/her mobile phone and can deposit, pay out or transfer money in another account directly by himself or through nearby agents and can cash out from nearest agent's outlets. For instance the Dutch Bangla Bank has 82035 agents facilitating mobile banking in the country (DBBL, 2014). This type of banking saves people's real time, cost and reduces hassles of queuing before traditional banks, not to emphasize its role in fostering economic and business development. BRAC Bank's mobile banking unit *bKash* signed an MOU with the Local Government Division and Access to Information (A2I) to allow entrepreneurs at Union Information & Service Centers (UISCs) to act as their agents and others are also following the same.

Railway ticketing is another transactional service that is currently available. Tickets can be purchased through internet by registering with some information such as cell phone number, e-mail address and then booking from available seats. Upon payment through VISA/Master/ Dutch-Bangla Bank Nexus Card the customers of Railway receive ticket details via e-mails. However, the printed ticket details have to be replaced with an e-ticket 15 minutes before travel in the designated counters showing the registered cell phone number and the card used for payment. Mobile providers such as Grameenphone and BanglaLink also provide railway e-ticket options to their subscribers.

It is evident that Bangladesh has recorded partial success in matters of transactional services. Efforts are currently afoot for ensuring full scale transactional services. Some of the developments in this regard include the formulation of Bangladesh Payment and Settlement Regulations, 2009 and establishment of the Controller of Certifying Authorities (CCA) Office for recruiting Certifying Authorities (for digital signatures). Such measures are expected to ensure secure online payment and help transformation towards transactional e-services (Bhuiyan, 2011).

Networked/Integrated Services

The networked or integrated stage is the most sophisticated level characterized by the integration of services and institutions aimed at removing physical barriers and offer most, if not all, public services spotlessly. It also enables the citizens to participate by involving in two-way open dialogues to express their views on public policy, law making, etc. and to receive responses. As noted, since 2010 Bangladesh has been striving towards integration of service delivery. Necessary acts and policies are being adopted with some limited implementation. For instance, Bangladesh e-governance Interoperability Framework (BD-eGIF) adopted by the Prime Minister's Office empowers a team to work for fulfilling the objectives of attaining efficiency, improved levels of services, and ensure cost effectiveness by eradicating the heaps of inconsistent information, incongruent data standards and ineffective communication among the government, businesses and citizens. In other words, it works for establishing one stop services across departments by bringing interoperability between key domains such as organisations, information and technology (Zaman, 2007; Bhuiyan 2012). The government's initiatives to establish the National Identity Registration Authority (NIRA) under an Ordinance in 2008 to provide 18 services to citizens such as passport, bank account and so on and consequently the enactment of National Identification Law in 2010 are all measures towards this end.

The e-government Interoperability Framework is aimed at facilitating a common standard framework among different ministries/divisions while developing their management information systems (MIS), websites, and portals. Development of Interoperability Framework will guarantee not only the compatible technologies across departments but also congruity between processes, policies and management, diverse stakeholders and interest groups to establish a coherent information system (Mahmood & Babul,

2009). Development of central databases as the National Voter ID, Birth Registration, Machine Readable Passport (MRP), Driving License, Tax Identification Number (TIN) make the issue of interoperability urgent since processes related to these databases scarcely follow any coherent standards. Towards interoperability a number of measures such as Unicode-compliant NIKOSH font (Bangla language) usage for preparing public document is suggested. Citizen Core Data Structure (CCDS) is another technical interoperability lately adopted by the Cabinet Division in July 2011. A major drive in this regard is the agreement between Bangladesh Election Commission (BEC) that prepares the National Identity Card and the NBR to share their information on national identity for validating the tax holder's information to prevent tax evasion (Bhuiyan, 2012). UNDP assisted Access to Information (A2I) Program under the Prime Minister's Office has been working on future plans that include interoperability as well as technical, operational and administrative issues.

Clearly, various e-government initiatives have changed the way public service was delivered in the past. In other words e-government has led to transformation of governance and service delivery processes. However, it has yet to deliver whole range of benefits given limited progress recorded thus far. Though web initiatives are abundant most of them are mere information type, some of them are interactive in nature. Only a handful of them are at transactional level and very few of them are in the connected/integrated stage. It is encouraging that a plethora of initiatives are underway to enhance the transactional and transformational services.

E-Services at the Grassroots Level: One-Stop Service Centres

In spite of the progresses and achievements in initiatives for online information and services the vast majority of the population especially those living in rural areas have remained largely unaffected. Though mobile-based applications have potentials to reach all, the same cannot be assumed for web-based ones. It is worth noting that nearly 70% of 150 million people in Bangladesh live in rural areas. The vast majority of them do not have capacity to purchase ICT. Also they lack ability to use the new technology as manifested in very high levels of illiteracy in the country. On the other hand, online availability of services and information poses a potential danger of digital divide (Islam, 2008).

Faced with such problematic economic and social realities, governments around the world often take recourse to leapfrogging in their development initiatives including e-government schemes to bypass mammoth infrastructural and management costs by adopting cheaper and convenient means. One such strategy, often known as quick-win, attempts to introduce e-governments through shared access points, spread mobile technologies to connect the masses, adopt public-private partnerships to curtail costs as well as permit private sectors to operate (UN, 2012; Karim 2010; Bhatnagar, 2004). The government of Bangladesh has also adopted few such quick win strategies to address the issue of digital divide and ensure the accessibility by all in the provision of online information and services. Table 1 provides a snapshot of some of the leading quick-win projects targeted to the people in the countryside. This section presents the developments at lower levels: the Union Information and Service Centre and District E-Service Centre - two most important initiatives aimed at addressing the digital divide and making services accessible to the rural poor.

Union Information and Service Centres

In a country like Bangladesh where ICT infrastructure is inadequate and the vast majority of people lack access to e-services as noted, e-government requires innovative solutions. Union Information

Table 1. Quick win initiatives for connecting rural masses

Quick Win Initiatives	Provider Ministry/Agency	Key Services	Main Beneficiaries	Comments
Promotion of e-Krishi through Agriculture Information and Communication Center (AICC), 2009	Ministry of Agriculture / Agriculture Information Service (AIS). Facilitated by officials and attended by clubs of farmers	ICT, print and audio-visual contents on agriculture	Farmers & agro business entrepreneurs	150 Union Parishads, 38000 direct users
Fisheries Information and Communication Centres (FICC), 2009	Ministry of Fisheries & Livestock. Facilitated by officials and attended by clubs of Fish Farmers	ICT, print and audio-visual contents on fisheries	Fish Farmers	20 centres across the country
Upazila Health Complex Health Line (UHCHL)	Ministry of Health & Family Welfare, mobile based application	Health Advice	Citizens	All upazilas in the country
Electronic Purjee Management System, 2009	Ministry of Industries/ Sugar mills	SMS based purchase order (Purjee).	200000 Sugarcane Farmers and 15 Sugar Mills.	15% increase in extraction; Awarded the Manthan Award in 2010
District E-Service Center (DESC), 2011	Deputy Commissioner's Office	37 types of services including land records	Citizens	Introduced in 64 districts
Union Information & Service Centres (UISC). Inaugurated in Nov. 2010.	Local Government Division (LGD)/ A2I and entrepreneurs under PPP model	Online information and services. Land copy, email, passport, electricity bill pay, mobile banking and commercial services.	Citizens especially in rural areas	4,501 Unions. Nearly 4 million people receiving services each month

Source: Compiled by authors from A2I, 2011.

& Service Centres (UISCs) represent a major attempt on part of the government to address this and to ensure that the benefits of e-government are shared widely. Driven by the desire of achieving the twin goals of Digital Bangladesh i. e. connecting citizens and delivering services to their doorsteps 4501 UISCs have been established across the country. In operation since 2010 this initiative is an attempt to translate the current government's vision of Digital Bangladesh by 2021.

Like other private tele-centers UISC is ICT enabled one-stop information service outlet operating at the union (the lowest tier of local government) level. It is designed to enhance the access of the rural poor to ICT and various governmental services - both online and off-line. It is equipped with computers, scanners, digital camera printer, internet connection, etc.- initially provided by the government. But, unlike its private counterpart the UISC is founded on public-private partnership model. Operated by two self-employed entrepreneurs (*uddoktas*), one male and one female, who are expected to make subsequent investment that it becomes an economically a vibrant model. The government provides the policy guidelines, training and supervision while the *Union Parishad* provides ICT equipment, the office and the furniture. However, to become economically viable the UISCs must demonstrate the continued earning from various services (Zaman, 2011).

UISCs currently offer two types of services such as government information and services and commercial services. Informational services include various livelihood information on agriculture, health, education and employment. UISCs also offer information on legal and human right aspects, environment, disaster management, science & technology, business and commerce. All such information can be downloaded from national e-content depository - the *e-Tathyakosh*. The *e-Tothyakosh* can be accessed online and offline with a CD version supplied to the *Uddakta*. On the other hand, commercial services range from simple email, word-processing, copying-printing-scanning to banking services. Table 2 shows the common services offered by UISCs, as found in the study areas in four districts.

Data collected from 154 service users in four districts suggests that there is a predominance of commercial services over e-government service. Only half of the UISCs studied could provide services of the later kind. The service delivery role of the UISCs has remained limited largely because they are yet to be connected to relevant government agencies to be able to offer e-government services. Also, despite having all other equipment UISCs lack powerful Internet connectivity. The few e-government services provided by UISCs are mainly in the form of utility bills, various certificates, government forms and documents. They do so by connecting themselves with websites of relevant government agencies. In the meantime, UISCs mostly offer commercial services on behalf of various private agencies with whom they have forged partnerships. Some of these partnered organizations also provide technical supports. At the forefront of such partnerships are private banks (e.g. the Dutch-Bangla Bank, Mercantile Bank, Trust Bank and BRAC Bank), life insurance companies (e.g. *Jibon Bima*), mobile phone companies (e.g. *Robi* and *BanglaLink*), NGOs (e.g. British Council, Practical Action, *Ankur* ICT Development Foundation), and troubleshooting support organizations (BCS, Cyber Cafe Association of Bangladesh). For instance, partnership with Dutch-Bangla Bank enables UISCs to work as an agent for mobile banking. Bangladesh Association of Software and Information Services (BASIS) is developing the district portal to provide back-end support to the UISC (Zaman, 2011).

Findings of the study suggest that where services are available especially the governmental ones, UISCs contribute to customer satisfaction through the reduction of distance, time and cost of services. People are able to obtain hassle-free government services without travelling long distance and assistance from intermediaries. It has facilitated easy access, increased transparency and

Table 2. Services offered and accessed at the UISC level

Information or Services Accessed	Male		Female		Total	
	Count	Row N%	Count	Row N%	Count	Column N%
Land Certificate Copy	12	100.0%	0	0.0%	12	7.8%
Electricity Bill Payment	3	30.0%	7	70.0%	10	6.5%
Applying for Passport	3	100.0%	0	0.0%	3	1.9%
Applying for overseas job (Malaysia)	13	100.0%	0	0.0%	13	8.4%
Government Forms download	2	100.0%	0	0.0%	2	1.3%
Education Information/ services(registration/admission	8	66.7%	4	33.3%	12	7.8%
Certificates(birth/death/inheritance/citizenship)	18	60%	12	40.0%	30	19.5%
Mobile banking	7	46.7%	8	53.3%	15	9.7%
Photocopying/compose/printing/laminating/ scanning, etc.	15	100.0%	0	0.0%	15	9.7%
Skype conversation	3	60.0%	2	40.0%	5	3.2%
Applying for job or job search	3	100.0%	0	0.0%	3	1.9%
Photoshoot	7	63.6%	4	36.4%	11	7.1%
E-mail or internet browsing	3	60.0%	2	40.0%	5	3.2%
Computer Training	6	35.3%	11	64.7%	17	11.0%
Others	1	100%	0	0.0%	1	0.6%

Source: Field Research

reduced the problems of corruption associated with government service delivery. An estimate shows that on a daily basis 300000 people receive services from these centres across Bangladesh (*The Daily Janakantha*, 3 Dec, 2011). Despite the multitude of problems such drop-outs of *Uddaktas* and lack of entrepreneurship among them, infrastructure problems especially slow internet and power breakdown, inadequate cooperation from *Union Parishad* and the absence of online service support from government offices the above figure suggests the growing popularity of UISC as an alternative channel for accessing governmental services. As a new initiative it holds enormous promise to redefine the nature of service delivery and broaden the access of ordinary citizens to government information and services in the future.

District E-Service Centres

In line with its campaign of Digital Bangladesh the current government has also established District E-Service Centres (DESCs) in all 64 districts (the most important administrative unit) of Bangladesh with the aim of making governmental services easily accessible to the people. Traditionally, the district administration has been the focal point for accessing government services by the people living both in rural and urban areas. But often access to services was difficult because of complex processes involved and multiple points at which these services were delivered. This created rooms for brokers and intermediaries who negotiated the services on behalf of their clients. DESCs are designed to put an end to public sufferings and inconveniences by providing them with easy access to all services from one point. Located in the Deputy Commissioner (DC)'s Office in each district DESC is expected to serve as a one-stop centre offering a range of governmental services via multiple tools and methods. Piloted first in Jessore in 2010 and later replicated in 10 other districts, the system was eventually rolled out across Bangladesh in November 2011 (A2I, 2011).

Under the DESC citizens can submit requests and documents over the counter in person or by mail or apply online. Upon receipt, application documents are scanned and the applicants are given a tracking number along with an automatic SMS message stating the delivery date. In between delivery and request, the status can also be known by sending SMS to 16345. Requests are logged into the system where their status is monitored by the Deputy Commissioner as well the officials in the Cabinet Division. The system was meant to bring efficiency in the delivery as well as benefit the citizens in reduction of time and cost as well as free them from the clutches of corrupt officials and intermediaries.

DESC is still at the early stage of its implementation. Though there are as many as 37 services on the list, none of them are currently available online. A few districts have introduced the land copy to be provided online without actually developing the digitized land records. Hence, upon receiving the request, the record room officials do it all manually and then scan it to preserve for future use. Research by authors in 4 districts finds that this process takes more time than in the past. The problem becomes more complicated when volumes of applications are received from various UISCs for action/processing. In Jessore the problem has been addressed by deploying additional staff in the record room. As a result, it reduced the time of delivery, and because of initial online management such as generation of tracking number and notification of the outcome through SMS, the influence of intermediaries and scope of corruption have significantly reduced. Also, UISCs in Jessore are able to collect land

copies by applying and paying online. The district has developed an online payment system from a locally developed software.

Despite limited progresses made and the prevalence of traditional methods of file management and processing etc. the significance of DESC cannot be underestimated. The computerization and associated developments have reduced the use of paper in the DC office since many intra and inter office communications can be done through online and through auto-generated SMS. Above all, as some districts are doing well other districts also feel it important to do something to uplift their image. For citizens, it is possible to apply for services without physically visiting the DC office: they can apply from UISCs, from post offices or from personal computers at home. But in that case chance of receiving a timely response is less than going to the DESC and receiving a tracking number. Yet, people do not need to stroll around counters or take recourse to intermediaries to identify them in the DC office since they can submit all kinds of applications from one-stop shop. Because of tracking number and digital management of applications the chances of application to go missing, as with the previous system, have reduced. In districts like Jessore where the top management is committed the system has shown promises of fast and efficient service delivery.

Thorny Issues and Closing Remarks

E-government is high on the governmental agenda. Numerous efforts made since the mid-1990s aimed at creating and strengthening ICT infrastructure, institutional and regulatory framework as well as web initiatives at various levels have marked a shift in governance and service delivery. These efforts have also helped Bangladesh raise her profile in e-government and online service delivery. However, when compared with the situation in other developing countries around the world this progress appears to be modest given that Bangladesh has not been able to go beyond informational and interactive stages, and in limited cases transactional services. Currently, Bangladesh's drives towards e-governance and online service delivery are handicapped by numerous barriers and challenges (see Faroqi & Siddiquee 2011; Siddiquee, 2013; Siddiquee & Faroqi, 2013).

One of the most formidable barriers to online service delivery in Bangladesh is country's poor ICT infrastructure and overall e-preparedness. In terms of global e-readiness Bangladesh ranks at 150th position (among 193 countries) (UN, 2012) which is an indication of the precarious situation in various aspects e-government preparedness. Bangladesh also ranks very low in terms of telecommunications infrastructure. With only 3.7% internet users, 0.61%, fixed phone users, 0.11% fixed internet subscribers and 0.04% broadband user per 100 inhabitants Bangladesh performs poorly even compared with her regional neighbors, as shown in the following table:

As shown in Table 3 Bangladesh is ahead of only Nepal in terms of infrastructure readiness. But Nepal has got higher percentage of internet users than Bangladesh. Bangladesh has the lowest percentage for internet users in the region when its web measure index is ahead of many of its neighbors (only behind India). This puts the country at a high risk of digital divide. Similarly, in the human capital index with adult literacy rate of 55.90% and gross enrolment ratio 48.70%

Bangladesh places itself in the 167th position (UN, 2012), only a little ahead of Pakistan, which also serves as the major source of digital divide.

UISCs and DECS are among the initiatives launched to tackle such problems and to transform service delivery at the grassroots level. Notwithstanding the fact that these initiatives are still at the early stage and they offer considerable prospects for the future the current experience shows that their effectiveness is reduced by a range of practical and local challenges. While inadequate infrastructure and integration with government agencies remains a major hurdle for UISCs to offer increased services to their clients, at times resistance from vested interests renders them ineffective. In one of the districts studied where the newly introduced land record service at UISC collapsed within few days due to resistance from record room staff at the district HQ with accord from the management. It was in the pretext that delivery under new system took more time and the UISCs could not provide the land records within the stipulated period. This is partly because in the absence of online payment system the UISC entrepreneurs have to visit the DC office to submit paper documents and affix required fees. In the process, as it appears, they have replaced the traditional intermediaries. But as this new role has threatened the vested interests that the intermediaries have traditionally served, the cooperation from local

Table 3. South Asia: Telecommunications infrastructure (per 100 population)

Country	Internet User	Fixed Phone User	Mobile Subscriber	Fixed Internet Subscriber	Fixed Broadband	Rank among 193 Members
Bangladesh	3.70%	0.61%	46.17%	0.11%	0.04%	161st
Bhutan	13.60%	3.62%	54.32%	0.93%	1.20%	139th
India	7.50%	2.87%	61.42%	1.53%	0.90%	145th
Maldives	28.30%	15.20%	156.50%	6.44%	4.92%	74th
Nepal	6.78%	2.81%	30.69%	0.28%	0.38%	167th
Pakistan	16.78%	1.97%	59.21%	2.17%	0.31%	135th
Sri Lanka	12%	17.15%	83.22%	1.21%	1.02%	116th

Source: UN Survey, 2012 compiled by authors.

bureaucrats was anything but satisfactory. They took longer time to process UISC requests which resulted in lack of confidence among the users and declining interest among the *uddaktas* to provide this service anymore. Two other districts are yet to develop system of offering land certificates through UISCs. The current level of development does not permit DESCs to deliver the services as envisaged. The government offices in the district level are virtually unconnected through intranet with each other let alone the connection with the lowest administrative unit, the *upazila*. E-mail and mobile based SMS are the only methods of communication between various units. Moreover, the current development only allows applications for services that are available in the DC office, not any other offices in the district. Moreover, there are problems of internet bandwidth since broadband allocation for each office is insufficient. 1 MBPS connection for DC office has to be shared by all officials and staff making it very slow and at times slower than mobile internets.

The above discussion presents a perplexing situation of e-government development in Bangladesh. Despite numerous efforts Bangladesh's progress has remained unsatisfactory. This is particularly true with advanced stages of egovernment development. In fact, as this chapter demonstrates, Bangladesh has failed to advance beyond basic and to some extent intermediate stages of e-government development. This means that the current progress falls short of what is required for providing enhanced online and integrated services to the population and for translating the vision of Digital Bangladesh into reality. As a developing country with a large population the majority of whom are poor and illiterate Bangladesh faces an enormous task of tackling challenges of e-government and making public services available online and for all. Since Bangladesh's problems are complex and multi-dimensional, there is no quick fix to such enormous challenges. What is needed is a sustained commitment on part of country's leadership and continuous drives to move the agenda forward with a robust implementation strategy in place. Given the arduous and stretched nature of the task, e-government must be seen as a journey rather than a destination.

REFERENCES

Access to Information. (A2I) Program. (2008). e-Governance in Bangladesh: Where we stand a Horizon Scan Report, 2007, Access to Information (A2I). Dhaka, Bangladesh: Prime Minister's Office & UNDP.

Access to Information. (A2I) Program. (2011). Bangladesh: Access to Information (A2I) Evaluation – A Report prepared for United Nations Development Program (UNDP). Dhaka, Bangladesh: Prime Minister's Office.

Backus, M. (2001). *E-Governance and Developing Countries: Introduction and Examples*. Institute for International Cooperation and Development (IICD) Research Report 3. Retrieved from http://www.iicd.org

Bangladesh Bank. (2014). *Home*. Retrieved from www.bb.org.bd

Bangladesh Enterprise Institute (BEI). (2010). *Realizing the Vision of Digital Bangladesh through e-government*. Retrieved from http://www.bei-bd.org/images/publication/whc4f4b6fd3c20ed.pdf

Bangladesh Public Service Commission (BPSC). (2014). *Home*. Retrieved from http://www.bpsc.gov.bd/

Bangladesh Telecommunications Regulatory Commission (BTRC). (2009). *Annual Report 2007-2008*. Retrieved from http://www.btrc.gov.bd/

Bekkers, V. (2013). E-government and innovation: The socio-political shaping of ICT as a source of innovation. In *Handbook of Innovations in Public Services*. Cheltenham, UK: Edward Elgar. doi:10.4337/9781849809757.00028

Bhatnagar, S. (2004). *E-government: From Vision to Implementation*. New Delhi: Sage Publications.

Bhuiyan, M. S. H. (2012). Towards Interoperable Government- A Case of Bangladesh. In Gil-Garcia et al. (Eds.), *Proceedings of 6th International Conference on Theory and Practice of Electronic Governance*. Albany, NY: ICEGOV.

Bhuiyan, S. H. (2011). Modernising Bangladesh public administration through E-governance: Benefits and challenges. *Government Information Quarterly*, (28): 54–65. doi:10.1016/j.giq.2010.04.006

Bureau of Manpower. Employment and Training (BMET). (2014). *Home*. Ministry of Expatriates Welfare and Overseas Employment. Retrieved from http://www.bmet.org.bd/BMET/index

Central Procurement Technical Unit (CPTU). (2014). *Home*. Ministry of Planning. Retrieved from http://www.cptu.gov.bd/

Department of Immigration and Passports (DIP). (2014). *Home*. Ministry of Home Affairs. Retrieved from http://www.dip.gov.bd/

Dhaka Metropolitan Police (DMP). (2014). *Home*. Bangladesh Police. Retrieved from http://www.dmp.gov.bd/

District E-Service Centres (DESC). (2014). *Home*. Retrieved from http://www.dhaka.gov.bd/

Dutch-Bangla Bank Limited (DBBL). (2014). *Mobile Banking*. Retrieved from http://www.dutchbanglabank.com/

Faroqi, M. G., & Siddiquee, N. A. (2011). Limping into the information age, challenges of E-Government in Bangladesh. *Journal of Comparative Asian Development*, 10(1), 33–61. doi:10.1080/15339114.2011.578473

Government of Bangladesh (GoB). (2002). *National Information and Communication Technology (ICT), Policy 2002*. Dhaka, Bangladesh: Ministry of Science and Information and Communication Technology.

Government of Bangladesh (GOB). (2009). *E-Government Bulletin January: Access to Information Program*. Dhaka, Bangladesh: Prime Minister's Office.

Government of Bangladesh (GOB). (2014). *National e-Tothyakosh, Bangladesh Home*. Retrieved from http://www.infokosh.bangladesh.gov.bd/index.php

Herman, P., & Cullen, R. (2006). E-government: Transforming the Government. In *Comparative Perspectives on E-government*. Lanham, MD: The Scarecrow Press.

Hoque, S. M. S. (2006). E-government in Bangladesh: A Scrutiny from Citizens Perspective. In R. Ahmad (Ed.), *The Role of Public Administration in Building a harmonious Society*. Academic Press.

Institute of Governance Studies (IGS). (2009). *Digital Bangladesh: The Beginning of Citizen-Centric E-Government?* BRAC University.

Islam, S. (2008). Towards a sustainable e-Participation implementation model. *European Journal of e-Practice, 5*.

Islam, S.M. (2013). Mobile Banking: An Emerging Issue in Bangladesh. *ASA University Review, 7* (1).

Karim, M. A. (2010). Digital Bangladesh for Good Governance. *Bangladesh Development Forum, Online Paper Dhaka*. Retrieved from http://www.erd.gov.bd/BDF2010/BG_%20Paper/BDF2010_Session%20VI.pdf

Lam, W. (2005). Integration challenges towards increasing e-government maturity. *Journal of E-Government*, *1*(2), 45–58. doi:10.1300/J399v01n02_04

Mahmood, I., & Babul, A. I. (2009). *E-Governance for Development: Bangladesh Perspectives*. Ministry of Public Administration. Retrieved from http://edem.todaie.gov.tr/yd29-eGOVERNANCE_FOR_DEVELOPMENT__BANGLADESH_PERSPECTIVES.pdf

Ministry of Agriculture (MoA). (2014). *Home*. Retrieved from http://www.moa.gov.bd/

Ministry of Education (MoE). (2014). *Home*. Retrieved from http://www.moedu.gov.bd/

Ministry of Health (MoH). (2014). *Home*. Retrieved from http://www.mohfw.gov.bd/

Moon, M. J. (2002). The evolution of e-government among municipalities: Rhetoric or reality. *Public Administration Review*, *62*(4), 424–433. doi:10.1111/0033-3352.00196

National Board of Revenue (NBR). (2014). *Home*. Retrieved from http://www.nbr-bd.org/

National Curriculum and Textbook Board (NCTB). (2014). *Home*. Retrieved from http://www.nctb.gov.bd/

National Web Portal of Bangladesh (NWPB). (2014). *Home*. Government of the People's Republic of Bangladesh. Retrieved from http://www.bangladesh.gov.bd/

Siddiquee, N. A. (2013). E-Government: The Dawn of Citizen-centric Public Administration? In *Public Administration in South Asia: India, Bangladesh and Pakistan*. London: Academic Press. doi:10.1201/b14759-19

Siddiquee, N. A., & Faroqi, M. G. (2013). E-Government in Bangladesh: Prospects and Challenges. In *From Government to E-Governance- Public administration in the Digital Age*. Hershey, PA: IGI Global.

United Nations. (UN). (2003). E-Government at the Crossroads (World Public Sector Report). New York: Department of Economic & Social Affairs.

United Nations. (UN). (2008). E-Government Survey: From E-Government to Connected Governance. New York: Department of Economic and Social Affairs.

United Nations. (UN). (2012). United Nations e-government survey, 2012. New York: Department of Economic and Social Affairs.

United Nations Development Program (UNDP). (2006). *Simplification of Public Utility Bill Payment System (Recommendation by the Technical Committee)*. Dhaka, Bangladesh: Access to Information Programme.

West, D. M. (2004). E-government and transformation of service delivery and citizens' attitude. *Public Administration Review*, *64*(1), 15–27. doi:10.1111/j.1540-6210.2004.00343.x

Zaman, A. U. (2011). *Union information & service centre (UISC), ICT enabled one-stop service outlet in Bangladesh*. Retrieved from http://community.telecentre.org/profiles/blogs/union-information-amp-service-centre-uisc-ictenabled-one-stop?xg_source=activity

Zaman, F. (2007, August 11). Addressing interoperability issues: Editorial. *The Daily Star*.

KEY TERMS AND DEFINITIONS

Digital Bangladesh: A slogan as well as an agenda for change introduced by the ruling *Awami League* as a key strategy for national development. The Digital Bangladesh agenda includes a digitised government, ICT enabled services, nation-wide internet connectivity and high-tech parks for businesses and IT professionals.

District E-Services Centres (DESCs): Represent governmental attempt aimed at making public services at the district level easily accessible to the people. There is one DESC in each of the 64 districts. Located at the Deputy Commissioner's office, DESCs are still at the early stage of implementation, but expected to serve as one stop service points providing as many as 37 governmental services online.

E-Government: Simply means the application of ICT in the public sector. It is a term used to mean the governmental system that delivers public services by using ICT as a tool.

The Stage Model: Used to explain the development and maturity of e-government. It postulates that a country has to go through a number of stages in its e-journey before it is able to deliver services in an integrated and seamless fashion.

Union Information & Service Centres (UISCs): One-stop service shops operating at the union level. These have been designed to enhance access of the rural poor to ICT and various governmental services. Housed at the local *Union Parishad* office compound currently there are 4501 UISCs across Bangladesh that offer a range of online and off-line service to rural communities especially those who lack access to ICT.

Union Parishad: The elected council running the lowest unit of local government in Bangladesh. Headed by a chairman *Union Parishad* is responsible for providing some basic services to the residents within its jurisdiction.

ENDNOTES

[1] Darrel West proposes a separate but similar model that involves four stages of e-government development: (1) the billboard stage, (2) the partial service delivery stage, (3) the portal stage with fully executable and integrated service delivery and (4) the interactive democracy with public outreach and accountability features (West, 2004).

[2] Bangladesh being a developing country and late starter of e-government, participation has remained a long term goal.

[3] Field research for this purpose was undertaken in four districts between April, 2013 and August, 2013. It entailed collection of data from relevant stakeholders in 16 UISCs through questionnaires and in-depth interviews.

[4] The ICT Policy 2009 envisions the ICT as a tool to bring about 'transparent, accountable and responsible government'. It seeks to develop human resources, enhance social equity and ensure cost-effective delivery of governmental services to support the national goal of becoming a middle-income country within 10 years and joining the ranks of developed nations within 30 years. On the other hand, the ICT Act 2009 provides legitimacy of the electronic records and digital signature. It is, in fact, a slightly modified version of ICT Act 2006 which remained unimplemented.

Chapter 12
Understanding ICT:
The Potential and Challenges for the Empowerment of Rural Women in Bangladesh

Nazmunnessa Mahtab
University of Dhaka, Bangladesh

Nehal Mahtab
Leeds Metropolitan University, UK

ABSTRACT

This chapter focuses on how e-Governance empowers women, specifically poor rural women. ICT for Development emerged as a new area of work in the mid-1990s at a time when the potential of new technologies was starting to be better understood. In poor countries, particularly rural women in Bangladesh, access to ICTs is still a faraway reality for the vast majority of these women as they are further removed from the information age, as they are unaware of the demonstrated benefit from ICTs to address ground-level development challenges. The barriers they face pose greater problems for the poor rural women, who are more likely to be illiterate, not know English, and lack opportunities for training in computer skills. Access to ICT can enable women to gain a stronger voice in their government and at the global level. ICT also offers women flexibility in time and space and can be of particular value to women who face social isolation, especially the women in the rural areas in Bangladesh. To represent the use of ICT, this chapter focuses on the use of "Mobile Phone" by the rural women of Bangladesh and how the use of mobile phones have helped in empowering rural poor women in Bangladesh.

DOI: 10.4018/978-1-4666-3691-0.ch012

INTRODUCTION

Defining E-Government

E-Government means different things to different people. Some simply define it as digital government information or a way of engaging in digital transformation with customers. (In present day Bangladesh the announcement/declaration of the Prime Minister, Sheikh Hasina, connotes this definition). For others e-Government simply consists of the creation of a web site where information about political and governmental issues are presented. (This is also true for the case of Bangladesh especially among the common citizens.) This is because they have the idea that they can have access to government information through the web site. These very narrow and limited ways of defining and conceptualizing e-Government restrict the range of potentials, challenges and opportunities it can offer. One of the many reasons for the failure of various e-Government initiatives is related to the limited definitions and vague and misunderstanding of the e-Government concept, processes and functions.

E-Government is a multi-dimensional, complicated and complex concept, which requires a broad definition and understanding in order to be able to design and implement a successful strategy. The advent of the Internet, digital connectivity, the explosion and use of e-commerce and e-business models in the private sector are pressuring public sector to rethink hierarchical bureaucratic organizational models. Customers, citizens and businesses are faced everyday with new innovative e-business and e-commerce models implemented by private sector and made possible by ICT tools and applications and so they are demanding the same from government organizations. (Osborne and Gaebler, 1992). According to them government requires to empower, rather than serve, to make a paradigm shift from hierarchy to teamwork and participation, to be vision and mission oriented and customer focused. Thus we find the worldwide Governments are faced with the potential and challenges of transformation and the need to modernize administration practices and management to a system of "change management practices." (Tapscott, 1996). Further Tapscott and Caston(1993) argued that ICT causes a "paradigm shift" introducing the age of network intelligence, reinventing businesses, governments and individuals. The traditional bureaucratic paradigm, characterized by internal productive inefficiency, functional rationality, departmentalization, hierarchical control and rule-based management (Kaufman, 1977) is being replaced by competitive, knowledge based economy requirements, such as: flexibility, network organization, vertical-horizontal integration, innovative entrepreneurship, organization learning, speed up in service delivery, and a customer driven strategy. These new paradigm thrust the shift toward e-Government paradigm emphasizing coordinated network building, external collaboration. and customer services through ICT.

E-Governance and Empowerment of Women

The examples of how e-Governance empowers women, specifically poor rural women and girls are very rare. However, theoretically it has shown that most research work had focused on the experience of ICT with women empowerment. Huyer and Sikoska suggested that any approach for women empowerment through ICT needs to support women individually and in groups deals with limitations first, and then with ICT issues. A critical issue for women empowerment through e-Governance is the need for local content with local language. In most developing countries E-Governance is still considered as a new paradigm even for men .(World Bank, 2006). In South and South-East Asia e-Governance started to improve the economic condition of women through micro-credit schemes, thus promoting economic empowerment; providing political consciousness and human rights and advancing political and social empowerment. Also projects like supporting secondary school scholarship and stipend programmes for rural poor girls in Bangladesh; Female farmers in Ghana, and Schoolnet Africa, SEWA in India are examples on how could e-governance empower women and girls (World Bank, 2006).

Information and Communication Technologies for Development (ICT4D)

This is a general term referring to the application of Information and Communication Technologies (ICT4D) within the fields of socioeconomic development, international development and human rights. The basic assumption behind this idea is that more and better information and communication enhances the development of society whether in the area to improve income, education, health, security, or any other aspect of human development. The concept of iCT4D can be interpreted as dealing with disadvantaged populations anywhere in the world, but is typically associated with applications in developing countries. Information and Communication technology (ICT) is becoming a need and a choice for both governments and citizens to survive in the digital economy, but there is a focus on ICT as a tool more than on the reality of people who will use it and the environment of use.

ICT for Development emerged as a new area of work in the mid-1990s at a time when the potential of new technologies was starting to be better understood. UNDP defines ICT to include both new and "old" technologies, and does not limit to the use of the Internet or personal computers. Many older technologies, such as the telephone and radio, are more acceptable to the poorest sectors of the population and are regaining importance largely due to the gradual convergence of old and new ICTs.(Hijab and Zambrano, 2007)

At the Fourth World Conference on Women in 1995, participants reflected on the issue of ICTs and gender, and the two issues were addressed in formal conference documents and in non-governmental forums. Likewise, At the World Summit on Information Society (WSIS) in 2003 and 2005, women explicitly addressed the issue of the use of ICTs for governance and their involvement in such forms of governance. However, both of these events demonstrated the need for more work, particularly in the areas of policy, capacity development and governance mechanisms, to help catalyse social and political change in this field. (Oxfam, 2005).

Around the world new information and communication technologies(ICTs) have changed the lives of individuals, organizations and indeed entire nations. No country and few communities have remained untouched by the 'information society.' The potential for e-Government in developing countries, however, remains largely unexploited, even though ICT is believed to offer considerable potential for the sustainable development of e-Government. Different human and technological factors, issues and problems pertain in these countries. ICT, in general is referred to as an "enabler" but on the other hand it should also be regarded as a challenge and a peril in itself. Moving away from these assertions and assumptions the aim of the paper is to identify and analyze the primary issues, potentials, opportunities and challenges that e-Government initiatives present for the developing countries specifically how women and their communities in developing countries have been influenced by ICTs. Taking case studies from different countries the paper focuses on how the use of ICT may lead to women's empowerment. In short this paper is going to assess the effects of ICTs on women's empowerment

Gender Dimensions of ICT

New technologies in the arena of information and communication, have been seen as a movement in the new age. However there is a common viewpoint that such technologies have only technical rather than social implications. The dramatic positive changes brought about by these information and communication technologies (ICTs), have not touched all groups of human community. The existing power relations starting from the family to society determine the enjoyment of benefits from ICTs. Consequently, these technologies are not gender neutral. So it is not possible to harness ICTs to serve larger goals of gender equality, empowerment and justice. More important is the issue of gender and women's equal right to access, use and shape ICTs.

Analysis of gender issues in ICT builds on previous gender analysis of technology. Technologies are socially constructed and thus have different impacts on women and man. (Hafkin,2002a). Information and communication technologies (ICTs) play a growing role in the world's societies, and in the present phase of globalization and the implementation of the free market philosophy. Women's capacity to exploit the potential of the new ICT and tools for empowerment is constrained in different ways. Some constraints are linked to factors that affect both women and men, including technical infrastructure, connection costs, computer literacy and language skills. These overall constraints are, however, exacerbated in many cases by gender-based determinants which practically disadvantage women. (Ibid).

In poor countries, particularly rural women in Bangladesh access to ICTs is still a faraway reality for the vast majority of these women as they are further removed from the information age, as they are unaware of the demonstrated benefit from ICTs to address ground-level development challenges. The barriers they face pose greater problems for the poor rural women, who are more likely to be illiterate, not know English, and lack opportunities for training in computer skills. Together with this, domestic responsibilities, cultural restrictions on mobility, lesser economic power further marginalize them from the information sector. Women need ICT for the same reason as men, to access information of importance, to

their productive, reproductive and community roles and to obtain additional resources. Access to ICT can enable women to gain a stronger voice in their Government and at the global level. ICT also offers women flexibility in time and space and can be of particular value to women who face social isolation, specially the women in the rural areas in Bangladesh. To represent the use of ICT this paper mainly focuses on the use of "Mobile Phone" by the rural women of Bangladesh.

As mobile penetration increased across the developing world, the entry of mobile phones in the hands of women caused reactions. In many cases, mobile phone ownership empowered women in myriad ways, economic gains, increased access to information, greater autonomy and social empowerment, and a greater sense of security and safety. (www. mobile active.org/mobiles-women-part-one-good)

But there is also a darker side. Targetting women with mobile phones have caused changes in gender dynamics and family expenditures and may relate to increases in domestic violence, invasion of privacy, or control by a male partner.

Rural Women in Bangladesh

Bangladesh is a country dominated by rural population. But even after forty years of Independence rural areas are marked by severe poverty, illiteracy, lack of adequate health services, lack of employment opportunities and over all types of backwardness. The condition of rural women in rural areas is worse as the gender based discrimination with strong socio-cultural roots are entrenched and pervasive. Due to the patriarchal character of the society, ability and capacity of the rural women to participate equally in the process of rural governance has been a big challenge for them.

Although the Constitution of Bangladesh recognizes the equality of all citizens irrespective of sex, tribe, and status, the reality on ground for women has always indicated the opposite. The situation, especially in the North and South-Eastern parts of the country, is such that the girl child is marginalized right from birth. Early adolescence is usually lost to cultural practices of early marriage. It is also a well known fact that many parents give preferential treatment to the boys, especially in matters concerning education (Bangladesh, like other South Asian countries, is a son –preference society). And that up till now in some areas girls are still made to live in their (the boys) shadows, denied education and other rights, and socially exploited. Their rights to attain womanhood before going into child bearing are being aborted and abused. To address this anomaly, respective Government's have taken the initiative to promote girl's education making it free till Level 12. But this laudable attempt is yet to achieve the much needed leverage effect and there continues to be a national gender disparity in basic education enrolment, retention and completion against girls. Whatever research statistics is found seems to present a positive picture regarding girls' education as the cases of "drop-outs" are not being reported due to early marriage which stops girls from receiving their education. Thus it is apparent that women in Bangladesh are inferior and dependent on men in many ways. When the girl reaches puberty or when she is usually dropped out of school her marriage will be arranged and the family has to pay 'dowry' to the groom's family to marry off their daughter. As a social custom the girl will thereafter pursue the rules of 'Purdah' and live in seclusion. Only very poor women are allowed to go outside to work and earn a living.(Hultberg, 2008). Although the Constitution provides for equal rights to women, women still suffer discrimination in all spheres of life and are victims of violence in the home, at the workplace and on the society level as well. (MOWCA, 2008)

DEFINITIONS AND CONCEPTUALIZATION OF EMPOWERMENT

The concept of women's empowerment appears to be the outcome of several important critiques and debates generated by women's movements throughout the world, but particularly by Third World feminists. In reference to women, particularly, the 'grassroots women,' the term 'empowerment has become popular during the 1980s. It has gained wider acceptance in the field of development in the 1990s. To describe the goal of development, empowerment has virtually replaced terms like 'welfare,' 'upliftment,' 'community participation,' 'and poverty alleviation.' (Batliwala, 1994, 127). However, it has been found that many people are still confused as to what the term actually implies in relation to social, economic and political arenas.

Paulo Freire (1973) did not use the term empowerment in emphasizing on education as a means of conscientizing and inspiring individual and group challenges to social inequality (Srtomquist, 2002). However, social activists from the South concerned with poverty saw empowerment as a local grass root endeavour with the aim of inspiring the poor to challenge their subordinated status. Mainstream development agencies used empowerment as synonymous with participation and development. Thus empowerment seems to fit many shoes. (Papart, Rai and Staudt, 2002).

During the past three decades, there has been a steadily increasing awareness of the need to empower women through measures to increase social, economic and political equality, and broader access to fundamental human rights, improvements in nutrition, basic health and education. Along with an increasing focus on women's empowerment a growing body of literature has emerged which seeks to define and operationalise the concept. A recent review (Malhotra et el, 2002) describes the diversity of this literature and highlights certain similarities in definitions of women's empowerment, although they use different terminology.

DEFINING EMPOWERMENT

Empowerment, especially for women, has been on the minds of a number of scholars and practitioners, most notably Srilatha Batliwala (1994), Naila Kabeer (1994, 2001), Jo Rowlands (1997), Gita Sen (1985), and Anju Malhotra (2002). For Batliwala empowerment is:

The process of changing existing power relations, and of gaining greater control over the resources of power. (Batliwala, 1994, 130)

Naila Kabeer (1994) also emphasizes on the centrality of empowerment for the struggle to achieve gender equality. Criticizing the liberal and Marxist emphasis on power over resources, institutions and decision making, she argues for a more feminist approach to power, one that emphasizes the transformative potential of power within. This power is rooted in self-understanding that can inspire women to recognize and challenge gender inequality in home and the community. (1994: 224-229). Like Batliwala, she focuses on collective grassroots participatory action and defines empowerment as:

the power to work with others to control resources, to determine agendas and to make decisions. (1994:229)

Kabeer (2001) offers a useful definition of empowerment. For her,

empowerment refers to the expansion in people's ability to make strategic life choices where this ability was previously denied to them.

In this definition choice is presented in terms of three interrelated dimensions that include resources (preconditions), agency (process) and achievements (outcomes).

Jo Rowlands (1997, 1998) focuses on a broader analytical perspective to the discussion on gender and empowerment. She argues that:

Empowerment is more than participation in decision making; it must also include processes that lead people to perceive themselves as able and entitled to make decisions. (1997:14)

Following all these definitions and discussions on women's empowerment, the notion of empowerment came to be most clearly articulated in 1985 by DAWN. According to them

Empowerment required transformation of structures of subordination through radical changes in law, property rights, and other institutions that reinforce and perpetuate male domination. (Sen and Grown, 1985)

As Malhotra (2002) says, nearly all these above definitions focuses on a change from relative powerlessness to greater equity in exercising power and she thus distinguishes 'empowerment' from the general concept of 'power', as exercised by dominant individuals or groups. According to her, to be considered 'empowered,'

women must be significant actors in the process of change.

This definition also helps to distinguish 'women's empowerment' from the related concepts of 'gender equality', or 'gender equity'. A change towards gender equality or greater gender equity would not be considered as 'empowerment' unless women had been agents of that change. (Malhotra, 2002).

These definitions of empowerment raise a number of concepts associated with the term. For example, power, domination, control, access, confidence, assertiveness, decision-making, agency and choice. To summarize the decisional aspects of the term, we may say that empowerment is:

- Having power to control over surroundings which effect women's lives.
- Agency, expressed in terms of women's ability to make decisions that affect outcomes of importance to themselves and their families, or women's control over their own lives and resources.
- Process, that is, the skill given to women to challenge and change her situation for better.

Among all these, 'power' is used as a reference point to understand 'empowerment.' The most conspicuous feature of the term empowerment is that it contains the word power, which may be broadly defined as control over material assets, intellectual resources, and ideology. In other words, it

can be said that Empowerment has generated new notions of power. Present day notions of power have evolved in hierarchical, male dominated societies and are based on divisive, destructive and oppressive values. It is not for women to take power and use it in the same exploitative and corrupt way. Rather women's empowerment processes must evolve a new understanding of power, and experiment with ways of democratizing and sharing power----building new mechanisms for collective responsibility, decision making and accountability, (Batliwala, 1994, 134).

At this point it is important to analyze Kabeer's understanding of the dimensions of empowerment including three issues of 'resources', 'agencies' and 'outcomes' all of which are also related to the concept of 'power,'

Resouces can be material, social or human, that is:

they refer not only to conventional economic resources, such as land, equipment, finance, working capital etc, but also to the various human and social resources which serve to enhance the ability to exercise choice. (Kabeer, 2001)

The second dimension of power relates to *"agency"*, that is the ability to define one's goals and act upon them.

Figure 1. Kabeer's dimensions of empowerment

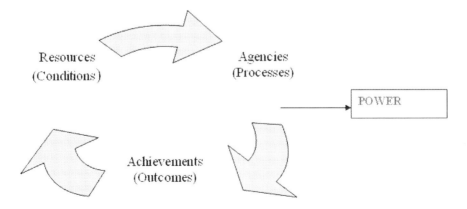

It also encompasses the meaning, motivation and purpose which individuals bring to their ability, the issue of agency, or the 'power within'. (Ibid, 2001)

Agency has both positive and negative meanings in relation to power. In the positive sense of 'power to', it refers to people's capacity to define their own life choices and to pursue their own goals, even in the face of opposition from others.

The negative meaning of agency implies the use of 'power over'. This means the capacity to override the agency of others, such as, through the use of coercion, fear, threat or violence.

As Kabeer (2001) points out further that 'resources' and 'agency' together constitute what Sen refers to as 'capabilities'……the potential that people have for living the lives they want, of achieving valued ways of living and doing, which ultimately leads to 'functionings' and 'achievements', that is the 'outcomes'.

UNDERSTANDING EMPOWERMENT

This paper begins with an understanding of the concept and issues involved in dealing with women's empowerment. Till today numerous books, papers, articles have been written based on empirical research studies in different parts of the world on the measurement of women's empowerment. On the basis of very limited findings from these studies, the present paper will focus on a paradigm shift of women's empowerment from changing the idea of micro-credit, micro-finance and poverty alleviation to achieving empowerment by the use of 'mobile phone' and the basic question addressed is how mobile phone can be used as instruments/ means of achieving empowerment of women, while on the other hand be an outcome/process/end of preventing/ combating violence against women. The paper is written on the basis of my own long time research experience, knowledge and teaching on women's issues and concerns specifically focusing on empowerment. Empowerment is a strategy that has as a primary goal and equitable redistribution of power and resources. As such the paper begins with "Empowerment is a process of transformation which enables a woman to identify her strengths, skills to challenge and change her situation, make own choices and decisions and control over her surroundings the effect her life," (Mahtab, 2011).

Figure 2. The method of women's empowerment can be seen in the following chart

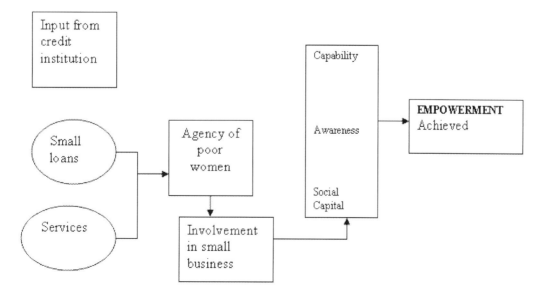

Although the main issue is on empowerment certain other relevant concerns are also discussed which helps in achieving empowerment. As such the paper concentrates on three main aspects of the Village Pay Phone. 1) How the use of the mobile has been an important component in reducing poverty; 2) How this very aspect of the use of mobile phone has increased violence within the family of the users and 3) How the village pay phone had led to the empowerment of the rural women . Finally the paper concludes with a new paradigm of women's empowerment which identifies that in today's world the most essential pre requisite for achieving women's empowerment is "VOICE." The use of the Village Pay Phone (MOBILE) are all interactive, interdependent and inseparable facets of the phenomenon of empowerment, without which women will remain 'disempowered.' It is in this backdrop that the use and contribution of women in the use of mobile phone to women's empowerment is to be assessed. In short, it evaluates the role of Village Phone (VP) in empowering the VP operators and its users.

INTRODUCTION OF (MOBILE) THE VILLAGE PAY PHONE

Before 1997, there was no telephone network in rural Bangladesh. Even in the rest of the country the level of connectivity was unsatisfactory with less than 0.39% tele-density (Bayes, 2001). It was then that Bangladesh initiated liberalization of the sector by awarding six cellular phone licenses to private business investors during 1989-1996. The USA-based entrepreneur Iqbal Quadir was the pioneer to float the idea of providing mobile telephones to the rural people of Bangladesh through an innovative, shared-access business model (Grameen Phone Annual Report, 2006). It is a profitable business arm of the Grameen Bank founded by Nobel laureate Muhammad Yunus. It was also in 1997 that the Grameen (Grameen meaning village) family members namely Grameen bank, grameen Phone and Grameen Telecom—jointly launched the Village Phone (VP) Programme. (Yusuf, Alam. 2011, Bhuiya, 2004).

During the early years although the Grameen Bank model distributed mobile phone to the women group members of the Grameen Bank, the women could hardly use it as they were unaware of its use and did not know actually the function or use of it. Automatically the use fell on their male counterparts, either their husbands, or their sons or other male members of the family. Gradually when the group members of Grameen Bank, usually the users of micro-credit schemes discussed the issue and came to learn about its use they became conscious and started using it as a small business concern which brought them income to pay their installments of the micro-credit programmes. To find out these issues the study was based on the following mechanisms.

METHODOLOGY OF THE STUDY

The methodology for data collection for the study consisted of a combination of a variety of procedures. For example, direct, face-to face interviews were taken from the women selected randomly from different out posts of Dhaka Division mainly covering the rural areas quite far away from the city, and those who have been members of Grameen Bank for a long time. This included the Districts of Tangail, Manikganj from where fifteen women were interviewed. Women VP owners, operators and users (both male and female) were covered in the interview.

Secondary sources were also included. Studies conducted by other researchers (Bayes, 2001, Richard, Ramirez, and Huq (2000), Aminuzzaman et el,(2002). Yusuf and Alam, (2011), and Hultberg (2008). These studies were consulted because they each covered different regions of Bangladesh and so their findings represented a comparative analysis of the situation of the use of Village Pay Phone by women in rural Bangladesh.

In addition to this three case studies are presented to focus on the three aspects of the study mentioned earlier. For example, one case study focused on the reduction of poverty by the use of Village Pay Phone; one case study demonstrated how the use increased violence in the family while one case study indicated a real example of how women could be empowered by the use of the mobile phone.

Finally, some success stories of the use of mobile phone in empowering women have been included from different countries.

REDUCTION OF POVERTY THROUGH VILLAGE PAY PHONE: WAVES OF CHANGES IN LIVES OF RURAL WOMEN

During our visit to the villages in Tangail district we interviewed ten women and found out how the use of the Grameen mobile phone helped these women in reducing poverty.

The Village Pay Phone was introduced by Quadir (the founder of Grameen Phone Limited (GP), the first mobile phone service provider in

Figure 3. Women empowerment through ICT

Bangladesh). It was opersted by villagers living in rural areas. Under the VPP system, the operator receives a loan from the Grameen Bank to buy a mobile phone from Grameen Telecom (GT). In 2007, the Village Pay Phones have been established in over 50,000 villages, in 61 of 64 districts of Bangladesh and the total number of VPPs had exceeded 297,079 (Grameen Bank, 2007, July, 31).

Eradicating extreme poverty and hunger along with promoting gender equality, and empowering women are two of the cornerstones of the Millennium Development Goals. While they are geared towards diverging areas and sectors, in many ways they are interlinked. Often women are left behind in the development bandwagon; their marginalization eventually leads them into poverty which is also a circle completed with hunger.

The strategy women used was that they lent their phone to be used by some men who utilized the phone by offering village people to use the phone to talk with relatives, usually those living outside the country, get their news and for this task the users were charged with an amount of money which was later delivered to the owners of the phone.

The outcome of renting mobiles to other people ensured the easy accessibility of mobile phones for all those poor people, especially those who could not otherwise afford them. This procedure was followed by five women who were interviewed and they collectively opined how this helped them to pay their installments to Grameen Bank for the phone and how it helped them to earn an additional source of income for their family and finally help them in combating the poverty level they were previously experiencing. In this case one issue was very clear that the phone was used by either the husband of the women or their sons. No outside people were allowed to use the phone. In this way some of the women have been able to start a small business of their own, by renting a small space where they could make use of the phone by those who needed it. Thus it became evident that the VPP service was introduced to determine the status of rural poor women to become a mini-entrepreneur, enhance skills and knowledge and improve economic and social status. (Aminuzzaman et el, 2003). A successful owner stated:

My life has totally been changed by the use of the Village Phone. When I first got the phone I started using it by letting other poor women to use the phone for talking to their relatives, where they were not allowed to go outside to commercial places because of social restrictions existing in their family. I charged a very small amount and could earn some income. However when my husband came to know about this he gave me the idea of letting him operate at an outside place where both women and men can come and use the phone. At first, I was a little hesitant as to be scared of not getting the money from my husband. But I was also aware that if I do not agree to his proposal he might totally stop me from using the phone for other women, and ultimately this would stop my earnings of an additional income. Realizing all these obstacles I agreed to let my husband operate the phone outside the family and this really brought luck to me. As I was a bit educated (at least I knew how to read and write and had some knowledge of numbers I could not be cheated by my husband. I did manage to make some profit from this mini- business adventure and used the profit to start other business both by my husband and myself.

Laily Begum, initially a hose wife of a day labourer of Village Patia in Dakhin Khan (Dhaka District) is the first woman whose life has been changed radically by Village Phone. With her husband's suggestion, Laily took loan from Grameen Bank and initiated her Village Phone enterprise through which she started earning Taka 20,000 to 25,000 per month and even managed to save a little. With the savings, she and her husband set up five shops, running some themselves and renting out the rest. That spelt an end to Laily's poverty. Her three children now go to school.

Rokeya is another village phone lady from Manikganj a little further down the city of Dhaka. She transformed her life a few years ago after buying a mobile phone, and to this day she is reaping the benefits of that purchase. *"Six years ago I was a simple housewife; I did not do anything except cooking, cleaning and looking after our children."* One day her husband fell ill and they did not have enough money to take him to the hospital. That was when the alarm really started ringing which drove her to step forward to self- reliance and village phone seemed to be the best option for her. Soon she was earning up to Taka 10,000 a month. *"This was the biggest decision of my life and I knew if it failed, my family would fall apart."*

Shilpi, now owes her middle class way of life to the mobile phone. *"Five years ago, I wanted to be more than just a housewife; so I purchased a mobile phone. Within weeks of taking out a loan, I was able to pay it back, and since then I have continued to make good money to this day."* She stated that most of her income comes from reload charges, which is a sizeable sum. Her husband, a police constable in the police station is proud of his wife. He says, *"The shop next to our house is now better known as* Bhabi's Dokan (In Bangladesh, "Bhabi" is usually addressed to elder brother's wife). *And I am being identified as her husband rather than people calling my wife."*

Rokeya, Shilpi and Laily are just a few of thousands, who have prospered through the village phone programme. Today, hundreds and thousands of women living in extreme poverty have been able to come out of the state of poverty and achieving their dreams. Laily Begum is the pioneer; she has led the way for women to do away with poverty, and bringing meaning to their lives. With this end n view, it is proved beyond doubt that even the illiterate poor women can confidently handle the state of the art of information technology, and can positively contribute in changing their lives. (The Daily Star, 2010).

EMPOWERMENT: A WEAPON TO COMBAT VIOLENCE

The boy is like the lamp of the family, and everybody wants it lit continuously; The woman realizes that her value goes up with the birth of a son and down with daughters. (Jasvinder Kaur, 2001)

VIOLENCE AGAINST WOMEN

Violence against women has become a common phenomenon. The 'culture of silence' surrounds violence against women and girls. Everywhere and in all ages, women have been victims of violence. Rape, murder, acid throwing, trafficking in women and children, coercion of various kinds, repression at home and outside, violence and murder for dowry have increased at an alarming rate. A cross-country comparison found that the incidence of domestic violence against women in Bangladesh was very high, with 47% of adult women reporting physical assault by a male partner. (UNFPA, 2000; UNDP, 2002).

Recent statistics on violence against women collected by UNICEF (2005), indicate the magnitude of the different forms of violence. Dowry and dowry related violence, such as acid attacks and murder are still prevalent. A recent report (UNHCHR,2005) stated that 165 women were killed in one year, 77 had acid thrown on them, and was divorced and 11 committed suicide over dowry demands.

Girls aged 14 to 17 are more likely to commit suicide, and attempt suicide than boys. The Bangladesh health and Injury Survey 2005, reported that more than 2200 children committed suicide in one year---or about six per day. Of those six four were females. Suicide is the biggest killer among this age group. (UNICEF, 2005).

Domestic violence remains a huge threat to the security of adolescent girls. A UNICEF report found that extreme physical abuse at home led to death accounted for more than 70% of the reported domestic violence cases involving young housewives and girls aged 13 to 18. (www.unicef. org/bangladesh).

Bangladesh gas one of the highest rates of child marriage in the world. More than two-thirds of adolescent girls are marr1ed aged between10 to 19. Nearly two in five girls aged 15 to17 are married, despite 18 being the legal age for marriage. (UNICEF, 2005)

According to the survey conducted by STEPS Towards Development, the majority of the reproductive aged women surveyed (60% urban, 61% rural) reported either being physically or sexually abused at some point in their lives. Women reported various health problems including working difficulties (18% urban, 24% rural); pain (26% urban, 36% rural), dizziness (44% urban, 64% rural) memory loss (13% urban, 20% rural). (ICDDRB, 2001).

According to the statement by ALRC, a Human Rights Organization in Bangladesh, 'in 2004, 267 women including one child were victimized due to dowry related matters. Among them 165 were killed, 77 tortured by acid violence and one were divorced and 11 committed suicide due to incessant demands of marriage.' On the basis of some leading newspaper in the last six months 21 girls were harassed or committed suicide or murdered because of 'eve teasing.'

According to a major study by ICDDRB:

- About 60% of women of reproductive age (15-49 years) had been physically or sexually abused during their lifetime;

- Two –thirds of the women never talked about their experience of violence and almost none accessed formal services for support;
- About 19% of women surveyed had expressed severe physical violence, defined as being hit with a fist or object, kicked or dragged, beaten up, choked, burnt, or threatened or injured with a weapon;
- 6% of maternal deaths are due to homicide and suicide related to rape and illegitimate pregnancy;
- 47% Bangladeshi women are abused by their partner;
- During the last three months, a report revealed by ASK (a rights based group) that 13 women committed suicide due to stalking and 8 people were killed for protesting stalking incidents;
- The report also found that 148 women were raped. Of them 27 were killed after they were violated while 10 committed suicide failing to stand humiliation;
- 11 female domestic helps died mysteriously while 4 others succumbed to their injuries after being tortured by their employers;
- Some 72 women were killed in domestic violence and 16 others committed suicide. 2 of a total of 67 women, subjected to torture for dowry, killed themselves according to the study report. (The Daily Star, April 01, 2011).

THE USE OF MOBILE PHONE AND VIOLENCE AGAINST WOMEN

The second dimension of this paper deals with how the use of mobile phone is causing a rise in committing violence against women. The UN General Assembly in its resolution 48/104

(1993) defines violence against women "as any act of gender violence that results in or is likely to result in, physical, mental or psychological harm or suffering to women, including threats of such acts, coercion or arbitrary deprivation of liberty, whether in public or private life…." (General Assembly, 1993).

The Beijing Platform for Action retakes the above definition and emphasizes that "in all societies, to a greater or lesser extent women and girls are subjected to physical, sexual and psychological abuse that cuts across times of income, class and culture'. (PfA, 1995).

The use of mobile phone is part of information communication technologies (ICT). ICT helps increasing violence against women (VAW) to today's digital Bangladesh. In the context of Bangladesh, the mobile technology is used by some group of people to perpetuate violence against women. VAW has become a common concern where mobile phone is playing a pivotal role. During the last decade, we have experienced that organizations working on violence advocacy or combating violence against women and girls have documented narratives from number of survivors whose abusers would use mobile technology to stalk them. It is important and also relevant to indicate on what types of violence women have been facing owing to the use of mobile phone. It portrays discrimination and manifestation of the unequal power relationship. At present mobile phone is another instrument for men to harass women. All are well known to acid violence, fatwa, rape wife beating, eve-teasing and domestic violence of all kinds. But by the haphazard and misuse of mobile technology, women are being abused sexually, mentally and physically as well. (Roy and Himu, 2011).

During our study in rural Bangladesh we found that quite a number of women were victims of extreme violence when they started taking loans from Grameen Bank for the use of mobile phone. These women were totally prohibited by their husbands to use the phone for any commercial purposes as some other women had the privilege to use their phones. So what did these women do? They usually made use of their phones when their husbands were out of the house and in this way they let other women use their phones I return of a very small amount of money, However, this did not remain unnoticed or hidden for a long time. When their husbands came to know about the issue they were beaten up, their phones were taken away by their husbands. In these cases the women faced a double burden of violence: 1) physical torture, beating by their husbands and 2) while not being able to repay the installments against the loan taken for the phone they were continuously harassed by the Grameen Bank people who used to come to collect the installments. They even suffered by being rejected by continuing to be group members and thus losing the opportunity of earning an income from the loan. As one women stated:

Seeing my neighbour earn a lot of money from the use of mobile phone I got motivated and interested to borrow a loan to buy a mobile phone and start a business of my own. Although I knew my husband was vehemently opposed to this very idea of women doing business I did this and usually started the work at home. While my husband was out some women from the neighbourhood would come to my house and use the phone to talk to their relatives, get information on health issues or even talk to their husbands living abroad. Soon the matter cam to be known by my husband when one day re returned early from work and saw other women using the phone. This aroused anger in him, he became furious and started torturing me by first throwing away the phone, breaking it into pieces, beating me, shaking my head and kicking me for not listening to him. Later on he even took away all the money that I could save by the use of the phone. He even went to the extent of suspecting me of letting other men come into the house and use the phone.

This case study reveals an abuse of power in a personal or family relationship, where one person attempts to control and dominate the other through physical, psychological and /or sexual violence or the threat of violence, or by controlling of the other person's finances, mobility or social life. It also indicates that abusive intimate partners are using technology for committing violence against women.

In rural Bangladesh young girls are also victims of violence by young boys through the use of mobile phones. The phenomenon of harassment and violence while they are going to schools is receiving increasing attention. Young girls are often given to carry phones by their families in cases of avoiding acts of violence by boys during their way to schools. However, it is often found that these girls become victims of violence by receiving calls from unknown from men and ultimately violated by these men. These often results in acts of suicide the girls, for not being able to face their families, receiving justice or being humiliated by the society. Sexual harassment and stalking against girls and young women in educational institutions is also an issue of increased attention in recent years in the urban society in Bangladesh. The case of eve teasing and stalking have taken a different turn in the society. As any girl or women is stalked the person who objects to this view is often killed. This has been the case of a school teacher being killed when he opposed to a girl student being stalked by a school boy . In another case a girl's mother was killed when she raised her voice against the boy who had teased her daughter while going to school; while still in another case a girl's grand father was killed when he wanted action the boy who had stalked her grand daughter. These are all instances of the misuse of obscene mobile phone calls when people are called to meet by using the phone.

Another part of the picture may be revealed by the use of mobile text message (SMS).Often the men accuse their spouses of receiving love messages. For example, one man has beaten his wife to death, the other divorced his wife while a third one shot his wife. Often the phenomenon is such that dirty men compose love songs and send sms (short message sent) triggered by the use of mobile phone. Sometimes younger women face greater trouble when their husbands or partner collect intimate video clips or photographs of their wives with other men. This usually occurs in wedding occasions or parties when old friends may have the opportunity to meet after several years and get involved in intimate relationships. Sometimes women often face great difficulty when they become entangled in mobile tracking practices by their husbands or inmates. Again in rural Bangladesh traffickers are using the mobile phone to communicate with and recruit victims who are usually young girls of poor fathers who do not deny to sell their daughters to the traffickers.

Women's participation in the development process—especially in areas such as family planning, environmental protection and education is crucial. Yet women are faced with violence, their ability to participate in these and other aspects of development is hampered. In many countries, including Bangladesh, husbands resist women's work outside the home, since they fear this may lead to women's empowerment.

"Violence against women derives essentially from the lower status accorded to women in the family and in society. It is abetted by ignorance, lack of laws to prohibit violence, inadequate efforts by public authorities to enforce existing laws, and absence of educational and other means to address its causes…….." (BPfA, 1995). Worldwide violence against women is an impediment to gender equality and women's empowerment. The only lasting solution is to reduce women's political and economic vulnerability, raising their social status and strengthening their ability to gain control over their own lives, that is empowering them.

Magar (2003) has tried to show the inter-relations and inter-connectedness between individual capacities, group capacities and achievements through a conceptual framework of women's empowerment as shown in Figure 4.

WOMEN'S EMPOWERMENT CONCEPTUAL FRAMEWORK

Rethinking Empowerment

The following discussions on different dimensions, paradigms of empowerment leads us to one conclusion the 'empowerment is very difficult to define and measure. Empowerment is a multidimensional phenomenon including literacy, education, women's status, health and violence. In this regard it is important to mention about the

pioneering study undertaken by BRAC Research Group that have identified an important indicator to measure empowerment, that is "VOICE."

This implies that the various dimensions or paradigms of empowerment becomes useless if women do not have the voice, that is voice defined in such a way that *it is heard and listened to.*

The study has focused on three issues which include: (Azim and Sultan, 2011)

1. Coming out of the Private: Women Forging Voices in Bangladesh;
2. Work for Pay;
3. Bodily Integrity.

All the three aspects of the study focuses on Women's Ability to Talk; (Mohsen, 2011);

Figure 4. Women's empowerment is an outcome of a process whereby individual attitudes (self esteem and self efficacy) and capabilities (knowledge and skills and political awareness), combined with collaborative actions (social and political participation), and reciprocally influenced by resources (information, material, and socio-psychological) result in a transformation to desired achievements (individual, group, and societal) (Magar, 2003)

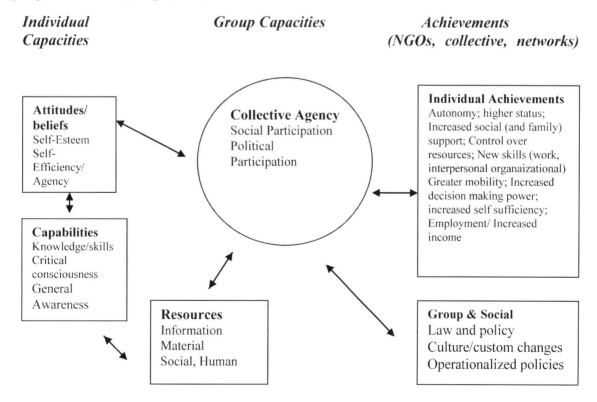

Changing Trends of Women's Employment (Sultan, 2011), Bodily Integrety of Honour Chastity, Beauty as Seen Belonging to Someone Else (Mahmud, 2011) with VOICE being heard and listened to. Empowerment has no meaning or pathway.

EMPOWERMENT FOR WOMEN is a powerful term. So summarizing the discussions on the different definitions given by different scholars, researchers we may say that:

Education, health, status of women, violence and voice are all interlinked. They appear in a *dialectical* relationship as follows:

- Education is the cornerstone of empowerment;
- Women's health is inextricably linked to social status;
- Health influences and ensures empowerment;
- Empowerment is a weapon to combat violence.

Education, women's status, health violence requires voice; voice determines and influences education, women's status, health, violence and all these elements are inseparable and influence one another.

Women are embracing the concept of empowerment because of their situations---their disempowerment and their unmet needs. As women have increasingly discovered their commonalities through access to education, improved health services, means to face and struggle for their rights and fight against violence, they have attempted to understand the global and local political, economic and cultural forces that shape these situations.

Today, empowerment has been recognized as a strategy to reduce inequity and redistribute power, which women, in particular are using to improve their situations.

Nobel Lautette Amartya Sen sees empowerment as 'freedom', defining empowerment as 'social, political, economic and ideological freedom; It is both collective and personal rather than individual. In fact the four concepts----education, health, freedom and empowerment are all integrally related, each capable of positively affecting the other. Women must have freedom and voice if they are to be empowered; the processes of education and empowerment lead to increased status and freedom and this in turn leads to their health and combating violence against them.

To summarize the discussion on the impact of ICT on women's empowerment the following issues are relevant:

- Empowerment is a complex phenomenon to measure because of its multi-dimensional aspects;
- A study by Ahmed, Islam, Hasan and Rahman(2006) found that, in Bangladesh, women's involvement in ICT industries and ICT based government organizations(GO) and non-government organizations(NGOs) have changed the behavioural aspects of women's life style and thereby affects the society as a whole;
- In another study on the impact of ICT intervention towards the development in Third World countries, Ashraf, Hanich and Swatman (2008) describe the situation in Bangladesh as the study showed there are positive prospects in Bangladesh in terms of ICT used by women for their empowerment;
- Information gathering has been noted as a pre-requisite for empowerment;
- Participation drives empowerment by encouraging people to be actively involved in the development process, contribute ideas, take the initiative to articulate needs and problems and assert their autonomy (Obayclu & Ogunlade, 2006);
- Successful case studies from many countries describe the use of ICT as a tool for the economic empowerment of women (Prasad& Sreedevi, 2007); participation in

Figure 5. The impact of mobile phone on women's empowerment

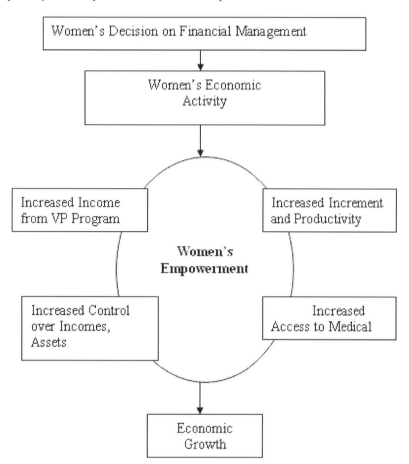

public life (Lennie, 2007), and enhancing women's skills and capabilities in society (Mitchell & Gillis, 2007). When used effectively, ICT can create better opportunities for women to exchange information, gain access to on-line education and to engage in e-commerce activities (Marcelle, 2002);

- ICT offer opportunities for direct, interactive communication even by those who lack skills, who are illiterate, lack mobility and have little confidence;
- The Village Pay Phone are operated by villagers living in rural areas of Bangladesh. The operator receives a loan from the Grameen Bank (GB) to purchase a mobile phone from Grameen Telecom (GT);
- Iqbal Qadir, the founder of Grameen Phone, remarked in a speech that " *a woman with a mobile phone becomes important in a village. This changes power distribution.*"

Some aspects of life which have a direct influence of ICT especially on women are:

- **Women's Increased Access to Job Market and Improved Entrepreneurship using ICTs:** Grameen telecommunications have explicit goal of helping Grameen Bank members shift from relatively low-yield traditional ventures, like animal husbandry into the technology sector by creating micro-enterprises that can both generate individual income and provide whole village phones. Village Phones have increased income and savings accumulation among phone owners, mostly women. Moreover, women entrepreneurs in other sectors apart from ICT are having more access to market information and as a result they enjoy distinct competency;

- **Increase of Average Household Income in Villages:** The women phone operators are generally poorer than the average villager is. However, the income that they earn is significant, generally accounting for 30-40% of household income and averaging US $ 300 per year in a country where average per capita income is US $ 286.

- **Women's Empowerment through Grameen Telecom:** Bangladesh has created a phone culture among women in the villages by enabling their access to communication tools from which they might otherwise be excluded. They have also shown that poor, largely uneducated women can master the skills and run a small business. Women phone operators have achieved economic and social empowerment within their households and communities.

- **Improved Governance:** ICT is also particularly useful in increasing the transparency and accountability of government, an application form from which women can particularly profit. One example demonstrates how women used ICT to call upon a national government and a local administration for greater accountability and transparency.

- **Easy Family Communication:** The use of mobile and internet even at home has given a wider opportunity to women in general to communicate with the world. Women re-

maining in close-doors or of a conservative atmosphere do have the privilege to know about, the whereabouts of their relatives and friends by the blessing of the ICT.

- **Breaking the Vicious Circles:** The particular strength of the programme is its capacity to empower women in social contexts. By bringing women for the first time in non-kin relation they strive to weaken the existing patriarchal society which entailed the total subservience of women.

- **Inclusion/ Participation:** The VP programme has enabled rural women----In this case, VP phone operators to directly participate in generating income for the household in a way that is less physically demanding and carries less risk than farming or animal husbandry. Furthermore, they can use the help of other family members in procuring services, thus increasing the overall welfare of the households.

- **Mobility:** The women who are involved in the programme have to attend meetings in NGOs are required to move from one place to another. Consequently this helps them in being involved to new ideas, knowledge and experiences through their interactions with the world outside their four walls of their homesteads.

It is evident that the development of ICT skills in women is found to produce perceptual changes in mental spaces, such as level of confidence, self-esteem, self-respect and freedom from domination or dependency of any type. If women's engagement in ICT is active and in-depth in terms of learning and education, then women could become more empowered. Moreover, poverty could be reduced in rural populations in Bangladesh and finally women can acquire the capacity to combat violence against them.

ICT 4D FOR WOMEN: SOME SUCCESS STORIES

This section of the paper presents some success stories of the use of ICTs in different countries through the use of Mobile Phone. It consists of a series of studies commissioned by the International Development research Center (IDRC) on the future of ICTs and Development.

As digital technologies open up new spaces and opportunities, there is a lot of optimism about empowerment of women, and alleviation of poverty and gender disparity. According to (http://www.itu.int/ITU-D/sis/Gender/1 the ITU, the Un agency for ITU issues:

Information and communication technologies (ICTs) can be used to close the gender gap by creating new jobs for impoverished women. Women, for example, have been at the forefront of the village phone movement, selling time to rural people too poor to own their own phones. ICTs can also be used to promote basic literacy and education for women and girls, provide job training and prepare women for careers in the ICT sector as well as to ensure health and safety.

As far as women's empowerment continues at the bottom of the pyramid, the issue has been more centered on mobile phones than on computer-related ICTs. (http;//en.wilipedia.org/wiki/Bottom of the pyramid).

Other reasons why the mobile phone has been relatively more gender responsive than the computer-related ICTs have been pointed out by stating that:

We find that women have already started appropriating the mobile phone, finding their own ways to overcome difficulties of literacy, language and costs, working together and using it as a tool for ex-

plaining their assets and capabilities with no need for technical training and back-up. Perhaps this is the best example of self-empowerment through utilizing new ITCs.(Macuveve & others,(http//www.idrc.ca/en/ev:137001-201:1-DO TOPIC.htmll)

Strategic uses of ICTs are being made in other key areas of empowerment, such as combating violence among women. A study by Stanford University Report by Dayoung Lee indicated that mobile phones lower a women's tolerance of domestic violence significantly by giving them greater connectivity and access. As Lee wrote:

Phones may empower women by giving them better access to social services. Given the privacy of talking on the phone, women can more easily report domestic violence or consult family planning agencies.(http://economics.stanford.edu/files/HonorsTheses/Theses 2009/Lee.%20D.%20 2009.pdf)

As mobile penetration increases across the developing world, the entry of mobile phones in the hands of women causes reactions. In many cases, mobile phone ownership empowers women in myriad ways: economic gains, increased access to information, greater autonomy and social empowerment, and a greater sense of security and safety.

Technology in the hands of women have been correlated with changes in asset ownership, spending decisions, negotiating power, within a household and changes in household dynamic. In a study on mobile phones and poverty reduction in Uganda, Kathleen Diga, a researcher on mobile technology and women, wrote that:

Ultimately, the mobile phone is a tool that enables citizens to communicate with family and friends, to save on transport costs, to identify and take advantage of economic opportunities and to react immediately to mitigate shocks and vulnerable situations.

Around the world people and organizations recognize the potential of mobile technology in development and are creating their own projects across multiple sectors, such as health, finance, media, democratic participation, empowerment and human rights. In India, the Self Employees Women's Association (SEWA) uses mobile phones to improve women's bargaining power and increases their incomes. Each day, SEWA sends agricultural workers SMS messages with community prices so they can determine when and where to get the best price for their products.

In rural Tamil Nadu, mobile provider *Uninor* enables female entrepreneurs to deliver ICT training to other women in the community.

In Bangladesh a woman who built an international tea empire (one that employs 1500 female farmers) credit much of her success to mobile technology.

My mobile phone has helped ne so much with the business- it is absolutely crucial for distribution and marketing. I don't have an office or showroom, so people just ring me on the mobile to place orders.

Finally, it is important to mention that in Bangladesh, the Grameen Bank took a focused approach to gender and development through their model of poverty reduction, serving as a source of micro-credit and literacy training, skills development, and health, family planning and political consciousness education directed at women. Grameen Phones is particularly noteworthy because of the economic empowerment that it has brought to the poor rural (largely uneducated) women. From among its more than two million borrowers, predominantly women, the Bank management selects Village Phone Operators to whom the phone is provided as an in-kind loan. The opera-

tors resell wireless phone services (incoming and outgoing) to fellow villagers.(Gender_and ITC/ Placing_Women's_Empowerment_Back_In).

Stories of this type are not rare. Across the developing world mobile phones contribute to economic gains, access to information, social empowerment and greater sense of security and safety.

CONCLUDING REMARKS: THE CHALLENGES AND FUTURE DIRECTIONS

As the paper and the following cases explain ICTs and policies to encourage the development of women can have profound implications for women in terms of employment, education, health and environmental sustainability and community development. Experience from recent policy efforts at the international level suggests that gender biases in the information society will persist for the foreseeable future. ICTs are clearly not 'gender-neutral' because women know and understand the importance of information and the power that the technology of mobile phone hold in terms of breaking out of systematic discrimination and indeed even gender violence in the household, workplace and village, especially if women organize themselves as indicated by NGO activities and programmes.

Having said all these positive aspects of the impact of ICT on women's empowerment today in Bangladesh the empowerment of women is fraught with new challenges that lie ahead in the sphere of ICTs. For example, the expansion and spread of ICT throughout the country specifically in the area of mobile phone companies have lead to a sharp decrease in the prices of the mobile phones together with the charges that they can make. The many and diverse companies working today include the AKTEL, Bangla Link, City Cell Warid etc. This had led to the competitiveness of the mobile phone scheme and it has become very difficult for the Village Pay Phone to operate on a profit basis as previously and this definitely has a profound effect on the purchase and utilization of the pay phone by the rural population in Bangladesh. A majority of the VP operators reported that they have been experiencing a dent in the competitive advantage they used to enjoy when there were no other service providers in the villages. The income of VP operators has fallen so much that they can no longer depend solely on their mobile phones to make a living.

Women have to be aware of the market forces both for the purchase and use as operators and many may be unable to do so due to their less knowledge and information gap. This will eventually affect their small micro-enterprises which they may be engaged in.

To conclude, *"it is important to point out that 'empowerment is typically conceptualized as a process, and therefore change is at its very essence. Once a resource, capacity, or form of agency becomes commonplace, it no longer distinguishes more empowered women from the less empowered women. Therefore, it is relevant that the measurement of empowerment must change and adapt to keep up with the elusive phenomenon." (Schuler, Islam, and Rottach, 2010)*

REFERENCES

Ahmed, A., Islam, D., Hasan, A. R., & Rahman, N. (2006). *Measuring Impact of ICT on Women in Bangladesh*. Retrieved March 27, 2008, from http://icc.ough.edu.cn/WorldComp2005/EEE4168.pdf

Aminuzzaman, S., Baldersheim, H., & Ishtiaq, J. (2002). *Talking Back! Empowerment and Mobile Phones in Rural Bangladesh: A Study of the Village Pay Phone of Grameen Bank*. Paper presented at the International Society for Third Sector Research (ISTR) Fifth International Conference Transforming Civil Society, Citizenship and Governance: The Third Sector in an Era of Global (Dis) Order Graduate School in Humanities. Cape Town, South Africa.

Ashraf, M. M., Hanisch, J., & Swatman, P. (2008). *ICT Intervention and Its Impact In Village Areas of Developing Country*. Paper presented at the IADIS International Conference e-Society. Algarve, Portugal.

Azim, F., & Sultan, M. (Eds.). (2010). *Mapping Women's Economic Empowerment*. Dhaka, Bangladesh: The University Press Limited.

Baltiwala, S. (1994). *Women's Empowerment in South Asia: Concepts and Practices*. New Delhi: Food and Agricultural Organization/Asia, South Asia Bureau of Adult Education.

Bayes, A. (2001). Infrastructura and Rural Development: Insights from a Grameen Bank Village Phone Initiative in Bangladesh. *Agricultural Economics, 25*(2), 261–272.

Daily Star. (2010, October 29). Article. *The Daily Star*.

Hafkin, N. (2002a). *Gender Issues in ICT Policy in Developing Countries: An Overview*. Retrieved from http//www.womensnet.org.za/gender-issues-ict-policy-developing-countries-an-overview

Hijab, N., & Zambrano, R. (2008). *Gender responsive E-Governance: Exploring the Transformative Potential*. New York: UNDP.

Hultberg, L. (2008). *Women Empowerment in Bangladesh: A Study of the Village Pay Phone Program. School of Education and Communication (HLK)*. Jonkoping University.

Huyer, S., & Sikoska, T. (2003). Overcoming Gender Digital Divide: Understanding ICT and Their Potential for the Empowerment of Women. *Instraw Research Paper Series, 1*, 17-57.

Kabeer, N. (2001). Resources, Agency, Achievements: Reflections on the Measurement of Women's Empowerment in Discussion: Women's Empowerment Theory and Practice. *Sida Studies, 3*.

Kaufman, H. (1977). *Red Tape: Its Origins, Uses and Abuses*. Washington, DC: Brookings Institution.

Lennie, J. (2002). Rural Women's Empowerment in a Communication Technology Project, Some Contradictory Effects. *Rural Society, 12*(3), 224–254.

Macueve, G., Mandlate, J., Ginger, L., Gaster, P., & Macome, E. (2009). *Women's Use of Information and Communication Technologies in Mozambique: A Tool for Empowerment*. IDRC.

Magar, V. (2003). Empowerment Approaches to Gender-Based Violence: Women's Courts in Delhi Slums. *Women Studies International Forum, 26*(6), 509-523.

Marcelle, G. M. (2002). *Information and Communication Technologies, (ICT) and Their Impact On The Use as an Instrument for the Advancement and Empowerment of Women*. Retrieved March 25, 2008 from http/www.un.org/womenwatch/draw/egn/ict2002/reports/ReportonlinePDF

Obayelu, A., & Ogundale. (2006). Anakyses of the uses of Information Communication Technology (ICT) for Gender Empowerment and Sustainable Poverty Alleviation in Nigeria. *International Journal of Education and Development using ICT, 2* (3).

Osborne, D., & Gaebler, T. (1992). *Reinventing Government: How the Entrepreneurial Spirit is Transforming the Public Sector*. Addison, Wesley.

Prasad, P. N., & Sreedevi, V. (2007). Economic Empowerment of Women Through Information Technology—A Case Study from an Indian State. *Journal of International Women's Studies, 8*(4), 107–119.

Roy, S., & Himu, T. A. (2011). How does the Use of Cellular Phone Commit Violence Against Women. *Higher Education of Social Sciences, 1*(1), 1013.

Schuler, S. R., Islam, F., & Rottach, E. (2010). Women's Empowerment Revisited: A Case Study from Bangladesh. *Development in Practice, 20*(7), 840–854. PMID:20856695

Tapscott, D. (1996). *The Digital Economy*. New York: McGraw Hill.

Tapscott, D., & Caston, A. (1993). *Paradigm Shift: The New promise of Information Technology*. New York: McGraw Hill.

World Bank. (2006). *Engendering Information & Communication Technologies Challenges and Opportunities for Gender-Equitable Development*. Retrieved from http://web.world bank.org/WEBSITE/EXTERNAL/TOPICS

Yusuf, M. A., & Alam, Q. (2011). Empowering Role of the Village Phone Program in Bangladesh: In Retrospect. Prospect: Journal of Information Technology Impact, 11(1), 35-50.

KEY TERMS AND DEFINITIONS

E-governance: E- governance is a multi dimensional concept. It may be simply defined as digital government information, or a way of transforming or engaging in technological transfer of information to clienteles or customers.

Empowerment of Women: This is defined as the capacity of the rural poor women in making their choices in their lives, that is, their right in decision making. It involves changing their lives, having greater control over resources of power.

Gender Dimensions: This refers to the social construct indicating the differences in roles and relations between women and men based on power. It also shows how technologies are not gender neutral and thus leads to the disadvantage of women in society.

ICT: This is Information and Communication Technologies within the fields of socio-economic development. It implies better information and communication and enhances the development in the area of education, health, human rights and security, or any other aspect of human development.

Mobile Phone: Defined as the technology used by rural women in Bangladesh and how this has helped them in reducing poverty, getting engaged in work outside their homes and eventually has provided the opportunity of getting empowered.

Poverty: Poverty means hunger; Poverty means lack of shelter; Poverty means lack of freedom, decision making power and non-representation from everything in life.

Violence against Women: This is a very common phenomenon among the rural poor women in Bangladesh. Violence arises due to poverty, subordination, lack of knowledge and mainly patriarchy. Violence occurs everywhere and in all ages. Rape, murder, acid throwing, dowry related murder are increasing at an alarming rate. It is through the use of ICT (mobile phone) that women are being able to combat the problem of violence.

Chapter 13
E–Governance Preparedness of Public Bureaucracy in Bangladesh

Md. Rokon-Ul-Hasan
Bangladesh Public Administration Training Centre, Bangladesh

Mobasser Monem
University of Dhaka, Bangladesh

ABSTRACT

In Bangladesh, there is an undeniable wave of awareness about e-governance at present. Therefore, it is high time that government prepare itself in terms of implementing e-governance in order to cope with the requirements of the fast changing global environment. As bureaucracy is one of the most vital pillars of government, it is imperative that it is well prepared to face the upcoming challenges of technological boost. This chapter assesses the preparedness level of bureaucracy from the perspective of e-governance implementation. Analysis of primary data reveals that the frequency of computer and Internet usage for official activities is also very low. Most of the officials do not have any formal ICT training, and those who have such training have covered only very elementary aspects. The overall readiness in terms of technical skills is found to be unsatisfactory. Existing laws, rules, and regulations are found to be very insufficient for smooth implementation of e-governance in Bangladesh.

1. INTRODUCTION

The concept of governance has evolved with the change in the role of the governments along with the increased participation of other stakeholders like market, civil society, NGOs and above all, the citizens in the overall policy formulation as well as implementation. Although primarily this phenomenon emerged in developed countries, 'governance' has become a key agenda even in the developing world as a result of direct and indirect forces of globalization. The advancement in Information and Communication Technology (ICT) has added new dimension to the governance arena and the concept of e-governance (electronic governance) has gained much focus in the dis-

DOI: 10.4018/978-1-4666-3691-0.ch013

course of governance. Bangladesh is no exception to the global trend of inclination towards ICT and e-governance has become an area of concern within the country of late.

The significance of 'e-governance' seems to have been identified by the state actors including the political leaders and bureaucrats along with the non-state counterparts. Now that the important stakeholders have consensus about the indispensability of e-governance from a normative viewpoint, it is equally important that actions are taken in accordance with well conceived short-term, medium-term and long-term action plans (Hoque, 2009). To materialize such plans, all the stakeholders need to be well prepared, and the bureaucracy is one of them. The e-governance readiness of the bureaucracy has got significant implication as far as the success of e-governance initiatives is concerned.

It is very important to realize that e-governance is not only a means to increase administrative efficiency but also a tool to enhance democracy by ensuring the citizens' participation in the policy making process. It also has to be recognized that technology is only a means to an end where the 'end' is citizen welfare by an improved governance mechanism. The preparedness of e-governance is a multifarious phenomenon that includes social, cultural, psychological, economic and legal aspects along with the most commonly perceived aspect of technology.

There is an undeniable wave of awareness about e-governance in the polity of Bangladesh at present. This awareness is, at least partially, motivated by one of the predominant political agenda of 'Digital Bangladesh' of the present government in power.[1] In spite of this 'wave' there is a common feeling among the conscious citizens that the manifestation of the vision is not clear to people, including the politicians and even the bureaucracy. Now, bureaucracy is the functioning machine that helps materialize the visions of the political executives of the government. No matter how sincere a political vision is,

if the bureaucracy is not involved in the process of policy formulation and implementation properly, the success of vision will be at stake. Therefore, it is imperative that the preparedness of the bureaucracy in terms of e-governance is assessed properly. Since the field level bureaucracy has a greater opportunity to interact with the citizens than the central bureaucracy, the preparedness at the field level is no less important than that of the central bureaucracy. An objective analysis of the situation in this regard will definitely provide invaluable insights about what needs to be done to materialize 'e-governance' on a priority basis.

Against the backdrop of significant advancement in Information and Communication Technology (ICT) and extensive globalization, e-governance is an issue on which all the stakeholders have a consensus to adopt. In spite of some success in this area there is no space for Bangladesh to be complacent. Achievement of true e-governance does not seem to be an easy task in the face of myriad of problems to embrace.

Although the government's ICT infrastructure at the Ministry/ Division level has significantly improved over the years, the inadequacy of ICT logistics in many government offices has been a concern of the researchers. A 2008 study by SICT (Support to ICT) programme found that 24% of the Departments, Corporations and Commissions have no PCs in their offices. The offices at the Ministry/ Division level generally all have Internet access shared over LAN. Internet connectivity at lower levels is sporadic. There is no government wide network yet in place - so government offices have to rely on Internet to relay data and messages. (BEI, 2010)

The existing policy and legal framework does not yet encompass a comprehensive guideline about e-governance implementation. Currently the e-Government policy framework is largely being driven by the ICT Policy, 2009 and the ICT Act, 2009. The present policy framework does not deal with some important issues. Few of such issues are, among others, technological standardization, data privacy and security and interoperability among shared service platform (to avoid duplication of effort) etc.

In absence of central e-Governance coordinating and monitoring entity, the tasks of prioritizing and controlling the quality of the e-governance projects remained as a challenge in Bangladesh (Hoque, 2009). E-Governance requires rethinking the standard operating procedure. The existing administrative rethinking mechanism is not aligned with the e-governance activities and plans. Such lack of coordination between administrative reform and e-governance is another challenge to fully utilization of e-Governance (Morshed, 2007).

Lastly, the readiness of the human resources of the government, who are supposed to be the first mover to achieve e-governance, is not beyond question. In the present scenario the extent and nature of training available for the government employees is not sufficient and appropriate (Hoque, 2009). Apart from the technical skills, there is another important issue of mindset of the bureaucrats towards the prospective changes to be offered by e-governance. Quite often members of bureaucracy are accused of having fear of losing authority on the event of e-governance initiatives.

The recent consciousness about information technology has paved the way for considering e-governance with utmost importance as a development option for Bangladesh. E-governance, if successfully implemented, will not only make the government processes effective and efficient, but would also facilitate transparency, accountability of all the counterparts; above all it will enhance democracy by ensuring citizens' participation in the governance system. Now that a part of the society is becoming vibrant about e-governance all the stakeholders of 'governance' system should be keen to capitalize on the sentience. To successfully do so, an assessment of the preparedness of central as well as of field level bureaucracy is a true necessity. This study seeks to examine the preparedness level of the bureaucracy and also to identify the major factors that affect e-governance preparedness of the bureaucracy based on the case of the Office of the Deputy Commissioner, Dhaka. It covers only class one officers, administrative officers (most commonly known as AOs who are class two officers) and the office assistants. It also includes some service seekers who are common citizens.

Brief Overview of Office of the Deputy Commissioner, Dhaka

Bangladesh comprises of 64 districts and Dhaka is one of them. The representative of central government at the district level is the Deputy Commissioner and his/ her office is the DC Office which is the area of study of this research. Office of the Deputy Commissioner (DC Office) is one of the most important offices of the country; and Dhaka being the capital of Bangladesh, Dhaka DC office is of utmost importance as far as service delivery and presence of government is concerned. A large number of people of all sections visit this office for getting various kinds of services on a regular basis. The Deputy Commissioner, Dhaka has five Additional Deputy Commissioners (ADCs) namely ADC (General), ADC (Revenue), ADC (Land Acquisition), ADC (Education and Development) and Additional District Magistrate (ADM). The DC plays two very important roles in addition to his role as deputy to the Commissioner. These two roles are District Magistrate (DM) and Collector. The role of DM is to oversee the executive magisterial functions within his jurisdiction whereas as 'Collector' he supervises the revenue collection system within the district. Therefore major functions of DC Office, Dhaka include Land management and Land Acquisition, Executive Magistracy, Supervision of Development Activities, Public Exams, National and other elections, treasury functions, Issuance of different types of licenses, Maintenance of Law and Order situations, etc.

2. THEORETICAL UNDERPINNINGS

The concept of e-governance describes the result for the addition of the prefix 'E' to governance, where E stands for electronic and has occasioned glaring transformations in the lexicon of governance and administration. It explains the import of information and tele-communications revolution in governance. E-governance thus implies the replacement of the Weberian principles of bureaucratic governance with the trends of horizontal, leaner, dynamic and networked governance. E-governance refers to the governance processes in which Information and Communications Technologies (ICTs) play active and significant roles for efficient and effective governance, and for making the government more accessible and accountable to the citizens. The concept has become an integral part of public sector transformation as ICTs have helped to deliver more modern services for citizens and businesses. It stimulates the emergence of Information Society, drives public sector transformation and help governments prepare for future models of public administrations (Gupta and Jain, 2010: 91 – 100).

In a detailed explication while describing a closely related but not to be interchanged concept, the World Bank (2004) aptly opines that e-government is

the use by government agencies of information technologies (such as Wide Area Networks, the Internet, and mobile computing) that have the ability to transform relations with citizens, businesses, and other arms of government. These technologies can serve a variety of different ends: better delivery of government services to citizens, improved interactions with business and industry, citizen empowerment through access to information, or more efficient government management.

The resulting benefits can be less corruption, increased transparency, greater convenience, revenue growth, and/or cost reductions.

Thus, the emphasis here is on use of information technologies in improving citizen-government interactions, while adopting cost-cutting approach to administration and evolving dependable cum most rewarding modes of revenue generation that can conduce to efficiency, accountability and transparency in public business.

In a similar vein, UNESCO (2008) defines governance as the exercise of political, economic and administrative authority in the management of a country's affairs, including citizens' articulation of their interests and exercise of their legal rights and obligations. Thus, the global scientific and cultural educational agency infers that e-governance may be understood as the performance of this governance via the electronic medium in order to facilitate an efficient, speedy and transparent process of disseminating information to the public, and other agencies, and for performing government administration activities.

This definition visualizes the use of the electronic medium in the exercise of authority in the management of a country's affairs along with articulation of citizens' interests leading to greater transparency and efficiency. While the Council of Europe (2009) has taken e-Governance to mean the use of electronic technologies in three areas of public action, viz:

- Relations between the public authorities and the civil society,
- Functioning of the public authorities at all stages of the democratic process (electronic democracy),
- The provision of public services (electronic public services).

In this light, the focus is on making use of electronic technologies with a view to encouraging better interaction between government and citizens, promoting democracy and providing public services.

Coming from a seemingly divergent perception, the American E-Government Act of 2002 (Section 3601) perceives electronic Government as the

use by the Government of web-based internet applications and other information technologies, combined with processes that implement these technologies to enhance the access to and delivery of Government information and services to the public, other agencies, and other Government entities.

The above submission can equally result in bringing about improvements in government operations that may include effectiveness, efficiency, service quality, and or transformation.

The perception also reflects the strategy of the United States' Government regarding the use of ICT in improving government operations on the one hand and enhancing the access and delivery of information and services to citizens and government entities on the other.

Basically, e-Governance is generally understood as the use of Information and Communications Technology (ICT) at all levels of the government in order to provide services to the citizens, interaction with business enterprises and communication and exchange of information between different agencies of the Government in a speedy, convenient, efficient and transparent manner. With a bid to domesticating the implementation of e-governance, Dr. APJ Abdul Kalam, former President of India in an inaugural address in 2009 presented at IIT Delhi during International conference on e-governance, visualized e-governance in the Indian context to mean:

A transparent smart e-Governance with seamless access, secure and authentic flow of information crossing the interdepartmental barrier and providing a fair and unbiased service to the citizen (Government of India, 2009).

E-governance therefore implies adoption of new ways and means for citizens to manage their own lives with the help of new Information and Communication Technologies (ICT). It is also the application of Information Technology to the process of government functioning in order to bring about simple, moral, accountable, responsive and transparent (SMART) Governance (Renu, 2003). Here, it involves the transformation from being a passive information and service provider to active citizen involvement. It can also be defined as giving citizens the choice of when and where they access government information and services (Renu, 2003b). Thus, e-governance is the process of using Information Technology for automating both the internal operations of the government and its external interactions with citizens and other businesses.

3. E-GOVERNANCE: A NEW PARADIGM?

Discussions on the evolution of public administration as an area of study dates back to 1887 with the seminal article by Woodrow Wilson entitled *"The Study of Administration"*. Based on emerging issues, Henry (1995) suggested five overlapping paradigms in the discipline to include the following in their orders of sequence:

Paradigm 1: Politics/administration dichotomy (1900-1926).
Paradigm 2: Principles of administration (1927-1937).

Paradigm 3: Public administration as Political Science (1950-1970).

Paradigm 4: Public administration as Management (1956-1970).

Paradigm 5: Public administration as Public Administration (1970-?).

The periods of the paradigms are obviously not specific and distinct as observed in the era of public administration as political science and public administration as management. Its overlapping form is further observed with the overstretching influence of the fifth paradigm which Henry could not assign borderline owing to its persistent relevance especially in intellectual discourses. However, Muinul-Islam and Saadudin Ahmed (2007:24-46) in their theoretical espouse on understanding e-governance carefully suggested a seemingly dependable borderline for the last epoch in evolutionary study and practice of public administration at the year 2000. This according to them is strongly rooted in the emergence of a new idea in the theories and practice of public administration following the coinage of the concept of *New Public Management* in 2001 by Christopher Hood in his article titled "*A public management for all seasons*" thereby introducing a paradigm shift in the discipline. Hence, the emergence of a sixth paradigm called Public Administration as New Public Management (NPM), (1991-?). It should be recalled that the idea that metamorphosed into the sixth paradigm was earlier discussed by some other scholars like Pollitt, Lan and Rosenbloom, Osborne and Gaebler under different names in the early 1990s.

What is more, advancements in technology which has over the past three decades occasioned unprecedented revolutions in information and communications technologies did not leave the realm of politics and governance untouched. It has steadily permeated the organization and structure of governments in both the developed and developing nations. Developments in information and communications technologies (ICTs) have greatly changed the pattern of both private and public conduct and businesses across the world with an inevitable process of converting information from analog to digital forms. This has fostered convenience and allowed government organisations to effectively store, analyze and retrieve information which is the hub of administration. The revolution grossly became more domineering with changes in telecommunications technology and the convergence of computers that resulted in the advent of the internet or World Wide Web (Bretschneider, 2003). The introduction of the internet and web presence in the 1990s has obviously ushered in a new dimension into the discipline with *Public Administration* getting to be studied as *E-governance:* another emerging paradigm that is gradually defining contemporary governance and administration. This is thus the seventh paradigm that is popping up soonest (Islam and Ahmed, 2007:29-46). Well, I guess practitioners and my colleagues in the academia will agree with me that ICTs has revolutionized the structure, processes and operations of public administration as being witnessed in the domain of contemporary politics (Nye, 1999), nature of government institutions (Foutain, 2001), improved performance management (Brown 1999), rate of red-tape reduction (Moon and Bretschneider, 2002) and, re-engineering public sector organizations (Anderson, 1999).

Seen as a check tool and fulcrum of efficiency, e-governance in administration invariably begets new models for policy formulation, new forms of citizenship, new patterns of political power configuration and class alignment, new options for economic development and provides improved platforms for connecting people with the political process. It thus engenders transparency and accountability, creates room for speedy information dissemination, and fosters greater citizens' participation and improved services in public administration. It equally reduces the cost of governance and provides greater links to more efficient ways of public service delivery (Agarwal and Rastogi, 2003).

4. E-GOVERNMENT AND E-GOVERNANCE: CRYSTALLIZING THE CONCEPTS

In the literature regarding 'e-governance', the term 'e-government' is profusely present, not surprisingly though. These two terms, as they appear, have significant interconnection although they do not mean the same thing. E-government is a narrower term of the two, referring to a transformation of the functions of the government to be driven primarily by ICT. The focus of the concept 'e-government' primarily lies in streamlining of the administrative processes with a view to achieving greater efficiency and effectiveness and secondarily on some online services to the citizens (Backus, 2001).

E-governance, however, is a broader term that includes transformation on at least four levels. First, it involves the transformation of the business of government (e-government). Secondly, it involves a transformation in the *operational definitions* of the principles upon which governance is founded, shifting towards increased participation, openness, transparency, and communication (Schiavo-Ocampo & Sundaram, 2001). Thirdly, it involves a transformation in the interactions between government and its (internal and external) clients, classified as government-to-citizen (G2C), government-to-business (G2B), government to its internal employee clients (G2E), government to other government institutional clients (G2G), and citizen-to-citizen (C2C). Finally, it involves a transformation of the society itself, through

the emergence of connections, as well as relations among (NGOs), built and sustained using electronic means (Pablo & Pan: 2002).

Researchers have a consensus of some sort about the scope of e-governance in a sense that most of them, if not all, have defined the boundary of e-governance beyond the government or e-government. Backus (2001) argues that by achieving the concrete objective of supporting and simplifying governance for all parties - government, citizens and businesses through online services and other electronic means, e-governance uses electronic means to support and stimulate good governance. So, conceptually it can be argued that 'e-government' is a prerequisite of 'e-governance' while it is also one of the actors of the overall 'e-governance' system. Hoque (2009) quotes Dobrica (2006) to state that e-governance aims to enable the interaction between government and citizens (G2C) (Government-to-Citizen), improve inter-agency relationships between G2G (Government-to-Government), and establish efficient relationship between the government and business enterprises (G2B) (Government-to-Business).

5. FORMS OF E-GOVERNANCE INTERACTIONS

Researchers have a consensus of some sort about the scope of e-governance in a sense that most of them, if not all, have defined the boundary of e-governance beyond the government or e-government. Backus (2001) argues that by achieving the concrete objective of supporting and simplifying governance for all parties - government, citizens and businesses through online services and other electronic means, e-governance uses electronic means to support and stimulate good governance. Application of ICTs in the processes of carrying out government functions facilitates interactions between different stake holders, levels of government as well as strata of persons/organizations in governance. These interactions may be described as follows:

- **G2C (Government-to-Citizen):** Involves interaction of individual citizens with the government. G2C allows government agencies to talk, listen, relate and continuously communicate with its citizens, supporting, in this way of accountability, democracy and improvements to public services. G2C allows customers to access government information and services instantly, conveniently from everywhere.

- **G2B   (Government-to-Business):** Involves interaction of business entities with the government. It includes e-transaction initiatives such as e-procurement and the development of an electronic marketplace for government helping businesses to become more competitive.

- **G2G   (Government-to-Government):** Involves interaction among government offices as well as governments of other countries. Governments depend on other levels of government within the state to effectively deliver services and allocate responsibilities. G2G focus online communication and cooperation among the government agencies and departments to share database, resources, pool skills and capabilities with a view to avoiding duplication and enhancing the efficiency and effectiveness of process.

- **G2E   (Government-to-Employee):** Involves interaction between the government and its employees. It gives employees the possibility of accessing relevant information regarding: compensation and benefit policies, training and learning opportunities, civil rights laws, etc. G2E refers also to strategic and tactical mecha-

nisms for encouraging the implementation of government goals and programs as well as human resource management, budgeting and accounting.

6. STAGES OF E-GOVERNANCE

In this paper the 'stages of e-government' will be interchangeably used with 'stages of e-governance'. Researchers and institutions have developed different models to describe various stages of e-government at different point of time. According to the United Nations' E-government Survey (2008), there are five stages of e-government evolution. These stages are as follows:

Stage 1 - Emerging: A government's online presence is mainly comprised of a web page and/or an official website; links to ministries or departments of education, health, social welfare, labour and finance may/may not exist. Much of the information is static and there is little interaction with citizens.

Stage 2 - Enhanced: Governments provide more information on public policy and governance. They have created links to archived information that is easily accessible to citizens, as for instance, documents, forms, reports, laws and regulations, and newsletters.

Stage 3 - Interactive: Governments deliver online services such as downloadable forms for tax payments and applications for license renewals.

Stage 4 - Transactional: Governments begin to transform themselves by introducing two-way interactions between 'citizen and government'. All transactions are conducted online.

Stage 5 - Connected: Governments transform themselves into a connected entity that responds to the needs of its citizens by developing an integrated back office infrastructure.

7. EVOLUTION OF E-GOVERNANCE IN BANGLADESH

Utilization of technology in service delivery is not a new phenomenon in Bangladesh. Initiatives were evident even more than one and a half decade ago. Since then, the concept of e-governance seems to have been conceived much better than ever before. Initially, there was a clear emphasis on building ICT infrastructure, possibly deemed as a pre-requisite to the delivery of e-citizen services. However, despite some successes, many of these e-government projects did not sustain in the long run due to lack of long-term visions for those projects, and myriad other challenges. Over time, the government modified its approach and undertook strategies to address some of those challenges. Increasing number of citizen centric e-services projects was gradually undertaken. The evolution of the concept of e-governance in Bangladesh can be viewed as the continuum of the three distinct phases as described below.

Phase I (Late 1990s to 2006): Infrastructure Building

Early efforts started in mid 1990s, when the government automated the railway ticketing system. Another notable project from this period was the e-birth registration project under Rajshahi City Corporation in 2001, which made the process significantly faster and more efficient. Another early success was the automation of BANBEIS, which included GIS mapping of all schools and detailed information regarding them (including logistics, teachers, etc.), enabling unprecedented efficiency in education planning.

This trend of infrastructure building and process automation continued in a more coordinated manner from 2002-03, with the formation of the Support to ICT (SICT) Task Force Project, a publicly funded implementation arm of the National ICT Task Force based at the Planning Commission. SICT functioned like an internal facilitator which conceptualized, planned and prioritized projects, and provided funding and technical assistance to line ministries to implement them. SICT undertook a total of 38 projects, approximately 63% of which were focused primarily on internal automation and infrastructure building, and has completed 34 so far (BEI, 2010).

Many of the projects initiated by the SICT or the line ministries themselves during this period did not sustain in the long run. In May 2008, a Review Committee formed by the Caretaker Government found that out of the 103 policy directives of 2002, only 8 were fully or largely accomplished, 61 were partially accomplished and 34 remained unaddressed (GoB, 2008).

It can easily be noticed, however, that each of these projects were essentially the automation of existing government processes. While these increased efficiency in the respective agencies, they were not necessarily targeted towards empowerment of citizens through easy and open access to information and government services.

Phase II (2006 to 2009): Isolated E-services

Since 2006, with the caretaker government taking over, a gradual shift was noticed in the approach to e-government. The top-down approach to planning was gradually being replaced by more participatory approach within different entities of the government. It was increasingly realized that without internal demand and ownership generated through a planning process, success with such projects, which required extensive change management, could not be achieved.

An entity, which played an important role in this shift, was the Access to Information (A2I) Programme at the Prime Minister's Office (PMO). The programme was initiated in 2006 with support from UNDP to support the e- government Cell at the PMO. Although A2I was not directly in charge of implementing e-government projects, it took significant initiatives to generate internal bureaucratic demand for e-government, such as the series of workshops which led to 53 e-citizen services being committed to by the secretaries of various ministries and divisions in June 2008. Similarly, 64 e-citizen services were later identified by Deputy Commissioners (DCs) for implementation. A2I also provided continuous technical support and consultation to these projects.

Despite this trend towards the provision of information and services to citizens, the e-services designed and implemented during this period were hardly adequate. Besides, the focal points for e-government at the ministries were all at the Joint Secretary level, with relatively little decision making power, and insufficient incentives for initiating e-government projects since they get transferred frequently.

Phase III (2010 and Onward): Beyond the Concept of Isolated Services

After all the efforts to provide electronic services in an isolated manner, it seems that the government has realized that e-governance is not only about providing e-services to citizens. The holistic picture is being dominant under the circumstances of advancements in other countries. Recent developments yield indications that e-government is moving to the next phase in Bangladesh, away from isolated e-services towards more integrated, connected and transactional e-services. The present government came to power with the pledge of building a "Digital Bangladesh", and has tried to keep consistent focus on this promise so far. This has resulted in a political climate highly supportive of and conducive to e-government projects. A recent initiative (in 2010), the Digital Innovation Fair, born out of the A2I program at the PMO, took this opportunity and showcased the various successful and ongoing projects undertaken by the Ministries, effectively putting government agencies in a competitive environment and giving citizens an unprecedented opportunity to witness what services the Government is providing,

thereby creating a demand for these services. Although one might term the initiative as a political showdown, the awareness building aspect as well as the positive competition among various ministries that entailed such effort can never be underestimated.

Apart from the political will, which is undoubtedly a critical element for success, several other favourable factors have also propitiously converged in recent times. Most ministries have undergone extensive internal process automation and infrastructure development projects, which are usually the most resource consuming, and most of these projects have been completed. There have also been demonstrated successes in the creation and deployment of e-services. All this sets the stage for integrating the front-end services with automated backend processes, through holistic planning, and improving the quality and efficiency of e-services.

8. METHODOLOGY

Assessing the e-governance preparedness and identifying the influencing factors is a matter of qualitative judgment. However, to prioritize actions to enhance such preparedness deserves some sort of quantitative evaluation. Therefore, a combination of qualitative and quantitative approach has been used to attain the objectives of this study. The data for this study were collected both from primary and secondary sources. Secondary data were drawn from the existing literatures such as books, newspaper reports, previous research works, seminar papers, reports etc. Primary data were collected through questionnaire survey. The respondents included the employees working at the Office of the Deputy Commissioner, Dhaka. To collect data, in-depth interviews were conducted through open ended semi structured questionnaire. Two sets of questionnaire have been used to collect primary data, one for the officials and the other for the citizens.

Due to resource constraints all the employees working in the Office of the Deputy Commissioner (DC), Dhaka could not be chosen as respondents. Therefore, *Stratified Random Sampling* was deliberately used to choose the respondents for the purpose of the questionnaire survey. Three strata were chosen from three categories of officials namely *class one officers*, *administrative officers (class two)* and the *office assistants*. Apart from the employees working at the DC office, some service seekers were also covered. A total of 65 (sixty five) respondents were chosen from the three strata mentioned above for the questionnaire survey.

9. THEORETICAL AND ANALYTICAL FRAMEWORK

As the objective of this study is to assess the preparedness level of bureaucracy in terms of e-governance, adoption of technology is a key issue. This adoption is likely to be affected by a number of factors. For the purpose of identifying those factors in developing an analytical framework for the research, a relevant theory namely *Technology Acceptance Model* has been used. This model is elaborated in the following sub section.

Technology Acceptance Model

The Technology Acceptance Model (TAM) represents one of the explanatory models that have influenced the theories of human behaviour most

(Venkatesh, Morris, Davis, & Davis, 2003). The TAM was specifically developed with the primary aim of identifying the determinants involved in computer acceptance in general; secondly, to examine a variety of information technology usage behaviours; and thirdly, to provide a parsimonious theoretical explanatory model (Davis, Bagozzi, & Warshaw, 1989). It is rooted in social psychology and draws on Fishbein's and Ajzen's (1975) Theory of Reasoned Action (TRA), which establishes that the intent to produce a behavior depends on two basic determinants: attitude toward behaviour and subjective norms. Subjective norms refer to the reasons for producing a certain behaviour or not and make the link between the latter and an expected result, whereas attitude toward behaviour refers to the positive or negative value the individual associates to the fact of producing the behaviour.

Technology Acceptance Model (TAM) attempts to explain why a user accepts or rejects information technology by adapting TRA. TAM provides a basis with which one traces how external variables influence belief, attitude, and intention to use. Two cognitive beliefs are posited by TAM: perceived usefulness and perceived ease of use. According to TAM, one's actual use of a technology system is influenced directly or indirectly by the user's *behavioural intentions*, *attitude*, *perceived usefulness* of the system, and *perceived ease of use* of the system. TAM also proposes that external factors affect intention and actual use through mediated effects on perceived usefulness and perceived ease of use.

Table 1. Profile of the questionnaire survey respondents

Questionnaire	Respondent Criteria	Number of Respondents	Total
Questionnaire	Class One Officers	15	65
	Administrative Officer/ Office Assistant	20	
	Service Seekers/ Citizen	**30**	
Total			**65**

The TAM suggests that attitude would be a direct predictor of the intention to use technology, which, in turn, would predict the actual usage of the technology. Davis and Venkatesh (1996) however, suggest that attitude would not play a significant role; rather, perceived ease of use (expectation that a technology requires minimum effort) and perceived usefulness (perception that the use of a technology can enhance performance of a task at hand) would determine the intention to use a technology.

The 'External Variables' segment of Figure-1 has an important significance on the construction of this analytical framework. This is to emphasize the fact that there are quite a number of factors that have the potential to influence the perceived ease of use and perceived usefulness so as to have an indirect bearing on the adoption of e-governance related systems that include both process and technology. Venkatesh and Davis (1996) focused on understanding the antecedents of the perceived ease of use. They concluded that computer self-efficacy acts as a determinant of perceived ease of use both before and after hands-on use and that the objective usability was found to be a determinant of ease of use only after direct experience with a system.

The above discussion clearly depicts that there are quite a number of factors that can influence the 'actual use' of any system. Technology Ac-

ceptance Model (TAM) provides an option, in the form of 'external variables', which offers researchers a space to develop a framework regarding the usage of any information technology related system. The analytical framework of this study described below is primarily based on the proposition of TAM, identifies few independent variables that are likely to have bearings upon the e-governance preparedness of public bureaucracy.

Analytical Framework

In accordance with the above mentioned model, five independent variables have been identified that may possibly affect the dependent variable *'e-governance preparedness'*. These independent variables are *Technical Skill, Infrastructure and Logistic Support, Policy and Legal Framework, Attitude,* and *Incentive on ICT Usage*. An analytical framework for the purpose of this study has been developed which is shown below:

Technical Skill of using any system is a factor that can affect the perceived ease of use of the concerned system. So, it can be included as one of the external variables mentioned in the Technology Acceptance Model (TAM). This is also applicable for another independent variable *Infrastructure and Logistic Support* which is very likely to affect the perceived ease of use of e-governance systems. *Policy and Legal Framework* related

Figure 1. Technology acceptance model (Davis, 1989)

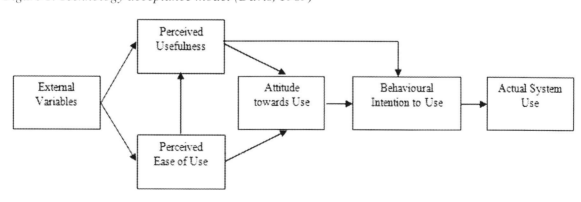

Figure 2. Analytical framework

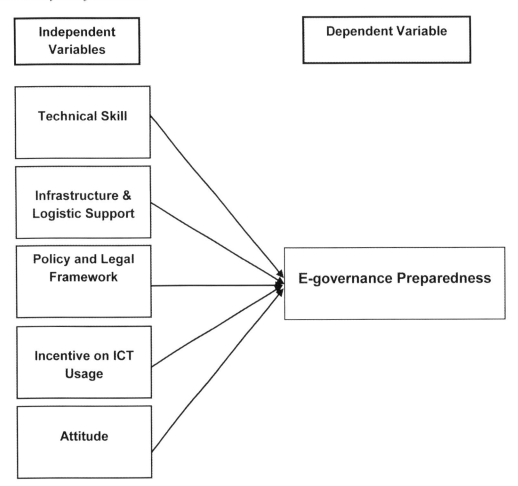

with e-governance is another external variable that can affect the perceived usefulness of the system. Another variable *Attitude* is also justified as an independent variable because it is also present in the TAM as an intermediate variable. The effect of the fifth independent variable (i.e., *Incentive*

on ICT Usage) on e-governance preparedness can be explained by Vroom's Expectancy Theory as it stipulates that a tendency to act in a specific way depends on the possible outcome. Therefore it can be argued that the bureaucrats' e-governance preparedness can be affected by the presence/absence of incentive on using ICT.

Table 2. Distribution of respondents by age (n = 35)

Age Group	Frequency	Percentage (%)
21 – 30	4	11%
31 – 40	23	66%
41 – 50	6	17%
51 – 60	2	6%

10. ANALYSIS OF THE FINDINGS OF THE QUESTIONNAIRE SURVEY

From the above distribution we find that most of the respondents (66%) fall in the age group of 31 to 40 years.

Logistics, Skill and Usage Level of Respondents

From Figure 3 it appears that 74% of the respondents have computer at home for their personal use.

According to the assessment of the respondents themselves about their comfort level in using computer, the response is quite mixed. Interestingly enough the maximum number of respondents (34%) rate themselves as 'very fluent' in using computer. The distribution is given in Table 3:

It is interesting to observe that the computer fluency along with the age of the respondents. Table 3 displays the matrix of age vs. computer fluency. It reveals in total 21 of the respondents are either 'fluent' or 'very fluent' and 17 of them are below 40 years of age. This implies that people of lower age tend to have better computer usage fluency.

In terms of access to computer at the office, the scenario is pretty ordinary. 31% of the respondents do NOT have access to computer at

Figure 3. Ownership of computer at home (n = 35)

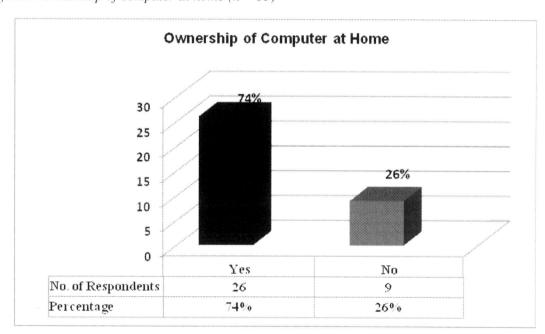

Table 3. Fluency of respondents in computer use (n = 35)

Fluency in Computer Use	Frequency	Percentage (%)
Not Fluent	4	11%
Moderately Fluent	10	29%
Fluent	9	26%
Very Fluent	12	34%

Table 4. Computer fluency vs. age group matrix (n=35)

Fluency in Computer Use/ Age Group	21-30	31-40	41-50	51-60
Not Fluent	0	1	2	1
Moderately Fluent	0	9	1	0
Fluent	1	6	2	0
Very Fluent	3	7	2	0

the workplace. Interestingly enough, of those who have access to computer, majority (26% of total respondents) share the computer among 3 persons. The computer sharing pattern is depicted in Figure 4 below:

Attempt to assess the computer usage frequency of the respondents is accompanied by a finding that majority (31%) of the respondents do not use computer for official purpose 'Almost Everyday' whereas 26% of them use minimum once everyday and 23% use computer almost everyday. It is notable that 11% of the respondents never use computer for official purpose. The computer usage frequency is shown below with a pie chart (Figure 5).

To show a clearer picture about the daily computer usage, the primary data (Table 5) reveals that 37% of the respondents use computer only for 30 minutes to 1 hour a day. The next big share (29%) indicates daily computer usage of less than 30 minutes which, of course, includes NO usage.

Availability of internet connection at home has a pretty balanced scenario. 51% (18 respondents) have internet connection at home whereas remaining 49% (17 respondents) do not have internet access at home.

From the respondents it was found out that internet is available at office premises although 37% of the respondents did not have internet access at their working terminal. However, the assessment about the speed of internet reveals that the users are more or less satisfied as 73% of the respondents termed the internet speed as 'moderate'. This is described in Figure 6.

While the speed of office internet connection is satisfactory, the internet usage frequency for official purpose is rather alarming. A total of 43% of the respondents admitted that they never use internet for official purpose. Figure 7 describes the internet usage pattern of the respondents for official purpose.

In case of e-mail usage, it was found out that 37% of the respondents did not have any personal e-mail address. More importantly 97% of the respondents did not have any official e-mail address either. As a matter of fact, the 3% respondent having official e-mail address amounts to a single person, i.e., the Deputy Commissioner. It is a significant piece of information that only the office head has an official electronic identity in the form of e-mail address. On the basis of earlier findings, the 60% of the respondents never uses

Figure 4. Computer ownership and sharing pattern at office (n = 35)

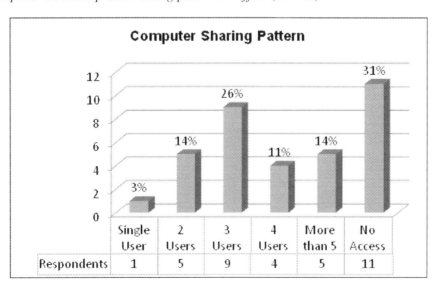

Figure 5. Frequency of computer use (n = 35)

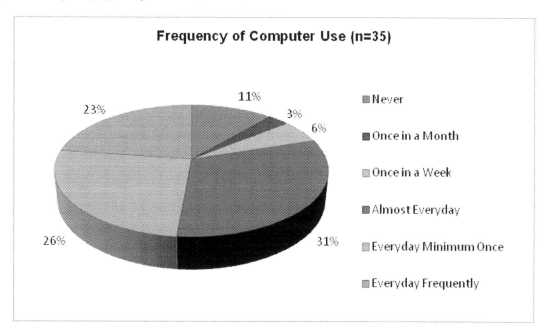

Table 5. Daily computer usage pattern (n = 35)

Daily Computer Usage	Frequency	Percentage
Less than 30 Minutes	10	29%
30 Min to 1 hour	13	37%
1 hour to 2 hours	6	17%
2 hours to 4 hours	4	11%
More than 4 hours	2	6%

e-mail for official purpose. Those who use e-mail had to share the official e-mail account of the Deputy Commissioner.

The respondents' exposure to Information and Communication Technology (ICT) related training was found to be as less as 23% (9 respondents) only. Even more importantly, of those 26%, 62.5% (5 respondents) termed their level of training as 'elementary'. 25% of them (2 respondents) termed it as 'mid-level'. The training scenario is depicted in Figure- 8. The content of the training, according to the respondents, included very fundamentals

of computer operation accompanied by basics of Microsoft Office applications, MS Word in particular.

Regulatory Aspects of E-governance

Majority (80%) of the respondents were unaware of any ICT related laws, rules or regulations. The respondents' perceptions about whether they are enforced to use ICT by any law, rules or regulations is noteworthy. About 91% of the respondents felt that they were not enforced by any such law or

Figure 6. Assessment about office Internet speed

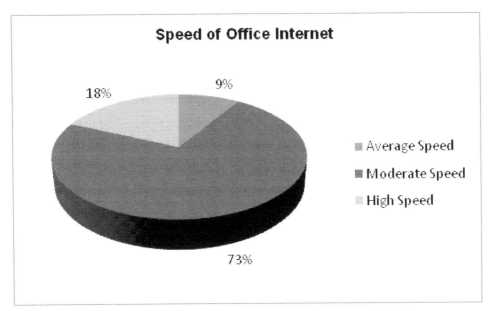

Figure 7. Frequency of Internet use in official work (n=35)

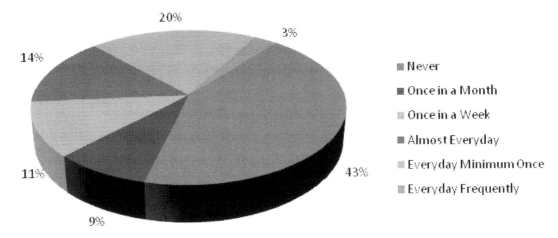

regulation to use ICT tools and techniques. Their opinion regarding the adequacy of ICT related laws, rules and regulations is also significant. 60% of the respondents believed that the existing regulatory framework was 'not sufficient' whereas 23% of them opined it to be 'very insufficient'. The overall picture about the perception is shown in Figure 9.

Incentive/Motivational Aspect of ICT Expertise

To enquire about the incentive provision as well as any motivational schemes, three specific questions were included in the questionnaire. The first two questions were about any possible 'financial benefit' and 'other type of benefit' for the officials

Figure 8. Level of ICT training of the respondents (n=8; 26% of 35 respondents)

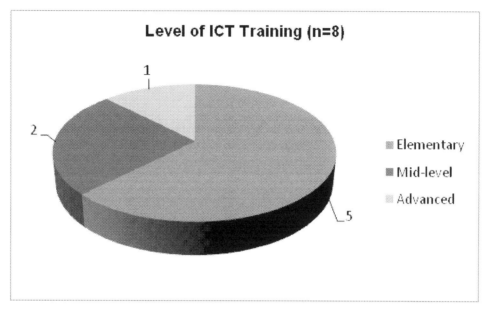

Figure 9. Opinion about adequacy of ICT law/ rules/ regulations (n=35)

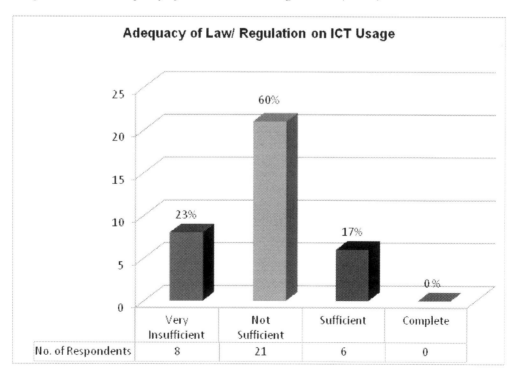

having ICT expertise. The respondents were 100% unanimous on these two issues, revealing that there was no such provision. However, in case of the third question, that enquired whether there is any positive impact of ICT expertise on the promotional prospect of the concerned officials, the finding is quite interesting.

As depicted in Figure 10, a significant 37% has a perception that any incumbent's ICT expertise leads to a positive impact on his/her promotional prospects. This finding is noteworthy because, in case of promotion, according to existing rules and regulations, there is no such provision that ICT expertise will have a direct influence. The response may have been so because of indirect influence in Annual Confidential Report (ACR) which is one of the factors considered in case of promotion.

Another significant finding is about the general evaluation mechanism of ICT expertise. In this case, 69% of the total respondents opined that ICT expertise is evaluated 'verbally along with additional work load'. 17% informed that it was not evaluated at all.

Service Aspect of E-Governance Preparedness

As regards to the extent of services provided electronically wherever possible, the respondents were asked whether they do have any provision of service through the official website. A significantly high 86% of the respondents told that they had no such service provision. The remaining 14% respondents mentioned that some of the services were provided through the websites. The superset of mentioned services included 'Daily Activity Information', 'Submission of Forms', 'Internet Service', 'Notice', 'Resolution', 'Complaint', 'Chalan Form', 'Vendorship List', 'Meeting Resolution' etc.

The responses about the services provided through website literally made another question redundant which enquired about availability of forms/ reports/ notices at the website. Actually the services mentioned in response to the first question were nothing but static forms and reports to be viewed by service seekers.

This fact is further validated by the perception of the respondents about utilization of available

Figure 10. Perception about effect of ICT expertise on promotion prospect (n=35)

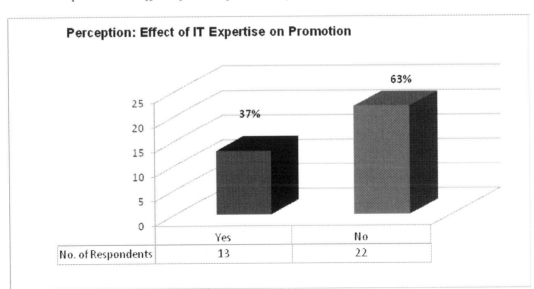

Figure 11. Opinion regarding evaluation of officials' ICT expertise (n=35)

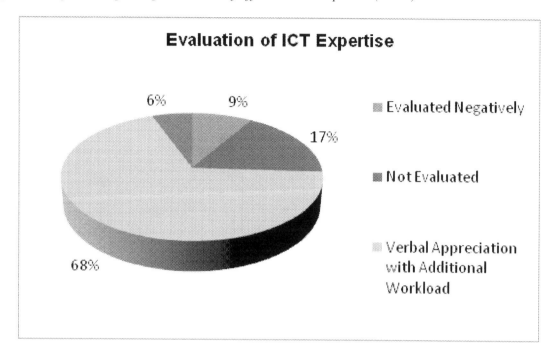

ICT facilities. Majority of the respondents (51%) opined that the utilization level was 'Low' whereas only 14% mentioned it to be 'High'. The opinion is described by Figure 12.

Holistic Picture of E-Governance Preparedness

Before going to the perception of the officials about the overall preparedness in terms of e-governance, one very important issue is mentionable. This is about the information on electricity load shedding in the study area during office hours. About 80% of the respondents informed that the daily load shedding during office hours varied between 2 to 4 hours. The response is graphically presented in Figure 13.

Considering the arithmetic mean to be the duration for each slot (i.e., 1.5 hours for 1 to 2 hr,

2.5 hours for 2 to 3 hours and so on) the average load shedding time is calculated to be 2.96 hours daily during office hours.

Lastly for the respondents' opinion about the overall e-governance preparedness of the office, the responses ranked the preparedness on a scale from 0 to 10. The responses are shown in a bar graph (Figure 14).

The average grading of the respondents is calculated to be 4.17 (out of 10), which indicates that the officials themselves did not rank the office's e-governance preparedness very high.

The respondents also gave their opinion about possible hindrances to e-governance implementation. The most highly rated cause identified was 'weakness of policy and regulatory framework' which was mentioned as one of the major causes by 83% of the respondents. The second highest ranked cause was the 'lack of infrastructure

Figure 12. Utilization of available ICT facilities (n=35)

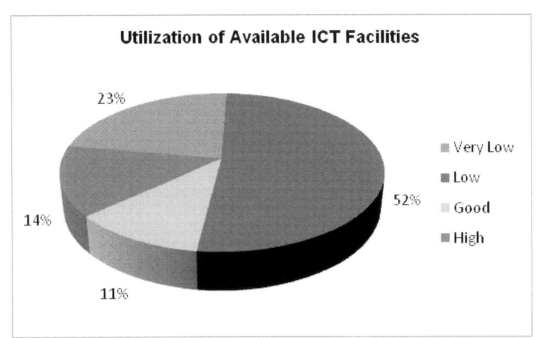

Figure 13. Duration of load shedding during office hours (n=35)

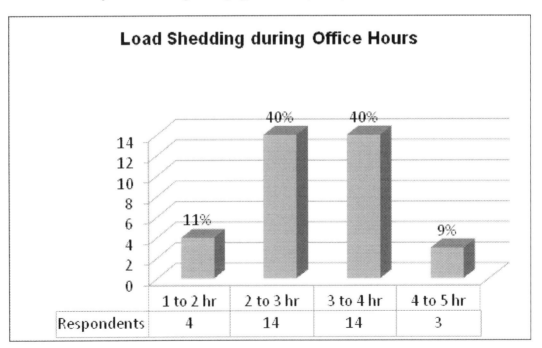

Figure 14. Perception about e-governance preparedness (n = 35)

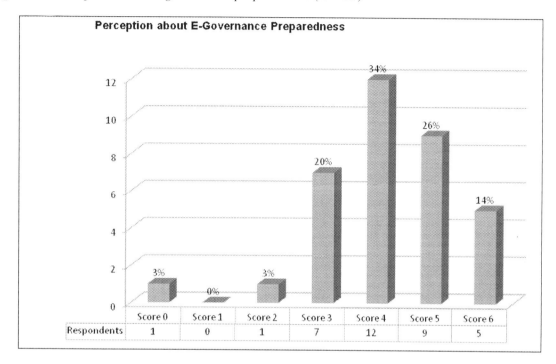

and logistics' having mentioned by 77% of the respondents. The other responses are mentioned in Figure 15.

Analysis of the Data

This section analyzes the primary data obtained from the questionnaire survey with reference to United Nations' Five Stage Model comprising of five stages namely *'Emerging'*, *'Enhanced'*, *'Interactive'*, *'Transactional'* and *'Connected'*. To assess the e-governance preparedness of the study area (Office of the Deputy Commissioner, Dhaka) the findings were compared with the key features of various stages of the aforementioned model. For the purpose of comparison, the main features of the UN model are listed in Table 6.

Quantitative Analysis with Reference to the Analytical Framework

This section attempts to evaluate the status of e-governance preparedness of the Office of the Deputy Commissioner, Dhaka in a quantitative manner with reference to the independent variables of the analytical framework and the measurable indicators associated with them. Although there is no quantitative benchmark to assess the preparedness as far as the UN's five stage model is concerned, it would be useful to validate the qualitative assessment about the findings and to have a holistic picture of the preparedness level.

The quantitative analysis is done by giving equal weight to all the indicators and calculating the scores obtained on the basis of the primary data obtained, both from the officials and the citizens. The scores are added up to obtain a total score of 8.18 out of 17 (Table 7).

Figure 15. Perception about hindrances to e-governance implementation

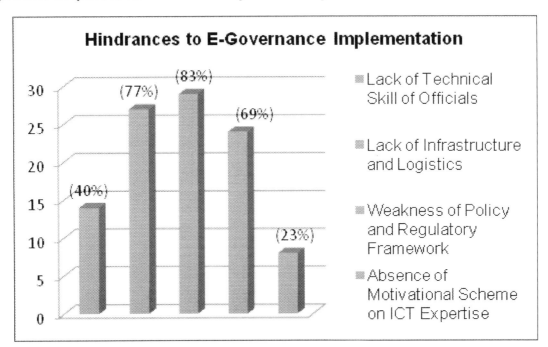

Table 6. Key features of various stages of UN model of e-governance maturity

Emerging	Web presence is established through official website. Information is limited, basic and static.
Enhanced	Increased information with more regular update. Dynamic nature of Content.
Interactive	Users can download forms, contact officials, and make appointments and requests.
Transactional	Users can actually pay for services or conduct financial transactions online.
Connected	Government as a connected entity to the needs of its citizens by developing an integrated back office infrastructure featuring horizontal and vertical connection among government agencies and with citizens.

Now converting the score of 8.18 on a scale of 10, it is found out that the obtained score is 4.81 [Conversion of Score (Out of 10) = (8.18×10)/17 = 4.81]. It is interesting to observe that this score is higher than both the values of ratings given by the officials and the citizens, the prior being 4.17 and the later being 3.3, both being out of a total score of 10.

As mentioned earlier, there is no quantitative benchmark for assessing the e-governance preparedness. Therefore a score of 4.81, or for that matter 4.17 or 3.3, does not conclusively indicate any specific level of preparedness as far as the UN's five stage model is concerned. However, the quantitative assessment rather provides clues to judge the preparedness level qualitatively. In this case, possibly the most intuitive conclusion is the office under consideration has not yet reached the halfway mark of what one may call the ultimate preparedness level in terms of e-governance, which is the 'connected' stage of the UN's five stage model for the purpose of this study.

Table 7. Quantitative evaluation as regards to independent variables and indicators

SL.	Independent Variables	Indicators	Score Obtained
1.	Technical Skill (Total Point 5)	Training and the contents	2.79
		Ownership of Computer for personal use	
		Fluency of Computer Operation	
		Internet connection at home	
		Personal e-mail	
2.	Infrastructure and Logistic Support (Total Point 4)	Power Situation	2.22
		Computer and Accessories at workplace	
		Internet connection at workplace	
		Internet Speed at office	
3.	Policy and Legal Framework (Total Point 2)	Opinion of Officials about Adequacy of ICT related Laws/ Rules/ Regulations	1.91
		Opinion of Citizens about Adequacy of ICT related Laws/ Rules/ Regulations	
4.	Incentive on ICT Expertise (Total Point 3)	Monetary benefit package on use of ICT at office	0.90
		Promotion prospect	
		Intangible benefits (like appreciation etc.)	
5.	Attitude (Total Point 3)	Citizens' Perception about Attitude	1.31
		Utilization of Existing ICT Facilities (Officials' Perspective)	
		Utilization of Existing ICT Facilities (Citizens' Perspective)	
		Total (Out of 17)	8.18

Correlations between Dependent and Independent Variables

Bi-variate Pearson's correlation analysis has been performed to identify whether there is any significant correlation between the independent and dependent variables. As mentioned earlier, for this study the dependent variable was 'E-governance Preparedness' and its dependency on the five independent variables have been examined with the help of SPSS. The results are shown in Table 8.

It is evident from the above table that 'Policy and Legal Framework' is the independent variable which have the highest correlation (Pearson's correlation, $r = 0.674$) with the e-governance preparedness level according to the responses of the respondents. The second strongest factor is 'Infrastructure and Logistic Support' having a correlation coefficient (r) of 0.626. This finding obtained from the Pearson's bi-variate correlation analysis is very much compliant with the direct responses of the respondents. It is interesting to

Table 8. Relationship between dependent and independent variables

Independent Variables	Correlation (r)
Technical Skill	0.476**
Infrastructure and Logistic Support	0.626**
Policy and Legal Framework	0.674**
Incentive on ICT Expertise	0.126**
Attitude	0.411**

** Correlation is significant at the 0.01 level

observe that incentive on ICT expertise has the minimum influence on the e-governance preparedness ($r = 0.126$). 'Technical Skill' has a reasonably moderate influence in this respect.

Qualitative Analysis of the Data Obtained

From the primary data obtained it is found out that the office under consideration has its web presence through the official website http://www.dcdhaka.gov.bd. Observation reveals that it provides significant amount of static data. So, it is evident that the office has definitely passed the criteria for the 'emerging' stage.

Now to compare with the benchmark of 'enhanced' stage, it is noteworthy that some of the respondents mentioned about complaint/suggestion mechanism through website which is also validated by observation of the website. Therefore, it can be concluded that the office has passed the criteria for 'enhanced' stage as well.

Evaluating against the third stage, i.e., the 'interactive' stage is quite intriguing because of some contradiction of gathered data from the officials. Only 14% of the officials claimed that the website has forms/ documents/ reports/ notices regarding their service. The percentage is pretty low; even if the claim is correct. The study reveals that the website does not host any forms on its own, rather have link to the national website for forms (http://www.forms.gov.bd). It also has got the resolutions of the 'Monthly Coordination Meeting' but paradoxically the resolution of the meetings held in November 2011 (accessed on 20 February 2012). So it is evident that it is not updated as expected. Of course the website does have notice of some important events, meetings etc. Therefore, it can be concluded that the office does not qualify all the criteria of the 'interactive' stage of e-governance and pass partially in this regard.

Although further evaluation seems unnecessary, it is worth identifying purposefully that the website does not provide any transactional services whereby the citizens can pay their various bills, payments etc. As a result, one can fairly conclude by saying that the office under consideration has not achieved any part of the 'transactional' stage of e-governance, let alone the 'connected' stage. To conclude about the assessment of the e-governance maturity of Office of the Deputy Commissioner, Dhaka it can be argued that the office is at the transition of the two stages of e-governance namely 'enhanced' and 'interactive'. This is to suggest that some elementary attributes of 'interactive' stage is found to be present in the area of the study while the essence of the stage is grossly absent. This implies that the office under consideration is trying to catch up with the 'interactive' stage but yet has a long way to achieve it. Based on these findings it can be argued that the e-governance preparedness level would be much lower among the bureaucrats posted at the regional and local level administration in Bangladesh.

11. CONCLUDING REMARKS

E-governance is the demand of the time in this era of technological excellence. In course of this study it has been observed that some sort of awareness about e-governance, ICT opportunities etc. has been present which was not there even a few years back. Whether the awareness is good enough is different issue but there is absolutely no doubt that people in general have begun to realize the importance of ICT. Even the common people who do not have much formal education, let alone technical skills, have started to recognize the importance of e-governance in ensuring good governance as well as welfare of people. The same thing is true for the officials working for the government; irrespective of their competence level in information technology and electronic governance system. Although the effort may not always be present, but government officials do admit the necessity of e-governance implementation. There may be some sort of pessimism among the officials, including the high-ups, about the success of the ICT initiatives due to different reasons; but they are consentient with the enlightened civilians about the necessity of **e**-governance.

Although the awareness of the government officials about the indispensability of e-governance is felt much stronger than before, the preparedness level does not show significant improvement, both at the individual and institutional level. At individual level the possible reasons might include lack of technological orientation (which in most cases induces fear of technology) and improper attitude towards change. At the institutional level the reasons behind low preparedness are even more serious which includes insufficiency of appropriate legal and regulatory framework, paucity of logistics and infrastructural support, and inadequacy of motivational mechanism for the skilled personnel.

E-governance is an important innovation for enhancing good governance and strengthening the democratic process and can also facilitate access to information, freedom of expression, greater equity, efficiency, productivity growth and social inclusion. Successful e-government initiatives can have demonstrable and tangible impact on improving citizen participation and quality of life as a result of effective multi-stakeholder partnerships. Bangladesh government need to develop appropriate policy; framework supported by legislation for e-governance, that are linked to strategic development objectives; enlist high-ranking political e-government champions; focus awareness, outreaching training efforts to the less privileged segment of targeted users, particularly women and neglected rural communities.

E-governance portends unparallel reforms in the processes and structures of public conduct, politics and administration. It offers many benefits to the government and its citizens with much potential for institutional and personal goal attainments. In Bangladesh, issues of massive poverty, weak democratic and bureaucratic institution in the hands of corrupt leadership could be

arrested with skillful application of e-governance models. Thus, the conception and application of e-governance with the dawn of digital societies is persistently turning the table in the study and practice of public administration. The discipline is fast shifting from the complex pawns of governance in variegated definitions by the institutions of global governance to electronically propelled reforms that are capable of engendering greater citizens' involvement in policy formulation, responsive governance and administration, and communized global best practices that are in-tune with environments of political systems. The governance of Bangladesh as well as the study and practice of public administration should, as a matter of national importance, be tailored towards proficient use and application of information and communications technologies.

REFERENCES

Agarwal, V. M. M., & Rastogi, L. (2003). *Enabling e-governance – Integrated citizen relationship management framework – The Indian perspective.* Retrieved from http://www.e11online.com/pdf/e11_whitepaper2.pdf

Aminuzzaman, M. S. (1991). *Introduction to Social Research.* Bangladesh Publishers.

Anderson, K. (1999). Re-engineering public sector organizations using information technology. In *Reinventing Government in the Information Age.* London: Routledge.

Backus, M. (2001). E-governance in developing countries. *IICD Research Brief, 1.*

Baum, C., & DiMaio, A. (2000). *Gartner's Four Phases of E-Government Model.* Gartner.

BEI. (2010). *Realizing the Vision of Digital Bangladesh through e-Government, July 2010.* Retrieved from www.bei-bd.org/downloadreports/view/48/download

Bretschneider, S. (2003). Information technology, e-government and institutional change. *Public Administration Review, 63*(6). doi:10.1111/1540-6210.00337

Brown, D. (1999). Information systems for improved performance management: Development approaches in US public agencies. In *Re-inventing Government in the Information Age*. London: Routledge.

Carter, L., & Bélanger, F. (2005). The utilization of e-government services: citizen trust, innovation and acceptance factors. *Information Systems Journal, 15*, 5–25. doi:10.1111/j.1365-2575.2005.00183.x

Council of Europe. (2009). *Strategy for Innovation and good governance at Local Level*. Brussels: Author.

Davis, F. D. (1989). Perceived usefulness, perceived ease of use, and user acceptance of information technology. *Management Information Systems Quarterly, 13*(3), 319–340. doi:10.2307/249008

Davis, F. D., Bagozzi, R. P., & Warshaw, P. R. (1989). User acceptance of computer technology: A comparison of two theoretical models. *Management Science, 35*, 982–1003. doi:10.1287/mnsc.35.8.982

Davis, F. D., & Venkatesh, V. (1996). A critical assessment of potential measurement biases in the technology acceptance model: Three experiments. *International Journal of Human-Computer Studies, 45*, 19–45. doi:10.1006/ijhc.1996.0040

Fishbein, M., & Ajzen, I. (1975). *Belief, attitude, intention and behaviour: An introduction to theory and research*. Reading, MA: Addison-Wesley.

Fountain, J. (2001). *Building the virtual state: Information technology and institutional change*. Washington, DC: Brookings Institution.

Grandon, E., Alshare, O., & Kwan, O. (2005). Factors influencing student intention to adopt online classes: A cross-cultural study. *Journal of Computing Sciences in Colleges, 20*(4), 46–56.

Gupta, P. R., & Jain, D. K. (2010). Road Map for E governance. In *Proceedings of ASCNT*. CDAC.

Henry, N. (1995). *Public Administration and public affairs* (6th ed.). Prentice-Hall.

Hood, C. (1991). A Public Management for All Seasons? *Public Administration, 69*(1). doi:10.1111/j.1467-9299.1991.tb00779.x

Hoque, M. M. (2009). *An Information System Planning Framework for E-Governance in Bangladesh*. Unpublished report.

Hoque, S. M. S. (2005). *E-Governance in Bangladesh: A Scrutiny from Citizens' Perspective*. Paper presented in Network of Asia-Pacific Schools and Institutes of Public Administration and Governance (NAPSIPAG) Annual Conference 2005. New York, NY.

Mahbubul, A. (2007). *E-Governance: Scope and Implementation Challenges in Bangladesh*. Retrieved from http://delivery.acm.org/10.1145/1330000/1328108/p246-alam.pdf

Moon, M., & Bretschneider, S. (2002). Can State Government Actions affect Innovation and its diffusion? An extended communication model and empirical test. *Technological Forecasting and Social Change, 54*(1).

Morshed, A. (2007). *E-governance: Bangladesh perspective*. Retrieved from http://unpan1.un.org/intradoc/groups/public/documents/APCITY/UNPAN02625.pdf

Muinul-Islam, M., & Saaduddin-Ahmed, A. M. (2007). Understanding e-governance: A theoretical approach. *Journal of Asian Affairs, 29*(4).

Mungania, P., & Reio, T. G., Jr. (2005). *If e-learners get there, will they stay? The role of e-learning self-efficacy.* Paper presented at the Academy of Human Resource Development International Conference (AHRD). Estes Park, CO.

Nye, J. (1999). Information technology and democratic governance. In *Democracy.com? Governance in Networked World.* Hollis, NH: Hollis.

Pablo, D. Z., & Pan, L. S. (2002). *A Multi-Disciplinary Analysis of E-governance: Where Do We Start?* Unpublished Report.

Park, S. Y. (2009). An analysis of the technology acceptance model in understanding university students' behavioral intention to use e-learning. *Journal of Educational Technology & Society, 12*(3), 150–162.

Renu, B. (2003a). *Electronic Gov-A key issue in the 21st century.* Electronic Governance Division, Ministry of Information Technology, Government of India.

Renu, B. (2003b). *E-governance in G2B and some major incliatives.* Dept. of Information Technology, Ministry of Communication and Information Technology.

Robbins, S. P., & Judge, T. A. (2008). Organizational Behavior. In S. P. Robbins, & T. A. Judge (Eds.), *Organizational Behavior* (13th ed.). Academic Press.

Schiavo-Ocampo, S., & Sundaram, P. (2001). *To Serve and Preserve: Improving Public Administration in a Competitive World.* Manila, Philippines: Asian Development Bank.

Taifur, S. (2006). *SICT's Steps Towards Good Governance Through ICTs: E-governance Strategies. Support to ICT Task Force program project (SICT), Ministry of Planning, Government of Bangladesh Press. UN e-Government Survey. (2008). From e-Government to Connected Governance.* New York: Author.

UNESCO. (2008). *E-governance and Accountability.* UNESCO.

Valentina, N. (2004). E – Government for Developing Countries: Opportunities and Challenges. *The Electrical Journal on Information Systems in Developing Countries, 18*(1), 1–24.

Venkatesh, V., & Davis, F. D. (1996). A model of the antecedents of perceived ease of use: Development and test. *Decision Sciences, 27*, 451–481. doi:10.1111/j.1540-5915.1996.tb01822.x

Venkatesh, V., Morris, M. G., Davis, G. B., & Davis, F. D. (2003). User acceptance of information technology: Toward a unified view. *MIS Quaterly, 27*(3), 425–478.

Wilson, W. (1887). *The Study of Administration.* Washington, DC: US Printing Office.

World Bank. (2008). *E-government.* Retrieved from http://go.worldbank.org

World Bank Group. (2004). *Report on Bangladesh.* Retrieved from http://www.worldbank.org/

KEY TERMS AND DEFINITIONS

E-Governance: E-governance refers to the governance processes in which Information and Communications Technologies (ICTs) play active and significant roles.

E-Government: It is a narrower term of the two, referring to a transformation of the functions of the government based on primarily by ICT.

G2B (Government-to-Business): Involves interaction of business entities with the government.

G2C (Government-to-Citizen): Involves interaction of individual citizens with the government.

G2E (Government-to-Employee): Involves interaction between the government and its employees.

G2G (Government-to-Government): Involves interaction among government offices as well as governments of other countries.

Paradigm: A conceptual framework, a way of explaining a phenomenon.

Public Bureaucracy in Bangladesh: Public bureaucracy in Bangladesh is characterized by its institutional rigidity, elitist nature and change resistant orientation.

ENDNOTES

[1] The Awami League government of Bangladesh before the election of 2009 included this idea of digital Bangladesh in their election manifest.

Chapter 14
Beyond the Digital Divide:
Language Factors, Resource Wealth, and Post–Communism in Mongolia

Undrah Buyan Baasanjav
Southern Illinois University – Edwardsville, USA

ABSTRACT

This chapter explores the interplay between society and Internet technology in the context of the developing former socialist country of Mongolia. This chapter goes beyond questions of access to the Internet and explores three factors of the global digital divide. First, this chapter explores how language factors such as non-Roman domain names and the use of the Cyrillic alphabet exacerbate the digital divide in the impoverished country of Mongolia. ICANN's initiation of international domain names is an initial development toward achieving linguistic diversity on the Internet. Second, this chapter explores how post-communist settings and foreign investment and aid dependency afflict Internet development. A rapid economic growth in Mongolia has increased access to mobile phones, computers, and the Internet; however, the influx of foreign capital poured into the mining, construction, and telecommunication sectors frequently comes in non-concessional terms raising concerns over the public debt in Mongolia.

INTRODUCTION

The discrepancy in Internet use between developed and developing countries is referred as the "global digital divide." In recent years, developing countries have exponentially increased their use of information and communication technology, especially mobile phones, and this increase has contributed to the rhetoric of the closing of the global digital divide. The World Bank (2012) reports that the number of mobile phone subscribers in developing countries rose by 1500 percent

from 2000 to 2010, from 4 persons per 100 to 72 in 2010 (p. 11). In some developing countries, more people have access to a mobile phone than to a bank or clean water (World Bank, 2012, p. 3). Yet, only 12.7% of the population in Sub-Saharan Africa and 9.4% of the population in South-Asia used the Internet in 2011, whereas in Europe 73.4% of population used the Internet (World Bank, 2013). Though the Internet is increasingly accessed on mobile phones, the rhetoric surrounding the closing the global digital divide based on increasing mobile phone use in developing

DOI: 10.4018/978-1-4666-3691-0.ch014

countries does more harm than good because this rhetoric reinforces the access-centered approach that oftentimes translates into policies that benefit multinational corporations (MNC) helping them tap into markets in developing countries. The access-centered and western-focused digital divide research has not deeply explored the language, political and cultural factors of the global digital divide.

Unlike mobile phones, Internet development directly reflects social and cultural settings and existing inequalities. In this chapter, I strive to explain the interplay between society and Internet technology in the context of the developing former socialist country of Mongolia. This chapter goes beyond questions of access to the Internet and explores three factors of the global digital divide. First, this chapter explores how language factors such as non-Roman domain names and the use of the Cyrillic alphabet exacerbate the digital divide in the impoverished country of Mongolia. Second, this paper explores how post-communist settings and foreign investment and aid dependency afflict Internet development.

THE CASE STUDY OF THE GLOBAL DIGITAL DIVIDE: THE INTERNET IN MONGOLIA

The Mongolian case demonstrates challenges typical to developing countries with unexploited natural resources and also has similarities to other former socialist countries with a communist past. A mining boom in the last decade, which lured foreign investment into Mongolia, brought a GDP growth of 17% in 2011 ("Before the gold rush," 2013, Feb 16). With a nomadic culture, a Buddhist tradition, and a communist past, Mongolia has a unique struggle with the digital divide. Mongolia is a Central Asian developing country landlocked between Russia and China with a small population of 2.7 million. Like many other developing countries, Mongolia has an emerging economy indicated by the GNI per capita of US$ 2,310. Internet use has grown steadily, yet only 16.4 individuals per 100 persons use the Internet in 2012 (ITU, 2013a).

Though access to the Internet has steadily been increasing as shown in Figure 1, for many

Figure 1. The growth in the percentages of Internet users, fixed phone users and mobile phone users in Mongolia

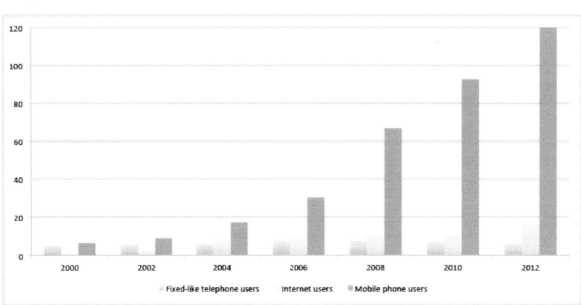

Mongolians the Internet is still a distant priority as shown by the 16.4 percent of people using the Internet in contrast to the use of mobile phones, which has almost saturated the market. The vastness of the territory and the underdeveloped infrastructure especially in the provinces of Mongolia have hindered access to the Internet for many Mongolians. The International Telecommunications Union (ITU) (2013b) showcases Mongolia as a country that made a great stride in increasing access to information communication technology. While the liberalization of the market in telecommunications services, especially in mobile phone services, has lured Korean and Japanese investors into the mobile phone services in Mongolia, the number of Internet users as can be seen in Figure 1 above has not caught up with the mobile phone services. While mobile phone services have rapidly improved along with the mining boom in Mongolia of the last decade, socially beneficial Internet applications such as e-government, e-health and online education still lag far behind.

The Mongolian case clearly shows the challenges of the global digital have-nots, and especially it helps us to understand the language factors of the global digital divide. Despite the relatively high literacy rate of 96% common to former socialist countries, Internet use is still low partly due to the low degree of English knowledge among Mongolians (Baasanjav, 2012). The Mongolian version of the Cyrillic alphabet, which has two extra vowels, Θ and Y, that do not exist in the Russian Cyrillic alphabet have caused many challenges for Mongolians until Microsoft released a Windows system incorporating the Unicode standard. Unicode standards are international standards for interchange, processing, and the display of multilingual characters sets and diverse written languages by providing "a repertoire of code points used in different scripts, including various classifications of character properties, and normalization rules" (ICANN, 2012, Feb 20, p.10). When a user types, for example, a Chinese ideograph for "hill" 山, a browser or search engine

software uniquely renders a Unicode code point of (U+5C71) regardless of the differences in platforms, software and language employing the Unicode standard. Digital divide scholars acknowledge the "symbolic power" of English, and refer to the great discrepancy of language representation on the Internet as one of the contributing factors to the global digital divide (Hobsbawm, 1996; Norris, 2001; Warschauer, 2003). The predominant use of English in the management of critical Internet resources (i.e., Internet domain names) limited non-English speaking Mongolians from fully benefiting from the Internet. The Internet Corporation for Assigned Names and Numbers (ICANN), the governing body of the Internet, approved in 2009 a new standard for fully internationalized domain names that use characters outside the range of the capital and small Roman letters from A to Z, the Arabic numbers of 0 to 9, and hyphens as used in the English language. Theoretically, international domain names consisting entirely of native character sets tend to benefit local companies and people who only speak their local languages and improve access to the Internet. Global digital divide research has rarely explored language factors like domain names, and this chapter strives to explore these factors.

Second, this chapter strives to locate the global digital divide within a context of Mongolian polity and economy. A recent mining boom in Mongolia fleshed out the tension between multinational corporations tapping into the country's natural resources and the relatively weak institutions of Mongolia, which have been transitioning since the democratic revolution of 1991. *The Economist* (2013, Feb 16), for instance, mentions how "resource nationalism" advocating the local control of mines is popular among politicians in Mongolia. Even though Mongolia is one the three legitimate democracies in Asia along with Japan and South Korea, Mongolia's relatively young liberal constitutional democracy is tested in connection to its commitment to a neo-liberal market economy which is guided by privatization and liberalization with a "hands-off" approach. The country's biggest mining project Oyu Tolgoi (Turquoise Hill) copper-and-gold mine is 66% owned by Rio Tinto, the British-Australian mining giant, and another lucrative coal mine Tavan Tolgoi was two-third owned by Canadian Ivanhoe mines ("Before the gold rush," 2013, Feb 16). Corruption is still widespread typical to developing countries with untapped natural resources, and the socialist legacy is still evident similar to Eastern European and former Soviet Union countries, which threw off both external domination by the Soviet Union and the repressive communist party control in the 1990s (Holmes, 1997, p. 14). According to the new Constitution of 1992, Mongolia is a democratic country characterized by the rule of law and the freedoms of speech, press, and information.

The role of media and the Internet in post-communist and developing countries has been debated among scholars. Some emphasize that media's and the Internet's democratic potential in expanding the public sphere (Zassoursky, 2004; Coleman & Kaposi, 2006), while others see a "marked degree of continuation" of old propagandistic media (Sparks & Reading, 1998). UNESCO (2007) reports that leaders in Mongolia strive to control information as they did during the socialist time, and media often serve as "a propaganda mouthpiece of political and business interests" due to their financial dependence (p.1). Even though access to the Internet and mobile phones is increasing, the communication policy in Mongolia for closing the digital divide is not comprehensive.

THE GLOBAL DIGITAL DIVIDE IN DEVELOPING AND POST-COMMUNIST COUNTRIES

The definition, the causes, and the consequences of the global digital divide are explained variedly. The term "digital divide" tends to dichotomize "haves," who have knowledge and resources to use the Internet, and "have-nots," who do not possess such knowledge and resources. On the global scale, the disparities in access to information technology and in the use of the Internet between developed and developing countries have been defined as the global digital divide (James, 2013; Norris, 2001; Stevenson, 2009; Qureshi, 2012; Warschauer, 2003).

The theoretical views on the global digital divide vary from the modernization and diffusion approach to the social equality perspective and the world society approach. The first perspective sees the Internet as a change agent in modernizing developing counties in the footsteps of developed countries and claims that the unlimited information available via the Internet and its two-way communication possibilities enrich and strengthen societies. In this perspective, technology like the Internet is adopted by different groups of societies over a certain period of time creating a trajectory of adoption. This trajectory of adoption starts slowly by earlier adopters, who have better social economic status (SES), better education and more resources than the general public, and after a certain period of time, the critical mass of people adopts the technology (Rogers, 2000). Then the rest of the society jumps on the band-wagon of adoption. However, it should be noted that developed nations reached the critical mass thanks to a great deal of policies that facilitated the diffusion of the Internet, and in many developing countries, the adoption pattern slowed down earlier than the trajectory of diffusion of radio and TV (James, 2007, 2013; DeMaggio et.al, 2004; Hargittai, 2003).

The opposing school of thought, under the broad umbrella of social constructivism and the social inequality perspective, claims that the relationship between society and technology is co-constitutive. The political, and social context in which technology is embedded tends to shape Internet development, and the scholars coming from this perspective tend to argue that new technology like the Internet exacerbates existing disparity in an already unequal society. Therefore, they suggest that Internet studies should go beyond the narrowly defined access issue to a broader context of social settings, local languages, literacy levels, as well as the existing disparity in media development (Carey, 2005; Slevin, 2000; Bellamy & Taylor, 1998; Van Dijk, 2006; and Warschaur, 2003). The great discrepancy of language representation on the Internet, and the geographical imbalance in Internet content production are the most complex issues of the global digital divide. "Global English" is a lingua franca in international communication and on the Internet, and it has become a new barrier to equal opportunity in developing countries because unequal access to learning English coincides with other social inequalities (Baasanjav, in press; Warschauer, 2003). The difference in language representation on the Internet reflects an existing asymmetry in content creation in old media between developed and developing countries (Hargittai, 2004), since new media production is oftentimes "repackaged," or "remediated" from traditional media onto the Internet. Since there are fewer textbooks and other forms of written knowledge in less developed countries like Mongolia, the global digital divide is exacerbated by the poorly developed old media and the lack of written knowledge available in print and other non-digital media in local languages. The issue of the lack of printed and produced knowledge is even more important in a former socialist country where information was censored because of communist party ideology.

The third perspective, the world society approach, in general derives from the political economy perspective and is critical of the underlying structural and ideological differences in the north-south divide. Researchers arguing from this perspective point out that global digital divide studies have been moving away from the inequality perspective toward the rhetoric of new market opportunities as the role of multinational corporations (MNC) rose in global media governance (Hamelink, 2002; O'Siochru, Girard, &

Mahan, 2002; Stevenson, 2007). The scholars of the world society perspectives criticize the modernity approach and the dominance of multinational corporations in international governance that reinforce the existing north - south divide. Dominated by MNC, international organizations tend to push forward the access-centered approach in developing countries that translates into a neo-liberal economic agenda when used without discretion. This agenda assumes that 1) economic development is accelerated with information technology; 2) the growth of ICT needs the investment of foreign companies; and 3) foreign companies invest when the market is liberalized. Since the majority of global technological research and development is concentrated in a few developed countries in order to solve the concerns and problems of rich countries, new technologies bring western technological domination and ideology (Hamelink, 2001; James, 2013). When developing countries follow the patterns of consumption of developed nations in an effort to catch up, the only people who benefit are the corporations in the developed countries (Hamelink, 2001). Furthermore, an access-centered and western-focused approach to the digital divide leaves unexamined specific social, and cultural aspects, and actual Internet content in developing countries (Hamelink, 2000; Slevin, 2000; Warschauer, 2003; Van Dijk, 2006).

The global digital divide should use a different discourse that takes into account the existing power dynamics between developed and developing countries, local social and political settings, cultural and linguistic diversity, and the influences of international aid and organizations. This chapter provides the analysis of these factors.

The Global Digital Divide in Transitioning Counties of the Former Second World

Media scholars are just now beginning to study the social and political consequences of the Internet in so called "third wave democracies"

(Coleman& Kaposi, 2006). The few studies that have examined Internet development in former socialist countries (Dimitrova & Beilock, 2005; Ifinedo & Singh, 2011; Kolko, Wei & Spyridakis, 2003; Herron, 1999; Boje & Dragulanescu, 2003; Walton, Yaacoubi & Kolko, 2012) mostly focus on access or lump together countries that are very different politically, economically and culturally. Digital divide studies have predominantly been access centered by asking: "How many people or households have access to the Internet?" Geographical location, income, age, race, and gender are often seen as the factoring variable of the digital divide.

In former socialist countries, information was tightly controlled and censored in all political, social and economic spheres of society. The communist parties built state-surveillance systems through democratic centralization, the nomenklatura system and various secret police institutions (Spark & Reading, 1998, p.32). The one party ideology, a centrally planned economy, and a preference for a certain type of cultural product all were expected. The repressive party-states purged counter-revolutionaries, religious and capitalist elements, and critical intelligentsia, yet brought somewhat egalitarian social service networks with free higher education and a social welfare system.

Though patterns of democracy development and new media adoption in these countries vary widely, some similar residual patterns seem to persist. In Mongolia, the leaders' desire to retain control of information, and to use the media to "agitate the masses" remains strong despite achievements such as the dismantlement of the censorship authority, the adoption of a new Law on Media, and a boom of independent media outlets (Munkhmandakh & Nielsen, 2001; UNESCO, 2007). Similarly, media perpetuate infused communist taste and nostalgia for communism in the Czech Republic (Klvana, 2004). The Czech Republic, Estonia, Slovenia, Hungary and Poland are among the most successful transitional economies

(TE) that are changing from a centrally planned economy to a market economy. These countries are characterized by "rapid economic liberalization, legal and institutional reforms, restructuring and privatization, and macroeconomic stabilization" (Ifinedo & Singh, 2011, p. 4). In these successful post communist countries the Internet is embraced and new media has contributed to open and free societies indicated by their democracy indexes (Coleman & Kaposi, 2006; Dutta, 2007; Ifinedo & Singh, 2011; Klvana, 2004). The situation is very different for other former socialist countries in Central Asia and Russia that reverted back to the authoritarian regimes. In these countries the Internet is tightly controlled. Ifinedo & Singh (2011) explored the determinants of the maturity of E-government projects in transitional economies in Eastern and Central Europe and point to factors such as national wealth, human capital, transparency indexes, and government efficiency as the determinants for successful E-government. Even though Mongolia did not revert to the authoritarian regime, the corruption index in Mongolia is high, and that lead to an ambiguous evaluation by the Transparency International (2010). New found wealth, relatively literate human capital, and a low level of transparency make the Mongolian case of the global digital divide similar to the Eastern and Central European countries. A burgeoning number of civil society institutions, an increasing information flow with more than 340 media outlets including online media (UNESCO, 2007) and the government's priority for the development of information and communication technologies (ICT4D) would suggest a conductive environment for the bridging of the digital divide in Mongolia (Baasanjav, 2011). Yet, communication practices in impoverished nations call for a different methodological approach, which takes into consideration different communication practices such the use of the Internet in public cafes, centers, and at work. Like in many other developing countries, the majority of Internet users in Mongolia are business subscribers. Furthermore, the social divide that exists between rural and urban areas and the institutional divide that exists between government organizations and educational institutions are the most evident forms of the digital divide in Mongolia (Baasanjav 2012). While government organizations, especially agencies in the capital, tend to have better Internet access, educational institutions like libraries and secondary schools, especially in the countryside, constitute obvious "have-nots" (Baasanjav, 2012). In former communist developing countries, where consumption was suppressed and the statistical data used to be fabricated for ideological reasons, discrepancies exist between the official numbers of Internet users and the actual number of users (Kolko, B, Wei, C. & Spyridakis, J.H, 2003; Warschaur, 2003). Since digital divide theory in general posits that those who use the Internet tend to be better educated and socially better off than those who do not use the Internet, people in remote places and less powerful organizations need to have policies to help them overcome these disparities. In the sections to follow, I'll discuss how the language factors, post-communistic settings, and foreign investment dependency factor into the global digital divide in Mongolia:

MONGOLIAN CYRILLIC ALPHABET USE AND CYRILLIC SCRIPT DOMAIN NAMES .MOH

The symbolic power of global English is explored in this chapter by examining the use of domain names and the challenges relating to the use of the Cyrillic alphabet in Mongolia. Historically, Mongolians used the *uighur alphabet* of an Arabic origin from thirteenth century untill 1941. The first Mongolian literary text written in the *uighur* script is *The Secret History of the Mongols* and depicts Chinghis Khan's (Genghis Khan) conquests. This *Uighur* script is written vertically and had twenty four letters, each letter having three different forms in the beginning, in the middle and at the

end of a word. In 1941, mostly due to pressure from Russia, the traditional Mongolian alphabet was abandoned and was replaced by the Cyrillic alphabet used in the Soviet Union. Because the Mongolian language is not related to Slavic languages, depicting, rendering, and interpreting the Mongolian language in Internet browsers, search engines and other apps in the Cyrillic script have been challenging problems for Mongolians. After the collapse of the Soviet Union, in 1991 the Mongolian Parliament attempted to revert back from the Cyrillic alphabet to the *uighur* script; however, this effort was proven to be unfeasible due to the economic downturn of the country. Since 1991, the *uigur* script is taught in schools in Mongolia, but Cyrillic remains the official written script in Mongolia. The Mongolian version of the Cyrillic alphabet has two extra vowels, Ө (barred O) and Y (straight Y), that do not exist in the Russian Cyrillic alphabet, and these two letters are often distorted on the Internet (Baasanjav, 2011). Even today, Mongolian Twitter users, for example, use different representations of these two characters. The initiation of Cyrillic script domain names invokes a couple of questions relating to the language factors of the global digital divide in Mongolia as discussed below.

The domain name system is an important part of global Internet governance, and the Internet Corporation for Assigned Names and Numbers (ICANN) ensures the stability of the current development of the Internet by issuing pro-competitive and legitimate domain names without violating trademarks and intellectual property rights. Domain names, textual names of web resources on the Internet, are descriptive markers with corresponding numerical addresses called Internet protocol (IP) addresses. When an end user types a web address or an email address, the domain names system (DNS) on the Internet resolves the entered web address into the IP address of the requested web host or email user addresses (Zook, 2000). Special computers on the Internet, called name servers, resolve a web resource address (e.g. www.

mol.mn) into an IP address (202.131.0.3 or an IP address block starting with 202.131). Domain names consist of top-level domain names placed at the very end, and sub-domain names separated by dots. Top-level domain names are also divided into generic top level domain names (gTLD) such as .com, .edu, .gov, .mil, .net, .org, .int, .asia, .africa and country code top level domain (ccTLD) names assigned to certain countries and territories such as .cn (China), .ru (Russia) and .mn (Mongolia) (Baasanjav, in press).

In 2009, ICANN approved a new standard for fully internationalized country-code domain names (IDN ccTLD) in different scripts other than the Roman alphabet, and since then has been approving and delegating IDN ccTLDs to local domain name registries and registrars through its fast-track process. Mongolia's two big neighbor states-- China and Russia--have played vital roles ICANN's initation of internatioalization of domain names, and have taken full control ove the resistration of their country-code domain names with .中国 and .рф suffixes respectively (Baasanjav, in press). The Mongolian Cyrillic script country-code top-level domain name .мон as of April 2014 is pending to be delegated by ICANN to Datacom Company, the only private domain name registrar of the .mn suffix. The initiation of IDN ccTLds consisting entirely of native character sets unquestionably increases business opportunities for local businesses.

One of the major challenges of implementing IDNs has been the introduction of different character sets in the domain name systems (DNS). Two relevant technical standards—Unicode and punycode -- need to be explained in relation to IDN ccTLDs. International standards for interchange, processing, and the display of multilingual characters sets and diverse written languages have resulted in Unicode standards, which provide "a repertoire of code points used in different scripts, including various classifications of character properties, and normalization rules" (ICANN, 2012, Feb 20, p.10). Cyrillic script characters in

general occupy code points ranging from U+0400 to U+04FF in the Unicode 6.2 standard, and the Mongolian language share the most of the Cyrillic characters with other languages written in Cyrillic. However, not all Cyrillic alphabets including two extra letters Өө (Unicode points U+04E8 and U+04E9) and Үү (Unicode points U+04AE and U+04AF) in the extended Cyrillic can be used in international domain names. These two vowels are frequently used in Mongolian and the limitation on the use of these characters in the Mongolian domain names might considerably limit the range of possible strings.

Furthermore, while country-code domain registries might recognize IDNs, the root file, a single and globally consistent list of top-level domain name assignments with pointers to authoritative name servers (NSs), do not recognize Unicode characters and still work only in the LDH (letters, digit and hyphen used in the Roman character set) characters (Froomkin, 2011; Mueller, 2002, 2010). Because of this hierarchical nature of the DNS, a standard called the International Domain Names in Applications (IDNA) was developed which converts Unicode character sets (U-label) to a "punycode" string in LDH characters sets (A-label) prefixed by 'xn.' For example, the Cyrillic name of Mongolia's IDN ccTLD .мон is represented in the string '(xn--l1acc).' The IDNA protocol also specifies rules for determining whether a code point can be included in a domain name (ICANN, 2012, Feb 20, p.10). The latest version is the IDNA2008 standard which incorporates more variances of IDNs (Baasanjav, in press). Variants are usually defined as visually identical domain names, and there is no script-wide variant in Cyrillic. Cyrillic shares many visually similar glyphs with the Roman, Greek, and the Perso-Arabic alphabets invoking security concerns surrounding spoofing, impersonation, and homograph attacks. That is why ICANN strongly cautions against mixed characters and confusable collisions due to visual similarities in IDNs (ICANN, 2011, Oct 6; ICANN, 2012,

Feb 20). One of the major stability and security concerns raised by the internationalized domain names has been the "spoofing" of domain names (Síthigh, 2010). The citibank.com web site can be impersonated by replacing the Roman letter c (Unicode character U+0107) with the Cyrillic letter c (Unicode character U+0301) thus luring bank customers to a false site. The two letters look alike and are homographs, and redirecting with malicious intends is called a homograph attack. IDNs make it easier for criminals to impersonate or spoof web sites by mixing different scripts leading to homograph attacks, phishing, and redirects in order to steal money, information, or goods. Variant issues arise mostly at the level of language in Cyrillic. Since the root cannot use language-sensitive rules in Cyrillic, domain names need to share aggregate defined variant rules (Baasanjav, in press; ICANN, 2012, Feb 20).

Non-western characters in domain name systems will unquestionably increase participation possibilities for non-western developing countries in Internet governance, which has historically been marginal. In the past, television and radio industries in the US bought .tv and .fm country code domain names from the developing nations of Tuvalu and the Federation of Micronesia and exploited these ccTLDs for businesses unrelated to those developing countries (Hrynyshin, 2008). Less developed countries like Mongolia tend to use ccTLDs almost three times more than gTLDs (Baasanjav, 2012). Even though Mongolian organizations seem to prefer to use .mn domain names partly due to the ease of working with the local domain name registrar and partly due to the perceived legitimacy of the nation-state in media governance in the country, they frequently use English words and acronyms in domain names (Baasanjav, 2012). These textual URL addresses are tailored for an audience with knowledge of the English language. In 2006, 74.5% of the sample of Mongolian web sites used English words or the acronyms in their textual URL addresses (Baasanjav, 2012). English remains a necessity

for Internet users and an amplifying factor of the global digital divide.

Furthermore, though the addition of Cyrillic domain names will allow for a more inclusive approach to bridging the digital divide for Mongolians who use the Cyrillic alphabet, it will also highlight a problem associated with the use of the Cyrillic alphabet. These problems range from digitizing Mongolian language library resources onto computer systems to a lack of Cyrillic alphabet possibilities in synchronous online chat environments. There is no software that recognizes the Mongolian Cyrillic alphabet, therefore the indexing of library resources falls behind in the digital form. In addition, when government officials try to take advantage of online chat features for discussing public issues with citizens, they tend to use the Roman alphabet which makes communication cumbersome for Mongolians who use the Cyrillic alphabet (Baasanjav, 2008). Initiating non-western alphabets domain names and setting culturally inclusive non-western alphabet standards have been important steps in achieving linguistic diversity on the Internet and overcoming the global digital divide in countries like Mongolia. This process requires deliberate efforts by international organizations and multilateral bodies to initiate and carry out new policies, otherwise small developing countries and people with diverse cultural heritages will be excluded.

THE INFLUENCE OF FOREIGN INVESTMENT THE SOCIALIST LEGACY ON MEDIA AND INTERNET DEVELOPMENT

The role of new media in Mongolia needs to be explored within the broader context of the economy and polity rather than specific problems pertaining to the use of the Internet. Mongolia is one of the fastest growing economies with a GDP growth of 17% in 2011 and 12% in 2011 thanks to its new found wealth in coal, gold and copper mines and the influx of foreign capital into the country (World Bank, 2013; "Before the gold rush," 2013, Feb 16). The mining boom seems to test Mongolia's 23-year-old democracy by asking whether or not the government will spend the new wealth on dealing with inequality and the poverty of its citizens, or fall into the "resource curse" that has afflicted many developing countries ("Steppe in an ugly direction," 2012). The International Monetary Fund reports that the number of people living below the poverty level fell by 10% in 2011 due to the government distribution of money from mining ("Before the gold rush," 2013, Feb 16). Yet, the mining industries in foreign countries are cautious of "resource nationalism" among politicians in the government and parliament of Mongolia that pushed a "strategic entities foreign-investment law" in November 2013 that tightened and delayed the mining deals of foreign companies. Mongolians strive to cope with drastic economic changes and navigate the complexities of rapid growth within a semi-open media environment, which still shows a marked degree of continuation of socialist media. People worry that big foreign investment will aggravate widespread corruption, as happened in the 1990s because of hasty privatization of state-owned businesses after the fall of communism ("Nomads no more," 23 Oct 2010). Below I discuss how the dependency on foreign aid and investment and the communist past of the country factor into the digital divide in Mongolia.

Dependency on foreign aid and investment has been a recurring concern for Mongolia. Prior to the democratic revolution, in the 1980's, aid from the Soviet and COMECON (an economic bloc of the former communist countries) made up one third of the gross domestic product of Mongolia. Between 1991 and 2002, international aid money provided by donor countries amounted to 2.9 billion US dollars according to the Economic Intelligence Unit (2005). By the year 2003, foreign aid per capita was $100 comprising some 20 percent of the gross national product, placing Mongolia in the category of the fifth most aid-dependent country

in the world. By 2012, Mongolia's economy was around six billion and GDP per capita was around 2,300 US dollars. The World Bank (2013) reports that public debt reached around 63% of GDP and alarmingly, the share of commercial external debt increased to 43 percent in 2012 from 0.2 percent in 2011, while the loans on concessional terms from multilateral creditors (e.g., WB, ADB and IMF) significantly dropped to 26 percent (World Bank, 2013, p. 24).

International donor aid money prior to the mining boom helped Mongolia to have a burgeoning number of civil society institutions and media outlets, and to initiate socially beneficial programs including programs that helped to close the digital divide (Baasanjav, 2011). International and donor organizations such as (UNDP), the Soros Foundation, the Canadian International Development and Research Center helped government, non-government and educational institutions in Mongolia, as well as the "have-nots" in rural Mongolia to increase access to information. Around 2000-2005, many non-governmental organizations and international non-government organizations created and maintained their web sites thanks to donor aid money and support (Baasanjav, 2012). The executive offices of government institutions of Mongolia- the Prime Minister's Cabinet, and ministries - established their online presence in many cases thanks to donors such as the United Nations Development Program UNDP, the Asian Development Bank, and the World Bank. The Parliament first established an Internet connection and created its web site in 1997 with the support of the Open Society Institution or the Soros Foundation, a philanthropic organization based in New York. Reflecting the immense role of international organizations, many institutions maintained their web sites in two languages - Mongolian and English – in order to provide the "right" information for donors.

The second wave of these projects focused on the "have-nots" in the countryside of Mongolia and educational and research institutions with little resources. The Citizens Information Centers funded by the UNDP and the Community Information Centers and Internet Schools in the provinces both supported by the Soros Foundation were examples. The sustainability of these projects raised questions due to the high cost of rural communication and the low purchasing power of people in rural Mongolia and in the institutions with less resources such as schools, and libraries. The geographical digital divide between the capital city and the rest of the country, as well as the institutional divide between organizations with political and economic power and the less powerful are evident in the Mongolian case. Government organizations in the capital, which are already "better-off" in Mongolia, benefit more from these international organizations' support than the other organizations. Rent-seeking behaviors of public officials and the opaqueness of using aid money sometimes led to actions which benefitted only the factional or private interests of politicians such as those selling computers at a lower rate, not the general public (Baasanjav, 2008). Yet, this donor aid money was instrumental in increasing access to information and the Internet in and created some socially beneficial programs for the digital have-nots in Mongolia.

The mining boom in Mongolia in recent years has changed the economy drastically influencing other sectors such as construction, service sectors and telecommunications. The International Telecommunications Union applauds Mongolia's great strides in increasing the percentage of household with a computer (from 24 per cent in 2011 to 30 per cent in 2012) and Internet access (from 9 per cent in 2011 to 14 per cent in 2012) (ITU, 2013b, p. 32). It seems that government policy focuses on access to information and communication technology, and pours international loans and investment into infrastructure and technologies that are rapidly changing and may soon be obsolete. The fact that the public debt reached 63% of GDP and the percentage of non-concessional term loans from foreign private investors are

increasing in the investment structure raises concerns over Mongolia's debt in the long run. This heavy investment in infrastructure and access to telecommunications services was the reason for Hamelink's (2001) warning that developing countries should not try to follow the pattern of consumption observed in developed countries. In the case of Mongolia, the government is investing loan money borrowed from foreign investors in ways that benefit some businesses more than the rest of society. Privatization and liberalization with the "hands-off" approach by the government in the 90's after the collapse of socialism created some competition and brought foreign ownership by Korea and Japan into the telecommunications sectors of Mongolia. And access to technology and the Internet is undoubtedly increasing following the economic boom; yet there seems to be little evidence for policies and programs that benefit Mongolian citizens beyond the "hands-off" market-driven and access centered approach.

Although Mongolian institutions are striving to use the Internet for social and political purposes, these processes are also being molded by old institutional routines and the challenges inherent in newly established institutions when dealing with rapid economic changes. Checks and balances between the key legislative and executive branches are still in flux, and when faced with new challenges, people's attitudes and organizational routines inherited from socialist institutions often persist. In 2001, the first Mongolian e-government web site *Open-Government* (www. open-government.mn) was created to facilitate dialogue on economic reform issues, but the project quickly shifted its focus to the legislative process by placing pending legislations, bills and other legislative documents on its web sites, and soliciting feedbacks from citizens using discussion forums (Baasanjav, 2008). The executive branch takeover by replicating the functions of *The Mongolian State Great Khural* (the Parliament) on the Internet indicated the fusion of legislative and executive powers that are typical in post-communist countries. The Mongolian Parliament, which once used to unanimously approve the bills created by the communist party apparatchiks, is transitioning to a law making institution and a representative governing branch. Furthermore, key organizations like the Parliament and political parties emphasize traditional media and in some cases this preference for traditional media is a reason for the weaker efforts to develop the Internet by Mongolian organizations. Traditional media--television, radio and newspapers, still seems to play a huge role in Mongolian society due to its nation-wide mass audience, which was cultivated by the ubiquitous socialist media. During the socialist time, government controlled information via television and newspapers had the function of propagandizing first, and controlling and censoring information second. Since there was no need to produce and create information, government institutions did not have professionals who could provide information for the public. The environment from the socialist past segued into "the information flow problem," that is "the difficulties in obtaining information" in Mongolian organizations (Baasanjav, 2008). Even though everyone - the government officials and the media - talk about the importance of openness of information, people are uninformed. Public officials in ministries are wary even of providing information to the e-Government web site team, using the excuse that "a draft is not finalized." A web master in the ministry has created a "black list" of departments and officials who "would not give information to be posted to the web site." The information flow problems are also coupled with the overall lack of library resources and educational materials. An acute shortage of funds for educational and research institutions also encourage media institutions to "recycle" information and content from socialist times. The shaping of Internet technology is not simply "a process of free and conscious choice" (Bellamy & Taylor, 1998, p.151), rather the use of the Internet is shaped and constrained by existing routines of organizations and by the uncertainty

of rapid economic changes. The Mongolian case shows that post-communist settings are impeding Internet development because of traditional ways, slow information flow, uninformed people, and a preference for traditional media.

CONCLUSION

This chapter aimed at bringing evidence of the global digital divide in the developing country of Mongolia to contribute to the global digital divide scholarship that goes beyond Internet access. A remote country like Mongolia is affected by the decisions made by global Internet governing organizations, as well as by foreign investment and multinational corporations. The world society approach to the global digital divide underlining the structural and symbolic power differences between developed and developing countries seems to suggest the necessity for deliberate steps to bridge the global digital divide by creating inclusive Internet governing practices and promoting linguistic diversity on the Internet. ICANN's initiation of international domain names is an initial development toward achieving linguistic diversity on the Internet. Developing international standards that are inclusive of Mongolia's Cyrillic alphabet into browsers, search engines, domain names and mobile applications help Mongolians use the Internet to communicate with each other more fully, and benefit from participating globally in Internet governance.

A rapid economic growth in Mongolia has also increased access to mobile phones, computers, and the Internet. However, the influx of foreign capital poured into the mining, construction, and telecommunication sectors frequently comes in non-concessional terms raising concerns over the public debt in Mongolia. The decline in international aid by multilateral organizations like the World Bank, the International Monetary Fund, and the Asian bank, and the increase in foreign private investment (Mining and telecommunications multinational corporations) might benefit foreign corporations more than Mongolians. The Mongolian government's economic policy though relatively *laissez-faire,* and resource and access centered, still shows a fusion of economic and political power in managing international investment and resource wealth. The lack of information, the paternalistic approach by the government, and the secrecy in society inherited from the socialist time, also amplifies "the difficulty of obtaining information" at all levels of Mongolian society.

REFERENCES

Baasanjav, U. (2008). Mediated political and social participation: The case study of Mongolian government and civil society institutions. *Journal of Information Technology & Politics, 4*(3), 41–60. doi:10.1080/19331680801915041

Baasanjav, U. (2011). Web use patterns for civic discourse: The case of Mongolian institutions. *Information Communication and Society, 14*(5), 591–618. doi:10.1080/1369118X.2010.513416

Baasanjav, U. (2012). Global digital divide: Language gap and post-communism in Mongolia. In A. Manoharan, & M. Holzer (Eds.), *E-Governance and civic engagement: Factors and determinants of e-democracy* (pp. 210–234). Hershey, PA: IGI Global.

Baasanjav, U. (in press). Linguistic diversity on the Internet: Arabic, Chinese and Cyrillic script top-level domain names. *Telecommunications Policy.* doi: 10.1016/j.telpol.2014.03.005

Bellamy, C., & Taylor, J. (1998). *Governing in the information age.* Buckingham, UK: Open University Press.

Boje, C., & Dragulanescu, N. G. (2003). Digital Divide in Eastern European Countries and its Social Impact. In *Proceedings of the 2003 American Society for Engineering Education Annual Conference & Exposition.* Retrieved Oct 30, 2010 from http://www.ndragulanescu.ro/publicatii/CP40.pdf

Carey, J. W. (2005). The historical pragmatism and the Internet. *New Media & Society, 7*(4), 443–455. doi:10.1177/1461444805054107

Coleman, S., & Kaposi, I. (2006). *New democracies, new media: What's new? A study of e-participation projects in third-wave democracies.* Retrieved August 14, 2006 from http://www.ega.ee/handbook/

Dimitrova, D. V., & Beilock, R. (2005). Where freedom matters: Internet adoption among the former socialist countries. *Gazette: The International Journal for Communication Studies, 67*(2), 173–187. doi:10.1177/0016549205050130

Dutta, S. (2007). Estonia: A sustainable success in networked readiness. In S. Dutta, & I. Mia (Eds.), *The global information technology report 2006–2007: Connecting to the networked economy* (pp. 81–90). New York: Palgrave Macmillan.

Economic Intelligence Unit. (2005). *Country profile 2005: Mongolia.* Retrieved September 20, 2005 from http://www.eiu.com/report_dl.asp?issue_id=139144599&mode=pdf

Economist. (2010, October 23). Nomads no more, Mongolia's mining boom. *The Economist,* p. 52.

Economist. (2012, April 28). Steppe in an ugly direction: Political shenanigans in Mongolia. *The Economist.*

Economist. (2013, February 16). Before the gold rush. *The Economist,* p, 46.

Hamelink, C. J. (2000). *The Ethics of Cyberspace*. London: Sage.

Hargittai, E. (2003). The digital divide and what to do about it. In D. C. Jones (Ed.), *The New Economy Handbook*. San Diego, CA: Academic Press.

Herron, E. J. (1999). Democratization and the development of information regimes: Internet in Eurasia and Baltics. *Problems of Post-Communism*, *46*(4), 56–68.

Hobsbawm, E. J. (1996). Language, culture, and national identity. *Social Research*, *63*, 1065–1081.

Holmes, L. (1997). *Post-communism: An introduction*. Durham, NC: Duke University Press.

Hrynyshyn, D. (2008). Globalization, nationality and commodification: The politics of the social construction of the internet. *New Media & Society*, *10*(5), 751–770. doi:10.1177/1461444808094355

ICANN. (2011, October 6). *IDN variant TLDs – Cyrillic script issues*. Retrieved from http://archive.icann.org/en/topics/new-gtlds/cyrillic-vip-issues-report-06oct11-en.pdf

ICANN. (2012, February 20). *A Study of issues related to the management of IDN variant TLDs* (Integrated Issues Report). Retrieved from http://www.icann.org/en/resources/idn/idn-vip-integrated-issues-final-clean-20feb12-en.pdf

Ifinedo, P., & Singh, M. (2011). Determinants of egovernment maturity in the transition economies of Central and Eastern Europe: 1. *Electronic Journal of E-Government*, *9*, 166.

ITU. (2013a). *ICT Facts and Figures 2013*. Retrieved April 5, 2014 from http://www.itu.int/en/ITU-D/Statistics/Pages/stat/default.aspx

ITU. (2013b). *Measuring the Information Society*. Retrieved April 5, 2014 from http://www.itu.int/en/ITU-D/Statistics/Pages/publications/mis2013.aspx

James, J. (2007). From origins to implications: key aspects in the debate over the digital divide. *Journal of Information Technology*, *22*, 284–295. doi:10.1057/palgrave.jit.2000097

James, J. (2008). Digital divide complacency: Misconceptions and dangers. *The Information Society*, *24*, 54–61. doi:10.1080/01972240701774790

James, J. (2013). The diffusion of IT in the historical context of innovations from developed countries. *Social Indicators Research*, *111*, 175–184. doi:10.1007/s11205-011-9989-0 PMID:23378682

Klvana, T. P. (2004). New Europe's civil society, democracy, and the media thirteen years after: The story of the Czech Republic. *The Harvard International Journal of Press/Politics*, *9*, 40–55. doi:10.1177/1081180X04266505

Kolko, B., Wei, C., & Spyridakis, J. H. (2003). Internet use in Uzbekistan: Developing a methodology for tracking information technology implementation success. *Internet Technologies and International Development, 1*(2).

Munkhmandakh, M., & Nielsen, P. E. (2001). The Mongolian media landscape in transition: A cultural clash between global, national, local and no nomads media. *NordiCom Review: Nordic Research on Media and Communication, 22*(2).

Norris, P. (2001). *Digital Divide: Civic Engagement, Information Poverty, and the Internet Worldwide*. Cambridge, UK: Cambridge UP. doi:10.1017/CBO9781139164887

Qureshi, S. (2012). As the global digital divide narrows, who is being left behind? *Information Technology for Development*, *18*(4), 277–280. doi:10.1080/02681102.2012.730656

Slevin, J. (2000). *The Internet and Society*. Cambridge, MA: Polity Press.

Sparks, C. S., & Reading, A. (1997). *Communism, Capitalism and the Media in Eastern Europe.* London: Sage.

Stevenson, S. (2009). Digital divide: A discursive move away from the real inequality. *The Information Society, 25,* 1–22. doi:10.1080/01972240802587539

Transparency International. (2010). *Corruption perceptions index 2010.* Retrieved Oct 30, 2010 from http://www.transparency.org/policy_research/surveys_indices/cpi/2010/results

UNESCO. (2007). *The Mongolian Media Landscape: Sector Analysis.* Retrieved April 5, 2014 from http://portal.unesco.org/ci/en/ev.php-URL_ID=25638&URL_DO=DO_TOPIC&URL_SECTION=201.html

United Nations Statistics Division (UNSD). (2008). *Mongolia: Country Profile.* Retrieved Oct 28, 2010 from http://data.un.org/CountryProfile.aspx?crname=MONGOLIA

Van Dijk, J. (2006). Digital divide research, achievements and shortcomings. *Poetics, 34,* 221–235. doi:10.1016/j.poetic.2006.05.004

Walton, R., Yaacoubi, J., & Kolko, B. (2012). What's it for? Expectations of internet value and usefulness in Central Asia. *Information Technologies and International Development, 8*(3), 69.

World Bank. (2012a). *Information and Communications for Development 2012: Maximizing Mobile.* Washington, DC: World Bank.

World Bank. (2012b). *Little Data Book on Information and Communication Technology.* Washington, DC: World Bank.

Zassoursky, I. (2004). *Media and power in post-soviet Russia.* Armonk, NY: M.E. Sharpe.

Zook, M. (2000). Internet metrics: Using host and domain counts to map the internet. *Telecommunications Policy, 24*(6/7).

KEY TERMS AND DEFINITIONS

Cyrillic Content on the Internet: Internet content written in the Cyrillic alphabet.

Domain Names: Textual names of web resources on the Internet, are descriptive markers with corresponding numerical addresses called Internet protocol (IP) addresses.

Global Digital Divide: The discrepancy in Internet use between developed and developing countries.

International Domain Names: Fully internationalized domain names that use characters outside the range of the capital and small Roman letters from A to Z, the Arabic numbers of 0 to 9, and hyphens.

Linguistic Diversity on the Internet: The inclusion of all languages in cyberspace including diversity in the naming and numbering system of the Internet.

Post-Communistic Characteristics: Characteristics such as the rise of nationalism, the revival of religion, the boom of independent media outlets, and institutional routines that were prevalent in former socialist countries and continue after the fall of communism.

Socially Beneficial Internet Applications: Services and information on the Internet provided by government and non-government organizations, as well as by individuals that benefit the general public.

***Uighur* Alphabet:** A script of an Arabic origin written vertically and had twenty four letters, each letter having three different forms in the beginning, in the middle and at the end of a word.

Unicode Standard: International standards for interchange, processing, and the display of multilingual characters sets and diverse written languages.

Chapter 15
Developing a Citizen–Centric eGovernment Model for Developing Countries:
Case of Kurdistan Region of Iraq

Hamid Jahankhani
Williams College, UK

Shareef M. Shareef
University of Salahaddin, Iraq

Mohammad Dastbaz
Leeds Metropolitan University, UK

Elias Pimenidis
University of East London, UK

ABSTRACT

This chapter presents an enhanced eGovernment stage model based on citizens' participation for improvements in the delivery of governmental services by putting citizens' insights and their requirements in the context of e-government development and the potential use of a multi-channel delivery of services for regional governments in developing countries. The model proposed is based on research done in the Kurdistan region of Iraq. This research identified missing elements in traditional eGovernment models that would prove essential for implementation in developing countries. These models usually propose five stages of development spanning from emergence to integration. The proposal here considers most of the limitations in two stages, namely initial and an enhancement stage with the advantage of decreasing the uncertainty of e-government implementation in the public sector by recognising the consequence of the institutional readiness, adoption processes, the needs of ICT tools, and the factors that influence the implementation process.

INTRODUCTION

eGovernment is a dynamic continuous service provision process which makes availability of services to the society via technology along with the potential of multi-channel delivery of services; such as internet, telephone, wireless devices, and other communication media, along with an effective management process (Shareef et al, 2011). As the range of eGovernment potential has grown and developed, the definition of eGovernment has developed with it.

DOI: 10.4018/978-1-4666-3691-0.ch015

The extant literature offers a number of different definitions about eGovernment. For instance, e-Government is defined as the use of information and communications technology (ICT) to transform government by making it more accessible, result-oriented, efficient, effective, and accountable (OECD, 2003). Such an implementation includes a range of activities from providing greater access to government information to promoting civic engagement in providing development opportunities. Gulick & Urwick (1937) defined eGovernment as the process of making activities and functions effectively and efficiently with and through other people.

Gil-Garcia & Martinez (2005) defined e-Government as the intensive use of IT for service provision to their citizens, and the enhancement of managerial efficiency and the encouragement of democratic values and mechanisms. This definition argues that the provision of services is not only through the use of technology, but also enhancing the management process in order to be more transparent and more efficient (Tan, 2006; Heeks, 2001). Holzer & Tae Kim (2005) identified that digital government provides services to citizens and digital democracy is the citizen's contributions to the government. EGovernment in broadest term involves offering better access to government information and encouraging civic engagement to provide development opportunities. Consequently, citizens, business, and government institutions are all benefiting from the electronic government system (World Bank Group, 2009). The important factors are related to citizens' demands and their perception to participate and utilise eGovernment services. It is essential to promote and allow citizens to communicate and participate in e-government. In this regard, Fang (2002) defined e-Governance as the direct contribution of the people in decision making

and participating in political activities such as e-democracy, and e-voting. In a broader definition eGovernance will cover parliament, Judiciary functions, government, citizens' contribution, political parties, and organizations.

Therefore, eGovernment is no longer seen as the simple provision of information and services through the Internet, but as a way of stakeholders interaction with government. eGovernment is also seen as a way to modernise and enhance the economical, political, and social relationship between government and stakeholders, (Apostolou et al, 2011). However, this interaction faces various technological, cultural, and economical obstacles, (Rose & Gant, 2010, Gupta et al, 2008, Sahraoui, 2005), with each state facing different hurdles such as; resistance to change, digital divide, privacy and security, (Conklin, 2007, Coursey et al, 2007, Ebrahim & Irani, 2005).

Most of the eGovernment initiatives across the globe focus on the organisation of the front office, and on the communication between governmental departments and citizens. In order to make government successful, back-office functions have to be taken into account. In reality, back-office functions are the significant part of any eGovernment system, and they quite often require information exchange and knowledge sharing between different department, and institutions. In order to achieve seamless operations at the back-office, the institutional structure for managing these operations is crucial.

The Kurdistan Regional Government (KRG) in Iraq focuses on the role of new technology to promote and develop public administration, and at the same time to improve the government's capability in supervising key activities in the reconstruction of Kurdish social life, infrastructure, services, increased political freedom and tangible improvements in the people's daily lives.

An Overview of the Iraqi Kurdistan

Kurdistan is a federal region of Iraq. It is a secular and democratic region with a parliamentary system of government. It comprises of three cities, namely; Erbil (capital), Suleymani, and Duhok. According to the Iraqi constitution that was approved by a national referendum held on 15 October 2005. The Kurdistan Region of Iraq (KRI) is located at the north of Iraq; it neighboured Iran to the east, Syria to the west, and Turkey to the north. The area of the region is about 40,643 Km^2 (see www.Krg.org) with an estimated population of approximately 4,910,742, (Kurdistan, 2007). A geographical map of Kurdistan is illustrated in Figure1. After the uprising of spring 1991, the Iraqi central government withdrew all the administrations of Kurdistan. This has created a power vacuum situation, but the Kurdish authority was able to build an administration by their efforts. They held an election in 1992, and made an accountability government.

KRG was formally established in 2003 and recognised by Iraqi constitution, has its own president, parliament, and government that consist of 19 ministries, and a prime minister. Kurdistan parliament comprises of various political parties that reflecting the variety of the region's citizens, and ethnic groups. Kurdistan was lagging behind in ICT prior to 1991. In terms of telecommunication infrastructure development, the growth of the wired telephone network throughout Iraq, especially Kurdistan was lagging behind; there was no mobile communication, and very little if any ICT in the institutions and schools.

In recent years, Kurdistan has moved to develop and use ICT as a tool to improve government services and citizen requirements. In this regard,

Figure 1. Geographical map of KRI

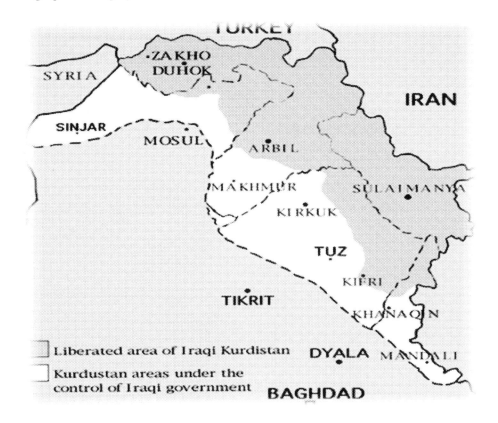

a cabinet post has been created to take charge of developing IT with the Kurdistan region. A broad Web Information site was designed and launched in the late 2002, and is organized by the department of foreign relations in the KRG. The website was situated as the government info-structure and designed as the information gateway for all the external and internal public in order to obtain information of government's activities and news (Shareef et al, 2012).

Critical Challenges Influence eGovernment Initiative in KRI

Lack of comprehensive ICT infrastructure and its availability to large sections of population there are number key challenges facing the eGovernment implementation in KRI. According to the head of the IT department at the council of ministries, the current government system is facing several challenges that should be solved to prepare for eGovernment initiative to be implemented, (Shareef et al, 2012). Furthermore, lack of interoperability (Zhao & Zhao, 2010) as well as lack of inter-institutions coordination between ministries and government institutions was identified as some

of the other key problems. This might make an eGovernment initiative difficult, because every ministry is carrying out projects independently without referring to other agencies or sharing the information with other related ministries to uptake the project successfully. The factors to focus on to avoid such challenges were also identified with the findings summarized in Table 1.

Technological Challenges

The extant literature is clear about the lack of ICT infrastructure and heterogeneous technologies will increase the digital divide (Mousavi et al, 2008). Therefore, ICT infrastructure is one of the fundamental challenges that are facing eGovernment implementation in developing countries (Heeks, 2008; Gupta et al, 2008). ICT infrastructures are well established in developed countries, but remain as one of the main challenges for developing countries; such as Iraq in general and Kurdistan in particular. The survey reveals that most of the institutions in the KRI are equipped with computers and Internet connection that will allow employees to use the technology and collaborate with other institutions (Shareef et al, 2011). How-

Table 1. E-Government challenges identified for KRI

Technological	Economical	Societal	Political
ICT infrastructure, heterogeneous technologies	High financial resources	Citizen awareness	Strategy vision and missions
IT and Internet skills	Cost, time, and effort during transaction	Human capacity building, Internet penetration	Policy issues and legislation
Computer and ICT literacy	Financial funding and, budgets	Culture attitude, poverty Partnership	Weak of education system policy
Capability, and Inter-operability of computer system		Interoperability collaboration of public/private, Resistance to change, Ease of access and usage	Leadership role, involve, support, motivate, and influence
International connection networks, and updated applications		Citizen participation, Poor of information quality and System acceptance, Social networks	Legal framework of public process of government, lack of standards
		Privacy, security, trust, and Level of stress. Citizens requirement and their views	Lack of management skills, and Data Protection

ever, only managers use the Internet and ordinary employees do not have access to the Internet. The research revealed that this is due to the nature of the centralised administration system along with the lack of knowledge by some of the managers and policy makers. Despite the connection of all ministries together via fibre optics, the level of collaboration, transactions and data exchanges were negligible.

Economic and Societal Challenge

The high financial resource is one of the primary challenges that face the eGovernment initiative (Rose & Grant, 2010). The traditional government channel services such as telephone and physically visiting offices in particular require more money for any government transaction (Aichholzer & Schmutzer, 2000). While the implementation of eGovernment systems are also require a considerable budget to create an efficient system. One of the important societal challenges is that of "trust". In many developing countries people do not trust their government, especially where there has been lack of democratic structure and practice, or instability of the political system.

Therefore building trust between government and the citizens becomes one of the fundamental challenges having an impact per se and influencing eGovernment implementation (Bannister & Connolly, 2011). To achieve the trust in government among stakeholders, citizens and other stakeholders will need to be partners in the eGovernment efforts. In this regard, Yu & Liu (2001) state that trust is becoming a vital issue in the design of information system. However, Eastlick et al. (2006) states that trust and commitment are mediating agents among entities online. Therefore, the desire for cultivating trust amongst stakeholders of eGovernment is considered as a primary principle in designing and evolving successful eGovernment systems.

The main feature of trust is how government can encourage stakeholders to use e-services and participate in the new system also how to increase the level of trust in government. Government requires and encourages its citizen to perform their transaction online that means placing their trust in government. In addition, Jahankhani (2004) points out that there are three kinds of trusts, these are: characteristic-based trust, process-based trust, and institutional-based trust. These types of trusts are vital in encouraging citizen participation in eGovernment systems and are beneficial for the continuous progress and evolution of electronic commerce. Al-Khouri & Bal (2006) also identify three schemes to solve the "trusted authentication medium" for eGovernment services, by utilising developed technology national ID schemes namely; smart card, biometrics and public key infrastructure (PKI). Furthermore, Dutton et al. (2005) argue that the privacy and security of citizen's information are vital issues to enhance trust in eGovernment services and suggested that to enhance trust technologies such as firewalls and authentication systems assist to evolve citizen trust in government website. Therefore, eGovernment models in the developing world should consider the issue of trust in government.

Privacy is a significant factor that needs to be carefully considered in the electronic government adoption; government gathers huge amounts of data form their citizens via daily transactions. This data will expand with growth in scope and popularity of eGovernment services. Managing this type of challenge is vital in order to encourage citizens to use eGovernment services, and build citizen's trust in the new system. The main concern of citizens is the privacy and security, when using their personal information to perform any transaction with eGovernment services. Particularly, businesses are concerned with public perceptions about the privacy and security of information on the Internet (Hiller & Bélanger, 2001).

In order to secure citizens' information it is necessary to know the security of information. Information security is the process of recognising events which have the possibility to experience harm or threat and taking actions against in order to eliminate and reduce this threat (Schechter, 2004). The security of information can be referred to the old time civilisations when civilisations began to take models in order to communicate freely without any risk of eavesdropping. For instance, the Egyptians began adopting cryptography in 3000 BC applying Hieroglyphics (Schneier, 1996) in order to hide writings from an unintended receiver.

The development of new technology has created various security methods to secure information to individuals, organisations, armies and nations. These methods are varied in terms of the context; some were based on rules, regulation, policies and mathematical approach and others based on pure cryptographic knowledge. For instance, in the early 1970s Bell and Lapadula model was developed (Bell & Lapadula, 1973), the model aims to secure the confidentiality of military information. Later, McLean (1990) introduced a new method of the security field expressing a threat of secret channels that permit a bypass of the security rules. Since the number of security models augmented, the challenges continued to increase and researchers continued to investigate to find out various solutions via new models and development of existing once.

The aims of some models were evolved to offer security across the boundaries of multiple organisations such as "Multilateral Model" (Sadeqhi and Stuble, 2005). Hence, information security has developed to be the vital factor and supporting constituent of the Internet spread.

In other words if stakeholders are not sure about the way that their information will be treated and have some privacy concerns they do not go online to conduct their transactions with government institutions. The government institutions should guarantee the citizen's personal and financial information would not be used against the citizens later. The government should also construct a secure strategic plan; the privacy policy standard and Data Protection Act to provide the legal framework.

EGovernment Stage Model for Regional Government in Developing Countries

The proposed eGovernment stage model is based on a citizen-centric approach. The model has been developed using an evolutionary approach and by taking onboard the key factors identified in the existing e-government models presented in the extant literature. The key difference of this model from the others is including all the elements and components that are required for an effective implementation of e-services in regional government in developing countries. The proposed model is based on both technological and public perspectives, but mainly focuses on a citizen's perspective. In each stage government plans a strategic roadmap, technical procedure, and financial and security procedures. The first element is the road map in which eGovernment administrator identifies the opportunities to design a suitable path way for every change and development. The second element is technological opportunity, which updates and installs new technology and their applications. The third concept is the security, which checks the system and builds a vigorous security system. The last element is the financial issues and resources required; an eGovernment administrator allocates financial resources for each stage to make sufficient systems able to move forward. At the end of each stage, the process should be evaluated and tested in order to identify the validity of the business process at each stage. The most vital challenge in this model is focused mainly on two stages that are different from other eGovernment stage models namely; initial and an enhancement stages also modifies other stages according to the KRG objectives and state's reality. These two stages are very important which have not been considered as a priority in eGovernment models by most of the academic researchers. The sketch of a proposed eGovernment stage model is illustrated in Figure 2.

Figure 2. Six stages model for e-government

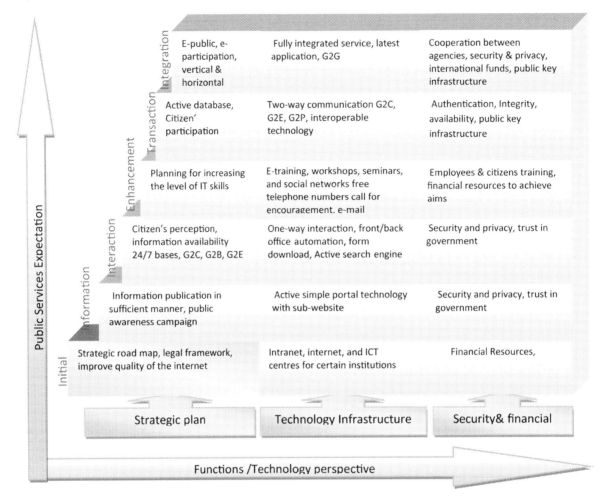

Initial Stage

Government at this stage sets up the technical infrastructure (Gupta et al, 2008; Al-Shafi & Weerakkody, 2008) such as; a networking system, Intranet and Internet, availability, and ICT centres, at least in some certain government institutions. Government attempts to draw a strategic roadmap for an eGovernment system for instance; infrastructure (intra-institutional network structure), legal framework, eGovernment administration, timescale, financial resources (budget), human infrastructure, security and the main objectives of the proposed system. Thereby, all government clerical staff will share that in order to reduce the design-reality divide (Ghalib & Heeks, 2008). The establishment of traditional multi-channel delivery of services such as; posting telephone centre, face-to-face, and others, in order to enable the entire stakeholders to benefit from government services, due to a lack of some traditional service channels in the KRI.

The government at this stage should guarantee the security of the network infrastructure, and improve the quality of the Internet that is a big concern.

Information Stage

At this stage, the government establishes a plan on how to provide information to its citizens seamlessly, and reasonable budget is allocated to execute this stage It also creates an appropriate portal or website and sub-websites for certain government institutions to put sufficient information online. This is to allow citizens to access some key information online such as; institution's objectives, rules, regulations, political issues, government activities, and news. The information should be presented in various languages such as international (English and/or French), national and, local. The typical recommendation is that professionals control the management of the site and highly skilled IT people to be able to update the information continually. The resources should be allocated professionally, and the website should be easy to use. Government should build a constructive institutional framework for managing the information portal at this stage. At this stage the information is not transactional.

The government should prepare and make the community aware of the system; therefore government should plan for processes on how encourage stakeholders to participate in the new system. This process requires suitable budget and technological support capability to be successful. The provision of guidance, notes and to make citizens aware of how and why to use the information online will go a long way to alleviate some of the problems and how the system will benefit them.

Interaction Stage

At this stage government plans to convince its citizens by providing suitable information and some e-services. Government interacts with the different stakeholders, including: citizens, business, employees and intra/interdepartmental. Citizens can access and download forms such as driving licence application forms, which imply one-way interaction. The government provides substantial, clear, useful and effective information on the web, and also offers electronic mail and other multiple channels to ease and improve the interaction process with stakeholders. Such interactions will arise via dedicated telephone lines, email; SMS contact numbers, feedback forms and downloadable forms online. Furthermore, government automates and develops back-office capabilities to enable employees to conduct and perform consumers' transactions rapidly and efficiently. To achieve the interaction stage effectively comprehensive security measures should be put in place. The government portal should include a section for citizens (citizen opinion) in order to enrich the information by their comments and suggestions regarding information availability and service provision. Some services could be provided through alternative multi-channel deliveries, such as providing direct contact with government employees through, telephone, e-mail and chat forums. These kinds of channels will consequently save time and cost, and may resolve some of the lack of transparency and bureaucracy culture. It may also result in reduced bribery and corruption activities which have plagued many government institutions and are a big concern to most regional governments in developing countries, whilst getting rid of waiting in long queues and paying money to get served.

Ehancement Stage

To embark on an eGovernment system, the government should prepare and assist the community to raise their IT skills and efforts for bridging the digital divide. This requires a comprehensive on how to encourage stakeholders to participate in training courses to reduce the digital divide. As well as requiring suitable budget and technical capability the implementation of this phase requires political commitments. At this stage, sufficient information and some e-services are uploaded on the website properly. Then, the guidance and promoting citizens' awareness (Calvin et al, 2008,

Coursey et al., 2007) continued at this stage. The government prepares citizens for the use of new information and services electronically. Enable provision of information regarding government such as, downloadable database, reports, policies, laws and regulation, along with some information and e-services. The government should encourage citizens to participate in eGovernment activities that will be a vital factor to the success of eGovernment process (Fitzgeral, 2005).

Transaction Stage

At this stage the eGovernment initiatives will concentrate on processing citizens' services online, from different government agencies. This requires technological capability along with designated applications to perform transaction. The focus is on putting an active database link to online services, enabling adequate security and confidentiality of information in the process. Here, the citizens transact with government online by filling forms and government replies with confirmation. For example, citizens who want to renew their licence, or pay tax and fines online. The online transaction facilities can be of great benefits to citizens, especially those living further away and/or not easy to access/difficult areas, saving time, effort and costs. The fifth stage is the start up of the eGovernment as an innovative entity changing the way citizens communicate with their government (Layne & Lee 2001). It is also the stage at which the government initiates two-way communication with its stakeholders, through various types of relationships, such as; Government-to-Citizen (G2C), Government-to-Business (G2B), Government-to-employees (G2E), Government-to-Government (G2G) and Government-to-Person (G2P). To achieve two-way communication effectively requires reasonable financial budget and human resources. At this stage, government provides services by using advanced technology along with the developed application and consideration to the authentication, integrity, and availability of e-services.

Integration Stage

After the successful implementation of the transaction stage, it is predicted that expectations and engagements of citizens will increase. Therefore, government should plan a road map on how to satisfy stakeholders and integrate e-service processes. The integration process allows government institutions to provide full services to its citizens and businesses online. In this case, the user will be placed at the centre of the development and the provision of electronic public services. All institutions will cooperate in a universal eGovernment website or portal with interconnected sub-websites for ministries and government institutions. The services will be accessible for citizens and will be able to receive all services online through this/these websites. Apart from that, government creates opportunity channels such as kiosk, blog, twitter, Face book, online polls, e-meeting, and others to enable citizens to state their viewpoints and opinion on the initiation of eGovernment implementations and the type of services desired. Hence this will lead to the transparent environment and provides equal opportunity to all citizens in the society along with social justice. The significant point, which should be considered by government authorities, is the cooperation between government institutions in order to speed up the efficiency of the information and e-services to the public.

Layne & Lee (2001), classified this stage into two stages; Vertical and Horizontal stages. On the vertical stage the local government/state government and the federal government system are connected for different services or functions of government. This therefore creates the interrelationship between regions and the federal government as

G2G. For example; a driver's license registration system at local level might be connected to the State system for checking. The State system is then connected to a national database of licenses in the federal system. In situations where systems are collaborating vertically, an individual fills in the business licence form in a region; this information will also exist on the federal government business license system. Consequently, any crime reported and recorded on state systems can be queried and be accessible from any city or federal state. The complete benefit of eGovernment will be recognised only when institutional changes have associated technology changes.

In the horizontal stage, various government institutions are able to interact with each other. The main feature at this stage is creating a database across different government institutions and making them communicate with each other and preferably share information. Therefore, the information provided by one institution will be propagated throughout all the government institutions. For example, when a citizen applies for a driving license after moving to another city, then he/she does not need to fill in the entire form again, because the basic residence record could be propagated to a different institutional service part of government. The majority of countries have failed to identify i.e. horizontal stage of eGovernment commonly across all public services in their countries (Shareef et al, 2012).

The significant feature in this stage is the creation of the relationship between government and citizens in the political process, such as e-democracy and e-voting. Stakeholders can suitably express their suggestions and opinions to contribute in political matters through various channels in order to establish e-democracy (Siau & Long, 2005) thus it will promote transparency and accountability. Furthermore, the cooperation between the academics, local government officers and other stakeholder's viewpoint is also another factor needed to ensure success of the system. The main challenge will be to meet the one stop services confidentiality. The eventual aim of eGovernment will be executed and all stakeholders of electronic government can benefit from one-stop government services. Table 2, provides a summarised list of challenges encountered at each stage.

Table 2. Summarized challenges in six stages model

E-government's stages	Challenges
Initial	Strategic plan, technological preparation; networking, internet, legal framework, network security
Information	Active website, and sector management adequately Resource allocation in sufficient way Sustainable Information updating Sufficient information to meet the citizens' requirements. Citizens awareness is essential
Interaction	Interactions, citizen perception, front/back office automation in certain agencies. Public policy provision, G2C, G2B, G2G
Enhancement	Emerging E-learning, G2C, G2E Lack of citizen knowledge, Culture attitude, Digital gap, and Privacy.
Transaction	Authentication and confidentiality Transaction between G2C, G2B, G2E and G2P.
Integration	Interrelationship G2G, cooperation among government institutions. The integration of federal government with its local and regional governments One-stop-shopping goal, e-democracy, and e-voting

Challenges Facing eGovernment Implementation in Developing Countries

Information and communications technology play a vital role in the running of every institution across the globe. Nevertheless, three out of five IT projects fail in terms of satisfying user requirements. Furthermore, most of the above also failed by exceeding their completion deadlines and or budgets. Such failings represent a substantial financial loss for the organizations involved. EGovernment projects face the same challenges as any other IT project, (Arif, 2008). Literature contains the results from various researches on the challenges in developing eGovernment systems such as; the lack of awareness, bureaucratic culture, government support, usability of websites, trust, human resource, and capacity building. All of the above can also be considered as key risks in IT projects of diverse types. Overcoming such challenges would therefore be the fundamental tests for citizens and government for any country planning to implement e-government.

Currently, most local, federal and state governments face severe hurdles in managing e-government, both in developing and developed countries. As far as literature is concerned, most of such challenges arise not from the application, but from the complexity of the infrastructure itself. Another key factor of failure in eGovernment management is that of poor management process inherent within the organization (Heeks, 2008). Proper management will improve the success of an eGovernment initiative. Lack of discipline and rigor of system management can also considerably contribute to the failure of the eGovernment system (Rose & Gant, 2010).

Another factor that can impact on eGovernment systems is the lack of interoperability among government institutions, where each institution sets up their own system without sharing data or information with the others. In addition, misunderstanding and lack of collaboration between the services and ICT may cause tension.

The interference of politicians in public administration might contribute to the failure of systems, particularly in developing countries. Politicians should support the development process in order to implement successful systems, (Shareef et al, 2011). The lack of direct contact can result in multiple iterations, weak leadership and poor IT skills employed in the eGovernment sector will also invoke failures in the eGovernment system. Moreover, lack of participation from business, employees, citizens, and others of different ICT means along with capabilities may influence failure in eGovernment systems. The cooperation of all stakeholders therefore is a key factor for a successful eGovernment system.

CONCLUSION

One of the key challenges that this research identifies for the development of eGovernment in KRI is the bureaucratic structures and processes in government bodies and public administration. Clearly this has a negative impact and broadens the gap between government and citizens.

This research has revealed that none of the currently available and reviewed eGovernment models take into account the specific particular issues facing developing countries. Most models that we reviewed did not recognise the requirement for encouraging, increasing awareness, of citizens and having an engagement plan with the e-government. They also merely concentrate on the transformation of government services rather than automation of the working procedure. In addition, most of the eGovernment models have not considered the potential of multi-channel delivery of services as an alternative form of communication with the government in the case of the failure of websites in order to enable stakeholders to utilise alternative and preferred channels for various cases. Most of the eGovernment models have not prioritised the automation of front/back office in certain government institutions at the early stages. This will assist the speeding up of transaction processing and might add to the success of the eGovernment system.

Therefore, an enhanced eGovernment stage model for regional governments in developing countries is proposed. The main contribution of this model emphasises the demand side (citizen-focused in terms of participation) and encourages public participation in service acquisition. The proposed model provides steps for eGovernment implementation of regional government in developing countries.

The most significant challenge in this model occurs mainly in two stages that are different from other eGovernment stage models, namely the initial and an enhancement. These two stages are very important and ones that have not been considered as a main priority of the models that proposed by any of the international organisations, consulting companies, and individual academic researchers. The other four stages are modified based on the eGovernment models in the literature along with the KRG objectives, state's reality and citizens' desires.

REFERENCES

Aichholzer, G., & Schmutzer, R. (2000). Organizational challenges to the development of electronic government. In *Proceedings of the 11th International Workshop on Database and Expert System Applications* (pp. 379-383). London: IEEE.

Al-Khouri, A. M., & Bal, J. (2006). Electronic government in the GCC countries. *International Journal of Social Sciences, 1*(2).

Al-Shafi, S., & Weerakkody, V. (2008). Adoption of wireless Internet parks: An empirical study in Qatar. In *Proceedings of the 5th European and Mediterranean Conference on Information Systems* (EMCIS). EMCIS.

Apostolou, D., Mentzas, G., Stojanovic, L., Thoenssen, B., & Pariente Lobo, T. (2011). A collaborative decision framework for managing changes in eGovernment services. *Government Information Quarterly, 28,* 101–116. doi:10.1016/j.giq.2010.03.007

Arif, M. (2008). Customer Orientation in eGovernment Project Management: A Case Study. *The Electronic. Journal of E-Government, 6*(1), 1–10.

Bannister, F., & Connolly, R. (2011). Trust and transformational government: A proposed framework for research. *Government Information Quarterly, 28*(2), 137–147. doi:10.1016/j.giq.2010.06.010

Bell, D., & Lapadula, L. (1973). Secure Computer System: Unified Exposition and Multics Interpretation. *Technical Report MTR-2997 Rev.1.*

Calvin, M. L. C., Lau, Y., & Pan, L. S. (2008). EGovernment implementation: A macro analysis of Singapore's eGovernment initiatives. *Government Information Quarterly, 25*(2), 239–255. doi:10.1016/j.giq.2006.04.011

Conklin, W. A. (2007). Barriers to Adoption of e-Government', System Sciences. In *Proceedings of the 40th Annual Hawaii International Conference on System Sciences.* IEEE.

Coursey, D., Yang, K., Kasserkert, K., & Norris, D. (2007). E-Gov Adoption in U.S. Local Governments: Bridging Public Management and Institutional Explanations in a Pooled Time Series Model. In *Proceedings of 9th Public Management Research Conference.* Academic Press.

Dutton, W., Guerra, A. G., Zizzo, J. D., & Peltu, M. (2005). The cyber trust tension in E-government: Balancing identity, privacy, security. *Information Polity*, *10*(1-2), 13–23.

Eastlick, M. A., Lots, L. S., & Warrington, P. (2006). Understanding online B-to-C relationships: An integrated model of privacy concerns, trust, and commitment. *Journal of Business Research*, *59*(8), 877–886. doi:10.1016/j.jbusres.2006.02.006

Ebrahim, Z., & Irani, Z. (2005). EGovernment adoption: Architecture and barriers. *Business Process Management Journal*, *11*(5), 589–611. doi:10.1108/14637150510619902

Fang, Z. (2002). EGovernment in Digital Era: Concept, Practice, and Development. *International Journal of the Computer, the Internet and Management*, *10*(2), 1-22.

Fitzgerald, G. N. R. (2005). The turnaround of the London Ambulance Service Computer Aided Dispatch system (LASCAD). *European Journal of Information Systems*, *14*(3), 244–257. doi:10.1057/palgrave.ejis.3000541

Ghalib, A., & Heeks, R. (2008). *Automating Public Sector Bank Transactions in South Asia: Design-Reality Gap Case Study No.1*. Retrieved from http://www.egov4dev.org/success/case/bankauto.shtml

Gil-García, J. R., & Martinez, M. J. (2005). *Exploring E-Government Evolution: The Influence of Systems of Rules on Organizational Action*. Retrieved from http://www.umass.edu/digitalcenter/research/working_papers/05_001gilgarcia

Gulick, L., & Urwick, L. (1937). *Papers on the Science of Administration*. New York: Institute of Public Administration.

Gupta, B., Dasgupta, B. I., & Gupta, A. (2008). Adoption of ICT in a government organization in a developing country: An empirical study. *The Journal of Strategic Information Systems*, *17*(2), 140–154. doi:10.1016/j.jsis.2007.12.004

Heeks, R. (2001). *Understanding e-governance for development*. Retrieved from http://unpan1.un.org/intradoc/groups/public/documents/NISPAcee/UNPAN015484.pdf

Heeks, R. (2008). *Success and Failure Rates of eGovernment in Developing/Transitional Countries: Overview*. Retrieved from http://www.egov4dev.org/success/sfrates.shtml

Hiller, J. S., & Belanger, F. (2001). Privacy Strategies for Electronic Government. In M. A. Abramson, & G. E. Means (Eds.), *EGovernment 2001*. Boulder, CO: Rowman and Littlefield.

Holzer, M., & Tae Kim, S. (2005). *Digital Governance in Municipalities Worldwide*. Retrieved from http://unpan1.un.org/intradoc/groups/public/documents/aspa/unpan022839.pdf

Jahankhani, H., & Varghese, M. K. (2004). The role of consumer trust in relation to electronic commerce. In *Proceedings of the 4th Annual Hawaii International Conference on Business*, (pp. 21-24). IEEE.

Kurdistan Regional Statistics Office. (2007). Retrieved from http://www.krso.net/detail.aspx?page=statisticsbysubjects&c=sbsPopulationLabor&id=361

Layne, K., & Lee, J. W. (2001). Developing fully functional e-government: A four stage model. *Government Information Quarterly*, *18*(2), 122–136. doi:10.1016/S0740-624X(01)00066-1

Mclean, J. (1990). *Security Models and Information Flow*. Retrieved from http://www.cs.cornell.edu/andru/cs711/2003fa/reading/1990mclean-sp.pdf

Mousavi, S. A., Pimenidis, E., & Jahankhani, H. (2008). Cultivating trust – An electronic government development model for addressing the needs of developing countries. *International Journal of Electronic Security and Digital Forensics*, *1*(3), 233–248. doi:10.1504/IJESDF.2008.020942

Organization for Economic Co-operation and Development (OECD). (2003). *The e-government imperative: Main findings*. Retrieved from http://www.oecd.org/dataoecd/60/60/2502539.pdf

Rose, R. W., & Grant, G. G. (2010). Critical issues pertaining to the planning and implementation of EGovernment initiatives. *Government Information Quarterly*, *27*(1), 26–33. doi:10.1016/j.giq.2009.06.002

Sadeqhi, A. R., & Stuble, C. (2005). Towards multilaterally secure computing platforms-with open source and trusted computing. *Information Security Technical Report*, *10*(2), 83–95. doi:10.1016/j.istr.2005.05.004

Sahraoui, S. (2005). eGovernment in the Arabian Gulf: Government transformation vs. government automation. In *Proceedings of the eGovernment Workshop '05 (e-GOV05)*. Academic Press.

Schechter, S. (2004). *Computer Security Strength & Risk: A Quantitative Approach*. (PhD Thesis). The Division of Engineering and Applied Sciences, Harvard University, Cambridge, MA. Retieved from http://www.eecs.harvard.edu/~stuart/papers/thesis.pdf

Schneier, B. (1996). *Applied Cryptography, Protocols, Algorithms and Source Code in C*. John Wiley & Sons, Inc.

Shareef, M. J., & Jahankhani, H. S. Arreymbi, & Pimenidis, E. (2011). The Challenges Influencing the Development and Adoption of e-Government Systems Initiatives in Developing Countries. In *Proceedings of First Global Conference on Communication, Science, and Information Engineering*. London: British Computer Society.

Shareef, S., Jahankhani, H., & Dastbaz, M. (2012). E-Government Stage Model: Based on Citizen-Centric Approach in Regional Government in Developing Countries. *International Journal of Electronic Commerce Studies*, *3*(1), 145–164.

Siau, K., & Long, Y. (2005). Synthesizing eGovernment stage models-a meta-synthesis based on meta-ethnography approach. *Industrial Management & Data Systems*, *105*(4), 443–458. doi:10.1108/02635570510592352

Tan, A. (2006). Mobile Web catching on. *ZDNet Asia*. Retrieved from http://www.zdnetasia.com/news/communications/0,39044192,39369023,00.htm

World Bank. (2009). *Information and communications for development, extending research and increasing impact*. Retrieved from http://books.google.co.uk/books

Yu, E., & Liu. (2001). Modelling Trust for System Design Using the i* Strategic Actors Framework. In R. Falcone, M. Singh & Y.H. Tan (Eds.), *Trust in Cyber-Societies – Integrating the Human and Artificial Perspectives* (LNAI), (vol. 2246, pp. 175–194). Berlin: Springer.

Zhao, J. J., & Zhao, Y. S. (2010). Opportunities and threats: A security assessment of state eGovernment websites. *Government Information Quarterly*, *27*(1), 49–56. doi:10.1016/j.giq.2009.07.004

KEY TERMS AND DEFINITIONS

E-Democracy: The use of ICT for political and governance processes through citizen engagement.

E-Government: Governments all over the world attempt to utilise Information and Communications Technology (ICT) to improve government's services provided to their stakeholders (citizen, business and government) in order to be more accessible, effective, efficient, and accountable.

Kurdistan Region of Iraq (KRI): Is located at the north of Iraq. After the uprising of spring 1991, the Iraqi central government withdrew all the administrations of Kurdistan. This has created a power vacuum situation, but the Kurdish authority was able to build an administration by their efforts. They held an election in 1992, and made an accountability government.

Kurdistan Regional Government (KRG): Kurdistan is a federal region of Iraq. It is a secular and democratic region with a parliamentary system of government. It comprises of three cities, namely; Erbil (capital), Suleymani, and Duhok. According to the Iraqi constitution that was approved by a national referendum held on 15 October 2005.

Management Framework: The E-Government strategy provides an assurance and coordinated approach for the departments to complete the projects.

Privacy: Government gathers huge amounts of data from their citizens via daily transactions. Managing this type of challenge is vital in order to encourage citizens to use eGovernment services, and build citizen's trust in the new system.

Stage Model: E-government naturally presents a number of challenges during implementation and therefore in order to help developers and administrators to think about the organization that they are developing the eGovernment for. Researchers have developed an approach based on stages of growth and development called stage model.

Chapter 16
Development of
E–Governance in Sri Lanka

Suran Dissanayake
Leeds Metropolitan University, UK

Lakshman Dissanayake
University of Colombo, Sri Lanka

ABSTRACT

Evolution of e-Governance concept in Sri Lanka can be traced back to 1983 because the Government of Sri Lanka for the first time recognized its obligation for ICT development by creating the National Computer Policy of 1983. The Information and Communication Technology Act No. 27 of 2003 came into existence in 2003 and the Information and Communication Technology Agency of Sri Lanka was established. In 2004, "e-Sri Lanka Development Project" was initiated. It included information infrastructure building, improvement of human resources in ICT, citizen-specific service delivery, creating a modern government using ICT for social and economic development, and endorsing Sri Lanka as a destination for ICT. The e-Sri Lanka initiative expects to use ICT to develop the economy of Sri Lanka by reducing poverty and thus improving the quality of life of its citizens. Presently, the government makes an effort in realizing this vision through six programme strategy schemes. This is explored in this chapter.

INTRODUCTION

The definition of e-Governance is influenced by various factors and dimensions. The word "electronic" in the term e-Governance indicates that the governance is driven by electronic technology. Therefore, e-Governance is government services among three areas, i.e. government to citizen, business and other governments utilizing information technology, communications and various individual systems. It may also incorporate internal aspects of government processes such as back office functions and internal interactions (Saugata and Masud, 2007). Although there are no boundaries in e-Governance, it can be stated that it can enable efficient, convenient and transparent services for a country and its citizens. Therefore the major beneficiaries of e-Governance are primarily citizens, businesses other interest groups and the government itself (Garson, 2006).

In a plight towards outreach to all citizens in society, many governments are exploring more

DOI: 10.4018/978-1-4666-3691-0.ch016

novel and responsive methods of interacting with and providing services to citizens. This new facet of service delivery termed as e-Governance is now reaching the more underdeveloped areas of the world with expansions in 3G and HSPA AND HASPA+ technologies that enable faster communication via the internet. In the most recent past, government websites used to only represent informative services but now they are migrating into an era where their purpose is to formulate relationships and actively engage with citizens, and other public and private organisations, establishing a culture of empowerment through engagement. Government institutions are slowly becoming more trustworthy and friendly to the people they serve taking away the previous perceptions of heightened bureaucracy. Utilising the capacity of the World Wide Web, governments are using websites to become more approachable and transparent to the communities (Bhatnagar 2003). The uptake of such endeavours by governments and the use of ICT can be regarded as their insight to the potential of ICT in communication and development.

On a global scale most governments began e-governance in the mid 1990s as method to rectify issues of administrative segments of the government itself and to use technology intensively to change the modes of operation in the system (Hague and Loader 1999) for higher accountability through transparency (Bhatnagar 2003). Most developing countries have a large digital divide which exists in the educated who can afford access to technology and information and the poor uneducated who do not (Basu, 2004)

Evolution of the E-Governance in Sri Lanka

In 2009, the Government of Sri Lanka introduced the following vision for the maxim use of Information and Communication Technology (ICT) for the development of the government sector:

To enable a more efficient and effective government and enhance government service access to create a more citizen centric government by adopting ICT (ICTA, 2009: 1)

However, the evolution of e-Governance concept in Sri Lanka extends its history to 1983 because the Government of Sri Lanka first acknowledged the necessity for ICT development by way of the National Computer Policy (COMPOL) of 1983. In this regard, the Natural Resources, Energy and Science Authority of Sri Lanka (NARESA) firstly took the initiative of formulating the National Computer Policy. Subsequently, the recognition of the COMPOL by the government paved the way to the founding of the Computer and Information Technology Council of Sri Lanka (CINTEC), which was named later as the Council for Information Technology - by a Parliamentary Act No. 10 of 1984, to function directly under the then President.

The most effective impact on the development of the e-Governance came with the establishment of the Information and Communication Technology Agency of Sri Lanka (ICTA) in July 2003 with the Information and Communication Technology Act No. 27 of 2003, (ICT Act). The CTA was recognized as the legal successor to CINTEC and regarded as the apex ICT institution which is currently performing under the Presidential Secretariat. The above mentioned Act empowered the ICTA to develop and deploy approaches and programmes in both Government and private sectors. This has steered programmes and policies on ICT, which are currently exemplified in the "e-Sri Lanka Development Project" which can be regarded as an important milestone of the development of e-governance in Sri Lanka. This project which was initiated during the period 2002-2005, intended to take the dividends of ICT to all sections of Sri Lankan society and thereby improve the socio economic development. This effort created a conducive environment where government could work in partnership with stakeholders to craft the required infrastructure, and set up e-government services.

In 2004, the Government of Sri Lanka further recognized "e-Sri Lanka Development Project" as the National Information Technology Action Plan of the Government, and reinforced ICTA's legal mandate by allowing ICTA to execute all the components of the e-Sri Lanka Development Project; empower ICTA to recommend to the Cabinet of Ministers the suitable regulatory and policy framework essential for the execution of the e-Sri Lanka expansion scheme and to sustain ICT development in Sri Lanka; and periodically assess the above programme components and make any modifications required in keeping with the Policy as approved by the government (ICTA, 2009: 5). Consequently the Information and Communication Technology (Amendment) Act, No. 33 of 2008 Act was able to empower ICTA to provide recommendations related to articulating of National ICT Policy Frameworks to the Inter-Ministerial Committee which would be submitted for approval by the Cabinet in Parliament.

To understand the presence of and use of e-governance in Sri Lanka, it is necessary to primarily understand the technological advance alongside the development of and expansion of the concept. This includes developments in the telecommunication's sector, changes in the methods how ICT has been used and arrangements made to reduce the digital divide throughout the country such as public policy development, access to information, ICT development, foreign aid, technology expansion and uptake of the public of internet based services. This article reviews these elements by analysing key trends that occurred during the past five years from 2007 - 2013.

E-governance in the Sri Lankan context is a concept that spans for about ten years. It is related to the increase of participation and empowerment of citizens (Hague and Loader 1999). It emerged as a strategy used by various governments throughout the recent past for improved delivery of service

at a lower cost due to simplified operations procedures (Fountain 2006). Sri Lankan Governments have realised e-governance as a vital too which can be used to create an information flow structure that enhances the ability for development opportunities. Until recently, this mode was utilised only through websites to encourage people's participation to government services as a supporting mechanism to the existing conventional procedures. Now e-governance structures which are in place not only act as an information service, but are an interactive service offered to the general public. The service now is extended to the mobile sectors as well.

Prior to 2005 Government websites were existent; however, they served a sole purpose of information dissemination. After the Tsunami disaster of 2004 a distinct change in the nature of the activities of the existing websites and other government bodies commenced. Most organizations which already had active websites focused on creating information dissemination related web services to aid in the relief, rehabilitation and reconstruction activities taking place at the time. Others followed suit and developed websites to assist in the same.

The telecommunications sector in Sri Lanka shifted to the 3G technology in 2005 with Dialog Telekom and Sri Lanka Telecom Mobitel in 2006 with both providing their customers broadband internet services. Until the introduction of mobile broadband, Sri Lankans only had access to public switched telephone network (PSTN) which create a dialed connection to an Internet service provider (ISP) via fixed telephone cables. The expansion of internet and connectivity marked a significant moment in the expansion of e-governance services provided by the government. It was at this stage that many mobile service providers were providing various service packages at cheaper monthly rentals. These were focused on the public as well as the private sector and included provision for internet usage which increased the number of users using the internet.

The various governments in Sri Lanka have seen the importance of ICT for the country since the beginning of the new millennia and in 2003 the initiative was institutionalized In terms of the Information and Communication Technology Act No. 27 of 2003, (ICT Act). This functioned under the Presidential Secretariat for a few years and then was moved to the Ministry of Telecommunication and Information Technology. The ICTA has been mandated to take all necessary measures to implement the Government's Policy and Action Plan in relation to ICT. In terms of Section 6 of the ICT Act, ICTA is required to assist the Cabinet of Ministers in the formulation of the National Policy on ICT and provide all information necessary for its formulation.

One of the most important steps taken by the e-Sri Lanka initiative is to use the ICT to develop the economy of Sri Lanka by reducing poverty and thus improving the quality of life of its citizens. The Government of Sri Lanka makes an effort in realizing this vision through six programme strategy scheme which covers ICT policy, Leadership, Institutional Development Programme, Information Infrastructure, Re-engineering Government, ICT Human Resource Development, ICT Investment and Private Sector Development and e-society. In this regard, the Government, private sector and other stakeholders make a combined effort by accepting that the ICT is the underpinning factor that allows a nation to construct a society with impartial distribution of knowledge and opportunity. Moreover, the Government also recognizes that the ICT as a key contributing factor of the competitive advantage of nations.

The Re-engineering Government project is aiming at providing citizen services in the most efficient manner by improving the way government works by re-engineering and technologically empowering government business processes. These programme tracks key and sustainable improvements in the Government of Sri Lanka's efficiency, transparency, effectiveness, and quality of services. In this regard, it will strengthen and develop fundamental governance and public management reforms as a complement and enabler of required solutions. This will be through public sector operations and processes being re-engineered through strategic implementation of ICT and also instigating innovative ICT based administrative guidelines sharing of data electronically amongst the various government departments, provision of up to date current data to citizens and businesses where the data and services are independent of distance and easy to access and user friendly, 24/7 operations to information sharing and handling, encapsulating transparency to government processes through ICT and access to information, placing the end user first and focusing on user based designs as opposed to the organisational method of work and ensuring service standards are constant and practiced throughout the government e-Governance programmes and initiatives.

The following picture depicts the governance process adopted by Re-Government project of the Government of Sri Lanka.

Present Status of the E-Governance in Sri Lanka

The Government of Sri Lanka, through its e-government project attempts its best to bring all the government services closer to the people. Presently, the Government Information Centre provides all the services accessible to the general public with distinctive A-Z index. For instance, it exhibits the steps required to obtain a birth certificate even for a child who is born in a remote village in Sri Lanka. Consequently, the e-Government program intends to make access to government services much more efficient through streamlined ICT-enabled processes. Presently, e-Governance software include employment both local and foreign, population and e-pensions etc.

The current government initiative is to use ICT as an avenue for empowerment of the rural sector through the e-Sri Lanka Development Initiative which is administered by the Presidential

Figure 1. Governance process adopted by Re-Government project
Source: http://www.icta.lk/en/e-sri-lanka.html

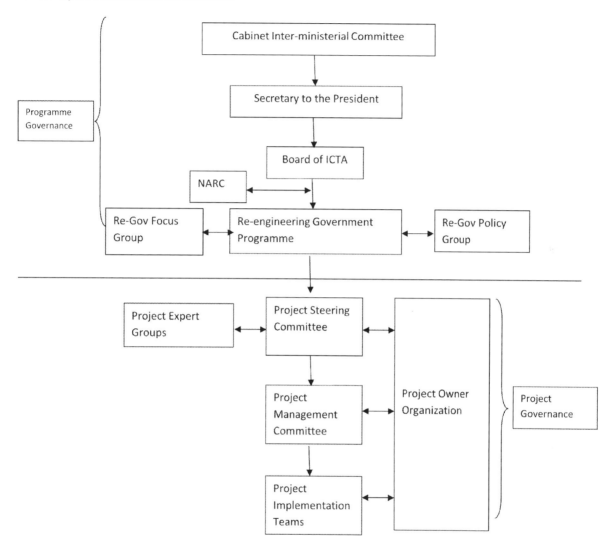

Secretariat is implemented by ICTA, promotes ICT development throughout the country and ensures benefits of technology are not limited to a privileged few. This programme has enabled the youth of the country with access to information with the Nenasala programme which is network of 720 centres located throughout the country which supplements the 3,500 IT labs in schools, across the country that has increased ICT literacy rates in the country from 4% in 2002 is over 40% in 2012. The e-Sri Lanka programme is moving the country towards the SMART Sri Lanka initiative of the Sri Lanka Government which proposes one portal for all services (ICTA, 2013).

In the most recent past, public private relationships such as those between the major telecommunications companies and government institutions have created a change in the development and management of websites and also the services rendered by these institutes. A leader in this segment has been Sri Lanka telecom Mobitel the government mobile telecommunications provider, who have in the past few years, signed NDAs with government organizations such as the Railways, Postal and Immigration departments among others to provide ICT related services to the general public. A significant achievement in this regard has been the electronic travel authorization system for applying visa to Sri Lanka which was developed and maintained by SLT Mobitel (ETA, 2013). Another area is the work with Sri Lanka Railways where the use of Mobiles to obtain ticketing services for the train system has been introduced to ensure ease of access to the railway services in Sri Lanka. Furthermore, endeavors such as the mLearning initiative which was developed by Mobitel in partnership with the University of Colombo to ensure further education to rural areas of the country (Mobitel,2013). Another recent development in this area is m-Chanelling in Government hospitals implemented jointly by the ICT Agency of Sri Lanka and Sri Lanka Mobitel inaugurated at the Dompe District Hospital (ICTA, 2013).

Other telecommunications service providers such as Dialog Axiata, the leading telecommunications service provider in the country has also embarked on providing mobile technology services to the public transport sector for bus ticketing services (Daily News, 2011).

Although most of these projects are fully functional while some are still in the testing phases, the implementation of such initiatives promotes the e-governance aspects of Sri Lanka.

The key areas of e-governance in Sri Lanka according the to the ICTA and these are; ICT policy, Leadership and Institutional Development, Information Infrastructure, Re-engineering Government, ICT Human Resources Capacity Building, ICT Investment and Private Sector Development and eSociety.

In this regard, the e-services which the government has offered can be viewed as follows, 7 administration related services which include finding local government representative data to

government transfer opportunities to grievance handling, 9 agrarian related services which include; permits for livestock import to crop recommendation and reservoir storage details amongst price verifications for produce, 12 employment and skills related services, 7 health related services, 5 national security relate d services and many more with a total of 68 services offered by 39 governmental organisations. All these services can be accessed from the main government eportal or from each organisations website (Government of Sri Lanka 2013).

Mobile e-governance initiatives that the government of Sri Lanka have developed deployed and manage are SMS services for Tea Small Holdings Development Authority, train schedule information, Registration of persons, police clearance applications, price related information for export goods and also domestic produce such as daily vegetable and fish prices, vehicle revenue licence related services and also water level related information of the main river systems. Mobile Application based services are available for the Postal service, all governmental organisation services and railway service. Most Government websites are now mobile compatible as well.

Although there exist many services for information dissemination and citizen participation, there is laps in the communication of such services to the public. Although many services are communicated to the public by the press during their launch events and also information regarding these are posted on walls of most government organizations, the key is to identify how much of these services are being used by the benefactors i.e. the general public. The statistics show that only 188,252 SMS related services, 73721 mobile applications were downloaded and 359 payment services where used up to August 2013 (Government of Sri Lanka eServices, 2013). This indicates that either the general public is unaware of the services, do not have the sufficient knowledge to use them (Heeks, 1999), do not have the infrastructure to use them or do not have a requirement for the services. It could be related to the lack of connectivity in developing countries (Odedra-Straub 2003) or poor IT infrastructures (Tapscott, 1996).

According to Computer Literacy Sri Lanka Report of 2009 of the department of Census and statistics of Sri Lanka, on average, computers are available in one out of ten households. The value 23.6% in urban which is one out of four households and 9.2% in the rural sector while it is 3.1% in the estate sector as of 2009 (CLS 2009). Additionally, according to the Telecommunications Regulatory Commission of Sri Lanka there are 1,693,513 fixed and mobile internet users and 20,234,698 mobile telephone users in the country (TRC, September 2013). This is indicative of the fact that further measure need to be taken to promote e-governance in Sri Lanka. This is in line with research that states that e-governance schemes only work if governing bodies take responsibility to make aware citizens though education related to the value of such programmes (Jaeger and Thompson, 2003).

CONCLUSION

In Sri Lanka, the ICTA will execute the e-Sri Lanka initiative including the five areas information infrastructure building, a supporting environment, improvement of human resources related to ICT, citizen specific service delivery, creating a modern government using ICT for social and economic development and endorsing Sri Lanka as a destination for ICT. A stakeholder fronted approach will be used by the Government of Sri Lanka in implementing this approach using focus groups and also including validations via public-private partnerships. Moreover the Government's attention is directed towards developing a conducive and essential environment to realize the objectives of 'e-Sri Lanka'. Therefore, focus shall be towards creating a pro-active policy and a regulatory environment which supports ICT reform and development, human capacity and

leadership development and promote efforts taken to the stakeholders. The information infrastructure programme which will be created in the future should be sufficient to handle and provide the general public access to modern communication and information which is inexpensive from any location at the time chosen by them thus promoting all Sri Lankans in the global community.

The Re-engineering Government programme showcases sustainable improvements in the Government of Sri Lanka's (GOSL) efficiency, transparency, effectiveness, and quality of services. In this respect, the Government will strengthen and develop fundamental governance and public management reforms. ICT HR Capacity Building programme is expected to assist Re-engineering Government by equipping employees with the required ICT, leadership and management skills and competencies. Furthermore, it is also intended to provide education and learning opportunities for all citizens by utilizing the ICT infrastructure being established by the Information Infrastructure programme.

The ICTA is committed to increase the consumption of ICT in public and private sectors within the country. Further it aims to associate Sri Lanka as priority choice in relation to ICT services and investments. Development of Information and Communication Technologies has made a noteworthy impact on the lives of the Sri Lankan people. Nonetheless, rural Sri Lanka, where the majority is still residing still need further assistance to obtain benefits from these developments. The overall aim the e-Society Programme is to endorse the novel use of ICT to provide the social and economic platform for the most vulnerable persons in Sri Lanka. However, in order to resourcefully accomplish the anticipated goals of the e-Sri Lanka initiative, it is important that policies and guidelines are created to ensure the best use of technology, effective consumption of up-to-date equipment and software innovations, guarantee systems adhere to standards, avoid replication, and promote interoperability and reuse.

REFERENCES

Ali, A. H. (2011). The Power of Social Media in Developing Nations: New Tools for Closing the Global Digital Divide and Beyond. *Harvard Human Rights Journal, 24*(1), 186–219.

Basu, S. (2004). E-Government and Developing Countries: An Overview. *International Review of Law Computers & Technology, 18*(1), 109–132. doi:10.1080/13600860410001674779

Bhatnagar, S. (2003). Access to Information: E-Government. In Hodess, Inowlocki, & Wolfe (Eds.), Global Corruption Report. Profile Books Ltd.

Business Dictionary. (2014). *Computer Literacy*. Retrieved from http://www.business-dictionary.com/definition/computer-literacy.html#ixzz33pThxtOf

Daily News. (n.d.). *Bus ticket booking Via Dialog mobiles*. Retrieved from http://archives.dailynews.lk/2001/pix/PrintPage.asp?REF=/2011/06/24/bus10.asp

Department of Census and Statistics. (2009). *Computer Literacy Statistics*. Retrieved from http://www.statistics.gov.lk/Newsletters/Publication1(Computer%20litalary).pdf

Department of Immigration & Emigration Sri Lanka. (2013). *Electronic travel Authorisation System*. Retrieved from http://www.eta.gov.lk/slvisa/

Fountain, J. (2006). Central Issues in the Political Development of the Virtual State. In *The Network Society: From Knowledge to Policy*. Washington, DC: Brookings Institution Press.

Government of Sri Lanka. (2013). *Services for Citizens 2013*. Retrieved from http://www.gov.lk/web/index.php?option=com_eservices&Itemid=271&lang=en

Hague, B., & Loader, B. D. (1999). *Digital Democracy: Discourse and Decision Making in the Information Age*. London: Routledge.

Hanseth, O. (2002). From systems and tools to networks and infrastructures – From design to cultivation. In *Towards a theory of ICT solutions and its design methodology implications*. Academic Press.

ICTA. (2011). *Annual Report, 2011*. Retrieved from http://www.icta.lk/images/icta/ICTA-Annual-Report-2011.pdf

ICTA. (2013a). *Lanka Gate Statistics, 2013*. Retrieved from http://www.gov.lk/web/images/eservstatis/lankagatestats_aug_2013.pdf

ICTA. (2013b). *m-Chanelling in Government hospitals, 2013*. Retrieved from http://www.icta.lk/en/icta/90-general/1370-mchanelling-in-government-hospitals.html

ICTA. (2013c). *Re-engineering Government (Re-Gov)*. Retrieved from http://www.icta.lk/programmes/re-engineering-government.html

Jaeger, P. T., & Thompson, K. M. (2003). e-Government around the world: Lessons, challenges, and new directions. *Government Information Quarterly, 20*, 389–394. doi:10.1016/j.giq.2003.08.001

Magoulas, G., Lepouras, G., & Vassilakis, C. (2007). *Virtual reality in the e-Society*. London: Springer.

Mobitel Corporate Website. (2013). *Value Added Services, 2013*. Retrieved from http://www.mobitel.lk/vas,jsessionid=588FD813388EB3EEC61B66FF37DD6F4B.liferay1

OECD Library. (2013). *OECD Factbook 2013: Economic, Environmental and Social Statistics*. Retrieved from http://www.oecd-ilibrary.org/sites/factbook-2013-en/08/02/02/index.html,jsessionid=11k47lbu37nuh.x-oecd-live-01?contentType=%2Fns%2FChapter%2C%2Fns%2FStatisticalPublication&itemId=%2Fcontent%2Fchapter%2Ffactbook-2013-65-en&mimeType=text%2Fhtml&containerItemId=%2Fcontent%2Fserial%2F18147364&accessItemIds

Raina, R. (2007). ICT Human Resource Development in Asia and the Pacific. In *Proceedings of Current Status, Emerging Trends, Policies and Strategies, Regional Forum on ICT Capacity Building: Where are we, where are we going and what will it take to fill the gap?* Incheon, Korea: Academic Press.

Rowley, J. (2006). An analysis of the e-service literature: Towards a research agenda. *Internet Research*, *16*(3), 339–359. doi:10.1108/10662240610673736

Telecommunications Regulatory Commission of Sri Lanka. (2013). *Information and Statistics, 2013*. Retrieved from http://www.trc.gov.lk/information/statistics.html

UNESCO. (2010). *eGovernance*. Retrieved from http://portal.unesco.org/ci/en/ev.php-URL_ID=3038&URL_DO=DO_TOPIC&URL_SECTION=201.html

World Bank. (2011). *e-Government*. Retrieved from http://web.worldbank.org/wbsite/external/topics/extinformationandcommunicationandtechnologies/extegovernment/0,contentMDK:20507153~menuPK:702592~pagePK:148956~piPK:216618~theSitePK:702586,00.html

KEY TERMS AND DEFINITIONS

Computer Literacy: Computer literacy is the rank of acquaintance with the fundamental hardware and software concepts that permit someone to make use of personal computers for data entry, word processing, spread sheets, and electronic communications (Business Dictionary, 2014).

Digital Divide: A digital divide is an economic and social gap between different categories of people in a population in their access to, use of, or knowledge of information and communication technologies (ICT) (Ali, 2011).

E-Governance: According to the UNESCO 'E-Governance is the public sector's use of information and communication technologies with the aim of improving information and service delivery, encouraging citizen participation in the decision-making process and making government more accountable, transparent and effective' (UNESCO, 2010).

E-Government: According to the World Bank, "E-Government" refers to the use by government agencies of information technologies (such as Wide Area Networks, the Internet, and mobile computing) that have the ability to transform relations with citizens, businesses, and other arms of government. These technologies can serve a variety of different ends: better delivery of government services to citizens, improved interactions with business and industry, citizen empowerment through access to information, or more efficient government management (WORLDBANK, 2011).

E-Services: Rowley (2006) defines e-services as: "…deeds, efforts or performances whose delivery is mediated by information technology. Such e-service includes the service element of e-tailing, customer support, and service delivery". It shows the utilization of Information and communication technologies in different areas of public services.

E-Society: E-society is a society that has one or more e-Communities engaged in the areas of e-governance related activities which employ information and communication technologies in order to realize a public interests and goals (Margoulas, Lepouras and Vassillakis, 2007).

ICT Human Resource Development: Raina (2007) mentioned that ICT is a skill intensive industry which needs development of human resources related to ICT with close monitoring and development in order to maintain and accelerate the current momentum of ICT led economic development and social transformation.

ICT Investment: According to OECD library 'ICT investment covers the acquisition of equipment and computer software that is used in production for more than one year…. This investment enabled new technologies to enter the production process, to expand and renew the capital stock, and to sustain economic growth' (OECD Library, 2013).

Information Infrastructure: Hanseth (2002) defines information infrastructure as 'a shared, evolving, open, standardized, and heterogeneous installed base'.

Re-Engineering Government -Sri Lanka: Re-engineering Government is a programme which pursues major and sustainable improvements in the Government of Sri Lanka's (GOSL) efficiency, transparency, effectiveness, and quality of services by 1 reinforcing and expanding fundamental governance and public management reforms as a complement and enabler of required solutions (ICTA, 2013).

Chapter 17
Rural–Urban Digital Divide in Romania

Virgil Stoica
Alexandru Ioan Cuza University of Iasi, Romania

Andrei Ilas
Independent Researcher, Romania

ABSTRACT

The last two decades witnessed the sudden raise in importance of Information and Communications Technology (ICT). Some societies have been quick to embrace the benefits of ICT, while others have used the new technologies in a rather limited way. A new term, "digital divide," was coined to describe the gap between the societies using ICT on a large scale and those with limited access. Much was written with respect to the causes of this gap. Factors such as socioeconomic conditions, geographical position, tradition, social and individual values are considered to play major roles in the creation of the digital divide. The vast majority of the studies have focused on the digital performance of cities with far less attention being paid to what was happening in the villages. Arguably, the villages would greatly benefit, and the existent data shows that in many societies a significant rural-urban digital divide is already in place. The goal of this chapter is to assess the urban-rural digital divide in Romania in terms of official website performances by evaluating five components: security and personal data protection, usability, content, type of services, and digital democracy. The authors conclude that in Romania the rural-urban digital divide is extremely large. Based on their conclusions, they offer suggestions for future studies and policies.

1. INTRODUCTION

It is obvious today that the information and communications technology (ICT) is restructuring the way our societies function. Under its influence, traditionally conservative areas are rapidly transforming (Susskind, 2008) and the very nature of

industrial production is changed with the users taking part in the products making (Bruns, 2008).

During the last two decades, e-governance rapidly advanced on the public agendas as it brought fresh promises of bureaucratic quickness and transparency. However, beyond the collective consensus that these promises are essential to a

DOI: 10.4018/978-1-4666-3691-0.ch017

good administration, there are numerous views with respect to the implementation of ICT and its side-effects. For example, although a country may be able to make impressive e-government progresses in a very short period of time (Misuraca et al., 2010), this could lead to a "re-ordering of the state's administrative structures and of government itself" (Lanzara, 2009) with unpredictable short and long-term consequences.

Despite its possible disruptive effect, the ICT is not arriving on an empty field and its effect should not be overestimated. The current features of administrations around the world had been drawn by the fiscal crisis of the 70's who invited the governments to "work better and cost less" (Denhardt, 2008). This finally led to the development of the New Public Management (NPM) that focused on providing public services using a business approach. Recently, the shortcomings of the NPM and the opportunities offered by ITC encouraged scholars to announce the NPM's death (Dunleavy et al., 2006) soon to be replaced by an 'e-paradigm'. At almost a decade after this bold announcement, the e-paradigm did not entirely replaced the old one, a sign that the transformation of bureaucracies around the world is rather incremental.

The e-governance is actually only one phenomenon in a much larger technological revolution that is transforming the very structure of our societies. While some societies fully embarked for this new 'industrial' adventure, others seem to prefer a limited use of the new technologies. As it has been the case throughout the entire modern history in the advent of new technologies, new disparities among societies are created. A new term, digital divide, has been coined to describe the newly appeared "gap between individuals, households, businesses and geographic areas at different socio-economic levels with regard both to their opportunities to access information and communication technologies and to their use of the

Internet for a wide variety of activities"(OECD, 2001). Put differently, the digital divide is about opportunities created or missed by having or using the new technology.

No doubt that in the "knowledge era" the ICT access is vital, but one should not fall in the trap of a technological determinism when explaining the digital divide (Malecki &Moriset, 2008). Indeed, when approaching the digital divide one should not overlook the classic discussion on social inequalities. In fact, the literature studying the ICT related evolutions has proved that the same 'old' factors are playing the significant in this phenomenon too. For instance, having internet connections at home is influenced by income, education, age, race and ethnicity (Mossberger, 2003). Also, while the gender is not reflected into an Internet access divide, the men tend to use more the Internet than the women (Fallows, 2005). The traditional difference between rural and urban is also reflected especially in developing countries where the rural access to Internet represents a problem (Mahan, 2007).

Out of the above literature review we may assert at a theoretical level that the tendency should be for the digital divide to mirror the social inequalities within a society. This is why we should probably agree that if the digital divide do not create, perpetuate or exacerbate social inequalities, the government intervention should not be considered a necessity (Rooksby & Weckert, 2004). In other words, closing the digital divide should be not possible without diminishing other persistent inequalities.

From this perspective, a comprehensive research on digital divide should always try to correlate the digital inequalities with other social inequalities. However, our research objective is more modest, to evaluate the urban - rural digital divide in Romania, in terms of official websites performances

2. AN OVERVIEW OF RURAL E-GOVERNMENT

The rural e-government can be defined as the digital interaction between government and the citizens living in rural areas, the businesses, and other governmental agencies operating in the same area. In fact, rural e-government is nothing but a part of e-government and should be always considered as included in any definition of e-government. However, from a practical point of view, rural e-government raises specific issues, especially in those society where the divide between cities and villages is still in place.

The literature is rather scarce when it comes to rural e-government. Several reasons may be behind this situation. Firstly, the rural e-government could look as a less appealing research theme when compared to national, urban or large cities e-government. Secondly, a large majority of the global rural population lives in poor countries where even basic Internet access is problematic. Thirdly, the population of well-developed countries living in rural areas declined other the years, with the differences between rural and urban being less noticeable. And finally, there is a surprising lack of e-government official data on rural areas.

The few existing researches on e-rural government are depicting the same image: a significant digital divide between rural and urban areas, especially in the developing countries where the access to Internet represents a problem (Gamage & Haplin, 2007; Mahan, 2007). But beyond this general image the researches on rural e-government do not fall into the same category. For instance, the study of e-government in a small Japanese village led the author to the conclusion that the local authorities are right to configure e-government "to address local need" (Thompson, 2002). Similarly, the authors of a paper on governmental actors behavior in rural Texas courts were drawing attention on the importance of adapting e-government to the mandate and responsibilities of the local actors (Doty & Erdelez, 2002). A research made on small US municipalities (less than 100,000 in population), concluded that "e-government adoption is a function of financial, technical, and human resources" (Schwester, 2011). The authors of a UK comparative study suggested that citizens' background is the main obstacle in accessing e-government services offered by a city, while the geographic location of a village is deterring it to offer quality e-government services altogether (Choudrie et al., 2005).

If it is to look at successful rural e-government projects, two countries – India and Australia, both with important parts of their population living in rural or remote areas, are usually mentioned in the literature. In India, where approximately 70% of over one billion population is living in rural areas, the projects are mostly regional and they are aiming to help farmers selling their products, obtaining information or establishing contact over the Internet (Gorla, 2009; Ranjini 2012). Australia has a relatively small rural population of 2.3 millions but scattered all over its immense territory (UN, 2010). In Australia the government launched two initiatives in the area of e-government health: Health-*Institute* – a public portal that provides health related information, and Australian Childhood Immunisation Register – a national electronic database (Henman, 2010).

Taking into consideration the suggestions and conclusions found in the literature, a new research on rural e-government could propose itself to weigh the importance of difference factors such as the economic development of a country, the national or regional policies, the size and location of the village or its financial, technical and human resources (Samah et al., 2010). Being one of the few of its kind, our research has the more limited goal of assessing the level of Romanian rural websites performance by comparing it to their urban counterparts. In order to achieve this goal, we need first to take a look at the national e-government and, hence, to understand the context in which Romanian rural e-government has to evolve.

3. E-GOVERNMENT IN ROMANIA

Romania has joined the European Union (EU) on 1st January 2007. In order to be admitted in EU and, later on, as a Member State, Romania had to comply with EU policies on e-government development by adopting laws, establishing national agencies and implementing national strategies (Table 1).

In 2006, the management component of the Strategic Institutional Plan for the period 2007-2009 has been adopted (MCIS, 2006). The document noticed that Romania had a particular situation when compared to other EU Member States. Hence, in a majority of EU states the existent unique fixed-line phone provider has been designated as universal internet provider due to the fact that it had a well-developed network. In Romania, although a monopolist fixed-line phone provider existed, it did not covered the entire territory. Therefore, the costs to connect a new home to this network would have been considerable. Moreover, a third part of Romania's territory is mountainous, a fact that makes the extension of the network even more difficult. Last but not least, a majority of Romanians had a low purchasing power and there were not enough budgetary resources to cover the costs for the universal service.

Table 1. Political statements, laws, and administrative bodies regarding e-Government

Year	Event
1991	The Government adopts an Act that establishes a framework for Romania`s evolution as information society.
1992	The National Commission of Informatics is created
1992	The White Book of Informatics is published
1995	The Government reiterates the goal of establishing an information society
1996	The National Strategy regarding the information society is published
2001	Law no. 544/2001 regulating free access to public information is adopted
2001	Law no. 455/2001 conferring equal legal value to the electronic signature as for the classic one is adopted
2001	Law no. 677/2001 establishing a framework for the use of data on private life is adopted
2002	Law no. 365/2002 establishing the foundations of e-commerce is adopted
2002	The Regulatory National Authority for Communications is created
2003	Law no. 161/2003 creating a system for fighting e-crime is adopted
2003	Law no. 304/2003 establishing legal provisions for contracts between internet providers and internet users is adopted
2004	The law no. 506/2004 extends the application of the Law no. 677/2001 with specific provisions regarding the electronic field.
2004	The first reference to e-government is included in a governing program.
2005	The National Authority for the Supervision of Personal Data Utilization is created.
2007	Law no. 109/2007 establishing a legal framework for the reuse of documents created by public authorities is adopted
2007	The Agency for Informational Society Services that controls informatics system for the national e-services is created.
2007	The Strategic Institutional Plan of the Ministry of Communications mentions, for the first time, the existence of the rural – urban digital gap.
2008	The National Center for Electronic Personalized Passports is created.
2009	A governing program that contains detailed plans for e-government improvements receives parliamentary support.
2012	A new governing program promises better broadband connections for disadvantaged areas
2013	The 2013-2016 governing program acknowledges the existence of the rural – urban digital divide, and announces measures to close it.

The same Strategic Institutional Plan noticed that more than 40% of Romanians are living in villages and estimated the digital gap between rural and urban as the multiple of a number from 10 to 15. The Plan indicated that for small communities the development of the fixed-line broadband connections could favour their economic and social integration. These communities could have the chance of accessing new goods and services and be part of digital economy and information society.

After one year, a new document on the management component of the Strategic Institutional Plan for the period 2008-2011 has been proposed by the same ministry (MCIS, 2007). This new document is enumerating the closing of the rural/urban digital gap among its objectives.

The governing programs from February and May 2012 are indirectly acknowledging this situation: the Romanian Government (RG) should support better broadband connections for disadvantaged areas (RG, 2012; RG 2013). However, there is no specification if these areas are rural areas or certain geographical regions of the country. The 2013-2016 governing program acknowledges the existence of the rural – urban digital divide, and announces measures to close it.

Despite this wide legislation, important number of governmental agencies, and generous national policies, the e-government in Romania is in an early stage of development (Stoica & Ilas, 2012). The e-Romania website designed to provide citizens access to all national, local, and rural administrative services was inactive for three years after its launch. The aforementioned website became functional only in January 2014. Despite a significant financial investment (over 12 million euros), the site is not performing well; it should be able to support around 50,000 simultaneous, but it seems it fails well before this number. (HN, 2014)

According to the Administrative and Regulatory National Authority for Communications (ARNAC), Romania has 3.8 millions fixed-line broadband connections with 2.8 millions in cities and the rest of one million in villages (ARNAC, 2013). The 2011 census organized by the National Institute of Statistics (NIS), is showing that in Romania 46.03% of Romanian population are living in villages (NIS, 2011). These data indicate that in the rural areas there are 11.0 fixed-line broadband connections per 100 inhabitants compared to 25.44 per city inhabitants. As can be seen in Table 2, the digital gap seemed to reduce over the last years, but the rural areas are still lagging behind the urban ones. (ARNAC, 2013)

4. PROJECTS TARGETING ROMANIAN RURAL AREAS

The Romanian government has been rather shy in directly addressing the rural-urban digital divide issue and in supporting e-government development in rural areas. However, the government was involved in projects, supported by USAID and the World Bank, that indirectly touched on these issues.

Starting with June, 2002, until September, 2005, USAID developed in Romania a project called *Romania Information Technology Initiative: Policy* (RITIP). When the project started, the ICTs market was poorly regulated and Romanians had little access to ICTs due to prohibitive prices.

Table 2. Fixed-line broadband connections in urban and rural areas in 2011 and 2013

	2011		2013	
	Urban	Rural	Urban	Rural
Fixed-line broadband connections [millions]	2.5	0.6	2.8	1.0
Fixed-line broadband connections/100 inhabitants	23.1	6.8	25.4	11.0

Therefore, the USAID's project was meant to assist Romania's Government in establishing a functional policy and regulatory framework for ICTs based on international best practices.

Within RITIP, Romanian government received legal and technical assistance in order to establish a regulatory and policy framework. In addition, RITIP offered training for Romanian regulators, gave the opportunity to public servants to meet with members of Federal Communications Commission and International Telecommunications Union, provided technical assistance in preparing the legislation for the reform in telecommunications and e-commerce, assisted with the setting-up of the National Regulatory Agency. At the request of Romanian officials, an e-Government guide for Romania public servants has been developed under the umbrella of the same project.

An additional RITIP's objective was to help with the expansion of rural access to telecommunications and Internet through assistance to Romanian government. Thus, several telecenters were designed and successfully launched in five underserved regions. Based on this pilot experience, RITIP recommended that the local authorities of each municipality should have the responsibility for telecenters' management. In September 2005, the government accepted these recommendations and, following a public procedure, installed 40 telecenters in rural localities with no or few telephone connections.

The World Bank asked the RITIP to share lessons learned regarding the design and implementation of telecenters. Based on this feedback, the World Bank approved in November 2005 a 60 million dollars projects called *Knowledge Economy Project* (KEP). The main objective of KEP was to accelerate the participation of knowledge disadvantaged communities in the knowledge-based society and economy in Romania. This project intended to establish at least 200 Local Community e-Networks based in schools and libraries for education, business and public communications in disadvantaged communities.

These e-Networks would operate under private management and are expected to achieve financial self-sustainability.

In order to improve digital literacy, the KEP aimed to establish at least 200 multi-purpose local e-networks (LENs). LENs should serve as "knowledge-centers", providing information, services and benefits to citizens and small businesses in disadvantaged communities. Approximately 45% of the most disadvantaged communities were eligible to participate in the project. A typology of 13 community types has been developed during project preparation (based on socio-economic, technological, education, and business factors). Communities prepared an application, including a three-year development plan indicating the level of public subsidy anticipated (central and local). Selected communities were determined through a competitive process, with their applications being evaluated accordingly to an agreed scoring matrix. LEN are public resources, available to communities, with access governed by a set of established and agreed rules. LENs are publicly owned, but from the outset open to private initiative. However, according to the Implementation Status & Results Report, released in 19th of August 2012 only 37 LCeNs were created, "the project progress towards project development objective beeing moderately satisfactory, while the overall implementation progress of the project remains unsatisfactory given the low levels of commitment and disbursement"(World Bank).

Development and promotion of e-government services was another component of KEP. The project financed the full-scale implementation and deployment of a small number of e-government services, intialy provided through LENs. This included the development of an appropriate infrastructure, implementation of a compatible legislative framework, development of an institutionalized and technological platform, and the training of human resources. An online system for notifications and authorizations for family associations and self-employed individuals is also included in this project. In a second phase, these services should be developed at a national level. However, the same report admited that " no progress have been made in implementing the e-government activites" (World Bank, 2012).

The KEP was also supposed to develop an integrated network for citizen status information and documentation. The project would finance the development of the "Public Community Services through the National System for the Personal Evidence". Citizens using LENs would have been able to apply online for birth and marriage certificates and enable individuals to update marriage status, deaths of family members, etc. Applicants should have been able to track the progress of their application online. Civil servants operating the system were trained in the selection of communities in which LENs have been established. However, according to the last Implementation Status & Results Report this activity has not started due to the insufficiency of budget (World Bank, 2012).

Another similar project is the Project RO-NET. The goal of the project is to build a national infrastructure in the poor areas of the country with the financial aid of European structural funds. Within this project, the Romanian Government launched in 2011 the National Broadband Strategy with the aim of increasing the number of households connected to the broadband to 80% before 2015. The Ministry for Informational Society acknowledged that the broadband access is rather limited in Romania, especially in the rural areas. The Ministry believes that this situation is triggered by the small number of computers in the rural areas and the reduced purchasing power of the rural households. (MSI, 2011). Although ambitious, and ultimately extremely useful, the project did not reach in three years the implementation phase.

It is clear from the data presented above that even the projects where external organisms have been or are involved are enjoying a limited success. It appears that both at national and local level the public officials are not able to contribute to the development of rural e-government.

5. RESEARCH METHODOLOGY

The specific aim of this paper is to evaluate the performance difference between the official web pages of cities and villages. In order to asses Romania's rural and urban website performances, we have evaluated official websites of Romanian villages and cities, closely following Mark Holzer and Seang-Tae Kim's model described in their study *Digital Governance in Municipalities Worldwide* (2005).

In Romania, there are 2856 rural settlements, and 308 towns and cities. At the time of the study, only 1128 of villages (39,49%) had functional web pages, compared with 237 cities (76.94%). Our research examines e-government performance following a five-level incremental model of e-government evolution: the first level is that of providing information, the second one adds the information exchange, followed by providing services, service integration and, in the end, political participation (Moon, 2002). The criteria used for assessing the villages' websites have five components: security and personal data protection, usability, contents, type of provided services, and digital democracy. The study used 98 measures, forty-three of them being dichotomous. For non-dichotomous questions (mostly 0/2 and few 0/3), a scale of 3 or 4 steps has been utilised (0,1, 2 or 0, 1, 2, 3), where: 0 indicates that the site provides no information regarding the asked question; 1 simply indicates that the information exists; 2 indicates that the information can be downloaded (files or folders, audio or video documents); and 3 indicates the possibility of on-line transactions (payments for goods or services, demands for licences, existence of certain data bases, use of electronic signature). The final score is the sum of all items, the maximum raw score being 219, and a maximum weighted score being 100. Weighting was necessary, because each of the five dimensions had a different number of questions (18 in the case of security and 20 for all other dimensions), as well as different scores (25, 32, 48, 59, 55). The five dimensions were given equal weight, not taking into account the number of questions used when assessing it. Thus, after weighting, each dimension was able to take on scores from 0 to 20.

The "security and personal data protection" has been operationalised through several concepts: public statements concerning personal data protection, authentication, encryption, the management of collected data and the use of cookies. Easy-to-understand and easy-to-use design, length of access page, structure, the extent to which it addresses particular target audiences, and the ability to search for information on the site were the concepts behind "usability's" operationalization. As for "contents", the accent was placed on the possibility of accessing recent information, official documents, reports, publications and audio/video materials. In the "services" category were included the transactions that might occur between local administration and citizens, or between local administration and business owners, as well as lodging requests for various authorisations (*E.g.* permits, licences). The "digital democracy" category was operationalised as it follows: instruments for citizens to provide feedback to local officials, debates on the village webpage concerning local public policies, and existence of a system for measuring citizen satisfaction and governmental performance.

This evaluation scale has been applied to a sample of Romanian rural communities that during the referring period (June 2 to June 15, 2013), had a functional webpage. A random sample of three rural and urban websites has been extracted out of each of the 41 Romania's counties (except the capital, Bucharest).

The process of data gathering has been accomplished with the aid of our undergraduate and master students of the Political Science Department of Alexandru Ioan Cuza University of Iasi. The evaluation grid included grading examples for each item, the operators being given detailed explanations on the grading system. In order to ensure the reliability of the instrument and its application, each website has been evaluated at least twice by different operators. If the difference between the scores was larger than 5 points (5% of the maximum value of the scale), the website underwent one more assessment.

6. RESULTS OF THE STUDY

Table 3 shows some descriptive statistics obtained from 246 surveyed web pages (123 from rural settlements and 123 from cities), for their general scores as well as for each of the five dimensions. It can be seen that the amplitude of scores is much

Table 3. General score and the scores for the five dimensions of Romanian rural and urban websites

	General Score		Security		Usability		Content		Services		Digital Democracy	
	Rural	Urban	Rural	Urban	Rural	Urban	Rural	Urban	Rural	Urban	Rural	Urban
Mean	11.67	18.86	0.34	1.09	7.44	9.40	2.49	4.30	0.80	2.42	0.60	1.78
Median	10.97	17.63	0.00	0.00	7.5	9,38	2.40	4.00	0.68	2.03	0.36	0.73
Standard Deviation	4.41	8.15	0.86	2.15	2.32	3.03	1.53	2.51	0.84	2.49	0.86	1.96
Minimum	2.60	4.78	0.00	0.00	1.25	3.13	0.00	0.00	0.00	0.00	0.00	0
Maximum	25.4	43.49	7.10	9.68	14.38	16.25	6.80	11.6	3.05	16.1	4.36	7.62
Confidence Interval (95%)	10.89-12.45	17.41-20.31	0.19-0.49	0.71-1.47	7.03-7.85	8.86-9.94	2.22-2.76	3.85-4.75	0.65-0.95	1.98-2.86	0.45-0.75	1.43-2.13

smaller in rural than in urban areas (22.8 versus 38.71), standard deviation being close to half, this is indicating an increased homogeneity of quality web pages in villages.

The highest score is obtained by the rural websites was 25.4, while the lowest score was 2.60. The same parameter for cities varies between 43.49 and 4.78. Taking into account that the maximum possible score is 100 and the fact that 119 out of 123 rural websites have scores lower than 20 (only 77 of urban websites are in the same situation), it is clear that Romanian rural e-government performance is very low.

The fact that the rural average score is only 11.67, and that 97 from 123 rural websites have obtained scores lower than 15 suggests that local authorities are only incidentally interested in e-government. Because our research examined only a sample and not all rural websites, the mean scores should be regarded as estimations. However, we can be 95% sure that the real mean of the general score is between 10.89 and 12.45 (Table 1).

Figure 1 presents the histogram of total scores distribution on class boundaries of 3 units. The average for rural global scores is 11.67 with a standard deviation of 4.41 and a median of 10.97. The fact that the median is lower than the average shows that the score distribution leans to the right; the few bigger scores are influencing the average score in such a way that it has a bigger value than the median. The category with most scores are those between 9 -12, where no less than 34 villages can be found, which is almost a third. The same shape of the histogram can be observed for urban websites. However, the chart for urban scores is skewed more to the right, 21 cities having a better performance than the best rural webpage.

When it comes to "security and personal data protection", the best sites barely reached 7.10 points of a maximum of 20 (Table 3). The average was 0.34 with a median of zero. In fact, 88 of the 123 rural web pages do not even mention personal data protection and 24 have only a very

Figure 1. Score distribution histogram for Romanian rural websites

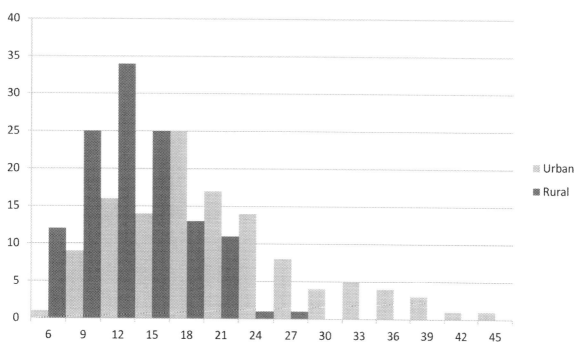

brief note. Only five sites are allowing users to fill in a form on their personal data protection. This absence of concern for information security could be triggered by the fact that the web administrators are seeing the webpages as a one-way platforms of providing information and, consequently, the personal data protection is not relevant.

The highest score for "usability", in the rural areas is 14.38 points of a maximum of 20. The average score for this dimension is 7.44 points with a standard deviation of 2.32; the median was 7.50 with an almost symmetrical distribution. Most websites have relatively brief access pages/ homepages of no more than two screens in length; the sitemap is absent for the majority of websites, but a navigation bar is available on each page. The homepage often displays useless photographs (E.g. mayors participating at different events), which further hinders the access. The audience is never targeted as groups (E.g. locals, tourists, business owners, elders, young people or individuals with special needs). Only few sites offer the opportunity of filling in online forms. Fourteen official pages have a search engine but without the option of sorting the results by relevance or by any other criterion. Twenty two of the websites show the date of latest update; for the rest, this date has to be inferred from the latest press release or document published.

The highest score for "contents" is 6.80 for villages, with an average of 2.49, a standard deviation of 1.53, and a median of 2.40. Most websites provide the City Hall address and some contact details, as well as a list (most time a partial one) of the local council decisions/resolutions. Some information on the local budget can be found only in 17 websites. A good part of information regards past events, while future ones are announced in a few words and are related, as a rule, to village's most festive moments (village holiday and religious celebrations).The minutes of the local council meetings are absent. Almost a third of the websites offers information in at least two languages (Romanian and English), but

there are several websites in three, four or even six languages (Romanian, English, French, Italian, Hungarian and German). Only one site presents information about possible natural disasters. No site offers access options for those with sight or hearing disabilities. There are no websites containing information related to day-to-day life aspects, such as traffic information in the area. The most surprising fact is that 20 rural websites have almost no information: only the name of the community and, in some cases, the address of the local council or the mayor's name. Some websites have menus, but without content.

The highest score for "online services" is 3.05 (Table 3) with an average of 0.80, a standard deviation of 0.84, and a median of 0.68. In fact, the websites of 42 rural settlements do not offer any online services. Other 30 websites are offering only one service: either for requesting information or for lodging complaints. Only 8 of the assessed web pages provide access to databases. We are aware of only one Romanian village, Luncavita, where the locals are paying their utility bills using the official webpage as a portal. The village decided to join the National System of Electronic Payment of Taxes and it is mainly the locals working in other countries or parts of Romania that using this system (Romania Libera, 2012).

The highest score on "digital democracy" is 4.36 points (Table 3). All the other websites obtained scores below 3.27. The average score for participation is 0.60, with a standard deviation of 0.86, and a median of 0.36. A number of 60 out of 123 websites offered no online feedback option. Only two websites are providing online forms for commentaries on local authorities' performance. Nine websites have discussion forums open to citizens, but local officials are rarely present. The websites do not have online opinion polls, do not offer a platform for a digital referendum or for an online petition.

The scores obtained for each dimension of the performance index are lower for rural than for urban (Table 4). The closest scores are on

Table 4. Rural and urban e-government differences by dimensions

	Rural	Urban	%
General score	11.67	18.86	61.61
Security	0.34	1.09	220.58
Usability	7.44	9.40	26.34
Contents	2.49	4.30	72.69
Services	0.80	2.42	202.50
Digital democracy	0.60	1.78	196.66

"usability" (7.44 for rural and 9.40 for urban, a difference of 26%). For the other dimensions, the urban scores are larger than the rural ones from 72% for "content", up to 220% for 'security". All differences are statistically significant.

When comparing the five dimensions score (Table 3), it can be noticed that "usability" obtained both the highest individual score (14.38 for rural, and 16.25 for urban) and the highest average score (7.44, respectively 9.40). The performance decreases drastically when assessing the "content" (2.49 and 4.30) and goes to merely insignificant for the other three dimensions: 0.80 for "services", 0.60 for "participation" and 0.34

for "security and personal data protection". For urban websites, these three dimensions scores very low (2.42, 1.78, and 1.09 from 20), but several times better than for rural websites. In other words, Romanian rural e-government scores relatively well on the technical dimension ("usability") but very poorly on the four substantive dimensions of e-government.

Romanian urban and rural e-government are identical when comparing the order of the scores obtained for each of the five dimensions: the best performance is obtained for "usability", followed in order by "contents", "services", "digital democracy" and "security" (Figure 2). This order

Figure 2. The five dimensions of e-government score, for rural and urban

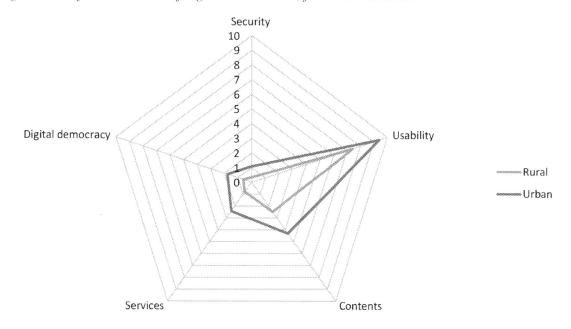

suggests what is happening behind the webpage. At some moment, the page is created with the goal of openness and attraction towards a great number of citizens ("usability"). It is, after all, a cheap way for local officials to reach the electors. Page is filled with some information to make it more attractive ("contents"), but without a preoccupation for e-services ("services"), for the feedback that citizen could provide ("digital democracy") or for protecting the data on citizen gathered while they are using the webpage ("security").

In order to analyze in depth the differences between rural and urban the sample of cities was divided into four groups: very small towns (under 10.000 inhabitants), small towns (10.001 to 50.000 inhabitants), mediums (50.001 to 100.000 inhabitants) and large ones (over 100.001 inhabitants). For the 21 very small cities, the mean score is 12.36. The same statistic is 15.02 for small cities (34 cities), 19.96 for medium size cities (44), and 27.97 for large cities (24). The null hypothesis states that there is no difference regarding the mean general score among the four groups of cities and the group of villages.

In order to test this hypothesis, we have applied an ANOVA test. P-value was almost zero which indicated that there are differences between the average scores obtained by each group. Which are the groups having significant differences in between? In order to find the answer to this question we used Tukey Kramer test which consists in successive comparisons between groups. As it may be observed in Table 5, at 0.05 degree of significance there are important differences between most groups, except the two pairs: mean scores for rural and very small and small cities are much alike – 11.67 and 12.36, as well as between very small cities an small cities – 12.36 and 15.02.

The same statistical test was used for the five dimensions of e-government score (Table 6). The image becomes clearer: only large cities scores every time better than other groups for each dimension; medium cities score better than smaller settlements for four dimensions (except

"security"), and small cities for two dimensions. These results are suggesting that, when it comes to e-government performance in Romania, size maters, and not the type of locality, if it is named village, town or city.

The differences between groups are being originated in administrative, financial and human capacities which are considerable bigger for large cities and much smaller for the others. A bigger budget permits additional founds either for the electronic communication department which administrates the official city web site, or for buying such services from the market. In addition, a larger city has a more complex personnel diagram that implies employees grounded in a variety of fields. Moreover, large cities are attracting personnel with higher qualification, better fitted for developing and maintaining an official website.

The differences from inside the groups might be explained based on officials' interest towards electronic government. However, these differences are much smaller between villages, only large and medium cities having among them some extreme values. For some incumbents of local power, official websites became, probably, instruments of political market free of any charge. Considering the five dimensions used in calculation of the global score, we may assert that "services" and "digital democracy" are the ones with lowest scores. This indicates that the official web page is often used only as a method of pointing out mayors' activities.

CONCLUDING REMARKS

The present study allows several conclusions regarding the Romanian rural – urban digital divide; it also suggests new directions of research.

Romanian Rural areas are older, less educated and poorer than the urban areas. This provides conditions for the existence of significant digital divide between urban and rural communities. The results of our research permit us to conclude that Romanian rural e-government is in an early

Table 5. Tukey Kramer outputs

Tukey Kramer Multiple Comparisons							
	Sample	Sample		Absolute	**Std. Error**	Critical	
Group	Mean	Size	Comparison	Difference	**of Difference**	Range	Results
1	11.67813	123	Group 1 to Group 2	16.29978	**0.85340672**	3.2941	**Means are different**
2	27.97792	24	Group 1 to Group 3	8.285960	**0.67179213**	2.5931	**Means are different**
3	19.96409	44	Group 1 to Group 4	3.351281	**0.74099176**	2.8602	**Means are different**
4	15.02941	34	Group 1 to Group 5	0.691393	**0.90297268**	3.4855	**Means are not different**
5	12.36952	21	Group 2 to Group 3	8.013825	**0.97046095**	3.746	**Means are different**
			Group 2 to Group 4	12.94850	**1.01958746**	3.9356	**Means are different**
Other Data			Group 2 to Group 5	15.60839	**1.14273771**	4.411	**Means are different**
Level of significance	0.05		Group 3 to Group 4	4.934679	**0.87324694**	3.3707	**Means are different**
Numerator d.f.	5		Group 3 to Group 5	7.594567	**1.01432297**	3.9153	**Means are different**
Denominator d.f.	241		Group 4 to Group 5	2.659888	**1.06142132**	4.0971	**Means are not different**
MSW	29.25103						
Q Statistic	3.86						

Table 6. General score and the scores for the five dimensions of Romanian rural and different types of cities

	General Score	**Security**	**Usability**	**Content**	**Services**	**Digital Democracy**
Rural	**11.678***	**0.350***	**7.462***	**2.501***	**0.804***	**0.596***
Very small cities	**12.369***	**0.553***	**6.892***	**2.580***	**1.447***	**0.986***
Small cities	15.029	**0.930***	8.369	**3.051***	**1.582***	1.521
Medium cities	19.964	**1.012***	10.07	4.763	2.647	1.634
Large cities	27.978	1.963	11.85	6.733	4.053	3.401

*At a level of significance of 0.05, means differences are not statistically relevant.

development phase. Despite the declared national interest for a rural e-government policy, the reality is not gratifying. There are very few laws and by-laws targeting local e-government and no national strategy is designed to close this gap and the rural authorities are lacking the necessary resources for improving their e-government capabilities.

In terms of infrastructure, the number of broad-band connections has increased in recent years in rural areas. But even if the gap concerning this indicator between villages and cities was reduced to some extent, it still remains very high.

On the supply side of government official web page content, the differences between the major towns and villages are The medium general score is 18.86 for cities and only 11.67 for villages. Our empirical research showed that only the dimensions of "usability" (7.44 out of 20 points) and "content" (2.49 out of 20 points) are registering significant scores. There is practically no concern for "security and personal data protection" (the mean score is 0.34). It is almost impossible to identify electronic services for rural communities (0.80), and citizens do not have online opportunities to express their opinion regarding the way the community is run (0.61). For the same dimensions, cities score much better: 9.40 for "usability", 4.30 for "content", 1.09 for "security", 2.42. for "services", and 1.78 for "digital democracy". All of these differences are statistically relevant. This suggests how local officials are seeing e-government. The webpage is probably used to attract citizens and to promote the local official. This is why "usability" obtained the highest score. In the same vein, "contents" obtained a reasonable score because some information has to be provided in order to keep the users on the page. This philosophy conducts to a lack of interest for e-services, for the citizens' feedback or for protecting personal data.

The analysis of localities size influence on web pages performance shows that the differences between villages and very small towns (up to 10,000 inhabitants) and even between villages and small towns (up to 50,000 inhabitants) are insignificant. In a larger perspective, the size does matter for Romanian e-government performance: a big city is more likely to score better that a medium city which in turn is more likely to score better than a small town, a very small town, or a village. Therefore, what really matters is not the name of the town or village, but the size of locality.

This last observation could lead to new practical approaches. In the absence of a national action plan on rural e-government, the villages and small towns could put together their resources and build a single webpage for several communities.

REFERENCES

Adams, N., Stubbs, V., & Woods, V. (2005). Psychological barriers to Internet usage among older adults in the UK. *Medical Informatics and the Internet in Medicine*, 30(1), 3–17. doi:10.1080/14639230500066876 PMID:16036626

Adriani, F., & Becchetti, L. (2003). Does the Digital Divide Matter? The role of ICT in cross-country level and growth estimates. *CEIS Tor Vergata Research Paper No. 4*. Retrived from http://ssrn.com/abstract=382983 or http://dx.doi.org/10.2139/ssrn.382983

ARNAC (Administrative and Regulatory National Authority for Communications). (2013). *Internet Access Services: Report of Statistical Data. January 1 - June 30, 2013*. Retrieved from file:///E:/Raport%20DS%20sem%20I%202013.pdf

Barry, A. (2001). *Political Machines: Governing a Technological Society*. London: The Athlone Press.

Benjamin, M. (2001). Re-examining the Digital Divide. In *Communications Policy in Transition: The Internet and Beyond* (pp. 321–348). Cambridge, MA: MIT Press.

Bruns, A. (2008). *Blogs, Wikipedia, Second Life, and Beyond*. New York: Peter Lang.

Chin, M. D., & Fairlie, R. W. (2004). *The determinants of the Global Digital Divide: A Cross-Country Analysis of Computer and Internet Penetration*. Cambridge, MA: National Bureau of Economic Research.

Choudrie, J., Weerakkody, V., & Jones, S. (2005). Realising e-government in the UK: Rural and urban challenges. *The Journal of Enterprise Information Management*, *18*(5), 568–585. doi:10.1108/17410390510624016

Compaine, B. (2001). *The Digital Divide: Facing a crisis or creating a mith?* Cambridge, MA: MIT Press.

Cullen, R. (2006). E-government and the Digital Divide. In *Comparative Perspectives on E-Government: Serving Today and Building for Tomorrow* (pp. 289–313). Lanham, MD: The Scarecrow Press.

Denhardt, R. B. (2008). *Theories of Public Organization*. Belmont, MA: Thomson Wadsworth.

Doty, P., & Erdelez, S. (2002). Information micro-practices in Texas rural courts: methods and issues for E-Government. *Government Information Quarterly*, *19*, 369–387. doi:10.1016/S0740-624X(02)00121-1

Dunleavy, P., Margetts, H., Bastow, S., & Tinker, J. (2006). *Digital Era Governance: IT Corporations, the State, and E-Government*. New York: Oxford University Press. doi:10.1093/acprof:oso/9780199296194.001.0001

Fallows, D. (2005). *How Women and Men use the internet*. Retrieved from http://www.pewinternet.org/Reports/2005

Ferr, E., Cantamessa, M., & Polucci, E. (2005). Urban Versus Regional Divide: Comparing and Classifying Digital Divide. In E-government: Towards electronic democracy (pp. 81-90). Springer.

Gamage, P., & Haplin, E. (2007). E-Sri Lanka: Bridging the digital divide. *The Electronic Library*, *25*(6), 693–710. doi:10.1108/02640470710837128

Gorla, N. (2009). A Survey of Rural e-Government Projects in India: Status and Benefits. *Information Technology for Development*, *15*(1), 52–58. doi:10.1002/itdj.20064

Hargittai, E. (2002). Beyond logs and surveys: In-depth measures of people's web use skills. *Journal of the American Society for Information Science and Technology Perspectives*, *53*(14), 1239–1244. doi:10.1002/asi.10166

Henman, P. (2010). *Governing Electronically: E-Government and the Reconfiguration of Public Administration, Policy and Power*. London: Palgrave Macmillan. doi:10.1057/9780230248496

HN. (2014). *Cum se lauda autoritatile ca portalul eRomania sustine peste 50.000 de utilizatori simultan, cand de fapt site-ul devine inaccesibil la 100 de cereri simultane*. Retrieved from http://economie.hotnews.ro/stiri-telecom-16800984-video-test-cum-lauda-autoritatile-portalul-eromania-sustine-peste-50-000-utilizatori-simultan-cand-fapt-site-devine-inaccesibil-100-cereri-simultane.htm

Holzer, M., & Kim, S. (2005). *Digital Governance in Municipalities Worldwide (2005): A Longitudinal Assessment of Municipal Websites Through the World*. Retrieved from www.andromeda.rutgers.edu/~egovinst/Website/researchpg.htm

ITU (International Telecommunication Union). (2011). *The World in 2011 – ICT Facts and Figures*. Retrieved from http://www.itu.int/ITU-D/ict/facts/2011/material/ICTFactsFigures2011.pdf

Lanzara, G. F. (2009). Building digital institutions: ICT and the rise of assemblages in government. In *ICT and Innovation in the Public Sector: European Studies in the Making of E-Government* (pp. 9–39). London: Palgrave Macmillan.

Layne, K., & Lee, J. (2001). Developing Fully Functional E-Government: A Four Stage Model. *Government Information Quarterly*, *18*(2), 122–136. doi:10.1016/S0740-624X(01)00066-1

Lazarus, W., & Mora, F. (2000). *Online content for low-income and underserved americans: The digital divide's new frontier*. Santa Monica, CA: The Children's Partnership.

Mahan, A. (2007). Conclusion: ICT and Pro-poor Strategies and Research. In *Digital Poverty: Latin American and Caribbean Perspectives* (pp. 141–156). Ottawa, Canada: International Development Research Center. doi:10.3362/9781780441115.007

Malecki, E. J., & Moriset, B. (2008). *The Digital Economy: Business organization, production processes, and regional developments*. London: Routledge.

MCSI (Ministry of Communications and Information Society). (2006). *Strategic Institutional Plan: Management Component*. Retrieved from http://www.mcsi.ro/Minister/Despre-MCSI/Unitatea-de-Politici-Publice/Documente-programatice# MCSI (Ministry of Communications and Information Society). (2007). *Strategic Institutional Plan: Budgetary Component*. Retrieved from http://www.mcsi.ro/Minister/Despre-MCSI/Unitatea-de-Politici-Publice/Documente-programatice# MSI (Ministry for Informational Society). (2011). *Proiectul RO-NET - Construirea unei infrastructuri naționale de broadband în zonele defavorizate, prin utilizarea fondurilor structural*. Retrieved from http://www.mcsi.ro/Minister/Proiect-Ro-NET/Documente-suport/Documente-suport# Milakovich, E. M. (2012). *Digital Governance: New technologies for Improving Public Service and Participation*. New York: Routledge.

Min, S.-J. (2010). From the Digital Divide to the Democratic Divide: Internet Skills, Political Interest, and the Second-Level Digital Divide in Political Internet Use. *Journal of Information Technology & Politics*, *7*(1), 22–35. doi:10.1080/19331680903109402

Misuraca, G., Rossel, P., & Glassey, O. (2010). Overcoming barriers to innovation in e-government: The Swiss way. In *Understanding e-government in Europe: Issues and challenges* (pp. 202–218). New York: Routlegde.

Moon, M. J. (2002). The Evolution of E-government Among Municipalities: Rhetoric or Reality. *Public Administration Review*, *62*(4), 424–433. doi:10.1111/0033-3352.00196

Mossberger, K., Tolbert, C., & Stansbury, M. (2003). *Virtual Inequality: Beyond the Digital Divide*. Washington, DC: Georgetown University Press.

NIS (National Institute of Statistics). (2011). *The Population and Housing Census of 2011*. Retrieved from http://www.recensamantromania.ro/rezultate-2

Norris, P. (2001). *Digital Divide: Civic Engagement, information poverty, and the internet worldwide*. New York: Cambridge University Press. doi:10.1017/CBO9781139164887

O'Hara, K., & Stevens, D. (2006). *Inequality.com: Power, poverty and the digital divide*. Oxford, UK: Oneworld Publications.

OECD. (2001). *Understanding the Digital Divide*. Paris: Organisation for Economic Co-operation and Development.

Ranjini, S. (2012). Innovation in services delivery in rural areas in India. *International Journal of Management Research and Review*, *2*(1), 143–153.

RG (Romanian Government). (2012). *Government Program*. Retrieved from http://www.gov.ro/upload/articles/117322/programul-de-guvernare-2012.pdf

RG (Romanian Government). (2013-2016). *Government Program*. Retrieved from http://gov.ro/fisiere/pagini_fisiere/13-08-02-10-48-52program-de-guvernare-2013-20161.pdf

Romania Libera. (2012). *Luncavita – The only village collecting local taxes online*. Retrieved from http://www.romanialibera.ro/actualitate/locale/luncavita-singura-comuna-care-incaseaza-impozitele-online-272501.html

Rooksby, E., & Weckert, J. (2004). Digital Divides: Their Social and Ethical Implications. In *Ethical and Policy Implications of Information Technology* (pp. 29–47). Hershey, PA: Information Science Publishing. doi:10.4018/978-1-59140-168-1.ch002

Samah, B., Shaffril, H., D'Silva, J., & Hassan, M. (2010). Information Communication Technology, Village Development and Security Committee and Village Vision Movement: A Recipe for Rural Success in Malaysia. *Asian Social Science*, 6(4), 136–144. doi:10.5539/ass.v6n4p136

Schwester, R. (2011). Examining the Barriers to e-Government Adoption. In *Leading Issues in e-Governmen* (pp. 32–50). Reading, UK: Academic Publishing International Ltd.

Sevron, L. (2002). *Bridging the Digital Divide: Technology, Community and Public Policy*. Malden, MA: Blakwell Publishing.

Stoica, V., & Ilas, A. (2009). Romanian Urban e-Government. Digital Services and Digital Democracy in 165 Cities. *Electronic. Journal of E-Government*, 7(2), 171–182.

Stoica, V., & Ilas, A. (2012). Is Romania Ready for Nation-Wide Public e-Services? Five Factors to Consider before Adopting an E-Government Public Policy. In *Handbook of Research on E-Government in Emerging Economies: Adoption, E-Participation, and Legal Frameworks* (pp. 717–732). Hershey, PA: IGI Global. doi:10.4018/978-1-4666-0324-0.ch037

Susskind, R. (2008). *The End of Lawyers? Rethinking the Nature of Legal Services*. Oxford, UK: Oxford University Press.

Thompson, C. S. (2002). Enlisting on-line residents: Expanding the boundaries of e-government in a Japanese rural township. *Government Information Quarterly*, 19, 173–188. doi:10.1016/S0740-624X(02)00093-X

UN (United Nations). (2010). *World Population Prospects, the 2010 Revision*. Retrieved from http://esa.un.org/unpd/wpp/Sorting-Tables/tab-sorting_population.htm

Van Dijk, J. (2005). *The deepening divide: Inequality in the information society*. London: Sage Publications.

Warschauer, M. (2003). *Technology and social inclusion: Rethinking the digital divide*. Cambridge, MA: MIT Press.

World Bank. (2012). Retrieved from http://www-wds.worldbank.org/external/default/WDSContentServer/WDSP/ECA/2012/08/19/ADB66A1A61526C0E85257A5F006C-CBCA/1_0/Rendered/PDF/ISR0Disclosabl01920120134540570042 3.pdf

KEY TERMS AND DEFINITIONS

E-Government Public Policy: A public policy intended to implement or improve ICTs or public services using ICTs.

E-Government Readiness: The readiness both of a society and of a government to use ICTs in order to provide information and services.

E-Government: Institutionalized practices and activities of public administration using ICTs to provide information and services to various social actors (including government).

E-Rural Government: The digital interaction between government and the citizens living in rural areas, the businesses, and other governmental agencies operating in the same area.

International Digital Divide: The existence of significant differences between states regarding the access and use of ICTs by citizens, business or public administration.

National Digital Divide: The existence of significant differences between regions or social classes regarding the access and use of ICTs by citizens, business or public administration.

Public policy: A multitude of governmental planned processes involving various actors, social context and values, a specific discourse, and different types of institutions, networks and organizations.

Chapter 18
ICTs and Their Impact on Women's Roles and Evolution within Developing Societies

Ana-Cristina Ionescu
Chamber of Commerce and Industry of Romania (CCIR), Romania

ABSTRACT

The Internet is definitely the most complex and dynamic technical and cultural phenomenon that humanity ever experienced. Nevertheless, despite its positive impact on the Western world, Web 2.0 has yet to prove its power in the undeveloped regions of the globe, where the Internet Era is still at its dawn. In developing countries, the barriers that women face, such as poverty or social imbalances, establish significant challenges that hinder connectivity and access to modern technologies. In this context, the chapter discusses the evolution of gender speech in relation to new Information and Communication Technologies (ICTs). The authors determine whether the declarations and plans for action that were issued subsequent to the 1995 Fourth World Conference on Women in Beijing enhanced the establishment of gendered policies on ICTs, particularly in the undeveloped regions of the world, and whether, in this way, they empower women, contribute to combating women's poverty, and promote gender equality.

INTRODUCTION

Every mental act is composed of doubt and belief, but it is belief that is the positive, it is belief that sustains thought and holds the world together - Søren Kierkegaard

As stated in the title, my chapter discusses the importance of ICTs for women's evolution within the *information* millennium, in an optimistic, yet realistic note, pointing out both the advancements

DOI: 10.4018/978-1-4666-3691-0.ch018

and shortcomings of the developments in this field. It may seem to some of you that this paper is a celebration of ICTs - especially the Internet. However, I prefer such feedback, rather than thinking later that young girls' fear to approach technologies in their careers, for example, is due also to my failure to point out and to explain the enormous potential of ICTs for women empowerment.

In addition to providing unlimited freedom to track down and to share information *in real time* (Flew, 2008), the Internet - a space less influenced by social norms and pressure compared with the outer world - transcends the biases of the traditional communities, enhances the creation of social capital and fosters relationships, ideas promoted extensively in the ICTs literature from the last 20 years (Rheingold, 1993; Stoll, 1995; Watson, 1997; Wellman, 2001).

The impact of Web 2.0 translates in the so-called cyber culture, a concept linked to the use of computer networks for communication, entertainment and business. Defined by its cognitive and social characteristics, rather than geographic ones, the cyber culture relies on establishing identity and credibility, while both concepts - desirable results of online interaction - are being used as pillars of the virtual communities (Rheingold, 1993).

I aim to highlight that for women all over the globe the online networking is liberating, as many of the relationships initiated through Computer Mediated Communication (CMC) do not limit to a virtual realm and transcend to a real-life setting (Parks and Floyd, 1996). Yet, developing countries have only 21.1 Internet users per 100 inhabitants as opposed to 71.6 Internet users per 100 inhabitants in the developed countries. The most severe situation is encountered in Africa, where only 9.6 users exist per 100 inhabitants (United Nations, 2011).

The perspective of this chapter is rather social, than technical, as I aim to emphasize the revolutionary potential of the Internet for human relations. Web 2.0 enhances interactions, impossible in the outer world and connects vast networks of

individuals, across large distances, at very little cost (Laurie et al., 2005; Girard, 2003). Subsequently, means of communication like e-mailing, online forums and discussion boards or blogs have contributed to raising awareness on women's rights both in the outer and virtual world.

Of course, gender is not a new topic or the belief that Internet enhances social equality (Miller, 1991; Veysey, 1978). However, such concepts are taboo even today in some parts of the world. While physical borders are cancelled online, women connect to discussion forums from everywhere and form trans-national communities via virtual networking to fight gender stereotyping and combat the social exclusion of a predominantly male-dominated world. The Internet enhanced women's ability to create their own information and share it online, and in real time, to control the content and distribution channels, and to propagate their messages to large audiences.

The purpose of this article is to provide a thorough analysis of the relevant literature in the field - feminist studies of new information and communication technologies, reports by international organizations such as UNESCO, United Nations or the International Telecommunications Union - and to create awareness for and identify solutions to overcome barriers that hinder women's access to and use of ICTs, while revealing the immeasurable potential of technologies for their empowerment.

WOMEN'S ACCESS TO AND USE OF ICTs

In addition to being a socially designed system of knowledge, technology is shaped by historical, cultural and political contexts (Edley & Houston, 2011). Technology, often understood as a technical tool that society can utilize and not like something that in itself is influenced by society, is considered to be gender neutral, although it affects differently the various sections of society. However, the gendered approach argues that technology is not neutral, but depends on cultural beliefs (Stahl, 2008) and wealth (Lee, 2006a). While opening new horizons, ICTs produce and perpetuate gender stereotypes and the corporate colonization of private and work life (Deetz, 1992).

Women's access to technology depends on their allegiance to different social identities such as class, ethnicity, caste, race or age which interact with gender. Reports on women and ICTs point out how having Internet access at home can empower women and influence their participation within the society and the labor market (Bernstein, 1999). It facilitates their access to knowledge and information, improves their skills, especially in the ICT field and helps them develop careers outside the home (ITU, 2010). The use of ICTs can make essential contributions to reducing poverty, increasing productivity, and stimulating innovation and economic transformation. Technologies provide women with access to critical information that helps them achieve better results and thus better living conditions (Fredriksson, 2011).

The existing power relations in different societies determine the usability of and the access to ICTs. The new ICTs communication infrastructure facilitates the achievement of networking in real time and, in this way, women are able to move beyond the patriarchal vision by expressing opinions on websites that tackle their concerns and, hence, increase their influence in relevant domains. Youngs (2000) notes, that women's access to the Internet has enhanced the creation of new global communities, with a focus on feminist issues, such as: violence against women; political, social and cultural rights; repression. Examples in this regard include women centres, meant to enhance online interaction between women in different parts of the world, irrespective of their class, ethnicity, race, age or wealth, like: Calgary's Women Centre in Canada (www.thirdagecommons.ca/resources/online-interaction-calgary-womens-centre), which provides electronic forums for senior women; the

Asia - Pacific online network of women in politics, governance and transformative leadership (www.onlinewomeninpolitics.org); Black business women online (http://mybbwo.com); Women's Information Network (http://thewinonline.com), which aims to eradicate illiteracy, poverty and hunger, militating for peace on the globe.

Still, in some parts of the world, even today technology is seen as a male preserve historically and women's access to ICTs is controversial and political. The most dramatic situation is encountered in the rural areas, where women have restricted access to ICTs because the basic infrastructure for such technologies is missing (Willis Arronowitz, 2011) and the costs of deployment are high. There, ICTs are used almost entirely by the husband, and women, the majority of them illiterate housewives, lack opportunities for training in computer skills. Domestic responsibilities, cultural restrictions on mobility, reduced income, and the lack of relevance to their existence, exclude them from the information sector.

In a world that constantly redefines its values to balance inequities, technologies need to be easily accessible and meaningful to different segments of populations, especially the ones in the developing societies, unable to keep up with advancements. Technological convergence holds immense potential for the improvement of life and liberty in some ways and can degrade it in others, as the same technology has the potential to be utilized both a weapon of social control and a means of resistance (Rheingold, 2002; United Nations, 2000). Google, for example, has developed sites in 190 domains, with a user interface translated into a total of 130 different languages, from Afrikaans to Zulu. Yet, Google is not the dominant search engine in every country where it exists. In India, Rediff, a Mumbai-based provider of online news, information, communication, entertainment, and shopping services is said to comply better with the needs of the local customers, with tailored services. This is a clear sign that the ICT industry needs to come up with a location-based approach that involves an in-depth analysis of cultural, legal, and regulatory aspects (Kelly and Blakesley, 2011).

In the urban areas, a culture that encourages women to pursue a career and attend higher education, the easy access to information through modern technologies like the Internet or mobile phones and the increasing tendency to adapt to the international trends, determine a different situation, as women have the possibility to find employment opportunities in the ICT industry. However, patterns of gender segregation apply to the ICT industry, as well, because men hold the majority of high-skilled, high value-added jobs, while women are concentrated in the low-skilled, lower value-added jobs, like work in call centers or teleworking. Out of the two categories of teleworkers, the well-educated with demanding jobs that necessitate entrepreneurial and specialized skills and the low-level workers who perform tasks like typing or data entry, women are most likely to integrate into the later, the separation being a gendered one (Dodge and Kitchin, 2001).

The simple inclusion of women in the information society does not mean that women assume more power in the ownership and control of new ICTs. To better understand the relation between women and ICTs, Lee (2006a) argues, quoting Margaret Gallagher (1981); Gill Kirkup (2001); Michele Martin (2002) that women should be analyzed in the light of unequal global wealth distribution, where they represent resources in the production, distribution, and consumption process of the information society. While discussing a gender-biased IT environment where women programmers follow a "gender script" to draft technologies and studies on gender and education that picture female students as not so interested in studying masculine subjects as technologies and computing, Lee (2006a) criticizes women's association with consumption of technologies and men's with production.

Discussing women's participation in ICTs, Robins (2002) wonders if *African Women Online are Just ICT Consumers?* She assesses that, while African women endeavor to extend their spheres of influence in political, economic and social life, we do not know if the ICTs - especially the internet - can determine a transformation or will reproduce the inequalities of the status quo. Her studies on Senegal, for example, aiming to determine the interconnections between gender, class and international trade with the new ICTs, point out that the solution to enhancing women's access to technologies lies in a better coordination of governmental and non-governmental initiatives with private capital interests, not in a naive celebration of ICT potential nor condemnation of a new digital colonialism.

Analyzing the problem of inadequate access to ICTs, Galperin and Mariscal (2007) point out the need to develop appropriate pro-poor ICT policies within the Latin American and Caribbean context. In their view, market reforms in this regard have accentuated the social and economic divides, failing to ensure the benefits of the Information Society. Hence, they discuss the necessity of a policy reform that builds upon the achievements of market liberalization efforts in the region, in accordance with the realities of the digital poverty concept that addresses the multiple dimensions of inadequate levels of access to ICT services by people and organizations, as well as the barriers to their productive use.

Recent reports highlight that the ICT sector fails to take full advantage of female potential. Women lack equal opportunities to apply for ICT jobs and consequently the opportunity of a better life - better salary and more attractive career opportunities than most other sectors. While the total employment growth for women scientists and engineers was around 6.2% per year from 2002 to 2007, global organizations highly recommend promoting equal training opportunities in

ICT-related fields for women to answer the new demands of the ICT sector, as they are skilled, capable, talented, and creative and bring innovation into the work place (European Commission, 2010; ITU, 2010).

The Situation Around the Globe: Some Figures

ICTs are understood as technologies that enhance communication and process information and its delivery electronically. The description comprises old and new ICTs, i.e. radio, television, telephones (fixed and mobile), computers and the Internet. Today extensive flows of information, capital, ideas, people and products are being provided via the various ICTs. Populations access to and use of ITCs contributes to both broad-based economic growth and specific development goals (UNDP-APDIP, 2004).

Although great progress has been achieved in point of access to and use of ICTs (see Table 1), there are still huge inequities between the western world and undeveloped and developing regions

- Africa, Asia and Latin America, according to Internet World Stats on continents provided within Table 2.

Developing countries have only 21.1 Internet users per 100 inhabitants as opposed to 71.6 Internet users per 100 inhabitants in the developed countries. In Africa, as a consequence of poverty and precarious living conditions, only 9.6 users per 100 inhabitants are online (United Nations, 2011). Yet, lack of connectivity is not the most severe problem, just the most visible and most tackled. In reality, Internet's expansion to populations is hindered by illiteracy or language barriers. While the dominant language on the Internet is English, at least 20 percent of the world's population speaks languages that are hardly encountered on the web. There are still places on earth where individuals have no access to electricity, never made a telephone call, and the number of illiterate adults is the double of people who are online (Girard, 2003). Although serious efforts are being made to overcome these situations, i.e. initiatives like Costa-Rica's National Program of Educational Informatics meant to enhance the access

Table 1. World's access to and usage of ICTs

	2000	2008
Access to ICTs		
Telephone lines (per 100 people)	16,2	18,9
Mobile cellular subscriptions (per 100 people)	12,3	60,8
Fixed broadband Internet subscribers (per 100 people)	2,3	8,7
Personal computers (per 100 people)	8,0	15,3
Usage of ICTs		
International voice traffic (minutes per person per month)	3,2	…
Mobile telephone usage (minutes per user per month)	195	282
Internet users (per 100 people)	6,8	23,9

Source: World Bank, 2010.

Table 2. World Internet users and population stats

World Regions	Population (2012 Est.)	Internet Users Dec. 31, 2000	Internet Users Latest Data	Penetration (% Population)	Growth 2000-2012	Users % of Table
Africa	1,073,380,925	4,514,400	167,335,676	15.6%	3,606.7%	7.0%
Asia	3,922,066,987	114,304,000	1,076,681,059	27.5%	841.9%	44.8%
Europe	820,918,446	105,096,093	518,512,109	63.2%	393.4%	21.5%
Middle East	223,608,203	3,284,800	90,000,455	40.2%	2,639.9%	3.7%
North America	348,280,154	108,096,800	273,785,413	78.6%	153.3%	11.4%
Latin America/ Caribbean	593,688,638	18,068,919	254,915,745	42.9%	1,310.8%	10.6%
Oceania/ Australia	35,903,569	7,620,480	24,287,919	67.6%	218.7%	1.0%
World Total	7,017,846,922	360,985,492	2,405,518,376	34.3%	566.4%	100.0%

Source: www.Internetworldstats.com

of populations to technologies (Villalobos and Monge-González, 2011), much more initiatives are necessary to democratize Internet usage and more programs aiming to expand access in rural areas need to be developed (Willis Arronowitz, 2011).

A means of overcoming gender inequality - fight social biases and change patriarchal mentalities, access to and use of technologies can improve women's role around the globe and support their evolution both at home and in their careers (ITU, 2011), as Internet empowers women and enlarges their participation in society and the labor market. ICTs enhance their access to knowledge and information, improve their skills, especially in the ICT field and help them develop careers (ITU, 2010). Yet, many of the tasks performed by women are badly remunerated and the percentage of women who managed to reach executive jobs is reduced.

Due to unequal access to resources (ITU, 2011), inequality in access to use of technologies between men and women is still significantly high both in undeveloped and developed countries. Women face barriers like poverty and illiteracy, socialization patterns or unequal access to education and training and, hence, have lower skills than men. In most countries analyzed by the ITU study, men represent a higher share of Internet users, excepting in New Zealand and Thailand, where the percent of women using the Internet is slightly higher than that of men.

Yet, gender differences in Internet use are not necessarily connected with the development levels. Significant gaps are noted both in developed and undeveloped countries: while in Azerbaijan, Turkey, Senegal and Russia men represent a quite larger per cent of the Internet users compared to women, also in the European Union or other western European countries, the difference between male and female Internet users is significant - 74 per cent of men and only 69 per cent of women are online in the EU, respectively 92 per cent of men versus 86 per cent of women in Switzerland (ITU, 2011).

The statistics within Table 3 provide an overview of the present situation around the globe.

THE EVER-INCREASING POTENTIAL OF THE INTERNET FOR WOMEN EMPOWERMENT

ICTs hold a great potential for the empowerment of women both from a cultural and economic point of view. Freedom of expression is a human

Table 3. The gender divide: women and men (aged 15 to 74) using the Internet

Country	Reference Year	Women	Men	Difference Women - Men
Australia	2009	78.2	78.7	-0.4
Azerbaijan	2010	35.5	53.4	-17.9
Belarus	2010	32.0	36.3	-4.3
Brazil	2010	37.5	38.0	-0.5
Chile	2009	39.1	43.5	-4.4
Costa Rica	2008	32.4	35.9	-3.5
Ecuador	2010	29.4	31.6	-2.2
Egypt	2009	17.6	22.8	-5.2
El Salvador	2009	11.6	14.0	-2.4
EU27	2010	68.5	74.0	-5.4
Honduras	2008	13.1	13.1	-0.1
Hong Kong, China	2009	69.2	75.3	-6.2
Iran (I.R.)	2009	11.7	15.4	-3.7
Israel	2009	64.2	68.7	-4.5
Japan	2009	83.8	87.5	-3.7
Korea (Rep.)	2009	78.5	86.9	-8.4
Macao, China	2009	53.7	59.9	-6.1
Mauritius	2008	20.1	23.2	-3.1
Mexico	2010	32.1	36.3	-4.2
New Zealand	2009	84.2	82.8	1.4
Paraguay	2008	14.6	15.9	-1.3
Peru	2008	27.8	35.5	-7.7
Qatar	2010	77.8	83.6	-5.7
Senegal	2009	9.3	18.3	-9.0
Singapore	2009	63.3	71.4	-8.1
Switzerland	2010	86.0	91.9	-5.9
Thailand	2010	21.6	20.3	1.3
Turkey	2010	29.9	50.1	-20.2
Ukraine	2009	16.8	19.6	-2.7
Uruguay	2009	39.7	40.5	-0.9

Source: ITU, 2011

right and, in our contemporary society, Internet access itself has become a human right (United Nations, 2011).

The Internet era, characterized by diversity of content, rapid transmission of information and interactivity, gave new valences to previously existing unilateral communication technologies, which are physically and socially limited. Web 2.0 enhanced women users not only to consume but also to produce information, as in the virtual space inequities are less pronounced. The *new* information, "always on the move, fluctuating between decipherability and indecipherability and indeterminate in its mobility" (Holmes, 2005, p. 10), describes a two-way reciprocity public sphere, enabled by the new ICTs.

Mansell and When (1998) point out two different categories of initiatives meant to enhance women's access to the benefits of ICTs: those generated by women themselves in using ICTs as tools of social and economic empowerment and those taken by national and international organizations to assure women's access to the benefits of the information society.

The Internet has the potential to change women's role in politics on a transnational level, as they can create nowadays, through these new technologies local and global political networks (Youngs, 2000). Online, women can communicate across cultures and network via virtual feminist communities - a means of survival and liberation. Turkle (1995, 1996, 1997) argues that human interaction in the virtual communities is safer than real-world one, to construct, test, and transform our complex identities, gathering of our shared presence on all the windows that open on the computer screen, while we are online. Within such communities women can connect with peers and share information, resources, and opinions on issues such as abuse and discrimination that they suffer in the outer environment (Weiss, 1995; Hawthorne, 1999).

A landmark initiative meant to enhance women's access to and use of new ICTs is the Women's Programme of the Association for Progressive Communications - APC, created in 1993, with a focus on fields like ecology, human rights, feminism, and the protection of minority groups (UNESCO, 1997). The programme was intended to increase women's participation in CMC, a chance to correct gender inequities when designing, implementing, and using the new ICTs. In West francophone Africa, Environnement et développement du tiers monde - synérgie genre et développement (ENDA-SYNFEV) promotes electronic communication for women's groups as

a tool for action, mostly in areas like health and human rights. In Southern Africa, Women's Net aims to facilitate women's access to resources and information by organizing gender sensitive training programmes and by strengthening the link between projects and organizations. In Asia, the Asian Women's Resource Exchange (AWORC) was established in 1998 to enhance electronic resource-sharing among women's information centres on the continent, to facilitate Internet literacy, and to promote activism among and between individual women and women's organizations. In Latin America, the Area Mujeres (Women's Programme) of the Latin American Information Agency (ALAI) was created in 1989 and carries out lobby and advocacy initiatives on the right to communicate, from a gender perspective. Its success is due to permanent and active dialogue with organizations that share its electronic communication and networking goals (United Nations, 2000).

Connectivity gained new valences in the era of cyberfeminism, as cyberfeminists - activists or networkers - utilize the Internet intensively in order to develop campaigns at both international and local levels (Hawthorne and Klein, 1999). An example in this regard is the International Women's Tribune Centre - IWTC (http://www.irc.nl/page/7049), which provides communication, information, education, and organizing support services to women's organizations and community groups working to improve the lives of women, particularly low-income women in Africa, Asia and the Pacific, Latin America and the Caribbean, Eastern Europe and Western Asia. IWTC focuses on five programme areas: human rights; advocacy and accountability with a focus on the Beijing plus Five meeting; information access and communication capacity-building; networking and organizational support. Significant efforts have been made also by the transnational feminist network (TFN), groups of women who work together for women's rights at a national and transnational level, like: The Sisterhood Is Global Institute (www.sigi.org), Women's Learning Partnership - WLP (http://www.learningpartnership. org), Women Living under Muslim Laws (http:// www.wluml.org) or The Association for Women's Rights in Development - AWID (http://www.awid. org). Emerged in the context of economic, political and cultural globalization, the TFNs, expression of global feminism, militate against inequalities, oppression, unsustainable economic growth and patriarchal controls over women.

Other successful initiatives in the area include: the publication in May 1999 of the world's first virtual women's newspaper, *Worldwoman*, intended to disseminate transnational news written by women to a wide global audience or the more recent Great Britain-based online journal, *International Journal of Gender, Science and Technology*, established in 2009. Significant efforts have been made also by international organizations. To support freedom of expression and the development of community media, plurality of content and opinion, and the training of media professionals, UNESCO has allocated, over the last thirty years, more than US$100 million to 1,200 projects in 140 countries via its International Programme for the Development of Communication (IPDC). Examples of initiatives include support for the Media Institute of South Africa to improve the quality of journalism in post-apartheid South Africa, the deployment of a women's media centre in Cambodia, and the training of the next generation of professional journalists in Mongolia (Souter, 2010).

Today, much more awareness on women's rights with respect to technologies by global feminists is needed. Yet, the prerequisite is that they *have to be part of the technology discussion* to be able to make their voices heard, to believe in and promote equal opportunities.

GENDER AND ICTS

The gender perspective analyses women as creators of information, enabled to spread their own messages in cyberspace, with significant echo in real world. Engendering ICT does not refer to a greater use of ICTs by women, but to facilitating women's access to the ICT system by transforming it. Measures in this regard include: ICT policies initiated by the government with strong gender perspectives and involvement of the civil society in gender equality related issues; considering gender related issues when drafting, implementing and evaluating ICT projects and policies; analyzing the differential impact of telecommunications/ ICTs on men and women (Gurumurthy, 2004).

Cyberspace allows individuals to redefine their selves - *gender identities* - without reshaping their bodies, while CMC represents a means to enhance the fluidity of gender constructions. The importance of CMC, "global conveyance of thought", for society does not reside in the mere capacity to distribute an unlimited quantity of information, but rather in its potential to enhance inter-personal communication (Barlow, 1996) and overcome discrimination (Lawley, 1993).

Historical Gender Milestones

The 1995 Beijing Declaration and Platform for Action

The advancements of the new ICTs in the early 1990s and fervent debate on the *information society* in the educational, business or political environment, at a national and international level, determined a stronger focus on the new technologies within the Fourth World Conference on Women, that took place in Beijing, between 4-15 September 1995, as compared to the first three events.

Gender equality in science and technology for development was one of the main subjects to be discussed by the United Nations Commission on Science and Technology for Development (UNC-STD), between 1993 and 1995. These meetings tackled the gendered relations that appear with the use of the advanced ICTs and highlighted the need for science and technology programs to consider explicitly their gender impact. UNC-STD included the outcomes in the "Declaration of Intent on Gender, Science, and Technology for Sustainable Human Development" and made the recommendation that governments adopt it in order to set a direction for the national politics and encouraged the countries which created committees to tackle gender related issues (Gender Working Group, 1995). In their research carried out in preparation of the Beijing Fourth World Conference on Women, UNCSTD identified an emerging gender divide, i.e. considerable gender differences in levels of access to, control of and advantages obtained from the technological developments (United Nations, 2005b).

In this regard, the Beijing Declaration and Platform for Action, adopted within the 1995 United Nations Fourth World Conference on Women was a cardinal initiative. The declaration emphasized the potential of the media to contribute to the advancement of women and fight stereotyping and inequality in women's access to and participation in ICTs (International Federation of Journalists, 2009). The document included a part dedicated to Women and the Media, the J section, with two strategic objectives: "to increase the participation and access of women to expression and decision-making in and through the media and new technologies of communication" and "to promote a balanced and non-stereotyped portrayal of women in the media" (United Nations, 1995, para. 238 and 242). Specifically, the governments of all nations were advised to enhance women's empowerment by: encouraging and recognizing women's (electronic and non-electronic) networks; supporting women's education, training and employment to ensure their equal access to all areas and levels of the media and to enable them to produce information through the use of new technologies and urging women to use new communication technologies in order to strengthen democratic participation (United Nations, 1995). The importance and potential of the new ICTs as

a means to enhance women's empowerment are highlighted from the very first paragraph, with optimism and hope:

During the past decade, advances in information technology have facilitated a global communications network that transcends national boundaries and has an impact on public policy, private attitudes and behavior, especially of children and young adults. Everywhere the potential exists for the media to make a far greater contribution to the advancement of women (The United Nations, 1995, para. 234).

Yet, the declaration also reveals that:

...few [women] have attained positions at the decision-making level or serve on governing boards and bodies that influence media policy. The lack of gender sensitivity in the media is evidenced by the failure to eliminate the gender-based stereotyping that can be found in public and private local, national and international media organizations (United Nations 1995, para. 235).

In order to change the projection of negative and degrading images of women in the media communications - electronic, print, visual and audio, which affect negatively women' participation in the society and reinforce their traditional roles, the declaration suggested that women should be empowered by enhancing their skills, knowledge and access to information technology. In this way, they will be able to combat the negative portrayals and that self-regulatory mechanisms for the media should be created in order to fight gender-biased programming.

Although the dominant idea, throughout the document, is the necessity to change the negative and degrading perception of women within the collective mental, in general and in the media, in particular, the Platform does not militate explicitly for developing women's critical thinking to better understand the economic and social impact of the new ICTs. The document describes the technologies as a neutral tool that women could benefit once they acquire the corresponding skills. Moreover, it does not analyze gender inequalities due to male oriented organizational cultures or the macroeconomic dimension of ICTs, nor the concentration of ownership and control of new ICTs. For example, within ICT companies there are practices which enhance gender inequality by limiting women to low status occupations. It is a well known fact that ICT companies perpetuate organizational cultures and work climates which do not lead to women fully participating on equal terms with their male colleagues, or equal empowerment and, moreover, they are said to advantage women who can perform the particular "masculine" behaviors (Marcelle, 2000). Women who work in male-dominated companies believe that masculine qualities are a requisite for being successful in their careers, as opposed to women who work in gender-integrated companies, who tend to see both traditionally feminine and traditionally masculine qualities as being important for their success (Lips, 2001).

The platform opposes the beneficial new ICTs to the mass media, which is seen as a vehicle that promotes degrading, offensive and stereotypi-cal images of women. However, the two are not separate entities as mass media utilizes the new technologies for content transmission, which includes unfortunately many times degrading images of women. According to the platform (Section A) poverty is the main cause for women's lack of access to economic resources, including technologies, while Section F points out that women should be given access to ICTs for economic empowerment. While the impact of the Platform is undoubtedly positive, a stronger focus is needed to determine the degree to which strategic objectives are corroborated into Member States' national action plans. Hyer et al. (2009) point out, quoting Bell et al. (1996), that women are underpowered to affect policy changes. The organizations that represent them are rarely involved in activities like policy advocacy, lobby, planning and oversight or invited to dialogue in issues related to gender concerns.

Strategies, Outcomes and Achievements Post - Beijing

The specific measures that Member States integrated within their national action plans after the Beijing meeting are listed in table 4 and will be further analyzed to determine the impact of the

Table 4. Measures implemented by member states following the 1995 Fourth World Conference on Women

Media content	Elimination of stereotypes of women in the mass media (25); The media promote gender-sensitive issues and positive women's roles and contribution (6); The media promote gender equality (7); Censorship of media content that is deemed harmful to women (2); The media to carry out publicity campaigns about gender issues (3).
Women's involvement in the media	More participation from women (the national action plans are usually unclear in indicating what kinds and levels of participation among which groups of women) (3); More women in media decision-making (12); Provide training for media women specialists (6)
Women and new ICTs	To encourage and recognize women's networks (1); To promote the information society (1); Enhance women's participation in ICTs (2)

Note: The number in brackets indicates the number of countries which included the measure in national action plan
Source: Lee (2006b)

Beijing Declaration and Platform for Action on women's role and empowerment in contemporary societies.

Statistics published by the UN Department of Public Information (United Nations, 1997b) revealed that the Fourth World Conference on Women in Beijing, resulted in agreement by 189 delegations on a five-year plan to enhance the social, economic and political empowerment of women, improve their health, advance their education and promote their reproductive rights. Moreover, over 100 countries have announced new initiatives to further the advancement of women as a result of the Beijing Women's Conference.

However, Section J failed to provide a critical and comprehensive understanding of women's relations to new ICTs, as none of the national action plans included all twelve areas laid out in the Platform, while only 46 out of 86 plans included women and the media as a critical area of concern, which made it the third least included area (United Nations, 1997a). Strategic Objective J.2 "Promote a balanced and non-stereotyped portrayal of women in the media" was more commonly included than Strategic Objective J.1 which aimed to encourage women's participation in new ICTs.

The progress made in the implementation of the Beijing platform was reviewed within the 2000 United Nations General Assembly Special Session (UNGASS) "Women 2000: Gender Equality, Development and Peace in the 21st Century" or Beijing +5 Review, which concluded that limited progress had been made in eradicating illiteracy, setting as objective a 50 per cent improvement in the levels of adult literacy by 2015, especially for women.

An online discussion on *Women and Media* was designed, moderated, and facilitated from November 8 - December 17, 1999 by WomenWatch, a United Nations initiative meant to measure progress and obstacle since the Fourth World Conference on Women and WomenAction (2000), a network of national, regional and international organizations focusing on Women and Media or Section J of the Beijing Platform for Action (BPFA). The project focused on the two key areas highlighted within the Section J as being critical: to increase the participation and access of women to expression and decision-making in and through the media and new ICTs and to promote a balanced and non-stereotyped portrayal of women in the media. Although the participants stated that very little has changed since 1995 regarding the way in which the women were portrayed in the media, the examples below highlight interesting best practices in several countries (WomenAction, 2000).

In Argentina, Women for Equal Rights have created a web page with a database on women in politics, in order to make women politicians visible to women in their country. As a result more women have graduated in communications, and are working in mainstream media, print, electronic, TV and radio. Women have gained confidence to analyze and give opinions on issues which until recently were considered male domains and some women journalists are in decision making positions at large newspapers, and in production of TV and radio news and information services and programmes.

Remarkable initiatives were deployed also in China, in 1996, where women journalists in Beijing built a network to monitor portrayal of women, and advocate women's participation in media, while in South Africa The Commission on Gender Equality and Women's net organized a media-worker training on using the Internet to research on gender, with the purpose of raising awareness on gender equality: the Zambia Association For Research and Development (ZARD) and the Media Women's Association (ZAMWA) have developed training programmes in gender awareness for media personnel.

Additional significant initiatives include: the Jamaican Broadcasting Commission (JBC), in the Caribbean island of Jamaica, committed itself to becoming the first Anglophone Caribbean country to end gender-silencing in the media. An important advancement in this regard, in the Asia Pacific region, is the tool kit developed by Isis International-Manila from a project initiated by the Asian Media Information and Communications Centre, whose primary focus is to gender-sensitize media practitioners by forcing them to revisit newsrooms policies and question the practices that define the construction of the news and other media productions (Isis, 1996).

Also, important women networking initiatives were developed. The Gender in Africa Information Network (GAIN), a global network committed to making indigenous information on women and gender valued, visible and accessible globally, enhances women's participation in the global information society, by providing them a dedicated forum with online support and information. In Zambia, the representative body of Women's NGOs manages an NGO media network, which was formed to maximize efficiency and impact of their work. The progress of the network determined relevant improvement on other forms of media, which are slowly moving away from portraying conservative gender role distinctions. Bridging technology gaps was also an objective, as there are still a lot of women around the globe who don't have access to the new ICTs but they are not necessarily excluded from the benefits of these technologies. In the disadvantaged areas of the world, women online can provide a valuable service in bridging technological gaps. A Vocational Institute for Rural Women in India distributed a newsletter in two remote districts in the state of Bihar, on weekdays, to women in the market.

However, despite of the various best practices presented, some participants stated that, in many countries, the ideas and initiatives from section J were difficult to implement because they involved a radical transformation of the systems in place, which obviously could not happen on the spot. Many participants mentioned access, training, resources and language as obstacles, especially in the disadvantaged areas of the world, while others discussed about policies which encouraged concentration of communication and information in certain areas. Another explanation, for technological isolation, referred to the psychological barriers to women's access to ICTs: lack of information about what benefits can be gained through the access to technologies and lack of self-confidence with regard to learning how to use these technologies.

Table 5 summarizes the recommendations resulting from the Women and Media (Section J, Beijing Platform for Action) online discussion focusing on *policy initiatives, ICT development, education and training, dissemination*, and *monitoring and research*, essential for our discussion, before moving on to the Bejing +10 and +15 progress analysis:

In 2005, Member States of the United Nations carried out a ten-year review of progress in implementation of the Beijing Declaration and Platform for Action at the 49th session of the Commission on the Status of Women, with seventy-six countries providing information on women and media. The report of the Secretary General reviewed the status of the implementation of the Beijing Platform for Action, based mainly on the results of a questionnaire to Member States in this regard - 134 responses, which aimed to point out the major achievements, gaps, challenges and priorities for further initiatives to secure full implementation.

The conclusions on section J -Women and the Media emphasized that in the absence of educational and training programmes, women still encounter social and cultural barriers and hence they are not able to access media career opportunities and benefit equal participation in the field. Much more efforts are needed to sensitize media policy makers on women's rights to equal participation and on the need to eliminate discrimination and stereotyping in all aspects of the media.

Table 5. Online discussion on Women and the Media (Section J, Beijing Platform for Action) - recommendations

Policy	• The launching of a broad debate on communication and democracy by the UN, involving the active participation of women, and for this purpose, convene a World Conference on Communication; • The UN, media and civil society organizations should promote the formulation and adoption of global ethical frameworks, based on gender equality; • Women's right to communicate should be included by the UN as one of its priorities in the agenda for the 21st century; • Donor agencies must develop long-range strategies for supporting greater connectivity for women; • Action should be taken not only around negative portrayal of women in conventional media, but in electronic and other new media; • Governments should promote positive discrimination for women in access to ICTs; • Women's organizations should lobby and advocate at within the ICT sector and government for adequate ICT gender policies.

ICT Development	• Priority and resources should be assigned to development of and women's access to the following technological tools:
	    o Affordable computer hardware, laptops, that do not require mains electricity (e.g. wind-up or solar), so that women can communicate from everywhere;
	    o User-friendly free software with low-tech hardware requirements, for women's ICT access in areas and social groups with scant technological resources;
	    o Gender-sensitive multi-language translation software (including non-Latin alphabet languages) adapted to social issues;
	    o Search engines and information systems focusing on gender issues.
	• Opportunities should be provided and promoted for women to merge newer technologies with other technologies.
	• Women's use of new participatory technologies should be promoted.

Education and training	National education systems and other players in the field of education should: 1. Increase and expand the gender sensitization of individuals and institutions from an early age; 2. Take measures to show young women and girls that technology is not beyond their grasp; 3. Develop training programmes for women's organizations in computing, information management and strategies for dissemination through the media; 4. Provide training to journalism students and journalists to better understand issues of concern to women, gender and the media.
Dissemination	Creation and dissemination of information on women needs to be supported via: • Initiatives that create women and gender-sensitive content for the Internet; • Regular information to media groups and other civil society organizations on issues related to women and media; • Alternative media could pool resources, at least in the area of dissemination, so as to reach wider audiences; • Information should be translated, reproduced and repackaged using electronic communications, newsletters, radio, popular theatre, etc; • Information relevant to the needs of rural women in local languages, via radio, audio visual and popular media; • Networks or of professional translators could be built to provide free or low-cost translation services to women's organizations; • Donors should provide increased and sustained support for women's media productions.
Monitoring and Research	• Regular and on-going media monitoring should be undertaken for gender bias/sensitivity and results shared with policymakers in media and society; • Donors should give increased and sustained support for on-going research and studies on the portrayal of women in the media; • A status report could be undertaken with UNESCO on progress on issues raised in the 1995 study on women and the media.

Source: WomenAction, 2000

The exchange of best practices was encouraged especially with countries that succeeded to improve the image of women, via media advertising and programming, establishing at the same time regulatory mechanisms on gender portrayal in the media. The report revealed that in the rural areas traditional media use was still the dominant means of information - radio or printed materials, while in the developing countries in many cases the local media outlets are often the only source of news on community issues such as employment or education.

The establishment of local, national and international women's media networks with the purpose to support women's involvement in media work was noted as an important development, while the expansion of ICT was seen as empowering for an increasing number of women who thus could contribute to knowledge-sharing, networking and electronic commerce activities. Yet, problems like the enduring negative stereotypes and portrayals of women in the media, the impact of poverty and illiteracy, the lack of computer literacy and language barriers were still persistent (United Nations, 2005c).

At its fifty-third session in 2009, the Commission on the Status of Women reviewed the implementation of the Beijing Declaration and Platform for Action (1995) and the outcomes of the twenty-third special session of the General Assembly (2000), at its fifty-fourth session in 2010. The General Assembly marked the 15th anniversary of the adoption of the Beijing Declaration and Platform for Action in a commemorative meeting during CSW. The focus was placed on sharing experiences and best practices, with the purpose of exceeding remaining obstacles and new challenges, including those related to the Millennium Development Goals.

The Report of the 54th Session of the Commission on the Status of Women (CSW) states that is difficult to envisage a clear global overview of women's current participation in the media and ICT sectors due to the lack of sex-disaggregated data and gender-specific indicators. Moreover, the lack of gender-sensitive policies in the media has led to employment inequalities, as women journalists do not benefit the same status like their male colleagues.

Although women are increasingly employed in the media, including at the senior level, they have not yet attained equality in terms of holding decision-making positions in the media industry. Overall, media coverage of gender equality issues in majority of countries is reduced. Media still reflects women's roles in a negative way, providing stereotyped images that picture women as victims, sex objects, weak personalities economically and emotionally dependant by the father or husband, while passive and unprofessional in the workplace.

Both traditional and new media release biased stories and news and reinforce in this way gender stereotypes, as they picture a world where women and girls hardly matter, especially in areas like politics, sports or economy. Therefore, changing the stereotyped images of women in commercials and the media remains a high priority in many countries. While the availability of ICTs has improved, women's access to technologies is unequal, especially in the rural areas. Even today women in many countries fail to benefit the full potential of ICTs due to language barriers, physical inaccessibility to public access centres for technologies and lack of relevant content (United Nations, 2010b).

However, perspectives seem promising, as the year 2010 brought in a commendable development, the creation of UN Women, the United Nations Entity for Gender Equality and the Empowerment of Women by the United Nations General Assembly. The initiative is part of the UN reform agenda and incorporates the important work of four previously distinct parts of the UN system which focused exclusively on gender equality and women's empowerment: Division for the Advancement of Women (DAW), International Research and Training Institute for the Advancement of Women (INSTRAW), Office of the Special Adviser on Gender Issues and Advancement of Women (OSAGI), United Nations Development Fund for Women (UNIFEM).

The World's Women 2010: Trends and Statistics report (United Nations, 2010a) points out progress regarding gender equality in areas like school enrolment, health, and economic participation. Still, the gender gap remains critical in areas such as decision-making, women's empowerment, and violence against women. The progress in education - in the literacy status of adult women and men around the world - is slow and uneven, with women still facing many disadvantages and representing two thirds of the world's 774 million adult illiterates, a figure that has not changed over the past two decades. As for poverty, the report points out that, at the household level, the data show that certain types of female-headed households are more likely to be poor than male-headed households of the same type. For example, in Latin America and the Caribbean and the more developed regions, households of lone mothers with children have higher poverty rates than those of lone fathers with children. Women's lack of access to and control over resources limits their development and accentuates their vulnerability to unfavorable social, economic and political evolutions, because they have less cash income than men, particularly in the less developed regions of Africa or Asia. Moreover, relevant proportions of married women in sub-Saharan Africa and Southern Asia have no control over household spending or the spending of their own cash earnings.

Yet, the aforementioned report calls for optimism as improvement in access to education will eventually raise literacy levels. Primary enrolment of girls and boys is increasing across the world and trends for less developed regions such as Africa and South-Central Asia are encouraging. However, gender disparities are significant, as from the total of 72 million children being out of school worldwide, 54 per cent are girls. Except for sub-Saharan Africa and Southern and Western Asia, a relevant improvement in women's enrolment is registered in tertiary education, where women's prevalence is higher than men's at a global level. However, the analysis of the various fields of study reveals gender inequalities in tertiary education as women, although predominant in fields like education, health and welfare, social sciences, humanities and art, are severely underrepresented in areas such as science and engineering.

In other words, women should have access not only to the new technologies, but also to education, research and settings where freedoms can be exercised. The inequalities between men and women are accentuated by the difficulties that women encounter in continuing their education. In traditional communities, the access to education is limited and many young girls never attend school or complete their education (United Nations, 2005a). Differences in this respect between men and women are particularly preeminent in the Arab States, in sub-Saharan Africa, and in South and West Asia, where a woman's access to education is obstructed by customs, local values, and lack of finances or employment.

Acquiring new technology skills offers women the perspective of financial independence, enhancing them to access fields that are traditionally male dominated. The empowerment of women may be encouraged by cooperative development or microcredit programmes, especially in the developing countries, once they overcome the cultural barriers, prominent especially in the Arab states (UNESCO, 2005).

FUTURE PERSPECTIVES

ITCs empowerment concurs significantly to reducing poverty, increasing productivity, and stimulating the economic transformation of women: better jobs and better living conditions (Fredriksson, 2011). Two major contemporary aspects condition the spread of the Internet: the availability of personal computers (PCs) and the prevalence of preexisting fixed telephone lines and cable (Rueda-Sabater & Garrity, 2011). Women in the most remote and traditional places are being connected to the world via innovative initiatives. In Afghanistan, in 2010, a mobile phone operator - MTN - enhanced mobile use among women by setting up women-only retail stores. The solution was tailored to the needs of a country where tradition prohibits women from interacting with men unrelated to them. At present, women represent 18 percent of Afghan mobile phone subscribers. In Nigeria, mobile phone use decreased transaction costs and saved time and money for the women running micro-enterprises by cutting out travel, previously necessary to identify buyers and negotiate prices. In the developing countries, which count for over 80 percent of all new subscriptions worldwide, over 1.5 billion mobile phones are currently in use and the number expected for 2015 is 2.5 billion. Mobile phones are used increasingly to access the Internet. A statistic from June 2009 reveals that in Kenya, for example, 99 percent of all Internet subscribers were at that time accessing the Internet via mobile phones (Fredriksson, 2011).

To understand correctly the tremendous implications of the gender divide we must *equally* analyze its three interdependent dimensions: *the technological divide* - significant disparities in infrastructure, *the content divide* - even today a great percent of the web-based information fails to meet the real needs of the various populations, while the online dominant English content excludes local voices and *the gender divide* - women and girls have less access to technologies then men and boys, because of the social biases, existent both in rich and poor societies. Certainly, more dedicated research is necessary and policies by international organizations tailored on local features, because for example what applies today in an ex communist eastern European country does not fit the profile of an isolated African community. More policy research on women and ICTs is necessary in developing countries, where reduced connectivity and poor access to and use of technologies are consequences of the lack of wealth and education (Girard, 2003; Lee, 2006a).

In rich or poor communities, women are not free to choose their roles in relation to ICTs. Changing the traditional patriarchal mentalities both in western and developing communities is the

greatest challenge that we are facing for centuries. It requires sustainable gendered ICTs policies by governments, intensive social and economic field analyses by civil society and private sector, media campaigns by women advocates of gender equality and most important a change of attitude by each and every women on all fifth continents. It's unacceptable in the third millennium for women to believe that their views don't receive the same level of attention as those expressed by men (see article dated August 25th, 2012 on Scotswomen and independence, in The Economist online edition[1]).

Very often CEOs state that they want to hire women and provide them with the same working conditions and career opportunities that men benefit. Yet, in the ICTs sector this perspective is almost inexistent, as only 11% of the Tech Executives are women as opposed to 89% men (Fidelman, 2012). Trying to elucidate why women are so underrepresented in the technology area, Fidelman (2012) discusses perceptions - women are not attracted to ICTs and define them as a male thing. Following discussions on women and ICTs with a group of 10 female business leaders, he concludes that the core of this problem resides in the childhood and high school/college periods, when women have to be encouraged more towards technical fields, while later the technical paths within organizations need to be better promoted among women, in the effort to destroy the myth of the male dominated technical careers.

And this myth is unacceptable! Studies on sex and intelligence reviewed by Fine (2010) reveal that there is no scientific evidence for innate biological differences between men and women's minds. In her book "Delusions of Gender: How Our Minds, Society, and Neurosexism Create Difference", Fine (2010) argues that, in fact, cultural and societal beliefs contribute to commonly perceived sex differences. She argues that differences between men and women have less to do with neurological differences and more with our own implicit gender stereotypes, pointing out that thoughts and attitudes often disagree with consciously held beliefs.

New ICTs can open huge opportunities for humanity, but only accompanied by measures that enhance individuals to utilize them: equal access to education and training, global access to information and consideration for linguistic diversity. Cyberspace offers an unlimited volume of resources for information and knowledge, new opportunities for expression and participation and most important huge potential for development (Dutton et al., 2011).

Looking back in time I have my own personal experiences very fresh in my mind - a young girl with no access to free technologies and just two predefined hours of tyrannical TV per day, living in pre-democratic Romania, before the fall of the communist system in 1989. But the totalitarian regime ended and so did the transition to democracy - hopefully - and television was overthrown once the new ICTs made their appearance. Today, Internet is an important engine for freedom, individuality, economic empowerment, culture and morality, at a global and local level. Access to the Internet translates into freedom to think outside patriarchal mentalities, liberty to decide on what is good and what is bad and most important freedom to exist equally as a woman or as a man in a world with no boundaries and less biases then the outer one.

In the near future, major endeavors are necessary to bring half the world population - including half of the female population - online by 2015 (ITU, 2010) and to ensure the development of a free, professional media and regulatory policies, substantiated on the four UNESCO key principles:

freedom of expression, quality education for all, universal access to information and knowledge, and respect for linguistic diversity (Berger, 2009).

Also, I do believe that the personal contribution of each of us to research, discussions or simply day-to-day dialogue is quintessential. I encourage women to be optimistic about their chances, give up the stereotypical way of thinking towards technologies and believe, because *belief creates behaviors* (Neale Donald Walsch).

REFERENCES

Barlow, J. P. (1996). *A Declaration of the Independence of Cyberspace.* Retrieved April 21, 2012, from http://www.eff.org/~barlow/Declaration-Final.html

Berger, G. (Ed.). (2009). *Freedom of Expression, Access to Information and Empowerment of People.* Paris, France: United Nations Educational, Scientific and Cultural Organization (UNESCO). Retrieved July 08, 2012 from http://unesdoc.unesco.org/images/0018/001803/180312e.pdf

Bernstein, D. R. (1999). Java, Women and the Culture of Computing. In *Proceedings of the 12th Annual Conference of the National Advisory Committee on Computing Qualifications.* Dunedin, New Zealand: Academic Press. Retrieved July 21, 2012 from http://turbo.kean.edu/~dbernste/naccq.html

Deetz, S. A. (1992). *Democracy in an Age of Corporate Colonization. Developments in Communication and the Politics of Every Day Life.* Albany, NY: State University of New York Press.

Dodge, M., & Kitchin, R. (2001). *Mapping Cyberspace.* New York: Routledge.

Dutton, W. H., Dopatka, A., Law, G., & Nash, V. (2011). *Freedom of connection, freedom of expression: The changing legal and regulatory ecology shaping the Internet.* United Nations Educational, Scientific and Cultural Organization (UNESCO), Communication and Information Sector, Division for Freedom of Expression, Democracy and Peace. Retrieved September 01, 2012 from http://unesdoc.unesco.org/images/0019/001915/191594e.pdf

Edley, P. P., & Houston, R. (2011). The More Things Change, the More They Stay the Same: The Role of ICTs in Work and Family Connections. In K. B. Wright, & L. M. Webb (Eds.), *Computer-Mediated Communication in Personal Relationships* (pp. 194–225). New York, NY: Peter Lang Publishing.

European Commission. (2010). *Women and ICT. Status Report 2009.* Information Society and Media. Retrieved April 15, 2012 from http://ec.europa.eu/information_society/activities/itgirls/doc/women_ict_report.pdf

Fidelman, M. (2012, May). *Here's the Real Reason There Are Not More Women in Technology.* Retrieved July 2, 2012 from http://www.forbes.com/sites/markfidelman/2012/06/05/heres-the-real-reason-there-are-not-more-women-in-technology/

Fine, C. (2010). *Delusions of Gender: How Our Minds, Society and Neurosexism Create Difference.* New York: W. W. Norton and Company.

Flew, T. (2008). *New Media: An introduction* (3rd ed.). Melbourne, Australia: Oxford University Press.

Fredriksson, T. (2011). The Growing Possibilities of Information and Communication Technologies for Reducing Poverty. In S. Dutta, & I. Mia, (Eds.), *The Global Information Technology Report 2010 – 2011* (pp. 69 - 79). Geneva, Switzerland: World Economic Forum and INSEAD. Retrieved June 17, 2012 from http://reports.weforum.org/global-information-technology-report/content/pdf/wef-gitr-2010-2011.pdf

Galperin, H., & Mariscal, J. (2007). *Digital Poverty: Latin American and Caribbean Perspectives.* International Development Research Centre: Practical Action Publishing. Retrieved December 15, 2011, from http://www.idrc.ca/openebooks/342-3/

Gender Working Group, United Nations Commission on Science and Technology for Development (UNCSTD). (1995). *Missing Links: Gender Equity in Science and Technology for Development.* Ottawa, Canada: International Development Research Centre in association with Intermediate Technology Publications and UNIFEM.

Girard, B. (2003). *The one to watch. Radio, new ICTs and interactivity.* Rome: Food and Agriculture Organization of the United Nations.

Gurumurthy, A. (2004). Gender and ICTs. London: Bridge, Institute of Development Studies (IDS).

Hawthorne, S. (1999). Connectivity: Cultural Practice of the Powerful or Subversion from the Margins. In S. Hawthorne, & R. Klein (Eds.), *Cyberfeminism: Connectivity, Critique and Creativity* (pp. 125–128). Melbourne, Australia: Spinifex.

Hawthorne, S. (1999). Cyborgs, Virtual Bodies and Organic Bodies: Theoretical Feminist Responses. In S. Hawthorne, & R. Klein (Eds.), *Cyberfeminism: Connectivity, Critique and Creativity* (pp. 213–250). Melbourne, Australia: Spinifex.

Hawthorne, S., & Klein, R. (1999). Introduction: Cyberfeminism. In S. Hawthorne, & R. Klein (Eds.), *Cyberfeminism: Connectivity, Critique and Creativity* (pp. 1–16). Melbourne, Australia: Spinifex.

Holmes, D. (2005). *Communication theory: Media, technology and society*. Thousand Oaks, CA: Sage Publications Inc.

Hyer, E. K., Ballif-Spanvill, B., Peters, S. J., Solomon, Y., Thomas, H., & Ward, C. (2009). Gender Inequities in Educational Participation. In D. B. Holsinger, & W. J. Jacob (Eds.), *Inequality in Education: Comparative and International Perspectives* (pp. 128–149). Dordrecht, The Netherlands: Springer.

International Federation of Journalists in cooperation with the United Nations Educational, Scientific and Cultural Organization (UNESCO). (2009). *Getting the Balance Right: Gender Equality in Journalism*. Brussels, Belgium: International Press Centre. Retrieved March 13, 2012 from http://unesdoc.unesco.org/images/0018/001807/180707e.pdf

International Telecommunication Union. (2010). *Measuring the Information Society: Version 1.01*. Geneva: ITU.

International Telecommunication Union. (2011). *Measuring the Information Society*. Geneva: ITU.

Internet World Stats. (n.d.). Retrieved January, 2014, from http://www.Internetworldstats.com/stats.htm

Isis. (1996). Women in the News: A Guide for Media. Retrieved January 2, 2012 from http://www.isiswomen.org/index.php?option=com_content&view=article&id=181:a-gender-equality-toolkit&catid=163:publications&Itemid=240

Kelly, J., & Blakesley, N. (2011). Localization 2.0. In S. Dutta, & I. Mia (Eds.), *The Global Information Technology Report 2010 - 2011* (pp. 119 - 127). Geneva, Switzerland: World Economic Forum and INSEAD. Retrieved June 17, 2012 from http://reports.weforum.org/global-information-technology-report/content/pdf/wef-gitr-2010-2011.pdf

Laurie, N., Andolina, R., & Radcliffe, S. (2005). Ethnodevelopment: Social Movements, Creating Experts and Professionalising Indigenous Knowledge in Ecuador. *Antipode, 37*(3), 470–496. doi:10.1111/j.0066-4812.2005.00507.x

Lawley, E. L. (1993). *Computers and the Communication of Gender*. Retrieved January 4, 2012, from http://www.itcs.com/elawley/gender.html

Lee, M. (2006a). What's missing in feminist research in new information and communication technologies? *Feminist Media Studies, 6*(2), 191–210. doi:10.1080/14680770600645168

Lee, M. (2006b). A feminist political economic understanding of the relations between state, market and civil society from Beijing to Tunis. *International Journal of Media and Cultural Politics, 4*(2), 221–240.

Lips, H. M. (2001). Social and interpersonal aspects. In J. Wor-ell (Ed.), *Encyclopedia of women and gender* (pp. 847–858). San Diego, CA: Academic Press.

Mansell, R., & When, U. (1998). Knowledge Societies: Information Technology for Sustainable Development. In *Innovative knowledge societies - Consequences of ICT strategies: The benefits, risks, and outcomes* (pp. 241–255). Oxford, UK: Oxford University Press.

Marcelle, G. M. (2000). *Gender, Justice and Information and Communication Technologies (ICTs).* Paper presented at the 44th Session of the Commission on the Status of Women. New York, NY.

Miller, T. (1991). *The Hippies and American Values.* Knoxville, TN: University of Tennessee Press.

Parks, M., & Floyd, K. (1996). Making Friends in Cyberspace. *The Journal of Communication, 46,* 80–97. doi:10.1111/j.1460-2466.1996.tb01462.x

Rheingold, H. (1993). *Daily Life in Cyberspace: The Virtual Community: Homesteading on the Electronic Frontier* (pp. 57–109). Reading, MA: Addison-Wesley.

Rheingold, H. (2002). *Smart Mobs: The next social revolution.* Cambridge, MA: Perseus Publishing.

Robins, M. B. (2002). Are African Women Online just ICT Consumers? *International Communication Gazette, 64*(3), 235–249. doi:10.1177/17480485020640030201

Rueda-Sabater, E., & Garrity, J. (2011). The Emerging Internet Economy: Looking a Decade Ahead. In S. Dutta & I. Mia (Eds.), *The Global Information Technology Report 2010 – 2011: Transformations 2.0* (pp. 33 - 47). Geneva, Switzerland: World Economic Forum and INSEAD. Retrieved June 17, 2012 from http://reports.weforum.org/global-information-technology-report/content/pdf/wef-gitr-2010-2011.pdf

Souter, D. (2010). *Towards inclusive knowledge societies: A review of UNESCO's action in implementing the WSIS outcomes.* United Nations Educational, Scientific and Cultural Organization (UNESCO), Communication and Information Sector. Retrieved July 6, 2012 from http://unesdoc.unesco.org/images/0018/001878/187832e.pdf

Stahl, B. C. (2008). *Information Systems: Critical Perspectives.* New York, NY: Routledge. doi:10.4324/9780203927939

Stoll, C. (1995). *Silicon Snake Oil: Second Thoughts on the Information Highway.* New York: Anchor Books.

Stoll, C. (1995, February 27). The Internet? Bah! *Newsweek.* Retrieved January 04, 2012, from http://www.newsweek.com/1995/02/26/the-InternetInternet-bah.html

Turkle, S. (1995). *Life on the Screen: Identity in the Age of the Internet.* New York: Simon & Schuster.

Turkle, S. (1996). Virtuality and its Discontents: Searching for Community in Cyberspace. *The American Prospect, 24,* 50–57.

Turkle, S. (1997). Multiple Subjectivity and Virtual Community at the End of the Freudian Century. *Sociological Inquiry, 67*(1), 72–84. doi:10.1111/j.1475-682X.1997.tb00430.x

UNESCO. (1997). *World Communication Report: The media and the challenges of the new technologies.* Paris, France: UNESCO Publishing.

UNESCO. (2005). *World Report: Towards Knowledge Societies.* Paris, France: UNESCO Publishing.

United Nations. (1995). *Report of the Fourth World Conference on Women.* New York: The United Nations.

United Nations. (1997a). Synthesized Report on National Action Plans and Strategies for Implementation of the Beijing Platform for Action. New York, NY: The United Nations, the Department of Public Information.

United Nations. (1997b). *Women at a glance.* New York, NY: The United Nations, the Commission on the Status of Women. Retrieved 25 July 2012 from http://www.un.org/ecosocdev/geninfo/women/women96.htm

United Nations. (2000). *The World's Women Trends and Statistics.* New York, NY: The United Nations.

United Nations. (2005a). *The World's Women 2005: Progress in statistics.* New York, NY: The United Nations.

United Nations. (2005b). *Women 2000 and beyond: Gender equality and empowerment of women through ICT. The United Nations.* Division for the Advancement of Women, Department of Economic and Social Affairs.

United Nations. (2005c). *Review of the implementation of the Beijing Platform for Action and the outcome documents of the special session of the General Assembly entitled Women 2000: Gender equality, development and peace for the twenty-first century (E/CN.6/2005/2). The United Nations: Economic and Social Council.* Commission on the Status of Women.

United Nations. (2010a). *The World's Women 2010 Trends and Statistics.* New York, NY: The United Nations.

United Nations. (2010b). *Review of the implementation of the Beijing Declaration and Platform for Action, the outcomes of the twenty-third special session of the General Assembly and its contribution to shaping a gender perspective towards the full realization of the Millennium Development Goals (E/2010/4*–E/CN.6/2010/2).* The United Nations Economic and Social Council, Commission on the Status of Women.

United Nations. (2011). *Report of the Special Rapporteur on the promotion and protection of the right to freedom of opinion and expression, Frank La Rue.* The United Nations Human Rights Council. Retrieved June 18, 2012, from http://documents.latimes.com/un-report-Internet-rights/

United Nations Development Programme-Asia Pacific Development Information Programme (UNDP-APDIP). (2004). *Information and Communications Technology for Development: A Sourcebook for Parliamentarians.* New Delhi, India: Elsevier. Retrieved January 18, 2012, from http://www.apdip.net/publications/ict4d/sourcebook.pdf

Veysey, L. R. (1978). *The Communal Experience: Anarchist and Mystical Communities in Twentieth-Century America.* Chicago, IL: University of Chicago Press.

Villalobos, V., & Monge-González, R. (2011). Costa Rica's Efforts Toward an Innovation-Driven Economy: The Role of the ICT Sector. In S. Dutta, & I. Mia (Eds.), *The Global Information Technology Report 2010 – 2011* (pp. 119 - 127). Geneva, Switzerland: World Economic Forum and INSEAD. Retrieved June 17, 2012 from http://reports.weforum.org/global-information-technology-report/content/pdf/wef-gitr-2010-2011.pdf

Watson, N. (1997). Why we argue about virtual community: A case study of the Phish.net fan community. In S. G. Jones (Ed.), *Virtual Culture* (pp. 102–132). Thousand Oaks, CA: Sage.

Weiss, P. A. (1995). Introduction: Feminist Reflections on Community. In P. A. Weiss, & M. Friedman (Eds.), *Feminism and Community*. Philadelphia, PA: Temple University Press.

Wellman, B. (2001). Community in the network society. *The American Behavioral Scientist, 45*(3), 476–495.

Willis Aronowitz, N. (2011). UN Declares Internet Access a Human Right: What Does This Really Mean? *Good Magazine*. Retrieved June 26, 2012, from http://www.good.is/post/un-declares-Internet-access-a-human-right-what-does-this-really-mean/

WomenAction. (2000). *United Nations General Assembly Special Session on Women* and *Report of online discussion on Women and Media*. Retrieved January 04, 2012, from http://www.womenaction.org/ungass/bpfa/ungass.html

World Bank. (2010). *The Little Data Book on Information and Communication Technology 2010*. Development Data Group and the Global ICT Department of the World Bank. Retrieved January 17, 2012 from http://siteresources.worldbank.org/EXTINFORMATIONANDCOMMU-NICATIONANDTECHNOLOGIES/Resources/LittleDataBook2010.pdf

Youngs, G. (2000). Internet policies and states. In C. Kramarae, & D. Spender (Eds.), *Routledge International Encyclopedia of Women: Global Women's Issues and Knowledge* (pp. 1154–1156). New York, NY: Routledge.

KEY TERMS AND DEFINITIONS

Cyber Feminism: Represents a cyber-community guided by the feminist philosophy and values which aims to enhance feminist interactions and initiatives in the virtual life.

Cyberspace: A global network which reunites IT infrastructures, telecommunications networks and computer processing systems to facilitate individuals a complete social cyber experience characterized by interactivity, ideas exchange and sharing information.

Gender Equality: Means equal valuing of the roles of women and men within societies. By reducing stereotypes, women and men can equally participate in and benefit the economic, social, cultural and political life.

Gender Stereotypes: Represent over-simple generalizations of the gender attributes, differences, and roles of women and men, which seldom reveal accurate information. When individuals express gender assumptions by default to others regardless of evidence to the contrary, they are perpetuating gender stereotyping. The most common female stereotypic role is that of a loving wife and mother, while the male one projects the husband as the financial provider of the family. These kinds of stereotypes are dangerous as they can negatively affect personal and professional growth.

Human Rights: Represent fundamental civil, political, economic, social and cultural rights that all people are entitled to regardless of nationality, sex, age, national or ethnic origin, race, religion or language. Human rights serve as trans-national norms to protect all individuals from political, legal and social abuses.

ICTs: Information and communications technologies - refer to all communication devices and applications utilized for producing and transmitting information. The ICT sector comprises: radio, television, cellular phones, computer and network hardware and software, satellite systems and the corresponding services and applications. Today, ICTs - especially Web 2.0 - are understood as a time -sharing function that would not only enhance many-to-many communication but also permit users to really benefit from the medium, to migrate from a mere sender-receiver model of communication towards one of interaction.

Online Networking: Depicts the set of activities related with generating and developing relationships online. The vast and generous cyber premises enhance us to learn about and connect with individuals that we don't have a chance to meet in real life.

Virtual Communities: Aim to reflect the cycle of a face-to-face society by enhancing people with similar interests to converge and unite across large distances through online means of interaction like: email, chat and public forms of communications like discussion forums, newsgroups or networking platforms. Online communities can overcome time, space, class, age and sex to create a society and, focused on social experiences, individuals can experience other cultures and environments, besides of those where they physically live in.

Web 2.0: Is associated with web applications - social networking platforms, blogs, wikis or video sharing sites - that facilitate interactive information sharing, interoperability, user-focused infrastructure and networking tools on the World Wide Web. These developments contributed essentially to changing the way women are perceived by the societies traditionally as web 2.0, unlike real life, enabled them to interact in a social media dialogue as creators of content and hence controllers of information within the virtual communities.

ENDNOTES

[1]   http://www.economist.com/node/21560899?fsrc=scn/fb/wl/ar/just-sayyes

Chapter 19
Medicare and Medicaid Services Online:
Government Initiatives Narrowing Online Access Inequalities

Mary Schmeida
Kent State University, USA

Ramona McNeal
University of Northern Iowa, USA

ABSTRACT

Government initiatives in the United States have been passed in an effort to increase citizen usage of e-government programs. One such service is the availability of online health insurance information. However, not all demographic groups have been equally able to access these services, primarily the poor and rural American. As more legislation is passed, including the advancement of broadband services to remote areas, infrastructure barriers are being removed, opening access to Medicare and Medicaid websites for these vulnerable groups. The purpose of this chapter is to analyze factors predicting the impact of recent government actions on citizen access to health insurance information online. This topic is explored using multivariate regression analysis and individual level data from the Internet and American Life Project. The findings suggest that healthcare needs and quality of Internet access may be playing a more important role in health insurance information services than other factors.

INTRODUCTION

Historic inequalities in Internet usage are narrowing; U.S. citizens are now more able and inclined to access online healthcare information online including insurance information from Medicare and Medicaid, and private health insurance sites.

Demographic factors such as age, education, income, and race/ethnicity have historically been found to create inequalities in Internet access and usage necessary to search online for information and services (Schmeida, & McNeal, 2007; Schmeida, & McNeal, 2009). However, federal and state government initiatives aimed at increasing

DOI: 10.4018/978-1-4666-3691-0.ch019

Internet usage across demographic groups show favorable improvement in narrowing disparities in Internet usage. The objective of this chapter is to explore the impact of government efforts to increase Internet searches for public and private health insurance information. This chapter uses empirical analysis of demographic and environmental factors that historically have been associated with Internet access inequalities to explore the extent that these inequalities have narrowed in online searches for insurance information on years 2008 through 2012.

BACKGROUND

The U.S. federal and state-local governments have adopted some form of electronic government practice to increase Medicare and Medicaid enrollment by broadening access to information and services through advanced communication technology such as the Internet. To improve access to these public health insurance programs, the federal government has established Web-based information on Medicare eligibility criteria, enrollment guidelines, public health service centers, among other information. States have also made considerable progress in Website technical development (West, 2005) with each of the 50 states providing residents with Medicaid online service information. These changes in government practices are part of a larger trend in information provision and management in the public sector. Starting with the Clinton Administration, all levels (federal, state and local) began adopting practices of electronic or e-government, which "refer to the delivery of information and services via the Internet or other digital means" (West, 2004, p. 2).

E-government policies were adopted under the Clinton Administration with hopes that the Internet could be used to deliver goods and services in a way that would reduce government cost and increase efficiency. These same goals helped motivate the passage of the *E-government Act 2002*, signed into

law by President George W. Bush on December 17, 2002. Despite the promises of e-government, there are factors that limited the potential for government savings through delivery of government services and information online. One such issue is the "two-systems" problem. Until the government can bring all citizens online, it will need to deliver services and information in two ways. The first is the traditional methods including face-to-face, phone and mail and second through electronic means. This will limit the potential for cost savings (Fountain, 2001).

In order to recoup money invested in e-government strategies, citizens would need to come online in greater numbers. More specifically, the government would need to address the "digital divide" or inequalities in Internet access and usage. Solving the digital divide is not simply a matter of providing Internet access. Belanger & Carter (2009) found that the two main reasons why citizens do not use e-government more often is the access divide and skills divide. Although they identify lack of Internet access as the main reason citizens do not use e-government services, they found that lack of technical skills was also a deterrent to e-government usage. Mossberger, Tolbert & Stansbury (2003) describe technology skills in terms of two broad categories. The first category is technical competencies that include the necessary skills to use hardware and software such as typing and using a mouse. The second category (information literacy) concerns the ability to determine which information to obtain from the Internet for specific tasks, related to basic literacy (Mossberger, Tolbert & Stansbury, 2003, pp. 38). Their research found that individuals lacking technical skills tended to be older, less educated, Latino, African American and less affluent. Early research on Internet access in the United States (National Telecommunications and Information Administration [NTIA] 2000) found a similar divide based on access. Those least likely to have Internet access were female, less affluent, older, less educated, African American or Latino, had mental or physical disabilities, were in a single parent household and resided in rural areas. In addition, Van Dijk (1999) argued that there is a third divide or psychological divide which could be described as limited Internet use because of mental barriers including lack of interest and fear of computers. Adams, Stubbs & Woods (2005) added need to the list of reasons why individuals go online. The found motivation was important to both Internet usage and developing technological skills.

While much of the literature focuses on individual level factors to explain inequalities in Internet usage there are also environmental level factors. The first issue is a rural/urban divide. Urban areas are more likely to attract Internet providers because of advantages related to technological, economics, infrastructure and geography (Gabel, 2007; Mack & Grubesic, 2009). The rural/urban divide has proven to be a difficult gap to close. The NTIA (2013; pp. 31-34) found that in 2011 there was considerable variation in Internet adoption by state. The percentage of households with broadband service by state ranged from 53% to 80%. The differences by state fell along the rural/urban divide with more urban states having greater broadband adoption. Finally, West and Miller (2006) found regional differences with certain regions having higher levels of Internet connectivity.

A recent report by the NTIA (2013) finds that Americans are coming online in greater numbers than ever. By 2011, 93% of the U.S. population lived in areas with broadband service. In addition, approximately 76% of households had computers and 72% had Internet service. Nevertheless some groups were less likely to go online than others. Those least likely to use the Internet were less affluent, older, less educated, African American or Latino and resided in a rural area. The most important reasons given for not using the Internet included lack of interest, too expensive and inadequate computer.

Starting with the Clinton Administration, the federal government began to adopt strategies to increase Internet use. Initial strategies sought to increase Internet usage by providing Internet access in public places including schools and libraries. Under the George W. Bush Administration the strategy changed to a focus on increasing technological literacy. His administration worked to reduce inequalities in usage by improving computer skills through directives in the No Child Left Behind Act (NCLB). Actions taken by the Obama administration again altered the federal response to the digital divide. Under this new approach grants and loans were made available to state and local communities to either update existing telecommunication infrastructure or to put into place necessary infrastructure to provide broadband service to areas that do not currently have broadband access or are underserved (McNeal, 2012). A number of these programs, under the three presidents, required cooperation from state and local government, and often required them to submit an application for various grants and loans. Some state and local governments have been more committed to expanding Internet access than others and have been more aggressive in applying for federal monies. This has resulted in an unintended consequence: the disparities in access is increasing by location with differences in access varying more greatly depending on action of government officials (Jaeger, Bertot, McClure & Rodriguez, 2007).

Medicare and Medicaid Outreach to the Uninsured and Underinsured

In addition to improving Internet access and use, government initiatives are also aimed at enrolling uninsured and underinsured Americans into the Medicare and Medicaid public health insurance programs, and into private-sector insurance plans. Medicare is the government health insurance program for people 65 years and older, disabled, and/ or with permanent kidney failure. Medicaid is the federal-state health insurance program designed to assist the poor, such as low-income children, poor parents, pregnant women, the elderly, and disabled (Centers for Medicare & Medicaid Services, 2013a). Several racial/ ethnic groups are disproportionately uninsured in the U.S., with Latinos leading all other groups (U.S. Department of Health and Human Services [US-DHHS], March 2014), African Americans more likely to be without health insurance than whites (USDHHS, December 2013), and rural Americans leading urban counterparts (USDHHS, September 2013). Recent federal legislation known as the Patient Protection and Affordable Care Act (ACA) was signed into law by President Barack Obama March 2010. This legislation represents steps toward reforming healthcare. Among its provisions is the protection of consumers from disapproved insurance practices, improving access to affordable healthcare insurance, improving the integrity of the Medicare program, expanding already existing health programs, such as the Medicare and Medicaid programs, and strengthening consumer rights (www.whitehouse.gov, 2014; Public Law 111-148, 2010). Under ACA, Americans are mandated to have health insurance, and those currently enrolled in public programs will see expanded coverage and cost savings. For example, it is reported that women enrolled in 2011 Medicare saved nearly $1.2 billion because of improvement in prescription coverage, and also received preventive services without cost-sharing in 2011 for Medicare (USDHHS, July 2013).

To improve access to public health insurance programs, the federal government has improved upon already established web-based information on Medicare eligibility criteria, enrollment guidelines, public health service centers, locating Medicare and/ or Medicaid service providers, among other information. The Centers for

Medicare and Medicaid Services holds online "Open Door Forums" giving stakeholders an opportunity to dialogue with CMS about policies and government initiatives related to Medicare and Medicaid, the Children's Health Insurance Program, and private-sector insurance options. One goal for ACA is to make health insurance coverage more affordable and accessible. During this time of change, the Internet is critical for aiding consumers to access new insurance information, including public health insurance and the many private sector health insurance plans now tailored to meet ACA requirements. Called the Health Insurance Marketplace or "exchange," the government has set up this website at www.healthcare.gov as a one-stop shopping place for insurance needs. However, not all Americans have access to the Internet and skills to obtain online information regarding new insurance rules. Rural Americans, for example have historically been disadvantaged to accessing the Internet for health information and to securing health insurance. As reported by the U.S. Department of Health and Human Services (September 2013) about one in five uninsured Americans are living in rural regions. The Health Insurance Marketplace is expected to expand insurance coverage options and create competition among insurers making insurance more affordable to all Americans, such as rural residents. However, the success of bringing rural Americans to health insurance coverage may to some extent be associated on their ability to access the information on the web.

Can Medicare and Medicaid outreach strategies for increasing enrollment improve through the use of the Internet? The adoption of e-government strategies, such as applying advanced communication technology does not necessarily guarantee successful outcomes. Success is dependent on many factors particularly government program consumers having both access to and use of the

Internet. This is evident from research exploring the impact of e-government practices established to help those most in need of Medicare and Medicaid services to receive them. Early studies show that Medicare and Medicaid websites had not been accessible to vulnerable groups. Those most in need of these Internet sites were not accessing them at home (Schmeida, 2005). Although earlier studies on Internet access were discouraging, later studies show some disparities narrowing for vulnerable population groups, such as the poor. In exploring differences across socioeconomic groups, Schmeida and McNeal (2007) found disparities in searching Medicare and Medicaid information online are narrowing as the elderly and poor, among those in greatest need for publicly subsidized health insurance, began accessing program information online. These changes mirror the spread of Internet access in the U.S. Although individuals who are elderly or less affluent were later than other groups to go online, once they did, they were more likely than their counterparts to take part in online searches for Medicare and Medicaid information. This finding suggests that online Medicare and Medicaid outreach strategies have the potential for increasing enrollment, but success is contingent on increasing Internet use. More recently, Schmeida & McNeal (2013) examined changes in online searches for health insurance information for the years 2002 through 2010. They found that disparities in online searches based on location have dissipated overtime. This suggests that government efforts to bring broadband services to geographically disadvantaged areas may be having some level of success. They also found that starting in the year 2008, younger individuals overtook older citizens in online searches for medical insurance. Although this finding initially seemed inconsistent with prior research, they were able to attribute it to the current economic climate with more individuals (both young and old) needing to rely on government programs such as Medicaid.

EMPIRICAL MODEL: DATA AND METHODS

Data

In examining the question of whether the Internet can help facilitate enrollment in Medicare and Medicaid, this chapter will rely on secondary data analysis or data collected by another entity. More specifically, the study utilizes the *Internet and American Life Daily Tracking Survey 2008, 2010* and *2012* conducted for the Pew Internet & American Life Project, by the Princeton Survey Research Associates. The Pew Internet & American Life Project is part of the Pew Research Center, a nonpartisan, nonprofit group that conducts studies and provides information regarding factors which shape American society. Pew surveys are random digit dial national telephone surveys limited to individuals 18 years or older and live in the continental United States. This study is based on three surveys conducted for the Internet and American Life Project in 2008 with a sample size (n) of 3,030; 2010 (n= 3,000) and 2012 (n= 3014).There are advantages and disadvantages associated with all forms of data analysis. One disadvantage associated with secondary data analysis is that the data was collected for a specific purpose and may not be ideally suited for other research. In general, these datasets are well suited for this study; it allowed for the usage of the same dependent variable across all three years of study however several independent variables changed overtime. As a result, care must be taken when discussing the impact of certain independent variables overtime.

Methods

Demographic and geographical factors associated with citizen online searches on Medicare or Medicaid public health insurance information are analyzed for each of these years using logistic regression analysis, and the trends for 2008 through 2012 are explored. Logistic regression analysis is used because the dependent variable is binary. Independent variables were selected based on findings from prior research on traditional citizen-initiated government contact and barriers to Internet usage. The dependent was constructed as a dummy variable using the question: "Have you ever searched for online information related to insurance, including private insurance, Medicare or Medicaid?" The variables are coded 1 for someone looking for health insurance information online and 0 otherwise. Because this question is broader than we wish and also included the possibility of searches for private insurance, two control variables were included for *Medicare* and *Medicaid* recipients. Each variable was coded 1 if the individual was receiving this form of government health insurance and 0 otherwise. These measures were not available in 2008 and are only included in the 2010 and 2012 models.

Explanatory or independent variables include *Income* measured on a 9-point scale where 1 indicated that family incomes ranges from $0 to $10,000 and 9 signifies a family income of $150,000 or more. *Education* is measured using a 7-point scale, ranging from eighth-grade education or less to post-graduate training/ professional training, which includes Masters/ Ph.D., law and medical school. Government research (NTIA, 2013) indicates that individuals who are more affluent and those with greater educational attainment are more likely to use the Internet. This does not guarantee that they are more likely to conduct Internet searches for government health insurance programs. Schmeida & McNeal, (2007) found that those with lower income levels are more likely to conduct online searches for Medicare and Medicaid information. This outcome can be explained by the literature on citizen-initiated government

contact (Sharp, 1986), which argues that citizens are more likely to contact government when they have a need or perceive a need.

Age is measured in years, and *Gender* is measured using a binary variable coded 1 for male and 0 for female. The literature on Internet usage provides little help in predicting the impact of gender on online searches and suggests that age will be negatively associated with online information searches. There is reason to believe however, that women would be more likely to conduct online searches for health care information. The National Alliance for Caregiving (2009) found that certain groups in the U.S. were more likely to conduct online searches for healthcare information. One group that stood out was women. This can be explained by the fact that women in the U.S. are more likely to take on the role of caring for elderly family members. To control for race and ethnicity, dummy variables were included for *African Americans*, *Asian Americans*, and *Latinos* with *non-Hispanic Whites* as the reference group. Because government research (NTIA, 2013) finds that Asian Americans and non-Hispanic Whites are more likely to have Internet access at home, they would be most likely to conduct Internet searches.

For the years 2008 and 2010, dummy variables were included for *No Home Internet Connection* and *Home Dialup Connection*, with broadband access at home as the reference group. For 2012, these controls were no longer available. This is to be expected; in 2007 approximately 11% of U.S. households were using dialup by 2011 the percentage had dropped to 2% (NTIA, 2013, pp. 20). These controls were included because research (Selwyn, 2004) argues that access to Internet service that is both more convenient and faster (such as home broadband) encourages greater use of the Internet and develops Internet skills. Because these variables were no longer available in 2012, a dummy variable was included for *Smartphone* coded 1 if an individual had a smartphone and 0 otherwise. Since smartphones are making Internet access more convenient, this measure is used as a proxy for quality of Internet access for the year 2012.

Because research on Internet access (NTIA, 2013) finds a persistent gap in urban/ rural areas, two dummy variables were included for the respondent's geographic area (*Suburban* and *Urban*) with rural as the reference group. Residents living in suburban and urban areas are expected to be more likely to conduct Internet searches compared to those living in rural areas. Dummy variables for the *Midwest, Northeast and West* regions were included to control for regional differences. The South was designated as the reference group because West and Miller (2006) found that this region has the lowest levels of Internet connectivity. Finally, the literature (McNeal, Hale, & Dotterweich, 2008; Sharp 1986; Thomas & Melkers, 1999) on citizen-initiated government contact indicates that individuals who contact government have a greater need for government services. To control for need, measurements for parents and individuals living with a chronic illness were included in the models. Parent is measured using a dummy variable coded 1 if the individual is a parent or guardian of a child under 18 and 0 otherwise. Chronic illness is coded 1 if the individual is living with a chronic illness such as kidney disease or cancer and 0 otherwise.

FINDINGS AND DISCUSSION

In Table 1, the dependent variable was coded so that higher scores are associated with increased likelihood of searching for information online. Since the dependent variable is binary, models are estimated using logistic regression. Table 1 presents the findings for 2008, 2010 and 2012 using the dependent variable: "Have you ever searched for online information related to insurance, including private insurance, Medicare or Medicaid?" Taken together, these tables suggest that individual-level variables play a larger role than geographic factors in determining who searches for health insurance information online.

There was limited support for the argument that income places an important role in Internet searches. This factor was only significant for the year 2008, where individuals with lower income levels were found to be more likely to search for health insurance information online. One variable that was found to be important was education. Across all three years, Internet searches for online health insurance information have been found more likely to done by individuals with higher education levels. This finding is expected, since these individuals are not only more likely to have Internet access but both greater technical and information literacy skills. Consistent across all three years of study was the finding that race/ ethnicity factors are not associated with Internet health insurance searches. This finding conflicts with trends (both past and recent) that indicate racial/ ethnic minorities are less likely to have Internet access but is consistent with research on online health searches (Schmeida & McNeal, 2013). Wattal et al (2011) provides a possible explanation. They argue that the spread of new technology is highly correlated with existing social classes in a society. Because concentrated areas of poverty are more prevalent among different ethnic and racial groups in the United States, you would expect that after controlling for variables such as education attainment and median family income differences in Internet usage based on race/ethnicity would disappear.

Women were found more likely to search for healthcare information in only the year 2008. Geographical differences including region and community type (urban, suburban and rural) were also not found to play a major role in Internet searches for health insurance information. This is despite trend studies finding that residents in rural areas and the South have less access to the broadband service. Quality of access was found to

Table 1. Public and private health insurance Internet searches, 2008-2012

Variables	Year 2008 β (se)	p>|z|	Year 2010 β (se)	p>|z|	Year 2012 β (se)	p>|z|
Environmental Variables						
Suburban	-.106(.216)	.623	.142(.157)	.365	.251(.165)	.128
Urban	**.535(.234)**	**.022**	.166(.162)	.306	.127(.173)	.459
Midwest	.137(.201)	.493	-.076(.144)	.599	.022(.153)	.883
Northeast	.006(.227)	.980	.007(.157)	.966	-.046(.156)	.769
West	.096(.212)	.650	-.161(.144)	.263	.223(.137)	.103
Individual Level Variables						
Age	**-.021(.006)**	**.000**	**- .011(.004)**	**.005**	**-.010(.004)**	**.020**
Male	**-.965(.162)**	**.000**	.043(.108)	.693	-.021(.108)	.848
Latino	-.329(.318)	.301	-.016(.164)	.921	-.002(.164)	.987
Black	-.361(.293)	.219	-.077(.145)	.598	-.207(.157)	.189
Asian	- .693(.582)	.232	-.054(.305)	.861	-.349(.291)	.231
Education	**.146(.058)**	**.012**	**.270(.039)**	**.000**	**.203(.033)**	**.000**
Income	**-.079(.042)**	**.063**	.022(.027)	.432	-.042(.027)	.117
Dial-up Connection	-.222(.241)	.358	**-.484(.234)**	**.039**	____	
No Home Internet Connection	**-2.35(.326)**	**.000**	**-2.29(.220)**	**.000**	____	
Chronic Illness	.098(.172)	.566	**.572(.119)**	**.000**	**.321(.119)**	**.007**
Parent	.007(.174)	.967	.098(.112)	.413	**.270(.118)**	**.022**
Medicaid Recipient	____		.141(.180)	.432	**.576(.165)**	**.000**
Medicare Recipient	____		-.097(.177)	.585	.156(.172)	.362
Smart Phone	____		____		**.496(.138)**	**.000**
Constant Pseudo R2	.0535(.437) .1678	.903	**-1.84(.297)** .1729	**.000**	**-2.71(.314)** .0681	**.000**
LR Chi²	214.40	.000	451.67	.000	162.19	.000
N	1279		2306		2255	

Sources: *The Internet and American Life Daily Tracking Survey December 2008, September 2010 Daily Tracking Poll and the 2012 Pew Health Tracking Survey.* Logistic regression estimates with standard errors in parentheses. Reported probabilities are based on two-tailed tests. Statistically significant coefficients at .10 or less in bold. "Have you ever searched for online information related to insurance, including private insurance, Medicare or Medicaid?"

be an important factor in online health insurance searches across all three years. For both 2008 and 2010, those individuals without home Internet access were less likely to conduct health insurance information searches. In addition, those who used dialup at home were less likely to do searches in 2010. Finally, those individuals with smartphones were more likely to conduct online searches.

Younger individuals were more likely to search for medical insurance information online across all three years. This finding is inconsistent with Schmeida & McNeal (2007) who found that older individuals were more likely to search for Medicare and Medicaid information online. The finding is however consistent with Schmeida & McNeal (2013) whose multiyears study found that younger individuals overtook older individuals in insurance searches in 2008. They suggested that this change in pattern could be explained by the current economic climate with more individuals (both young and old) needing to rely on government programs such as Medicaid. This argument follows Adams, Stubbs & Woods (2005) who argue that need or motivation was important to both Internet usage and developing technological skills. Other variables also suggest that economic conditions are an important motivation for online searches for insurance information. Although neither measure of need (parent and chronic illness) were statistically significant for all three years, they increasingly became important factors as the U.S. moved into the" Great Recession" and following its after effects. The same can be said for the controls for Medicare and Medicaid recipients. Although neither variable was significant in 2010, Medicaid recipient was a relevant factor in 2012. The aftermath of the "Great Recession" is likely to be felt for some time. The Centers for Medicare and Medicaid Services (2013b) found that state and local government expenditures on healthcare consumed 30% of their revenue. This percentage is the largest since the government began collecting this data in 1987 and is expected to continue to represent a large percentage of state and local government budgets.

FUTURE RESEARCH DIRECTIONS

The results from this study diverge from earlier research on Internet health insurance studies and contradict what we expect based on trend studies that chart Internet usage. Early trend studies on Internet usage and access in the United States showed disparities based on age, income, education, race, ethnicity, dual/single parent households, urban/ rural areas, primary language spoken at home, and mental or physical disabilities. Initially, gender was also a factor but was found to disappear by 2002 (NTIA, 2013). Of these factors, the

rural/ urban divide has proven to be one of the more difficult to close. The findings of this study do not mesh well with the expected outcomes that could be drawn from trend studies on Internet access and usage. This study suggests that using health insurance websites is primarily based on education levels, need and quality of access (speed and convenience). One reason that education may be important is because it is a predictor of both Internet access and information literacy. Another explanation has been suggested by West (2005). Although nation statistics suggest that many Americans read at an 8th grade reading level or less, his examination of government websites (both state and federal) from 2001 to 2003 found that the average reading level was at an eleventh grade level. This suggests that although there has been effort across three presidents to bring more citizens online, there also must be an effort to ensure that citizens can use government websites once they are online. Although many studies have focused on the digital divide and overcoming it, future research may wish to consider the impact of usability of government websites on the expansion of government services and information online.

One caveat to consider when examining the outcome of this study is that certain control variables were not available throughout the three years of consideration. One variable that changed was the measure for quality of Internet access. For 2008 and 2010, two dummy variables were used; one for no Internet access at home and the other for dialup access at home. For 2012, possession of a smartphone was used as a proxy for quality of Internet access. This change was necessary because very few individuals in the United States use dialup anymore. Quality of access (speed and convenience) was found to be significant predictors of searching online health insurance websites regardless of the measure used. This suggests that future studies should consider the impact of technical advances on Internet adoption and usage including cloud computing, and mobile technology.

Finally, this study indicates that need (possibly in response to the downturn of the economy) may have driven more people online to look for health insurance information. Researchers need to be aware of happenings such as changes in the economy that might impact citizen behavior. One such event is currently taking place in the United States. Policy implementation of the Patient Protection and Affordable Care Act (ACA) on improving Medicare and Medicaid enrollment is in an early stage. This Act has potential to mobilize interest / motivation in searching for public and/ or private insurance online, particularly since government websites have become more "user friendly" in informing the general public on insurance. What demographic groups respond to Medicare and Medicaid outreach efforts online? The adoption of e-government strategies, such as applying advanced communication technology to enhance ACA policy implementation does not necessarily guarantee successful outreach outcomes. Success is dependent on many factors particularly government consumers having both access to and use of the Internet. Further study is needed to determine the impact of the ACA.

CONCLUSION

This chapter began with the question, "has the effort of three presidental administrations to address the digital divide also helped bring vulnerable citizens online to Medicare and Medicaid insurance information?" This study built on earlier research that found that government action was making a difference. Among this earlier research was Schmeida and McNeal (2007) who found the elderly and poor, were among those most likely to search for subsidized health insurance online, despite being least likely to have Internet access. The findings from this research are different. Although they are not necessarily discouraging, they lead us to conclude that factors which were not in the forefront of previous research are now some of the more important predictors of accessing online Medicare and Medicare insurance information.

Three concepts stood out: quality of access(speed and convenience), education and need. The finding that education was significant across all three years of this study may simply result from the fact that it is associated with both Internet access and information literacy. It might also be an indicator that given that more Americans than ever are coming online, the government should refocus its efforts on making certain that government websites are user friendly. West (2005) found that despite the fact that many Americans read at an 8th grade level or lower, the average reading levels of government websites was 11th grade. While it is necessary to bring citizens online to realize the full potential of e-government programs, it's just as important to guarantee they can use government websites. The quality of access available was statistically significant regardless of how this concept was measured. We are going through a period of rapid changes in information technology (IT) including mobile technology and cloud computing. In order to encourage citizens to use e-government instead of conventional means of interacting with government, it might be necessary to develop strategies that allow citizens to take greater advantages of the newest technology. For example, in the case of healthcare information; the government might consider developing applicable apps. Finally, citizens appeared to be seeking out information on subsidized health insurance in the aftermath of the economic downturn or Great Recession. This reminds researchers and government officials that they must be cognizant of social, economic and political events that could have a direct or indirect impact on e-government usage. The next event that should influence online insurance searches is the implementation of the Patient Protection and Affordable Care Act (ACA) which is in its early stages.

REFERENCES

Adams, N., Stubbs, V., & Woods, V. (2005). Psychological barriers to Internet usage among older adults in the U.K. *Medical Informatics and the Internet in Medicine*, *30*(1), 3–17. doi:10.1080/14639230500066876 PMID:16036626

Belanger, F., & Carter, L. (2009). The impact of the digital divide on e-government use. *Communications of the ACM*, *52*(4), 132–135. doi:10.1145/1498765.1498801

Centers for Medicare & Medicaid Services. (2013a). *Medicare program - general information*. Retrieved July 12, 2013, from http://www.cms.gov/

Center for Medicare & Medicaid Services. (2013b). *National health expenditure accounts: Sponsored highlights*. Retrieved February 19, 2014, from http:// www.cms.gov/Research-Statistics-Data-and-Systems/Statistics-Trend-and-Reports/NationalHealthExpendData/National-HealthAccountsHistorical.html

Fountain, J. (2001). *Building the virtual state: Information technology and institutional change*. Washington, DC: Brookings Institution Press.

Gabel, D. (2007). Broadband and universal service. *Telecommunications Policy*, *31*, 327–346. doi:10.1016/j.telpol.2007.05.002

Jaeger, P., Bertot, J., McClure, C., & Rodriguez, M. (2007). Public libraries and Internet access across the United States: A comparison by state from 2004 to 2006. *Information Technology and Libraries*, *26*(2), 4–14.

Mack, E., & Grubesic, T. (2009). Forecasting broadband provision. *Information Economics and Policy*, *21*, 297–311. doi:10.1016/j.infoecopol.2009.08.001

McNeal, R. (2012). State response to Obama's broadband access policy: A study in policy implementation. In *Public Sector Transformation through E-Government: Experiences from Europe and North America*. Routledge.

McNeal, R., Hale, K., & Dotterweich, L. (2008). Citizen-government interaction and the internet: Expectations and accomplishments in contact, quality and trust. *Journal of Information Technology & Politics*, *5*(2), 213–229. doi:10.1080/19331680802298298

McNeal, R., & Schmeida, M. (2007). Electronic campaign finance reform in the American states. In *The encyclopedia of digital government* (Vol. 3, pp. 624–628). Idea Group Publishing.

Mossberger, K., Tolbert, C., & McNeal, R. (2007). *Digital citizenship: The internet, society and participation*. Cambridge, MA: MIT Press.

Mossberger, K., Tolbert, C., & Stansbury, M. (2003). *Virtual inequality: Beyond the digital divide*. Washington, DC: Georgetown Press.

National Alliance for Caregiving. (2009). *Caregiving in the U.S. 2009*. Retrieved June 8, 2013, from http://www.caregiving.org/data/Caregiving_in_the_US_2009_full_report.pdf

National Telecommunications and Information Administration. (2000). *Falling through the net: Toward digital inclusion: A report on Americans access to technology tools*. Retrieved October 14, 2005, from http://www.ntia.doc.gov/files/ntia/publications/fttn00.pdf

National Telecommunications and Information Administration. (2013). *Exploring the digital nation: America's Emerging online* experience. Retrieved February 19, 2014, from http://www.ntia.doc.gov/report/2013/exploring-digital-nation-americas-emerging-online-experience

Public Law 111-148. (2010). *Patient Protection and Affordable Care Act.*

Schmeida, M. (2005). *Telehealth innovation in the American states.* Ann Arbor, MI: ProQuest.

Schmeida, M., & McNeal, R. (2007). The telehealth divide: disparities in searching public health information online. *Journal of Health Care for the Poor and Underserved, 18*, 637–647. doi:10.1353/hpu.2007.0068 PMID:17675719

Schmeida, M., & McNeal, R. (2009). Demographic differences in telehealth policy outcomes. In *Handbook of Research on Distributed Medical Informatics and E-health.* Idea Group Publishing.

Schmeida, M., & McNeal, R. (2013). Bridging the inequality gap to searching Medicare and Medicaid information online: An empirical analysis of e-government Success 2002 through 2010. In J. Ramon Gil-Garcia (Ed.), *E-Government Success around the World: Cases, Empirical Studies, and Practical Recommendations.* IGI Global. doi:10.4018/978-1-4666-4173-0.ch004

Selwyn, N. (2004). Reconsidering political and popular understandings of the digital divide. *New Media & Society, 6*(3), 341–362. doi:10.1177/1461444804042519

Thomas, J. C., & Melkers, J. (1999). Explaining citizen-initiated contacts with municipal bureaucrats: Lessons from the Atlanta experience. *Urban Affairs Review, 34*(5), 667–690. doi:10.1177/10780879922184130

U.S. Department of Health & Human Services. (2013a). *The Affordable Care Act and African Americans.* Retrieved March 30, 2014, from http://www.hhs.gov/healthcare/facts/factsheets/2012/04/aca-and-african-americans04122012a.html

U.S. Department of Health & Human Services. (2013b). *The Affordable Care Act and women.* Retrieved March 30, 2014 from http://www.hhs.gov/healthcare/facts/factsheets/2012/03/women03202012a.html

U.S. Department of Health & Human Services. (2013c). *The Affordable Care Act- what it means for rural America.* Retrieved March 30, 2014, from http://www.hhs.gov/healthcare/facts/factsheets/2013/09/rural09202013.html

U.S. Department of Health & Human Services. (2014) *The Affordable Care Act and Latinos.* Retrieved March 30, 2014 from http://www.hhs.gov/healthcare/facts/factsheets/2012/04/aca-and-latinos04102012a.html

Van Dijk, J. (1999). *The network society, social aspects of new media.* London: Sage.

Wattal, S., Hong, Y., Mandviwalla, M., & Jain, A. (2011). *Technological diffusion in the society: Digital divide in the context of social class.* Paper presented at the Hawaii International Conference on System Sciences. Hawaii, HI. www.whitehouse.gov. (2014). *Health care that works for Americans.* Retrieved March 31, 2014 from www.whitehouse.gov/healthreform/healthcare-overview

West, D. (2004). E-government and the transformation of service delivery and citizen attitudes. *Public Administration Review, 64*(1), 15–27. doi:10.1111/j.1540-6210.2004.00343.x

West, D. (2005). *Digital government: Technology and public sector performance.* Princeton, NJ: Princeton University Press.

West, D., & Miller, E. (2006). The digital divide in public e-health: barriers to accessibility and privacy in state health department web sites. *Journal of Health Care for the Poor and Underserved, 17*, 652–667. doi:10.1353/hpu.2006.0115 PMID:16960328

ADDITIONAL READING

Al-Sobhi, F., Weerakkody, V., & El-Haddadeh, R. (2012). Building trust in e-government adoption through an intermediary channel. *International Journal of Electronic Government Research, 8*(2), 91–106. doi:10.4018/jegr.2012040105

Bennett, M. D. (2003). *A broadband world: the promise of advanced services*. Washington, DC: Alliance for Public Technology & the Benton Foundation.

Bertot, J., & Jaeger, P. (2008). The E-government paradox: Better customer service doesn't necessarily cost less. *Government Information Quarterly, 25*(3), 134–154.

Bimber, B. (1999). The Internet and citizen communication with government: Does the medium matter? *Political Communication, 16*(4), 409–428. doi:10.1080/105846099198569

Bimber, B. (2003). *Information and American democracy: technology in the evolution of political power.* Cambridge University Press. doi:10.1017/CBO9780511615573

Chen, Y., & Dimitrova, D. (2006). Electronic government and online engagement: citizen interaction with government via Web portals. *International Journal of Electronic Government Research, 2*(1), 54–76. doi:10.4018/jegr.2006010104

Dugdale, A., Daly, A., Papandrea, F., & Maley, M. (2005). Accessing e-government: Challenges for citizens and organizations. *International Review of Administrative Sciences, 71*(1), 109–118. doi:10.1177/0020852305051687

Evans, D., & Yen, D. C. (2006). E-government: Evolving relationships of citizens and government, domestic, and international development. *Government Information Quarterly, 23*, 207–235. doi:10.1016/j.giq.2005.11.004

Fountain, J. E. (2008). Bureaucratic reform and e-government in the United States: An institutional perspective. In A. Chadwick, & P. N. Howard (Eds.), *Routledge handbook of Internet politics* (pp. 99–113). New York: Routledge.

Goldsmith, S., & Eggers, W. D. (2004). *Governing by network: the new shape of the public sector.* Washington, DC: Brookings Institution Press.

Hargittai, E., & Hinnant, A. (2008). Digital inequalities: Differences in young adults' use of the Internet. *Communication Research, 35*(5), 602–621. doi:10.1177/0093650208321782

Ho, A. T.-K. (2002). Reinventing Local Governments and the E-Government Initiative. *Public Administration Review, 62*(4), 434–444. doi:10.1111/0033-3352.00197

Jaeger, P., & Bertot, J. (2010). Transparency and technological change: ensuring equal and sustained public access to government information. *Government Information Quarterly, 27*(4), 371–376. doi:10.1016/j.giq.2010.05.003

Jayakar, K., & Park, E. (2012). Funding public computing centers: Balancing broadband availability and expected demand. *Government Information Quarterly, 29*(1), 50–59. doi:10.1016/j.giq.2011.02.005

Kernaghan, K. (2005). Moving toward the virtual state: Integrating services and service channels for citizen-centered delivery. *International Review of Administrative Sciences, 71*(1), 119–131. doi:10.1177/0020852305051688

Kettl, Don. (2002). *The transformation of governance: public administration for twenty-first century America.* Baltimore, MD: The Johns Hopkins University Press.

Layne, K., & Lee, J. (2001). Developing fully functional e-government: a four stage model. *Government Information Quarterly*, *18*(2), 122–136. doi:10.1016/S0740-624X(01)00066-1

Lenhart, A., Purcell, K., Smith, A., & Zichuhr, K. (2010). *Social media & mobile use among teens and young adults*. PEW Research Center. Retrieved October 24, 2011, from http://pewinternet.org/Reports/2010/social-media-and-young-adults.aspx

Levy, F., & Murnane, R. (1996, May). With what skills are computers a complement? *The American Economic Review*, *86*(2), 258–262.

Mayer-Schonberger, V., & Lazer, D. (Ed.). (2007). Governance and information technology: from electronic government to information government. Cambridge, MA: MIT Press.

McNeal, R., Tolbert, C., Mossberger, K., & Dotterweich, L. (2003). Innovating in digital government in the American states. *Social Science Quarterly*, *84*(1), 52–70. doi:10.1111/1540-6237.00140

Norris, P. (1999). *Critical citizens: global support for democratic governance*. Oxford: Oxford University Press. doi:10.1093/0198295685.001.0001

Ong, C., & Wang, S. (2009). Managing citizen-initiated email contacts. *Government Information Quarterly*, *26*(3), 498–504. doi:10.1016/j.giq.2008.07.005

Putnam, R. (2000). *Bowling alone: the collapse and revival of American community*. New York: Simon & Schuster. doi:10.1145/358916.361990

Rappoport, P. N., & Kridel, D. J., & Taylor, L.D. (2002). The demand for broadband: access, content, and the value of time. In R.W. Crandall & J.H. Alleman, (Ed.) Broadband: should we regulate high-speed internet access? (pp. 57-82). Washington, D.C.: AEI Brookings Joint Center for Regulatory Studies.

Rose, W., & Grant, G. (2010). Critical Issues pertaining to the planning and implementation of e-government initiatives. *Government Information Quarterly*, *27*(1), 26–33. doi:10.1016/j.giq.2009.06.002

Servon, L. J., & Nelson, M. K. (2001). Community technology centers: narrowing the digital divide in low-income urban communities. *Journal of Urban Affairs*, *23*(3-4), 279–290. doi:10.1111/0735-2166.00089

Southwest Rural Health Research Center. (2010). *Rural healthy people 2010: a companion document to healthy people 2010*. Volume 1. College Station, TX: The Texas A & M University System Health Science Center, School of Rural Public Health, Southwest Rural Health Research Center. Retrieved March 2014, from http://www.srph.tamhsc.edu/centers/rhp2010/publications.htm

Stover, S. (1999). *Rural internet connectivity*. Rural Policy Research Institute. Retrieved June 21, 2000, from http://www.rupi.org

Stovers, S., Chapman, G., & Walters, J. (2004). Beyond community networking and CTCs: Access, development, and public policy. *Telecommunications Policy*, *28*(7-8), 465–485. doi:10.1016/j.telpol.2004.05.008

Thomas, J. C. (1982). Citizen-initiated contacts with government agencies: a test of three theories. *American Journal of Political Science*, *26*(3), 504–522. doi:10.2307/2110940

Tolbert, C. J., Mossberger, K., & McNeal, R. (2008). Innovation and learning: measuring e-government performance in the American states 2000-2004. *Public Administration Review*, *68*(3), 549–563. doi:10.1111/j.1540-6210.2008.00890.x

Tong, R. (2007). Gender-based disparities east/west: rethinking the burden of care in the United States and Taiwan. *Bioethics*, *21*(9), 488–499. doi:10.1111/j.1467-8519.2007.00594.x PMID:17927625

Van Dijk, J., & Hacker, K. (2003). The digital divide as a complex and dynamic phenomenon. *The Information Society*, *19*(4), 315–326. doi:10.1080/01972240309487

Walsh, E. O. (2001). The truth about the digital divide. In B. Compaine (Ed.), *The digital divide: facing a crisis or a myth?* (pp. 279–284). Cambridge, Mass.: MIT Press.

KEY TERMS AND DEFINITIONS

Community Technology Center (CTC): A public building including schools and libraries where citizens can go for computer access and training.

Digital Divide: Persistent gaps in Internet access based on demographic factors such as age, income and education.

Electronic Government (E-Government): The delivery of information and services online.

E-Rate: Created by the passage of the Telecommunications Act of 1996, this federal program was set up as a $2.25 billion annual fund to help defray the cost of Internet service to schools and libraries by providing discounts for connectivity costs for the Internet.

Health Insurance Marketplace: Also called the "exchange" it is a one-stop shopping place for healthcare insurance information with a website at www.healthcare.gov.

Information Literacy: The ability to determine which information found on the Internet is appropriate for a specific task.

Medicaid: Public health insurance program sponsored by the US government for the impoverished of all age groups, for the blind, disabled, and medically needy considered impoverished. It is the second largest US public health insurance program.

Medicare: Public health insurance program sponsored by the US government for persons under 65 years and certain disability, age 65 or older, and all age groups with End-State Renal Disease. It is the largest US public health insurance program.

Patient Protection and Affordable Care Act: Public Law 111-148, signed into law by President Barack Obama March 2010. This legislation enables comprehensive reform set to improve healthcare insurance coverage for Americans, strengthen consumer rights and protections, improve access to healthcare, improve quality of care, and build the integrity of the Medicare program.

Technical Competency: Necessary skills to use hardware and software, such as typing and using a mouse. through the Internet or other digital means.

Chapter 20
The Role of E–Health in Developing Nations

Shane O'Hanlon
University of Limerick, Ireland

ABSTRACT

Many developing nations have begun to introduce elements of e-Health to improve service provision. This chapter provides an account of work in the area including case studies where pioneers have utilised modern mobile technologies to quickly and efficiently introduce new mHealth interventions, despite being resource-limited and having a heavy disease burden. Telemedicine has become well established, linking these nations with specialists in centres of excellence. Obstacles such as cost, inadequate infrastructure, data security, and the lack of a trained health informatics workforce need to be resolved. Several innovative solutions have been put forward: satellite broadband access for the most remote areas, international sponsorship initiatives, use of open source software, and exchange programmes for staff education. There is strong support from the World Health Organization and other international bodies, as development of the eHealth agenda has the potential to help ease access barriers and improve provision of healthcare in developing countries. This is explored in this chapter.

E-HEALTH: DEFINITION, SCOPE AND FUNDING

e-Health as a term has been in use for many years, but even up to recently there was little agreement as to what exactly it encompasses. Oh and colleagues (2005) noted that it was in widespread use, but found over 50 unique definitions in the literature. There is broad agreement that it involves the use of information and communication technology for provision of healthcare. This obviously has a very large scope and includes many areas such as

telemedicine, telecare, electronic health records, clinical decision support systems and more recently the concept of m-Health (mobile Health). With the shift towards smartphone technology, m-Health has gained in significance and it is likely that many newer applications will be developed in this area. This has particular relevance for developing countries as the traditional reliance on desktop computing appears to be waning and the opportunities for mobile technologies are increasing. Considering that many of these countries are spread over large geographical areas that are

DOI: 10.4018/978-1-4666-3691-0.ch020

often difficult to access, m-Health may be the most economical way of introducing e-Health interventions.

e-Health has broad support from governments, non-government organisations, industry and healthcare providers. There are some major funding initiatives in progress with the aim of stimulating development and uptake. For example, the European Commission's (EC) seventh research framework programme has a total budget of more than €50 billion, with prioritisation for e-Health. The World Health Organization (WHO) has urged member states to reach communities, including vulnerable groups, with e-Health services appropriate to their needs (World Health Organization, 2005). They also publish a yearly Compendium showcasing innovative technology for low-resource settings.

Unfortunately, e-Health currently lacks a system of international coordination, and many countries are involved in disparate efforts. Additionally, many e-Health projects are not conducted as part of a research trial, or take the form of small pilot studies. There is still a need for policymakers to encourage joined-up thinking across different nations and to coordinate efforts to minimise duplication and foster exchange of ideas. This would also help to increase the evidence base and to demonstrate that e-Health can be useful for the end user in developing countries.

EVOLUTION AND EVIDENCE

As early as 1969, computers were predicted to be a solution for the growing demands of healthcare provision (Barnett & Sukenik, 1969). Although the capabilities of technology have improved exponentially since then, there is still a need for better evidence for the effectiveness of e-Health solutions. The WHO resolution on e-Health speaks about "the potential impact that it could have" and the EC notes that e-Health will provide "better, more efficient healthcare services for all".

Although it seems logical, there is however an inherent danger in assuming that e-Health will have benefits for patients. For example, one study reported an unexpected increase in mortality when a computerised provider order entry (CPOE) system was introduced in a paediatric hospital (Han et al., 2005). It has been suggested that socio-technical change may have been responsible for this result (O'Hanlon 2011). It demonstrates the importance of considering usability when designing these systems, and of performing careful evaluations when implementing them (Catwell & Sheikh, 2009). Thankfully a more recent similar project demonstrated a significant reduction of 20% in mortality (Longhurst et al., 2010).

Recently the first systematic review of the evidence for e-Health was published (Black et al., 2011). The authors noted that despite support from policymakers and "techno-enthusiasts", there was only a small amount of evidence to substantiate claims being made about their effectiveness. In particular they found no evidence that they were more cost-effective. This has serious implications when considering the use of e-Health in developing nations as there is an opportunity cost involved. If governments begin to fund e-Health interventions it may be at the expense of other services that may arguably be cheaper and more effective. There is a need for a more robust evidence-base before this can be recommended. In particular there should be more emphasis on what these interventions can achieve in resource-limited environments.

E-HEALTH APPLIED TO DEVELOPING NATIONS

It has been estimated that the developing world consists of over 5 billion people in 127 countries (Wootton, 2008). Healthcare in developing nations can be disorganised, underfunded and lacking in resources. These countries incur almost 80% of all deaths related to chronic diseases (World Health Organization, 2005). Geneva: WHO; 2005. [Aug

1;2010]. WHO Facing the Facts: The Impact of Chronic Disease in the Americas.) In many cases this is because of poor access to healthcare as well as unhealthy living conditions. The management of chronic disease requires regular contact with health services and the availability of skilled health professionals. One of the main objectives of e-Health is to increase access to healthcare. For those in the developing world there is a significant access barrier that could potentially be addressed by interventions such as telemedicine and m-Health. Bringing expertise to rural and remote areas could be achieved by using handheld diagnostic aids, decision support systems and telemedicine links with major centres. There are already some examples of these systems, detailed in the case studies later in this chapter.

Lack of infrastructure has been a challenge in delivering internet-based solutions in resource-limited areas. However the arrival of the mobile internet has transformed the playing field. It is no longer necessary to lay down thousands of miles of cable to bring a connection to remote areas. The leapfrog effect has allowed some developing countries to skip the expensive and time-consuming fixed-line infrastructure development of the late 20th century and go directly to implementation of satellite or long-distance wireless systems (Sinha, 2005). Internet access is now possible anywhere in the world, and with it the potential to bring knowledge and expertise to anyone.

It is important that any country that begins development of e-Health systems first considers the needs of its people. The current and future healthcare and public health requirements must be evaluated and this should be the main driver for implementation. This goal-directed system can then be assessed on whether it achieves its aims. As the country's needs evolve, the system can then be adjusted.

Likewise, e-Health can be a benefit to workers in the health service of developing countries. There is a widespread shortage of medical personnel so making most efficient use of resources is a vital priority. One way in which e-Health is helpful is in extending the reach of medical education. Doctors and other professionals need to continuously update their skills and knowledge, something that is difficult to achieve in resource-poor nations. By tapping into international knowledge bases and e-learning modules it is possible to stay abreast of recent evidence and practice.

M-HEALTH

At the forefront of the e-Health drive is m-Health, the use of mobile technologies to assist with healthcare provision. This has the potential to deliver e-Health interventions to areas with access difficulty, which makes it particularly useful for roll-out in the developing world. This appears to be already in progress. In one major international survey of m-Health, 77% of low-income countries reported at least one m-Health initiative, compared with 87% of high-income countries (World Health Organization, 2011).

This is helped by the fact that 64% of all mobile phone users can now be found in the developing world (United Nations, 2007). Using this technology appears to be acceptable and convenient. For example, one study reported that the majority of patients surveyed were willing to participate in outreach programmes designed to improve their illness self-care via automated telephone messaging (Piette et al., 2010).

m-Health can be used to help provide access to e-Health technologies, but it can also be used to deliver solutions by itself. There are examples of using m-Health to gather data at multiple locations and send it to a central e-Health programme where targeted intervention can be made; and also projects where m-Health itself provides the benefit. It is useful to examine some case studies that demonstrate the point.

Case Study 1: Text to Change

Text to Change (TTC) was an initiative in Uganda with the goal of improving health education through text messaging (Text to Change, 2008). A three month pilot phase was put in place with the specific aim of increasing public knowledge around AIDS, and changing behaviour. The text messages encouraged people to seek voluntary testing and counselling for HIV/AIDS. The means of education was through an interactive quiz which was sent to users. When a wrong answer was given, the system sent users the correct response so that they could improve their knowledge. The incentive was to offer free airtime to users. Additionally, for those who went to test centres via TTC the service was free.

In total the quiz was sent to 15,000 mobile phone subscribers, and the uptake rate was 17.4%. At the test centres, it was noted that the quiz directly resulted in a 40% increase in patients who came in for testing.

As well as this positive outcome, the project had other spin-off benefits. The responses to the quiz allowed organisers to gather information about the level of knowledge around HIV/AIDS and highlighted particular areas where there were gaps in understanding. This should be useful for directing any future educational projects. Participants were also more informed about the location of their local test centre, and about the services offered. One of the more useful outcomes was the discovery by the project team that respondents reported a fear of HIV testing because they perceived it to be lacking in confidentiality and also accuracy. This suspicion of testing helps explains why uptake rates might be low, and can be targeted as an area where more work is needed.

The sponsors also reported benefit as they were able to highlight this measure as part of the development of their corporate social responsibility, and the testing centre benefited through increased throughput. Both of these outcomes were important as the project relies on funding for future operation.

m-Health can also facilitate local collection of data on a small level, with immediate transfer to a regional centre where it can be aggregated into a powerful dataset. This can be particularly useful in countries that cover a large area, or with significant rural populations. Real-time tracking of diseases can transform service planning and help to quickly intervene to reduce spread.

Case Study 2: Remote Data Collection

Dengue is a mosquito-borne illness that is prevalent in many areas. Tracking the spread of the virus is important to inform public health authorities so that response planning can be co-ordinated. A project in Brazil called Data Gathering was put in place to contain the spread of the infection (UN Foundation-Vodafone Foundation Partnership, 2009). The aim was to equip field officers with a solution which would allow them to monitor local infection rates and provide for central collation of the resultant data in real-time. Customised questionnaires were created and administered via mobile phone. When agents had entered all their data it was sent wirelessly to the server, with a GPS (Global Positioning System) record of the location of the data originator.

As there was an immediate improvement in service provision with this project, it was unsurprising to see positive user feedback. It was noted that the application was easier and more practical than the previous situation. There was also a reduction in the time spent gathering data. The organisers noted the importance of usability, as if field agents did not see it benefiting their work they would be much less likely to use it. There was a visible result in that immediate up-to-date data was available to guide health authorities. Previously the response time after gathering data and collating it manually would have been 2-3 months. In the event of an outbreak, it would not have been possible to put response measures in place until it may have been too late. The new system provides for immediate action, with the possibility of intervening on the same day as the data is gathered.

TELEMEDICINE

Telemedicine, like other branches of e-Health, has had its successes and failures. In the 1990s the South African government attempted to institute a national telemedicine system, but failed (Mars, 2009). Likewise a $5.5 million project in Malaysia had to be withdrawn for redesign (Wootton & Tahir, 2004). More recently there have been several success stories and there now exists a reasonable amount of evidence that telemedicine can be of benefit to patients and healthcare providers. Most of this comes from research in western countries and there has been relatively little work done in resource-poor nations. In a recent review of telemedicine in the developing world, Wootton & Bonnardot (2010) found that store-and-forward systems were the most common type, with email the most frequently seen modality. The quality of reports was weak, suggesting that little research exists for its effectiveness as a tool in these countries.

Despite this, telemedicine is now well established in some developing countries. It has been used by clinicians to gain access to second opinions, specialist advice, and to share knowledge. It has also been suggested as a potential tool to coordinate disaster response. It was employed following the Armenian earthquake in 1988 to allow cooperation between medical teams in Armenia and Russia (Houtchens et al., 1993). A satellite link was put in place that allowed medical teams

on site to obtain advice from experts. Over a 12 week period, 209 patients were discussed and the diagnosis was altered in 26%.

Telemedicine has also been used for medical education where there are access difficulties. For example the RAFT (Réseau en Afrique Francophone pour la Télémédecine) network extending across 10 French-speaking countries allows the communication and sharing of medical information via videoconference (Geissbuhler, Bagayoko, & Ly, 2007). The system has been used by physicians in the developing world to consult colleagues, follow educational courses and access information from databases and libraries. Another example is the WHO Pacific open learning network, which uses asynchronous education.

It has been noted that only 0.1% of the potential demand for telemedicine referral services is being met at the moment (Wootton, 2008). This may be because doctors are too busy to use it; are not willing to be seen to ask for help; don't feel they can get an appropriate answer; or do not value the service. One solution is to set up intra-national telemedicine networks, where the expert advice comes from a tertiary referral centre within the same country (Wootton, 2008). The aim would then be to improve health outcomes, be cost-effective and sustainable, and act as a model for other countries to follow. Having a national solution also reduces dependence on other countries and avoids reluctance that may be associated with seeking help from someone outside the country.

Case Study 3: Remote Monitoring

Remote monitoring is one area of e-Health where there is evidence of benefit to patients. In chronic conditions such as heart failure, being able to transmit data to providers can help to improve control and reduce hospital admissions (Schmidt, 2010).

The Chinese Aged Diabetic Assistant (CADA) (CADA Project, 2008) is a form of health monitoring at a distance. Diabetes is a chronic condition which requires regular contact with health services in order to prevent serious and sometimes life-threatening complications. In developing nations such as China there has been a recent surge in the prevalence of diabetes, mainly due to lifestyle changes. This project developed a self-management system with two different components: a remote monitoring tool and a patient education feature. As blood sugar levels need to be observed regularly to ensure that the disease is under control, users are trained to enter their results into an enabled smartphone which allows doctors to track their progress. This facilitates intervention once readings go outside set parameters. The project software is provided without charge to encourage uptake.

The education component sends recommendations and guidelines that help diabetic control. For example, physical activity, weight, dietary advice are provided. The system also educates users about optimal blood sugar levels and what to expect if levels need intervention, such as increased medication dosage. This approach is user-centred and practical and solves problems that are of immediate relevance. A project such as this also has the advantage of helping service users and providers. It allows healthcare teams to monitor the response to treatment changes and helps to predict future healthcare needs.

Case Study 4: Swinfen Charitable Trust

The Swinfen Charitable Trust set up an email telemedicine system in 1998 in order to provide access to specialty opinion for hospitals in developing countries. It has the aim of assisting poor, sick and disabled people in the developing world by establishing these links (Wootton, Menzies, & Ferguson, 2009). The specialists who provide advice and support do so on a voluntary basis. The system uses a hybrid email/web messaging communications format that provides for secure transmission of clinical data and sometimes im-

ages. Store and forward telemedicine is used. Hospitals in countries such as Iraq, Afghanistan, Pakistan and Kuwait have benefited from the service.

The system has proved to be very useful and efficient, with a median response time of 19 hours. It is limited in how much it can be used because the need for access to the internet. Despite this, in the first 8 years almost 1,500 referrals were received. In a review of cases, the trust found that telemedicine was considered to have assisted with the diagnosis in all cases (median score 5 on a five-point scale from 1, not helpful at all to 5, very good/excellent). The specialist advice given was considered helpful in all except one case and the outcome for the patient was considered to be good in 15 of the cases (68%). The authors felt that the system was successful and delivered significant benefits for both the referring clinician and the patient. They advised that a low cost solution such as this should be considered before more expensive technology is contemplated.

BARRIERS

The main barriers to implementing e-Health in the developing world are lack of equipment, lack of information technology skills and the costs involved (Ouma & Herselman, 2008). Apart from these, there are other challenges for governments in the developing world. As is the case in many career areas, there has been a 'brain-drain' of professionals involved in information technology, informatics and healthcare towards the western world. Globally there is a relatively small health informatics-trained workforce so there is a need for universities and other institutions to produce more qualified individuals. Although there has been a successful rollout of mobile communications technology in many countries, the skills-base has not remained, with experts often brought in from abroad on short-term contracts. Exchange programmes between developing and developed countries could be a major help, and sponsorship opportunities for willing and motivated individuals would help to alleviate the shortage.

Engaging stakeholders is a major challenge. While school enrolment and literacy rates remain low, engagement with and development of e-Health services may remain poor (Kirigia, Seddoh, Gatwiri, Muthuri, & Seddoh 2005). Cultural diversity means that traditional health services may not be the primary point of access for people requiring care. Many are suspicious of orthodox health approaches and may not engage with providers. As well as patients, it can be difficult to involve politicians and achieve widespread local support. The introduction of technology can add new challenges as the resultant socio-technical change can be unpredictable. It alters how patients interact with their health service, and this may result in some people rejecting the change.

In terms of finances and resources it is always a challenge to set up new e-Health projects. As most are developed with seed funding there is usually a short defined period of activity. Project managers need to quickly demonstrate success and a positive outcome in order to successfully obtain long-term funding. This sustainability challenge is a major issue for e-Health in the developing world. Use of open source software where possible is helpful, as it allows users to avoid the costs involved with licensing and upgrade of products (Drury, 2005). It is also vital that all funds are accounted for and that there is transparency in how and where they are used.

Scalability is another difficulty since projects that are implemented locally on a pilot basis may prove much more difficult to organise on an expanded level. This poses a problem for continuity as the lack of funding can mean interruptions and prolonged time-lags between related projects. One strategy that has recently been proposed for telemedicine is the IBOT strategy: Initiate-Build-Operate-Transfer (Latifi, 2011). This includes assessment of healthcare needs, development

of educational programmes, establishment of a nationwide telemedicine network, and integration of the telemedicine program into healthcare infrastructure. The author also proposes that such programmes are transferred to government control once established. Involving local leadership has also been highlighted as an important step towards ensuring organisational success (Fraser & Blaya, 2010).

A final important consideration is whether e-Health interventions in developing countries target the appropriate population. For example, using m-Health necessarily means that only those with mobile phones will be able to access such projects. It is likely that communities with high rates of chronic disease, and the greatest access requirements, will have significantly lower rates of mobile phone ownership. In one South American study, patients with lung disease and arthritis, and those over 70 years of age were found to be less likely to have a mobile phone (Piette, Mendoza-Avelares, Milton, Lange, & Fajardo, 2010). This is typical of the exact population that needs most help. We must be careful not to exclude those who can benefit most, by designing projects that address this paradox.

ETHICAL AND LEGAL CONSIDERATIONS

As well as the ethical problem of possibly excluding those who most need an intervention, e-Health entails other ethical considerations that must be addressed in designing projects. The issue of opportunity cost as mentioned earlier must not be allowed to result in deterioration in the *status quo*. Diverting funds to exciting but unproven technology may cause hardship in a service that is already under pressure. The quality of technology is also an issue, in particular where donated equipment or software is concerned. If an e-Health intervention is provided it must be of reasonable quality to ensure that it can fulfil its purpose. For example monitors must be of adequate resolution to make a diagnosis where imaging is concerned. Accepting inferior quality simply because it is free is unethical.

There are legal challenges, especially where cross-border interventions such as telemedicine are concerned (Istepanian & Lacal, 2003). For example a specialist in the United States who provides a free opinion on a patient in Kenya may be liable for any harm that occurs due to misdiagnosis. It appears that in such a hypothetical situation there may be difficulty in predicting what the outcome may be. This poses a barrier to anyone who is interested in helping such a service but would expect to be indemnified. Is it ethical that doctors can participate in patient care, even at a distance, and not be responsible for the outcome? It is also questionable whether patients can be deprived of their right to seek recourse in the courts by any agreement or precondition. Some health conditions are also unsuitable to be assessed by telemedicine, requiring inpatient treatment (Mechael, 2006).

Information privacy is a human right and there is no doubt that e-Health can pose a threat to this. Transmission of sensitive health information such as HIV status requires high-level security and encryption (Todrys & Mechael, 2008). Access control should be used to limit the ability to view the data to only those people who are directly involved in care. There is also the issue of obtaining consent from patients to process their data electronically. Many countries have diverging opinions on this, and many have no laws to govern the area. There is concern that adequate policy and legal frameworks have not been put in place in some areas (Willyard, 2010). E-Health projects need to have considered these legal issues before being put in place (Healy, 2008).

As can be seen, there is a need for a well-established regulatory framework in e-Health to address many of these issues. There is a role for a supra-national body such as the World Health Organization here. The testing of e-Health interventions is also vital to reduce the risk of harm to the minimum possible. There is as yet no agreement as to how this should be done.

FUTURE RESEARCH DIRECTIONS

In the developed world there is already a clear need for more research to show the benefits of e-Health. In comparison, very little research has been conducted to investigate the effects of e-Health on health provision in low-income nations. This is extraordinary considering the possibility that such projects may have an even greater effect on service users in these areas. Health services in many countries are underfunded, poorly organised and in need of more equipment and workers. E-Health has the potential to address many of the deficiencies seen in such systems. The challenges to setting up research include access block, lack of comparative health outcome data before the intervention, and lack of business and political will. In addition there are few links built up with western academics which might be expected to foster such an exchange of research ideas.

In the coming years, policymakers in the developing world need to actively seek out co-operation with partners who have already implemented e-Health technologies. This would help to provide longevity and increase confidence that projects would show permanent results. It has been estimated that fewer than 10 per cent of the telemedicine experiments carried out in developing countries in the twentieth century were a success; that 45 per cent were abandoned after a year; and that the remainder were wound down after three years of effort (Healy, 2008). The World Health Organization has been posited as an important stakeholder that should develop a knowledge-base and promote catalytic e-Health activities (Mechael, 2007).

Economic analyses also need to be built into e-Health interventions used in the developing world. Both private and charitable donors need to demonstrate that there is an economic argument for implementing e-Health. Positive results will in turn increase the likelihood of further investment. There is a possibility that micro-financing may help here also, at least to provide projects with small amounts of initial funding.

In all of this, it is easy to forget the patient. Projects that are technology-driven and do not take the end user into account seem likely to fail. As e-Health emphasises the importance of patient-centred healthcare, it is necessary that qualitative studies are undertaken to explore their experiences (Wootton, Vladzymyrskyy, Zolfo, & Bonnardot 2011). As in medicine, it is often by talking to the patient rather than looking at the results, that one gleans the most useful information.

CONCLUSION

e-Health has much potential to help ease access barriers and to improve provision of healthcare in developing countries. There are several examples of small projects that have been successful, but many of these run for a defined period of time on a pilot level. There is a clear need for more co-ordinated effort in this area, and to increase sustainability and scalability by planning projects with clear outcomes and involving the end user in the evaluation. Major stakeholders need to leverage successful pilot projects to build a knowledge-base of effective solutions. Patients should be involved in the development of these projects. Several barriers exist including financial challenges, legal and ethical difficulties and the ongoing requirement to demonstrate evidence for efficacy. However projects such as the Swinfen Charitable Trust have shown that even with few resources a positive outcome is possible for end users. In order to help further development, steps must be taken to increase the informatics workforce and for developed nations to exchange knowledge and skills. Achieving this may make e-Health a very fruitful area in the developing world.

REFERENCES

Barnett, G. O., & Sukenik, H. J. (1969). Hospital information systems II. In J. F. Dickson III, & J. H. U. Brown (Eds.), *Future goals of engineering in biology and medicine*. New York: Academic Press.

Black, A. D., Car, J., Pagliari, C., Anandan, C., & Cresswell, K., Bokun, et al. (2011). The Impact of e-Health on the Quality and Safety of Health Care: A Systematic Overview. *PLoS Medicine*, *8*(1), e1000387. doi:10.1371/journal.pmed.1000387 PMID:21267058

CADA Project. (2008). Retrieved October 2, 2012, from http://www.cadaproject.com

Catwell, L., & Sheikh, A. (2009). Evaluating e-Health Interventions: The Need for Continuous Systemic Evaluation. *PLoS Medicine*, *6*(8), e1000126. doi:10.1371/journal.pmed.1000126 PMID:19688038

Drury, P. (2005). E-health: A model for developing countries. *Health International*, *2*(2), 19–26.

Fraser, H. S. F., & Blaya, J. (2010). Implementing medical information systems in developing countries, what works and what doesn't. In *Proceedings of American Medical Informatics Association Annual Symposium,* (pp. 232–236). AMIA.

Geissbuhler, A., Bagayoko, C. O., & Ly, O. (2007). The RAFT network: 5 years of distance continuing medical education and tele-consultations over the Internet in French-speaking Africa. *International Journal of Medical Informatics*, *76*(5-6), 351–356. doi:10.1016/j.ijmedinf.2007.01.012 PMID:17331799

Han, Y. Y., Carcillo, J. A., Venkataraman, S. T., Clark, R. S. B., Watson, R. S., & Nguyen, T. C. et al. (2005). Unexpected increased mortality after implementation of a commercially sold computerized physician order entry system. *Pediatrics*, *116*(6), 1506–1512. doi:10.1542/peds.2005-1287 PMID:16322178

Healy, J. (2008). *Implementing e-Health in Developing Countries Guidance and Principles.* Retrieved from http://www.itu.int/ITU-D/cyb/app/docs/e-Health_prefinal_15092008.pdf

Houtchens, B. A., Clemmer, T. P., Holloway, H. C., Kiselev, A. A., Logan, J. S., & Merrell, R. C. et al. (1993). Telemedicine and international disaster response: Medical consultation to Armenia and Russia via a Telemedicine Spacebridge. *Prehospital and Disaster Medicine, 8*(1), 57–66.

Istepanian, R., & Lacal, J. (2003). *Emerging Mobile Communication Technologies for Health: Some Imperative notes on m-Health.* Paper presented at The 25th Silver 59 Anniversary International Conference of the IEEE Engineering in Medicine and Biology Society. Cancun Mexico.

Kirigia, J. M., Seddoh, A., Gatwiri, D., Muthuri, L. H. K., & Seddoh, J. (2005). E-health: Determinants, opportunities, challenges and the way forward for countries in the WHO African Region. *BioMed Central Public Health, 5,* 137. doi:10.1186/1471-2458-5-137 PMID:16364186

Latifi, R. (2011). Initiate-build-operate-transfer - A strategy for establishing sustainable telemedicine programs not only in the developing countries. *Studies in Health Technology and Informatics, 165,* 3–10. PMID:21685579

Longhurst, C. A., Parast, L., Sandborg, C. I., Widen, E., Sullivan, J., & Hahn, J. S. et al. (2010). Decrease in hospital-wide mortality rate after implementation of a commercially sold computerized physician order entry system. *Pediatrics, 126*(1), 14–21. doi:10.1542/peds.2009-3271 PMID:20439590

Mars, M. (2009). Telemedicine in South Africa. In R. Wootton, N. G. Patil, R. E. Scott, & K. Ho (Eds.), *Tele-Health in the Developing World* (pp. 222–231). London: Royal Society of Medicine Press.

Mechael, P. (2006). *Exploring Health-related Uses of Mobile Phones: An Egyptian Case Study.* (Doctoral dissertation). London School of Hygiene and Tropical Medicine, London, UK. Retrieved from http://www-personal.umich.edu/~parkyo/site/paper%20abstracts/PatriciaMechaelMobilePhonesWellBeingEgypt2.pdf

Mechael, P. (2007). *Towards the Development of an mHealth Strategy: A Literature Review.* Retrieved from http://mobileactive.org/files/file_uploads/WHOHealthReviewUpdatedAug222008_TEXT.pdf

O'Hanlon, S. (2011). *The dangers of e-Health.* Paper presented at the Meeting of HEALTHINF. Rome, Italy.

Oh, H., Rizo, C., Enkin, M., & Jadad, A. (2005). What is e-Health (3), a systematic review of published definitions. *Journal of Medical Internet Research, 7*(1), e1. doi:10.2196/jmir.7.1.e1 PMID:15829471

Ouma, S., & Herselman, M. E. (2008). E-health in Rural Areas: Case of Developing Countries. *International Journal of Biological and Life Sciences, 4*(4).

Piette, J. D., Mendoza-Avelares, M. O., Milton, E. C., Lange, I., & Fajardo, R. (2010). Access to Mobile Communication Technology and Willingness to Participate in Automated Telemedicine Calls Among Chronically Ill Patients in Honduras. *Telemedicine Journal and e-Health, 16*(10), 1030–1041. doi:10.1089/tmj.2010.0074 PMID:21062234

Schmidt, S., Schuchert, A., Krieg, T., & Oeff, M. (2010). Home telemonitoring in patients with chronic heart failure: A chance to improve patient care? *Deutsches Ärzteblatt International, 107*(8), 131–138. PMID:20300221

Sinha, C. (2005). *Effect of Mobile Telephony on Empowering Rural Communities in Developing Countries.* Paper presented at the meeting of International Research Foundation for Development (IRFD) Conference on Digital Divide, Global Development and the Information Society. New York, NY.

Text to Change. (2008). Retrieved October 1, 2012, from http://www.texttochange.org

Todrys, K., & Mechael, P. (2008). *The Ethics of Telemedicine in Africa: The Millennium Villages Project Experience.* Paper presented at Mobile Communications and the Ethics of Social Networking. Budapest, Hungary.

UN Foundation-Vodafone Foundation Partnership. (2009). mHealth for Development: The Opportunity of Mobile Technology for Healthcare in the Developing World. Washington, DC: Author.

United Nations Department of Economic and Social Affairs, Division for Public Administration and Development Management. (2007). Compendium of ICT Applications on Electronic Government: Vol. 1. *Mobile Applications on Health and Learning.* New York: United Nations.

Willyard, C. (2010). Electronic records pose dilemma in developing countries. *Nature Medicine, 16*(3), 249. doi:10.1038/nm0310-249a PMID:20208497

Wootton, R. (2008). Telemedicine support for the developing world. *Journal of Telemedicine and Telecare, 14,* 109–114. doi:10.1258/jtt.2008.003001 PMID:18430271

Wootton, R., & Bonnardot, L. (2010). In what circumstances is telemedicine appropriate in the developing world? *Journal of the Royal Society of Medicine Short Reports, 1*(5), 37. doi:10.1258/shorts.2010.010045 PMID:21103129

Wootton, R., Menzies, J., & Ferguson, P. (2009). Follow-up data for patients managed by store and forward telemedicine in developing countries. *Journal of Telemedicine and Telecare, 15*(2), 83–88. doi:10.1258/jtt.2008.080710 PMID:19246608

Wootton, R., & Tahir, M. S. M. (2004). Challenges in launching a Malaysian teleconsulting network. In P. Whitten, & D. Cook (Eds.), *Understanding Health Communications Technologies.* San Francisco, CA: Jossey-Bass.

Wootton, R., Vladzymyrskyy, A., Zolfo, M., & Bonnardot, L. (2011). Experience with low-cost telemedicine in three different settings: Recommendations based on a proposed framework for network performance evaluation. *Global Health Action, 4.*

World Health Organization. (2005a). *Resolution WHA 58.28 on e-Health.* Retrieved from http://apps.who.int/gb/ebwha/pdf_files/WHA58/WHA58_28-en.pdf

World Health Organization. (2005b). *WHO Facing the Facts: The Impact of Chronic Disease in the Americas.* Geneva: WHO.

World Health Organization. (2011). *mHealth New horizons for health through mobile technologies.* Retrieved from http://www.who.int/goe/publications/goe_mhealth_web.pdf

KEY TERMS AND DEFINITIONS

Developing Countries: Nonindustrialised poor countries that seek to develop their resources by industrialisation.

E-Health: The use of information technology to improve healthcare.

Healthcare: The organised provision of medical care to individuals or to a community.

Informatics: The study of information and communication technology.

Information and Communication Technology: The use of computers to collect, process and transfer information.

Leapfrog Effect: A theory of development where inferior steps are skipped in order to progress to the most modern technologies.

M-Health: The use of mobile devices and technology to enhance the provision of healthcare.

386

Compilation of References

AA.VV. (2014, February 25). Smartmatic permite re-sultados electorales en tiempo récord en Ecuador. *IT/Users Magazine.* Retrieved March 11, 2014 from http://itusersmagazine.com/category/e-government/

Abaday, A. (2010). E-devlet'le memur işsiz mi kalacak? *Ntvmsnbc.* Retrieved March 21 from http://www.ntvmsnbc.com/id/25072060/

Abdelsalam, H. M., Reddick, C. G., ElKadi, H. A., & Gama, S. (2012). Factors affecting perceived effectiveness of local e-government in Egypt. *International Journal of Information Communication Technologies and Human Development, 4*(1), 24–38. doi:10.4018/jicthd.2012010102

Abramowicz, W., Bassara, A., Filipowska, A., Wisniewski, M., & Zebrowski, P. (2006). Mobility implications for m-government platform design. *Cybernetics and Systems: An International Journal, 37*(2-3), 119–135. doi:10.1080/01969720500428255

Abramson, M. A., & Morin, T. L. (2003). E-government: A progress report. In *E-government 2003.* New York: Rowman& Littlefield Publishers, Inc.

Accenture. (2002). *E-government leadership – Realizing the vision.* Retrieved from www.accenture.com/xd/xd.asp?it=enWeb&xd=industries%5Cgovernment%5Cgove_welcome.xml

Accenture. (2009). *From e-government to e-governance: Using new technologies to strengthen relationships with citizens.* Dublin, Ireland: Institute for Health and Public Service Value.

Accenture. (2014). *Digital government pathways to delivering public services for the future: A comparative study of digital government performance across 10 countries.* Retrieved from http://nstore.accenture.com/acn_com/Accenture-Digital-Government-Pathways-to-Delivering-Public-Services-for-the-Future.pdf

Access to Information. (A2I) Program. (2008). e-Governance in Bangladesh: Where we stand a Horizon Scan Report, 2007, Access to Information (A2I). Dhaka, Bangladesh: Prime Minister's Office & UNDP.

Access to Information. (A2I) Program. (2011). Bangladesh: Access to Information (A2I) Evaluation – A Report prepared for United Nations Development Program (UNDP). Dhaka, Bangladesh: Prime Minister's Office.

Acquisti, A., & Gross, R. (2006). Imagined communities: Awareness, information sharing, and privacy on the Facebook. In P. Golle & G. Danezis (Eds.), *Proceedings of 6th Workshop on Privacy Enhancing Technologies* (pp. 36–58). Cambridge, UK: Robinson College.

Adams, N., Stubbs, V., & Woods, V. (2005). Psychological barriers to Internet usage among older adults in the UK. *Medical Informatics and the Internet in Medicine, 30*(1), 3–17. doi:10.1080/14639230500066876 PMID:16036626

Adriani, F., & Becchetti, L. (2003). Does the Digital Divide Matter? The role of ICT in cross-country level and growth estimates. *CEIS Tor Vergata Research Paper No. 4.* Retrived from http://ssrn.com/abstract=382983 or http://dx.doi.org/10.2139/ssrn.382983

Agarwal, V., Mittal, M., & Rastogi, L. (2003). *Enabling e-Governance – Integrated citizen relationship management framework – The Indian perspective, India.* Retrieved from http://www.e11online.com/pdf/e11_whitepaper2.pdf

AGPD (Spanish Data Protection Agency) and INTECO. (2009). *Study on data privacy and security in the Social Networks.* Retrieved from https://www.agpd.es/portalweb/canaldocumentacion/publicaciones/common/Estudios/estudio_inteco_aped_120209_redes_sociales.pdf

Ahmed, A., Islam, D., Hasan, A. R., & Rahman, N. (2006). *Measuring Impact of ICT on Women in Bangladesh.* Retrieved March 27, 2008, from http://icc.ough.edu.cn/WorldComp2005/EEE4168.pdf

Ahn, M. J., & Bretschneider, S. (2011). Politics of E-Government: E-Government and the Political Control of Bureaucracy. *Public Administration Review, 71,* 414–424. doi:10.1111/j.1540-6210.2011.02225.x

Aichholzer, G., & Schmutzer, R. (2000). Organizational challenges to the development of electronic government. In *Proceedings of the 11th International Workshop on Database and Expert System Applications* (pp. 379-383). London: IEEE.

Ajzen, I. (1991). The theory of planned behavior. *Organizational Behavior and Human Decision Processes, 50*(2), 179–211. doi:10.1016/0749-5978(91)90020-T

Akman, I., Yazici, A., & Arifoglu, A. (2002). *E-government: Turkey profile.* Paper presented at the Second International European Conference on e-Government. Oxford, UK.

Akther, M. S., Onishi, T., & Kidokoro, T. (2007). E-government in a developing: Citizen-centric approach for success. *International Journal of Electronic Governance, 1*(1), 38–51. doi:10.1504/IJEG.2007.014342

AlAwadhi, S., & Morris, A. (2008). The Use of the UTAUT Model in the Adoption of E-Government Services in Kuwait. In *Proceeding of the 41st Hawaii International International Conference on Systems Science* (HICSS-41 2008). Waikoloa, HI: IEEE Computer Society.

Alawneh, A., Al-Refai, H., & Batiha, K. (2013). Measuring user satisfaction from e-government services: Lessons from Jordan. *Government Information Quarterly, 30*(3), 277–288. doi:10.1016/j.giq.2013.03.001

Alcaide Muñoz, L., López Hernández, A. M., & Rodríguez Bolívar, M. P. (2012). La investigación en e-Gobierno referida a economías emergentes: Evolución y tendencia futuras. CLAD. *Reforma y Democracia, 54,* 95–126.

Alexander, K. (2012). 2 Firms to replace IBM on Texas' data consolidation effort. *American-Statesman.* Retrieved from http://www.statesman.com/news/texas-politics/2-firms-to-replace-ibm-on-texas-data-2233786.html

Alford, J. (1998). A Public Management Road Less Traveled: Clients as Co-producers of Public Services. *Australian Journal of Public Administration, 57*(4), 128–137. doi:10.1111/j.1467-8500.1998.tb01568.x

Alford, J. (2000). Why Do Public-Sector Clients Coproduce? Toward a Contingency Theory. *Administration & Society, 34*(1), 32–56. doi:10.1177/0095399702034001004

Alford, J. (2002). Defining the Client in the Public Sector: A Social-Exchange Perspective. *Public Administration Review, 62*(3), 337–346. doi:10.1111/1540-6210.00183

Alford, J. (2009). *Engaging Public Sector Clients: From Service Delivery to Co-production.* New York: Palgrave Macmillan. doi:10.1057/9780230235816

Ali, M., Weerakkody, V., & El-Haddadeh, R. (2009). The impact of national culture on e-government implementation: A comparison case study. In *Proceedings of the Fifteenth Americas Conference on Information Systems.* AIS. Retrieved from http://dspace.brunel.ac.uk/bitstream/2438/3660/1/Culture%20and%20eGov_Final.pdf

Ali, A. H. (2011). The Power of Social Media in Developing Nations: New Tools for Closing the Global Digital Divide and Beyond. *Harvard Human Rights Journal, 24*(1), 186–219.

Alican, F. (2007). Experts without expertise: E-society projects in developing countries – The case of Turkey. *Information Polity, 12*(4), 255–263.

Alican, F. (2010). Can information technology contribute to social peace? The case of southeastern Turkey. *Information Polity, 15*(3), 189–198.

Al-Khouri, A. M., & Bal, J. (2006). Electronic government in the GCC countries. *International Journal of Social Sciences, 1*(2).

Al-Shafi, S., & Weerakkody, V. (2008). Adoption of wireless Internet parks: An empirical study in Qatar. In *Proceedings of the 5th European and Mediterranean Conference on Information Systems* (EMCIS). EMCIS.

AL-Shehry. A. (2008). *Transformation towards e-government in the Kingdom of Saudi Arabia: Technological and organisational perspectives*. (Doctoral dissertation). The School of Computing, CCSR, De Montfort University. Retrieved from https://www.dora.dmu.ac.uk/bitstream/handle/2086/2418/e-thesis%20transformation%20to%20e-government.pdf?sequence=1

Aminuzzaman, S., Baldersheim, H., & Ishtiaq, J. (2002). *Talking Back! Empowerment and Mobile Phones in Rural Bangladesh: A Study of the Village Pay Phone of Grameen Bank*. Paper presented at the International Society for Third Sector Research (ISTR) Fifth International Conference Transforming Civil Society, Citizenship and Governance: The Third Sector in an Era of Global (Dis) Order Graduate School in Humanities. Cape Town, South Africa.

Aminuzzaman, M. S. (1991). *Introduction to Social Research*. Bangladesh Publishers.

Andersen, K., Francesconi, E., Grönlund, A., & Engers, T. (2011). Electronic Government and the Information Systems Perspective. In *Proceeding of the Second International Conference, EGOVIS 2011*. New York, NY: Springer.

Andersen, N. A. (2009). *Power at Play: The Relationships between Play, Work and Governance*. Palgrave Macmillan. doi:10.1057/9780230239296

Anderson, G. L., Herr, K., Nihlen, A. S., & Noffke, S. E. (2007). *Studying Your Own School: An Educator's Guide to Practitioner Action Research*. Corwin Press.

Anderson, K. (1999). Reengineering public sector organizations using information technology. In R. Heeks (Ed.), *Reinventing Government in the Information Age*. London: Routledge.

Andersson, S., & Heywood, P. M. (2009). The politics of perception: use and abuse of transparency international's approach to measuring corruption. *Political Studies, 57*(4), 746–767. doi:10.1111/j.1467-9248.2008.00758.x

Anka. (2006). E-Devlet Projesi MERNIS coktu. *E-memleketim*. Retrieved December 10, 2010 from http://www.ememleketim.com/haberler/haber.asp?hbr=247

Anonymous. (2007). İnternet bankacılığı işlemleri hukuki açıdan geçersiz. *Hürriyet*. Retrieved December 10, 2010 from http://hurarsiv.hurriyet.com.tr/goster/haber.aspx?id=5894815&tarih=2007-02-05

Anonymous. (2009a). Uluslar Tek eDevlet Aginda. *Yeni Safak*. Retrieved December 10, 2010 from http://www.edevletmerkezi.org/sitetr/basinda_edem/haber5.html

Anonymous. (2009b). E-devlet modül eğitim ödülü verildi. *Siirtliler.net*. Retrieved November 24, 2011 from http://www.siirtliler.net/goster.asp?nereye=yazioku&ID=125&Siirt_haberleri

Anonymous. (2010a). E-devlette yasanan zorluklar ortadan kalkiyor. *MDevlet*. Retrieved December 10, 2010 from http://www.mdevlet.org/2010/01/e-devlette-yasanan-zorluklar-ortadan-kalkiyor/

Anonymous. (2010b). Emekli Adayina e-Devlet Surprizi. *Gazeteport*. Retrieved December 10, 2010 from http://www.gazeteport.com.tr/EKONOMI/NEWS/GP_803120

Anonymous. (2010c). Sigorta bilgilerini öğrenmek için şifre şartı geldi, çalışanlar mağdur oldu. *Saglik Aktuel*. Retrieved December 10, 2010 from http://www.saglikaktuel.com/haber/sigorta-bilgilerini-ogrenmek-icin-sifre-sarti-geldi,-calisanlar-magdur-oldu-13905.htm

Anonymous. (2010d). SGK İle İlgili Kişisel Bilgilere 1 Kasım'dan beri ulaşılamıyor. *ShowHaber*. Retrieved December 10, 2010 from http://www.showhaber.com/sgk-ile-ilgili-kisisel-bilgilere-1-kasimdan-beri-ulasilamiyor-365126.htm

Anonymous. (2010e). E-devlet de çökertildi! *BHaber*. Retrieved December 10, 2010 from http://bhaber.net/haber/11116-e-devlet-de-kertildi.html

Anonymous. (2010f). İçişleri Bakanlığı 11 İlde E-İmza Uygulaması Başlattı. *ShowHaber*. Retrieved December 10, 2010 from http://www.showhaber.com/icisleri-bakanligi-11-ilde-e-imza-uygulamasi-baslatti-333521.htm

Anonymous. (2010g). E-devlete geçiş:Bazı sorunlar ve çözüm önerileri. *Bir iyilik.* Retrieved December 11, 2010 from http://www.biriyilik.com/odevler-kaynaklar/iktisat-isletme-ve-ekonomi/e-devlete-gecis-bazi-sorunlar-ve-cozum-onerileri-31741.html

Anonymous. (2010h). Şanlıurfa Türkiye'ye örnek oldu. *Şanlıurfa.com.* Retrieved December 11, 2010 from http://www.sanliurfa.com/news_detail.php?id=17030

Anonymous. (2010i).Teknoloji hayal gücüyle besleniyor. *Koç Sistem.* Retrieved December 10, 2010 from http://www.kocsistem.com.tr/tr/rop14.aspx

Anonymous. (2011). *Testimony.* Retrieved April 5, 2011 from http://democrats.energycommerce.house.gov/sites/default/files/image_uploads/Testimony_05.04.11_Spafford.pdf.

Anonymous. (2014). *Complexity metrics.* Retrieved April 12, 2014 from http://www.aivosto.com/project/help/pm-complexity.html

Antin, J., & Churchill. (2011). *Badges in Social Media: A Social Psychological Perspective.* Paper presented at the Gamification Workshop, CHI2011. New York, NY.

Apostolou, D., Mentzas, G., Stojanovic, L., Thoenssen, B., & Pariente Lobo, T. (2011). A collaborative decision framework for managing changes in eGovernment services. *Government Information Quarterly, 28,* 101–116. doi:10.1016/j.giq.2010.03.007

Appelbaum, S. H. (1997). Socio-technical systems theory: An intervention strategy for organizational development. *Management Decision, 35*(6), 452–463. doi:10.1108/00251749710173823

Arango, T., & Yeginsu, C. (2014). *Amid Flow of Leaks, Turkey Moves to Crimp Internet.* Retrieved April 12, 2014 from http://www.nytimes.com/2014/02/07/world/europe/amid-flow-of-leaks-turkey-moves-to-crimp-internet.html?_r=0

Arif, M. (2008). Customer Orientation in eGovernment Project Management: A Case Study. *The Electronic. Journal of E-Government, 6*(1), 1–10.

ARNAC (Administrative and Regulatory National Authority for Communications). (2013). *Internet Access Services: Report of Statistical Data. January 1 - June 30, 2013.* Retrieved from file:///E:/Raport%20DS%20sem%20I%202013.pdf

Arslan, A. (2009). *Cross-cultural analysis of European e-government adoption* (MPRA Paper No. 20705). Retrieved from http://mpra.ub.uni-muenchen.de/20705/1/MPRA_paper_20705.pdf

Ashraf, M. M., Hanisch, J., & Swatman, P. (2008). *ICT Intervention and Its Impact In Village Areas of Developing Country.* Paper presented at the IADIS International Conference e-Society. Algarve, Portugal.

Atkinson, D. R. (2003). *Network Government for the Digital Age.* Washington, DC: Progressive Police Institute.

Atkins, S. E. (1988). Subject trends in library and information science research 1975-1984. *Library Trends, 36*(4), 633–658.

Avgerou, C. (2000). Recognising alternative rationalities in the deployment of information systems. *The Electronic Journal on Information Systems in Developing Countries, 3*(7), 1–15.

Avgerou, C., & Walsham, G. (2000). *Information Technology in Context: Studies from the Perspective of Developing Countries.* London: Ashgate.

Aviv, A., Gibson, K., Mossop, E., Blaze, M., & Smith, J. (2010). *Smudge Attacks on Smartphone Touch Screens.* Retrieved April 12, 2014 from https://www.usenix.org/legacy/event/woot10/tech/full_papers/Aviv.pdf

Azim, F., & Sultan, M. (Eds.). (2010). *Mapping Women's Economic Empowerment.* Dhaka, Bangladesh: The University Press Limited.

Baasanjav, U. (2008). Mediated political and social participation: The case study of Mongolian government and civil society institutions. *Journal of Information Technology & Politics, 4*(3), 41–60. doi:10.1080/19331680801915041

Baasanjav, U. (2011). Web use patterns for civic discourse: The case of Mongolian institutions. *Information Communication and Society, 14*(5), 591–618. doi:10.1080/1369118X.2010.513416

Baasanjav, U. (2012). Global digital divide: Language gap and post-communism in Mongolia. In A. Manoharan, & M. Holzer (Eds.), *E-Governance and civic engagement: Factors and determinants of e-democracy* (pp. 210–234). Hershey, PA: IGI Global.

Baasanjav, U. (in press). Linguistic diversity on the Internet: Arabic, Chinese and Cyrillic script top-level domain names. *Telecommunications Policy*.

Backus, M. (2001). *E-governance and developing countries: introduction and examples* (Research Report, No. 3). International Institute for Communication and Development (IICD). Retrieved from editor.iicd.org/files/report3.doc

Backus, M. (2001). E-governance in developing countries. *IICD Research Brief, 1*.

Baev, V. (2005). Social and Philosophical aspects of E-governance Paradigm Formation for Public Administration. *Razon Y Palabra, 42*.

Bailey, M. T. (1992). Do physicists use case studies? Thoughts on public administration research. *Public Administration Review, 52*(1), 47–55. doi:10.2307/976545

Balcı, A., & Medeni, T. (2010). E-Government Gateway Development in Turkey: Some Challenges and Future Directions for Citizen Focus. In E. Downey, C. D. Ekstrom, & M. A. Jones (Eds.), *E-Government Website Development: Future Trends and Strategic Models*. Hershey, PA: IGI Global. doi:10.4018/978-1-61692-018-0.ch010

Baltiwala, S. (1994). *Women's Empowerment in South Asia: Concepts and Practices*. New Delhi: Food and Agricultural Organization/Asia, South Asia Bureau of Adult Education.

Bangladesh Bank. (2014). *Home*. Retrieved from www.bb.org.bd

Bangladesh Enterprise Institute (BEI). (2010). *Realizing the Vision of Digital Bangladesh through e-government*. Retrieved from http://www.bei-bd.org/images/publication/whc4f4b6fd3c20ed.pdf

Bangladesh Public Service Commission (BPSC). (2014). *Home*. Retrieved from http://www.bpsc.gov.bd/

Bangladesh Telecommunications Regulatory Commission (BTRC). (2009). *Annual Report 2007-2008*. Retrieved from http://www.btrc.gov.bd/

Bannister, F. (2012). *Case Studies in e-Government*. Reading, MA: Academic Publishing International.

Bannister, F., & Connolly, R. (2011). Trust and transformational government: A proposed framework for research. *Government Information Quarterly, 28*(2), 137–147. doi:10.1016/j.giq.2010.06.010

Bannister, F., & Connolly, R. (2012). Forward to the past: Lessons for the future of e-government from the story so far. *Information Polity, 17*(3-4), 211–226.

Barlow, J. P. (1996). *A Declaration of the Independence of Cyberspace*. Retrieved April 21, 2012, from http://www.eff.org/~barlow/Declaration-Final.html

Barnett, G. O., & Sukenik, H. J. (1969). Hospital information systems II. In J. F. Dickson III, & J. H. U. Brown (Eds.), *Future goals of engineering in biology and medicine*. New York: Academic Press.

Barry, A. (2001). *Political Machines: Governing a Technological Society*. London: The Athlone Press.

Bartle, R. (2004). *Designing virtual worlds*. Indianapolis, IN: New Riders Publishing.

Barzelay, M. (2001). *The New Public Management: Improving Research and Policy Dialogue*. New York: Sage.

Basu, S. (2004). E-government and developing countries: An overview. *International Review of Law Computers & Technology, 18*(1), 109–132. doi:10.1080/13600860410001674779

Baum, C., & Maio, D. (2000). *Gartner's four phases of e-government model*. Gartner's Group.

Bayes, A. (2001). Infrastructura and Rural Development: Insights from a Grameen Bank Village Phone Initiative in Bangladesh. *Agricultural Economics, 25*(2), 261–272.

BEI. (2010). *Realizing the Vision of Digital Bangladesh through e-Government, July 2010*. Retrieved from www.bei-bd.org/downloadreports/view/48/download

Bekkers, V. (2013). E-government and innovation: The socio-political shaping of ICT as a source of innovation. In *Handbook of Innovations in Public Services*. Cheltenham, UK: Edward Elgar. doi:10.4337/9781849809757.00028

Bekkers, V., & Homburg, V. (2007). The myths of e-government: Looking beyond the assumptions of new and better government. *The Information Society, 23*(5), 373–382. doi:10.1080/01972240701572913

Belanger, F., & Carter, L. (2009). The impact of the digital divide on e-government use. *Communications of the ACM, 52*(4), 132–135. doi:10.1145/1498765.1498801

Bell, D., & Lapadula, L. (1973). Secure Computer System: Unified Exposition and Multics Interpretation. *Technical Report MTR-2997 Rev.1.*

Bellamy, C. (2000). The politics of public information systems. In G. D. Garson (Ed.), *Handbook of public information systems* (pp. 85–98). New York, NY: Marcel Dekker.

Bellamy, C., & Taylor, J. (1998). *Governing in the information age*. Buckingham, UK: Open University Press.

Belt, D. (2014). We need an exit strategy for Facebook. *GovLoop*. Retrieved from http://www.govloop.com/profiles/blogs/we-need-an-exit-strategy-for-facebook?elq=4032ae94bb34426b8c0b2cf075679922&elqCampaignId=4352

Bendapudi, N., & Leone. (2003). Psychological Implications of Customer Participation in Co-Production. *Journal of Marketing, 67*(1), 14–28. doi:10.1509/jmkg.67.1.14.18592

Benjamin, M. (2001). Re-examining the Digital Divide. In *Communications Policy in Transition: The Internet and Beyond* (pp. 321–348). Cambridge, MA: MIT Press.

Benjamin, S. M. (2006). Evaluating e-rulemaking: Public participation and political institutions. *Duke Law Journal, 55*(5), 893–941.

Berger, G. (Ed.). (2009). *Freedom of Expression, Access to Information and Empowerment of People*. Paris, France: United Nations Educational, Scientific and Cultural Organization (UNESCO). Retrieved July 08, 2012 from http://unesdoc.unesco.org/images/0018/001803/180312e.pdf

Berlin, S., Raz, T., Glezer, C., & Zviran, M. (2009). Comparison of estimation methods of cost and duration in IT projects. *Information and Software Technology, 51*(4), 738–748. doi:10.1016/j.infsof.2008.09.007

Bernstein, D. R. (1999). Java, Women and the Culture of Computing. In *Proceedings of the 12th Annual Conference of the National Advisory Committee on Computing Qualifications*. Dunedin, New Zealand: Academic Press. Retrieved July 21, 2012 from http://turbo.kean.edu/~dbernste/naccq.html

Bertot, J. C., Jaeger, P. T., & Grimes, J. M. (2010). Using ICTs to create a culture of transparency: E-government and social media as openness and anti-corruption tools for societies. *Government Information Quarterly, 27*(3), 264–271. doi:10.1016/j.giq.2010.03.001

Bertucci, G. (2008). *UN e-Government Survey: From e-Government to Connected Governance*. New York: United Nations, Division for Public Administration and Development Management.

Bhatnagar, S. (2003). Access to Information: E-Government. In Hodess, Inowlocki, & Wolfe (Eds.), Global Corruption Report. Profile Books Ltd.

Bhatnagar, S. (2004). *E-government: From Vision to Implementation*. New Delhi: Sage Publications.

Bhatnagar, S. C. (1999). *E-government: Opportunities and Challenges*. Ahmadabad, India: Indian Institute of Management.

Bhatnagar, S. C. (2001). *Philippine Customs Reform*. Washington, DC: World Bank.

Bhatnagar, S. C., & Singh, N. (2010). Assessing the Impact of E-Government: A Study of Projects in India e government. *Information Technologies & International Development, 6*(2), 109–127.

Bhogle, S. (2008). E-governance. In A.-V. Anttiroiko (Ed.), *Electronic Government: Concepts, Methodologies, Tools and Applications*. Hershey, PA: IGI Global. doi:10.4018/978-1-59904-947-2.ch006

Bhuiyan, M. S. H. (2012). Towards Interoperable Government- A Case of Bangladesh. In Gil-Garcia et al. (Eds.), *Proceedings of 6th International Conference on Theory and Practice of Electronic Governance*. Albany, NY: ICEGOV.

Bhuiyan, S. H. (2011). Modernising Bangladesh public administration through E-governance: Benefits and challenges. *Government Information Quarterly*, (28): 54–65. doi:10.1016/j.giq.2010.04.006

Bidyarthi, H. M., & Srivastava, A. K. (2008). Citizen's perspectives of e-governance. In A. Ojha (Ed.), E-Governance in Practice (pp. 69-76). Secunderabad, India: SIGeGOV.

Bingham, R. D., & Bowen, W. (1994). Mainstream public administration over time: A topical content analysis of public administration review. *Public Administration Review*, *54*(2), 204–208. doi:10.2307/976531

Bing, S. (1992). The Reform of Mainland China's Cadre System—Establishing a Civil Service. *Issues & Studies*, *28*, 23–43.

Bishop, M. (2006). *Computer security – Arts and science*. Reading, MA: Addison-Wesley.

Black, A. D., Car, J., Pagliari, C., Anandan, C., & Cresswell, K., Bokun, et al. (2011). The Impact of e-Health on the Quality and Safety of Health Care: A Systematic Overview. *PLoS Medicine*, *8*(1), e1000387. doi:10.1371/journal.pmed.1000387 PMID:21267058

Blackberry. (2011). *Blackberry developers documents*. Retrieved April 12, 2014 from http://www.blackberry.com/developers/docs/7.0.0api/net/rim/device/api/io/nfc/se/SecureElemen.html

Blau, P. M. (1964). *Exchange and power in social life*. New York: John Wiley.

Bogost, I. (2011). *Gamification is Bullshit: My position statement at the Wharton Gamification Symposium*. Retrieved from http://www.bogost.com/blog/gamification_is_bullshit.shtml

Boje, C., & Dragulanescu, N. G. (2003). Digital Divide in Eastern European Countries and its Social Impact. In *Proceedings of the 2003 American Society for Engineering Education Annual Conference & Exposition*. Retrieved Oct 30, 2010 from http://www.ndragulanescu.ro/publicatii/CP40.pdf

Bostrom, R. P., & Heinen, S. (1977). MIS problems and failures: A socio-technical perspective, part II: The application of the socio-technical theory. *Management Information Systems Quarterly*, *1*(4), 11–28. doi:10.2307/249019

Bovaird, T. (2007). Beyond Engagement and Participation – User and Community Co-production of Public Services. *Public Administration Review*, *67*(5), 846–860. doi:10.1111/j.1540-6210.2007.00773.x

Bovaird, T., & Löffler. (2003). Evaluating the Quality of Public Governance: Indicators, Models and Methodologies. *International Review of Administrative Sciences*, *69*(3), 313–328. doi:10.1177/0020852303693002

Bovaird, T., & Löffler. (2007). Assessing the Quality of Local Governance: A Case Study of Public Services. *Public Money & Management*, *27*(4), 293–300. doi:10.1111/j.1467-9302.2007.00597.x

Bovens, M., & Zouridis, S. (2002). From street-level to system-level bureaucracies: How information and communication technology is transforming administrative discretion and constitutional control. *Public Administration Review*, *62*(2), 174–184. doi:10.1111/0033-3352.00168

Boyd, D., & Ellison, N. (2008). Social Network Sites: Definition, History and Scholarship. *Journal of Computer-Mediated Communication*, *13*(1), 210–230. doi:10.1111/j.1083-6101.2007.00393.x

Bozeman, B. (2007). *Public values and public interest: Counterbalancing economic individualism*. Washington, DC: George Washington Press.

Brainard, L. (2003). Citizen organizing in cyber- space. *American Review of Public Administration*, *33*(4), 384–406. doi:10.1177/0275074003257430

Brainard, L., & McNutt, J. (2010). Virtual government-citizen relations: Informational, transactional, or collaborative? *Administration & Society*, *42*(7), 836–858. doi:10.1177/0095399710386308

Brandsen, T., & Pestoff. (2006). Co-production, the Third Sector and the Delivery of Public Services: An Introduction. *Public Management Review*, *8*(4), 493–501. doi:10.1080/14719030601022874

Breen, M. (1999). Counterrevolution in the infrastructure – A cultural study of technscientific impoverishment. In *Ethics and electronic information in the 21st century* (pp. 29–45). West Lafayette, IN: Purdue University Press.

Bretschneider, S. (2003). Information technology, e-government, and institutional change. *Public Administration Review, 63*(6). doi:10.1111/1540-6210.00337

Brewer, G. A., Neubauer, B. J., & Geiselhart, K. (2006). Designing and Implementing E-Government Systems: Critical Implications for Public Administration and Democracy. *Administration & Society, 38*(4), 472–499. doi:10.1177/0095399706290638

Brown, D. (1999). Information systems for improved performance management: Development approaches in U.S. public agencies. In R. Heeks (Ed.), *Reinventing Government in the Information Age*. London: Routledge.

Brown, D. (2005). Electronic Government and Public Administration. *International Review of Administrative Sciences, 71*(2), 241–254. doi:10.1177/0020852305053883

Bruckman, A. (1999). *Can Educational Be Fun?* Paper presented at the Game Developer Conference. San Jose, CA.

Brudney, J., & Selden, S. (1995). The adoption of innovation by smaller local governments: The case of computer technology. *American Review of Public Administration, 25*(1), 71–86. doi:10.1177/027507409502500105

Bruns, A. (2008). *Blogs, Wikipedia, Second Life, and Beyond*. New York: Peter Lang.

Bruns, A. (2009). From Prosumer to Produser: Understanding User-Led Content Creation. In *Proceedings of Transforming Audiences 2009*. London: Academic Press.

Bryer, T. A. (2013). Public participation in regulatory decision-making: Cases from Regulations.org. *Public Performance & Management Review, 37*(2), 263–279. doi:10.2753/PMR1530-9576370204

Burawoy, M. (1979). *Manufacturing consent: Changes in the labor process under monopoly capitalism*. Chicago, IL: University of Chicago Press.

Bureau of Manpower. Employment and Training (BMET). (2014). *Home*. Ministry of Expatriates Welfare and Overseas Employment. Retrieved from http://www.bmet.org.bd/BMET/index

Burger-Helmchen, T., & Cohendet. (2011). User Communities and Social Software in the Video Game Industry. *Long Range Planning, 44*, 317–343. doi:10.1016/j.lrp.2011.09.003

Burke, B. (2014, April 4). Gartner Redefines Gamification. *Gartner*.

Burke, B. (2013, January 21). The Gamification of Business. *Forbes*.

Business Dictionary. (2014). *Computer Literacy*. Retrieved from http://www.businessdictionary.com/definition/computer-literacy.html#ixzz33pThxtOf

Caba Pérez, M. C., Rodríguez Bolívar, M. P., & López Hernández, A. M. (2010). Transparency and E-government in developing countries. The case of Latin-American municipalities. In *Citizens and E-Government: Evaluating Policy and Management* (pp. 158–183). Hershey, PA: IGI Global. doi:10.4018/978-1-61520-931-6.ch009

Caba, C., Rodríguez, M. P., & López, A. M. (2008). E-Government process and incentives for online public financial information. *Online Information Review, 32*(3), 379–400. doi:10.1108/14684520810889682

Cáceres, S. (2004). *Observatorio de la Sociedad de la Información: Un mundo de brechas y puentes digitales*. Retrieved Feb. 5, 2014 from http://fundacionorange.es/areas/28_observatorio/pdfs/DEF_20.pdf

CADA Project. (2008). Retrieved October 2, 2012, from http://www.cadaproject.com

Calista, D., & Melitski, J. (2007). E-government and e-governance: Converging constructs of public sector information and communications technologies. *Public Administration Quarterly, 31*(1), 87-99, 101-120.

Callanan, M. (2005). Institutionalizing Participation and Governance? New Participative Structures in Local Government in Ireland. *Public Administration, 83*(4), 909–929. doi:10.1111/j.0033-3298.2005.00483.x

Calvin, M. L. C., Lau, Y., & Pan, L. S. (2008). EGovernment implementation: A macro analysis of Singapore's eGovernment initiatives. *Government Information Quarterly, 25*(2), 239–255. doi:10.1016/j.giq.2006.04.011

Cameron, B. D. (2005). Trends in the Usage of ISI Bibliometric Data: Uses, Abuses, and Implications. *Portal: Libraries and the Academy, 5*(1), 105–125. doi:10.1353/pla.2005.0003

Campos Freire, F. (2008). Las redes sociales trastocan los modelos de los medios de comunicación tradicionales. *Revista Latina de Comunicación Social, 63*(2), 287–293.

Canadian International Development Agency. (2007). *Knowledge-Sharing Plan*. Retrieved February 19, 2008, from http://www.acdi-cida.gc.ca/CIDAWEB/acdicida.nsf/En/EMA-218122154-PR4

Canturk, S. (2010). E-kimlik Kartlarina Ayar. *Sabah.* Retrieved December 10, 2010 from http://www.sabah.com.tr/Gundem/2010/10/16/ekimlik_kartlarina_nasirli_parmak_ayari

Capgemini & IDC. (2011). *E-government benchmarking in 2011*. Brussels: European Commission, Directorate General for Information Society and Media.

Capgemini. (2007). *The user challenge benchmarking the supply of online public services*. Diegem, Belgium: Author.

Carey, J. W. (2005). The historical pragmatism and the Internet. *New Media & Society, 7*(4), 443–455. doi:10.1177/1461444805054107

Cariño, L. V. (2006, January-October). From traditional public administration to governance: Research in NCPAG, 1952-2002. *Philippine Journal of Public Administration*.

Carrizales, T., Holzer, M., Seang-Tae, K., & Chan-Gon, K. (2006). Digital governance world-wide: A longitudinal assessment of municipal websites. *International Journal of Electronic Government Research, 2*(4), 1–23. doi:10.4018/ jegr.2006100101

Carrizales, T. (2008). Functions of e-government: A study of municipal practices. *State and Local Government Review, 40*(1), 12–26. doi:10.1177/0160323X0804000102

Carter, L., Schaupp, L. C., & Evans, A. (2008). *Antecedents of e-File adoption: The US Perspective*. Retrieved April 20, 2009 from://ieeexplore.ieee.org/stamp/stamp.jsp?arnumber=04438920

Carter, L., & Bélanger, F. (2005). The utilization of e-government services: citizen trust, innovation and acceptance factors. *Information Systems Journal, 15*, 5–25. doi:10.1111/j.1365-2575.2005.00183.x

Carter, L., & McBride, A. (2010). Information privacy concerns and e-government: A research agenda. *Transforming Government: People. Process and Policy, 4*(1), 10–13.

Castells, M. (2005). The Network Society: From Knowledge to Policy. In *The Network Society: From Knowledge to Policy* (pp. 3–22). Washington, DC: Center for Transatlantic Relations.

Castells, M. (2009). *The rise of the network society: The information age*. Chichester, UK: Wiley-Blackwell. doi:10.1002/9781444319514

Catwell, L., & Sheikh, A. (2009). Evaluating e-Health Interventions: The Need for Continuous Systemic Evaluation. *PLoS Medicine, 6*(8), e1000126. doi:10.1371/journal.pmed.1000126 PMID:19688038

Çayhan, B. E. (2008). Implementing e-government in Turkey: A comparison of online public service delivery in Turkey and the European Union. *The Electronic Journal on Information Systems in Developing Countries, 35*(8), 1–11.

Cejudo, G. M. (2008). Explaining change in the Mexican public sector: The limits of New Public Management. *International Review of Administrative Science, 74*(1), 111–127. doi:10.1177/0020852307085737

Center for Medicare & Medicaid Services. (2013b). *National health expenditure accounts: Sponsored highlights*. Retrieved February 19, 2014, from http:// www.cms.gov/Research-Statistics-Data-and-Systems/Statistics-Trend-and-Reports/NationalHealthExpendData/NationalHealthAccountsHistorical.html

Centers for Medicare & Medicaid Services. (2013a). *Medicare program - general information*. Retrieved July 12, 2013, from http://www.cms.gov/

Central Procurement Technical Unit (CPTU). (2014). *Home*. Ministry of Planning. Retrieved from http://www.cptu.gov.bd/

Cerrillo, A. (2008). e-Administración. Barcelona, Spain: UOC.

Chadwick, A., & May, C. (2003). Interaction between States and Citizens in the Age of the Internet: e-Government in the United States, Britain and the European Union Governance. *An International Journal of Policy and Administration, 16*, 271–300. doi:10.1111/1468-0491.00216

Chandler, D. (1995). *Technological or Media Determinism*. Retrieved September 18, 2008 from http://www.aber.ac.uk/media/Documents/tecdet/tecdet.html

Chang, Y. W., & Huang, M. H. (2012). A study of the evolution of interdisciplinarity in Library and Information Science: Using three bibliometric methods. *Journal of the American Society for Information Science and Technology, 63*(1), 22–33. doi:10.1002/asi.21649

Chan, O. J. (2005). Enterprise Information Systems Strategy and Planning. *The Journal of American Academy of Business, 6*(2), 148–153.

Chin, M. D., & Fairlie, R. W. (2004). *The determinants of the Global Digital Divide: A Cross-Country Analysis of Computer and Internet Penetration*. Cambridge, MA: National Bureau of Economic Research.

Choudrie, J., Weerakkody, V., & Jones, S. (2005). Realising e-government in the UK: Rural and urban challenges. *The Journal of Enterprise Information Management, 18*(5), 568–585. doi:10.1108/17410390510624016

Cialdini, R. (2001). Harnessing the science of persuasion. *Harvard Business Review, 79*(9), 72–79.

Cialdini, R. (2001). *Influence: Science and Practice* (4th ed.). Allyn & Bacon.

Ciborra, C. (2005). Interpreting e-government and development: Efficiency, transparency or governance at a distance? *Information Technology & People, 18*(3), 260–279. doi:10.1108/09593840510615879

Cichonski, P., Millar, T., Grance, T., & Scarfone, K. (2012). Computer security incident handling guide. *NIST Special Publication, 800*, 61.

Cilingir, D., & Kushchu, I. (2004). E-government and m-government: Concurrent leaps by Turkey. In D. Remenyi (Ed.), *Proceedings of European Conference on E-Government (ECEG),* (pp. 813-821). Reading, UK: Academic Conferences International.

Cisco. (2014). *Cisco 2014 Annual Security Report*. Retrieved April 12, 2014 from http://www.cisco.com/web/offers/lp/2014-annual-security-report/index.html

Clark, P. B., & Wilson. (1961). Incentive Systems: A Theory of Organizations. *Administrative Science Quarterly, 6*, 129–166. doi:10.2307/2390752

Cloud Computing: Benefits, Risks and Recommendations for information security. (2009). Retrieved April 12, 2014 from http://www.enisa.europa.eu/act/rm/files/deliverables/cloud-computing-risk-assessment

Cocosila, M., Serenko, A., & Turel, O. (2011). Exploring the management information systems discipline: A scientometric study of ICIS, PACIS, and ASAC. *Scientometrics, 87*(1), 1–16. doi:10.1007/s11192-010-0331-4

Coglianese, C. (2004). E-rulemaking: Information technology and the regulatory process. *Administrative Law Review, 56*, 353–402.

Cohen, T. (2013). Rough Obamacare rollout: 4 reasons why. *CNN*. Retrieved from http://www.cnn.com/2013/10/22/politics/obamacare-website-four-reasons

Cohen, J. E. (2006). Citizen satisfaction with contacting government on the internet. *Information Polity, 11*(1), 51–65.

Coleman, S., & Kaposi, I. (2006). *New democracies, new media: What's new? A study of e-participation projects in third-wave democracies*. Retrieved August 14, 2006 from http://www.ega.ee/handbook/

Coleman, J. S. (1990). *Foundations of Social Theory*. Cambridge, MA: Belknap Press of Harvard University Press.

Compaine, B. (2001). *The Digital Divide: Facing a crisis or creating a mith?* Cambridge, MA: MIT Press.

Compeau, D. R., Higgins, C. A., & Huff, S. (1999). Social cognitive theory and individual reactions to computing technology: A longitudinal study. *Management Information Systems Quarterly, 23*(2), 145–158. doi:10.2307/249749

Conklin, W. A. (2007). Barriers to Adoption of e-Government', System Sciences. In *Proceedings of the 40th Annual Hawaii International Conference on System Sciences*. IEEE.

Cooper, P. J. (2009). *The war against regulation from Jimmy Carter to George W. Bush*. Lawrence, KS: University Press of Kansas.

Corrêa, I., & Claussen, M. V. (2011). Políticas de transparencia en la administración pública brasileña. *Revista CLAD: Reforma y Democracia, 51*, 129–152.

Council of Europe. (2009). *Strategy for Innovation and good governance at Local Level*. Brussels: Author.

Coursey, D., Yang, K., Kasserkert, K., & Norris, D. (2007). E-Gov Adoption in U.S. Local Governments: Bridging Public Management and Institutional Explanations in a Pooled Time Series Model. In *Proceedings of 9th Public Management Research Conference*. Academic Press.

Coursey, D., & Norris, D. F. (2008). Models of e-government: Are they correct? An empirical assessment. *Public Administration Review, 68*(3), 523–536. doi:10.1111/j.1540-6210.2008.00888.x

Craig, W. J., Harris, T. M., & Weiner, D. (Eds.). (2002). *Community participation and geographic information systems*. London: Taylor & Francis.

Csikszentmihlyi, M. (2008). *Flow: The Psychology of Optimal Experience*. Harper Collins.

Cullen, R. (2006). E-government and the Digital Divide. In *Comparative Perspectives on E-Government: Serving Today and Building for Tomorrow* (pp. 289–313). Lanham, MD: The Scarecrow Press.

D'agostino, M., Schwester, R., Carrizales, T., & Melitski, J. (2011). A study of e-government and e-governance: An empirical examination of municipal websites. *Public Administration Quarterly, 35*(1), 3–25.

Dada, D. (2006). E-readiness for developing countries: Moving the focus from the environment to the users. *The Electronic Journal of Information Systems in Developing Countries, 27*(6), 1–14.

Dada, D. (2006). The failure of e-government in developing countries: A literature review. *The Electronic Journal on Information Systems in Developing Countries, 26*(7), 1–10.

Daily News. (n.d.). *Bus ticket booking Via Dialog mobiles*. Retrieved from http://archives.dailynews.lk/2001/pix/PrintPage.asp?REF=/2011/06/24/bus10.asp

Daily Star. (2010, October 29). Article. *The Daily Star*.

Dam, N., Evers, V., & Arts, F. A. (2005). Cultural user experience issues in e-government: Designing for a multicultural society. In P. V. Besselaar & S. Koizumi (Eds.), *Digital Cities III – Third International Digital Cities Workshop*, (pp. 310-324). Amsterdam, The Netherlands: Springer. doi: 10.1007/11407546_18

Danziger, J. N. (1979). Technology and productivity: A contingency analysis of computers in local governments. *Administration & Society, 11*(2), 144–171. doi:10.1177/009539977901100202

Davis, F. D., Bagozzi, R. P., & Warshaw, P. R. (1989). User acceptance of computer technology: A comparison of two theoretical models. *Management Science, 35*(8), 952–1002. doi:10.1287/ mnsc.35.8.982

Davis, F. D. (1989). Perceived usefulness, perceived ease of use, and user acceptance of information technology. *Management Information Systems Quarterly, 13*(3), 319–340. doi:10.2307/249008

Davis, F. D., Bagozzi, R. P., & Warshaw, P. R. (1989). User acceptance of computer technology: A comparison of two theoretical models. *Management Science, 35*, 982–1003. doi:10.1287/mnsc.35.8.982

Davis, F. D., & Venkatesh, V. (1996). A critical assessment of potential measurement biases in the technology acceptance model: Three experiments. *International Journal of Human-Computer Studies, 45*, 19–45. doi:10.1006/ijhc.1996.0040

Davison, M. R., Wagner, C., & Ma, C. K. L. (2005). From government to e-government: A transition model. *Information Technology & People, 18*(3), 280–299. doi:10.1108/09593840510615888

Dawes, S. S. (2002). *The Future of E-Government.* Retrieved July 3, 2008, from www.vinnova.se/upload/EPiStorePDF/vr-06-11.pdf

De Kervenoael, R., Palmer, M., & Cakici, M. (2010). Exploring civil servant resistance to m-government: A story of transition and opportunities Turkey. In A. A. El-Masry, & A. G. Abdel-Wahab (Eds.), *Mobile Information Communication Technologies Adoption in Developing Countries: Effects and Implications* (pp. 134–160). Hershey, PA: IGI Global. doi:10.4018/978-1-61692-818-6.ch010

De Marez, L., Vyncke, P., Berte, K., Schuurman, D., & De Moor, K. (2007). Adopter segments, adoption determinants and mobile marketing. *Journal of Targeting. Measurement & Analysis for Marketing, 16*(1), 78–95. doi:10.1057/palgrave.jt.5750057

Deal & Key. (1998). *Corporate Celebration: Play, Purpose, and Profit at Work.* Berrett-Koehler.

Deane, A. (2003). *Increasing Voice and Transparency Using ICT Tools: E-Government, E-Governance.* Washington, DC: World Bank.

Deci, E. L. (1975). *Intrinsic Motivation.* New York: Plenum. doi:10.1007/978-1-4613-4446-9

Dedeoglu, A. O. (2004). The symbolic use of mobile telephone among Turkish consumers. *Journal of Euromarketing, 13*(2-3), 143–162. doi:10.1300/J037v13n02_08

Deetz, S. A. (1992). *Democracy in an Age of Corporate Colonization. Developments in Communication and the Politics of Every Day Life.* Albany, NY: State University of New York Press.

Defense Advanced Research Projects Agency (DARPA). (2014). *History.* Retrieved from http://www.darpa.mil/About/History/History.aspx

Delemaza, G., & Ochsenius, C. (2010). Redes de participación institucional y gobernanza democrática local: El caso de los presupuestos participativos en Chile. *Revista CLAD: Reforma y Democracia, 46,* 215–246.

De-Miguel-Molina, M. (2009). E-Government in Spain: An Analysis of the Right to Quality E-Government. *International Journal of Public Administration, 33*(1), 1–10. doi:10.1080/01900690903178454

De-Miguel-Molina, M., & Ripoll-Soler, C. (2012). Marketing e-government to citizens. In *From Government to E-Governance: Public Administration in the Digital Age* (pp. 75–92). Hershey, PA: IGI Global. doi:10.4018/978-1-4666-1909-8.ch006

Denhardt, R. B. (2008). *Theories of Public Organization.* Belmont, MA: Thomson Wadsworth.

Department of Census and Statistics. (2009). *Computer Literacy Statistics.* Retrieved from http://www.statistics.gov.lk/Newsletters/Publication1(Computer%20litalary).pdf

Department of Immigration & Emigration Sri Lanka. (2013). *Electronic travel Authorisation System.* Retrieved from http://www.eta.gov.lk/slvisa/

Department of Immigration and Passports (DIP). (2014). *Home.* Ministry of Home Affairs. Retrieved from http://www.dip.gov.bd/

Deterding, S. (2012, July-August). Gamification: Designing for Motivation. *Forum: Social Mediator,* 14-17.

Deterding, S. Dixon, Khaled, & Nacke. (2011). *Gamification: Toward a Definition* Paper presented at the CHI 2011 Gamification Workshop. New York, NY.

Deterding, S. O'Hara, Sicart, Dixon, & Nacke. (2011). *Using Game Design Elements in Non-Gaming Contexts.* Paper presented at the CHI 2011 Gamification Workshop. New York, NY.

Deterding. (2011). *From game design elements to gamefulness: Defining gamification.* MindTrek.

Devlet Planlama Teşkilatı (State Planning Organization). (2006). *Bilgi Toplumu Stratejisi (Information Society Strategy). Ratified by the High Planning Council (Decision No. 2006/38) on 11 July 2006 and promulgated in the Official Gazette (No. 26242) on 28 July 2006.* Ankara, Turkey: Author.

Devlet Planlama Teşkilatı (State Planning Organization). (2010). *Bilgi Toplumu Stratejisi Eylem Planı (2006-2010), Değerlendirme Raporu, Rapor No: 5* (Information Society Strategy Action Plan (2006-2010), Evaluation Report, Report No: 5). Ankara, Turkey: Author.

Dhaka Metropolitan Police (DMP). (2014). *Home.* Bangladesh Police. Retrieved from http://www.dmp.gov.bd/

Díaz Piraquive, F. N. et al. (2014). ICT as a Means of Generating Knowledge for Project Management. In *Proceedings in Complexity* (pp. 617–629). Springer. doi:10.1007/978-94-007-7287-8_50

Dimitrova, D. V., & Beilock, R. (2005). Where freedom matters: Internet adoption among the former socialist countries. *Gazette: The International Journal for Communication Studies, 67*(2), 173–187. doi:10.1177/0016549205050130

District E-Service Centres (DESC). (2014). *Home.* Retrieved from http://www.dhaka.gov.bd/

DNAIndia. (2013, October 5). Retrieved April 28, 2014, from http://www.dnaindia.com/world/report-bangladesh-nepal-to-use-indian-system-for-missing-children-1898872

Dodge, M., & Kitchin, R. (2001). *Mapping Cyberspace.* New York: Routledge.

Domínguez, A., Saenz-de-Navarrete, de-Marcos, Fernández-Sanz, Pagés, & Martínez-Herráiz. (2013). Gamifying Learning Experiences: Practical Implications and Outcomes. *Computers & Education, 63,* 380–392. doi:10.1016/j.compedu.2012.12.020

Donovan, L. (2012). *The Use of Serious Games in the Corporate Sector: A State of the Art Report.* Dublin, Ireland: Learnovate Centre.

Dorling, A., & McCaffery, F. (2012). The Gamification of SPICE. In *Software Process Improvement and Capability Determination* (pp. 295–301). Academic Press. doi:10.1007/978-3-642-30439-2_35

Dotson, K. (2011). *Turkey Hit by Further Anonymous Hacks and Data Leaks.* Retrieved April 12, 2014 from http://siliconangle.com/blog/2011/07/08/turkey-hit-by-further-anonymous-hacks-and-data-leaks/

Doty, P., & Erdelez, S. (2002). Information micro-practices in Texas rural courts: methods and issues for E-Government. *Government Information Quarterly, 19,* 369–387. doi:10.1016/S0740-624X(02)00121-1

Drury, P. (2005). E-health: A model for developing countries. *Health International, 2*(2), 19–26.

Dugdale, A. (2004). *E-Governance: Democracy in Transition.* National Institute for Governance Report.

Dul, J., & Hak, T. (2007). *Case Study Methodology in Business Research.* Burlington, MA: Butterworth-Heinemann.

Dunleavy, P., Margetts, H., Bastow, S., & Tinker, J. (2006). *Digital Era Governance: IT Corporations, the State, and E-Government.* New York: Oxford University Press. doi:10.1093/acprof:oso/9780199296194.001.0001

Dunleavy, P., Margetts, H., Bastow, S., & Tinkler, J. (2005). New Public Management is dead – Long live digital-era governance. *Journal of Public Administration: Research and Theory, 16*(3), 467–494. doi:10.1093/jopart/mui057

Dutch-Bangla Bank Limited (DBBL). (2014). *Mobile Banking.* Retrieved from http://www.dutchbanglabank.com/

Dutta, S. (2007). Estonia: A sustainable success in networked readiness. In S. Dutta, & I. Mia (Eds.), *The global information technology report 2006–2007: Connecting to the networked economy* (pp. 81–90). New York: Palgrave Macmillan.

Dutton, W. H., Dopatka, A., Law, G., & Nash, V. (2011). *Freedom of connection, freedom of expression: The changing legal and regulatory ecology shaping the Internet.* United Nations Educational, Scientific and Cultural Organization (UNESCO), Communication and Information Sector, Division for Freedom of Expression, Democracy and Peace. Retrieved September 01, 2012 from http://unesdoc.unesco.org/images/0019/001915/191594e.pdf

Dutton, W., Guerra, A. G., Zizzo, J. D., & Peltu, M. (2005). The cyber trust tension in E-government: Balancing identity, privacy, security. *Information Polity, 10*(1-2), 13–23.

Easley, D., & Ghosh. (2013). *Incentives, Gamification, and Game Theory: An Economic Approach to Badge Design.* Paper presented at EC'13. Philadelphia, PA.

Eastlick, M. A., Lots, L. S., & Warrington, P. (2006). Understanding online B-to-C relationships: An integrated model of privacy concerns, trust, and commitment. *Journal of Business Research, 59*(8), 877–886. doi:10.1016/j.jbusres.2006.02.006

Ebrahim, Z., & Irani, Z. (2005). E-government adoption: Architecture and barriers. *Business Process Management Journal, 11*(5), 589–611. doi:10.1108/14637150510619902

ECI. E.I.U. (2010). The Economist Intelligence Unit's Index of Democracy 2010. *The Economist.*

Economic Intelligence Unit. (2005). *Country profile 2005: Mongolia.* Retrieved September 20, 2005 from http://www.eiu.com/report_dl.asp?issue_id=139144599&mode=pdf

Economist. (2000, June 22). A survey of government and the Internet The next revolution. *The Economist.*

Economist. (2000, June 24). The Next Revolution – A survey of government and the internet. *The Economist*, p. 3.

Economist. (2010, October 23). Nomads no more, Mongolia's mining boom. *The Economist*, p. 52.

Economist. (2012, April 28). Steppe in an ugly direction: Political shenanigans in Mongolia. *The Economist.*

Economist. (2013, February 16). Before the gold rush. *The Economist*, p, 46.

Edelenbos, J., & Klijn, E. H. (2007). Trust in complex decision-making networks: A theoretical and empirical exploration. *Administration & Society, 39*(1), 25–50. doi:10.1177/0095399706294460

Edley, P. P., & Houston, R. (2011). The More Things Change, the More They Stay the Same: The Role of ICTs in Work and Family Connections. In K. B. Wright, & L. M. Webb (Eds.), *Computer-Mediated Communication in Personal Relationships* (pp. 194–225). New York, NY: Peter Lang Publishing.

Edmiston, K. (2003). State and local e-government: Prospects and challenges. *American Review of Public Administration, 33*(1), 20–45. doi:10.1177/0275074002250255

e-EAP (e-Europe Action Plan). (2005). Retrieved December 10, 2010 from http://ec.europa.eu/information_society/eeurope/2002/news_library/documents/eeurope2005/eeurope2005_en.pdf

Ehsan, M. (2004). Origin, Ideas and Practice of New Public Management: Lessons for Developing Countries. *Administrative Change, 31*(2), 69–82.

Ekeh, P. P. (1974). *Social Exchange Theory: The Two Traditions.* London: Heinemann.

Elkadi, H. (2013). Success and failure factors for e-government projects: A case from Egypt. *Egyptian Informatics Journal, 14*(2), 165–173. doi:10.1016/j.eij.2013.06.002

Ellison, N., Steinfield, C., & Lampe, C. (2007). The Benefits of Facebook Friends: Social Capital and College Students' Use of Online Social Network Sites. *Journal of Computer-Mediated Communication, 12*(4), 1143–1168. doi:10.1111/j.1083-6101.2007.00367.x

Elwood, S. (2008). Grassroots groups as stakeholders in spatial data infrastructures: Challenges and opportunities for local data development and sharing. *International Journal of Geographical Information Science, 22*(1), 71–90. doi:10.1080/13658810701348971

ENISA. (2014). *Top Ten Smartphone Risks.* Retrieved 12 April, 2014 from http://www.enisa.europa.eu/act/application-security/smartphone-security-1/top-ten-risks

EU. (2004). eGovernment Research in Europe. *European Commission.* Retrieved from http://europa.eu.int/information_society/programmes/egov_rd/text_en.htm

European Commission. (2003). Linking-up Europe: The importance of interoperability for e-Government services. *European Commission.* Retrieved July 20, 2007, from http://europa.eu.int/ISPO/ida/

European Commission. (2010). *Women and ICT. Status Report 2009.* Information Society and Media. Retrieved April 15, 2012 from http://ec.europa.eu/information_society/activities/itgirls/doc/women_ict_report.pdf

European Union. (2012). *EU Data Protection Directive 95/46/EC*. Retrieved April 12, 2014 from http://eur- lex.europa.eu/LexUriServ/LexUriServ.do?uri=CELEX:31995L0046:en:HTML

Eurostat. (2007). *E-government on-line availability*. Retrieved April 12, 2014 from http://epp.eurostat.ec.europa.eu/statistics_explained/index.php/E-government_statistics

Evci, C., Ciliz, K., Anarim, E., & Sankur, B. (2004). *Wireless networks in Turkey: A jewel in the crowd*. Alcatel Telecommunications Review.

Executive Office of the President. (2009). *Cyberspace policy review: Assuring a trusted and resilient information and communication infrastructu*re. Retrieved from http://www.whitehouse. gov/assets/documents/Cyberspace_Policy_Re- view_final.pdf

Fallows, D. (2005). *How Women and Men use the internet*. Retrieved from http://www.pewinternet.org/Reports/2005

Fang, Z. (2002). EGovernment in Digital Era: Concept, Practice, and Development. *International Journal of the Computer, the Internet and Management, 10*(2), 1-22.

Faroqi, M. G., & Siddiquee, N. A. (2011). Limping into the information age, challenges of E-Government in Bangladesh. *Journal of Comparative Asian Development, 10*(1), 33–61. doi:10.1080/15339114.2011.578473

Ferguson, M. (2001). e-Government- A strategic Framework for public services in the information age. London: Society of IT Management.

Ferr, E., Cantamessa, M., & Polucci, E. (2005). Urban Versus Regional Divide: Comparing and Classifying Digital Divide. In E-government: Towards electronic democracy (pp. 81-90). Springer.

Festinger, L. (1954). A theory of social comparison processes. *Human Relations, 7*(2), 117–140. doi:10.1177/001872675400700202

Fidelman, M. (2012, May). *Here's the Real Reason There Are Not More Women in Technology*. Retrieved July 2, 2012 from http://www.forbes.com/sites/markfidelman/2012/06/05/heres-the-real-reason-there-are-not-more-women-in-technology/

Fine, C. (2010). *Delusions of Gender: How Our Minds, Society and Neurosexism Create Difference*. New York: W. W. Norton and Company.

Fineman, S. (2006). On Being Positive: Concerns and Counterpoints. *Academy of Management Review, 31*, 270–291. doi:10.5465/AMR.2006.20208680

Finger, M., & Langenberg, T. (2007). Electronic governance. In A. V. Anttiroiko, & M. Malkia (Eds.), *Encyclopedia of Digital Government* (Vol. 2). Hershey, PA: Idea Group Reference.

Finquelievich, S. (2005). *E-política y e-gobierno en América Latina*. [E-politics and e-government in Latin America]. Buenos Aires, Argentina: LINKS A.C. Retrieved from http://www.links.org.ar/infoteca/E-Gobierno-y-E-Politica-en-LATAM.pdf

Fishbein, M., & Ajzen, I. (1975). *Belief, attitude, intention and behaviour: An introduction to theory and research*. Reading, MA: Addison-Wesley.

Fiss, P. C., & Zajac, E. J. (2004). The diffusion of ideas over contested terrain: The (non) adoption of shareholder value among German firms. *Adminstration Science Quarterly, 49*, 501–534.

Fitchard, K. (2013). *Ericsson: Global smartphone penetration will reach 60% in 2019*. Retrieved March 31, 2014 from http://gigaom.com/2013/11/11/ericsson-global-smartphone-penetration-will-reach-60-in-2019/

Fitzgerald, G. N. R. (2005). The turnaround of the London Ambulance Service Computer Aided Dispatch system (LASCAD). *European Journal of Information Systems, 14*(3), 244–257. doi:10.1057/palgrave.ejis.3000541

Fleming & Sturdy. (2011). 'Being yourself' in the electronic sweatshop: New forms of normative control. *Human Relations, 64*(2), 177–200. doi:10.1177/0018726710375481

Fleming. (2009). *Authenticity and the Cultural Politics of Work: New Forms of Informal Control*. Oxford University Press.

Flew, T. (2008). *New Media: An introduction* (3rd ed.). Melbourne, Australia: Oxford University Press.

Fluegge. (2008). *Who Put the Fun in Functional? Fun at Work and its Effects on Job Performance*. (PhD thesis). University of Florida.

Flynn, N. (2012). *Public Sector Management*. London: SAGE.

Fogg, B. J. (2009). *A behavior model for persuasive design*. Paper presented at Persuasive 2009, 4th International Conference on Persuasive Technology. Claremont, CA.

Fogg. (2003). *Persuasive Technology: Using Computers to Change What We Think and Do*. Morgan Kaufmann.

Fogg, B. J. (2002). *Persuasive technology: Using computers to change what we think and do*. Ubiquity.

Fountain, J. (2001). *Building the virtual state: Information technology and institutional change*. Washington, DC: Brookings Institution.

Fountain, J. (2006). Central Issues in the Political Development of the Virtual State. In *The Network Society: From Knowledge to Policy*. Washington, DC: Brookings Institution Press.

Fox, J., & Bailenson, J. N. (2009). Virtual self-modelling: The effects of vicarious reinforcement and identification on exercise behaviours. *Media Psychology, 12,* 1–25. doi:10.1080/15213260802669474

Fraser, H. S. F., & Blaya, J. (2010). Implementing medical information systems in developing countries, what works and what doesn't. In *Proceedings of American Medical Informatics Association Annual Symposium,* (pp. 232–236). AMIA.

Fredriksson, T. (2011). The Growing Possibilities of Information and Communication Technologies for Reducing Poverty. In S. Dutta, & I. Mia, (Eds.), *The Global Information Technology Report 2010 – 2011* (pp. 69 - 79). Geneva, Switzerland: World Economic Forum and INSEAD. Retrieved June 17, 2012 from http://reports.weforum.org/global-information-technology-report/content/pdf/wef-gitr-2010-2011.pdf

Freeman, R. E. (1984). *Strategic Management: A stakeholder approach*. Boston: Pitman.

Fukuyama, F. (1995). *Trust: The Social Virtues and the Creation of Prosperity*. New York, NY: Free Press.

Fung, A. (2004). *Empowered Participation: Reinventing Urban Democracy*. Princeton, NJ: Princeton University Press.

Furuholt, B., & Wahid, F. (2008). E-government challenges and the role of political leadership in Indonesia: The case of Sragen. In *Proceedings of the 41st Hawaii International Conference on System Sciences*. Washington, DC: IEEE Computer Society. doi: 10.1109/HICSS.2008.134

Gabel, D. (2007). Broadband and universal service. *Telecommunications Policy, 31,* 327–346. doi:10.1016/j.telpol.2007.05.002

Galperin, H., & Mariscal, J. (2007). *Digital Poverty: Latin American and Caribbean Perspectives*. International Development Research Centre: Practical Action Publishing. Retrieved December 15, 2011, from http://www.idrc.ca/openebooks/342-3/

Gamage, P., & Haplin, E. (2007). E-Sri Lanka: Bridging the digital divide. *The Electronic Library, 25*(6), 693–710. doi:10.1108/02640470710837128

Ganapati, S. (2011). Uses of Public Participation Geographic Information Systems Applications in E-Government. *Public Administration Review, 71,* 425–434. doi:10.1111/j.1540-6210.2011.02226.x

Gao, X., Song, Y., & Zhu, X. (2013). Integration and coordination: Advancing China's fragmented e-government to holistic governance. *Government Information Quarterly, 30*(2), 173–181. doi:10.1016/j.giq.2012.12.003

Garfield, E. (1972). Citation analysis as a tool in journal evaluation. *Science, 178*(4060), 471–479. doi:10.1126/science.178.4060.471 PMID:5079701

Garrido, M., Lavin, C., & Peña, N. R. (2014). Detecting Usability Problems and Offering Lines of Solutions: An Instrument' Proposal for Measuring Usability in Online Services. *IEEE Latin America Transactions, 12*(1), 9–16. doi:10.1109/TLA.2014.6716486

Garson, D. G. (2003). Toward and information technology research agenda for public administration. In *Public information technology: Policy and management issues* (pp. 331–357). Hershey, PA: Idea Group Publishers.

Garson, D. G. (2008). The promise of digital government. In *Digital government: Principles and best practices* (pp. 2–15). Hershey, PA: Idea Group Publishing.

Garson, G. D. (2006a). *Public Information Technology and E-governance: Managing the Virtual State*. Sudbury, MA: Jones and Bartlett.

Gatautis, R. (2010). Creating public value through e-Participation: Wave project. *Economics and Management,* (15), 483-490.

Geissbuhler, A., Bagayoko, C. O., & Ly, O. (2007). The RAFT network: 5 years of distance continuing medical education and tele-consultations over the Internet in French-speaking Africa. *International Journal of Medical Informatics, 76*(5-6), 351–356. doi:10.1016/j.ijmedinf.2007.01.012 PMID:17331799

Gender Working Group, United Nations Commission on Science and Technology for Development (UNCSTD). (1995). *Missing Links: Gender Equity in Science and Technology for Development*. Ottawa, Canada: International Development Research Centre in association with Intermediate Technology Publications and UNIFEM.

Gerodimos, R. (2006). Democracy and the Internet: Access, Engagement and Deliberation. *Systematics. Cybernetics and Informatics, 3*(6), 26–31.

Ghalib, A., & Heeks, R. (2008). *Automating Public Sector Bank Transactions in South Asia: Design-Reality Gap Case Study No.1*. Retrieved from http://www.egov4dev.org/success/case/bankauto.shtml

Ghose, R. (2001). Use of information technology for community empowerment: Transforming geographic information systems into community information systems. *Transactions in GIS, 5*(2), 141–163. doi:10.1111/1467-9671.00073

Ghyasi, A. F., & Kushchu, I. (2004). *Uses of mobile government in developing countries, unpublished*. Mobile Government Lab.

Gichoya, D. (2005). Factors Affecting the Successful Implementation of ICT Projects in Government. *The Electronic. Journal of E-Government, 3*(4), 175–184.

Giddens, A. (1976). *New rules of sociological method*. New York: Basic Books.

Giddens, A. (1979). *Central problems of social theory: Action, structure and contradiction in social analysis*. Berkeley, CA: University of California Press.

Giddens, A. (1984). *The constitution of society: Outline of the theory of structure*. Berkeley, CA: University of California Press.

Gil-García, J. R., & Martinez, M. J. (2005). *Exploring E-Government Evolution: The Influence of Systems of Rules on Organizational Action*. Retrieved from http://www.umass.edu/digitalcenter/research/working_papers/05_001gilgarcia

Gil-Garcia, R. J. (2012). *Enacting electronic government success: An integrative study of government-wide websites, organizational capabilities, and institutions*. New York, NY: Springer. doi:10.1007/978-1-4614-2015-6

Girard, B. (2003). *The one to watch. Radio, new ICTs and interactivity*. Rome: Food and Agriculture Organization of the United Nations.

Goldstein, N., Cialdini, R., & Griskevicius, V. (2008). A room with a viewpoint: using social norms to motivate environmental conservation in hotels. *The Journal of Consumer Research, 35*(3), 472–482. doi:10.1086/586910

Gomes de Souza, C., & Azevedo Ferreira, M. (2013). Researchers profile, co-authorship pattern and knowledge organization in information science in Brazil. *Scientometrics, 95*(2), 673–687. doi:10.1007/s11192-012-0882-7

González, R. et al. (2013). Design of an Open Platform for Collective Voting through EDNI on the Internet. In *E-Procurement Management for Successful Electronic Government Systems*. Hershey, PA: IGI Global.

Google. (2012). *ClientLogin for Installed Applications*. Retrieved April 12, 2014 from http://code.google.com/apis/accounts/docs/AuthForInstalledApps.html

Google. (2013). *Google Wallet Security*. Retrieved April 12, 2013 from http://www.google.com/wallet/how-it-works-security.htm

Google. (2014). *Google Seek For Android*. Retrieved April 12, 2014, from http://code.google.com/p/seek-for-android/

Gordon, M. D. (1982). Citation Ranking versus Subjective Evaluation in the Determination of Journal Hierarchies in the Social Sciences. *Journal of the American Society for Information Science American Society for Information Science, 33*(1), 55–57. doi:10.1002/asi.4630330109

Gorla, N. (2009). A Survey of Rural e-Government Projects in India: Status and Benefits. *Information Technology for Development, 15*(1), 52–58. doi:10.1002/itdj.20064

Gotembiewsky, R. T. (1977). *Public Administration as a developing discipline, part I: Perspectives on past and present.* New York: Marcel Dekker.

Gouscos, D., Kalikakis, M., Legal, M., & Papadopoulou, S. (2007). A general model of performance and quality for one-top e-Government service offerings. *Government Information Quarterly, 24*(4), 860–885. doi:10.1016/j.giq.2006.07.016

Government Accountability Office. (2010a). *Cybersecurity: Progress made but challenges remain in defining and coordinating the comprehensive national initiative.* Washington, DC: U.S. Government Printing Office.

Government Accountability Office. (2010b). *Cyberspace policy: Executive branch is making progress implementing 2009 policy review recommendations, but sustained leadership is needed.* Washington, DC: U.S. Government Printing Office.

Government Accountability Office. (2011). *Cybersecurity human capital: Initiatives need better planning and coordination.* Retrieved from http://www.gao.gov/assets/590/586494.pdf

Government of Bangladesh (GoB). (2002). *National Information and Communication Technology (ICT), Policy 2002.* Dhaka, Bangladesh: Ministry of Science and Information and Communication Technology.

Government of Bangladesh (GOB). (2009). *E-Government Bulletin January: Access to Information Program.* Dhaka, Bangladesh: Prime Minister's Office.

Government of Bangladesh (GOB). (2014). *National e-Tothyakosh, Bangladesh Home.* Retrieved from http://www.infokosh.bangladesh.gov.bd/index.php

Government of Sri Lanka. (2013). *Services for Citizens 2013.* Retrieved from http://www.gov.lk/web/index.php?option=com_eservices&Itemid=271&lang=en

Government Printing Office. (2010). *The patient protection and affordable healthcare act.* Retrieved from http://www.gpo.gov/fdsys/pkg/PLAW-111publ148/pdf/PLAW-111publ148.pdf

Grandon, E., Alshare, O., & Kwan, O. (2005). Factors influencing student intention to adopt online classes: A cross-cultural study. *Journal of Computing Sciences in Colleges, 20*(4), 46–56.

Grauman, B. (2012). *Cyber-security: The vexed question of global rules: An independent report on cyber preparedness around the world.* Retrieved from http://www.mcafee.com/us/resources/re- ports/rp-sda-cyber-security.pdf?cid=WBB048

Greenwich. (2001). *Fun and Gains: Motivate and Energize Staff with Workplace Games, Contests and Activities.* McGraw- Hill.

Gregerman. (2000). *Lessons from the Sandbox: Using the 13 Gifts of Childhood To Rediscover the Keys to Business Success.* McGraw-Hill.

Groh, F. (2012). Gamification: State of the Art, Definition and Utilization. In *Proceedings of the 4th Seminar on Research Trends in Media Informatics Institute of Media Informatics.* Ulm University.

Gronlund, A. (2007). Electronic government. In A. V. Anttiroiko, & M. Malkia (Eds.), *Encyclopedia of Digital Government* (Vol. 2). Hershey, PA: Idea Group Reference.

Gubbins, M. (2004). Global IT spending by sector. *Computing, 8*, 28.

Gülaçtı, E. (2009). *Elektronik İmza ve Güvenlik.* Tubitak, Uekae.

Gulick, L., & Urwick, L. (1937). *Papers on the Science of Administration.* New York: Institute of Public Administration.

Gupta, P. R., & Jain, D. K. (2010). Road Map for E governance. In *Proceedings of ASCNT.* CDAC.

Gupta, B., Dasgupta, B. I., & Gupta, A. (2008). Adoption of ICT in a government organization in a developing country: An empirical study. *The Journal of Strategic Information Systems*, *17*(2), 140–154. doi:10.1016/j.jsis.2007.12.004

Gupta, M. P., & Jana, D. (2003). E-government evaluation: A framework and case study. *Government Information Quarterly*, *20*, 365–387. doi:10.1016/j.giq.2003.08.002

Gurumurthy, A. (2004). Gender and ICTs. London: Bridge, Institute of Development Studies (IDS).

Hafkin, N. (2002a). *Gender Issues in ICT Policy in Developing Countries: An Overview*. Retrieved from http//www.womensnet.org.za/gender-issues-ict-policy-developing-countries-an-overview

Hague, B., & Loader, B. D. (1999). *Digital Democracy: Discourse and Decision Making in the Information Age*. London: Routledge.

Hahm, C. (2008). South Korea's Miraculous Democracy. *Journal of Democracy*, *19*(3), 128–142. doi:10.1353/jod.0.0005

Halvorsen, K. (2003). Assessing the effects of public participation. *Public Administration Review*, *63*(5), 535–543. doi:10.1111/1540-6210.00317

Hamari & Eranti. (2011). Framework for designing and evaluating game achievements. In *Think Design Play: The fifth international conference of the Digital Research Association* (DIGRA). Hilversum, The Netherlands: DiGRA/Utrecht School of the Arts.

Hamari, J., Koivisto, J., & Sarsa, H. (2014). Does Gamification Work? A Literature Review of Empirical Studies on Gamification. In *Proceedings of the 47th Hawaii International Conference on System Sciences*. IEEE.

Hamari, J. (2013). Transforming Homo Economicus into Homo Ludens: A Field Experiment on Gamification in a Utilitarian Peer-to-Peer Trading Service. *Electronic Commerce Research and Applications*, *12*, 236–245. doi:10.1016/j.elerap.2013.01.004

Hamari, J., & Järvinen, A. (2011). Building customer relationship through game mechanics in social games. In M. Cruz-Cunha, V. Carvalho, & P. Tavares (Eds.), *Business, Technological and Social Dimensions of Computer Games: Multidisciplinary Developments*. Hershey, PA: IGI Global. doi:10.4018/978-1-60960-567-4.ch021

Hamelink, C. J. (2000). *The Ethics of Cyberspace*. London: Sage.

Hanberger, A. (2003). Democratic implications of public organizations. *Public Organization Review*, *3*(1), 29–54. doi:10.1023/A:1023095927266

Hanna, N. K. (2009). E-government in developing countries. *Information Policy*. Retrieved from http://www.i-policy.org

Hanna, N. (2010). *Transforming Government and Building the Information Society: Challenges and Opportunities for the Developing World*. New York, NY: Springer.

Hanseth, O. (2002). From systems and tools to networks and infrastructures – From design to cultivation. In *Towards a theory of ICT solutions and its design methodology implications*. Academic Press.

Han, Y. Y., Carcillo, J. A., Venkataraman, S. T., Clark, R. S. B., Watson, R. S., & Nguyen, T. C. et al. (2005). Unexpected increased mortality after implementation of a commercially sold computerized physician order entry system. *Pediatrics*, *116*(6), 1506–1512. doi:10.1542/peds.2005-1287 PMID:16322178

Haque, A. (2001). GIS, public service, and the issue of democratic governance. *Public Administration Review*, *61*(3), 259–265. doi:10.1111/0033-3352.00028

Haque, M. S. (2002). E-governance in India: Its impacts on relations among citizens, politicians and public servants. *International Review of Administrative Sciences*, *68*, 231–250. doi:10.1177/0020852302682005

Hardy, C. A., & Williams, S. P. (2011). Assembling e-government research designs: A transdisciplinary view and interactive approach. *Public Administration Review*, *71*(3), 405–413. doi:10.1111/j.1540-6210.2011.02361.x

Hargittai, E. (2002). Beyond logs and surveys: In-depth measures of people's web use skills. *Journal of the American Society for Information Science and Technology Perspectives*, *53*(14), 1239–1244. doi:10.1002/asi.10166

Hargittai, E. (2003). The digital divide and what to do about it. In D. C. Jones (Ed.), *The New Economy Handbook*. San Diego, CA: Academic Press.

Haricharan, S. (2005). *Knowledge Management in the South African Public Sector*. Retrieved July 5, 2008 from http://www.ksp.org.za/holonl03.htm

Harrison, D. A., Mykytyn, P. P., & Riemenschneider, C. K. (1997). Executive decision about adoption of information technology in small business: Theory and empirical tests. *Information Systems Research, 8*(2), 171–195. doi:10.1287/ isre.8.2.171

Harris, T. M., & Weiner, D. (1998). Empowerment, marginalization and community-integrated GIS. *Cartography and Geographic Information Science, 25*(2), 67–76. doi:10.1559/152304098782594580

Hawthorne, S. (1999). Connectivity: Cultural Practice of the Powerful or Subversion from the Margins. In S. Hawthorne, & R. Klein (Eds.), *Cyberfeminism: Connectivity, Critique and Creativity* (pp. 125–128). Melbourne, Australia: Spinifex.

Hawthorne, S. (1999). Cyborgs, Virtual Bodies and Organic Bodies: Theoretical Feminist Responses. In S. Hawthorne, & R. Klein (Eds.), *Cyberfeminism: Connectivity, Critique and Creativity* (pp. 213–250). Melbourne, Australia: Spinifex.

Hawthorne, S., & Klein, R. (1999). Introduction: Cyberfeminism. In S. Hawthorne, & R. Klein (Eds.), *Cyberfeminism: Connectivity, Critique and Creativity* (pp. 1–16). Melbourne, Australia: Spinifex.

Hazlett, S. A., & Hill, F. (2003). E-government: The realities of using IT to transform the public sector. *Managing Service Quality, 13*(6), 445–452. doi:10.1108/09604520310506504

Healy, J. (2008). *Implementing e-Health in Developing Countries Guidance and Principles*. Retrieved from http://www.itu.int/ITU-D/cyb/app/docs/e-Health_prefinal_15092008.pdf

Heeks, R. (2001). *Understanding e-governance for development*. Retrieved from http://unpan1.un.org/intradoc/groups/public/documents/NISPAcee/UNPAN015484.pdf

Heeks, R. (2002). *eGovernment in Africa: Promise and Practice* (Working Paper 13). iGovernment.

Heeks, R. (2003). *e-Government Special – Does it Exist in Africa and what can it do?* Retrieved September 30, 2007, from http://www.balancingact-africa.com/news/back/balancing-act93.html#headline

Heeks, R. (2003). *Most eGovernment-for-Development Projects Fail: How Can Risks be Reduced?* (iGovernment Working Paper Series, No 14). Manchester, UK: IDPM, University of Manchester.

Heeks, R. (2008). *Success and Failure Rates of eGovernment in Developing/Transitional Countries: Overview*. Retrieved from http://www.egov4dev.org/success/sfrates.shtml

Heeks, R., Gao, P., & Ospina, A. (2010). *Delivering coherent ICT policies in developing countries*. Manchester, UK: Centre for Development Informatics, University of Manchester, e-Development Briefing No. 14. Retrieved from http://www.sed.manchester.ac.uk/idpm/research/publications/wp/di/short/CDIBriefing14PolicyCoherence.pdf

Heeks, R. (2001). *Reinventing Government in the Information Age*. London: Routledge.

Heeks, R. (2002). *Failure, Success and Improvisation of Information Systems Projects in Developing Countries. Institute for Development Policy and Management (IDPM)*. University of Manchester.

Heeks, R. (2002). Information systems and developing countries: Failure, success, and local improvisations. *The Information Society, 18*(2), 101–112. doi:10.1080/01972240290075039

Heeks, R., & Bailur, S. (2007). Analyzing e-government research: Perspectives, philosophies, theories, methods, and practice. *Government Information Quarterly, 24*(2), 243–265. doi:10.1016/j.giq.2006.06.005

Heggestuen, J. (2013). *One In Every 5 People In The World Own A Smartphone, One In Every 17 Own A Tablet*. Retrieved March 31, 2014, from http://www.businessinsider.com/smartphone-and-tablet-penetration-2013-10

Heintze, T., & Bretschneider, S. (2000). Information technology and restructuring in public organizations: Does adoption of information technology affect organizational structures, communications, and decision making? *Journal of Public Administration: Research and Theory, 10*(4), 801–830. doi:10.1093/oxfordjournals.jpart.a024292

Heinze, N., & Hu, Q. (2005). *e-Government Research: A Review via the Lens of Structuration Theory*. Paper presented at the Ninth Pacific Asia Conference on Information Systems (PACS2005). Bangkok, Thailand.

Hemsath & Yerkes. (1997). *301 Ways to Have Fun at Work*. Berrett-Koehler.

Henman, P. (2010). *Governing Electronically: E-Government and the Reconfiguration of Public Administration, Policy and Power*. London: Palgrave Macmillan. doi:10.1057/9780230248496

Henning, E., Van Rensburg, W., & Smit, B. (2004). *Finding your way in Qualitative Research*. Pretoria, South Africa: Van Schaick.

Henry, N. (1995). *Public Administration and public affairs* (6th ed.). Prentice-Hall.

Herbig, P., & Dunphy, S. (1998). Culture and innovation. *Cross Cultural Management: An International Journal, 5*(4), 13–21. doi:10.1108/13527609810796844

Herman, P., & Cullen, R. (2006). E-government: Transforming the Government. In *Comparative Perspectives on E-government*. Lanham, MD: The Scarecrow Press.

Herron, E. J. (1999). Democratization and the development of information regimes: Internet in Eurasia and Baltics. *Problems of Post-Communism, 46*(4), 56–68.

Hershfield, H. E., Goldstein, D. G., Sharpe, W. F., Fox, J., Yeykelis, L., Carstenson, L., & Bailenson, J. N. (2011). Increasing Saving Behavior Through Age-Progressed Renderings of the Future Self. *JMR, Journal of Marketing Research, 48*, 23–37. doi:10.1509/jmkr.48.SPL.S23 PMID:24634544

Herzig, P. Ameling, & Schill. (2012). A Generic Platform for Enterprise Gamification. In *Proceedings of Joint Working Conference on Software Architecture & 6th European Conference on Software Architecture* (pp. 219-223). Academic Press.

Hienerth, C., Keinz, & Lettl. (2011). Exploring the Nature and Implementation Process of User-Centric Business Models. *Long Range Planning, 44*, 344–374. doi:10.1016/j.lrp.2011.09.009

Hijab, N., & Zambrano, R. (2008). *Gender responsive E-Governance: Exploring the Transformative Potential*. New York: UNDP.

Hiller, J. S., & Belanger, F. (2001). Privacy Strategies for Electronic Government. In M. A. Abramson, & G. E. Means (Eds.), *EGovernment 2001*. Boulder, CO: Rowman and Littlefield.

Hindman, M. (2009). *The myth of digital democracy*. Princeton, NJ: Princeton University Press.

HN. (2014). *Cum se lauda autoritatile ca portalul eRomania sustine peste 50.000 de utilizatori simultan, cand de fapt site-ul devine inaccesibil la 100 de cereri simultane.* Retrieved from http://economie.hotnews.ro/stiri-telecom-16800984-video-test-cum-lauda-autoritatile-portalul-eromania-sustine-peste-50-000-utilizatori-simultan-cand-fapt-site-devine-inaccesibil-100-cereri-simultane.htm

Ho, A. (2002). Reinventing Local Governments and the E-Government Initiative. *Public Administration Review, 62*(4), 434–444. doi:10.1111/0033-3352.00197

Hobsbawm, E. J. (1996). Language, culture, and national identity. *Social Research, 63*, 1065–1081.

Holden, S. H., Norris, D. F., & Fletcher, P. D. (2003). Electronic government at the local level: Progress to date and future issues. *Public Performance and Management Review, 26*(3), 1–20.

Holliday, I., & Kwok, R. C. V. (2004). Governance in the information age: Building e-government in Hong Kong. *New Media & Society, 6*(4), 549–570. doi:10.1177/146144804044334

Holliday, I., & Yep, R. (2005). E-Government in China. *Public Administration and Development, 25*, 239–249. doi:10.1002/pad.361

Holmes, D. (2005). *Communication theory: Media, technology and society*. Thousand Oaks, CA: Sage Publications Inc.

Holmes, L. (1997). *Post-communism: An introduction*. Durham, NC: Duke University Press.

Holzer, M., & Kim, S. (2003). *Digital governance in municipalities worldwide: An assessment of municipal we sites throughout the world.* Newark, NJ: The E-Governance Institute/National Center for Public Productivity. Retrieved from http://un-pan1.un.org/intradoc/groups/public/documents/ aspa/unpan012905.pdf

Holzer, M., & Kim, S. (2005). *Digital Governance in Municipalities Worldwide (2005): A Longitudinal Assessment of Municipal Websites Through the World.* Retrieved from www.andromeda.rutgers.edu/~egovinst/ Website/researchpg.htm

Holzer, M., & Tae Kim, S. (2005). *Digital Governance in Municipalities Worldwide.* Retrieved from http://unpan1.un.org/intradoc/groups/public/documents/aspa/ unpan022839.pdf

Hood, C. (1983). The Tools of Government. London: Basingstoke.

Hood, C. (1991). A Public Management for All Seasons. *Public Administration, 69,* 3–19. doi:10.1111/j.1467-9299.1991.tb00779.x

Hood, C., Peters, & Wollmann. (1996). Sixteen Ways to Consumerize Public Services: Pick 'n Mix or Painful Trade-offs? *Public Money & Management, 16,* 43–50. doi:10.1080/09540969609387944

Hoque, M. M. (2009). *An Information System Planning Framework for E-Governance in Bangladesh.* Unpublished report.

Hoque, S. M. S. (2005). *E-Governance in Bangladesh: A Scrutiny from Citizens' Perspective.* Paper presented in Network of Asia-Pacific Schools and Institutes of Public Administration and Governance (NAPSIPAG) Annual Conference 2005. New York, NY.

Hoque, S. M. S. (2006). E-government in Bangladesh: A Scrutiny from Citizens Perspective. In R. Ahmad (Ed.), *The Role of Public Administration in Building a harmonious Society.* Academic Press.

Houtchens, B. A., Clemmer, T. P., Holloway, H. C., Kiselev, A. A., Logan, J. S., & Merrell, R. C. et al. (1993). Telemedicine and international disaster response: Medical consultation to Armenia and Russia via a Telemedicine Spacebridge. *Prehospital and Disaster Medicine, 8*(1), 57–66.

Hrynyshyn, D. (2008). Globalization, nationality and commodification: The politics of the social construction of the internet. *New Media & Society, 10*(5), 751–770. doi:10.1177/1461444808094355

Hu, G., Lin, H., & Pan, W. (2013). Conceptualizing and Examining E-Government Service Capability: A Review and Empirical Study. *Journal of the American Society for Information Science and Technology, 64*(11), 2379–2395. doi:10.1002/asi.22921

Hui, G., & Hayllar, M. R. (2010). Creating Public Value in E-Government: A Public-Private-Citizen Collaboration Framework in Web 2.0. *Australian Journal of Public Administration, 69,* 120–131. doi:10.1111/j.1467-8500.2009.00662.x

Hultberg, L. (2008). *Women Empowerment in Bangladesh: A Study of the Village Pay Phone Program. School of Education and Communication (HLK).* Jonkoping University.

Human Organization. (1959). Banana Time: Job Satisfaction and Informal Interaction. *Human Organization, 18,* 158–168.

Humeyra, P. (2014). *Turkey begins espionage investigation after Syria leak.* Retreved April 12, 2014 from http://www.reuters.com/article/2014/03/29/us-turkey-electionidUSBREA2R12X20140329

Huotari & Hamari. (2011). *Gamification from the perspective of service marketing.* Paper presented at CHI 2011. New York, NY.

Huotari, K., & Hamari, J. (2012). Defining gamification: a service marketing perspective. In *Proceedings of the 16th International Academic MindTrek Conference.* Tampere, Finland: ACM Press.

Hurriet Daily News. (2013). *Istanbul's Kadıköy offers free Wi-Fi on streets.* Retrieved from http://www.hurriyetdailynews.com/istanbuls-kadikoy-offers-free-wi-fi-on-streets. aspx?pageID=238&nID=55204&NewsCatID=341

Hurriet Daily News. (2014). *Turkey ranks second in Internet censors: Report.* Retrieved from http://www.hurriyetdailynews.com/turkey-ranks-second-in-internet-censors-report.aspx?pageID=238&nID=62219&News CatID=339

Huyer, S., & Sikoska, T. (2003). Overcoming Gender Digital Divide: Understanding ICT and Their Potential for the Empowerment of Women. *Instraw Research Paper Series, 1*, 17-57.

Hwang, M., Li, C., Shen, J., & Chu, Y. (2004). Challenges in e-government and security of information. *Information & Security, 15*(1), 9–20.

Hyer, E. K., Ballif-Spanvill, B., Peters, S. J., Solomon, Y., Thomas, H., & Ward, C. (2009). Gender Inequities in Educational Participation. In D. B. Holsinger, & W. J. Jacob (Eds.), *Inequality in Education: Comparative and International Perspectives* (pp. 128–149). Dordrecht, The Netherlands: Springer.

ICANN. (2011, October 6). *IDN variant TLDs – Cyrillic script issues.* Retrieved from http://archive.icann.org/en/topics/new-gtlds/cyrillic-vip-issues-report-06oct11-en.pdf

ICANN. (2012, February 20). *A Study of issues related to the management of IDN variant TLDs* (Integrated Issues Report). Retrieved from http://www.icann.org/en/resources/idn/idn-vip-integrated-issues-final-clean-20feb12-en.pdf

ICTA. (2011). *Annual Report, 2011.* Retrieved from http://www.icta.lk/images/icta/ICTA-Annual-Report-2011.pdf

ICTA. (2013). *Electronic Communications Market in Turkey.* Retrieved April 12, 2014 from http://eng.btk.gov.tr/kutuphane_ve_veribankasi/pazar_verileri/2013_Q2_ECM_MarketData.pdf

ICTA. (2013a). *Lanka Gate Statistics, 2013.* Retrieved from http://www.gov.lk/web/images/eservstatis/lanka-gatestats_aug_2013.pdf

ICTA. (2013b). *m-Chanelling in Government hospitals, 2013.* Retrieved from http://www.icta.lk/en/icta/90-general/1370-mchanelling-in-government-hospitals.html

ICTA. (2013c). *Re-engineering Government (Re-Gov).* Retrieved from http://www.icta.lk/programmes/re-engineering-government.html

IETF. (2012). Retrieved April 12, 2014 from http://tools.ietf.org/html/draft-ietf-websec-strict-transport-sec-02

Ifinedo, P. (2005). Measuring Africa 's e-readiness in the global networked economy: A nine-country data analysis. *International Journal of Education and Development Using ICT, 1*(1), 1–19.

Ifinedo, P., & Singh, M. (2011). Determinants of egovernment maturity in the transition economies of Central and Eastern Europe: 1. *Electronic Journal of E-Government, 9*, 166.

Im, T. (2011). Information Technology and Organizational Morphology: The Case of the Korean Central Government. *Public Administration Review, 71*(3), 435–443. doi:10.1111/j.1540-6210.2011.02227.x

Im, T., Porumbescu, G., & Lee, H. (2013). ICT as a buffer to change: A case study of the Seoul Metropolitan Government's Dasan Call Center. *Public Performance Management Review, 36*(3), 436–455. doi:10.2753/PMR1530-9576360303

Im, T., Shin, H. Y., Hong, E. Y., & Jin, Y. G. (2007). IT and Administrative Innovation in Korea. *Korean Journal of Policy Studies, 21*(2), 1–17.

Im, T., Shin, H. Y., & Jin, Y. (2007). IT and administrative innovation in Korea: How does IT affect organizational performance? *Korean Journal of Policy Studies, 21*(2), 1–17.

Institute of Governance Studies (IGS). (2009). *Digital Bangladesh: The Beginning of Citizen-Centric E-Government?* BRAC University.

Intelligence, G. S. M. A. (2014). *Mobile data usage on the rise in the Middle East.* Retrieved April 12, 2014 from https://gsmaintelligence.com/analysis/2013/07/mobile-data-usage-on-the-rise-in-the-middle-east/393/

International Federation of Journalists in cooperation with the United Nations Educational, Scientific and Cultural Organization (UNESCO). (2009). *Getting the Balance Right: Gender Equality in Journalism.* Brussels, Belgium: International Press Centre. Retrieved March 13, 2012 from http://unesdoc.unesco.org/images/0018/001807/180707e.pdf

International Telecommunication Union. (2010). *Measuring the Information Society: Version 1.01.* Geneva: ITU.

International Telecommunication Union. (2011). *Measuring the Information Society*. Geneva: ITU.

International Telecommunication Union. (2012). *Measuring the information society 2012*. Geneva: International Telecommunication Union.

Internet World Stats. (n.d.). Retrieved January, 2014, from http://www.Internetworldstats.com/stats.htm

Irani, Z. et al. (2014). Visualising a knowledge mapping of information systems investment evaluation. *Expert Systems with Applications, 41*(1), 105–125. doi:10.1016/j.eswa.2013.07.015

Isis. (1996). Women in the News: A Guide for Media. Retrieved January 2, 2012 from http://www.isiswomen.org/index.php?option=com_content&view=article&id=181:a-gender-equality-toolkit&catid=163:publications&Itemid=240

Islam, S. (2008). Towards a sustainable e-Participation implementation model. *European Journal of e-Practice, 5*.

Islam, S.M. (2013). Mobile Banking: An Emerging Issue in Bangladesh. *ASA University Review, 7* (1).

Istepanian, R., & Lacal, J. (2003). *Emerging Mobile Communication Technologies for Health: Some Imperative notes on m-Health.* Paper presented at The 25th Silver 59 Anniversary International Conference of the IEEE Engineering in Medicine and Biology Society. Cancun Mexico.

ITU (International Telecommunication Union). (2011). *The World in 2011 – ICT Facts and Figures.* Retrieved from http://www.itu.int/ITU-D/ict/facts/2011/material/ICTFactsFigures2011.pdf

ITU. (2013). *Key ICT indicators for developed and developing countries and the world.* Retrieved April 6, 2014 from http://www.itu.int/en/ITU-D/Statistics/Documents/statistics/2013/ITU_Key_2005-2013_ICT_data.xls

ITU. (2013a). *ICT Facts and Figures 2013.* Retrieved April 5, 2014 from http://www.itu.int/en/ITU-D/Statistics/Pages/stat/default.aspx

ITU. (2013b). *Measuring the Information Society.* Retrieved April 5, 2014 from http://www.itu.int/en/ITU-D/Statistics/Pages/publications/mis2013.aspx

Jackson, W. (2012). Could you continue to operate under cyberattack? *Government Computer News.* Retrieved from http://gcn.com/Articles/2012/02/27/Cybereye-operating-while-under-attack.aspx?Page=2

Jaeger, P. T. (2005). Deliberative democracy and the conceptual foundations of electronic government. *Government Information Quarterly, 22*(4), 702–719. doi:10.1016/j.giq.2006.01.012

Jaeger, P. T., & Thompson, K. M. (2003). E-government around the world: Lessons, challenges, and future directions. *Government Information Quarterly, 20*, 389–394. doi:10.1016/j.giq.2003.08.001

Jaeger, P., Bertot, J., McClure, C., & Rodriguez, M. (2007). Public libraries and Internet access across the United States: A comparison by state from 2004 to 2006. *Information Technology and Libraries, 26*(2), 4–14.

Jahankhani, H., & Varghese, M. K. (2004). The role of consumer trust in relation to electronic commerce. In *Proceedings of the 4th Annual Hawaii International Conference on Business*, (pp. 21-24). IEEE.

Jakobsson, M. (2011). The achievement machine: Understanding Xbox 360 achievements in gaming practices. *Game Studies, 11*, 1.

James, J. (2007). From origins to implications: key aspects in the debate over the digital divide. *Journal of Information Technology, 22*, 284–295. doi:10.1057/palgrave.jit.2000097

James, J. (2008). Digital divide complacency: Misconceptions and dangers. *The Information Society, 24*, 54–61. doi:10.1080/01972240701774790

James, J. (2013). The diffusion of IT in the historical context of innovations from developed countries. *Social Indicators Research, 111*, 175–184. doi:10.1007/s11205-011-9989-0 PMID:23378682

Janssen, M., Scholl, H., Wimmer, M., & Hua Tan, Y. (2011). *Electronic Government: 10th International Conference.* New York, NY: Springer.

Johnson, I. (1997). Redefining the Concept of Governance. Gatineau, Canada: Political and Social Policies Division, Policy Branch, Canadian International Development Agency (CIDA).

Johnson, S. (1998). The internet changes everything: Revolutionizing public participation and access to government information through the internet. *Administrative Law Review, 50*(2), 277–337.

Joia, L. A. (2004). Developing government to government enterprises in Brazil: A heuristic model drawn from multiple case studies. *International Journal of Information Management, 24*(2), 147–166. doi:10.1016/j.ijinfomgt.2003.12.013

Jorgensen, D. J., & Klay, E. W. (2007). Technology-driven change and public administration: Establishing essential normative principles. *International Journal of Public Administration, 30*, 289–305. doi:10.1080/01900690601117770

Julnes, P., & Johnson, D. (2011). Strengthening efforts to engage the Hispanic community in citizen-driven governance: an assessment of efforts in Utah. *Public Administration Review, 71*(2), 221–231. doi:10.1111/j.1540-6210.2011.02333.x

Jungherr, A. (2012). Online Campaigning in Germany: The CDU Online Campaign for the General Election 2009 in Germany. *German Politics, 21*, 317–340. doi:10.1080/09644008.2012.716043

Kaaya, J. (2004). Implementing e-Government Services in East Africa: Assessing Status Through Content Analysis of Government Websites. *The Electronic. Journal of E-Government, 1*(2), 39–54.

Kabeer, N. (2001). Resources, Agency, Achievements: Reflections on the Measurement of Women's Empowerment in Discussion: Women's Empowerment Theory and Practice. *Sida Studies, 3*.

Kahraman, C., Demirel Cetin, N., & Demirel, T. (2007). Prioritization of e-government strategies using a SWOT-AHP analysis: The case of Turkey. *European Journal of Information Systems, 16*, 284–298. doi:10.1057/palgrave.ejis.3000679

Karim, M. A. (2010). Digital Bangladesh for Good Governance. *Bangladesh Development Forum, Online Paper Dhaka*. Retrieved from http://www.erd.gov.bd/BDF2010/BG_%20Paper/BDF2010_Session%20VI.pdf

Karim, M. R. A. (2003). Technology and improved service delivery: Learning points from the Malyasian experience. *International Review of Administrative Sciences, 69*.

Karokola, G., Yngström, L., & Kowalski, S. (2012). Secure e-government services: A comparative analysis of e-government maturity models for the developing regions–The need for security services. *International Journal of Electronic Government Research, 8*(1), 1–25. doi:10.4018/ jegr.2012010101

Katz, M. L., & Shapiro, C. (1985). Network externalities, competition, and compatibility. *The American Economic Review, 75*(3), 424–440.

Kaufman, E. (2005). E-democracia local en la gestión cotidiana de los servicios públicos: Modelo asociativo (público – privado) de gobierno electrónico local. In S. Finquelievich (Ed.), E-política y e-gobierno en América Latina (pp. 130-150). Buenos Aires, Argentina: LINKS A.C.

Kaufman, H. (1977). *Red Tape: Its Origins, Uses and Abuses*. Washington, DC: Brookings Institution.

Kelly, J., & Blakesley, N. (2011). Localization 2.0. In S. Dutta, & I. Mia (Eds.), *The Global Information Technology Report 2010 - 2011* (pp. 119 - 127). Geneva, Switzerland: World Economic Forum and INSEAD. Retrieved June 17, 2012 from http://reports.weforum.org/global-information-technology-report/content/pdf/wef-gitr-2010-2011.pdf

Kerwin, C. M., & Furlong, S. R. (2011). *Rulemaking: How government agencies write law and make policy* (4th ed.). Washington, DC: CQ Press.

Kettl, D. F. (2000). The Transformation of Governance: Globalization, Devolution, and the Role of Government. *Public Administration Review, 60*(6), 488–497. doi:10.1111/0033-3352.00112

Kim, B. J., Kavanaough, A. L., & Hult, K. M. (2011). Civic engagement and internet use in local governance: Hierarchical linear model for understanding the role of local community groups. *Administration & Society, 43*(7), 807–835. doi:10.1177/0095399711413873

Kinzie, M. B., & Joseph, D. R. D. (2008). Gender differences in game activity preferences of middle school children: Implications for educational game design. *Educational Technology Research and Development, 56*, 643–663. doi:10.1007/s11423-007-9076-z

Kirigia, J. M., Seddoh, A., Gatwiri, D., Muthuri, L. H. K., & Seddoh, J. (2005). E-health: Determinants, opportunities, challenges and the way forward for countries in the WHO African Region. *BioMed Central Public Health, 5*, 137. doi:10.1186/1471-2458-5-137 PMID:16364186

Kleinberg, J. (2008). The Convergence of Social and Technological Networks. *Communications of the ACM, 51*(11), 66–72. doi:10.1145/1400214.1400232

Klvana, T. P. (2004). New Europe's civil society, democracy, and the media thirteen years after: The story of the Czech Republic. *The Harvard International Journal of Press/Politics, 9*, 40–55. doi:10.1177/1081180X04266505

Knack, S., & Keefer, P. (1997). Does Social Capital Have An Economic Payoff? A Cross-Country Investigation. *The Quarterly Journal of Economics, 112*(4), 1251–1288. doi:10.1162/003355300555475

Koehn, D. (2003). The nature of and conditions for online trust. *Journal of Business Ethics, 43*, 3–19. doi:10.1023/A:1022950813386

Kolko, B., Wei, C., & Spyridakis, J. H. (2003). Internet use in Uzbekistan: Developing a methodology for tracking information technology implementation success. *Internet Technologies and International Development, 1*(2).

Korac-Kakabadse, A., & Korac-Kakabadse, N. (1999). Information technology's impact on the quality of democracy: Reinventing the democracy vessel. In *Reinventing government in the information age: International practice in IT-enabled public sector reform* (pp. 211–228). London: Routledge.

Kotler, P., & Kartajaya, S. (2011). *Marketing 3.0.* Madrid: LID.

Kotler, P., & Lee, N. (2006). *Marketing in the public sector.* Upper Saddle River, NJ: Wharton School Publishing.

Kovacic, Z. J. (2005). The impact of national culture on worldwide e-government readiness. *Informing Science Journal, 8*, 143–158.

Kromidhan, E. (2012). Strategic e-government development and the role of benchmarking. *Government Information Quarterly, 29*(4), 573–581. doi:10.1016/j.giq.2012.04.006

Kumar, R., & Best, M. (2006). Impact and Sustainability of E-Government Services in Developing Countries: Lessons Learned from Tamil Nadu, India. *The Information Society, 22*, 1–12. doi:10.1080/01972240500388149

Kumar, V., Mukerji, B., Butt, I., & Persaud, A. (2007). Factors for Successful e-Government Adoption: A Conceptual Framework. *The Electronic. Journal of E-Government, 5*(1), 63–76.

Kumas, E. (2007). E-devlet kapısı ve risk değerlendirme metodolojisi. *Turkiye'de Internet Konferansi, 12.*

Kuran, N. H. (2005). *Türkiye icin E-devlet modeli.* Istanbul, Turkey: Bilgi Universitesi Yayınları.

Kurbanoglu, S. (2004). An overview of information literacy studies in Turkey. *The International Information & Library Review, 36*(1), 23–27. doi:10.1016/j.iilr.2003.07.001

Kurdistan Regional Statistics Office. (2007). Retrieved from http://www.krso.net/detail.aspx?page=statisticsbysubjects&c=sbsPopulationLabor&id=361

Kushchu, I., & Kuscu, H. (2003). From e-government to m-government: Facing the inevitable. In *Proceeding of European Conference on E-Government* (ECEG), (pp.253-260). Reading, UK: Academic Conferences International.

Kushchu, I. (2007). *Mobile Government: An Emerging Direction in E-Government.* Hershey, PA: IGI Publishing. doi:10.4018/978-1-59140-884-0

Lam, W. (2005). Barriers to e-government integration. *The Journal of Enterprise Information Management, 18*(5), 511–530. doi:10.1108/17410390510623981

Lam, W. (2005). Integration challenges towards increasing e-government maturity. *Journal of E-Government, 1*(2), 45–58. doi:10.1300/J399v01n02_04

Landsbergen, D., Coursey, D. H., Loveless, S., & Shangraw, R. F. Jr. (1997). Decision quality, confidence and commitment with expert systems: an experimental study. *Journal of Public Administration: Research and Theory, 7*(1), 131–158. doi:10.1093/oxfordjournals.jpart.a024336

Lannon, J., & Halpin, E. (2013). *Responding to cross border child trafficking in south Asia: An analysis of the feasability of a technological enabled missing children alert system.* Bangkok, Thailand: Plan International.

Lan, Z., & Anders, K. K. (2000). A Paradigmatic View of Contemporary Public Administration Research: An Empirical Test. *Administration & Society, 32*(2), 138–165. doi:10.1177/00953990022019380

Lanzara, G. F. (2009). Building digital institutions: ICT and the rise of assemblages in government. In *ICT and Innovation in the Public Sector: European Studies in the Making of E-Government* (pp. 9–39). London: Palgrave Macmillan.

Latifi, R. (2011). Initiate-build-operate-transfer - A strategy for establishing sustainable telemedicine programs not only in the developing countries. *Studies in Health Technology and Informatics, 165*, 3–10. PMID:21685579

Latour, B. (1993). *We Have Never Been Modern.* Cambridge, MA: Harvard University Press.

Laurie, N., Andolina, R., & Radcliffe, S. (2005). Ethnodevelopment: Social Movements, Creating Experts and Professionalising Indigenous Knowledge in Ecuador. *Antipode, 37*(3), 470–496. doi:10.1111/j.0066-4812.2005.00507.x

Lawley, E. (2012, July-August). Games as an Alternate Lens for Design. *Social Mediator*, 16-17.

Lawley, E. L. (1993). *Computers and the Communication of Gender.* Retrieved January 4, 2012, from http://www.itcs.com/elawley/gender.html

Layne, K., & Lee, J. (2001). Developing fully functional E-government: A four stage model. *Government Information Quarterly, 18*, 122–136. doi:10.1016/S0740-624X(01)00066-1

Lazarus, W., & Mora, F. (2000). *Online content for low-income and underserved americans: The digital divide's new frontier.* Santa Monica, CA: The Children's Partnership.

Lecy, J. D., Mergel, I. A., & Schmitz, H. P. (2013). Networks in public administration: Current scholarship in review. *Public Management Review.* doi: doi:10.1080/14719037.2012.743577

Lee, B. (2014). Window Dressing 2.0: Constituency-Level Web Campaigns in the 2010 UK General Election. *Politics, 34*, 45–57. doi:10.1111/1467-9256.12029

Lee, C. P., Chang, K., & Stokes Berry, F. S. (2011). Testing the development and diffusion of e-government and e-democracy: A global perspective. *Public Administration Review, 71*(3), 444–454. doi:10.1111/j.1540-6210.2011.02228.x

Lee, G., & Perry, J. L. (2002). Are computers boosting productivity? A test of the paradox in state governments. *Journal of Public Administration: Research and Theory, 12*(1), 77–102. doi:10.1093/oxfordjournals.jpart.a003525

Lee, M. (2006a). What's missing in feminist research in new information and communication technologies? *Feminist Media Studies, 6*(2), 191–210. doi:10.1080/14680770600645168

Lee, M. (2006b). A feminist political economic understanding of the relations between state, market and civil society from Beijing to Tunis. *International Journal of Media and Cultural Politics, 4*(2), 221–240.

Legge, J. S. Jr, & Devore, J. (1987). Measuring Productivity in U.S. Public Administration and Public Affairs Programs 1981-1985. *Administration & Society, 19*(2), 147–156. doi:10.1177/009539978701900201

Lenhart, A., & Fox, S. (2009). *Twitter and status updating.* Washington, DC: Pew Internet & American Life Project.

Lenihan, D. G. (2005). Realigning governance: From e-government to e-democracy. In *Practicing e-government: A global perspective* (pp. 250–288). Hershey, PA: Idea Group. doi:10.4018/978-1-59140-637-2.ch012

Lenk, K., & Traunmüller, R. (2002). Electronic government: Where are we heading? In R. Lenk & B. Traunmüller (Eds.), *Electronic Government: First International Conference, EGOV 2002* (pp. 173–199). New York: Springer.

Lennie, J. (2002). Rural Women's Empowerment in a Communication Technology Project, Some Contradictory Effects. *Rural Society, 12*(3), 224–254.

Leskovec, J., Adamic, L., & Huberman, B. (2006). The Dynamics of Viral Marketing. In *Proceedings of the 7th ACM Conf. on Electronic Commerce* (pp. 228-237). ACM.

Lessig, L. (1999). *Code and other laws of cyber-space.* New York: Basic Books.

Lewin, K. (1952). *Field theory in social science: Selected theoretical papers by Kurt Lewin.* London: Tavistock.

Lin, C.-P., & Bhattacherjee, A. (2008). Elucidating individual intention to use interactive information technologies: The role of network externalities. *International Journal of Electronic Commerce, 13*(1), 85–108. doi:10.2753/JEC1086-4415130103

Lio, M. C., Liu, M. C., & Ou, Y. P. (2011). Can the internet reduce corruption? A cross-country study based on a dynamic panel data models. *Government Information Quarterly, 28*(1), 47–53. doi:10.1016/j.giq.2010.01.005

Liou, K. T. (2007). E-Government Development and Chinn's Administrative Reform. *International Journal of Public Administration, 31*, 76–95. doi:10.1080/01900690601052597

Lips, H. M. (2001). Social and interpersonal aspects. In J. Wor-ell (Ed.), *Encyclopedia of women and gender* (pp. 847–858). San Diego, CA: Academic Press.

Llagostera, E. (2012). On Gamification and Persuasion. In *Proceedings of SBGames 2012.* XISBGames.

Löffler, E. Parrado, Bovaird, & Van Ryzin. (2008). If you want to go fast, walk alone: If you want to go far, walk together: Citizens and the co-production of public services. Paris: Ministry of Budget, Public Finance and Public Services.

Löfstedt, U. (2005). E-Government – Assessment of current research and some proposals for future direction. *International Journal of Public Information Systems, 1*(1), 39–52.

Longhurst, C. A., Parast, L., Sandborg, C. I., Widen, E., Sullivan, J., & Hahn, J. S. et al. (2010). Decrease in hospital-wide mortality rate after implementation of a commercially sold computerized physician order entry system. *Pediatrics, 126*(1), 14–21. doi:10.1542/peds.2009-3271 PMID:20439590

Lundin, Paul, & Christensen. (2000). *Fish! A Remarkable Way to Boost Morale and Improve Results.* Hyperion Books.

Lusch, R. F., & Vargo. (2006b). *The Service-dominant Logic of Marketing: Dialog, Debate, and Directions.* New York: M. S. Sharpe.

Lusch, R. F., & Vargo. (2006a). Service Dominant Logic: Reactions, Reflections and Refinements. *Marketing Theory, 6*, 281–288. doi:10.1177/1470593106066781

Mack, E., & Grubesic, T. (2009). Forecasting broadband provision. *Information Economics and Policy, 21*, 297–311. doi:10.1016/j.infoecopol.2009.08.001

Macnamara, J., Sakinofsky, P., & Beattie, J. (2012). E-electoral Engagement: How Governments Use Social Media to Engage Voters. *Australian Journal of Political Science, 47*, 623–639. doi:10.1080/10361146.2012.731491

Macueve, G., Mandlate, J., Ginger, L., Gaster, P., & Macome, E. (2009). *Women's Use of Information and Communication Technologies in Mozambique: A Tool for Empowerment.* IDRC.

Madon, S. (2004). Evaluating the developmental impact of e-governance initiatives: An exploratory framework. *The Electronic Journal on Information Systems in Developing Countries, 20*(5).

Magar, V. (2003). Empowerment Approaches to Gender-Based Violence: Women's Courts in Delhi Slums. *Women Studies International Forum, 26*(6), 509-523.

Magoulas, G., Lepouras, G., & Vassilakis, C. (2007). *Virtual reality in the e-Society*. London: Springer.

Mahan, A. (2007). Conclusion: ICT and Pro-poor Strategies and Research. In *Digital Poverty: Latin American and Caribbean Perspectives* (pp. 141–156). Ottawa, Canada: International Development Research Center. doi:10.3362/9781780441115.007

Mahbubul, A. (2007). *E-Governance: Scope and Implementation Challenges in Bangladesh*. Retrieved from http://delivery.acm.org/10.1145/1330000/1328108/p246-alam.pdf

Mahmood, I., & Babul, A. I. (2009). *E-Governance for Development: Bangladesh Perspectives*. Ministry of Public Administration. Retrieved from http://edem.todaie.gov.tr/yd29-eGOVERNANCE_FOR_DEVELOPMENT__BANGLADESH_PERSPECTIVES.pdf

Mahmood, Z. (2013). *E-Government Implementation and Practice in Developing Countries*. Hershey, PA: IGI Global. doi:10.4018/978-1-4666-4090-0

Malecki, E. J., & Moriset, B. (2008). *The Digital Economy: Business organization, production processes, and regional developments*. London: Routledge.

Manoharan, A. (2013). A study of the determinants of county e-Government in the United States. *American Review of Public Administration, 43*(2), 159–178. doi:10.1177/0275074012437876

Mansell, R., & When, U. (1998). Knowledge Societies: Information Technology for Sustainable Development. In *Innovative knowledge societies - Consequences of ICT strategies: The benefits, risks, and outcomes* (pp. 241–255). Oxford, UK: Oxford University Press.

Mao, E., Srite, M., Thatcher, J. B., & Yaprak, O. (2005). A research model for mobile phone service behaviors: Empirical validation in the U.S. & Turkey. *Journal of Global Information Technology Management, 8*(4), 7–29.

Marcelle, G. M. (2000). *Gender, Justice and Information and Communication Technologies (ICTs)*. Paper presented at the 44th Session of the Commission on the Status of Women. New York, NY.

Marcelle, G. M. (2002). *Information and Communication Technologies, (ICT) and Their Impact On The Use as an Instrument for the Advancement and Empowerment of Women*. Retrieved March 25, 2008 from http//www.un.org/womenwatch/draw/egn/ict2002/reports/ReportonlinePDF

Marche, S., & McNiven, J. D. (2003). E-Government and E-Governance: The Future isn't what it used to be. *Canadian Journal of Administrative Sciences, 20*(1), 74–86. doi:10.1111/j.1936-4490.2003.tb00306.x

Margolis, M., & Resnick, D. (2000). *Politics as usual: The cyberspace revolution*. Thousand Oaks, CA: Sage Publications.

Markus, M., & Robey, D. (1988). Information technology and organizational change: Causal structure in theory and research. *Management Science, 34*(5), 583–698. doi:10.1287/mnsc.34.5.583

Marschall, M. J. (2004). Citizen Participation in the Neighbourhood Context: A New Look at the Co-production of Local Public Goods. *Political Research Quarterly, 57*(2), 231–244. doi:10.1177/106591290405700205

Mars, M. (2009). Telemedicine in South Africa. In R. Wootton, N. G. Patil, R. E. Scott, & K. Ho (Eds.), *Tele-Health in the Developing World* (pp. 222–231). London: Royal Society of Medicine Press.

Mayer, R. C. Davis, & Schoorman, F.D. (1995). An integrative model of organizational trust. Academy of Management Review, 20, 709-734.

McCall, M. K. (2003). Seeking good governance in participatory-GIS: A review of processes and governance dimensions in applying GIS to participatory spatial planning. *Habitat International, 27*(4), 549–573. doi:10.1016/S0197-3975(03)00005-5

McCue, C., & Roman, A. V. (2013). E-procurement: Myth or reality? *Journal of Public Procurement, 12*(2), 221–248.

McGonigal, J. (2011). *Reality is Broken: Why Games Make Us Better and How They Can Change the World.* Penguin Press.

McGraw, G. (2005). *Software security.* Reading, MA: Addison-Wesley.

Mclean, J. (1990). *Security Models and Information Flow.* Retrieved from http://www.cs.cornell.edu/andru/cs711/2003fa/reading/1990mclean-sp.pdf

McNeal, R. (2012). State response to Obama's broadband access policy: A study in policy implementation. In *Public Sector Transformation through E-Government: Experiences from Europe and North America.* Routledge.

McNeal, R., Hale, K., & Dotterweich, L. (2008). Citizen-government interaction and the internet: Expectations and accomplishments in contact, quality and trust. *Journal of Information Technology & Politics*, *5*(2), 213–229. doi:10.1080/19331680802298298

McNeal, R., & Schmeida, M. (2007). Electronic campaign finance reform in the American states. In *The encyclopedia of digital government* (Vol. 3, pp. 624–628). Idea Group Publishing.

MCSI (Ministry of Communications and Information Society). (2006). *Strategic Institutional Plan: Management Component.* Retrieved from http://www.mcsi.ro/Minister/Despre-MCSI/Unitatea-de-Politici-Publice/Documente-programatice#

MCSI (Ministry of Communications and Information Society). (2007). *Strategic Institutional Plan: Budgetary Component.* Retrieved from http://www.mcsi.ro/Minister/Despre-MCSI/Unitatea-de-Politici-Publice/Documente-programatice#

MSI (Ministry for Informational Society). (2011). *Proiectul RO-NET - Construirea unei infrastructuri naționale de broadband în zonele defavorizate, prin utilizarea fondurilor structural.* Retrieved from http://www.mcsi.ro/Minister/Proiect-Ro-NET/Documente-suport/Documente-suport#

Milakovich, E. M. (2012). *Digital Governance: New technologies for Improving Public Service and Participation.* New York: Routledge.

Mechael, P. (2006). *Exploring Health-related Uses of Mobile Phones: An Egyptian Case Study.* (Doctoral dissertation). London School of Hygiene and Tropical Medicine, London, UK. Retrieved from http://www-personal.umich.edu/~parkyo/site/paper%20abstracts/PatriciaMechaelMobilePhonesWellBeingEgypt2.pdf

Mechael, P. (2007). *Towards the Development of an mHealth Strategy: A Literature Review.* Retrieved from http://mobileactive.org/files/file_uploads/WHO-HealthReviewUpdatedAug222008_TEXT.pdf

Meijer, A. J. (2011). Networked Coproduction of Public Services in Virtual Communities: From a Government-Centric to a Community Approach to Public Service Support. *Public Administration Review*, *71*, 598–607. doi:10.1111/j.1540-6210.2011.02391.x

Mekler, E. Bruhlmann, Opwis, & Tuch. (2013). Disassembling Gamification: The Effects of Points and Meaning on User Motivation and Performance. In *Proceedings of CHI 2013: Changing Perspectives*, (pp. 1137-1142). Paris, France: ACM.

Mergel, I. (2013). A framework for interpreting social media interactions in the public sector. *Government Information Quarterly*, *30*(4), 327–334. doi:10.1016/j.giq.2013.05.015

Mergel, I. A., & Schweik, M. (2012). The Paradox of the Interactive Web in the U.S. Public Sector. In E. Downey, & M. A. Jones (Eds.), *Public Service, Governance and Web 2.0 Technologies: Future Trends in Social Media* (pp. 266–289). Hershey, PA: IGI Global. doi:10.4018/978-1-4666-0071-3.ch017

Meshur, H. F. A. (2007). *Information and Communication Technologies (ICT) and the Changing Nature of Work: Anytime, Anyplace, Anywhere.* Selcuk University.

Mhlanga, B. (2006). Information and Communication Technologies (ICTs) Policy for change and the Mask for Development: A Critical Analysis of Zimbabwe's e-Readiness Survey Report. *The Electronic Journal on Information Systems in Developing Countries, 28*(1), 1–16.

Milakovich, M. E. (2012). *Digital governance: New technologies for improving public service and participation.* New York, NY: Routledge.

Millard, J. (2006). User attitudes to e-government citizen services in Europe. *International Journal of Electronic Government Research, 2*(2), 49–58. doi:10.4018/jegr.2006040103

Miller, T. (1991). *The Hippies and American Values.* Knoxville, TN: University of Tennessee Press.

Ministry of Agriculture (MoA). (2014). *Home.* Retrieved from http://www.moa.gov.bd/

Ministry of Education (MoE). (2014). *Home.* Retrieved from http://www.moedu.gov.bd/

Ministry of Health (MoH). (2014). *Home.* Retrieved from http://www.mohfw.gov.bd/

Min, S.-J. (2010). From the Digital Divide to the Democratic Divide: Internet Skills, Political Interest, and the Second-Level Digital Divide in Political Internet Use. *Journal of Information Technology & Politics, 7*(1), 22–35. doi:10.1080/19331680903109402

Misuraca, G., Rossel, P., & Glassey, O. (2010). Overcoming barriers to innovation in e-government: The Swiss way. In *Understanding e-government in Europe: Issues and challenges* (pp. 202–218). New York: Routlegde.

Mobitel Corporate Website. (2013). *Value Added Services, 2013.* Retrieved from http://www.mobitel.lk/vas,jsession id=588FD813388EB3EEC61B66FF37DD6F4B.liferay1

Moe, R. (1994). The ''Reinventing Government'' Exercise: Misinterpreting the Problem, Misjudging the Consequences. *Public Administration Review, 54*(2), 111–122. doi:10.2307/976519

Mollick, E. & Rothbard. (2013). *Mandatory Fun: Gamification and the Impact of Games at Work* (The Wharton School Research Paper Series). http://dx.doi.org/10.2139/ssrn.2277103

Montola, Nummenmaa, Lucero, Boberg, & Korhonen. (2009). Applying game achievement systems to enhance user experience in a photo sharing service. In *Proceedings of the 13th International MindTrek Conference: Everyday Life in the Ubiquitous Era.* New York, NY: ACM.

Moodley, S. (2003). The challenge of e-business for the South African apparel sector. *Technovation, 23*(7), 557–570. doi:10.1016/S0166-4972(02)00002-0

Moon, J. M. (2002). The evolution of e-government among municipalities: Rhetoric or reality? *Public Administration Review, 62*(4), 424–433. doi:10.1111/0033-3352.00196

Moon, J. M., & Bretschneider, S. (2002). Does perception of red tape constrain IT innovativeness in organizations: Unexpected results from simultaneous equation model and implications. *Journal of Public Administration: Research and Theory, 12*(2), 273–292. doi:10.1093/oxfordjournals.jpart.a003532

Moon, M. J., Lee, J., & Roh, C. Y. (2014). The evolution of internal IT applications and e-government studies in public administration: Research themes and methods. *Administration & Society, 46*(1), 3–36. doi:10.1177/0095399712459723

Moon, M. J., & Stuart, B. (1997). Can state government actions affect innovation and its diffusion? An Extended Communication Model and Empirical Test. *Technological Forecasting and Social Change, 54*(1), 57–77. doi:10.1016/S0040-1625(96)00121-7

Moon, M., & Bretschneider, S. (2002). Can State Government Actions affect Innovation and its diffusion? An extended communication model and empirical test. *Technological Forecasting and Social Change, 54*(1).

MOPAS. (2011). *E-government plans for 21st century.* Korean Ministry of Public Administration and Security.

Moral, C. (2009). Türkiye Bölgede Lider Olmaya Aday. *BThaber.* Retreived December 10, 2010 from http://www.bthaber.com.tr/haber.phtml?yazi_id=705000782

Morgan, D., & Cornwell, S. (2011). Contractors describe scant pre-launch testing of U.S. healthcare site. *Reuters.* Retrieved from http://www.reuters.com/article/2013/10/25/us-usa-healthcare-idUSBRE99M0VD20131025

Morgeson, F. V., VanAmburg, D., & Mithas, S. (2011). Misplaced Trust? Exploring the Structure of the E-Government-Citizen Trust Relationship. *Journal of Public Administration: Research and Theory*, 21(2), 257–283. doi:10.1093/jopart/muq006

Morshed, A. (2007). *E-governance: Bangladesh perspective*. Retrieved from http://unpan1.un.org/intradoc/groups/public/documents/APCITY/UNPAN02625.pdf

Mossberger, K., Tolbert, C., & McNeal, R. (2007). *Digital citizenship: The internet, society and participation*. Cambridge, MA: MIT Press.

Mossberger, K., Tolbert, C., & Stansbury, M. (2003). *Virtual inequality: Beyond the digital divide*. Washington, DC: Georgetown Press.

Mota, F. P. B., & Filho, J. R. (2011). Public e-procurement and the duality of technology: A comparative study in the context of Brazil and of the state of Paraiba. *Journal of Information Systems and Technology Management*, 8(2), 315–330. doi:10.4301/S1807-17752011000200003

Mousavi, S. A., Pimenidis, E., & Jahankhani, H. (2008). Cultivating trust – An electronic government development model for addressing the needs of developing countries. *International Journal of Electronic Security and Digital Forensics*, 1(3), 233–248. doi:10.1504/IJESDF.2008.020942

Muhlberger, P., Stromer-Galley, J., & Webb, N. (2011). Public policy and obstacles to virtual agora: Insights from the deliberative e-rulemaking project. *Information Polity*, 16, 197–214.

Muinul-Islam, M., & Saaduddin-Ahmed, A. M. (2007). Understanding e-governance: A theoretical approach. *Journal of Asian Affairs*, 29(4).

Mullen, H., & Horner, D. S. (2004). Ethical problems for e-government: An evaluative framework. *Electronic Journal of E-Government*, 2(3), 187–196.

Mungania, P., & Reio, T. G., Jr. (2005). *If e-learners get there, will they stay? The role of e-learning self-efficacy*. Paper presented at the Academy of Human Resource Development International Conference (AHRD). Estes Park, CO.

Munkhmandakh, M., & Nielsen, P. E. (2001). The Mongolian media landscape in transition: A cultural clash between global, national, local and no nomads media. *NordiCom Review: Nordic Research on Media and Communication, 22*(2).

Nam, T. (2011). Whose e-democracy? The democratic divide in American electoral campaigns. *Information Polity*, 16(201), 131–150.

Nam, T. (2012). Citizens' attitudes toward Open Government and Government 2.0. *International Review of Administrative Sciences*, 78, 346–368. doi:10.1177/0020852312438783

Naralan, A. (2008). Türkiye'de E-Devlet Güçlükleri. *EKEV Akademi Dergisi*, 12(37), 27–40.

National Alliance for Caregiving. (2009). *Caregiving in the U.S. 2009*. Retrieved June 8, 2013, from http://www.caregiving.org/data/Caregiving_in_the_US_2009_full_report.pdf

National Board of Revenue (NBR). (2014). *Home*. Retrieved from http://www.nbr-bd.org/

National Curriculum and Textbook Board (NCTB). (2014). *Home*. Retrieved from http://www.nctb.gov.bd/

National Telecommunications and Information Administration. (2000). *Falling through the net: Toward digital inclusion: A report on Americans access to technology tools*. Retrieved October 14, 2005, from http://www.ntia.doc.gov/files/ntia/publications/fttn00.pdf

National Telecommunications and Information Administration. (2013). *Exploring the digital nation: America's Emerging online* experience. Retrieved February 19, 2014, from http://www.ntia.doc.gov/report/2013/exploring-digital-nation-americas-emerging-online-experience

National Web Portal of Bangladesh (NWPB). (2014). *Home*. Government of the People's Republic of Bangladesh. Retrieved from http://www.bangladesh.gov.bd/

Needham, C. (2007). Realising the Potential of Co-production: Negotiating improvements in public services. *Social Policy and Society*, 7(2), 221–231.

Nelson, M. J. (2012). Soviet and American Precursors to the Gamification of Work. In *Proceedings of MindTrek 2012*. Tampere, Finland: ACM. doi:10.1145/2393132.2393138

Ng, K. (2010). Turkey's GCIO reveals success of citizen ID. *Asia Pacific FutureGov*. Retrieved December 10, 2010 from http://www.futuregov.asia/articles/2010/mar/02/Turkey-GCIO-reveals-success-citizen-ID/

NHS. (2011). *Breast Screening Programme Annual Review*. London: NHS.

Nicholson, S. (2012). A User-Centered Theoretical Framework for Meaningful Gamification. Paper Presented at Games+Learning+Society 8.0. Madison, WI.

NIS (National Institute of Statistics). (2011). *The Population and Housing Census of 2011*. Retrieved from http://www.recensamantromania.ro/rezultate-2

NIST Computer Security. (2009). Retrieved December 10, 2009 from http://csrc.nist.gov/publications/nistpubs/800-57/sp800- 57_PART3_key-management_Dec2009.pdf

Nord, J. H., & Nord, G. D. (1995). MIS research: Journal status and analysis. *Information & Management*, 29(1), 29–42. doi:10.1016/0378-7206(95)00010-T

Normann, R. (2002). *Services Management*. Chichester, UK: John Wiley & Sons.

Norris, D. F. (2003). Leading edge information technologies and American local governments. In *Public information technology: Policy and management issues* (pp. 139–169). Hershey, PA: Idea Group Publishers.

Norris, D. F. (2010). E-government 2020: Plus ça change, plus c'est la meme chose. *Public Administration Review*, 70, s180–s181. doi:10.1111/j.1540-6210.2010.02269.x

Norris, D. F., & Kraemer, K. L. (1996). Mainframe and PC computing in American cities: Myths and realities. *Public Administration Review*, 56(6), 568–576. doi:10.2307/977255

Norris, D. F., & Moon, M. J. (2005). Advancing E-Government at the Grassroots: Tortoise or Hare? *Public Administration Review*, 65(1), 64–75. doi:10.1111/j.1540-6210.2005.00431.x

Norris, P. (2001). *Digital divide: Civic engagement, information poverty, and the internet worldwide*. Cambridge, UK: Cambridge University Press. doi:10.1017/CBO9781139164887

Nurdin, N., Stockdale, R., & Scheepers, H. (2010). Examining the role of the culture of local government on adoption and use of e-government services. In M. Janssen, W. Lamersdorf, J. Pries-Heje, & M. Rosemann (Eds.), E-government, e-services and global processes (pp. 79-93). Brisbane, Australia: IFIP. doi: 10. 1007/978-3-642-15346-4_7

Nye, J. S. (2002). Information technology and democratic governance. In E. C Kamarck, E. C., & J. S. Nye (Eds.), Governance.com: Democracy in the information age (pp. 1-16). Washington, DC: Brookings Institution Press.

Nye, J. Jr. (1999). Information Technology and Democratic Governance. In E. C. Karmarck, & J. Nye Jr., (Eds.), *Democracy.com? Governance in Networked World*. Hollis, NH: Hollis Publishing Company.

O'Hanlon, S. (2011). *The dangers of e-Health*. Paper presented at the Meeting of HEALTHINF. Rome, Italy.

O'Hara, K., & Stevens, D. (2006). *Inequality.com: Power, poverty and the digital divide*. Oxford, UK: Oneworld Publications.

Obayelu, A., & Ogundale. (2006). Anakyses of the uses of Information Communication Technology (ICT) for Gender Empowerment and Sustainable Poverty Alleviation in Nigeria. *International Journal of Education and Development using ICT, 2* (3).

Odabaş, Ç. (2005). Stratejik Yönetim ve E-Devlet. *Sayıştay Dergisi*, 55, 83–94.

OECD Library. (2013). *OECD Factbook 2013: Economic, Environmental and Social Statistics*. Retrieved from http://www.oecd-ilibrary.org/sites/factbook-2013-en/08/02/02/index.html,jsessionid=11k47lbu37nuh.x-oecd-live-01?contentType=%2Fns%2FChapter%2C%2Fns%2FStatisticalPublication&itemId=%2Fcontent%2Fchapter%2Ffactbook-2013-65-en&mimeType=text%2Fhtml&containerItemId=%2Fcontent%2Fserial%2F18147364&accessItemIds

OECD. (2001). *Understanding the Digital Divide*. Paris: Organisation for Economic Co-operation and Development.

OECD. (2003). *The e-Government Imperative*. Paris: OECD e-Government Studies.

Office of Management and Budget. (2013). *Fiscal year 2012: Report to congress on the implementation of the federal information security management act of 2002*. Retrieved from http://www.whitehouse.gov/sites/default/files/omb/assets/egov_docs/fy12_fisma_0.pdf

Oh, H., Rizo, C., Enkin, M., & Jadad, A. (2005). What is e-Health (3), a systematic review of published definitions. *Journal of Medical Internet Research*, *7*(1), e1. doi:10.2196/jmir.7.1.e1 PMID:15829471

Oinas-Kukkonen, H., & Harjumaa, M. (2009). Persuasive systems design: Key issues, process model, and system features. *Communications of the Association for Information Systems*, *24*(1), 28.

ONTSI (Spanish Telecommunications and Information Society Observatory). (2009). *White Paper on Digital Contents in Spain 2008*. Retrieved from http://observatorio.red.es/contenidos-digitales/articles/id/2662/libro-blanco-los-contenidos-digitales-espana-2008.html

Oprescu, F., Jones, C., & Katsikitis, M. (2014). From games to gamified workplaces: From games to gamified workplaces. *Psychology (Savannah, Ga.)*, *5*(14).

Organisation for Economic Co-Operation and Development. (2003). *Promise and problems of e-democracy – Challenges of online citizen engagement*. Paris: OECD.

Organisation for Economic Co-Operation and Development. (2009). *Rethinking e-government services: User-centred approaches*. Paris: OECD Publishing.

Organization for Economic Co-operation and Development (OECD). (2001). *Understanding the Digital Divide*. Paris: OECD Publications. Retrieved from http://www.oecd.org/dataoecd/38/57/1888451.pdf

Organization for Economic Co-operation and Development (OECD). (2003). *The e-government imperative: Main findings*. Retrieved from http://www.oecd.org/dataoecd/60/60/2502539.pdf

Orlikowski, W. J. (1992). The duality of technology: Rethinking the concept of technology in organizations. *Organization Science*, *3*(3), 398–427. doi:10.1287/orsc.3.3.398

Orlikowski, W. J. (2000). Using technology and constituting structures: A practice lens for studying technology in organizations. *Organization Science*, *11*(4), 404–428. doi:10.1287/orsc.11.4.404.14600

Orlikowski, W. J., & Baroudi, J. J. (1991). Studying Information Technology in Organizations: Research Approaches and Assumptions. *Information Systems Research*, *2*(1), 1–28. doi:10.1287/isre.2.1.1

Osborne, D., & Gaebler, T. (1992). *Reinventing Government: How the Entrepreneurial Spirit is Transforming the Public Sector*. Addison, Wesley.

Osborne, S. (2006). The new public governance. *Public Management Review*, *8*(3), 377–387. doi:10.1080/14719030600853022

Osborne, S. P. (Ed.). (2010). *The New Public Governance? Emerging Perspectives on the Theory and Practice of Public Governance*. London: Routledge.

Osborne, S. P., & Brown, L. (2011). Innovation, public policy and public services delivery in the UK: The word that would be king? *Public Administration*, *89*(4), 1335–1350. doi:10.1111/j.1467-9299.2011.01932.x

Osborne, S. P., McLaughlin, K., & Chew, C. (2010). Relationship Marketing, relational capital and the governance of public services delivery. In S. P. Osborne (Ed.), *The New Public Governance?* (pp. 185–199). New York: Routledge.

Osimo, D. (2008). *Web 2.0 in government: Why and how? (JRC Scientific and Technical Reports)*. European Commission.

Ostrom, E. (1996). Crossing the Great Divide: Coproduction, Synergy and Development. *World Development*, *24*(6), 1073–1087. doi:10.1016/0305-750X(96)00023-X

Ouma, S., & Herselman, M. E. (2008). E-health in Rural Areas: Case of Developing Countries. *International Journal of Biological and Life Sciences*, *4*(4).

OWASP. (2014a). *Cloud Top 10*. Retreved April 12, 2014 from https://www.owasp.org/index.php/Category:OWASP_Cloud_%E2%80%90_10_Project

OWASP. (2014b). *Top 10 mobile risks*. Retrieved 12 April, 2014 from https://www.owasp.org/index.php/OWASP_Mobile_Security_Project#tab=Top_Ten_Mobile_Risks

OWASP. (2014c). *Web Services*. Retrieved April 12, 2014 from https://www.owasp.org/index.php/Web_Services

Ozcan, Y. Z., & Kocak, A. (2003). Research note: A need or a status symbol? Use of cellular telephones in Turkey. *European Journal of Communication, 18*(2), 241–254. doi:10.1177/0267323103018002004

Pablo, D. Z., & Pan, L. S. (2002). *A Multi-Disciplinary Analysis of E-governance: Where Do We Start?* Unpublished Report.

Pacific Council on International Policy (PCIP). (2002). *Roadmap for E-government in the Developing World*. Los Angeles, CA: The Working Group on E-Government in the Developing World. Retrieved form http://www.pacificcouncil.org/pdfs/e-gov.paper.f.pdf

Paharia, R. (2012, July-August). Gamification Means Amplifying Intrinsic Value. *Social Mediator, 17*.

Parajuli, J. (2007). A Content Analysis of Selected Government Web Sites: A Case Study of Nepal. *The Electronic. Journal of E-Government, 5*(1), 87–94.

Park, C. O., & Joo, J. (2010). Control over the Korean Bureaucracy: A review of the NPM civil service reforms under the Roh Moon-Hyun Government. *Review of Public Personnel Administration, 30*(2), 189–210. doi:10.1177/0734371X09360183

Park, S. Y. (2009). An analysis of the technology acceptance model in understanding university students' behavioral intention to use e-learning. *Journal of Educational Technology & Society, 12*(3), 150–162.

Parks, M., & Floyd, K. (1996). Making Friends in Cyberspace. *The Journal of Communication, 46*, 80–97. doi:10.1111/j.1460-2466.1996.tb01462.x

Parks, R. B., Baker, Kiser, Oakerson, Ostrom, Ostrom, … Wilson. (1981). Consumers as Co-producers of Public Services: Some Economic and Institutional Considerations. *Policy Studies Journal: the Journal of the Policy Studies Organization, 9*(7), 1001–1011. doi:10.1111/j.1541-0072.1981.tb01208.x

Payne, A. F., Storbacka, K., & Frow, P. (2008). Managing the co-creation of value. *Journal of the Academy of Marketing Science, 36*(1), 83–96. doi:10.1007/s11747-007-0070-0

Peled, A. (2001). Do computers cut red tape? *American Review of Public Administration, 31*(4), 414–435. doi:10.1177/02750740122065027

Perry 6. (2004). *E-governance – Styles of political judgment in the information age polity*. New York: Palgrave.

Perryer, C., Scott-Ladd, B., & Leighton, C. (2012). Gamification: Implications for workplace intrinsic motivation in the 21st century. *AFBE Journal*, 371-381.

Pestoff, V. Brandsen, & Verschuere (Eds.). (2012). New Public Governance, the Third Sector and Co-production. London: Routledge.

Pestoff, V. (2006). Citizens and Co-Production of Welfare Services: Childcare in Eight European Countries. *Public Management Review, 8*(4), 503–519. doi:10.1080/14719030601022882

Pestoff, V. (2012). Co-production and Third Sector Social Services in Europe—Some Crucial Conceptual Issues. In *New Public Governance, the Third Sector and Co-production* (pp. 13–34). London: Routledge.

Piaget, J. (1960). General Problems of the Psychological Development of the Child. In *Discussion on Child Development*[). New York: International Universities Press.]. *Proceedings of the World Health Organization Study Group on Psychological Development of the Child, 4*, 3–27.

Piedra-Calderón, J. C., González, R., & Rainer, J. J. (2013). IT Projects & Their Specific Elements. *La Pensee, 75*(12).

Piette, J. D., Mendoza-Avelares, M. O., Milton, E. C., Lange, I., & Fajardo, R. (2010). Access to Mobile Communication Technology and Willingness to Participate in Automated Telemedicine Calls Among Chronically Ill Patients in Honduras. *Telemedicine Journal and e-Health, 16*(10), 1030–1041. doi:10.1089/tmj.2010.0074 PMID:21062234

Pink. (2009). *Drive: The surprising truth about what motivates us.* Riverhead Books.

Piro, G. et al. (2014). Information centric services in Smart Cities. *Journal of Systems and Software, 88*, 169–188. doi:10.1016/j.jss.2013.10.029

Plouffe, C. R., Hulland, J. S., & Vandenbosch, M. (2001). Research report: Richness versus parsimony in modeling technology adoption decisions – Understanding merchant adoption of smart card-based payment system. *Information Systems Research, 12*(2), 208–222. doi:10.1287/isre.12.2.208.9697

Plümper, T., & Radaelli, C. M. (2004). Publish or perish? Publications and citations of Italian political scientists in international political science journals, 1990-2002. *Journal of European Public Policy, 11*(6), 1112–1127. doi:10.1080/1350176042000298138

Pollitt, C. J. (2011). Mainstreaming Technological Change in the Study of Public Administration: A Conceptual Framework. *Public Policy and Administration.* doi:10.1177/0952076710378548

Port Turkey. (2013). *Internet economy of Turkey to grow 19% until 2017.* Retrieved April 12, 2014 from http://www.portturkey.com/internet/5097-internet-economy-of-turkey-to-grow-19-until-2017

Porter, M. (1991). *La Ventaja Competitiva de las Naciones.* Barcelona, Spain: Plaza & Janés.

pour le Développement de l'Administration Electronique, A. (ADAE). (2007). *MAREVA methodology guide: Analysis of the value of ADELE projects.* Dubai, UAE: Fourth High Level Seminar on Measuring and Evaluating E-government.

Power, M. (1997). *The audit society: Rituals of verification.* Oxford University Press.

Pralahad, C. K., & Ramaswamy. (2004). *The Future of Competition: Co-creating Unique Value with Customers.* Boston: Harvard Business School Press.

Prasad, P. N., & Sreedevi, V. (2007). Economic Empowerment of Women Through Information Technology—A Case Study from an Indian State. *Journal of International Women's Studies, 8*(4), 107–119.

Prebisch, R. (1962). The Economic Development of Latin America and its Principal Problems. *Economic Bulletin for Latin America, 7*(1), 1–22.

Prince, A. (2005). Introduciéndonos en y a las campañas políticas online. In S. Finquelievich (Ed.), E-política y e-gobierno en América Latina (pp. 43-54). Buenos Aires, Argentina: LINKS A.C.

Public Law 111-148. (2010). *Patient Protection and Affordable Care Act.*

Qureshi, S. (2012). As the global digital divide narrows, who is being left behind? *Information Technology for Development, 18*(4), 277–280. doi:10.1080/02681102.2012.730656

Raab, C. (1997). Privacy, information and democracy. In *The governance of cyberspace: Politics, technology and global restructuring.* London: Routledge. doi:10.4324/9780203360408_chapter_10

Raadschelders, J. C. N., & Lee, K. H. (2011). Trends in the Study of Public Administration: Empirical and Qualitative Observations from Public Administration Review, 2000-2009. *Public Administration Review, 71*(1), 19–33. doi:10.1111/j.1540-6210.2010.02303.x

Raessens, J. (2006). Playful Identities, or the Ludification of Culture. *Games and Culture, 1*(1), 52–57. doi:10.1177/1555412005281779

Raina, R. (2007). ICT Human Resource Development in Asia and the Pacific. In *Proceedings of Current Status, Emerging Trends, Policies and Strategies, Regional Forum on ICT Capacity Building: Where are we, where are we going and what will it take to fill the gap?* Incheon, Korea: Academic Press.

Ranjini, S. (2012). Innovation in services delivery in rural areas in India. *International Journal of Management Research and Review, 2*(1), 143–153.

Ray, R., & Kozameh, S. (2012). La economía de Ecuador desde 2007. Washington, DC: Centre for Economic and Policy Research (CEPR).

Reddick, C. (2005). Citizen interaction with e-government: From the streets to servers? *Government Information Quarterly, 22*, 38–57. doi:10.1016/j.giq.2004.10.003

Reddick, C. G. (2011). Customer Relationship Management (CRM) technology and organizational change: Evidence for the bureaucratic and e-Government paradigms. *Government Information Quarterly, 28*(3), 346–353. doi:10.1016/j.giq.2010.08.005

Reddick, C. G., Abdelsalam, H. M., & Elkadi, H. (2011). The influence of e-government on administrative discretion: The case of local governments in Egypt. *Public Administration and Development, 31*(5), 390–407. doi:10.1002/pad.615

Reeves, B., & Read. (2009). *Total Engagement: Using Games and Virtual Worlds to Change the Way People Work and Business Compete.* Harvard Business School Press.

Renu, B. (2003a). *Electronic Gov-A key issue in the 21st century.* Electronic Governance Division, Ministry of Information Technology, Government of India.

Renu, B. (2003b). *E-governance in G2B and some major incliatives.* Dept. of Information Technology, Ministry of Communication and Information Technology.

ResmiGazete. (2006). Yüksek Planlama Kururu Kararı. *Elektronik Resmi Gazete, 26242.*

Rethemeyer, K. R. (2006). Policymaking in the age of internet: Is the internet tending to make policy networks more or less inclusive? *Journal of Public Administration: Research and Theory, 17*(2), 259–284. doi:10.1093/jopart/mul001

RG (Romanian Government). (2012). *Government Program.* Retrieved from http://www.gov.ro/upload/articles/117322/programul-de-guvernare-2012.pdf

RG (Romanian Government). (2013-2016). *Government Program.* Retrieved from http://gov.ro/fisiere/pagini_fisiere/13-08-02-10-48-52program-de-guvernare-2013-20161.pdf

Rheingold, H. (1993). *Daily Life in Cyberspace: The Virtual Community: Homesteading on the Electronic Frontier* (pp. 57–109). Reading, MA: Addison-Wesley.

Rheingold, H. (2002). *Smart Mobs: The next social revolution.* Cambridge, MA: Perseus Publishing.

Rigby, S., & Ryan. (2011). *Glued to Games: How Video Games Draw Us In and Hold Us Spellbound.* Praeger.

Riley, T. B., & Riley, C. G. (2003). E-governance to e-democracy - Examining the Evolution. In *International Tracking Survey Report 2003.* Riley Information Services.

Robbins, S. P., & Judge, T. A. (2008). Organizational Behavior. In S. P. Robbins, & T. A. Judge (Eds.), *Organizational Behavior* (13th ed.). Academic Press.

Robins, M. B. (2002). Are African Women Online just ICT Consumers? *International Communication Gazette, 64*(3), 235–249. doi:10.1177/17480485020640030201

Rodríguez, M. P., Alcaide, L., & López, A. M. (2010). Trends of e-Government research: Contextualization and research opportunities. *International Journal of Digital Accounting Research, 10*, 87–111. doi:10.4192/1577-8517-v10_4

Roman, A.V., & Miller, H. (2013). New questions for e-government: Efficiency but not (yet?) democracy. *International Journal of Electronic Government Research, 9*(1), 65-81. doi: 10.4018/ jegr.2013010104

Roman, A. V. (2013a). Framing the questions of e-government ethics: An organizational perspective. *American Review of Public Administration.* doi:10.1177/0275074013485809

Roman, A. V. (2013b). Public policy and financial management through e-procurement: A practice oriented normative model for maximizing transformative impacts. *Journal of Public Procurement, 13*(3), 337–363.

Roman, A. V. (2013c). The mental revolution of public procurement specialists: Achieving transformative impacts within the context of e-procurement. In N. Pomazalová (Ed.), *Public sector transformation processes and Internet public procurement: Decision support systems* (pp. 1–16).

Romania Libera. (2012). *Luncavita – The only village collecting local taxes online*. Retrieved from http://www.romanialibera.ro/actualitate/locale/luncavita-singura-comuna-care-incaseaza-impozitele-online-272501.html

Romzek, B. S., & Johnston, J. M. (2005). State social services contracting: Exploring the determinants of effective contract accountability. *Public Administration Review*, *65*(4), 436–449. doi:10.1111/j.1540-6210.2005.00470.x

Rooksby, E., & Weckert, J. (2004). Digital Divides: Their Social and Ethical Implications. In *Ethical and Policy Implications of Information Technology* (pp. 29–47). Hershey, PA: Information Science Publishing. doi:10.4018/978-1-59140-168-1.ch002

Rosentraub, M. S., & Sharp. (1981). Consumers as Producers of Social Services: Coproduction and the Level of Social Services. *Southern Review of Public Administration*, *4*, 502–539.

Rose, R. W., & Grant, G. G. (2010). Critical issues pertaining to the planning and implementation of EGovernment initiatives. *Government Information Quarterly*, *27*(1), 26–33. doi:10.1016/j.giq.2009.06.002

Rothig, P. (2010). *WiBe 4.0 methodology: Economic efficiency assessments in particular with regard to the use of information & communication technology*. Berlin: Federal Ministry of the Interior.

Rowley, J. (2006). An analysis of the e-service literature: Towards a research agenda. *Internet Research*, *16*(3), 339–359. doi:10.1108/10662240610673736

Roy, D. (1952). Quota restriction and goldbricking in a machine shop. *American Journal of Sociology*, *57*, 427–442. doi:10.1086/221011

Roy, J. (2011). The promise (and pitfalls) of digital transformation. In R. P. Leone, & F. L. K. Ohemeng (Eds.), *Approaching Public Administration: Core Debates and Emerging Issues*. Toronto, Canada: Edmond Montgomery Publications.

Roy, S., & Himu, T. A. (2011). How does the Use of Cellular Phone Commit Violence Against Women. *Higher Education of Social Sciences*, *1*(1), 1013.

Rueda-Sabater, E., & Garrity, J. (2011). The Emerging Internet Economy: Looking a Decade Ahead. In S. Dutta & I. Mia (Eds.), *The Global Information Technology Report 2010 – 2011: Transformations 2.0* (pp. 33 - 47). Geneva, Switzerland: World Economic Forum and INSEAD. Retrieved June 17, 2012 from http://reports.weforum.org/global-information-technology-report/content/pdf/wef-gitr-2010-2011.pdf

Ruhode, E., Owei, V., & Maumbe, B. (2008). *Arguing for the Enhancement of Public Service Efficiency and Effectiveness through e-Government: The Case of Zimbabwe*. Paper presented at the IST-Africa 2008 Conference. Windhoek, Namibia.

Ruth, S., & Doh, S. (2007). Is E-Government Ready for Prime Time? *IEEE Internet Computing*, *11*(2), 80–82. doi:10.1109/MIC.2007.42

Ryan, R. M., & Deci. (2000). Self-determination theory and the facilitation of intrinsic motivation, social development, and well-being. *The American Psychologist*, *55*, 68–78. doi:10.1037/0003-066X.55.1.68 PMID:11392867

Sadeqhi, A. R., & Stuble, C. (2005). Towards multilaterally secure computing platforms-with open source and trusted computing. *Information Security Technical Report*, *10*(2), 83–95. doi:10.1016/j.istr.2005.05.004

Sahay, S. (1997). Implementation of information technology: A space-time perspective. *Organization Studies*, *18*(2), 229–260. doi:10.1177/017084069701800203

Sahin, A., Temizel, H., & Temizel, M. (2010). Türkiye'de demokrasiden e-demokrasiye geçiş süreci ve karşılaşılan sorunlar. *E-demokrasi*. Retrieved December 11, 2010 from http://www.e-demokrasi.org/index.php?option=com_content&view=article&id=31:tuerkiyede-demokrasiden-e-demokrasiye-geci-suereci-ve-karlalan-sorunlar&catid=7:makaleler&Itemid=21

Sahraoui, S. (2005). eGovernment in the Arabian Gulf: Government transformation vs. government automation. In *Proceedings of the eGovernment Workshop '05 (eGOV05)*. Academic Press.

Samah, B., Shaffril, H., D'Silva, J., & Hassan, M. (2010). Information Communication Technology, Village Development and Security Committee and Village Vision Movement: A Recipe for Rural Success in Malaysia. *Asian Social Science, 6*(4), 136–144. doi:10.5539/ass.v6n4p136

Saroka, R., & Poggi, E. (2005). Software de código abierto en la administración pública. In S. Finquelievich (Ed.), E-política y e-gobierno en América Latina (pp. 183-199). Buenos Aires, Argentina: LINKS A.C.

Savage, S. (2007). *Police Reform: Forces for Change.* Oxford, UK: Oxford University Press.

Saxena, K. B. C. (2005). Towards excellence in e-governance. *International Journal of Public Sector Management, 18*(6), 498–513. doi:10.1108/09513550510616733

Schechter, S. (2004). *Computer Security Strength & Risk: A Quantitative Approach.* (PhD Thesis). The Division of Engineering and Applied Sciences, Harvard University, Cambridge, MA. Retrieved from http://www.eecs.harvard.edu/~stuart/papers/thesis.pdf

Schelin, S. H. (2003). E-Government: An overview. In G. D. Garson (Ed.), *Public information technology: Policy and management issues* (pp. 120–137). Hershey, PA: Idea Group Publishing.

Schiavo-Ocampo, S., & Sundaram, P. (2001). *To Serve and Preserve: Improving Public Administration in a Competitive World.* Manila, Philippines: Asian Development Bank.

Schilling, M. A. (2000). Decades ahead of her time: Advancing stakeholder theory through the ideas of Mary Parker Follett. *Journal of Management History, 6*(5), 224–242. doi:10.1108/13552520010348371

Schmeida, M. (2005). *Telehealth innovation in the American states.* Ann Arbor, MI: ProQuest.

Schmeida, M., & McNeal, R. (2007). The telehealth divide: disparities in searching public health information online. *Journal of Health Care for the Poor and Underserved, 18,* 637–647. doi:10.1353/hpu.2007.0068 PMID:17675719

Schmeida, M., & McNeal, R. (2009). Demographic differences in telehealth policy outcomes. In *Handbook of Research on Distributed Medical Informatics and E-health.* Idea Group Publishing.

Schmeida, M., & McNeal, R. (2013). Bridging the inequality gap to searching Medicare and Medicaid information online: An empirical analysis of e-government Success 2002 through 2010. In J. Ramon Gil-Garcia (Ed.), *E-Government Success around the World: Cases, Empirical Studies, and Practical Recommendations.* IGI Global. doi:10.4018/978-1-4666-4173-0.ch004

Schmidt, S., Schuchert, A., Krieg, T., & Oeff, M. (2010). Home telemonitoring in patients with chronic heart failure: A chance to improve patient care? *Deutsches Ärzteblatt International, 107*(8), 131–138. PMID:20300221

Schneier, B. (1996). *Applied Cryptography, Protocols, Algorithms and Source Code in C.* John Wiley & Sons, Inc.

Scholl, H. J. (2009). Profiling the EG research community and its core. In M. A. Wimmer, H. J. Scholl, M. Janssen, & R. Traunmüller (Eds.), *Electronic government: 8th international conference, EGOV 2009* (pp. 1-12). Berlin: Springer-Verlag.

Scholl, J. H. (2001). *Applying Stakeholder Theory to E-Government: Benefits and Limits.* Boston: IFIP, Kluwer Academic Publishers.

Schuler, S. R., Islam, F., & Rottach, E. (2010). Women's empowerment revisited: A case study from Bangladesh. *Development in Practice, 20*(7), 840–854. doi:10.1080/09614524.2010.508108 PMID:20856695

Schweitzer, D., Boleng, J., Hughes, C., & Murphy, L. (2009). *Visualizing Keyboard Pattern Passwords.* Retrieved April 12, 2014 from cs.wheatoncollege.edu/~mgousie/comp401/amos.pdf

Schwester, R. (2011). Examining the Barriers to e-Government Adoption. In *Leading Issues in e-Governmen* (pp. 32–50). Reading, UK: Academic Publishing International Ltd.

Scott, J. (2006). E the people: Do U.S. municipal government web sites support public involvement? *Public Administration Review, 66*(3), 341–353. doi:10.1111/j.1540-6210.2006.00593.x

Seddon, P. B. (2005). Are ERP Systems a Source of Competitive Advantage? *Strategic Change, 14*(5), 283–293. doi:10.1002/jsc.729

Selwyn, N. (2004). Reconsidering political and popular understandings of the digital divide. *New Media & Society*, *6*(3), 341–362. doi:10.1177/1461444804042519

Seng, W. M., Jackson, S., & Philip, G. (2010). Cultural issues in developing E-Government in Malaysia. *Behaviour & Information Technology*, *29*(4), 423–432. doi:10.1080/01449290903300931

Senplades. (2013). *National Development Plan/National Plan for Good Living, 2013-2017*. Quito.

Sevron, L. (2002). *Bridging the Digital Divide: Technology, Community and Public Policy*. Malden, MA: Blakwell Publishing.

Shane, S. (1993). Cultural influences on national rates of innovation. *Journal of Business Venturing*, *8*(1), 59–73. doi:10.1016/0883-9026(93)90011-S

Shareef, M. J., & Jahankhani, H. S. Arreymbi, & Pimenidis, E. (2011). The Challenges Influencing the Development and Adoption of e-Government Systems Initiatives in Developing Countries. In *Proceedings of First Global Conference on Communication, Science, and Information Engineering*. London: British Computer Society.

Shareef, S., Jahankhani, H., & Dastbaz, M. (2012). E-Government Stage Model: Based on Citizen-Centric Approach in Regional Government in Developing Countries. *International Journal of Electronic Commerce Studies*, *3*(1), 145–164.

Sharma, S. K., & Gupta, J. N. D. (2004). Web services architecture for m-government: Issues and challenges. *Electronic Government*, *1*(4), 462–474. doi:10.1504/EG.2004.005921

Sherfinski, D. (2012). Virginia ditchedDMV customer service overhaul after spending $28M. *The Washington Times*. Retrieved from http://www.washingtontimes.com/news/2012/apr/3/virginia-ditched-dmv-customer-service-overhaul- aft/?page=1

Sherman, R. (2007). *Class Acts: Service and Inequality in Luxury Hotels*. University of California Press.

Siau, K., & Long, Y. (2005). Synthesizing eGovernment stage models-a meta-synthesis based on meta-ethnography approach. *Industrial Management & Data Systems*, *105*(4), 443–458. doi:10.1108/02635570510592352

Siddiquee, N. A. (2013). E-Government: The Dawn of Citizen-centric Public Administration? In *Public Administration in South Asia: India, Bangladesh and Pakistan*. London: Academic Press. doi:10.1201/b14759-19

Siddiquee, N. A., & Faroqi, M. G. (2013). E-Government in Bangladesh: Prospects and Challenges. In *From Government to E-Governance- Public administration in the Digital Age*. Hershey, PA: IGI Global.

Sieber, R. E. (2000). Conforming (to) the opposition: The social construction of geographical information systems in social movements. *International Journal of Geographical Information Science*, *14*(8), 775–793. doi:10.1080/136588100750022787

Singer, H. W. (1950). U.S. Foreign Investment in Underdeveloped Areas: The Distribution of Gains between Investing and Borrowing Countries. *The American Economic Review*, *40*, 473–485.

Sinha, C. (2005). *Effect of Mobile Telephony on Empowering Rural Communities in Developing Countries*. Paper presented at the meeting of International Research Foundation for Development (IRFD) Conference on Digital Divide, Global Development and the Information Society. New York, NY.

Slevin, J. (2000). *The Internet and Society*. Cambridge, MA: Polity Press.

Smith, A., Schlozman, K., Verba, S., & Brady, H. (2009). The Internet and Civic Engagement. *Pew Internet*. Retrieved from http:// www.pewinternet.org

Snellen, I. (2007). E-Government: A Challenge for Public Management. In E. Ferlie, L. E. Lynn, & C. Pollitt (Eds.), *The Oxford handbook of public management*. New York: Oxford University Press.

Softpedia. (2013). *Hackers Claim to Have Breached Turkey's Ministry of Finance, Data Leaked.* Retrieved April 12, 2014 from http://news.softpedia.com/news/Hackers-Claim-to-Have-Breached-Turkey-s-Ministry-of-Finance-Data-Leaked-364642.shtml

Souter, D. (2010). *Towards inclusive knowledge societies: A review of UNESCO's action in implementing the WSIS outcomes.* United Nations Educational, Scientific and Cultural Organization (UNESCO), Communication and Information Sector. Retrieved July 6, 2012 from http://unesdoc.unesco.org/images/0018/001878/187832e.pdf

Sparks, C. S., & Reading, A. (1997). *Communism, Capitalism and the Media in Eastern Europe.* London: Sage.

SSLSNIFF. (2014). Retrieved April 12, 2014 from http://tools.ietf.org/html/draft-ietf-websec-strict-transport-sec-02

Stahl, B. C. (2005). The ethical problem of framing e-government in terms of e-commerce. *The Electronic. Journal of E-Government, 3*(2), 77–86.

Stahl, B. C. (2008). *Information Systems: Critical Perspectives.* New York, NY: Routledge. doi:10.4324/9780203927939

Stake, R. E. (1995). *The Art of Case Study Research.* Thousand Oaks, CA: Sage Publications.

Stallman, R. (1995). Are computer property rights absolute? In *Computers, ethics & social values* (pp. 115–119). Upper Saddle River, NJ: Prentice Hall.

Stanforth, C. (2007). Using Actor-Network Theory to Analyze E-Government Implementation in Developing Countries. The Massachusetts Institute of Technology Information Technologies and International Development, 3(3), 35–60.

Stanimirovic, D., & Vintar, M. (2013). Conceptualization of an integrated indicator model for the evaluation of e-government policies. *Electronic. Journal of E-Government, 11*(2), 293–307.

Stanley, W. J., & Weare, C. (2004). The effects of Internet use on political participation. *Administration & Society, 36*(5), 503–527. doi:10.1177/0095399704268503

State Planning Organization. (2006a). *Information Society Strategy (2006-2010).* Retrieved December 10, 2010 from http://www.bilgitoplumu.gov.tr/eng/docs/Information_Society_Strategy.pdf

State Planning Organization. (2006b). *Information Society Strategy (2006-2010) Action Plan.* Retrieved December, 2010 from http://www.bilgitoplumu.gov.tr/eng/docs/Action_Plan.pdf

Stevenson, S. (2009). Digital divide: A discursive move away from the real inequality. *The Information Society, 25,* 1–22. doi:10.1080/01972240802587539

Stoica, V., & Ilas, A. (2009). Romanian Urban e-Government. Digital Services and Digital Democracy in 165 Cities. *Electronic. Journal of E-Government, 7*(2), 171–182.

Stoica, V., & Ilas, A. (2012). Is Romania Ready for Nation-Wide Public e-Services? Five Factors to Consider before Adopting an E-Government Public Policy. In *Handbook of Research on E-Government in Emerging Economies: Adoption, E-Participation, and Legal Frameworks* (pp. 717–732). Hershey, PA: IGI Global. doi:10.4018/978-1-4666-0324-0.ch037

Stoll, C. (1995, February 27). The Internet? Bah! *Newsweek.* Retrieved January 04, 2012, from http://www.newsweek.com/1995/02/26/the-InternetInternet-bah.html

Stoll, C. (1995). *Silicon Snake Oil: Second Thoughts on the Information Highway.* New York: Anchor Books.

Stutzman, F. (2006). An Evaluation of Identity-Sharing Behavior in Social Network Communities. In *Proceedings of the 2006 iDMA and IMS Code Conference.* International Digital and Media Arts Journal.

Stutzman, F., Gross, R., & Acquisti, A. (2012). Silent Listeners: The Evolution of Privacy and Disclosure on Facebook. *Journal of Privacy and Confidentiality, 4*(2), 7–41.

Sung, H-Y., & Hwang. (2013). A Collaborative Game-Based Learning Approach to Improving Students' Learning Performance in Science Courses. *Computers & Education, 63,* 43–51. doi:10.1016/j.compedu.2012.11.019

Sungu, E., Sungu, H., & Bayrakci, M. (2008). *E-inclusion: Providing services towards an information society for all.* Paper presented at the 8th International Educational Technology Conference. New York, NY.

Susanto, T. D., & Goodwin, R. (2013). User acceptance of SMS-based e-government services: Differences between adopters and non-adopters. *Government Information Quarterly, 30*(4), 486–497. doi:10.1016/j.giq.2013.05.010

Susskind, R. (2008). *The End of Lawyers? Rethinking the Nature of Legal Services.* Oxford, UK: Oxford University Press.

Taifur, S. (2006). *SICT's Steps Towards Good Governance Through ICTs: E-governance Strategies. Support to ICT Task Force program project (SICT), Ministry of Planning, Government of Bangladesh Press. UN e-Government Survey. (2008). From e-Government to Connected Governance.* New York: Author.

Tan, A. (2006). Mobile Web catching on. *ZDNet Asia.* Retrieved from http://www.zdnetasia.com/news/communications/0,39044192,39369023,00.htm

Tapscott, D. (1995). Leadership Needed in Age of Networked Intelligence. *Boston Business Journal, 11*(24), 15.

Tapscott, D. (1996). *The Digital Economy.* New York: McGraw Hill.

Tapscott, D., & Caston, A. (1993). *Paradigm Shift: The New promise of Information Technology.* New York: McGraw Hill.

Tapscott, D., & Williams, D. (2006). *Wikinomics: How mass collaboration changes everything.* New York: Portfolio, Penguin.

Taşçı, B. (2010). Aradiginiz e-Devlet'e ulasilamiyor. *HTEKONOMI.* Retrieved October 12, 2010 from http://ekonomi.haberturk.com/teknoloji/haber/541303-aradiginiz-e-devlete-ulasilamiyor

Teerling, M. L., & Pieterson, W. (2010). Multichannel marketing: An experiment on guiding citizens to the electronic channels. *Government Information Quarterly, 27*, 98–107. doi:10.1016/j.giq.2009.08.003

Telecommunications Regulatory Commission of Sri Lanka. (2013). *Information and Statistics, 2013.* Retrieved from http://www.trc.gov.lk/information/statistics.html

Tellis, W. (1997). Introduction to Case Study. *Qualitative Report, 3*(2).

Text to Change. (2008). Retrieved October 1, 2012, from http://www.texttochange.org

Thomas, J. C., & Melkers, J. (1999). Explaining citizen-initiated contacts with municipal bureaucrats: Lessons from the Atlanta experience. *Urban Affairs Review, 34*(5), 667–690. doi:10.1177/10780879922184130

Thompson, C. S. (2002). Enlisting on-line residents: Expanding the boundaries of e-government in a Japanese rural township. *Government Information Quarterly, 19*, 173–188. doi:10.1016/S0740-624X(02)00093-X

Thompson, F., & Jones, L. (2008). Reaping the Advantages of Information and Modern Technology: Moving from Bureaucracy to Hyperarchy and Netcentricity. *International Public Management Review, 9*(1), 148–192.

Thompson, R. L., Higgins, C. A., & Howell, J. M. (1991). Personal computing: Toward a conceptual model of utilization. *Management Information Systems Quarterly, 15*(1), 125–143. doi:10.2307/249443

Thornton, P. H. (2002). The rise of the corporation in a craft industry: Conflict and conformity in institutional logics. *Academy of Management Journal, 45*, 81–101. doi:10.2307/3069286

Thornton, P. H. (2004). *Markets from culture: Institutional logics and organizational decisions in high education publishing.* Standford, CA: Stanford University Press.

Thorp, J. (1998). *The information paradox: Realizing the business benefits of information technology.* Toronto, Canada: McGraw Hill Ryerson.

Todays Zaman. (2014). *FATİH project distributes tablet PCs.* Retrieved April 12, 2014 from http://www.todayszaman.com/news-339699-fatih-project-distributes-tablet-pcs.html

Todrys, K., & Mechael, P. (2008). *The Ethics of Telemedicine in Africa: The Millennium Villages Project Experience*. Paper presented at Mobile Communications and the Ethics of Social Networking. Budapest, Hungary.

Torenli, N. (2006). The 'other' faces of digital exclusion: ICT gender divides in the broader community. *European Journal of Communication, 21*(4), 435–455. doi:10.1177/0267323106070010

Torrejón, A. (2005). *Observatorio de la Sociedad de la Información: Algunas reflexiones sobre las ciudades del siglo XXI*. Retrieved Feb. 5, 2014 from http://fundacionorange.es/areas/28_observatorio/pdfs/DEF_26.pdf

Torres, L., Pina, V., & Royo, S. (2005). E-government ant the transformation of public administration in EU countries: Beyond NPM or just a second wave of reforms? *Online Information Review, 29*(5), 531–553. doi:10.1108/14684520510628918

Transparency International. (2010). *Corruption perceptions index 2010*. Retrieved Oct 30, 2010 from http://www.transparency.org/policy_research/surveys_indices/cpi/2010/results

Tseng, T. T. Y. (2008). A study of e-government system effectiveness: Applying structuration theory to context-aware ICT applications in public organisations. *International Journal of Electronic Business, 6*(4), 405–432. doi:10.1504/IJEB.2008.020677

Tseng, Y. H., & Tsay, M. Y. (2013). Journal clustering of library and information science for subfield delineation using the bibliometric analysis toolkit: CATAR. *Scientometric, 95*(2), 503–528. doi:10.1007/s11192-013-0964-1

TSI. (2008). *ICT Usage Survey on Households*. Turkish Standards Institute.

TUIK. (2007). *ICT usage survey on households and individuals*. Ankara, Turkey: Turkish Statistical Institute.

Turkle, S. (1995). *Life on the Screen: Identity in the Age of the Internet*. New York: Simon & Schuster.

Turkle, S. (1996). Virtuality and its Discontents: Searching for Community in Cyberspace. *The American Prospect, 24*, 50–57.

Turkle, S. (1997). Multiple Subjectivity and Virtual Community at the End of the Freudian Century. *Sociological Inquiry, 67*(1), 72–84. doi:10.1111/j.1475-682X.1997.tb00430.x

TURKSAT. (2008). Retrieved December 10, 2010 from http://www.turksat.com.tr/english/index.php/e-Government-/e-Government-Gateway-Project/What-is-e-Government-Gateway-Project.html

TURKSTAT. (2012). *Information and communication technology (ICT) usage survey on households and individuals*. Retrieved April 12, 2014 from http://www.turkstat.gov.tr/PreHaberBultenleri.do?id=10880

TUSIAD. (2010). *Türkiye İçin E-devlet Yönetim Modeline Doğru: Mevcut Durum Değerlendirmesi ve Öneriler, Report*. Author.

U.S. Congress. (2002). *2002 E-Government Act*. US: Author.

U.S. Department of Health & Human Services. (2013a). *The Affordable Care Act and African Americans*. Retrieved March 30, 2014, from http://www.hhs.gov/healthcare/facts/factsheets/2012/04/aca-and-african-americans04122012a.html

U.S. Department of Health & Human Services. (2013b). *The Affordable Care Act and women*. Retrieved March 30, 2014 from http://www.hhs.gov/healthcare/facts/factsheets/2012/03/women03202012a.html

U.S. Department of Health & Human Services. (2013c). *The Affordable Care Act- what it means for rural America*. Retrieved March 30, 2014, from http://www.hhs.gov/healthcare/facts/factsheets/2013/09/rural09202013.html

U.S. Department of Health & Human Services. (2014) *The Affordable Care Act and Latinos*. Retrieved March 30, 2014 from http://www.hhs.gov/healthcare/facts/factsheets/2012/04/aca-and-latinos04102012a.html

Uçkan, Ö. (2003). *E-devlet,-demokrasi ve e-yönetişim modeli: Bir ilkesel öncelik olarak bilgiye erişim özgürlüğü*. Retrieved December 11, 2010 from http://www.stradigma.com/turkce/haziran2003/print_09.html

UN (United Nations). (2010). *World Population Prospects, the 2010 Revision.* Retrieved from http://esa.un.org/unpd/wpp/Sorting-Tables/tab-sorting_population.htm

UN Foundation-Vodafone Foundation Partnership. (2009). mHealth for Development: The Opportunity of Mobile Technology for Healthcare in the Developing World. Washington, DC: Author.

UNDESA. (2002). *Plan of Action - e-government for Development.* Government of Italy, Ministry for Innovation and Technologies. Retrieved from www.palermoconference2002.org

UNESCO. (1997). *World Communication Report: The media and the challenges of the new technologies.* Paris, France: UNESCO Publishing.

UNESCO. (2005). *World Report: Towards Knowledge Societies.* Paris, France: UNESCO Publishing.

UNESCO. (2007). *The Mongolian Media Landscape: Sector Analysis.* Retrieved April 5, 2014 from http://portal.unesco.org/ci/en/ev.php-URL_ID=25638&URL_DO=DO_TOPIC&URL_SECTION=201.html

UNESCO. (2008). *E-governance and Accountability.* UNESCO.

UNESCO. (2010). *EGOVERNANCE.* Retrieved from http://portal.unesco.org/ci/en/ev.php-URL_ID=3038&URL_DO=DO_TOPIC&URL_SECTION=201.html

Unisys. (2012). *United States security index.* Retrieved from http://www.unisyssecurityindex.com/usi/us

United Nations Department of Economic and Social Affairs, Division for Public Administration and Development Management. (2007). Compendium of ICT Applications on Electronic Government: Vol. 1. *Mobile Applications on Health and Learning.* New York: United Nations.

United Nations Development Program (UNDP). (2006). *Simplification of Public Utility Bill Payment System (Recommendation by the Technical Committee).* Dhaka, Bangladesh: Access to Information Programme.

United Nations Development Programme-Asia Pacific Development Information Programme (UNDP-APDIP). (2004). *Information and Communications Technology for Development: A Sourcebook for Parliamentarians.* New Delhi, India: Elsevier. Retrieved January 18, 2012, from http://www.apdip.net/publications/ict4d/sourcebook.pdf

United Nations Statistics Division (UNSD). (2008). *Mongolia: Country Profile.* Retrieved Oct 28, 2010 from http://data.un.org/CountryProfile.aspx?crname=MONGOLIA

United Nations World Public Sector Report. (2003). *E-Government at the Crossroads.* Author.

United Nations. (1995). *Report of the Fourth World Conference on Women.* New York: The United Nations.

United Nations. (1997a). Synthesized Report on National Action Plans and Strategies for Implementation of the Beijing Platform for Action. New York, NY: The United Nations, the Department of Public Information.

United Nations. (1997b). *Women at a glance.* New York, NY: The United Nations, the Commission on the Status of Women. Retrieved 25 July 2012 from http://www.un.org/ecosocdev/geninfo/women/women96.htm

United Nations. (2000). *The World's Women Trends and Statistics.* New York, NY: The United Nations.

United Nations. (2003). *World Public Sector Report 2003: E-Government at the Crossroads.* New York: United Nations.

United Nations. (2005a). *The World's Women 2005: Progress in statistics.* New York, NY: The United Nations.

United Nations. (2005b). *Women 2000 and beyond: Gender equality and empowerment of women through ICT. The United Nations.* Division for the Advancement of Women, Department of Economic and Social Affairs.

United Nations. (2005c). *Review of the implementation of the Beijing Platform for Action and the outcome documents of the special session of the General Assembly entitled Women 2000: Gender equality, development and peace for the twenty-first century (E/CN.6/2005/2). The United Nations: Economic and Social Council.* Commission on the Status of Women.

United Nations. (2008). *E-Government Survey Report.* Retrieved June 10, 2008, from unpan1.un.org/intradoc/groups/public/documents/UN/UNPAN028607.pdf

United Nations. (2010). *E-government survey 2010: Leveraging e-government at a time of financial and economic crisis.* New York: United Nations.

United Nations. (2010a). *The World's Women 2010 Trends and Statistics.* New York, NY: The United Nations.

United Nations. (2010b). *Review of the implementation of the Beijing Declaration and Platform for Action, the outcomes of the twenty-third special session of the General Assembly and its contribution to shaping a gender perspective towards the full realization of the Millennium Development Goals (E/2010/4*–E/CN.6/2010/2).* The United Nations Economic and Social Council, Commission on the Status of Women.

United Nations. (2011). *Report of the Special Rapporteur on the promotion and protection of the right to freedom of opinion and expression, Frank La Rue.* The United Nations Human Rights Council. Retrieved June 18, 2012, from http://documents.latimes.com/un-report-Internet-rights/

United Nations. (2012). *United Nations e-government survey 2012 e-government for the people.* New York: United Nations.

United Nations. (2012). *United Nations E-Government Survey 2012: E-Government for the People.* New York: United Nations.

United Nations. (2012a). *UN public administration programme: Data center.* Retrieved from http://un-pan3.un.org/egovkb/datacenter/countryview.aspx

United Nations. (2012b). *United Nations e-government survey 2012: E-government for the people.* New York: The United Nations Department of Economic and Social Affairs.

United Nations. (Department of Economic and Social Affairs). (2003). *UN global e-government survey 2003.* New York, NY: Author. Retrieved from http://unpan1.un.org/intradoc/groups/public/documents/un/unpan016066.pdf

United Nations. (Department of Economic and Social Affairs). (2010). *E-government survey 2010: Leveraging e-government at a time of financial and economic crisis.* New York, NY: Author. Retrieved from http://www.unpan.org/egovkb/global_reports/08report.htm

United Nations. (UN). (2003). E-Government at the Crossroads (World Public Sector Report). New York: Department of Economic & Social Affairs.

United Nations. (UN). (2008). E-Government Survey: From E-Government to Connected Governance. New York: Department of Economic and Social Affairs.

United Nations. (UN). (2012). United Nations e-government survey, 2012. New York: Department of Economic and Social Affairs.

University, U. L. M. (2014a). *Google's ClientLogin implementation.* Retrieved April 12, 2014 from http://www.uni-ulm.de/in/mi/mitarbeiter/koenings/catching-authtokens.html

University, U. L. M. (2014b). *Google vulnerability of Client Login account credentials on unprotected.* Retrieved April 12, 2014 from http://www.uni-ulm.de/in/mi/mitarbeiter/koenings/catching-authtokens.html

UNPAN (United Nations). (2010). *United Nations e-government survey 2008: From e-government to connected governance.* New York: United Nations.

Ustun, A., Yazici, A., Akman, I., & Arifoglu, A. (2008). *Mobile government in Turkey: Investigating drivers and barriers.* Paper presented at the European Conferences on e-Government (ECEG). Lausanne, Switzerland.

Uzoka, F. E., Shemi, A. P., & Seleka, G. G. (2007). Behavioural Influences on E-Commerce Adoption in a Developing Country Context. *The Electronic Journal of Information Systems in Developing Countries, 31*(4), 1–15.

Valentina, N. (2004). E – Government for Developing Countries: Opportunities and Challenges. *The Electrical Journal on Information Systems in Developing Countries, 18*(1), 1–24.

Van Dijk, J. (1999). *The network society, social aspects of new media*. London: Sage.

Van Dijk, J. (2005). *The deepening divide: Inequality in the information society*. London: Sage Publications.

Van Dijk, J. (2006). Digital divide research, achievements and shortcomings. *Poetics, 34*, 221–235. doi:10.1016/j.poetic.2006.05.004

Vargo, S. L., & Lusch. (2004). Evolving to a New Dominant Logic for Marketing. *Journal of Marketing, 68*, 1–17. doi:10.1509/jmkg.68.1.1.24036

Vekatesh, V., & Davis, F.D. (n.d.). A theoretical extension of the technology acceptance model: Four longitudinal field studies. *Management Science, 45*(2), 186-204.

Vekatesh, V., & Speier, C. (1999). Computer technology training in the workplace: A longitudinal investigation of the effect of the mood. *Organizational Behavior and Human Decision Processes, 79*(1), 1–28. doi:10.1006/obhd.1999.2837 PMID:10388607

Velicu, B. C. (2012). Creating a citizen centric administration through eGovernment in Romania. *Romanian Journal of Political Science, 12*(2), 103–129.

Venkatesh, V., & Davis, F. D. (1996). A model of the antecedents of perceived ease of use: Development and test. *Decision Sciences, 27*, 451–481. doi:10.1111/j.1540-5915.1996.tb01822.x

Venkatesh, V., Morris, M. G., Davis, G. B., & Davis, F. D. (2003). User acceptance of information technology: Toward a unified view. *MIS Quaterly, 27*(3), 425–478.

Vergeer, M., Hermans, L., & Sams, S. (2013). Online social networks and micro-blogging in political campaigning: The exploration of a new campaign tool and a new campaign style. *Party Politics, 19*, 477–501. doi:10.1177/1354068811407580

Verschuere, B., Brandsen, & Pestoff. (2012). Co-production: The State of the Art in Research and the Future Agenda. *Voluntas: International Journal of Voluntary and Nonprofit Organizations*, 1-19.

Veysey, L. R. (1978). *The Communal Experience: Anarchist and Mystical Communities in Twentieth-Century America*. Chicago, IL: University of Chicago Press.

Vigoda, E. (2002). From responsiveness to collaboration: Governance, citizens, and the next generation of public administration. *Public Administration Review, 62*(5), 527–540. doi:10.1111/1540-6210.00235

Villalobos, V., & Monge-González, R. (2011). Costa Rica's Efforts Toward an Innovation-Driven Economy: The Role of the ICT Sector. In S. Dutta, & I. Mia (Eds.), *The Global Information Technology Report 2010 – 2011* (pp. 119 - 127). Geneva, Switzerland: World Economic Forum and INSEAD. Retrieved June 17, 2012 from http://reports.weforum.org/global-information-technology-report/content/pdf/wef-gitr-2010-2011.pdf

Vocino, T., & Elliott, R. H. (1982). Journal Prestige in Public Administration: A Research Note. *Administration & Society, 14*(1), 5–14. doi:10.1177/009539978201400101

Vygotsky, L. S. (1978). *Mind in society: The development of higher psychological processes*. Cambridge, MA: Harvard University Press.

Walton, R., Yaacoubi, J., & Kolko, B. (2012). What's it for? Expectations of internet value and usefulness in Central Asia. *Information Technologies and International Development, 8*(3), 69.

Wang, H., & Sun. (2011). Game reward systems: Gaming experiences and social meanings. In C. Marinka, K. Helen, & W. Annika (Eds.), *Proceedings of the DiGRA 2011 Conference: Think design play*. DiGRA.

Wang, H. J., & Lo, J. (2013). Determinants of citizens' intent to use government websites in Taiwan. *Information Development, 29*(2), 123–137. doi:10.1177/0266666912453835

Wanjiku, R. (2008). Still waiting for Madaraka PC. *Computerworld Kenya: The Voice of IT Management*. Retrieved November 2, 2010 from http://www.computerworld.co.ke/articles/2008/09/30/still-waiting-madaraka-pc

Warschauer, M. (2003). *Technology and social inclusion: Rethinking the digital divide*. Cambridge, MA: MIT Press.

Watson, N. (1997). Why we argue about virtual community: A case study of the Phish.net fan community. In S. G. Jones (Ed.), *Virtual Culture* (pp. 102–132). Thousand Oaks, CA: Sage.

Watson, R., & Mundy, B. (2001). A strategic perspective of electronic democracy. *Communications of the ACM, 44*(1), 27–30. doi:10.1145/357489.357499

Wattal, S., Hong, Y., Mandviwalla, M., & Jain, A. (2011). *Technological diffusion in the society: Digital divide in the context of social class*. Paper presented at the Hawaii International Conference on System Sciences. Hawaii, HI. www.whitehouse.gov. (2014). *Health care that works for Americans*. Retrieved March 31, 2014 from www.whitehouse.gov/healthreform/healthcare-overview

Weerakkody, V., Janssen, M., & Dwivedi, Y. K. (2011). Transformational change and business process reengineering (BPR): Lessons from the British and Dutch public sector. *Government Information Quarterly, 28*(3), 320–328. doi:10.1016/j.giq.2010.07.010

Weiss, P. A. (1995). Introduction: Feminist Reflections on Community. In P. A. Weiss, & M. Friedman (Eds.), *Feminism and Community*. Philadelphia, PA: Temple University Press.

Welch, E. W., Hinnant, C. C., & Moon, M. J. (2004). Linking citizen satisfaction with e-government and trust in government. *Journal of Public Administration: Research and Theory, 15*, 371–391. doi:10.1093/jopart/mui021

Wellman, B. (2001). Community in the network society. *The American Behavioral Scientist, 45*(3), 476–495.

Werbach, K., & Hunter. (2012). *For the Win: How Game Thinking Can Revolutionize Your Business*. Philadelphia, PA: Wharton Digital Press.

West, D. M. (2004). E-government and the Transformation of Service Delivery and Citizen Attitudes. *Public Administration Review, 64*(1). doi:10.1111/j.1540-6210.2004.00343.x

West, D. M. (2005). *Digital government: Technology and public sector performance*. Princeton, NJ: Princeton University Press.

West, D. M. (2007). *Global E-Government*. Providence, RI: Brown University.

West, D., & Miller, E. (2006). The digital divide in public e-health: barriers to accessibility and privacy in state health department web sites. *Journal of Health Care for the Poor and Underserved, 17*, 652–667. doi:10.1353/hpu.2006.0115 PMID:16960328

Westrup, C., & Al-Jaghoub, S. (2008). *Nation states, networks of flows and ICT-enabled development: Learning from Jordan*. Manchester, UK: Development Informatics Group, Institute for Development Policy and Management, University of Manchester, Working Paper Series, Paper No. 33. Retrieved from http://www.sed.manchester.ac.uk/idpm/research/publications/wp/di/documents/di_wp33.pdf

Whittington, R. (2003). The work of strategizing and organizing: For a practice perspective. *Strategic Organization, 1*(1), 117–125. doi:10.1177/1476127003001001221

Wigand, D. L. (2012). Communication and Collaboration in a Web 2.0 World. In E. Downey, & M. A. Jones (Eds.), *Public Service, Governance and Web 2.0 Technologies: Future Trends in Social Media* (pp. 1–18). Hershey, PA: IGI Global. doi:10.4018/978-1-4666-0071-3.ch001

Wikström, S. (1996). The Customer as Co-producer. *European Journal of Marketing, 30*(4), 6–19. doi:10.1108/03090569610118803

Willis Aronowitz, N. (2011). UN Declares Internet Access a Human Right: What Does This Really Mean? *Good Magazine*. Retrieved June 26, 2012, from http://www.good.is/post/un-declares-Internet-access-a-human-right-what-does-this-really-mean/

Willyard, C. (2010). Electronic records pose dilemma in developing countries. *Nature Medicine, 16*(3), 249. doi:10.1038/nm0310-249a PMID:20208497

Wilson, F. (1999). Cultural control within the virtual organization. *The Sociological Review, 47*, 672–694. doi:10.1111/1467-954X.00191

Wilson, J. Q. (1973). *Political Organizations*. New York: Basic Books.

Wilson, W. (1887). *The Study of Administration*. Washington, DC: US Printing Office.

Wire. (2014). Retrieved from http://www.wired.co.uk/news/archive/2014-03/27/turkey-youtube-ban

Wolcott, P., & Cagiltay, K. (2001). Telecommunications, liberalization and the growth of the internet in Turkey. *The Information Society*, *17*(2), 133–141. doi:10.1080/019722401750175685

WomenAction. (2000). *United Nations General Assembly Special Session on Women* and *Report of online discussion on Women and Media*. Retrieved January 04, 2012, from http://www.womenaction.org/ungass/bpfa/ungass.html

Wootton, R., Vladzymyrskyy, A., Zolfo, M., & Bonnardot, L. (2011). Experience with low-cost telemedicine in three different settings: Recommendations based on a proposed framework for network performance evaluation. *Global Health Action*, *4*.

Wootton, R. (2008). Telemedicine support for the developing world. *Journal of Telemedicine and Telecare*, *14*, 109–114. doi:10.1258/jtt.2008.003001 PMID:18430271

Wootton, R., & Bonnardot, L. (2010). In what circumstances is telemedicine appropriate in the developing world? *Journal of the Royal Society of Medicine Short Reports*, *1*(5), 37. doi:10.1258/shorts.2010.010045 PMID:21103129

Wootton, R., Menzies, J., & Ferguson, P. (2009). Follow-up data for patients managed by store and forward telemedicine in developing countries. *Journal of Telemedicine and Telecare*, *15*(2), 83–88. doi:10.1258/jtt.2008.080710 PMID:19246608

Wootton, R., & Tahir, M. S. M. (2004). Challenges in launching a Malaysian teleconsulting network. In P. Whitten, & D. Cook (Eds.), *Understanding Health Communications Technologies*. San Francisco, CA: Jossey-Bass.

World Bank Group. (2004). *Report on Bangladesh*. Retrieved from http://www.worldbank.org/

World Bank. (2006). *Engendering Information & Communication Technologies Challenges and Opportunities for Gender-Equitable Development*. Retrieved from http://web.world bank.org/WEBSITE/EXTERNAL/TOPICS

World Bank. (2008). *E-government*. Retrieved from http://go.worldbank.org

World Bank. (2009). *Information and communications for development, extending research and increasing impact*. Retrieved from http://books.google.co.uk/books

World Bank. (2010). *The Little Data Book on Information and Communication Technology 2010*. Development Data Group and the Global ICT Department of the World Bank. Retrieved January 17, 2012 from http://siteresources.worldbank.org/EXTINFORMATIONANDCOMMU-NICATIONANDTECHNOLOGIES/Resources/Little-DataBook2010.pdf

World Bank. (2011). *e-GOVERNMENT*. Retrieved from http://web.worldbank.org/WBSITE/EXTERNAL/TOP-ICS/EXTINFORMATIONANDCOMMUNICATION-ANDTECHNOLOGIES/EXTEGOVERNMENT/0,con tentMDK:20507153~menuPK:702592~pagePK:14895 6~piPK:216618~theSitePK:702586,00.html

World Bank. (2012). Retrieved from http://www-wds.world-bank.org/external/default/WDSContentServer/WDSP/ECA/2012/08/19/ADB66A1A61526C0E85257A5F-006CCBCA/1_0/Rendered/PDF/ISR0Disclos-abl019201201345405700423.pdf

World Bank. (2012a). *Information and Communications for Development 2012: Maximizing Mobile*. Washington, DC: World Bank.

World Bank. (2012b). *Little Data Book on Information and Communication Technology*. Washington, DC: World Bank.

World Economic Forum. (2010). *The Global Competitiveness Report 2010-2011*. Geneva, Switzerland: Author.

World Economic Forum. (2011). *The Global Information Technology Report 2010-2011*. Geneva, Switzerland: Author.

World Health Organization. (2005a). *Resolution WHA 58.28 on e-Health*. Retrieved from http://apps.who.int/gb/ebwha/pdf_files/WHA58/WHA58_28-en.pdf

World Health Organization. (2005b). *WHO Facing the Facts: The Impact of Chronic Disease in the Americas*. Geneva: WHO.

World Health Organization. (2011). *mHealth New horizons for health through mobile technologies*. Retrieved from http://www.who.int/goe/publications/goe_mhealth_web.pdf

Xu, Y. (2011). *Literature Review on Web Application Gamification and Analytics* (CSDL Technical Report 11-05). CSDL.

Yang, G. (2003). The Internet and civil society in China: A preliminary assessment. *Journal of Contemporary China, 12*, 453–475. doi:10.1080/10670560305471

Yang, K. (2011). Emergent accountability and structuration theory: Implications. In G. Frederickson, & M. Dubnick (Eds.), *Public Accountability and Its Promises* (pp. 269–281). Armonk, NY: M. E. Sharpe.

Yee, N., Bailenson, & Ducheneaut. (2009). The Proteus effect: Implications of transformed digital self-representation on online and offline behavior. *Communication Research, 36*(2), 285–312. doi:10.1177/0093650208330254

Yeloğlu, H. O., & Sağsan, M. (2009). The diffusion of e-government innovations in Turkey: A conceptual framework. *Journal of US-China Public Administration, 6*(7), 17–23.

Yildirim, M. (2010). Yanlışlığı düzeltmek gerek. *EGA*. Retrieved December 10, 2010 from www.ega.com.tr/haber_detay.php?haber_id=48

Yildiz, M., & Kuban, A. (2011). *Discourses of E-Government: An Inductive Analysis*. Paper presented at the EGPA Conference. New York, NY.

Yildiz, M. (2007). E-government research: Reviewing the literature, limitations, and ways forward. *Government Information Quarterly, 24*(3), 646–665. doi:10.1016/j.giq.2007.01.002

Yildiz, M. (2007). The state of mobile government in Turkey: Overview, policy issues, and future prospects. In I. Kushchu (Ed.), *Mobile Government: An Emerging Direction in E-Government*. Hershey, PA: IGI Publishing. doi:10.4018/978-1-59140-884-0.ch013

Yoon, S. H. (1996). Power online: A poststructuralist perspective on computer-mediated communication. In C. Ess (Ed.), *Philosophical perspectives on computer-mediated communication* (pp. 171–196). Albany, NY: State University of New York Press.

Youngs, G. (2000). Internet policies and states. In C. Kramarae, & D. Spender (Eds.), *Routledge International Encyclopedia of Women: Global Women's Issues and Knowledge* (pp. 1154–1156). New York, NY: Routledge.

Yu, E., & Liu. (2001). Modelling Trust for System Design Using the i* Strategic Actors Framework. In R. Falcone, M. Singh & Y.H. Tan (Eds.), *Trust in Cyber-Societies – Integrating the Human and Artificial Perspectives* (LNAI), (vol. 2246, pp. 175–194). Berlin: Springer.

Yuan, L., Xi, C., & Xiaoyi, W. (2012). Evaluationg the readiness of government portal websites in China to adopt contemporary public administration principles. *Government Information Quarterly, 29*(3), 403–412. doi:10.1016/j.giq.2011.12.009

Yucel, I. H. (2006). *Türkiye'de Bilim Teknoloji Politikaları ve İktisadi Gelişmenin Yönü. Sosyal Sektörler ve Koordinasyon Genel Müdürlüğü*. Devlet Planlama Teşkilatı.

Yusuf, M. A., & Alam, Q. (2011). Empowering Role of the Village Phone Program in Bangladesh: In Retrospect. Prospect: Journal of Information Technology Impact, 11(1), 35-50.

Zaho, D., & Rosson, M. (2009). How and Why People Twitter: The Role that Microblogging Plays in Informal Communication at Work. In *Proceedings of the ACM International Conference on Supporting Groupworth* (pp. 243-252). New York: ACM Press.

Zaman, A. U. (2011). *Union information & service centre (UISC), ICT enabled one-stop service outlet in Bangladesh*. Retrieved from http://community.telecentre.org/profiles/blogs/union-information-amp-service-centre-uisc-ictenabled-one-stop?xg_source=activity

Zaman, F. (2007, August 11). Addressing interoperability issues: Editorial. *The Daily Star*.

Zassoursky, I. (2004). *Media and power in post-soviet Russia*. Armonk, NY: M.E. Sharpe.

Zhang, J. (2002). Will the government serve the people? The development of Chinese e-government. *New Media & Society, 4*, 163–184. doi:10.1177/14614440222226325

Zhao, J. J., & Zhao, Y. S. (2010). Opportunities and threats: A security assessment of state eGovernment websites. *Government Information Quarterly, 27*(1), 49–56. doi:10.1016/j.giq.2009.07.004

Zheng, Y., & Heeks, R. (2008). *Conceptualising information culture in developing countries*. Manchester, UK: Development Informatics Group, Institute for Development Policy and Management, University of Manchester, Working Paper Series, Paper No. 34. Retrieved from http://www.sed.manchester.ac.uk/idpm/research/publications/wp/di/documents/di_wp34.pdf

Zhou, Z., & Hu, C. (2008). Study on the e-government security risk management. *International Journal of Computer Science and Network Security, 8*(5), 208–213.

Zhu, M., Huang, & Contractor. (2013). Motivations for self-assembling into project teams. *Social Networks, 35*(2), 251–264. doi:10.1016/j.socnet.2013.03.001

Zichermann, G., & Cunningham. (2011). *Gamification by Design: Implementing Game Mechanics in Web and Mobile Apps*. Sebastopol, CA: O'Reilly Media.

Zook, M. (2000). Internet metrics: Using host and domain counts to map the internet. *Telecommunications Policy, 24*(6/7).

About the Contributors

Edward Francis Halpin is Professor in Social and Human Rights Informatics and co-chair of the Digital Research Centre at Leeds Metropolitan University. He has a background in politics, community development, peace, human rights, e-Government/e-Governance, and social informatics/information management. For his PhD, he studied the use and application of information and information technology for human/child rights, and he has an MA in Public Policy. He worked as an expert for the European Parliament Scientific and Technical Options (STOA) Unit, is an Associate Schumann Fellow, having researched at the European University in Florence, Member of the Chartered Institute of Library and Information Managers, and a Fellow of the Royal Society for the Arts. Edward is Chair of the Geneva-based Human Rights Information and Documentation Systems International (HURIDOCS), an international NGO helping human rights organisations use information technologies and documentation methods to maximise the impact of their advocacy work.

David Griffin is a senior lecturer in Information Systems at Leeds Metropolitan University. His research interests include e-government, social innovation, and youth participation. Before becoming an academic, he spent 20 years working in local government IT as a project manager and a chief business analyst. He is a member of the editorial board of the *Electronic Journal of e-Government*.

Carolynn Rankin, PhD, is currently a Visiting Fellow in the Faculty of Arts, Environment, and Technology at Leeds Metropolitan University. Carolynn worked as an information management specialist for 20 years before moving into professional education in 2000. At Leeds Metropolitan University, she was Postgraduate Course Leader in the School of Information Management and in the School of Applied Global Ethics. Carolynn has interdisciplinary research interests, exploring the connections between civil society, social justice, and access to literacy and learning via libraries. Her current research projects include a longitudinal evaluation of the development of the Sister Libraries programme for the International Federation of Library Associations (IFLA). Carolynn's professional activities include the role of External Examiner for the Chartered Institute of Library and Information Professionals (CILIP) Professional Registration Board, and Assessor for CILIP Accreditation for Learning Providers. She is a member of the IFLA Standing Committee Library Theory and Research Section. Carolynn has co-authored and edited many publications. Her book titles include *Library Services from Birth to Five: Delivering the Best Start* and *Library Services for Children and Young People: Challenges and Opportunities in the Digital Age,* both published by Facet; *Professionalism in the Interdisciplinary Early Years Team* published by Continuum; and *Communication, Language, and Literacy from Birth to Five* published by Sage.

Lakshman Dissanayake received his Bachelors' Degree in Development Studies from the University of Colombo, obtaining First Class Honours in 1977. He holds a Postgraduate Diploma in Population Studies from the University of Colombo, Masters Degree in Demography from the Vrije Universiteit Brussel, and PhD from the University of Adelaide. Lakshman Dissanayake is Senior Professor in the Department of Demography, University of Colombo. He is also a Visiting Professor at the Faculty of Health and Social Sciences, Leeds Metropolitan University in United Kingdom. He is also an Adjunct member of the Australian Population and Migration Research Centre, The University of Adelaide in Australia. He was the former Dean of the Faculty of Graduate Studies, founder Director of the Colombo University Community Extension Centre, former Rector of the Sri Palee Campus of the University of Colombo. In the above capacities, he served as a member of the Senate and the Governing Council of the University of Colombo. Lakshman Dissanayake's expertise includes regional demography, regional development planning, health demography, and post-disaster reconstruction. He has published books, book chapters, and numerous research articles in local and internationally reputed journals.

Nazmunnessa Mahtab is Professor in the Department of Women and Gender Studies, University of Dhaka. She is also one of the founding members involved in the establishment of the Department. She had been a teacher in the Department of Public Administration, University of Dhaka since 1972. After graduating from the University of Dhaka, she pursued a Master's Degree in Politics, with specialization in Public Administration from the London School of Economics and Political Science (LSE), University of London, in 1975. She completed her PhD from the University of Delhi, India in 1982. She also did her Postdoctoral Research as a Senior Fulbright Scholar from George Washington University, Washington D.C. in 1989. Dr. Mahtab served as the Chairperson of the Department of Public Administration from 1986-1989 and Chairperson of the Department of Women and Gender Studies from 2003-2006. She has been working on women's issues and concerns for more than three decades, and has conducted many research works on diverse aspects of women's lives. Her areas of specialization include: Women and Poverty, Gender, and Development; Violence Against Women; CEDAW and Women's Rights; Gender and Governance; Women in Public Policy; and Leadership and Empowerment of Women. She is associated with many women's organizations, both at home and abroad. Dr. Mahtab possesses the experience and expertise of working as a Gender Consultant with the Government as well as with many international agencies, such as the UNDP, UNFPA, UNICEF, ILO, WHO, USAID. She has worked with many NGOs assisting them in developing a Gender Policy for their respective organizations. Dr. Mahtab also participated in gender training programs first as a trainee and later on as a trainer. She has participated in national and international seminars and conferences both at home and abroad and has written extensively on women's issues and problems. She has published three books: *Women in Bangladesh: From Inequality to Empowerment* (2007); *Introduction to Women and Gender Studies: Selected Texts on Issues and Concepts* (2011); *Women, Gender, and Development: Contemporary Issues* (2012).

* * *

Fuat Alican is a citizen of the world, enjoying exposure to various cultural paradigms, including prominent ones in Europe and the Americas. Born in Istanbul, Turkey, he has pursued an international career, both academically and professionally, with his pursuits taking him to the United States, the United Kingdom, and Latin America. He did his undergraduate and graduate work in the United States, followed by doctoral studies in Costa Rica, in economic and administrative sciences. Currently working as a researcher, lecturer, and management consultant, he is a leading expert in information and communication technologies, with a particular specialty in the software sector. His work background also includes multinational experience in the banking industry, specifically with Citigroup and Salomon Smith Barney. Alican is the author of numerous well-received publications, including books as well as articles, in the fields of economics, technology, and international politics. He also serves as Vice President at CIFOCICA.

Alberto Asquer is Lecturer of Public Policy and Management (Distance Learning) at SOAS, University of London. His research is mainly focused on organisational change in the public sector, innovation policy, and the political economy of liberalisation, privatisation, and re-regulation of public services. Some of his works have been published in *Governance, International Public Management Journal, Public Management Review*, and *Annals of Public and Cooperative Economics*. He was visiting fellow at the European University Institute and at CESIfo, Munich.

Undrah Buyan Baasanjav is an Assistant Professor in the Department of Mass Communications at Southern Illinois University Edwardsville. She received her PhD from Ohio University and taught at Michigan Technological University and Temple University. Her research and teaching focus on new media, gender and online gaming, and mediated political and social processes with an emphasis on Mongolia and post-communist countries. Dr. Baasanjav's scholarly work appears in the journals *Information, Communication, and Society, The Journal of Information Technology and Politics, New Media and Society, Explorations in Media Ecology, The Online Journal of Space Communication, Journal of Online Learning and Teaching,* and *Telecommunications Policy,* and in books by Routledge, Blackwell, and IGI Global.

Manuel Pedro Rodríguez Bolívar is Professor in Accounting at the University of Granada. He has authored numerous articles in international journals, among them we can highlight *Public Money & Management, Government Information Quarterly, Public Administration and Development, Online Information Review, International Review of Administrative Sciences, American Review of Public Administration, ABACUS, International Public Management Journal, Journal of Environmental Policy & Planning, Lex Localis, Journal of Local Self Government,* and *Administration & Society*. He has been also the author of several book chapters published in Routledge, Kluwer Academic Publishers, Springer, and IGI Global, and is author of full-length books published by the Ministry of Economy and Finance in Spain. He is also editor of books in Springer and Associate Editor in leading international journals.

Rubén González Crespo received a PhD in Software Engineering from Pontifical University of Salamanca (Spain). He is the Director of the Research Group of Society and Information Technologies, director adjunct of the Engineer Dept. in International University of La Rioja (Spain), and Technical Adviser of the Government of Panama.

Mohammad Dastbaz is the Dean of the Faculty of the Arts, Environment, and Technology, Leeds Metropolitan University. In 1994, Mohammad joined Kingston University, developing innovative multimedia-based learning systems, which led to his appointment as Principal Lecturer in the School of Computing and Mathematical Sciences at London South Bank University. In 2002, he joined the University of Greenwich as the Head of Information Systems and Multimedia. Before joining Leeds Met, he worked at the University of East London as their Dean of School of Computing, IT, and Engineering. Professor Mohammad Dastbaz completed his first degree in Electrical and Electronic Engineering, going on to complete a PhD in the "Design, Development, and Evaluation of Multimedia-Based Learning Systems" at Kingston University. He is an active researcher with over 60 reviewed journal and conference papers as well as a number of books and book chapters, and he has led and developed research projects totaling over £5M.

Ronan de Kervenoael is a Marketing Lecturer at Sabanci University in Turkey and network Lecturer at Aston University. His wider research interests lie under the umbrella of consumer behaviour and retailing, including the study of social, cultural, and technological transformations in how consumers (re)organize their lives and become producers of their experiences. His work has been published in *Environment & Planning A, World Development, Service Industries Journal, Telecommunication Policy.*

Suran Dissanayake's career commenced in 2005 with the Human Rights Commission of Sri Lanka (HRCSL), and he was assigned to work with the Internal Displacement programme affiliated with the UNHCR as an Information Officer. Suran acted as a liaison between Government, I/NGOs, beneficiaries, and other stakeholders in information dissemination. In 2006, Suran joined as Program Officer with the HRCSL's UNDP affiliated Disaster Relief Monitoring Programme, where he coordinated international and national programmes and also administered the complaints mechanism for human rights violations and coordinated the development rehabilitation programmes for both war-affected and tsunami-affected communities. During this tenure, Suran was also part of an editorial team and functioned as a co-editor of the IDP newsletter produced by the Brookings-Bern Project for Internal Displacement affiliated to the University of Berne. Suran also assisted in the production of national and international reports and contributed to the writing of guidelines on tsunami-related, conflict-related, and other humanitarian issues in Sri Lanka. In 2009, after graduating from Leeds Metropolitan University with BA Hons in Business Administration, Suran joined Mobitel Pvt Ltd, the National Telecommunications Service Provider in Sri Lanka and was assigned to the marketing division. Here, Suran functioned as a Product Manager for Value Added Services (VAS) and then for Mobitel Enterprise Solutions. Currently, Suran is studying for an MBA at Leeds Metropolitan University.

Mohammad Ehsan is an Associate Professor of Public Administration at the University of Dhaka, Bangladesh. He has also previously taught at the Shahjalal University of Science and Technology, Bangladesh and at Dalhousie University, Canada. He was educated at the University of Dhaka, Bangladesh; University of Bergen, Norway; and Carleton University, Canada. He is currently finishing his doctoral program at Dalhousie University, Canada. He published several books, chapters, encyclopedia entries, and articles in refereed journals. His current research focus is on public sector management, ethics and anti-corruption, democratic consolidation, digital governance, and policy and program evaluation.

Md. Gofran Faroqi graduated in Sociology from the University of Dhaka and started his career in the Bangladesh civil service. He served in both field administration and the secretariat level in different capacities. He was promoted as a Senior Assistant Secretary and was the Upazila Nirbahi Officer (UNO) in Lakhai of Habiganj district. He completed his Master of Public Administration from Flinders University, Australia in 2009. Currently, he is pursuing PhD at the Department of Politics and Public Policy, Flinders University. He has published several papers in international journals and contributed chapters to edited volumes. His major areas of research interest are public management, contemporary issues in public policy, governance and politics, accountability issues in GO/NGO sectors, and e-governance.

Andrei Ilas received a degree in Civil Law and a Doctorate in Political Sciences in Romania. He taught for eight years European Law and Comparative Politics at Alexandru Ioan Cuza University of Iasi, where he held a tenured position. During the past five years, he published peer-reviewed articles and participated in conferences on various e-government subjects. Andrei is currently pursuing a legal career in Ontario, Canada.

Ana-Cristina Ionescu is Director of Chamber Representation Division within the Chamber of Commerce and Industry of Romania (CCIR). She holds a BA in Communication and Public Relations from the National School of Political and Administrative Studies and a MS in International Business Studies from the Economical Studies Academy, Bucharest, Romania. She spent the last 10 years working in the European Chamber System, as a head of Foreign Affairs and Protocol, Deputy Director of a chamber practices division, head of a training center, within the CCIR. Her work in the Chamber System has been focusing on providing support services for companies (export promotion, internationalization, etc.), business development, training, EU-financed projects, events organizing. Her fields of expertise are foreign affairs, social sciences, Information and Communication Technologies (ICTs), chambers systems, corporate social responsibility, gender equality, innovation and innovative entrepreneurship. Her writings include a chapter on CSR and innovation for SMEs, several articles on ITC and gender-based rights and a co-authored chapter on Leadership in Science and Technology, with Dr. Richard A. Stein.

Muhammad Muinul Islam is an Assistant Professor in the Department of Public Administration in Jahangirnagar University, Bangladesh. Before he joined this university, he was a lecturer in the Department of Government and Politics in Asian University of Bangladesh and a Research Associate for a non-profit organization, VAB (Volunteers Association for Bangladesh). Apart from teaching, he did consultancies for USAID, EU, FAO, UNDP, and IFC. Mr. Islam completed his bachelor (Hons.) and Master's degree in public administration from University of Dhaka, Bangladesh. He has also completed an MPA degree from Andrew Young School of Policy Studies at Georgia State University, USA under Fulbright scholarship. His research interest includes different issues of public policy and governance, public budgeting and finance, and e-governance. He published several books, chapters, encyclopedia entries, and articles in refereed journals. He has also contributed and presented papers in different national and international conferences.

Hamid Jahankhani is the Director or research and Consultancy Development at Williams College. He gained his PhD from the Queen Mary College, University of London. In 2000, he moved to the University of East London to become the Professor of Information Security and Cyber Criminology at the university. Professor Jahankhani's principal research area for a number of years has been in the field of information security and digital forensics. In partnership with the key industrial sectors, he has examined and established several innovative research projects that are of direct relevance to the needs of UK and European information security, digital forensics industries, Critical National Infrastructure, and law enforcement agencies. Most of his research work in the field has been manifested in a number of ways so that it contributed significantly to the measures governments must take to protect the security of information on the Internet, the implications of cyber-crime in large corporations and individuals, resilience issues and threat assessment, risk analysis and the formulation of security policies, vulnerability assessment and forensics investigation of mobile devises. He is a respected international figure in the field of electronic security and digital forensics.

Nehal Mahtab, PhD, is currently working as a Senior Lecturer in School of Human Resources and Organizational Behavior at Leeds Business School, Leeds Metropolitan University, UK. Before joining at Leeds Metropolitan, Nehal was an Assistant Professor at the Department of Finance, University of Dhaka, Bangladesh, where he worked from 1999. Nehal has experience teaching in different universities in UK, USA, and Bangladesh. After graduating from the University of Dhaka, he pursued his second Master's Degree in Management Information Systems as a Fulbright Scholar from Duquesne University, USA. He completed his PhD from Leeds Metropolitan University, UK in 2013. Nehal is currently the Course Leader for the Undergraduate Business and Human Resources Management course at Leeds Metropolitan University and also a Member of the Academic Board of the Faculty of Business and Law. He has been working on Strategic Management, HR, ICT, and Gender issues and concerns for the last five years, and has conducted research works on these areas. His areas of specialization include: Strategic Alignment of Decision Making, Reward Management, Strategic HRM, ICT and Governance, Gender and Development, and Gender and Governance. Nehal is associated with the Chartered Institute of Personnel and Development (CIPD) as an Affiliate Member. He possesses the experience and expertise of working as a Consultant with the SEDF (a wing of the World Bank), UNDP, and ILO. Nehal also participated in different training programs pertaining to HR, ICT, and Gender. He is a Microsoft Office Specialist. Nehal has participated in national and international seminars and conferences both at home and abroad in his areas of expertise and interest.

Ramona McNeal is an associate professor in the Department of Political Science at the University of Northern Iowa. Her chief research interest is the impact of technology on participation, including its relationship to voting, elections, and public opinion. She also studies e-government, campaign finance reform, telehealth and telecommunication policy. She has published work in a number of journals including the *Journal of Information Technology & Politics*, *Social Science Quarterly*, *Political Research Quarterly*, *Government Information Quarterly*, and *Telemedicine and e-Health*. She is a co-author of *Digital Citizenship: The Internet, Society and Participation* (MIT Press, 2007) with Karen Mossberger and Caroline Tolbert.

María de Miguel Molina has a Law MSc from the Faculty of Law, Valencia University, and a Management PhD from the Management Department, Universitat Politècnica de València in Spain. She is an associate professor of Public Administration and Strategy at the Management Department, Faculty of Business Administration and Management, Universitat Politècnica de València. She is the director of the Master's program, Product and Service Management. Currently, she is the Head of Studies at the Faculty of Business Administration. Her main interests in the public management field are e-government, marketing strategies, and the different types of collaboration between higher education institutions. She is a member of the Spanish and Latin American Network Derechotics, which collaborates with the Valencian Institute of Public Administration.

Mobasser Monem is a Professor of Public Administration at University of Dhaka. He has his Doctoral degree in Public Management from the University of London, United Kingdom. He has worked on various aspects of public sector governance with particular focus on public sector management, local governance, and public policy. Dr. Monem has published extensively in academic journals at home and abroad on issues and areas relevant to public sector management, local governance, public sector service delivery, and institutional capacity building. He has worked as a consultant for UNDP, UNICEF, DANIDA, DFID, World Bank, JICA, KOICA, SIDA, and USAID.

Laura Alcaide Muñoz is Lecturer in Accounting in the Financial Economic and Accounting Department of the University of Granada. She is interested in how e-Government has favoured the process of reform and modernization of Public Administrations, making them more transparent, democratic, and participatory. Nowadays, her research topic is focused on how e-government allows citizens to connect with their policy makers and public managers and the increasingly frequent use of social networks. In addition, she is interested in financial sustainability in public sector. She has been author of articles published in *International Journal of Digital Accounting Research, Administration & Society, International Public Management Journal, Public Money and Management,* and *Lex Localis-Journal of Local Self Government,* and book chapters from IGI Global and Routledge-Taylor & Francis.

Shane O'Hanlon is a hospital physician and medical educator who also works in clinical informatics. He has a strong interest in e-Health and the use of informatics to improve medical care. He holds a Certificate in Human Rights Law and a MSc in Health Informatics. He is an executive member of the Health Informatics Society of Ireland and teaches at the University of Limerick, Ireland. He has worked as a medical volunteer in Malawi and St Lucia. He has presented papers on e-Health at national and international conferences and was a member of the program committee for HEALTHINF 2013.

Jungho Park received his Ph.D. from the Graduate School of Public and International Affairs at University of Pittsburgh in 2013. He is an associate research fellow at Korea Institute of Public Administration (KIPA). His research interests are centered on organizational behaviors (i.e., public service motivation) and citizens' attitudes toward public policies in the sense of policy noncompliance. His recent researches are focused on the citizens' trust in government and policy compliance and human resource polices in public sector.

Elias Pimenidis started his career with an undergraduate degree in Mechanical Engineering from the University of Strathclyde before he was awarded an MSc in Systems Engineering by the University of Wales (Cardiff). In 2001, Elias successfully completed and was awarded the prestigious Fellowship in Manufacturing Management at Cranfield University. The full academic cycle was completed with the award of a PhD ("Risk-Based Analogy for E-Business Estimation") by the University of Abertay Dundee. His main research interests are in the areas of project management (software and heavy engineering projects), risk management, e-Government development projects, Web-services and the security, and application of digital identification systems. His consulting role with a number of industrial organizations (primarily overseas) keeps him in continuous contact with challenges at the cutting edge of implementation and use of new technologies.

Gregory Porumbescu received his PhD from the Graduate School of Public Administration at Seoul National University in 2013. His research primarily relates to information and communications technology, transparency and accountability, and public opinion. His work has appeared in *The Journal of Public Administration Research and Theory*, *Public Administration Review*, and *Public Performance and Management Review*.

Carlos Ripoll Soler is an industrial engineer, having graduated from the Industrial Engineer School, Universitat Politècnica de València. He also has an MBA from the Faculty of Business Administration and Management, Universitat Politècnica de València, and he is a doctorate student in the Business Administration Doctorate Program at the Faculty of Business Administration and Management, Universitat Politècnica de València. His doctoral thesis project is focused on the different types of collaboration between higher education institutions. He is the director of the area of the Valencia Campus of Excellence at the Universitat Politècnica de València.

Md. Rokon-Ul-Hasan is currently working as the Deputy Director at the Bangladesh Public Administration Training Centre in Savar, Dhaka. He is a member of Bangladesh Civil Service (Administration Cadre). He had his Master in Public Policy and Governance from the North South University in 2011. Prior to that, he had MBA from the University of Dhaka and his Bachelor's degree in Electrical Engineering from the Bangladesh University of Engineering and Technology (BUET). His major research interests include governance, e-governance, public-private partnership, and civil service reform.

Alexandru V. Roman, PhD, is an Assistant Professor of Public Administration at California State University San Bernardino. His research interests include public management, public procurement, e-government, and public corruption.

Ephias Ruhode is a lecturer in the Information Technology Department at the Cape Peninsula University of Technology (CPUT) in Cape Town, South Africa. Prior to joining CPUT in 2007, he had worked in Zimbabwe for 13 years in various capacities as Lecturer in Computing, Analyst Programmer, ICT Operations Manager, and Software Development Manager. He holds a Doctor of Technology Degree in Information Technology from CPUT, an MBA Degree and undergraduate qualification in Computer Studies. He also received further training in computer technology in Japan and India. His research interest is Information Systems Development for Development (ISD4D), e-Government, e-Business, and e-Health.

José Manuel Saiz-Alvarez is PhD in Economics and Business Administration, Autonomous University of Madrid (Spain), and PhD in Sociology, Pontifical University of Salamanca (Spain). He has also studied at the Royal Complutense College at Harvard and University of South Florida (USA), University Lumière-Lyon II (France), and Tallinn University (Estonia). He is the Academic Director for Business Administration Doctoral Studies, Nebrija University (Spain). Professor Saiz-Alvarez has published widely, in Spanish and English, and some of his works has been translated into Polish, and he is Visiting Professor at TEC de Monterrey (Mexico and Peru), the Catholic University of Santiago de Guayaquil (Ecuador), and EAN University (Colombia).

Mary Schmeida, PhD, has served as a researcher for several organizations in the United States and is also affiliated with Kent State University, USA. She holds a Doctoral degree in Political Science, Public Policy. Her research areas of expertise are information technology and mobile health, telehealth, social and welfare policy in the U.S., healthcare reform policy, mental health policy, and rural health disparities. Her research has been published in scholarly books and journals and presented to national and international professional audiences.

Shareef M. Shareef is currently working as a head of Software Engineering department at the college of Engineering at the University of Salahaddin-Erbil. He received MSc in Digital Communications Networks in 2005 from London Metropolitan University with distinction. He has worked as an expert in the ICT Centre at the Ministry of Higher Education and Scientific Research in Kurdistan Region of Iraq in 2007. He joined the School of Architecture, Computing and Engineering at the University of East London as a PhD student in April 2009. He is an active researcher in the area of e-government and cloud computing initiatives in developing countries. He has published various papers along with participation in reviewing various conferences such as European Conference on E-Government (ECEG). He is also a member of many professional bodies in his area of specialisation, such as IET, and a Fellow of Higher Education Academy (FHEA).

Noore Alam Siddiquee is currently the Head, Department of Politics and Public Policy within the School of Social and Policy Studies at Flinders University, Australia. Dr. Siddiquee taught public policy and administration, politics and governance at various institutions of higher learning in Bangladesh, Malaysia, and Brunei for over 15 years before joining Flinders in 2006. He has undertaken consultancies for various institutions and published extensively in areas of public sector management/governance and reform. His publications include 2 books and over 60 articles in various journals of international repute. His most recent book, *Public Management and Governance in Malaysia: Trends and Transformations* (Routledge), was published in 2013. Major areas of his current research interest include public sector management and reform, e-governance, public accountability and ethics, decentralisation, local governance, and development. He has also supervised a large number of doctoral theses.

Virgil Stoica is PhD in Political Science and Associate Professor at Alexandru Ioan Cuza University of Iasi, Romania, Faculty of Philosophy, Social, and Political Sciences, where he holds a tenured position. He is the Head of Political Science Department, and he teaches Public Policy and Political Science Research Methods (for undergraduate students), Public Policy Analysis and Electronic Governance (for graduate students). During the last years, he published articles and participated to conferences on various e-government subjects. He also has research interest in public policies, local government, and political elites.

Vasileios Yfantis is a researcher at Ionian University in Greece and Lulea University of Technology in Sweden. He has presented conference papers in both Europe and Africa and is co-author of the book *Leveraging Developing Economies with the Use of Information Technology: Trends and Tools* (IGI Global). The main areas of his research interests are Information Communications Technology, e-Tourism, Digital Divide in Developing Countries, e-Government, and the Digital Entertainment Industry.

446

Index